"*The Routledge Handbook of Global and Digital Governance Crossroads* offers a compelling panoramic view of governance in our digital world. The handbook synthesizes wisdom from around the globe, delivering strategic insights on how to harmonize the needs of diverse stakeholders with emerging digital realities. Bringing together a unique blend of theory and practice, the editors have curated a wealth of knowledge that spans corporate to faith-based sectors, offering a blueprint for stakeholder-driven governance in the twenty-first century."

—**Jim Lecinski,** *Marketing Professor at Northwestern University's Kellogg School of Management and Former Google Vice-President*

"Never before has the need for this book been so urgent. Breaking down and communicating the interconnected landscape of economics, politics, and ethical/environmental sustainability to illuminate the deficiencies in current governance structures is a crucial step to resolving the most pressing crises of our time."

—**Nicholas Davies, Sustainability Consultant,** *Former Senior Policy Specialist for UK Parliament's Environmental Audit Committee*

"*The Routledge Handbook of Global and Digital Governance Crossroads* is as important as it is unsettling. Drawing on various global cases, it offers us fascinating reflections based on cross-sector and cross-country contexts. This collection illuminates the complex set of relations that articulates an increasingly embedded digital social life and the ensuing challenges demanded by its governance. Is it indeed possible to build in the near future normative structures capable of forging effective social contracts that promote prosperity, freedom, and peace for all? The book provides various fascinating answers, options, and concrete possibilities, making it a required reading for anybody who cares about the future of humankind."

—**Zander Navarro,** *Sociology Professor and Participatory Governance Researcher, Brasilia, Brazil*

"This volume offers fresh perspectives on institutional building that spans across domains, making it relevant to a wide range of experts across sectors and disciplines. This work offers innovative blueprints on good governance in the digital and AI era, much needed if we are to continue our commitment to democratic and global systems."

—**Payal Arora,** *Utrecht University Professor and Author of the Next Billion Users*

"The need to align business objectives with environmental and societal impact has never been greater. As we navigate self-regulation to the EU legislations, data transparency and governance are vital to underpin business operations. This book brings together a great number of insightful interdisciplinary perspectives on the fundamental need for good governance."

—**Shailja Dube,** *Institute of Positive Fashion Lead at British Fashion Council*

"In today's landscape of global interdependence, strong and consistent governance across borders is key to achieving an equitable and peaceful future. Bringing together such a diversity of authors, all experts in their respective governance fields, provides a uniquely relevant overview and gives me hope that the collaborative leadership I would like to envision can exist in our time."

—**Arizona Muse,** *American Fashion Supermodel, Global Sustainability Activist, and Founder of Dirt Charity Foundation*

"This unique and timely Handbook will expand our comprehension of the interplay of critical themes at the core of how our world is governed. Across a range of key sectors and levels, its authors masterfully integrate theoretical and practical insights, from their own work, to offer us smart tools and strategies for achieving human-centered development that is inclusive and equitable, while addressing the downside of the digital revolution."

—**Jeff Thindwa,** *Former Manager for Open and Collaborative Governance at the World Bank*

THE ROUTLEDGE HANDBOOK OF GLOBAL AND DIGITAL GOVERNANCE CROSSROADS

This handbook maps and analyzes cross-sector (public–corporate–social–community–faith) governance theories, models, and practices as they are evolving in a digital world. It studies human, cultural, societal, institutional interactions and challenges in a digitally enabled world, especially in the context of post-crisis resilience and agility. Every global crisis forces societies and nations to realign while addressing deeper structural and cultural issues in governance. The Covid-19 pandemic has necessitated swift local-to-global governance responses for timely digital innovations for health crisis interventions, economic recovery, and societal equity. While every nation-state is developing global pandemic responses in a digitally enabled world, the deeper crisis of human, institutional, and societal governance deficit is also evident. This handbook documents digital governance innovations that enhance stakeholder engagement and inclusion for resilient, accountable, and effective governance across sectors. This volume reflects on a range of theoretical frameworks adapted for understanding global and digital governance. It looks at international governance collaborations; corporate governance reform; education governance innovations; public sector and urban governance; health system governance, sustainability, and environmental governance; community and faith-based governance; and digital, cultural, and creativity governance. This book is unique, as it presents important work on post Covid-19 digital and democratic governance and brings together holistic—interdisciplinary and inter-sectoral—perspectives from the Global North and Global South, engaging the leading scholars, practitioners, businesses, and civil society. It will be of interest to multi-sector institutions and global audiences: governments, corporates, social sector institutions, digital entrepreneurs, students and researchers, academic professionals, policy-makers, public and private sector institutional leaders, and organizational and entrepreneurial innovators interested in the field of governance.

Preeti Shroff-Mehta currently serves as the Professor and Director of Executive Education Program at The Northwestern University—Medill School, USA. She is the Associate Editor for the Journal of Sustainable Marketing (JSM). Her teaching and research focus on Circular Economy and Sustainability, Integrated Marketing Communications, Change Management Leadership, Digital Media Business and Strategy, Luxury Branding, Place Branding, and

Women's Leadership Paths. She is the Senior Advisor for Institute for Development Impact (I4DI), Washington DC—GATES Foundation and MARS INC. supported initiative on Sustainable and Inclusive Global Supply Chains. She has served as Dean of MICA—The School of Ideas (Management, Marketing, Creative Communications) India; and Dean—School for International Training (SIT), World Learning in Washington DC and Vermont, USA. She worked as Director for Democratic Governance and Civil Society Capacity Development with World Learning in Washington, DC, and led international development programs in Africa, Asia, the Middle East, Europe, and Latin America in collaboration with the World Bank, United States Agency for International Development (USAID), the United Nations (UN), the Ford Foundation, and many other international agencies. Her academic teaching also includes SAIS—Johns Hopkins and the University of Maryland, USA.

Jagdish N. Sheth is Charles H. Kellstadt Professor of Business, Goizueta Business School, Emory University, USA. He is globally known for his scholarly contributions in consumer behavior, relationship marketing, competitive strategy, and geopolitical analysis. He has over fifty years of experience in teaching and research at the University of Southern California, the University of Illinois at Urbana-Champaign, Columbia University, MIT—Massachusetts Institute of Technology, and Emory. He is the recipient of all four top awards given by the American Marketing Association (AMA). Additionally, he received the Global Innovation Award and the Marion Creekmore Award, both from Emory University. Dr. Sheth has been an advisor to numerous corporations all over the world. He has authored or coauthored more than 350 papers and numerous books.

John Garrison is an accomplished international development professional with extensive experience in program management, participatory approaches, and strategic communications. He retired from the World Bank in December 2015 after working for twenty years as a civil society specialist, and he continues to work there as a senior consultant. He spent the first five years coordinating outreach to civil society in the Bank's office in Brasilia, Brazil, was the head of the Bank's Global Civil Society Team, and worked with the Inspection Panel in Washington, DC.

Shailendra Raj Mehta has just completed a seven-year term as President and Director and Distinguished Professor of Innovation and Entrepreneurship at MICA, in Ahmedabad, India. He is currently the O.P. Jindal Distinguished University Professor at O.P. Jindal Global University and Vice Chairman at the Indian Institute of Advanced Studies, Shimla. Earlier, he headed Auro University and Ahmedabad University. Before that, he had stints at Duke CE and the Indian Institute of Management Ahmedabad (joint appointment), and Purdue University, where he taught Economics and Strategic Management. He has done extensive research in Entrepreneurship, Industrial Organization, Information Economics, and Experimental Economics. His research has been the subject of a full-length review by *The Economist*. His work on creating world-class universities has been discussed around the world and profiled in multiple languages. He is rated as one of the top researchers in the field of strategy in India. His BA and MA are from Delhi University (St. Stephen's College and Delhi School of Economics respectively), his MPhil is from Balliol College, Oxford, and his Ph.D. is from Harvard.

THE ROUTLEDGE HANDBOOK OF GLOBAL AND DIGITAL GOVERNANCE CROSSROADS

Stakeholder Engagement and Democratization

Edited by Preeti Shroff-Mehta, Jagdish N. Sheth, John Garrison, and Shailendra Raj Mehta

Routledge
Taylor & Francis Group
LONDON AND NEW YORK

Designed cover image: Getty Images

First published 2025
by Routledge
4 Park Square, Milton Park, Abingdon, Oxon OX14 4RN

and by Routledge
605 Third Avenue, New York, NY 10158

Routledge is an imprint of the Taylor & Francis Group, an informa business

British Library Cataloguing-in-Publication Data
A catalogue record for this book is available from the British Library

ISBN: 978-1-032-16087-0 (hbk)
ISBN: 978-1-032-32659-7 (pbk)
ISBN: 978-1-003-31607-7 (ebk)

DOI: 10.4324/9781003316077

Typeset in Sabon
by Apex CoVantage, LLC

CONTENTS

FIGURES

TABLES

BOXES

CONTRIBUTORS

Sarah Angold is a textile pioneer and sustainability professional. She is a sought-out industry futures ambassador recognized for her enduring transformation initiatives. As an accredited sustainability expert from the University of Cambridge, she holds cross-disciplinary expertise in material innovation, circularity, and supply-chain transparency, contributing to UK parliamentary roundtables and international conferences while championing sustainable fashion education and innovation.

Christina Bartholomew is a U.S.-qualified attorney, Advanced Higher Education Teaching Fellow for Sustainable Business at INSEEC U, and Co-Founder of Stories Evolved, an international boutique consulting and advisory services firm that helps organizations cut through the ESG noise and articulate a north star for their future, built on an understanding of what ESG-related challenges, trends, and opportunities mean for their business and its stakeholders. Through her work designing certified sustainability education, events, and programming in partnership with the UN Global Compact, the Federal Bar Association, Fordham Law School, and the University College London, Christina is a leading voice in the legal sustainability community and has been invited to speak and moderate discussions at Legal ESG Summits in London and New York, the American Bar Association's Corporate Counsel Seminar, Weightmans Law Firm's Annual Partnership Summit, and law firms throughout the United States, the United Kingdom, and Africa, including Herbert Smith Freehills, ENSafrica, DAC Beachcroft, Webber Wentzel, and Impact International. She was educated at the University of Cambridge—Institute for Sustainability Leadership and the University of Texas School of Law, where she served as Executive Editor of the *Texas Journal of Women and the Law*. She received a B.A. in English literature from the University of Virginia. As a citizen of the United States, EU, and the United Kingdom—and London-based since 2007—she offers a truly global perspective.

Abhijit Bhaduri is Chief Executive Officer (CEO) of Abhijit Bhaduri & Associates. He is a prominent leadership and personal branding coach. He has managed global learning and development at Microsoft. He has a storied history of advising a spectrum of clients, from Fortune 100 firms to start-ups. As a top-rated learning expert and influential voice in talent management, Bhaduri is also a bestselling author with a substantial following on social media and contributes to leading publications in the business and HR spheres.

Nadereh Chamlou is currently a nonresident senior fellow at the Atlantic Council and an international development advisor. She is a former senior advisor of the World Bank, where he had over a thirty-three-year career. She held managerial, technical, coordination, and advisory positions in diverse fields such as economic management, corporate governance, private sector development, financial markets, environment, infrastructure, and gender. Her regional experience extends to Latin America, South Asia, East Asia, Europe, the Middle East, and North Africa. She has authored seminal publications, is a frequent speaker at international conferences, and serves on the boards of several organizations promoting research, empowerment, and innovation. She was educated at Georgetown University's School of Foreign Service and Graduate School for Economics. She is the recipient of the International Alliance for Women's 2015 "Making a Difference" Global Award.

Drissia Chouit was a former consultant to UNESCO. She is Full Professor of Comparative Linguistics, Communication, and Media Studies, Member of the Research Laboratory LaRCIGALS, and Representative of Moulay Ismail University of Meknes, Morocco, to the UNESCO-UNITWIN University Network on Media and Information Literacy and Intercultural Dialogue. She was globally elected as Co-Chair of the International Steering Committee (ISC) for the UNESCO Media and Information Literacy (MIL) Alliance for the term 2023–2025. She is Founding Member of MEDEA, Mediterranean Europe and Africa, which was launched in October 2023, and she is Director and Host of the series International E-Seminars on Contemporary Issues in Media and Information Literacy, with ten years' experience in diplomacy and international relations. As a fervent advocate of Media and Information Literacy for All, she has over twenty years' experience in teaching media and information literacy, with a focus on news literacy, information literacy in the digital age, fighting disinformation and extremism, and the power of language and communication. She has a number of publications and invited talks, both as a linguist and as a media and information literacy expert.

Hyesun Choung received her Ph.D. from the University of Wisconsin-Madison. She is an assistant professor in the Department of Communication at Michigan State University. Her research centers on human–artificial intelligence (AI) interactions, with an emphasis on the ethical and trust implications of AI technologies.

Barak Cohen is the owner and chief operating officer of his family's fourth-generation recycling business, based in Atlanta, GA. Prior to returning to his hometown of Atlanta, Barak spent ten years in Jerusalem and held a range of senior positions in the cultural and public policy sectors. Barak served as Deputy Director for Development and International Relations at The Israel Museum, Jerusalem (IMJ), Israel's largest cultural institution and home to the State of Israel and Jewish people's most important cultural treasures. Barak was responsible for maintaining and expanding the museum's base of support and collections through a network of seventeen "International Friends" organizations across the globe. Prior to joining the Museum, Barak served as Advisor for Foreign Affairs and Media to the Mayor of Jerusalem, developing strategy and implementing the international engagement and public relations priorities of the Jerusalem Municipality. He was the mayor's speechwriter and the municipality's international spokesman. Before joining the mayor's advisory team, Barak served as Director for International Outreach at the Israel Democracy Institute, a leading Israeli think tank. Prior to his time in Jerusalem, Barak was Assistant Director of the Anti-Defamation League's Southeast Region and worked as Wilderness Emergency Medical Technician (WEMT). Barak holds a BA in cultural anthropology from the University of Vermont and an MA in conflict research from the Hebrew University of Jerusalem, and he currently serves as a member of the Birthright Foundation's Ambassador's Council and as a board member of Congregation Ohr HaTorah in Atlanta.

Prabu David is currently serving as the dean and professor at Michigan State University. He is a dynamic leader in the field of communication. With a rich background that includes being a newspaper reporter and a researcher in advertising and public relations, his experiences have deeply informed his approach to education. David is dedicated to fostering an environment where the art and science of communication thrive, benefiting both society and his students. His academic contributions, particularly in multitasking and health communication, are recognized in leading journals, reflecting his commitment to advancing the field.

Jaya Deshmukh is an industry expert with over twenty years of experience in the field of corporate and stakeholder change management, with extensive expertise in managing change in complex organizational contexts. Jaya is Director of Change Management at the leading consulting firm and serves as the Chief Strategy Officer and Chief of Staff to the CEO at Colt Technology Services based in the United Kingdom. As the Provost and Senior VP for Academic Affairs at the Rochester Institute of Technology, Prabu David is an accomplished communication professional with a wealth of experience. With a background as Dean at Michigan State University and leadership roles at Washington State University and Ohio State University, he is a recognized figure in communication arts and sciences, specializing in AI ethics, machine learning, and artificial intelligence.

Ashutosh Dutt is Associate Professor contributing to the area of digital strategies and business analytics at MICA. He has more than nineteen years of experience. For the first five years of his career, he worked in the IT, marketing research, and data analytics industry, after which he has been in academics. He also consults the current Delhi government and the Delhi Commission for Women on matters of research and analysis. His courses include quantitative techniques, marketing analytics, machine learning, multivariate data analysis, marketing research, online research, and pricing research. He pioneered the marketing analytics specialization at MICA and led it for the first three years of its constitution. At MICA, he chaired many administrative initiatives at MICA, including admissions, the flagship PGP Programme, and MICA's International Annual Conference, ICMC. He currently leads the Centre for Learning and Innovative Pedagogy, a center of excellence at MICA. He also leads the Data Science and Business Analytics specialization at MICA. Having consulted brands like Symphony Coolers, House of MG, and organizations like the Gujarat Forest Department and the Delhi Dialogue Commission, he has rich consulting experience.

Bart W. Édes is an analyst, advisor, and public speaker on international development and trade, strategic foresight, and Asia's economic transformation. Édes is a distinguished fellow at the Asia Pacific Foundation of Canada and Professor of Practice at McGill University's Institute for the Study of International Development. Between 2001 and 2020, he held various leadership positions at the Asian Development Bank (ADB) with responsibility for strategy and knowledge in areas including ICT for development, civil society engagement, governance, and public sector management. Immediately prior to joining ADB, Édes served as a principal administrator for communications at Support for Improvement in Governance and Management in Central and Eastern Europe, a joint initiative of the Organization for Economic Cooperation and Development and the European Union supporting public administration reform in transition countries. He is the author of *Learning From Tomorrow: Using Strategic Foresight to Prepare for the Next Big Disruption*.

Henry Falk is Adjunct Professor of Environmental Health at the Rollins School of Public Health, Emory University. He has extensive experience, having served as Director of the Coordinating Center for Environmental Health and Injury Prevention at the Centers for Disease Control and Prevention (CDC) from 2005 to 2009. With a background in medicine and public health, he continues to contribute as Principal of Falk Consulting, LLC, and he has maintained a long-standing association with the Harvard T. H. Chan School of Public Health.

Alessandro Galtieri is Deputy General Counsel and Group Data Protection Officer at Colt, a global network and data center services company. He brings expertise in high-tech and legal domains, with qualifications in England, Ireland, and Italy. Engaging in professional committees, he serves on the Law Society's Technology and Law Committee, contributes to CLOC as a UK Council Member, and participates in ACC Europe's Diversity, Equity, and Inclusion Working Group and the Society for Computers and Law's Sustainability and ESG Committee.

John Garrison is an accomplished international development professional with extensive experience in program management, policy analysis, and strategic communications, primarily with the World Bank in Washington, DC. His diverse background spans across civil society, government, and academic sectors, showcasing his adeptness in grant-making and civil society engagement. With significant expertise in development issues ranging from environmental protection to health and rural advancement, Garrison has been at the forefront of pioneering participatory approaches and leveraging communications to amplify social impact.

Andrew Gibson is Assistant Professor of Philosophy of Education and Co-Director of the Cultures and Academic Values in Education (CAVE) research center at Trinity College Dublin. He is a review editor for the journal *LATISS: Learning and Teaching*, is on the editorial board for Philosophy and Theory in Higher Education, and is on the international advisory board of the Centre for Higher Education Futures (CHEF) research center, Aarhus University, Denmark. He has consulted for the OECD on country reviews of Ireland, Austria, and the Netherlands. His research focuses on the philosophy of higher education and the critical policy studies of higher education.

Björn-Sören Gigler heads the Data Economy and Blockchain Programs at GIZ GmbH and teaches political economy at Georgetown University. His work intersects digital transformation and international political economy, with a focus on GovTech and digital strategies for climate and inclusion.

Aimée Girdwood is a globally experienced sustainability expert, lawyer, and educator passionate about working with leaders and teams to drive responsible, purpose-led, and thriving organizations. With over seventeen years of international advisory, consulting, and legal experience, she focuses on working with organizations and their people to understand how they interact with and impact the world around them and the specific risks and opportunities sustainability presents. In addition, Aimée designs and implements appropriate strategies, policies, and upskilling initiatives to drive proactive leadership and long-term organizational sustainability and resilience.

Sanjay Gupta is Distinguished Professor of Accounting and Information Systems. He served as Eli and Edythe L. Broad Dean at Michigan State University, transforming the Broad College through strategic plans, innovations, and fundraising, elevating its global and national rankings. As a renowned scholar in corporate and individual tax policy, Gupta's leadership and expertise extend to prestigious roles, including Chair of the Department of Accounting and Information Systems and Faculty Director at Arizona State University's W. P. Carey School of Business.

Yan Han is the founder of Think Culture Foundation and leads International Business at Topline Consulting Group, bringing over twenty years of global experience in the Australia and China markets. As a "global citizen," Yan brings with her rich experience from Topline's China market, with unique and proven models built around innovative and digitally advanced practices. She has expertise in strategic planning, financial and risk management, joint ventures and alliances, new market development, and operations management.

Michael A. Harnar is a seasoned evaluation generalist with over twenty years of experience in diverse domains, from academia to technology assessment. As Assistant Professor at Western Michigan University, he's launched innovative educational programs and led the administrative evolution of a Ph.D. program in evaluation. Harnar combines his academic expertise with practical know-how as a project manager for a leading open-access journal, exemplifying his capacity to drive change and disseminate knowledge at the intersection of multiple disciplines.

Ellen Hazelkorn is Joint Managing Partner, BH Associates, Joint Editor of Policy Reviews in Higher Education, and Professor Emeritus at Technological University Dublin (Ireland). She is affiliated with the Centre for Global Higher Education, Oxford, and the Centre for International Higher Education, Boston College. She was Vice President at Dublin Institute of Technology (now TU Dublin) (1995–2008), Policy Advisor to, and Board Member of, the Higher Education Authority (Ireland) (2011–2017), and Consultant to the OECD (2001–2010). Over the past twenty years, Ellen has been a member of various government and tertiary education boards and has worked with UNESCO, the European Commission, and the World Bank providing advice to governments and institutions. Ellen has published over 200 peer-reviewed articles, book chapters, short articles and blogs, and policy papers. She is internationally recognized for her writings and analysis of university rankings.

Varsha Jain is the AGK chair, professor of marketing, and co-chairperson of research and dissertation at MICA, India. She is an associate editor (AE) at four "A" journals: the *Journal of Consumer Behaviour* (JCB), the *Journal of Advertising Research*, the *Journal of Consumer Marketing*, and the *Australasian Marketing Journal*. She received the best AE award from JCB in 2022. She is the vice chair of international relations, higher education, the special interest group, and the American Marketing Association (AMA), USA. She has authored over 140 publications, including multiple papers in A* and A journals, including the *European Journal of Marketing*, the *International Journal of Information Management*, the *Journal of Advertising Research*, the *Journal of Consumer Behavior*, the *Journal of Consumer Marketing*, and the *Journal of Business Research*. In her global research career, she is a visiting guest at Emory Business School, Atlanta, USA, and a visiting scholar at Greenwich University, London, and The Medill School, Northwestern University, USA. She is also a co-editor for special issues related to AI, social-media influencers, and Metaverse for JCB, due in 2023.

Amy Catherine Jersild brings nearly twenty-five years of expertise as an international development evaluation consultant, with a focus on development effectiveness and sustainable practices. Pursuing a Ph.D. at Western Michigan University, she has honed her skills in diverse roles, from academia to advising global entities like UNDP. Her work spans multiple continents and languages, reflecting her versatile and impactful career in international development.

Phalgun Kompalli is an Indian entrepreneur based out of New York. Currently, he is Co-Founder of upGrad, which is Asia's largest integrated learning skilling and workforce development company and has enrolled more than ten million learners from more than hundred countries. Prior to upGrad, Phalgun was Principal at The Parthenon Group, an education-strategy-consulting firm, where he was involved in advising large education conglomerates and investment funds on their growth and investment strategy in education. He has done significant work in the field of higher education and technology-enabled learning across India, the United States, Brazil, Africa, and Southeast Asia. Prior to Parthenon, Phalgun worked at Opera Solutions, an analytics firm that consults Fortune 500 companies on their revenue and cost optimization initiatives through data analytics. Phalgun completed his bachelor's degree in technology at IIT Delhi. He's originally from Hyderabad. He has been awarded the title of Forbes 30 under 30 Asia for consumer Tech in 2018 and was named the "BW Education 40 under 40 Achiever" by Business World in 2020.

Mayank Kumar is an education maven and accomplished entrepreneur. He is one of the sharpest minds leading the ed-tech revolution in India. Mayank is the co-founder and managing director of one of Asia's largest integrated learning skilling and workforce development majors—upGrad, which has enrolled over ten million learners worldwide. Mayank has spent most of his professional career in the education sector, where he has been involved in deals with over a billion dollars flowing into the sector. He has served as VP—Education at Bertelsmann, Europe's largest media and education conglomerate, where he oversaw the education strategy and its multi-million-dollar investments in India. Prior to joining Bertelsmann, Mayank was Senior Principal at The Parthenon Group, where he advised clients in the education sector on market potential, growth and market entry strategies, investment decisions, and revenue- and profit-uplift strategies. He participated in deals worth US$1 billion flowing into the education sector. He worked with global clients across all geographies, including China, South-East Asia, the Middle East, India, and South America. He has also worked at the Tata Strategic Group, advising Tata's strategic direction. His efforts were instrumental in making upGrad's India business model deliver high-impact results, which, in turn, has helped the brand rank 43rd under the FT Asia-Pacific High-Growth Companies 2021 List in partnership with Nikkei Asia and Statista. The brand has also been on the GSV Global EdTech 150 List in 2022.

Diana Laurillard is Professor of Learning with Digital Technology at the UCL Knowledge Lab. She leads innovative research in learning design and digital interventions for numeracy. With a past role spearheading e-learning strategy for the UK government and teaching technologies at The Open University, she now focuses on CPD massive open online courses (MOOCs) and developing digital tools for educators. Diana is a proponent of teaching as a design science, a concept central to her recent book and her work on the Learning Designer tool.

Parker Lemal-Brown (he/him) is a writer, producer, and strategy consultant. Parker was the first Head of Marketing for the social enterprise Sumbon and worked as a copywriter in Dakar, Senegal. He has worked in creative development and production for Netflix, Amazon, Universal, and Shondaland, as well as on the series Transparent, Bluff City Law, and Bridgerton. Parker recently wrote an episode for Grease: Rise of the Pink Ladies on Paramount Plus. He worked as a strategy consultant for Northwestern University, and he is a professional coach with individuals, universities, and companies on strategic marketing and brand development. Parker is currently pursuing a master's degree in communication science at the University of Amsterdam to further explore the power of data-driven and digital storytelling for global and social impact.

Katherine H. Mann is a researcher and Deputy Head of the Digital Transformation Cluster at Georgetown University. She specializes in digital development and its implications for governance, human development, and poverty.

Katherine Marshall is Senior Fellow at the Berkley Center for Religion, Peace, and World Affairs and Professor of the Practice of Development, Conflict, and Religion. She has nearly four decades of experience in global development. As the executive director of the World Faiths Development Dialogue and with a background at the World Bank, she is specialized in the intersection of religion and development, contributing to influential publications and serving on the boards of various NGOs.

Dr. Shailendra Raj Mehta has just completed a seven year term as President and Director and Distinguished Professor of Innovation and Entrepreneurship at MICA, in Ahmedabad, India. He is currently the O.P. Jindal Distinguished University Professor at O.P. Jindal Global University and Vice Chairman at the Indian Institute of Advanced Studies, Shimla. Earlier, he headed Auro University and Ahmedabad University. Before that, he had stints at Duke CE and the Indian Institute of Management Ahmedabad (joint appointment), and Purdue University, where he taught Economics and Strategic Management. He has done extensive research in Entrepreneurship, Industrial Organization, Information Economics, and Experimental Economics. His research has been the subject of a full-length review by the Economist. His work on creating world-class universities has been discussed around the world and profiled in multiple languages. He is rated as one of the top researchers in the field of strategy in India. His BA and MA are from Delhi University (St. Stephen's College and Delhi School of Economics respectively), his MPhil is from Balliol College, Oxford, and his Ph.D. is from Harvard.

Sandeep Menon is the managing director of Workato in India. He orchestrates the expansion of a prominent workflow automation and iPaaS platform, drawing on more than twenty-five years of experience in digital transformation and fintech. Adept at building and transforming businesses, he is actively involved as an advisor to ExchangeConnect, a board member of MICA, and the Hon. Secretary of the Wildlife Association of South India. Holding a Chevening Gurukul Fellowship and being an alum of MICA Business School, Sandeep is passionate about creating lasting institutions and sustainable growth.

Altaf Merchant is Gary E. and James A. Milgard Endowed Dean and Professor of Marketing at the University of Washington Tacoma's Milgard School of Business. With a focus on advertising, branding, and cross-cultural marketing, his research delves into nostalgia and brand heritage. He contributes as a senior research fellow and distinguished professor internationally, holds editorial positions in leading journals, and brings practical industry insights from his past roles in brand management at major multinationals.

Joshua A. Muskin, over the last forty-five years, has worked domestically and internationally with myriad institutions dedicated to creating better futures for children and families and communities. This journey has taken him from the classrooms of suburban Philadelphia to remote refugee settlements in Sudan and to many other locations in the Americas, Africa, Europe, and Asia. Focusing on education, Muskin has combined work with classroom teachers, local authorities, communities, and central system leaders to improve the quality of delivery and relevance of education outcomes, engaging with classroom instruction, learning assessment, gender equity and inclusion, technical and vocational training, literacy, and many other aspects. He has well supported economic development, gender equality, agriculture, WASH, refugee relief, and integrated community development, among others. Dr. Muskin majored in French literature at Dartmouth College and holds master's and Ph.D. degrees in development planning from the University of Pennsylvania.

K. V. Ramani received his Ph.D. in operations research from Cornell University, USA, 1977. He is Adjunct Professor at MICA after retiring from the Indian Institute of Management, Ahmedabad, where he worked from 1977 to 2018. One of his major contributions to IIM-Ahmedabad was the establishment of the Centre for Management of Health Services (CMHS) in 2003. As a visiting professor, Dr. Ramani has also taught in the management schools at Cornell University, USA (1999–2000); Florida International University, USA (1984–1986); the National University of Singapore (1991–1992 and 1995–1996); and Leeds University, (2003–2006). He has been a research scholar at the University of Texas, Austin, USA; the University of Western Sydney, Australia; Warwick University, UK; and the Helsinki School of Business Administration, Finland. He was the founding director of the Indian Institute of Public Health, Gandhinagar, Gujarat (2008).

John Redwood III is a distinguished World Bank Environment Specialist with a storied career spanning over twenty years. As an alumnus of Harvard University and UC Berkeley, where he graduated in social sciences and earned his master's and Ph.D. degrees in city and regional planning and economic development, John has contributed his expertise as a consultant to multiple multilateral development banks, focusing on sustainable development and environmental policy.

Rodrigo Martínez Romero was born in Mexico City in 1986. He is a co-founder of the Spiritual Politics Lab (SPlab), a start-up member of the Humanities Venture Lab at the University of Amsterdam. The SPLab is the research and innovation branch of the School of Conscious Politics (SCP) foundation, where he collaborates with trainers, artists, spiritual leaders, and researchers to test, innovate, and experiment with heart-driven political leadership education curriculums. The SCP provides learning spaces to support changemakers to resignify their relationship with politics and the political world, embark on learning journeys to actualize their spiritual and political potential, and unleash sacred activist projects to bring social healing to diverse local territories. What do we need politics to see and do from a space of love, hope, and evolution? As a lover of questions, Rodrigo aspires to keep growing as a spiritual-driven, social justice-minded, artistic entrepreneur. What is success? Currently expressing the art of being guided not by ego or market demands but by the wisdom of self to creatively restore balance and health to our social systems. Rodrigo holds a BA in international relations from El Colegio de Mexico and an MSc in leadership and change management from the Free University of Amsterdam.

Montserrat Koloffon Rosas, a Ph.D. student at Vrije Universiteit Amsterdam, investigates the effectiveness of international environmental regimes using complexity science. Focused on multi-stakeholder partnerships and Sustainable Development Goals, her research utilizes system dynamics simulation methods. With a background in political science, Montserrat has experience in climate strategy evaluation, consulting for local governments, and internships at institutions like the EU-LAC Foundation and the Mexican Embassy in Berlin.

Parth Salunke is presently a doctoral scholar at MICA, India, and his research interest lies at the intersection of consumer behavior, branding, and digital transformations in marketing. He is a visiting scholar at the University of Washington—Milgard School of Business, USA (2023). In the past, he has worked as BD, marketing executive, and market researcher for more than four years in his corporate career and loves consulting start-up business around his expertise in marketing. Research piqued his interest early in his career, and he has received the Research Excellence Award at MICA in 2022 and the Best Research Paper Award, five times, in International Research Conferences, the most recent prestigious American Marketing Association Winter Conference, the Best Paper Award—Runner Up in 2023, and the Best Methodology Paper Award in 2023 from the Marketing, Strategy and Policy Conference held in the United Kingdom. He also serves as an ad hoc reviewer for the *Journal of Consumer Behaviour*, USA (A Journal). He has received more than seventy accolades for his passion for public speaking and was awarded the Sarvajanik Vidya Sadak Award in 2018 and the Outstanding Aspirant Award in 2020 for his commendable performance in his educational career.

Ronnie Screwvala embarked on his entrepreneurial journey with Cable TV in India, later seizing an opportunity in toothbrush manufacturing, ultimately establishing one of India's largest operations. Despite setbacks and a failed foray into TV Home Shopping, he persisted, transforming UTV into a thriving media and entertainment giant before divesting it to The Walt Disney Co in 2012. Perception in most cases is larger than reality, and so in spite of so many failures, *Newsweek* termed him the Jack Warner of India, *Esquire* rated him one of the seventy-five most influential people of the twenty-first century, and *Fortune* as Asia's twenty-five most powerful and ranked seventy-eight among hundred most influential people in the world on Time 100. Having lived it and seen the misconception that it's all about quick success and that failure is to frown on, he authored a book *Dream With Your Eyes Open* as his commitment to champion entrepreneurship and evangelize failure. In his second book *Skill It, Kill It*, Ronnie has gone more candid and shared personal anecdotes and observations from his many failures and few successes to give readers an insider's view of the "invisible" skills, which can cut years off their learning curve. Ronnie in his second innings decided to deepen his commitment to making India a better place through a focus on two of the largest sunrise sectors—online education and the not-for-profit rural/social space. He is Co-Founder and Chairperson of upGrad which zeros in on the massive online education market and the fact that learning for every working professional is now a lifelong commitment. He and his wife Zarina are Co-Founders of The Swades Foundation, which is committed to empower one million lives in rural India every five to seven years through a 360-degree model spanning water, sanitation, health, education, and livelihood to lift them out of poverty permanently. Ronnie's passion lies in storytelling through movies with his brand RSVP. He also owns three sports teams under U Mumba in kabaddi, volleyball, and football, despite never having played any of the sports himself.

John S. Seberger is a Postdoctoral Research Associate within the College of Communication Arts and Sciences at Michigan State University. Collaborating closely with Dean Prabu David, he is part of an interdisciplinary team that bridges ComArtSci with the College of Engineering, contributing to the growing synergy between communication and technology.

Beheruz N. Sethna is President Emeritus and Regent's Professor at the University of West Georgia. He is an esteemed figure in the higher education sector. His tenure is marked by expertise in statistical data analysis, public speaking, leadership, marketing, and research. As a Columbia University alumnus, Sethna's distinguished career reflects a commitment to academic excellence and leadership in education.

Jagdish N. Sheth is Charles H. Kellstadt Professor of Business at Goizueta Business School, Emory University. He is globally known for his scholarly contributions in consumer behavior, relationship marketing, competitive strategy, and geopolitical analysis. He has over fifty years of experience in teaching and research at University of Southern California, University of Illinois at Urbana-Champaign, Columbia University, MIT, and Emory. Dr. Sheth is a recipient of the 2020 Padma Bhushan Award for literature and education, one of the highest civilian awards given by the Government of India. He is Fellow of the Academy of International Business (AIB), the Association of Consumer Research (ACR), the American Psychological Association (APA), and the American Marketing Association (AMA). He is Distinguished Fellow of the Academy of Marketing Science (AMS) and the International

Engineering Consortium. He is the recipient of all four top awards given by the American Marketing Association (AMA). Additionally, he received the Global Innovation Award and the Marion Creekmore Award, both from Emory University. Dr. Sheth has been an advisor to numerous corporations all over the world. He has authored or coauthored more than 350 papers and numerous books. He is Founder of Center for Telecommunications Management (CTM) at University of Southern California (USC), Founder and Chairman of India, China, and America (ICA) Institute, which analyzes the trilateral relationship and its impact on geopolitics, security, trade, and investment, and Founder and Chairman of the Academy of Indian Marketing (AIM) which supports research and scholarship among Indian scholars in marketing and management.

Preeti Shroff-Mehta is a senior global professional with over thirty years of global experience in international development management and higher education. She currently serves as the Professor and Director of Executive Education Programs at Medill School—Northwestern University, USA. Her global research and teaching focus on the circular economy, business sustainability, change management, women's leadership, and strategic communications. She has served as Dean of MICA—The School of Ideas in India, and SIT—World Learning in Washington, DC, and Vermont. She has a strong background in international development management with global institutions, including the World Bank, USAID, UN, and has taught graduate courses at SAIS—Johns Hopkins and the University of Maryland, USA.

Sukaran Thakur is Principal Partner at ICE Studios Consulting LLP and Director at the Heritage Group, based in Manali, Himachal Pradesh. At ICE Studios, Sukaran leads the strategy practice working with brands and organizations like Pfizer, USAID, Axis Bank, and HUL. Sukaran has previously worked as the Brand Head for Wills Lifestyle (WLS) at ITC and as Marketing Manager for the Luxury Portfolio at L'Oreal, managing the brands Lancôme, Kiehl's, Giorgio Armani, Ralph Lauren, Yves Saint Laurent, and Diesel. Sukaran was also a part of the Management Advisor Council at Deloitte India-US. He completed his bachelor's degree in applied computer science at Delhi University and followed that with a double master's degree in brand management from MICA, Ahmedabad, and in business law from NLS, Bangalore. Sukaran is also adjunct faculty in the Business Management and Communications Area at MICA; a visiting faculty at NIAM Jaipur, FLAME Pune, and Symbiosis Nagpur; and a guest faculty at Northwestern-Medill, along with being a subject-matter expert for upGrad and SpeakIn. As an academician, his areas of work and research are culture and communications, brand narratives, storytelling, semiotics, and artificial intelligence.

Tine Vekemans holds the Ācārya Mahāprajña Chair for Jain Studies which was established at Ghent University in 2022. Additionally, she is a senior postdoctoral research fellow funded by Ghent University's Special Research Fund (BOF). Over the past decade, Tine's research touched upon diverse aspects of modern and contemporary Jainism, including Jain migration history, changing lay-mendicant relations, Jainism in the digital age, and processes of knowledge transfer in the Jain diaspora. Broader recurring themes in her work include religious, cultural, and societal change, diversity and cosmopolitanism, the impact of migration as well as digital media on religion, culture, and learning. Her research approach often combines ethnography with textual study and/or media analysis, but always starts from practices and experiences of Jains. In addition to specialist courses on Jainism and research methodologies, she teaches introductory level courses on South Asian History and Current Affairs.

Vijay Viswanathan is Associate Dean and Professor at Northwestern University's Medill School, specializing in Integrated Marketing Communications. Transitioning from a seasoned marketer to academia, he brings a wealth of experience in market research, data analysis, and digital marketing strategies. With a strong educational foundation, including a Ph.D. in business from Emory University, he has conducted extensive research for various sectors such as financial services, retail, and media.

Arpan Yagnik is a Ph.D. graduate in media and communication from Bowling Green State University. He is a dedicated advocate for menstrual health, addressing inequality through scholarly work and practical initiatives. His impactful contributions include the "Keep It Flowing!" campaign, providing free menstrual hygiene products, and advancing research in health and development communication, with a growing interest in advertising and marketing, particularly in FMCG products within the Fem Care division.

Gad Yair is working in the Department of Sociology and Anthropology at the Hebrew University of Jerusalem, where he specializes in cultural sociology with a focus on higher education and science. His research spans across social theories and the social life of diverse cultures, including Israeli, German, American, and French.

FOREWORD

Global and Digital Governance Crossroads: Stakeholder-Driven Sustainable Democratization, or Digital Divide, Autocracy, and Inequality

The global and digital transformation has deeply impacted governance across public, corporate, and social sectors. Growing access to technology has enabled diverse stakeholders to enter and influence political, social, economic, education, health, and environmental governance. The millennial and Gen Z populations are becoming more vocal in the digital world to demand sustainable and inclusive governance. The circular economy and environmental, social, and governance (ESG) sustainability strategies and compliance are now a requirement for assessing public and private sector organizations' societal impact. On the other hand, the rise of authoritarianism is raising serious concerns regarding the use of digital platforms to control data and undermine individual privacy. Growing income inequality, exacerbated by the pandemic, is a matter of serious concern around the world. Are we now standing at the crossroads of digital and global governance, where there are opportunities for access and inclusion and, at the same time, global threats of inequality, autocratic control, and exclusion?

How do we choose the future path for digital and global governance, especially in the post Covid-19 world, after the virus exposed the social, economic, education, health, and environmental risks and vulnerabilities prominent among the world's population? That is the central question posed by this handbook. The renewal of the "social contract" between the state and society for governance reform and digital transformations for citizens is an urgent need. Governance centralization will be challenged by multiple stakeholders' demands for inclusion, and for representation of millions of people living in the periphery.

As the CEO of the Open Government Partnership, I lead a partnership of seventy-five countries, a growing number of local governments, and thousands of civil society organizations working together to transform governance by enhancing transparency, participation, inclusion, and accountability, so governments better serve their citizens.

I am delighted to acknowledge this timely and critical handbook, which addresses important issues pertaining to global and digital governance. This is a unique post Covid-19 global primer that brings together cross-sector and cross-country experiences by addressing global and digital governance transformations across six governance sectors and themes: international, corporate, education, community sustainability and health, digital-culture-creativity, and faith-based governance.

At the heart of this handbook is a central question: How do we build trust and engage with multiple stakeholders while standing at the unsteady crossroads of global governance in the data-driven and digitally enabled world? On the one hand, digital platforms and tools have encouraged inclusion and direct representation of marginalized voices and multiple stakeholders in global economy and governance. On the other hand, misinformation campaigns and autocratic forces are creating a divided world of fear, control, and violence by invading stakeholder and user privacy and security. Digital freedom and access include and exclude multiple stakeholder groups at the same time.

The array of chapters across the six thematic parts combine to underline that, in the digital and global era, the social contract between government and citizens needs renewal to ensure multi-stakeholder engagement for achieving democratic ideals such as fairness, equity, and justice. Some highlights are given below, as summarized by the authors:

1. Many international institutions are building digital capacity to be responsive to decentralization and democratization. Sustainability, diversity, and inclusion are the driving forces in a digitally enabled world. However, trust in governments is at the lowest point in history, and that demands accountability and responsiveness for multi-stakeholder engagement in global–local governance.
2. Corporate governance is transforming rapidly as a result of technology and data-driven platforms, consumers, products, and markets. The pressure is on to adopt digital transformation, nonhierarchical structures, and cross-functional sustainability innovations. Grief management is a top priority for global-to-local employee support. Co-governance with employees and consumers is the evolving brand of corporate governance.
3. Education institutions are transforming in the post Covid-19 digital era to evolve as hybrid learning platforms for lifelong education and skill building. The role of emerging ed-tech platforms is also critical in ensuring universal and on-the-job learning for all employees and workers. How we ensure academic freedom and creativity in education design, policy, structures, and governance in the digital era is the key challenge, as well as the key opportunity, to reforming education to better suit our changing world.
4. Digital and creative communications are powerful and require strategic approaches, especially across multimedia platforms. Media literacy, data, and information management together present an important strategy for risk management in the digital economy era for both countries and institutions. But they require better leadership structures to build trust and ensure accountability across public, private, and social sector institutions in the era of artificial intelligence (AI) and the metaverse. Such a strategy necessitates the evolution of creative management approaches to build trust and more inclusive governance. Value-driven ethical governance conversations and education will be critical for future global and digital governance.
5. The Covid-19 pandemic exposed severe gaps and weaknesses in global health systems. Ongoing environmental disasters are a reminder of the evolving global risks for climate and agriculture, economy and livelihoods, and societal sustainability. How do we develop sustainable governance ethics, policies, and practices in the era of human and AI

intersections in our daily lives? It is imperative to integrate UN sustainability goals and ESG standards in business management, investor relations, and customer engagement.

6. The digital world has deeply impacted faith-based governance around the world. Spiritual and religious communities around the world are now connecting using digital platforms and tools. At the same time, the separation of state and religion is getting blurred, as autocratic governments mobilize constituencies based on religious identities and harness the power of the internet to weaken democratic standards. An examination of faith-based and multi-faith governance is critical for democratization and inclusion.

The four co-editors of this handbook—Preeti Shroff-Mehta, Jagdish N. Sheth, John Garrison, and Shailendra Raj Mehta—combine many years of global to grassroots governance and management experience, and they have done a remarkable job in compiling expert author contributions and voices from around the world to address the opportunities and challenges in global and digital governance. This has resulted in a particularly rich handbook and important contribution to the field.

Sanjay Pradhan

PREFACE AND ACKNOWLEDGMENTS

This handbook is a collaborative and compassionate project focused on analyzing the global contexts of digital, public, private, and societal governance. It captures challenges as well as opportunities at the intersection of human and digital governance for institutional transformations and resilience. We extend our deepest gratitude to the numerous institutions, staff, editors, and expert authors from around the globe who have tirelessly contributed to bringing this project to fruition.

The idea of this handbook originated at MICA—The School of Ideas in Ahmedabad, India. MICA has sponsored and supported all phases of conceptualization and development. The editorial team would like to acknowledge support, guidance, and resources provided by MICA President and Director Shailendra Raj Mehta, MICA Governing Council, and MICA staff/faculty/student community for ongoing knowledge sharing and administrative support. We were also fortunate to have the wise and able presence of the dynamic co-editorial team members—Preeti Shroff-Mehta (Northwestern University), Jagdish N. Sheth (Emory University), John Garrison (World Bank), and Shailendra Raj Mehta (MICA—The School of Ideas)—who made this book's research journey meaningful and exciting. Every co-editor brought unique insights, experiences, and perspectives on stakeholder-driven global and digital governance. We are all grateful for the learning and insights derived while working as the group of co-editors and are deeply indebted to our family members for their unconditional support and understanding. The ongoing demands and coordination required, especially during the Covid and Post-Covid era, to complete this project were significant.

We all have learned and evolved along with the handbook development, which coincided with painful realities and constraints of the Covid-19 pandemic, including the loss of colleagues and extended family members. This book's research and coordination experience underscored the importance of self-governance during very difficult pandemic years. We extend our special acknowledgment to all authors and the publisher team for their consistent support and patience as we navigated six thematic parts and thirty-four chapter contributions for this timely and important handbook. We are indebted to Ms. Shoma Choudhary and her team from Routledge publishers, who gave us timely guidance for the development and completion of this handbook. We thank and wish the best for all book proposal and chapter reviewers from around the world.

This publication would not have been possible without the diligence and consistent support of our expert editor Marcelo Agudo. He has worked tirelessly despite his hectic schedule to be responsive to all editors and chapter authors across industry, government, and academic sectors. We thank him for his knowledge, insights, and suggestions to edit the entire handbook and make all chapters relevant and accessible for all readers. We were also fortunate to have Parker Lemal-Brown, an experienced editor and screenplay writer who coordinated research for multiple chapters, chapter structures and organization, and editing in the early stages of this project. We are honored to have received the foreword written by Sanjay Pradhan. We are also honored to have received the foreword written by Sanjay Pradhan, a highly respected scholar and practitioner in global governance and international development. We will continue to learn from his valuable work on global and local governance reforms.

This handbook's research and support staff team from MICA's President/Director and Dean's offices, who provided invaluable research and coordination support throughout this project include Rushvi Bhow, Sukruti Phatak, Devika Menon, Suhair Killiyath, and Pooja Sharma. We wish them all well in their ongoing academic and professional journeys. Jagdish N. Sheth would specifically like to thank Conor Harty for his extraordinary editorial support and Ángel Harris for her outstanding administrative support. John Garrison would like to acknowledge and thank the colleagues from the World Bank who contributed the foreword and compelling and interesting chapters on a wide range of topics on global governance. These chapters embody many years of experience, challenges, and lessons learned working in the leading institution on international development.

All chapters in this book have taught us a great deal about the complexities of human, institutional, and societal governance in an era, where conflicts and wars persist around the world. We all must work together to strengthen inclusive, collaborative, peaceful, and democratic governance to build human, communal, institutional, and societal capabilities. Change management requires that we govern with compassion to create a better world and opportunities for all. We sincerely hope that each chapter in this handbook will help readers understand and learn different dimensions of governance from self to societal across various sectors.

This handbook will be helpful for educators in their ongoing research and teaching on global and digital governance reform and change management. Industry and international leaders will be able to understand and apply global perspectives on digital, data, and human governance for shaping New Age organizations. Policy-makers will be able to derive insights on how different sectors and stakeholders are engaged in governance and need to be represented for strengthening institutional and societal governance reforms. All learners of global, digital, and democratic governance will enjoy diverse perspectives and inputs across all chapters and learn from outstanding contributions from expert authors from around the world.

Preeti Shroff-Mehta, Jagdish N. Sheth,
John Garrison, and Shailendra Raj-Mehta

INTRODUCTION

Shailendra Raj Mehta

Institutions are complex entities that are an integral part of society and shape its evolution. Their complexities come from both the explicit and implicit rules of engagement, and the number and diversity of stakeholders they need to address. Governance of institutions forms an integral part of their functioning and their design. Usually, scholarly literature focuses only on particular kinds of institutions in a narrowly defined domain or sector. Unusually, this book focuses on institutions across various domains encompassing the entire length and breadth of societies. This book includes corporate, educational, digital, health and environmental, community, faith-based, and multilateral institutions. Its uniqueness lies in the fact that it addresses governance issues across such a wide variety of domains. Therefore, we need a definition of governance that is general enough to encompass all of them.

So here is our definition—governance is the process by which an organization is accountable to all its internal and external stakeholders and through which it addresses, communicates, and harmonizes their needs and concerns. Multiple facets are embedded in this definition. First of all, every organization must explicitly be aware of all the stakeholders that it addresses. Second, it must identify their concerns. Third, it must determine the contradictions in the concerns of various stakeholders. Fourth, it must harmonize these concerns. Fifth, it must determine the degree to which these expectations have been fulfilled. And finally, it must communicate to the stakeholders that their concerns have been addressed.

Naturally different kinds of institutions face different kinds of challenges, determined, among other things, by their type, size, and context. Similar kinds of institutions face similar kinds of challenges, and much can be learned by analyzing the governance patterns of different classes of institutions. However, different types of institutions often address the same stakeholders. Seeing how different institutions address the same stakeholder can be pretty revealing. A proper study of such interactions provides immense scope for cross-fertilization. This is what our book is all about, and this is what makes it unique.

The editors focused the book on institutions' digital transformations to unite a book with such a broad scope. Unprecedented technological advancements have characterized the present era, resulting in the proliferation of digital platforms, exponential growth in computing power, an explosion of big data, the widespread use of artificial intelligence, and

DOI: 10.4324/9781003316077-1

Corporations	Individuals	Government	Civil Society Organizations	Tech Platforms	Media	Regulators	Educational Institutions	Minorities	Teachers	Students	Religious Groups	Professional Bodies	Multilateral Organizations	Influencers
x	x	x											x	
x			x										x	
x		x	x											
	x	x	x	x										
		x	x										x	
x	x				x	x								
x								x						
x	x					x								
x	x													
x	x					x								
x	x			x		x								
		x					x		x	x				
x						x	x			x				
							x		x	x				
							x	x	x	x				
						x	x	x	x					
		x					x				x			
		x					x						x	

Figure 0.1 Stakeholder Matrix
Source: Created by Shailendra Raj Mehta.

		Theoretical and Conceptual Frameworks
1	**International Governance Collaborations**	
1.1.	"Promoting Good Governance in a Digital Era: The Case for Deliberative Democratic Evaluation" - Amy Catherine Jersild & Michael A Harnar	Social Contract for Good Governance: Multi-Staekholderism Reflecting UN- SDGs
1.2.	"FROM THE STREETS TO THE BOARDROOM: The Growing Presence of Civil Society in Global Governance" - John Garrison	Civil Society Staekholder Engagement
1.3.	"How Social Movements are Harnessing Technology to Decentralize Governance" - Bart Édes	Digital Era Social Movements, "Hectivism"
1.4.	"Can Digital Innovations be a Gamechanger for Enhanced Openness, Accountability and Responsiveness of International Development?" - Bjorn-Soren Gigler	Open Development Appraoch, Citizen feedback
1.5.	"Global Environmental And Climate Change Governance" - John Redwood	Climate Change and Global Governance
2	**Corporate Governance**	
2.1.	"The Future of Corporate Governance in the Digital Age" - Jagdish N. Sheth	Self-Regulated Digital Age Governance
2.2.	"Corporate Board Governance in a Digital World" - Vijay Viswanathan	Digital Era Corporate Board Governance - Agency and Stewardship Theories
2.3.	"Digital Brand Governance" - Sukaran Thakur	Digital Brand Governance
2.4.	`"GRIEF – THE EMOTION HR MUST ADDRESS" - Abhijit Bhaduri	Grief Governance
2.5.	"A CONCEPTUAL FRAMEWORK OF BRAND CO-GOVERNANCE IN THE DIGITAL AGE" - Altaf Merchant, Varsha Jain, Parth Salunke	Brand Co-Governance in the Digtial Era
2.6.	"Digital Marketing Development & Governance – China Model" - Yan Han	Government Policy Framework for Private Sector Digtial Transformation
3	**Education Governance Reform**	
3.1.	"The Role Of Governance In Opening Up Digital Innovation In Teaching And Learning" (working title) - Diana Laurillard	Conversational Learning in the Digital World, Knowledge Eco-Systems
3.2.	"Education Governance in the Digital Era: User- Centric Program Strategy and Innovations" - Ronnie Screwvala, Mayanak Kumar, Phalgun Kompali	Skills Economy, E-Learning for Higher Productivity, Life-Long Learning in the Digital Era
3.3.	"Governing for Self-Governance in Education" (working title) - Joshua Muskin	Heterogenous Education Governance - Creative and Collaborative Education Adminstration, Teach on Roads and Not Rails
3.4.	"Digital Governance - A Flexible Online Learning Model" - Shailendra Raj Mehta, Preeti Shroff-Mehta, Ashutosh Dutt	Traditional to Flexible On-Line Leaarning Model, Peer- Driven Staekholder Creativity and Collaboration
3.5.	"University Governance in an Uncertain Age: The Changes . . . and the Unchanging" - Beheruz N. Sethna	Hippocratic Oath Driven University Governance - Do No Harm
3.6.	"Political Culture and Educational Governance: Covid-19 and the Limits of Decentralization in Israeli Education" - Gad Yair	Education Quality Governance: Centralisation and Decentralisation
3.7.	"Governing Global Higher Education and Science – IONAs and ever-renewing webs of interconnection" - Ellen Hazelkorn, Andrew Gibson	Governing International Networks in Education: The Functional Institutional Approach and The Conflict Theory Approach

Theoretical and Conceptual Frameworks

Source: Created by Preeti Shroff-Mehta.

	Corporations	Individuals	Government	Civil Society Organizations	Tech Platforms	Media	Regulators	Educational Institutions	Minorities	Teachers	Students	Religious Groups	Professional Bodies	Multilateral Organizations	Influencers
						x									
	x	x	x		x										
	x														
	x	x													
	x	x	x												
	x	x	x												
	x	x	x	x			x								
	x												x		
	x	x					x								
	x	x	x												
			x										x	x	
												x		x	
		x			x							x			x
		x										x			
		x			x							x			x
		x										x			
	19	18	13	5	5	2	8	7	3	4	4	6	2	6	2

Figure 0.1 (Continued)

		Theoretical and Conceptual Frameworks
4	**Digital, Culture and Creativity Governance**	
4.1.	"Media And Information Literacy For Post Covid-19 Governance: Promoting Peace And Intercultural Dialogue Through Language And Communication" - Drissia Chouit	Language, Communication and Information Literacy for Peace Building, Communication Awareness Levels
4.2.	"Trust In AI And A Multilevel Governance Approach" - Prabu David, Hysen Choung, John S. Seberber	Trust and Virtue Ethics for AI Governance
4.3.	"4P4R MODEL OF CREATIVITY GOVERNANCE" - Arpan Yagnik, Rodrigo Martínez Romero, Montserrat Koloffon Rosas	4P4R Model for Creative and User Ready Governance
4.4.	"Peer Driven Governance in the Digital Era" - Sandeep Menon, Preeti Shroff-Mehta	Peer Driven Open Governance in the Digital World
4.5.	"The Case For Data As A New Common Good – The Example Of Water" - Jaya Deshmukh, Alessandro Galtieri	Data Governance for Common Global Good
4.6.	"Leadership and Governance in a Digital Economy" - Prabhu David, Preeti Shroff-Mehta, Sanjay Gupta	Being to Becoming - Values Driven Leadership
5	**Health and Environmental Sustainability Governance**	
5.1.	"Sustainable Futures: Developing A Governance Framework For Transition In The Fashion Industry And Beyond" - Sarah Angold	Fit for Purpose Sustainable International Governance
5.2.	"Global Governance Futures: Digital Transformation And Democratic Reform" - Aimee Girdwood, Christina Bartholomew	Legal Dimensions of ESG for Transformational Governance
5.3.	"ESG Maturity Mapping: Sustainability in Legacy to Start-Up Organisations" - Preeti Shroff-Mehta, Prof. Vijay Viswanathan	Profit to Purpose in Start-up to Legacy Companies: ESG-I for Self-Awareness and Sustainability Leadership
5.4.	"Health Systems Governance" - KV Ramani	Crisis Contexts of Health Governance: Governance Triangle of Government, Service Providers, and Beneficiaries
5.5.	"Climate Change, Health, and Governance—The Ultimate Challenge" - Henry Falk	Multi-Sector Climate Change and Health Governance Framework
6	**Community and Faith-based Governance**	
6.1.	"Digital Transformation And Democratic Reforms- Religions At Tables: Contributing To Global Governance" - Katherine Marshall	Inter-Faith Governance for Peace and Sustainability
6.2.	"Googling Religious Guidance- Digitally Renegotiated Lay-Ascetic Relations In Contemporary Jainism" - Tine Vekemans	Borderless Religion, Priest and People: Faith in the Digital and Social Media Era (Jain Faith)
6.3.	"5-Dimensional Matrix Of Faith-Based Governance" - Arpan Yagnik	Five Dimensions of Faith Based Governance for Self-Consciousness and Harmony
6.4.	"Torah Transmission In A Digital Age" - Barak (Bart) Cohen	Religious Digital Cretives (Jewish Faith)
6.5.	Islam and Global Governance - Nadereh Chamlou	Islamic Faith, Finance and Gender Equality
	34 papers, 15 types of stakeholders that they address, and key concepts/frameworks in each chapter	

high-speed connectivity. These factors have profoundly impacted every institution, leaving none untouched. Covid-19 added another layer of complexity to the mix. We need new structures and concepts to navigate this new and transformed landscape. Additionally, the increasing interconnectedness brought about by globalization calls for a fresh approach.

The chapters included in this volume address concerns related to sovereignty, ethics, security, equity, fairness, inclusivity, and transparency. They delve into these issues and aim to provide concepts and case studies that can stimulate a new kind of conversation across different domains. This interdisciplinary dialogue will foster the cross-fertilization of ideas and facilitate the development of standard solutions.

We hope that a diverse range of readers, including corporate executives, civil society organizations, multilateral organizations, citizen groups, regulatory and government agencies, policy-makers, and academics, will find this book engaging and informative.

The overall picture is as follows. A total of thirty-four separate chapters address fifteen distinct stakeholders. When we combine all the stakeholders that are addressed in this book, we come up with the following list: multilateral organizations, corporations, individuals (as citizens and consumers), governments, civil society organizations, media, regulators, educational institutions, minority groups, teachers, students, religious groups, professional bodies, and influencers. Every stakeholder is addressed in multiple chapters.

As a result, as one look at the figure would indicate, there is diversity both within a class of institutions and across classes of institutions. This book studies them both. It is instructive to see the numbers. Corporations as a stakeholder are addressed by nineteen of the chapters in the present volume, individuals as consumers or citizens are addressed in eighteen of those chapters, and the government is addressed in thirteen of the chapters. Tech platforms, civil society organizations, regulators, educational institutions, minorities, teachers, students, religious bodies, and multilateral organizations are addressed by three to eight chapters each. The list tapers off with the media, professional bodies, and influencers, which are addressed by two chapters each.

As a result, researchers as well as practitioners will find much that is thought-provoking when they analyze how a particular stakeholder is handled in a variety of related or unrelated contexts. The editors would like to believe that an examination of this 34 × 15 matrix will provide enough food for thought and could contribute to both better research and better practice. If this is indeed the case, then our efforts would have been successful.

Each section editor for each of the six parts has provided their own summary, which encapsulates a unique perspective about that part. Readers are strongly urged to read these part summaries before dipping into the individual chapters. We provide another set of summaries in this introduction section to provide the overview, and it is on the basis of this overall view that the 34 × 15 matrix has been created. Therefore, readers of this book may also profit by going through this overall summary that ties together the various chapters and parts.

Part 1 Covers International Governance Collaborations

In "Promoting Good Governance in a Digital Era: The Case for Deliberative Democratic Evaluation," Amy Catherine Jersild and Michael A. Harnar present deliberative democratic evaluation as a framework for promoting good governance. They base this approach on the principles of inclusion, dialogue, and deliberation. By examining motivation, control, knowledge, and legitimacy of the participants, they formulate a 3 × 4 matrix. Their application of this approach to the fast fashion industry, accompanied by a comprehensive discussion, offers deep insights. Stakeholders include multilateral organizations, corporations, consumers, and government.

"From the Streets to the Boardroom: The Growing Presence of Civil Society in Global Governance," by John Garrison, begins with defining civil society organizations (CSOs). CSOs encompass voluntary and community organizations that exist in a space separate from governments and corporations, yet larger than both. The author contends that CSOs' involvement is essential for effective global governance, asserting that optimal decision-making can only be achieved through collaboration between civil society, government, and the corporate sector. Using his involvement in a similar collaborative effort at the World Bank as an example, Garrison provides valuable lessons in overcoming the inevitable misunderstandings that arise in such settings. Stakeholders include multilateral organizations, CSOs, and corporations.

In "How Social Movements Are Harnessing Technology to Decentralize Governance," Bart W. Édes discusses how the Covid-19 pandemic has fostered the re-evaluation of various established assumptions. He highlights the dual aspects of this period: the substantial challenges to be tackled, and the wealth of opportunities presented by emerging technologies. Notably, he points out how young people are harnessing social media and similar technologies to engage in social movements, illustrating both the potential and the difficulties of this new form of engagement. Stakeholders include CSOs, governments, and corporations.

Björn-Sören Gigler and Katherine H. Mann's chapter, "Can Digital Innovations Be a Game Changer for Enhanced Openness, Accountability, and Responsiveness in International Development?" explores how technology can facilitate openness. They characterize openness as involving data accessibility, human-centric design, decentralization, digital technology usage, multi-stakeholder coalitions, and real-time citizen feedback. This openness can subsequently foster collaborative governance, and they provide numerous examples to substantiate their points. Stakeholders include Government, Platforms, and Individual Citizens.

In "Global Environmental and Climate Change Governance," John Redwood addresses one of our era's most crucial challenges—climate change. He provides a historical overview of key events from the UN Conference on Human Environment in June 1972 in Stockholm, the Montréal Protocol on Ozone in 1987, Rio Earth Summit in June 1992, COP 17 in Durban, South Africa in December 2011, to the Paris Climate Agreement of December 2015. His candid appraisal illuminates both the successes and shortcomings of governance in this context. Stakeholders include Governments and Multilateral Organizations.

Part 2 Focuses on Corporate Governance

In "The Future of Corporate Governance in the Digital Age," Jagdish N. Sheth chronicles the evolution from Industry 1.0 (the Industrial Revolution) through Industry 4.0 (the Knowledge Age). He argues that the current structures must transition from hierarchical governance to distributed governance. He also mentions how technology drastically restructures work and employment relationships, predicting that by 2028, freelancers and contract workers might comprise half of the U.S. workforce. Such a shift presents a governance challenge. Drawing from the agricultural sector, which traditionally has had an amorphous labor force and is prone to mismanagement, he predicts significant issues if most workers become akin to agricultural laborers. He briefly outlines the necessary responses from the media, regulators, and corporations. Stakeholders include corporations individuals/employees, regulators, and media.

Another chapter by Vijay Viswanathan examines the history of corporate governance, emphasizing issues relevant in the digital era, with a particular focus on the role of gender and minorities in the boardroom. Stakeholders include corporations and minorities.

In his chapter, Sukaran Thakur discusses how corporations, like humans, now have digital identities. This evolution allows consumers to interact directly with brands, and brands to respond. However, this also increases the potential for misunderstanding. Thakur argues that while individuals can manage their personal brands, corporate digital strategy should be formulated and implemented at the corporate level with robust risk management systems. He suggests tying a portion of employee salaries to digital initiative progress and criticizes regulators for lagging behind the evolving ecosystem. Stakeholders include corporations, employees, and regulators.

Abhijit Bhaduri, in his chapter "Grief—The Emotion HR Must Address," highlights the necessity of incorporating grief governance into HR practices, especially in the wake of widespread losses caused by the Covid-19 pandemic. He debunks several myths about grief, including the notion that grief is solely personal, time heals everything, tears are a sign of weakness, and emotions have no place in the workplace. Stakeholders include corporations and employees.

In their chapter on "A Conceptual Framework of Brand Co-Governance in the Digital Age," Altaf Merchant, Varsha Jain, and Parth Salunke concentrate on brand creation and engagement. They analyze three forms of digital interactions: between brands, between users, and between brands and users. They suggest moderators focus on curbing impulsive behaviors, developing efficient information filtering strategies, and finding effective ways to collaborate with regulators to create compelling brand experiences in the digital realm. Stakeholders include corporations, employees and regulators.

Yan Han, in "Digital Marketing Development and Governance: The China Model," examines the rapidly growing Chinese economy, which has been at the forefront of digital marketing innovation. Han highlights the unique features of the Chinese Digital Marketing Model, particularly the interconnectedness of physical and virtual infrastructures. Han reveals some startling statistics, including the fact that 99.6 percent of Internet users in China access the Internet on their mobile phones. The study emphasizes interactions with platforms. Stakeholders include corporations, consumers, regulators, and platforms.

Part 3 Focuses on Education Governance Reform

In her chapter, "The Role of Governance in Opening Up Digital Innovation in Teaching and Learning," Diana Laurillard explores the potential of combining online and on-ground learning to enhance educational outcomes. She introduces the "Conversational Framework," which emphasizes interaction between the teacher's and student's concepts and actions. The implementation of this framework, along with robust governance, can significantly improve the system's efficiency and responsiveness, address global educational inequities, and facilitate the United Nations' Sustainable Development Goals (SDGs). Stakeholders include students, teachers, government, and universities.

In "Education Governance in the Digital Era: User-Centric Program Strategy and Innovations," the co-founders of upGrad, Ronnie Screwvala, Mayank Kumar, and Phalgun Kompalli, discuss their business model and technology. They detail their approach to lifelong learning, emphasizing inclusivity, personalization, industry-relevant curriculum, and mentoring. Their methods have made upGrad, one of the world's most valuable ed-tech companies. Stakeholders include corporations, mature students, and regulators.

Joshua A. Muskin's "Governing for Self-Governance in Education" introduces an integrated framework for education governance. Combining top-down and bottom-up approaches, his model balances broad goal setting, resource allocation, and quality definition from above with locally responsive pedagogical choices and inclusive measures. Stakeholders include teachers, educational institutions, and students.

Shailendra Raj Mehta, Preeti Shroff-Mehta, and Ashutosh Dutt, in "Digital Governance—A Flexible Online Learning Model," describe how they innovated their pedagogical approach in response to Covid-19. The authors introduce a 30/45/36/6 model that caters to online learners' unique needs and present evidence that students and faculty welcomed this framework. Stakeholders include students, faculty, and colleges.

In "University Governance in an Uncertain Age: The Changes . . . and the Unchanging," Beheruz N. Sethna shares insights from his lifelong experience in education, arguing for the autonomy of institutions and emphasizing the value of the U.S. accreditation model. Stakeholders include faculty, universities, and regulators.

Gad Yair's chapter, "Political Culture and Educational Governance: Covid-19 and the Limits of Decentralization in Israeli Education," discusses the segmented Israeli school system and the repercussions of its historical evolution. Yair reveals the surprising shortcomings within two major segments of the Israeli educational system, tracing their roots to decentralization efforts. Stakeholders include schools, religious bodies, and government.

Finally, "Governing Global Higher Education and Science: IONAs and Ever-Renewing Webs of Interconnection" by Ellen Hazelkorn and Andrew Gibson discusses international organizations, networks, and associations (IONAs). The authors argue for a nuanced understanding of the historical evolution of these global institutions, which significantly influence modern education. Stakeholders include multilateral organizations, governments, and universities.

Part 4 Focuses on Digital, Cultural, and Creativity Governance

In "Media and Information Literacy for Post Covid-19 Governance: Promoting Peace and Intercultural Dialogue Through Language and Communication," Drissia Chouit delves into the importance of communication. She emphasizes that mastering communication involves not only critical thinking but also emotional intelligence. Chouit further analyzes how politicians and interest groups utilize and manipulate language to further their agenda, which holds significant implications for media management. Stakeholders include the media.

In their chapter "A Multilevel Framework for AI Governance," Hyesun Choung, Prabu David, and John S. Seberger delve into a specific aspect of technology governance—artificial intelligence (AI). They highlight the necessity of building trust in AI systems and underscore that technology is deemed trustworthy when it is functional, reliable, and helpful. For potentially destructive technology like AI, principles of benevolence, transparency, fairness, and human oversight must be ingrained. Stakeholders include individuals, corporations, governments, and technology platforms.

In "4P4R Model of Creativity Governance," Arpan Yagnik, Rodrigo Martínez Romero, and Montserrat Koloffon Rosas introduce the 4P4R model of governance. They suggest that this model, which combines ancient wisdom traditions with modern knowledge, is exemplified by current female heads of state. Stakeholders include corporations.

Sandeep Menon in his chapter "Peer Driven Governance in the Digital Era," explore traditional and digital governance differences in terms of data and information access, user control, and community building. The open-source data model and digital democratization have turned the entire governance institution-centered regulatory regime on its head, enabling a community-led development process by which a strong peer group can access and manage data and information for multiple users and stakeholders. This chapter provides an early insight into how various digital world governance models could be implemented through peer-to-peer review and social agreements backed up by technology and automation as opposed to traditional, institution-led enforcement models. Stakeholders include corporations, user groups, and individuals.

In "The Case for Data as a New Common Good: The Example of Water," Jaya Deshmukh and Alessandro Galtieri discuss data governance. They advocate viewing data as a renewable resource, akin to water, as opposed to the traditional analogy of data being compared to oil. By adopting the middle ground between extreme individualistic and communitarian views, they cite examples from several countries to demonstrate successful models of data governance. Stakeholders include corporations, individuals, and government.

In "Leadership and Governance in a Digital Economy," Prabu David, Preeti Shroff-Mehta, and Sanjay Gupta tackle multiple themes, including the creation of value by stakeholders, power relationships, public sentiments, and environmental and social governance. Their primary focus, however, lies in exploring the role of values in leadership and governance. They draw from the teachings of Aristotle, Buddha, and Confucius to elucidate the importance of character, compassion, courage, justice, honesty, and temperance. Stakeholders include corporations, individuals, and government.

Part 5 Delves into Health and Environmental Sustainability Governance

In the intriguing chapter "Sustainable Futures: Developing a Governance Framework for Transition in the Fashion Industry and Beyond," Sarah Angold scrutinizes the practices of the fast fashion industry in the United Kingdom. Fast fashion involves the rapid production and discarding of clothing, not due to wear and tear but rather due to changing trends. The United Kingdom discarded roughly one million tons of clothing in 2017 alone. Globally, the fashion sector produced 2.1 billion metric tons of greenhouse gasses, approximating the combined emissions of the United Kingdom, France, and Germany. To address this issue, consumers, manufacturers, regulators, and the government must work together to minimize waste and recycle materials, supporting a circular economy. Key challenges include formulating common definitions and standards, aligning governance norms for corporate accountability, and securing government funding and political will. Case studies include the analysis of the Textiles 2030 program by waste charity WRAP, the Green Claims Code by the UK Government, and the 2019 Fixing Fashion report of the UK Parliament. Stakeholders include civil society organizations, government, regulators, individuals/consumers, and corporations.

Aimée Girdwood and Christina Bartholomew's chapter, "Promoting Long-Term Healthy and Sustainable Businesses Through Responsible and Proactive Legal Practice," explores the legal profession's role in implementing environmental and social governance (ESG). They present three maturity levels of ESG: compliance, proactive avoidance of negative

ESG impacts, and optimal responsibility, where firms become part of the solution to global challenges. Stakeholders include professional bodies and corporations.

Preeti Shroff-Mehta, Sukaran Thakur, Vijay Viswanathan, and Parker Lemal-Brown's chapter, "ESG Maturity Mapping: Sustainability in Legacy, New Age, and Start-Up Organizations," examines ESG approaches among start-ups and established corporations. They note that if start-ups consider ESG governance early, it can profoundly shape their future evolution. Stakeholders include corporations, individuals/customers, and regulators.

K. V. Ramani, in his chapter "Health System Governance," discusses the impact of the Alma Ata Declaration of 1978—"Health for All" on the governance of health systems. He argues that health governance should be intertwined with broader socioeconomic governance. He specifically discusses fairness in health-care financing and surveys the global differences in health expenditures and the private sector's role. Stakeholders include government, corporations, and individuals/citizens.

Henry Falk's chapter, "Climate Change, Health, and Governance: The Ultimate Challenge," explores the health implications of climate change and the need for effective climate change governance. Policy-makers must acknowledge that simply presenting scientific findings is not enough to facilitate change and must address the complexities of this issue. This chapter highlights case studies from the United States, among others, concluding with actions individuals and communities can take. Stakeholders include governments, multilateral agencies, and professional and scientific bodies.

Part 6 Delves into Community and Faith-Based Governance

"Digital Transformation and Democratic Reforms—Religions at Tables: Contributing to Global Governance," by Katherine Marshall, discusses the minimal presence of religious establishments in global deliberative bodies, despite 84 percent of the world's population being religiously affiliated. Having worked with the World Bank on such interactions, Marshall's chapter provides unique insights into this subject. Incorporating religious establishments into global governance could greatly contribute to peace among nations. Stakeholders include religious groups and multilateral organizations.

In "Googling Religious Guidance: Digitally Renegotiated Lay–Ascetic Relations in Contemporary Jainism," Tine Vekemans studies the impact of the internet on the governance of Jainism, one of the world's oldest religions with a small follower base. Vekemans sheds light on how digitalization has transformed the way Jains, particularly monks and nuns, interact with their laity. Online platforms, YouTube channels, and digital intermediaries have revolutionized the connection between the Jain community worldwide. Stakeholders include religious organizations, digital platforms, individuals, and influencers.

Arpan Yagnik's "Five-Dimensional Matrix of Faith-Based Governance" presents the dimensions of (1) ignorance versus arrogance, (2) apathy versus sympathy, (3) other-centered versus self-centered, (4) human versus planet-centered, and (5) alternate reality versus actual reality. He suggests that faith-based governance must strive to strike a balance within these dimensions. Stakeholders include religious groups and individuals/the public.

Barak Cohen's "Torah Transmission in a Digital Age" examines the digitalization of the Hebrew Bible or Torah. In-person interactions are no longer a necessity for studying the Torah, thanks to the rise of digital platforms and religious digital creatives. Cohen analyzes platforms like Sefaria, Torah Anytime, My Jewish Learning, and Chabad, which have grown in popularity and influence. Stakeholders include digital platforms, individuals, influencers and religious groups.

In the insightful study "Islam and Global Governance," Nadereh Chamlou discusses the influence of Quranic principles and Prophet Mohammed's life on Islamic governance. She analyzes the divergence in interpretation depending on the emphasis on Mecca or Medina period of the Prophet's life. Chamlou also addresses Islamic perspectives on free markets and women's roles, pointing out the inconsistencies between the Islamic tenets and their application in Islamic societies. Stakeholders include religious groups and individuals/ citizens.

In summary, the comprehensive contributions and compilation provide powerful insights for understanding theory and practice of Global and Digital Governance. At the heart of global and digital transformations impacting institutional and societal governance is the need to: create AI/ technology governance frameworks and ethics; better understand human and technology intersections; build capacity for data driven analysis and insights; and strengthen leadership for inclusive governance approaches for engaging with all stakeholders.

The summaries previously clearly identify the stakeholders that are addressed in each chapter. By skimming through the summaries and consulting the stakeholder table included here, the reader can quickly zero in on how issues pertaining to any specific stakeholder are addressed in a variety of contexts. Effective and responsive governance structures cannot be achieved without this context sensitivity. By broadening the understanding of context sensitivity to include a wide variety of domains, the book highlights pathways towards more effective governance structures. If ideas from one domain can enrich the ideas in other domains through cross-fertilisation, then this book will have fulfilled its purpose.

PART 1

Global Democratic Governance

In the last two decades, governance throughout the world has undergone significant changes and reforms. As this handbook compellingly describes, the breathtaking expansion of digital technologies and social media is further enabling the transformation of governance. Governance, from the local to the global levels, is becoming more transparent and accountable through the use of digital technologies. This first part of the *Global Democratic Governance* provides a useful contextual framework for these transformations occurring at the global and local levels. The five chapters discuss the origins, architecture, and characteristics of the global governance landscape and provide illustrative case studies in several key areas such as emergence of civil society, climate change, and local development.

Chapter 1, by Amy Catherine Jersild and Michael A. Harnar, focuses on the emergence in the early 1990s of the concepts of good governance, defined by strong institutions and the promotion of democratic ideals such as fairness, equity, and justice. It also describes the concept of "multistakholderism"—the emerging governance model involving multiple actors from civil society and the private sectors. It analyzes the fast fashion industry as an example of how this new governance approach could be applied to promote greater value-chain equity and sustainability in line with the United Nations' Sustainable Development Goals.

In the next chapter, John Garrison examines the origins of civil society and its unprecedented emergence in the global governance sphere over the past three decades. While most governance structures at the global level were established and dominated by governments over centuries, in last decades, civil society organizations (CSOs) have flourished by participating in UN conferences, organizing global advocacy networks, and engaging multilateral development banks. This chapter provides an in-depth and illustrative case study on relations between CSOs and the World Bank, which evolved from being adversarial to more collaborative over the past thirty years.

Following this trend, the chapter by Bart W. Edés focuses on how social movements are utilizing technology to decentralize governance worldwide. This chapter discusses recent changes and opportunities that emerged in the wake of the Covid-19 pandemic, leading

DOI: 10.4324/9781003316077-2

social movements to adopt digital media to create awareness and garner support among a wider audience. This chapter highlights the increasing role of energetic, tech-savvy youth leaders who use tools such as "hacktivism" to influence public opinion on their causes. This chapter concludes by discussing the social issues that could give rise to similar activism in the future.

In his chapter, John Redwood focuses on the worrying and impending impacts of climate change on our planet and the global governance mechanisms established to address global temperature rise. It describes the evolution of the most important environmental and climate conferences and treaties over the past few decades and highlights the central role played by UN agencies; conventions on biodiversity, desertification, and climate change; and other multilateral environmental agreements. Lastly, it argues that despite these laudable efforts, global environmental and climate change governance goals are still falling short of what is needed to reduce the threat of climate change.

The final chapter, by Björn-Sören Gigler and Katherine H. Mann, highlights how global digital technology initiatives are leading to more democratic governance at the local level. Digital innovations, such as interactive mapping and crowdsourcing, provide unprecedented opportunities to make local development more transparent and accountable. This chapter presents a theoretical model for the emerging open development approach to governance and several case studies of citizen-feedback programs in developing countries enabled by information and communications technology and geared to improving the quality and delivery of government services. The chapter concludes with some early lessons learned and the privacy challenges and operational obstacles these citizens' feedback programs face in practice.

These five chapters highlight common themes that underpin the transformation of governance at the global to local levels. These include the expansion of participation and inclusion within governance frameworks for traditionally excluded segments such as civil society organizations and Indigenous peoples. Much of this change is being propelled by the use of digital technology, the internet, and social media. The chapters also point to the gap between ideal notions or theoretical approaches to governance, on the one hand, and the reality of governance and implementation challenges, on the other hand. It is during times of great upheaval such as we are currently experiencing, however, that historic opportunities materialize to bridge the gap between the desired vision and practical attainment. Finally, this part underscores the power public opinion has in democratizing governance, while also noting its limits, as governments are often able to disregard these pressures.

1
PROMOTING GOOD GOVERNANCE IN A DIGITAL ERA

The Case for Deliberative Democratic Evaluation

Amy Catherine Jersild and Michael A. Harnar

Introduction

Good Governance

Former UN Secretary-General Kofi Annan defined good governance as "ensuring respect for human rights and the rule of law, strengthening democracy, and promoting transparency and capacity in public administration." In his often-cited remark, he proclaimed the importance of good governance as "perhaps the single most important factor in eradicating poverty and promoting development" (UN General Assembly Official Records 1998, para. 114, 13).

The World Bank defined good governance as "the manner in which power is exercised in the management of a country's economic and social resources for development" (World Bank 1992, 1). The Sustainable Development Goals (SDGs)—an interconnected, holistic set of seventeen goals to address social development, environmental protection, and economic growth—make reference to good governance in goal sixteen, "Promote peaceful and inclusive societies for sustainable development, provide access to justice for all and build effective, accountable and inclusive institutions at all levels."

These definitions, along with the SDGs, relay governance as a vital part of a sustainable, fair, inclusive, and equitable development approach. Equated with good governance is the building of strong institutions that promote the democratic ideals of fairness and equity within societies. The World Bank's use of the word *power* to define good governance conveys vying and competing interests within society, and a finite resource base that needs to be protected and managed intentionally and mindfully. The SDGs focus on inclusivity, justice, and security conveys a government's mediating and protective function toward its citizens as part of the social contract between government and its citizens—the tacit consent of citizens to submit to their government in exchange for the maintenance of social order. The social contract is a feature of the relationship between the governed and the governors, and it serves as a value of democratic representation.

DOI: 10.4324/9781003316077-3

Both the World Bank and the United Nations' good governance frameworks convey a similar focus on rule of law, transparency, participation, and accountability. The World Bank's Worldwide Governance Indicators, which reports on indicators for over 200 countries, include voice and accountability, political stability and absence of violence, government effectiveness, regulatory quality, rule of law, and control of corruption. The United Nations identified a framework of nine areas to describe good governance: participation, accountability, transparency, responsiveness, equity and inclusion, effectiveness and efficiency, rule of law, and a consensus orientation.

Struggles Facing Good Governance

The complexity of governance within nation-states is multiplied at the global level, where multilateral cooperation is paramount for effectively tackling cross-border issues and carrying out the SDGs themselves, for the good and welfare of all of the world's people and the environment. Multiple transnational problems require a concerted and coordinated effort among nation-states. The example of the Covid-19 pandemic has presented a particular challenge as a disease that knows no borders within a world of nation-states bound by trade policies, treaties, patents, and a growing sense of protectionism and guarded borders. As Masaya Llavaneras Blanco and Antulio Rosales (2020) state, "there is an underlying contradiction between the reality of a phenomenon that sees no borders, and a political system that relies on and reifies borders as defense mechanisms" (p. 4). Furthering the difficulty is the valuing of profits over the humanitarian need to vaccinate the world's population quickly, pitting market interests against humanitarian aims.

The growing protectionism among nation-states presents another governance challenge for cross-border migration. With more than 270 million international migrants in the world (UN Population Division 2019), all nations serve as a source, transit, or destination country. As governments have moved toward protectionist policies in managing their borders, migration flows around the world have increased steadily due to a variety of reasons, including economic disparity, climate change, and war and unrest. While agreements have been formulated, such as the Global Compact on Migration and the Global Compact on Refugees, challenges to decision-making among UN member states are often due to claims of sovereignty and a desire for other states to not meddle in internal affairs.

Furthermore, a single entity for international migration governance—one congruous to the World Trade Organization for matters of international trade—does not exist. Instead, international migration is the concern of multiple intergovernmental organizations.

And finally, climate change, the most existential threat of our times, presents a very pressing challenge for global governance. Unprecedented wildfires, rising temperatures and sea levels, and increased drought have resulted from a disregard for and abuse of natural resources. Governments have tried to address emissions of greenhouse gasses through global forums, but government action is not bold enough and environmental scientists claim the world is running out of time.

From Multilateralism to "Multistakeholderism"

For the past fifteen years, global governance frameworks have moved away from the nation-state as the primary actor in governing vis-à-vis multilateral debates and decision-making within the United Nations, to a multistakeholder approach involving both governmental and nongovernmental actors (Gleckman 2018). Following an agreement made by the UN Secretary-General and the World Economic Forum (WEF) in 2019, the private sector's interest to lead and contribute to policy-making at the global level has been officially sanctioned through the creation of multistakeholder groups organized to address policy and programs. The agreement reflects the WEF's interest in redefining corporate purpose and expanding its influence.[1]

This controversial trend has challenged the traditional notion of governments as sole governing bodies, granting the private sector greater influence in policy-making. At the practical level, it also presents problems and challenges for democratic ideals in decision-making. The role of nongovernmental actors as stakeholders conveys a set of interconnected relationships, with all members having a stake in an issue, problem, organization, or entity, and expecting to gain value from the interaction. This contrasts with the notion of citizen constituents, who wield a more passive role of influence and representation in governance. It also contrasts with the ideals of democracy, with nonelected actors participating in decisions affecting the social and economic welfare of people across the globe. While the participation of multiple actors in a decision-making process would appear to be democratic, the extent to which these actors are chosen to represent a group of people in making decisions that affect their social and economic welfare challenges the notion of a democratic and transparent process.

Furthermore, the power dynamic among members of the stakeholder groups is uneven, as are the relationships between the stakeholder groups and those outside the group whom they purport to represent. The chair of the stakeholder group holds a powerful position, selecting (or excluding) participants, controlling levels of transparency, and promoting policies and standards that could benefit markets while bypassing accountability checks (Gleckman 2018; Brooks and Kumar 2021). A lack of a democratic process in the formation of the group and the uneven and conflicting levels of power and representation within and outside the group raise questions about multistakeholderism's role in traditional definitions of good governance.

The agreement made by the United Nations and WEF took place within the context of a wider global movement of neoliberal policies, motivated by a regard for government as ineffective and lacking innovation and the private sector as innovative and overregulated by government (Mazzucato 2015, 2018). The number of wealthy philanthropists has skyrocketed, increasing their wealth even as economies are shrinking. Nearly half of the 76,000 private foundations in the United States alone were founded within the past ten years, suggesting an increased interest by the private sector in influencing social development issues and financing interventions that support more market-centric solutions.

The response has been divided. Political theorist Wendy Brown (2015) has characterized the growing influence of the private sector as the "economization" of our lives. She argues that this economization has made us market actors who think in economic terms, whether it concerns public or private matters. Neoliberalism has effectively hallowed out democratic ideals within society, she argues, chipping away at a sense of community and challenging notions of what may constitute the common or public good. In contrast, proponents of these developments hail the efficiency of private sector methods and approaches and yearn to apply them to the social sector, claiming the multilateralist approach of the United Nations as a failure on addressing the significant global problems of our time.

The Example of Multistakeholderism in the Technology Industry

Nation-states govern and relate to each other across the globe within a dramatically evolving context of technological advances. Technology as a tool has increasingly shaped our role as both citizens and consumers within our societies and has been used by governments in their daily operations, including delivery of services to citizens. The government's publishing of data has given citizens full and free access to information in a way that a relatively short time ago was unheard of. Such a change may be viewed as bridging a gap between government and citizens, giving people greater access to information and making government more transparent. The change may also be regarded as enabling citizens to better evaluate their own government.

Yet the shift to greater technological use has challenged the abilities of governments to effectively govern, with benefits experienced by some but not all constituents. The population's knowledge and access to technology is uneven, impacting equitable access to services. Furthermore, the use of technology in the workplace has shaped the world of work in different ways, providing a challenge to govern the labor market. With the overwhelming amount of data available and its prevalence within society, and with policy-makers well behind the technological advances in the field, the capacity and understanding of policy-makers to safeguard its population's data are also elusive (Keith 2018; Wright 2018; Tucker 2020).

Calls for a new social contract have been put forward with warnings about safeguarding our data and safeguarding democracy itself. As Kevin Keith (2018) of the *Guardian* states:

> This is the conversation the world has to have as the value of data is intrinsically linked to the value we place in each other. Only a new social contract that encompasses digital will enable us to fulfill its potential and expand the definition of us, strengthen democracy and ultimately improve lives.

Within the technology sector, the movement toward multistakeholder governance from multilateralism is vibrant and developed in terms of interest and participation. The United Nations has heralded private and public partnerships within the industry, bringing private actors to the table with an interest to share decision-making power. In 2015, it extended the Internet Governance Forum for another ten years, with the interest to involve governments, the private sector, civil society, international organizations, and technical and academic communities. Co-chaired by two private sector actors and well-known philanthropists Jack Ma and Melinda Gates, its 2019 report details various aspects of the industry in need of addressing, including equitable access to technology.

How might such multistakeholder processes best contribute toward good governance? How can such a process be democratic with a set of diverse actors, including some driven by profits and some representing its citizenry? Our purpose is to explore an evaluation approach for good global governance that facilitates discussion of competing values and supports understanding of sustainable and democratic outcomes, in support of the SDGs. In the next sections, we discuss evaluation as a practice and what it offers, discussing one approach in particular: deliberative democratic evaluation and its application among diverse stakeholders within the fast fashion industry.

Evaluation Within a Global Economy

Evaluation as a Human Need and Interest

We have a natural inclination to evaluate on an everyday basis, whether determining which clothes are best to wear in the morning or which restaurant serves better food for dinner. Beyond the everyday evaluative decision-making in which we all engage, evaluation reflects a human need to connect with other people. Indeed, in our capacity as citizens, we strive to connect with other fellow citizens to debate whether something of consequence, be it a program within our community or a policy recently adopted by our local government, is good and works well for ourselves and our community.

This debate is the essence of democracy itself, as claimed by political theorist Chantal Mouffe (2000). She speaks to a "dissociative conception of politics" in which the political is inherently conflicting and antagonistic. Conflict drives the democratic process and is central to its function. She argues that the main task for a democracy is to provide institutions that mediate this conflict in a way that does not lead to civil war.

In alignment with Mouffe's definition of democracy, some evaluation theorists (House 1980, 2006, 2015a, 2015b, 2016, 2019; House and Howe 1999, 2000a, 2000b, 2003; Greene 2003; Julnes 2012a, 2012b) consider evaluation a practice that promotes argument and contestation in support of democracy. At its most basic level, evaluation is a natural means for engaging in dialogue and debate. When people come together, evaluation ensues.

This natural inclination to evaluate as citizens concerns that which is regarded as the public domain. The evaluation theorist Peter Dahler-Larsen (2019) refers to this domain as "basically all of the matters connecting us in a society, as they represent our common destiny. The public thing stands between us and connects us, because what you do with it influences my life" (p. 2). This reflects Jürgen Habermas' concept of the German term Öffentlichkeit (public sphere), the social sites or arenas where ideas are articulated and negotiated, as well as the collective body constituted by "the public" (1989).

In the process of such participation, we engage in basic human sense-making, naturally describing and classifying our understanding of a program or policy under consideration. We then try to understand how something happens and why, and, finally, to value inquiry, that is, evaluation, or the process of attributing a value to that particular program or policy. When we contribute resources, such as via taxes to our government, we naturally want to take part in the evaluation of the use of those resources in the res publica (Mark, Henry, and Julnes 2000).

Similarly, at the global level, we are concerned about problems that we as global citizens all have a stake in—that of the well-being of the planet and the world's people. Those problems that transcend the human construct of borders, such as climate change and public health, are in need of a system of governance that is supported by evaluation to identify sound and impactful interventions.

Evaluation Purpose and Definition

A widely accepted definition of evaluation among theorists and practitioners is the process of determining the merit, worth, or value of something, whether it be a program, personnel, or product (Scriven 1991). The merit of a program, for example, refers to the intrinsic value it has in meeting the needs of its intended audience, whereas determining the worth involves assessing the program's extrinsic value to those outside the program and to society.

Evaluation is concerned with making judgments as to whether a program, policy, or product is good or bad by applying a set of defined criteria and standards to form an evaluative conclusion. Determining criteria helps define what is, for example, good, bad, worthy, unworthy, effective, or ineffective. Criteria are based on values; the values certain stakeholders may hold are reflected in the criteria chosen to evaluate. Evaluators are concerned with making these values explicit in arriving at evaluative conclusions regarding merit, worth, and value (Schwandt 2015).

As a value-laden profession, evaluation is an inherently political exercise. Evaluative conclusions will inform choices that reflect a value for one path over another in any given context. Where resources are limited, which is more often the case than not, these values are political.

Ultimately, as a practice concerned with values, evaluation is regarded as a means for improving a problem or situation, and ultimately a means for bettering society. Evaluation theorist Thomas Schwandt (2015; Schwandt and Gates 2016) argues that the focus of evaluation should be not only the question of whether something works or not, which is typically how evaluation is used, but also how it works and whether a particular intervention is indeed the right approach to addressing a problem. Asking the value-laden question of whether we are doing the right thing and ultimately, what kind of society we want to live in are more pertinent questions for evaluation. Evaluation can and should be a tool to use by policy-makers and citizens at all levels of society to answer such questions.

House and Howe (2000a, 2000b, 2003) echo this sentiment, arguing that evaluation should be an institution in and of itself that supports the realization of democratic exchanges within society and the realization of democracy itself. We discuss their evaluation approach, deliberative democratic evaluation (DDE), below.

Democratic Approaches to Evaluation as a Means to Promote Good Governance

The DDE approach developed by House and Howe has its roots in Barry MacDonald and Rob Walker's (1977) work in the United Kingdom. Its origin lies in a recognition of value pluralism, an embracing of case-study research involving politically sensitive relationships, and with the central questions of who controls the pursuit of new knowledge, and who has access to it. MacDonald's (1977) work was in direct response to the kind of evaluation practiced at the time, which he characterized as bureaucratic and autocratic. In these contested approaches, the evaluator had a distinctly close role to the evaluation commissioner. A bureaucratic approach accepted the values of those who hold office with the aim to please the commissioner of the evaluation. Autocratic evaluation offered external validation of policy, guided by the key concept of "the responsibility of office." As House and Howe would later state, "evaluation is too important to society to be purchased by the highest bidder or appropriated by the most powerful interest" (2000a, 4).

House and Howe (1999, 2000a, 2000b, 2003; House 2006) describe the DDE approach as a framework with three requirements: all relevant stakeholder views, values, and interests must be included in the evaluation; there must be a thorough discussion between stakeholders and the evaluator to explore these views, values, and interests; and there must be a thorough deliberation by all parties involved to reach conclusions. These conclusions may be jointly constructed with the evaluator. DDE can be characterized as what Thomas Schwandt and Emily Gates (2021) describe as a democratic, civic-led framework to evaluation that enables exploration of competing values among diverse stakeholders on complex societal problems.

The first requirement or principle of DDE is that inclusion of all interests is mandatory. Evaluation aspires to be an accurate representation of social reality, not an instrument to further the interest of some stakeholders over others. The interests of all stakeholder groups are central to the evaluation, as the interests of all parties would be represented in a democratic institution or process. Through engagement with all stakeholder groups, the consideration of all interests, values, and perspectives is then reflected in the evaluation. The evaluator should be able to justify why one criterion is chosen over another based on this engagement, ultimately enabling the evaluation to provide a basis of discussion that is not biased toward any particular interest.

The second DDE principle is dialogue. In order to be a deliberative democratic evaluation, a power balance must be realized where the voices of all stakeholders involved can be heard, and where discussion itself, as House and Howe (2003) warn, "should be based on consideration of merit, not on the status of participants" (p. 82). Revealing all the voices and their interests and perspectives, stakeholders may debate, argue, and perhaps change their minds. Balancing power relationships among stakeholders is an important and challenging task for the evaluator. House and Howe (2003) also note that evaluative conclusions are emergent from these discussions. The dialogue can be used to debate findings, and through these debates, evaluative conclusions are then forged.

The third DDE principle is deliberation. House and Howe (2003) describe deliberation as fundamentally a cognitive process that is grounded in reason, evidence, and principles of valid argument—all critical to the evaluative process. The evaluator's expertise is particularly crucial in deliberation. House and Howe (2003) note that values, perspectives, and interests are examined through a rational process. "Evaluation is a process for determining the validity of claims, claims that are emergent and transformed through deliberation into evaluative conclusions" (p. 83). In contrast to the individually focused model of evaluating for consumer choice, the evaluation of public programs and policies is a collective choice derived from collective deliberation. This approach to deliberation requires what House and Howe (2003) call "reciprocity of consciousness" among participants and a rough equality in levels of power in order to debate honestly about their collective ends.

The DDE approach is not without its critics, who claim that it is unworkable in practice and too idealistic in its aims. Operationalizing it—managing the various and competing interests among stakeholders—is challenging. Theorists of agonistic pluralism, for example, reject the Habermasian idea of a rational consensus achieved through deliberation alone. There will always be irreconcilable differences among divergent social identities within any multicultural society.

Yet proponents of DDE speak of the framework as a regulative ideal to work toward, despite the challenges to fully realize its goals. The effort to work toward this regulative ideal is indeed an effort to support democracy and democratic processes themselves, which often are messy and sometimes unattainable. Engaging in this process is a means toward realization of greater democratic ideals within a community, one that may improve over time if not fully impactful at any given time.

Operationalizing Deliberative Democratic Evaluation: Promoting Good Governance in the Fast Fashion Industry

The fast fashion industry is a global industry involving some of the world's most profitable corporations ("brands") engaged in sourcing the labor of primarily women in some of the world's poorest nations, such as Bangladesh, Cambodia, Ethiopia, and Haiti. Migrant labor is also used by middle-income countries; Jordan, for example, employed 75 percent of its 65,000 workers from South Asian countries in 2015.[2] Fast fashion is discussed in-depth in several other chapters in this book, giving readers insight into the industry's dynamics involving a range of stakeholders with varying interests and agendas, as well as its negative impact on the environment.

Clothing is exported to wealthier countries through trade agreements that give favor to developing countries, enabling them to benefit their economies and continue responding to the demand—for example, contributing to and participating in the system (industry). The stakeholders within this system include governments in supply and demand countries, the brands that are contracting factories in the supply countries, the employers operating these factories, the employees working in the factories, and the trade unions and employers' associations representing the interests of their respective parties within each country.

The demand for fast fashion lies among people in wealthy countries, hungry for cheap and expendable clothing. This has created a dynamic whereby the factories (supply) are pressured to provide at a cheaper rate, thus driving workers' wages down. In addition, as discussed in the other chapters, the industry is responsible for polluting the environment with toxic chemicals in its supply chain. The discarding of clothing by those in demand countries, when ready to buy something new, also adversely impacts the environment.

In the following sections, we explore the application of DDE to a hypothetical fast fashion industry multistakeholder committee mandated by the UN Secretary-General: to identify ways the industry is contributing toward the SDGs and ways it may be running contrary to the objectives and values of the SDGs and to identify possible interventions to enable the industry to better contribute toward the SDGs.

Applying Critical Systems Heuristics Within a DDE Framework

To apply the three principles of DDE to the hypothetical multistakeholder committee, we use critical systems heuristics (CSH) as a tool for engaging critically in the valuing process. CSH offers a means to systematically identify, criticize, and justify assumptions and to be critically reflective about valuing (Ulrich 2012; Gates 2018). In the hypothetical example herein, CSH helps make transparent the choices around inclusion, dialogue, and deliberation for a multistakeholder United Nations–mandated committee.

Critical systems thinking, which emerged in the 1980s, produced several strands, including CSH and total systems intervention. While the latter is focused on theoretical and methodological pluralism, CSH focuses on the normative core of professional practice (Midgley 2007; Ulrich 2012; Gates 2018). CSH is versatile and has been used within or in addition to other approaches, such as Participatory Rural Appraisal, and as a discursive framework for mediating conversation for team-building exercises (Ulrich and Reynolds 2010).

CSH focuses on four source areas of influence: motivation, control, knowledge, and legitimacy. Collectively, they describe the boundaries by which an issue or problem can be framed or viewed.

1. Sources of motivation: where a sense of purposefulness and principled value comes from.
2. Sources of control: where the necessary resources and power are located.
3. Sources of knowledge: where sufficient expertise and experience is assumed to be available.
4. Sources of legitimacy: where social and legal approval is assumed to reside.

There are twelve CSH questions in total, three within each of the four source areas of influence, designed to make explicit the judgments on which we often rely, either consciously or unconsciously. In helping to bound conversations on an issue and to check assumptions, the questions help to both understand an intervention within a given situation (the system in which it resides) and to design interventions for improvement (Ulrich and Reynolds 2010). The twelve questions are presented and discussed within the next section on operationalizing DDE for a multistakeholder committee focused on the fast fashion industry.

Application of DDE Framework and CSH Tool to the Fast Fashion Industry

Discussion below is organized around each of the three DDE principles of inclusion, dialogue, and deliberation, with CSH embedded within. We also explore using technology with the aim to enhance the process and maximize effectiveness in addressing such a complex problem as the fast fashion industry. The three DDE principles largely outline a series of steps in a process of forming a committee, discussing and debating context, and deliberating over which steps to take. Yet it is not a linear one; the three principles may feature in each step of the process, and the process itself may go backward and forward before concluding.

Inclusion

Addressing the social roles of stakeholders within the fast fashion industry (system) is the domain of the DDE principle of inclusion. The CSH questions across each of the four sources of influence (motivation, control, knowledge, and legitimacy) that are most relevant to the inclusion principle involve bounding committee members' understanding of all concerned actors and their level of influence and power. The DDE principle of inclusion highlights the importance of both committee make up and representation and explores levels of power and influence in an effort to prepare for dialogue and deliberation.

Given the fast fashion industry involves dynamics of monetary profit, human rights, market forces of supply and demand, and cross-border relationships, committee leadership should represent differing interests. Effective leadership rests on an understanding of the process, a genuine commitment to participation and representation, and a commitment to the committee's mandate of evolving the industry in better support of the SDGs.

Representatives of each stakeholder group should be invited to participate as committee members. In the fast fashion industry, these include governments of supply and demand countries, corporations (brands), enterprise associations within the supply countries, and labor unions within the supply countries. A survey of the association membership, both labor and enterprise, would help explore the context on the ground of each participating supply country and enable insight into the lives of those participants in the industry who may not be fully represented by their respective associations. The migrant woman factory worker employed in the industry, for example—with her perspective on her situation and influence in the supply country, as well as her situation in her country of origin—is a vital voice to capture.

Addressing CSH questions related to social roles within the industry in the four areas of influence—motivation, control, knowledge, and legitimacy—will bring out differing perspectives and interests. These questions are detailed in Table 1.1.

The private sector may claim they are the ultimate beneficiary, or the governments in the supply countries given the contribution of the industry to jobs and economic growth within their countries. The less powerful stakeholder group of workers may venture to lay claim to this status given they themselves earn a living from producing the actual product for sale. Or one may argue that the consumers in the demand countries are the beneficiaries. Discussing an ultimate beneficiary is a challenging conversation, revealing what values may be at play among the stakeholder groups and will require renegotiation based on criteria developed during the inclusion phase. The evaluator will need to give a critical lens to the discussion and serve as the committee's social conscience in coming to an answer.

A critical question for the multistakeholder committee is how the environment will be represented. In a process of determining stakeholder inclusion and engaging in discussion and deliberation over the boundaries of a system, how will the environment, an actor within the system at risk of harm, be included and protected?

Dialogue

A continued objective among the stakeholders is to level the playing field; therefore, the tentative responses to the questions presented in Table 1.1 should then be tested for their validity. How confident are we as a committee that the boundary judgments in question are right? How might we defend them if needed? What alternative judgments might be more appropriate? Engaging in this dialogue promotes impartiality among stakeholders, with the evaluator taking a careful facilitation role. It may also lead to a draft set of criteria for evaluative judgment as to the extent to which the industry is contributing toward the SDGs and where improvements need to be made. Furthermore, actual and ideal maps may also be filled out as part of an ongoing exercise during the evaluation, as shown in Table 1.2.

Table 1.1 CSH Questions on Social Roles

Source areas of influence	*Social roles (stakeholders)*
Motivation	*Beneficiary:* Who ought to be/is the intended beneficiary of the system?
Control	*Decision-maker:* Who ought to be/is in control of the conditions of success of the system?
Knowledge	*Expert:* Who ought to be/is providing relevant knowledge and skills for the system?
Legitimacy	*Witness:* Who ought to be/is representing the interests of those negatively affected by but not involved with the system?

Source: Authors.

Table 1.2 Sources of Influence: Social Roles (Stakeholders), Role-Specific Concerns (Stakes), and Key Problems (Stakeholding Issues)

Sources of influence	*Social roles (stakeholders)*	*Role-specific concerns (stakes)*	*Key problems (stakeholding issues)*
Motivation			
Control			
Expertise			
Legitimization			

Source: Authors.

Given the extreme power differentials between stakeholders, particularly that of employer and worker, and the need to cultivate and lift up all voices to be heard equally, the experience of Fishkin et al. (2018) in using deliberative polling with a multistakeholder committee focused on internet governance can be instructive. Deliberative polling may enable a fuller expression of voices among stakeholders at the outset, particularly where there are strong capitalist motivators such as profits at odds with other values of sustainability and safeguarding the environment. It involves using a stratified random sample of committee participants, or perhaps an extended group. Opinions may be collected before and after deliberation on a particular topic as a means to support dialogue among members. The poll may focus on several topics for debate, such as the industry's impact on the environment or the state of worker's conditions and wages within the industry. Polling at the start of the dialogue, and then at the end, can identify any shifts in opinion and value among participants.

We envision an online town hall where stakeholders engage in dialogue over the results generated through the polling. Research findings on the industry may also be presented for discussion. These may include the level of pollutants emitted by the industry into the environment over a yearly basis; impact these pollutants may have on people and the environment; measures, if any, taken by the industry to address pollution over time; trends in real wages for workers over time; profits earned by factories and brands over time; and the industry's contribution to each supply country's gross domestic product (GDP) over time. A clear picture of where costs exist within the industry (both people and environment) and where profits go will be presented for discussion. Reference to the SDGs should be made during discussion where appropriate.

The evaluator may wish to then introduce the CSH questions relevant to the dialogue phase, detailed in Table 1.3.

In facilitating dialogue in response to these CSH questions, the evaluator may explore the idea of a mission statement for the industry as a means of articulating a purpose. And, within the context of a newly articulated mission statement, identifying what and whose knowledge is of value. Exploring where harm occurs within the industry, means by which to address that harm, and mechanisms for all actors involved to be accountable can also be discussed.

The discussion may also focus on how sustainability is defined for the industry. What is the balance between shaping the demand and delivering on the supply so that the industry can function in a sustainable way? What might that look like in terms of production? How

Table 1.3 CSH Questions on Specific Concerns (Stakes)

Source areas of influence	*Specific concerns (stakes)*
Motivation	*Purpose:* What ought to be/is the purpose of the system?
Control	*Resources:* What conditions of success ought to be/are under the control of the system?
Knowledge	*Expertise:* What ought to be/are relevant new knowledge and skills for the system?
Legitimacy	*Emancipation:* What ought to be/are the opportunities for the interests of those negatively affected to have expression and freedom from the worldview of the system?

Source: Authors.

Table 1.4 CSH Questions on Key Problems (Stakeholding Issues)

Source area	*Key problems (stakeholding issues)*
Motivation	*Measurement of improvement:* What ought to be/is the system's measure of success?
Control	*Decision environment:* What conditions of success ought to be/are outside the control of the decision-maker?
Knowledge	*Guarantor:* What ought to be/are regarded as assurances of successful implementation?
Legitimacy	*Worldview:* What space ought to be/is available for reconciling differing worldviews regarding the system among those involved and affected?

Source: Authors.

can the industry contribute toward realization of the SDGs? Discussing boundaries and how the problem is framed once all stakeholder groups are identified addresses this second DDE principle.

Deliberation

Reimagining the industry based on honest debate grounded in reason, evidence, and principles of valid argument about its collective ends characterizes the deliberative phase of the process. CSH questions across the four areas of influence that are pertinent to the deliberative phase are presented in Table 1.4.

For the fast fashion industry, these questions may translate as: What does success look like with our new framework? How would we know if we have achieved it? What is outside our industry's control? How might we influence it? How can we all as contributors and benefactors of the system be accountable to our re-envisioning of success? And where do tensions still exist? How best to manage these tensions in an open and transparent way? How can those affected best participate?

Re-envisioning the industry as an "ideal map" (Table 1.5) is part of the deliberative process. Discussion around roles and responsibilities for the ideal map, and how

Table 1.5 Summary of Multi-Stakeholder Committee Approach in the Fast Fashion Industry Using a DDE Framework With CSH Embedded Within

DDE principles	*Main objective*	*CSH boundary critique: those involved*			*CSH boundary critique: those impacted*
		Motivation	*Power*	*Knowledge/expertise*	*Legitimization*
Inclusion (stakeholders)	All perspectives identified within the industry; leveling the playing field so there is no bias toward any particular interest; exploring issues of benefactor, those who are negatively affected, those who hold power of knowledge and expertise; exploring the industry as is from multiple perspectives	*Who benefits and who does not? Where is there harm in the industry and who/what is harmed? Who should benefit?*	*How is success defined within the industry from all participating perspectives? How is this success shared? How should success be defined within the industry? And how should it be shared?*	*Whose knowledge is valued and within what context? Where ought knowledge be valued within the industry?*	*Who represents those interests negatively affected? Is there legitimate representation within this relationship? How can this be improved?*
Dialogue (stakes)	Voices of all perspectives are heard; consideration is on merit not on status of participants; debate on what the industry could/should be; reconsidering the industry in light of the SDGs	If we considered the entire industry as an intervention with the purpose of contributing toward the common good (SDGs), what would our mission statement be? What values would we hold relevant? How would this change our industry as it is currently constructed?	How do we change the element of harm within our system/industry? How can we hold ourselves accountable to each other and to our mission? What is external and out of our control? What elements are within our control?	In articulating our mission statement and ways we can/will contribute toward realization of the SDGs, what new knowledge and skills are relevant and should be prized within our industry/system?	How would we characterize our newly revised worldview and are there elements outside our system that may be adversely affected? If so, how can they be free of our worldview?
Deliberation (stakeholding issues)	Honest debate grounded in reason, evidence and principles of valid argument about collective ends (contribution toward SDGs) for the industry; leveling of power among voices; reimagining the industry	What does success look like with our new framework? How would we know if we have achieved it?	What is outside our industry's control? How might we influence it?	How can we all as individual contributors and benefactors of the system be accountable to our re-envisioning of success?	Where do tensions still exist? How best to manage these tensions in an open and transparent way? How can those affected best participate?

Source: Authors.

stakeholders are to be accountable to each other, is an important part of the deliberation process. Specific interventions might be identified in the form of capacity development initiatives, projects, or programs, and policy development and implementation. Lastly, the UN global governance indicators or the World Bank governance framework discussed above may be applied to identify how well governance has been improved through the DDE process using CSH and to ensure the government has a strong role in the ideal map for the industry.

Challenges and Constraints: Evaluating With Validity

Validity refers to the extent to which a process and its results are viewed as credible. All evaluations are concerned with validity; the democratic evaluator will have to manage particular concerns and constraints, which include time, resources, level of commitment, and power differentials among stakeholders. The democratic evaluator is at the center of the process, facilitating discussion, leading participants in examining and critiquing boundaries, and embracing the political dimensions of the system under examination. The extent to which the DDE evaluator is able to manage this process of engaging with diverse and conflicting interests of multiple stakeholders will directly relate to the validity of the outcome in the eyes of the participants.

Constraints of time and resources among stakeholders are real in practice and often difficult to budget for, particularly with regard to stakeholders' time and participation. A genuine commitment to the principles of the process needs to be fostered in order to address time and resources, and, in the case of our example discussed above, an acknowledgment of problems and an imbalance within the industry, as well as an interest to improve, particularly by those holding greater levels of power. Preparation prior to the start of the inclusion process to cultivate these levels of commitment may contribute toward greater success rather than solely relying on such commitment naturally occurring through the participatory, dialogic process.

Representation may be a challenge as well, especially in the case of the fast fashion industry. Trade unions, particularly those in Jordan, for example, where 75 percent of the workforce is migrant labor from South Asia, have different (discriminatory) policies for its foreign members as compared to Jordanians. Likewise, employers' associations may more fully represent certain factories more than others within any given country, and there may be an imbalance of power and influence within these institutions. The deliberative polling initiative discussed above is one means for addressing this constraint.

Finding a level playing field given the power differentials, particularly between employers and employees, and brokering their various agendas, is not an easy task for the evaluator, even for the more experienced. This is particularly the case within the fast fashion industry where greater profits are typically desired by those with most power, which may directly conflict with values of workers' rights and environmental safeguarding. This will need to be very well planned, and the evaluator will likely need support. An evaluation team assisting the main evaluator would have a better ability of handling such conflict instead of a lone evaluator working with the committee.

Furthermore, enabling all parties, particularly those with limited power, such as employees, to speak truthfully may be a constraint. In the context of a given work environment, employees could feel they will risk their jobs if they speak out. One way to counteract this and minimize the challenge would be to have employees who are not directly employed by employers as participants in the process. Another possibility would be to adopt the approach of Cheryl MacNeil (2000), who found that conducting interviews with diverse stakeholders in the context of a psychiatric hospital prior to the deliberative forums was helpful in framing the different voices into the conversation. She also conducted interviews after the forum to allow for a debriefing and reflection on their experience during the forum. MacNeil believes this is an ethical imperative on the part of the evaluator, where debriefing helps build trusting relationships between stakeholders.

Conclusion

We have put forward a democratic evaluation approach, using critical systems heuristics and an example of a multistakeholder committee focused on a complex international issue, with the intent to think critically at the systems level, and with the overall objective of fostering democracy, supporting good governance, and contributing toward the achievement of the SDGs. We have argued that evaluation as a human need and interest can and should be at the core of good governance. Evaluation should be used as a means of promoting greater democratic processes, contributing toward improved and sustainable outcomes for both people and planet, thereby contributing toward the betterment of society and environment. Inclusion, dialogue, and deliberation are central concepts that should be central to, and critically assessed throughout, the process.

Evaluation can serve multiple purposes. It can be used to assess needs within a given context, identify problems, support or improve on an intervention underway (formative evaluation), or make judgments about the effectiveness and efficacy of an intervention at its conclusion (summative evaluation). Herein, we describe evaluation as an organizing tool to guide good governance efforts by holding democratic ideals as central to measures of good governance.

The challenge of weakened governing capacity among governments across the globe is a critical issue to our well-being as a planet. Where nonrepresentational interests that are based on a value for profit-making and blind to inequities and environmental degradation challenge democratic and sustainable interests for both people and planet, efforts to promote good governance are critical. Evaluation, we argue, is at the core of this effort.

Key Discussion Areas

- The role of governmental and nongovernmental actors in governance.
- The emergence of stakeholder-centric governance.
- The need for constant discussion and deliberation (evaluation) to determine the best governance approach toward the betterment of society and the planet.
- Fashion industry in detail and multistakeholderism in the industry.
- Approaches to promoting good governance in the fast fashion industry.

Notes

1 Refer to the Statement on the Purpose of a Corporation, released in 2019 and, as of 2021, signed by 181 CEOs, from the Business Roundtable website: https://opportunity.businessroundtable.org/ourcommitment/ (accessed February 24, 2023). Further discussion can be found at Business Roundtable, "Business Roundtable Redefines the Purpose of a Corporation to Promote 'An Economy That Serves All Americans'," August 19, 2019, www.businessroundtable.org/business-roundtable-redefines-the-purpose-of-a-corporation-to-promote-an-economy-that-serves-all-americans.

2 See Better Work's Jordan webpage for more information, https://betterwork.org/where-we-work/jordan/ (accessed February 23, 2023).

References

Blanco, Masaya Llavaneras, and Antulio Rosales. 2020. "Global Governance and COVID-19: The Implications of Fragmentation and Inequality." *E-International Relations*, May 20, 2020, www.e-ir.info/pdf/83300 (accessed February 24, 2023).

Brooks, Sally, and Arun Kumar. 2021. "Why the Super-Rich Will Not Be Saving the World: Philanthropy and 'Privatization Creep' in Global Development." *Business & Society* (December 2021): 1–6.

Brown, Wendy. 2015. *Undoing the Demos: Neoliberalism's Stealth Revolution.* New York: Zone Books.

Dahler-Larsen, Peter. 2019. *Quality: From Plato to Performance.* Cham, Switzerland: Palgrave Macmillan.

Fishkin, James S., Max Senges, Eileen Donahoe, Larry Diamond, and Alice Siu. 2018. "Deliberative Polling for Multistakeholder Internet Governance: Considered Judgments on Access for the Next Billion." *Information, Communication & Society* 21(11): 1541–54.

Gates, Emily F. 2018. "Toward Valuing with Critical Systems Heuristics." *American Journal of Evaluation* 39(2): 201–20.

Gleckman, Harris. 2018. *Multistakeholder Governance and Democracy: A Global Challenge.* London: Routledge.

Greene, Jennifer. 2003. "War and Peace . . . and Evaluation." *Studies in Educational Policy and Educational Philosophy*, www.tandfonline.com/doi/abs/10.1080/16522729.2003.11803869 (accessed February 24, 2023).

Habermas, Jurgen. 1989. *The Structural Transformation of the Public Sphere: An Inquiry into a Category of Bourgeois Society.* Cambridge: Polity Press/MIT.

House, Ernest R. 1980. *Evaluating with Validity.* Thousand Oaks, CA: Sage.

———. 2006. "Democracy and Evaluation." *Evaluation* 12(1): 119–27.

——— 2015a. "The Politics of Evaluation and the Evaluation of Politics." *Evaluation* 21(4): 492–96.

———. 2015b. *Evaluating: Values, Biases, and Practical Wisdom.* Charlotte, NC: Information Age.

———. 2016. "Values in Evaluation." *American Journal of Evaluation* 37(1): 104–8.

———. 2019. "Evaluation with a Focus on Justice." *Theorists' Models in Action: A Second Look. New Directions for Evaluation* 163: 61–72.

House, Ernest, and Kenneth Howe. 1999. *Values in Evaluation and Social Research.* Thousand Oaks, CA: Sage.

———. 2000a. "Deliberative Democratic Evaluation." *New Directions for Evaluation* 85: 3–12.

———. 2000b. "Deliberative Democratic Evaluation in Practice." In *Evaluation Models: Viewpoints on Educational and Human Services Evaluation*, edited by D. L. Stufflebeam, G. F. Madaus, and T. Kettaghan. Boston: Kluwer Academic Publishers.

———. 2003. "Deliberative Democratic Evaluation." In *International Handbook of Educational Evaluation*, edited by T. Kellaghan and D. L. Stufflebeam. Boston: Kluwer Academic Publishers.

Julnes, George. 2012a. "Managing Valuation." *New Directions for Evaluation* 133: 3–15.

———. 2012b. "Developing Policies to Support Valuing in the Public Interest." *New Directions for Evaluation* 133: 109–29.

Keith, Kevin. 2018. "We Need to Build a New Social Contract for the Digital Age." *The Guardian*, April 4, 2018.

MacDonald, Barry. 1977. "A Political Classification of Evaluation Studies in Education." In *Beyond the Numbers Game: A Reader in Educational Evaluation*, edited by D. Hamilton, D. Jenkins, C. King, B. MacDonald, and M. Parlett. London: Macmillan.

MacDonald, Barry, and R. Walker. 1977. "Case-Study and the Social Philosophy of Educational Research." In *Beyond the Numbers Game: A Reader in Educational Evaluation*, edited by D. Hamilton, D. Jenkins, C. King, B. MacDonald, and M. Parlett. London: Macmillan.

MacNeil, Cheryl. 2000. "Evaluator as Steward of Citizen Deliberation." *American Journal of Evaluation* 23(1): 45–54.

Mark, Mel, Gary Henry, and George Julnes. 2000. *Evaluation: An Integrated Framework for Understanding, Guiding and Improving Policies and Programs*. San Francisco: Jossey-Bass.

Mazzucato, Mariana. 2015. *The Entrepreneurial State: Debunking Public Versus Private Sector Myths*. New York: Public Affairs.

———. 2018. *The Value of Everything: Making and Taking in the Global Economy*. London: Penguin.

Midgley, G. 2007. "Systems Thinking for Evaluation." In *Systems Concepts in Evaluation: An Expert Anthology*, edited by B. Williams and I. Imam. Point Reyes, CA: Edge Press of Inverness.

Mouffe, Chantal. 2000. *The Democratic Paradox*. London: Verso.

Schwandt, Thomas. 2015. *Evaluation Foundations Revisited: Cultivating a Life of the Mind for Practice*. Stanford, CA: Stanford University Press.

Schwandt, Thomas, and Emily F. Gates. 2016. "What Can Evaluation Do? An Agenda for Evaluation in Service of an Equitable Society." In *Evaluation for an equitable society*, edited by Stewart I. Donaldson and Robert Picciotto. Charlotte, NC: Information Publishing Age.

———. 2021. *Evaluating and Valuing in Social Research*. New York: Guilford Press.

Scriven, Michael. 1991. *The Evaluation Thesaurus*. Newbury Park, CA: Sage.

Tucker, Ian. 2020. "Roger McNamee: 'Facebook Is a Threat to Whatever Remains of Democracy in the US'." *The Guardian*, July 26, 2020, www.theguardian.com/technology/2020/jul/26/roger-mcnamee-facebook-is-a-threat-to-whatever-remains-of-democracy-in-the-us (accessed February 24, 2023).

Ulrich, Werner. 2012. "CST's Two Ways: A Concise Account of Critical Systems Thinking," https://wulrich.com/downloads.html (accessed October 15, 2021).

Ulrich, Werner, and M. Reynolds. 2010. "Critical Systems Heuristics." In *Systems Approaches to Managing Change: A Practical Guide*, edited by M. Reynolds and S. Holwell. London: Springer.

UN General Assembly Official Records. 1998. "Report of the Secretary-General on the Work of the Organization," https://digitallibrary.un.org/record/1487773?ln=en (accessed September 15, 2021).

United Nations Population Division. 2019. "International Migrant Stock 2019," www.un.org/en/development/desa/population/migration/data/estimates2/estimates19.asp (accessed September 28, 2021).

United Nations Secretary-General High Level Panel on Digital Cooperation. 2019. "The Age of Digital Interdependence: Report of the High Level Panel on Digital Cooperation," www.un.org/en/pdfs/DigitalCooperation-report-for%20web.pdf (accessed October 16, 2021).

World Bank. 1992. *Governance and Development*. Washington, DC: International Bank for Reconstruction and Development, https://documents1.worldbank.org/curated/en/604951468739447676/pdf/multi-page.pdf (accessed October 16, 2021).

World Economic Forum. 2019. "World Economic Forum and UN Sign Strategic Partnership Framework," www.weforum.org/press/2019/06/world-economic-forum-and-un-sign-strategic-partnership-framework/ (accessed September 28, 2021).

Wright, Morgan. 2018. "Congress is Clueless About Facebook—and That Should Make Us Panic." *Hill*, April 12, 2018, https://thehill.com/opinion/technology/382792-congress-is-clueless-about-facebook-and-that-should-make-us-panic (accessed February 24, 2023).

2
FROM THE STREETS TO THE BOARDROOM

The Growing Presence of Civil Society in Global Governance

John Garrison

Introduction

Over the past thirty years, global governance has become more inclusive due to the growing presence of civil society organizations (CSOs) within global governance spaces traditionally reserved only for governments and the private sector. Civil society constitutes the "third sector" and represents the vast majority of citizens and organizations around the world; thus, their increased participation in global governance can make global institutions more democratic and legitimate. CSOs from a plethora of sectors and thematic areas are now present in policy dialogue tables at the United Nations, multilateral development banks, and business councils at the global level. The greater visibility and participation of CSOs in these institutions have made them more transparent and accountable.

This chapter will begin by defining what is civil society and how its presence has evolved from the local and national levels to the global sphere over the past three decades. It will then explore the evolving relationship between the World Bank (WB) and civil society to illustrate the growing importance of civil society in a leading global institution. A relationship which once was characterized by miscommunication, conflict, and street protests has evolved into an interactive and increasingly collaborative relationship based on policy dialogue, program consultations, and even operational collaboration. The WB and CSOs not only dialogue frequently around still contentious issues and consult on policies and programs but also collaborate with the Bank funding CSO development efforts and inviting CSOs into Bank governance mechanisms. This chapter will analyze the major policy issues, distinct engagement phases, and key actors which led to this historic evolution and its impact on the broader global landscape. Finally, this chapter will analyze the paradoxical twists and improbable advances in these relations and share lessons and insights learned from this historic process.

Defining Civil Society

Civil society is still an evolving and little understood term. Political science literature agrees that there are three distinct sectors in countries around the world. The first sector

DOI: 10.4324/9781003316077-4

is composed of governments; all 197 countries recognized by the United Nations have governments ranging widely from democracies and dictatorships to monarchies. The second sector is the private sector; nearly all of these countries also have a formally recognized private sector, with the exception of several communist countries, such as Cuba and North Korea, that do not acknowledge the existence of a private sector. The third and largest sector is civil society, which is by its very nature quite diffuse and the largest of the three sectors. A common definition of civil society is the associational life operating in the space between the state and market, including individual participation, and the activities of nongovernmental, voluntary, and community organizations (Edwards 2011).

Until recently, this sector had been known by other names, such as nongovernmental, not-for profit, charities, or private voluntary. The term civil society, which is more inclusive, was introduced several decades ago by well-known academics who study the third sector. Today, the term is used within the United Nations, among multilateral development banks such as the World Bank, and by most democratic governments. Some governments, generally dictatorships or one-party states, still deny the existence of civil society within their countries as they deny the notion of a third and independent sector that represents the vast majority of their population and can hold such governments to account (Hall 1995).

Civil society encompasses a broad range of constituencies, including nongovernmental organizations (NGOs), community-based organizations (CBOs), labor unions, foundations, faith-based organizations, Indigenous people's organizations (IPOs), and youth groups. While NGOs may be the best known of these constituencies due to their visibility as policy activists, other constituencies such as CBOs are much larger. While some estimates point to the existence of several million NGOs worldwide, tens of millions of community organizations exist across the world, such as rural cooperatives, women's groups, and slum associations. While most civil society constituencies have informal governance structures, some such as labor unions elect their leadership through regular voting. The International Trade Union Confederation, for instance, represents over 207 million workers worldwide (Eberly 2000).[1]

CSOs carry out different roles and perform a variety of activities, ranging from policy advocacy and research to service provision. CSOs work in countless thematic areas such as disasters, education, environment, and human rights. Their services also vary enormously and include operating schools and health clinics, managing conservation units, training farms, building houses, and marketing handicrafts. While policy-advocacy CSOs such as Amnesty International and Greenpeace may be better known, service-provision CSOs such as Save the Children and the International Rescue Committee are much larger and numerous. Some international CSOs such as CARE work in more than one hundred countries and reach over ninety million people worldwide.[2]

Evolution of Governance

Governance occurs on many levels: local (village or community level); sub-regional (within countries as determined by geography and/or ethnicity); national (within country borders), regional (e.g., Africa, Europe), and global. Governance began at the local village or community level many millennia ago, long before countries were ever established. The great majority of CSOs operate today at the local level, representing their constituencies (e.g., small farmers, slum dwellers, women, youth) and providing services such as soup kitchens, rural cooperatives, and youth centers. Due to the existence of such a capillary web of organizations, the local level affords the best opportunity for democratic governance, in which citizens can participate in the decision-making process for their own organizations and local governments. Within countries with authoritarian national governments, local governance faces difficult obstacles. Sometimes, the flourishing of local participatory governance can be a harbinger of a broader democratic movement at the national level. Such was the example in Brazil, where more participatory approaches at the local level, as exemplified by participatory budgeting processes in Southern Brazil, led to the dawning of democracy at the national level in the late 1980s (World Bank 2000).

At the national level, history shows that democratic governance occurs when all three sectors—government, the private sector, and civil society—participate fully in decision-making related to political issues, public policies, and budget formulation. These three sectors also participate, within their own roles and comparative advantages, in implementing, monitoring, and evaluating government policies, economic activities, and social services. Most of the more democratic countries worldwide have active civil society sectors with large national networks of NGOs, labor unions, foundations, and professional associations who participate actively in both the social and economic sectors. A study by the Center for Civil Society at Johns Hopkins University in the United States showed that the non-profit sector accounts for 4.5 percent of gross domestic product (GDP) in sixteen countries researched (Solomon 2013).[3]

At the global level, however, democratic governance trails the other two spheres, and the three-legged societal stool is the least balanced. Governments have traditionally dominated global governance, and the private sector is well represented. Through conquering armies, diplomacy, or trade agreements, governments have had ongoing relations with each other for many millennia. Governments formed military alliances among themselves from the dawn of history to protect themselves or project their influence. One of the first known military alliances was the Peloponnesian League led by Sparta in the sixth century BC. A more recent example is the North Atlantic Treaty Organization (NATO), which represents thirty European and North American nations. Governments also forged trade agreements and treaties centuries ago to facilitate the exchange of goods and services, culminating with the World Trade Organization established in 1995. Finally, governments began to establish regional or global associations of nations. The first global association of nations was the League of Nations established in 1919, which evolved into the United Nations in 1945.

The private sector has also had a long-standing presence in the international level as exemplified by the creation of the International Chambers of Commerce in 1919. Its presence in the global governance sphere, however, is more recent, as exemplified by the United Nations' Global Compact created in 1999 to encourage corporate social responsibility among its over 9,500 member companies. Civil society, however, is the newest and least represented sector at the global level of governance.

Emergence of Civil Society in Global Governance

Civil society has only recently begun to participate in global governance. CSOs first began to attend global UN conferences in large numbers beginning in the 1970s. These included the First World Conference on Women in Mexico City in 1975, Environment and Development Summit in Rio de Janeiro in 1992, and World Conference in Human Rights in Durban in 2001. The United Nations was the first space where civil society began to exercise its right to be present and influence policy decisions at the global level, followed by the international finance organizations (IFIs). In the 1970s, CSOs began to criticize and campaign against the World Bank and other IFIs. As a result, UN agencies and IFIs established policies and offices to engage CSOs by increasing information disclosure, policy dialogue, and programmatic consultations. Some UN agencies and IFIs even began to provide grants to CSOs and include them in their governance structure. Organizations such as the International Labor Organization, the UN Program on HIV/AIDS, and Climate Investments Funds invited CSO representatives to sit on their decision-making bodies—although their level of participation, through voice and/or vote, varied among the organizations (Florini 2000).

As a result, CSOs began to organize international networks and associations in order to be more effectively represented at the global level. Among the first global civil society networks to be established in 1993 was Civicus, which brings together CSOs and their networks to strengthen citizen action and civil society. Civicus has held over a dozen global gatherings with hundreds of CSO representatives from around the world to share experiences, discuss trends, and network. They also publish the Annual State of Civil Society Report, which provides a useful update on the latest trends of the sector worldwide (Heinrich 2008).[4] Of the civil society movements at the global level that have emerged over the past two decades, the best known of these was the anti-globalization movement, which began with protests during the World Trade Organization's Ministerial Conference held in Seattle in 1989. The anti-globalization movement led to the establishment of the World Social Forum (WSF), a counter event to the World Economic Forum (WEF), which annually gathers leading business leaders in Davos. The WSF held its first annual gathering in Porto Alegre, Brazil, in 2001, bringing together tens of thousands of civil society activists to debate and discuss alternative policies to unfair and marginalizing globalization trends. Since then, over twenty global forums and many regional forums have been held around the world.[5] Broad networks have emerged around thematic areas such as HIV/AIDS, education, health, and the environment. Two examples of these are the global HIV/AIDS movement, which advocates for increasing funding for AIDS research and treatment, and the Climate Action Network, which advocates for increased climate change mitigation and resilience efforts.

World Bank Case Study

Relations between civil society and the World Bank were largely adversarial at their start but have evolved over the past thirty years into being more collaborative today. As a result, the World Bank experience exemplifies well the emergence of civil society in the global governance sphere. And because the World Bank has always served as a bellwether among IFIs, examining how WB-CSO relations have improved reflects more broadly on these trends among other IFIs.

For the first two decades after the World Bank was established in 1947, the institution rarely interacted directly with civil society. While the Bank did have some contact with communities as project beneficiaries of large social development projects in such areas as primary education, community health, and rural development, this contact was largely passive and did not produce any significant engagement. Beginning in the 1970s, however, the World Bank became a lightning rod for civil society criticism through media campaigns and street protests. Civil society criticism emerged with a focus on such large development projects with negative environmental and social impacts. The Bank did not yet have environmental and social safeguard policies in place, and thus projects related to large dam construction, road building in fragile ecosystems, and forced land relocation harmed thousands of impoverished communities throughout the world.

Two iconic projects exemplified the newfound civil society activism against the World Bank. One was the Narmada Dam Project in India, in which the expansion of a large hydroelectric project resulted in the displacement of tens of thousands of poor farm families without providing any compensation or relocation assistance. The second project was the Polonoroeste Project in Brazil, which involved, among various development activities, paving a highway through the Amazonian rainforest. While, on its surface, it was a simple highway improvement project, it led to widespread deforestation and encroachment into Indigenous lands by thousands of small farmers from Southern Brazil who migrated into the area.

With time, advocacy CSOs also began to campaign against the Bank's macroeconomic policies, which they claimed generated rather than alleviate poverty. Known as the Washington Consensus, these WB policies included structural adjustment, loan conditionalities, privatization of state-run companies, and trade liberalization. CSOs claimed that this one-size-fits-all approach led to growing national debt, unemployment, higher food prices, and school users in many developing countries. The lack of access to information and even physical access to the Bank buildings were other targets of criticism by advocacy CSOs. Most Bank policy papers, sectoral studies, and project documents were not in the public domain, and CSO activists, academics, and average citizens could not access them. The most notorious of these confidential documents were the Country Assistance Strategies. It seemed contradictory to CSOs and other stakeholders that, while the Bank was funded by taxpayers in developed countries, citizens in developing countries could not know how the Bank intended to spend billions of dollars in their countries.

CSOs also had limited access to Bank offices, and those few who visited were physically escorted throughout the building. This lack of access led to street protests by CSOs during the semi-annual Spring and Fall Meetings held in Washington, DC. It was the only way they could seem to get the attention of Bank managers and staff about their policy concerns. The best known protests occurred in Madrid in 1994 (in which Greenpeace unfurled an anti-WB banner in one of the main halls), in Prague in 2000 (in which militants of the Black Block threw bricks at buses carrying Bank and International Monetary Fund staff), and in Washington in 2002 (where protestors blocked streets and forced Bank staff to sleep in their offices for several nights).

These campaigns were led by a relatively small but cohesive coalition of policy-advocacy CSOs from the United States, Europe, and a dozen developing countries such as Brazil, India, the Philippines, and South Africa. Well-known NGOs such as Bank Information Center, Development Group for Alternative Policies, and the Bretton Woods Project were established during this period to monitor and try to influence the Bank. They also formed coalitions to engage the Bank, such as the Fifty Years Is Enough Campaign, whose goal was to shut down the Bank as it was celebrating fifty years of existence.

Engagement Begins

Engagement with civil society began in earnest in the mid-1990s during the tenure of World Bank President James Wolfensohn. He was the most influential Bank leader since Robert McNamara in the early days of the Bank. Wolfensohn led the transformation by introducing pro-poor macroeconomic policies, funding new areas such as HIV/AIDS prevention and environmental protection, and diversifying staff. It was in the area of civil society engagement, however, where his actions were perhaps the boldest. Wolfensohn not only began to engage CSOs directly and constructively but expanded the Bank's contact with a broader range of sectors, including trade unions, youth, and faith-based organizations. Wolfensohn changed the underlying way civil society was viewed within the Bank by promoting a better understanding of CSOs and lending legitimacy to their engagement.

To understand and better document how the Bank began to increase its engagement with civil society, it developed a Civil Society Engagement Continuum, which provides a useful visual tool to understand how engagement occurred and developed (World Bank 2012, xviii). There are five steps to WB-CSO relations: information dissemination, policy dialogue, program consultations, operational collaboration, and institutional partnership (see Figure 2.1). With each level of engagement, the nature of the interactivity and influence in decision-making increases. As indicated below, most Bank–civil society relations to date have been concentrated at the first three levels of the engagement continuum.

At the information disclosure level, substantial changes were undertaken when the Bank adopted a comprehensive Access to Information policy in 2010, making the great majority of Bank data, reports, and project documents available to download from the Bank's website, generally free of charge. This includes the Country Assistance Strategy (renamed as the Country Partnership Framework), which had been the focus of CSO critique in the past. Not only did it became a public document, but consultation with civil society on its content is now a requirement. In addition, bank offices are also more accessible to CSOs and other

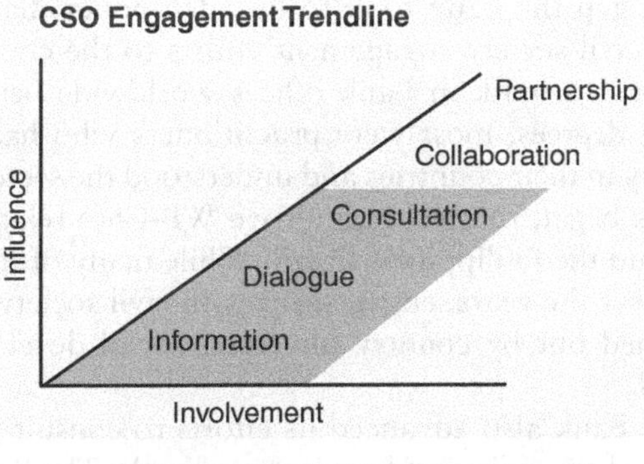

Activity	Nature of Interactivity	Level of Decision Making	Expected Outputs
Information access and dissemination	One-way	None	Better informed outside stakeholders
Policy dialogue	Two-way	None	Both sides better informed
Policy and progammatic consultation	Two-way	Low	Views of stakeholders taken into account
Collaboration	Two-way	Shared	Shared goals and action (short term, ad hoc)
Partnership	Two-way	Equal	Common goals and action (long term, institutional)

Figure 2.1 Civil Society Engagement Continuum
Source: World Bank (2012).

stakeholders today, as CSO representatives are frequently invited to attend policy meetings at Bank offices in Washington and in country offices. The Civil Society Policy Forum, held during the Fall and Spring Meetings, attracts over 800 CSO participants twice a year (World Bank 2012, 4).

The initial efforts at policy dialogue between the World Bank and civil society began in 1982 with the establishment of the World Bank–NGO Committee, a loose-knit group of CSOs and Bank staff who convened once or twice a year to discuss issues of concern to the civil society such as structural adjustment, third world debt, and environmental safeguards. These meetings would generally last all day and involve several dozen NGO representatives and a dozen Bank staff, including senior staff and sometimes the Bank president. This joint committee lasted for two decades and played a crucial role in beginning the process of improving Bank–civil society relations, which would accelerate and deepen over time.

The Bank also expanded the dialogue to other sectors beyond NGOs in 1995 with the arrival of Wolfensohn, including trade unions, foundations, youth groups, faith-based groups, peoples with disabilities, and LGBT groups. This expansion process often began through the holding of initial dialogue meetings and, in many cases, led to the establishment of new units within the Bank to take this engagement forward. In the case of the trade unions, for instance, the Bank's Labor Economics Department began holding yearly high-level meetings between the Bank president and the head of the International Trade Union Confederation. The faith-based unit began to dialogue with dozens of religious leaders from different faiths on the nexus between religion and development. The outreach to foundations unit was able to negotiate co-financing arrangements between the Bank and several foundations on vaccines and social accountability initiatives (World Bank 2012, 69).

The other important step the Bank took to broaden policy dialogue with civil society was to decentralize the civil society engagement efforts to the country level. Some eighty liaison officers were hired to work in Bank offices worldwide beginning in 1996. While some had social science degrees, most were practitioners who had long-term experience working with civil society in their countries and understood the sector well. The contracting of these Liaison Officers began to quickly improve WB-CSO relations in many countries such as Brazil, Kenya, and the Philippines, Brazil. While many of these liaison officer positions were phased out over the years, engagement with civil society has now become more mainstream and is carried out by country directors, social development specialists, and other country office staff.

Beyond dialogue, the Bank also advanced its efforts to consult with civil society on its policy documents, sectoral strategies, and project proposals. The Bank defines consultation as being more formal and binding than dialogue, as the Bank commits to incorporating the recommendations received during consultation meetings. In the 1990s, the Bank published guidelines and began offering training courses to Bank staff on how to effectively consult with civil society (World Bank 2007). It also embarked on detailed and comprehensive consultations of key new policies such as involuntary resettlement, extractive industries, and good governance. Some of these consultation processes, such as the one carried out on the environmental and social performance standards in the 2010s, took several years and involved dozens of consultation meetings worldwide with hundreds of CSO representatives. Consultations were also initiated around research and sector studies such as the annual World Development Reports on emerging development topics. They were also decentralized to the country level, where the Bank office consulted on the Country Partnership Framework strategy, although the scope and breadth of these varied among countries.

Advances over the past three decades on the fourth step of the engagement continuum, operational collaboration, involved working jointly with CSOs on one-time or short-term activities such as hosting events, undertaking research, and financing small projects. In Washington, for instance, the Bank collaborated with World Learning, who provided facilitators and technical experts, to co-deliver a one-day training module to Bank staff on why and how to engage with civil society. This program trained over 600 Bank staff from 2007 to 2014 on the rationale, methodology, and expected results of engaging civil society (World Bank 2012, 41).

As mentioned above, a groundbreaking example of operational collaboration occurred when the Bank provided thousands of grants to support CSO-managed projects at the local level. The Bank first began providing small grants directly to CSOs (rather than through governments) in the early 1980s, when it first established the Small Grants Program. These funds were intended to finance events, training, and other short-term activities at the local level and were managed by the country office. At its height, it disbursed some US$2.5 million per year and funded CSO projects in some sixty countries worldwide (World Bank 2012, 44). Over time, the Bank began to experiment with grant funding for specific thematic areas such as extractive industries, community development, and climate change. In the 1990s, over a dozen grant funds, some of these administered directly by the Bank and others jointly with government bilateral agencies through trust funds, disbursed over US$100 million per year. The most recent grant fund to be established in 2012 was the Global Partnership for Social Accountability (GPSA), which funds civil society strengthening, social inclusion, and public accountability projects in several dozen countries (World Bank 2012, 14)

Another significant advance in terms of operational collaboration occurred when CSOs were invited to join decision-making bodies of several Bank or trust fund boards as active observers or in some cases as voting members. These included the Global Partnership for Education, Global Agriculture and Food Security Program, Climate Investment Funds, and more recently the GPSA. Providing CSOs a "seat at the table" was an important milestone: it demonstrated to Bank staff and member governments that civil society is an important stakeholder that should have a vote—not only a voice—within a few of the Bank's governance mechanisms.

The fifth step of the engagement continuum, institutional partnerships, lags behind the others. These relations take longer to develop and require greater institutional commitment by all sides. Partnerships are characterized by organizational agreements to implement longer-term programmatic partnerships in which partners have joint decision-making responsibility, including joint management and co-funding commitments. Well-known examples of institutional partnerships were established with the World Wildlife Fund in the 1990s to promote sustainable forestry and with the Gates Foundation to fund the Global Alliance for Vaccines and Immunizations in 2000. The GPSA also involved an institutional partnership with the Ford Foundation, which provided funding and was a voting member on its steering committee.

The World Bank's expansion of civil society engagement was also reflected among other IFIs during this period. IFIs such as the Inter-American Development Bank, Asian Development Bank, and International Monetary Fund launched their own civil society engagement policies and programs. The scope of these outreach policies and programs varied depending on institutional characteristics and regional context. The Interamerican Development Bank (IDB), for instance, established CSO Advisory Committees in nearly all countries in Latin

America, while the International Monetary Fund mandated that its staff consult with civil society when carrying out Article IV Consultations country economic surveillance visits (International Monetary Fund 2015). The CSO engagement staff and units of these IFIs, together with several UN agencies, even set up an informal network of civil society liaison staff, which met annually for nearly two decades to exchange information, discuss trends, and share lessons related to civil society engagement.

Engagement Lessons and Insights

As discussed above, civil society–World Bank relations have changed and improved substantially over the past thirty years. The underlying question to be answered is whether this relationship has resulted in improving the quality of Bank policies and positively impacted the outcomes of Bank-financed projects at the local level. A second question is what lessons and insights have been learned that can perhaps be extended more broadly to global governance, and whether these relations can be further improved going forward.

Regarding what impact these closer relations have had on the Bank, much evidence exists to affirm that the Bank has benefited greatly from the initial advocacy campaigns by CSOs decades ago and more recently through closer relations. Important policies and practices in the areas of pro-poor macroeconomic development, environmental and social safeguards, HIV/AIDS prevention, and climate change all were adopted and/or accelerated due to pressure from civil society. The Bank is a more diverse and inclusive institution in terms of gender, ethnicity, and sexual orientation, because of outside pressure from civil society on these issues. The Bank is also a more transparent and accountable institution today because CSOs pushed for greater transparency through the access of information policies, and more accountable due to the establishment of its two compliance mechanisms—the Inspection Panel and the Compliance Advisor and Ombudsman—which CSOs played a key role in helping to establish. At the country level, the greater interaction with civil society through greater policy dialogue, ongoing consultations, and collaboration has enlarged and improved the Bank's institutional footprint by enriching its contacts beyond government and the private sector. Being in touch with broader society has made the Bank a more responsible and inclusive lending institution in these countries. Rather than crediting these changes all to outside pressure, it is more accurate to ascribe them to a "push-pull" process in which internal reform-minded leadership and the reforms they spearheaded within the Bank complemented the external pressure for change.

CSOs have, likewise, benefitted from these improved relations by becoming more knowledgeable about the Bank, having greater access to Bank documents, and collaborating with the Bank on various programs. Advocacy CSOs have benefitted from the closer contact by developing more focused and effective strategies to influence the institution. An example of this is how CSOs today work more closely with government representatives on the Bank board to change Bank policies, instead of largely relying on trying to sway Bank management as they did in the past. Likewise, countless service-provision CSOs in developing countries have benefitted from attending Bank events, collaborating with Bank operational programs, and receiving Bank grants. NGOs, community associations, Indigenous people's organizations, and others have received millions of dollars via small grants to provide services in the areas of education, social inclusion, and environment.

This engagement process has generated numerous lessons and insights about how change occurred at the Bank and the important role civil society played in this process. Some of this analysis also applies to the global governance context and how civil society has influenced other international institutions. When this process began, both the Bank and civil society had many misperceptions about each other. CSOs often had a conspiratorial view of the Bank, conjuring all sorts of Machiavellian intentions in its actions, even when the Bank blundered through faulty policies and/or problem projects. This was the case, for instance, with the Polonoroeste project in Brazil, which was so poorly designed and implemented that it led to unintended deforestation. Some CSOs assumed that the Bank was intentionally wanting to promote the widespread destruction of Amazonian forests to support agricultural production schemes. To quote Hanlon Razor's adage, however, one should "never attribute to malice that which is adequately explained by stupidity."

Likewise, the Bank had a limited understanding of civil society, which led to wrong assumptions and also encouraged conspiratorial views about the role of civil society. When feeling under attack by CSO media campaigns and street protests, some Bank managers and staff assumed that CSO advocacy networks represented civil society as a whole. In reality, these policy activists, and especially those that focused on the Bank, represent an infinitesimal percentage of the broad sector. Some also attributed negative intentions to the CSOs, thinking that they did not really care about the environment or the plight of the poor, but rather undertook these advocacy campaigns against the Bank so they could cynically raise money from foundations such as the Mott and Ford Foundations.

A good deal of miscommunication and cultural differences between Bank staff and CSO activists often impeded effective dialogue and reinforced negative stereotypes on both sides. It was common for both sides to want to undermine the messenger so they could ignore the message. In the case of the Bank, they often sought to criticize the credibility and seriousness of the CSO activists so they could discount the policy messages they espoused. Bank staff would sometimes scoff at the fact that the CSOs were not economists, did not understand the complexity of the Bank's economic policies, and had left-leaning ideas which were unrealistic or simply erroneous. They also resented the fact that CSOs always tried to take the "moral high ground" on such issues as human rights in order to unfairly criticize the Bank.

The CSOs, for their part, often expressed disdain for what they considered were stodgy and arrogant "suits" they often met with at the Bank. They felt that Bank managers and staff were overly bureaucratic, unwilling to steer from corporate messaging to express their own views, and did not understand or empathize with the plight of poor people in developing countries. For this reason, it was common for CSO activists to demand meetings with senior Bank staff, even the president himself, as they felt that it was a waste of time to meet with Bank technical staff who they felt were clueless and had no power to make decisions. They felt, further, that since many Bank staff were educated in prestigious universities such as Oxford and Harvard and/or were from developing country elite classes, they were unqualified to be effective pro-poor global development actors. In short, it was quite paradoxical that both sides viewed the other as arrogant and incompetent for quite different but self-reinforcing reasons.

In addition, a technical versus political disconnect existed in the early dialogue meetings between the WB and CSOs. It was not uncommon to witness dialogue meetings in which Bank economists would present their corporate presentations while CSO sociologists or community activists would ignore the economic arguments and graphs to focus, instead, on political analysis and anecdotal evidence of poverty. While "technocratic" Bank staff saw these meetings as a way of sharing data and having a technical discussion about how sound

Bank policies and projects were, CSO activists saw these dialogue meetings as an opportunity to have a political discussion about how misguided Bank policies and projects were.

Some of this miscommunication was also generated because Bank staff and CSO activists espoused different sets of facts and differing world views. The Bank tended to focus on macroeconomic trends and CSOs focused on micro-social conditions. Thus, it was not uncommon for Bank economists to point to positive economic growth trends in a given developing country while CSOs would bemoan the continued plight of the poor in that same country. In a sense, both parties were correct in their analysis, but they were analyzing different realities and levels. This asymmetrical macro- versus micro-approach seems to be quite common in global governance spaces between CSOs and IFIs. Over time, however, as the Bank and CSOs increased their engagement, learned to communicate more effectively, and increased mutual trust, the quality and level of policy dialogue began to improve.

Another insight gleaned from the Bank's bumpy attempts to engage civil society is that it often did the right things for the wrong reasons and at other times the wrong things for the right reasons. In other words, wrong-headed policies sometimes led to positive outcomes, while well-designed policies sometimes led to unintended negative consequences. A clear example of the former situation was the policy engagement process the Bank undertook with CSOs around structural adjustment. The Structural Adjustment Participatory Review Initiative was a groundbreaking, multi-year participatory research program geared to analyzing the impacts of the Bank's structural adjustment policies in over twelve countries (World Bank 2004, 3). While it was launched in 1997 by the Bank as a way of deflecting persistent criticism of Bank macroeconomic policies, it actually helped the Bank and CSOs better understand each other's positions and reach common understanding on the negative consequences macroeconomic policies were having on the poor. It also led the Bank to adopt more pro-poor macroeconomic policies such as the Poverty Reduction Strategy Papers.

An example of where well-intended policies led to unintended consequences was the Joint Facilitation Committee (JFC) outreach initiative launched in the early 2000s. The JFC was composed of leading CSO organizations and senior Bank managers established to deepen policy dialogue and consolidate relations. While on paper it seemed like a good idea to bring together leading NGOs, foundations, trade unions, faith-based organizations, and other constituencies to engage in the Bank, in practice it led to a good deal of miscommunication, posturing on all sides, and wasted energy until it was disbanded in 2005.

The methodology of "who, how, when, and where" offers another lesson for WB-CSO engagement. While it took the Bank quite a long time, it eventually learned that the approach and methodology employed not only mattered but could often determine the quality and results of the engagement initiative. In other words, the devil was in the details when it came to planning its outreach efforts to civil society. Sometimes the best designed and planned policy consultation events would be derailed by overlooked details such as who convened the event, where it was held, how much time was allotted, and whether preparatory documents (and in which languages) were shared with participants before the meeting. An analogous yet counterintuitive lesson for a technocratic institution such as the Bank is that style is equally and sometimes even more important than substance in these engagement events with civil society.

The Bank also learned that providing feedback on the results of the dialogue and consultation meetings is quite important. While this practice may seem obvious from a methodological perspective, it took the Bank a long time to understand its value and adopt it. In the early days of engagement, so much time and effort was spent organizing outreach events that scant attention was paid to meeting follow-up efforts including reporting back on the results of the meeting. Over time, however, Bank staff learned that informing participants about what was presented and discussed during the meeting, and more importantly what actions might have been adopted by the Bank as a result, was just as and even perhaps more important than the meeting itself. It became clear that disseminating results not only allowed the Bank to close the so-called feedback loop, but it also represented the crucial accountability component of the outreach process. Today, the Bank regularly disseminates summaries of the meetings held via email or website. In the case of lengthy consultation processes, such as on the new environmental and social standards, there are dozens of meeting reports posted on the Bank's website and even a table which shows which recommendations were adopted.[6]

Way Forward

These lessons lead to the final question of whether World Bank–civil society relations can be further mainstreamed and scaled up within the institution. As this chapter demonstrated, relations between the World Bank and civil society have advanced considerably on the three first levels of the engagement continuum—information sharing, policy dialogue, and programmatic consultation—but there has been less progress on the final two levels of operational collaboration and institutional partnerships. The two final levels may be harder to achieve, as they require structural policy changes to allow CSOs to receive increased grant funding, co-manage programs, and participate more fully in the Bank's governance spaces. Many government shareholders at the Bank (particularly those from developing countries) seem reluctant to provide civil society with this level of participation any time soon.

As discussed previously, important advances were achieved in these relations during the tenure of President Wolfensohn. Since Wolfensohn's departure in 2005, the intensity of the engagement process has slowed considerably. President Robert Zoellick (2007–2012) did introduce several important measures such as adapting the Access to Information Policy, engaging CSOs on food security and environmental issues, and establishing the GPSA, but subsequent Bank presidents have reduced the level of engagement with civil society. A case in point is the global Civil Society Team which has seen its visibility lowered within the institution and its outreach, research, and communication activities reduced. Fortunately, however, the advances achieved so far are cumulative and many, such as the Civil Society Policy Forum, cannot be reversed. In addition, civil society demand for increased participation in Bank affairs will not go away and this pressure will invariably result in further advances in the future. Just as it took the issues of gender equity and environmental conservation many decades to gain credibility and be mainstreamed within the Bank, it will still take some time for civil society engagement to be equally mainstreamed. Further advances in these relations will need to wait for new leadership at the top committed to this reform agenda.

Conclusion

The experience of the World Bank demonstrates that the presence and influence of civil society will continue to expand in the global governance sphere. This increase will continue to make global governance structures more transparent and accountable. Eventually civil society should have a seat in the governing councils of more UN agencies and perhaps even on the boards of the World Bank and other IFIs. This may seem improbable to some, but CSOs weren't even recognized as a formal sector at the global level until several decades ago. Today there is no major global policy-making process that does not have the presence and voice of civil society advocating for its positions. Thus, the participation of civil society will very likely become more institutionalized through participation in governing councils and boards in the coming decades. Civil society represents the great majority of citizens and organizations in the world, and only once they have a seat at the table will decisions made at the global level become more democratic and legitimate.

Key Discussion Areas

- Emergence and role of civil society in global governance.
- Review of World Bank experience to understand how the engagement with civil society intensified and became consolidated.
- Insights and lessons on the improbable process of more constructive engagement between the World Bank and civil society and its implications for other global governance spaces.

Notes

1 See "International Trade Union Confederation," www.ituc-csi.org (accessed February 24, 2023).
2 "CARE," www.care.org (accessed February 24, 2023).
3 The sixteen countries studied were Australia, Belgium, Brazil, Canada, the Czech Republic, France, Israel, Japan, Kyrgyzstan, Mexico, Mozambique, New Zealand, Norway, Portugal, Thailand, and the United States.
4 "CIVICUS Global Alliance," www.civicus.org/index.php (accessed February 24, 2023).
5 "World Social Forum," https://wsf2021.net (accessed February 24, 2023).
6 World Bank, "Review and Update of the World Bank Safeguard Policies," https://consultations.worldbank.org/consultation/review-and-update-world-bank-safeguard-policies (accessed February 24, 2023).

References

Eberly, Don, ed. 2000. *The Essential Civil Society Reader*. Oxford: Rowman & Littlefield Publishers.
Edwards, Michael, ed. 2011. *The Oxford Handbook on Civil Society*. Oxford: Oxford University Press.
Florini, Ann, ed. 2000. *The Third Force: The Rise of Transnational Civil Society*. Washington, DC: Carnegie Endowment for International Peace.
Hall, John. 1995. *Civil Society: Theory, History, Comparison*. Cambridge: Polity Press.
Heinrich, Finn, and Lorenzo Fioramonti. 2008. *CIVICUS Global Survey of the State of Civil Society: Volume 2: Comparative Perspectives*. Bloomfield, CT: Kumarian Press.
International Monetary Fund. 2015. *Guidance Note for Surveillance Under Article IV Consultation*. Washington, DC: IMF, May 2015, www.imf.org/external/np/pp/eng/2015/031915.pdf (accessed February 24, 2023).
Solomon, Lester. 2013. "The State of Global Civil Society and Volunteering: Latest Findings from the Implementation of the UN Nonprofit Handbook." Working Paper No. 49, Johns Hopkins University Center for Civil Society Studies, Baltimore.
World Bank. 2000. *From Confrontation to Collaboration: Civil Society–Government–World Bank Relations in Brazil*. Brasilia: World Bank.

———. 2004. *World Bank–Civil Society Relations—Review of Fiscal Years 2002–2004*. Washington, DC: World Bank.
———. 2007. *Consultations with Civil Society: A Sourcebook Working Document*. Washington, DC: World Bank.
———. 2012. *World Bank–Civil Society Relations—Review of Fiscal Years 2010–2012*. Washington, DC: World Bank.

3

HOW SOCIAL MOVEMENTS ARE HARNESSING TECHNOLOGY TO DECENTRALIZE GOVERNMENT

Bart W. Édes

Introduction

During the Covid-19 pandemic, the world witnessed a rapid acceleration in internet connectivity as people sought out virtual contact with others while living under government-imposed restrictions on commerce and mobility. In the year leading up to July 2022, the number of active social-media users worldwide increased by 227 million to reach nearly three-fifths of the world population (Data Reportal 2022). Some of these new social-media users, together with more experienced netizens, joined online discussions and debates on public policy issues, engaged in online advocacy, and built virtual coalitions. Individual citizens gained access to policy deliberations that, in pre-pandemic times, were held in person among smaller groups of elite decision-makers.

As I and John Garrison, a co-editor of this book, observed, almost 1,400 civil society representatives participated in the online Civil Society Policy Forum held during the virtual meetings of the World Bank and International Monetary Fund in October 2020—nearly double the number of civil society delegates who normally participate in person at the annual forum. Most of the new participants were activists from developing countries who would not have had the budget to travel to the headquarters of the two host institutions in Washington, DC. There was also a marked increase in the number of leaders from civil society organizations in the Global South who spoke at the twenty or so virtual policy dialogue sessions (Édes and Garrison 2021).

Prominent think tanks analyzing international affairs, geostrategic trends, development finance, trade, and economic and social policy shifted their expert panel discussions from primarily in-person events to online webinars. Suddenly, anyone with an internet connection could tune into publicly accessible discussions, pose questions, and inject views without having to be physically situated in the city where the think tank is headquartered. Attendance at such events often soared from a few dozen individuals before the pandemic to hundreds.

Covid-19 shook up the political arena, opening the door to government actions that would have been hard to fathom just months earlier, including massive spending programs aimed at cushioning the blow of the pandemic on people and businesses. The combined

DOI: 10.4324/9781003316077-5

health and economic crises led many to reflect on humanity's broken relationship with the environment and problems in society that were exacerbated by the spread of the virus, including inequality, racial discord, lack of adequate health care, and mental illness.

As in past crises, activists perceived new possibilities for driving meaningful change in government policies, priorities, and spending. The drastically changed circumstances caused by the pandemic created new policy space for bold action. Many of the new government spending programs not only addressed the short-term pain and disruption caused by the pandemic but also strengthened social protection systems and sought to green economies for years to come.

At the same time, the potential community of internet-enabled activists soared, along with the use of video platforms and social-media apps connecting people across the globe. Paul Engler, director of the Los Angeles-based Center for the Working Poor, observed that social movement organizers found themselves in a " 'moment of the whirlwind,' in which the standard rules of how politics works are turned on their head" (Engler 2020). Ashish Kothari, a founder of the Indian environmental group Kalpavriksh, observed:

> [W]e have been handed an incredible opportunity to right many historic wrongs. One is with regard to how we have treated our earthly home. And the other is regarding how our economies and politics have marginalized vast sections of humanity, the ones disproportionately suffering the consequences of multiple global crises. And the two are connected.
>
> *(Kothari 2020)*

The average person alive today enjoys access to far more information than ever before. People can educate themselves and form opinions on developments taking place in their communities, on the national scale, in distant lands, and at the global level. They can acquire a good understanding of economic, political, and social developments. Furthermore, they possess multiple means of expressing their views on those developments and connecting with others who share their views and desire for change. That all said, as online activism for a more just and sustainable world has grown, so have efforts by entrenched powers and malevolent actors to curtail its influence. I address this point later in the chapter.

Growing Mistrust of Government and Democracy

Over the past few decades, people around the world have lost trust in government. Researchers at the Centre for the Future of Democracy at the University of Cambridge studied data on global attitudes toward democracy over several decades in 154 countries. They concluded that 2019 featured the highest level of democratic discontent since 1995, the year when detailed stocktaking of global political sentiment began. In the United States, public trust in government is now near an historic low (Pew Research Center 2022).

Roberto Stefan Foa, a university lecturer in politics and public policy at the University of Cambridge, led a study on young people's views of democracy. The study found that, around the world, satisfaction with democracy is declining steepest among eighteen- to thirty-four-year-olds. Foa observes that "this is the first generation in living memory to have a global majority who are dissatisfied with the way democracy works while in their twenties and thirties" (Foa 2020). Skepticism about supranational governance has also been widespread. Discontent with the European Union and its legislative and regulatory arms contributed to the British vote for Brexit. Former U.S. President Donald Trump spoke for many Americans when he railed against organizations ranging from the North Atlantic Treaty Organization to UN bodies and the World Trade Organization, arguing that they were not acting in the interests of the United States and its citizens and relied too much on American financial support.

While facing increased public mistrust, governments have struggled to keep up with the rapid pace of technological change and scientific discovery. That pace only accelerated during Covid-19 times. Powerful companies became even more powerful in the early 2020s, challenging the ability of national and subnational governments, and international organizations, to develop coherent regulations for global tech titans that play a huge role in setting standards for the devices people use in their daily lives, data privacy, and access to information and news.

What do these developments suggest for the future of global governance and international rule-making? The role of sovereign states, and of intergovernmental organizations that enjoy the backing of such states, will continue to hold a central place for the foreseeable future. Yet their power will continue to be rivaled by many large corporations. In the second quarter of 2021, Microsoft recorded a 47 percent increase in year-on-year profits, which rose to US$16.5 billion. Both Microsoft and Apple each had a market cap of nearly US$2.5 trillion at the end of October 2021.

In the years ahead, governments, particularly authoritarian ones, will very likely continue to censor and control messages for change that they find threatening. They will marshal the forces of the state to silence those who support causes they find threatening. Yet while governments can successfully clamp down on coalitions demanding a better world, they can't do it everywhere, and not all of the time. Technology has strengthened the hand of social movements. Even some oppressive regimes will adapt and respond to the demands of certain social movements, in part to curry international favor and bolster their reputations, but also to preserve their power.

In the case of the private sector, corporations running powerful social-media platforms increasingly find that despite their enormous wealth, they, like governments, need to respond to public opinion when sufficient numbers mobilize around a cause and press their elected representatives to change their behavior. Public opinion fed into the decision of Facebook to create an independent Oversight Board in 2020 to help it make decisions about speech and online safety. Large multinational enterprises, sovereign states, and intergovernmental organizations will not be alone in determining the future rules by which we live. Increasingly, citizen networks and coalitions will grow into broader social movements that play a role in determining how the market and society should function.

Across the world, political and economic powers have gradually moved to the international level. The internet has enabled social movements to follow that transition and operate across borders. Influential actors are finding, sometimes with surprise, that they can be held accountable for their actions. Civic groups with little resources can mobilize support and public attention against a far more powerful competitor more easily and independently than in the past (Van Laer and Van Aelst 2009).

Social Movements in Action

The anti-globalization movement (a global social justice movement) of the 1990s made use of the internet to oppose free trade agreements, deregulation of financial markets, and the growing political power of multinational corporations. Filipinos organized "People Power 2" via phone text messages urging people to attend massive rallies calling for the resignation of President Joseph Estrada in January 2001. Arab Spring protesters made active use of digital media to condemn corruption and demand democratic reforms between 2010 and 2012. These were all significant movements rallying millions of people online and in person. Current-day activism builds on these historical precedents while harnessing a substantially deeper reservoir of technological platforms and tools, as well as higher rates of internet access that provide access to many more potential allies.

Examples of significant modern-day movements are all around us. They include those advocating for environmental sustainability and climate action, an end to gender-based violence, and more responsive and inclusive democracy. These movements come in many forms and structures and work at various geographical levels. Paul Engler, an instructor in protest methods, notes that in the early days of the pandemic, communities around the United States created Facebook Groups and Google Docs to coordinate mutual aid. Religious congregations, community organizations, labor unions, and neighborhood associations quickly organized activities to support members of their communities negatively impacted by Covid-19.

Once every year, sometime between the months of May and June, thousands of Singaporeans gather in their city-state's Hong Lim Park to display support for LGBT rights, inclusiveness, and diversity. Government restrictions imposed to curtail the spread of Covid-19 prevented large physical gatherings in 2020 and 2021. As a result, organizers turned the event into a livestreamed program, which yielded some benefits. Livestreaming speeches and musical performances could reach a larger audience and avoid the imposition of government conditions, such as a ban on participation by noncitizens in assemblies requiring a police permit. Launched as a local event in 2009, PinkDot events have sprung up in cities around the world, including Hong Kong, London, Penang, Salt Lake City, and Toronto.

Cross-border collaboration on issue advocacy accelerated in 2020 and 2021, argues Elaine Thomas, a social development specialist who has worked for two decades in developing countries of Africa and Asia. She cites the example of disability rights: Philippine civil society groups advocating for the interests of people with disabilities in their country became more involved in the global movement for disability rights, and they became more integrated into a network of allied organizations in Southeast Asia.[1]

The shocking police murder of George Floyd in May 2020 in the U.S. state of Minnesota spurred a massive wave of civic action under the banner of Black Lives Matter, a decentralized social and political movement protesting against police brutality and racially motivated violence against Black people. Although concentrated in the United States, the movement inspired calls for racial justice in many other countries. Institutions in public, private, and nonprofit sectors responded with new initiatives and investments. By late August 2021, the fifty largest U.S. public companies and their foundations collectively committed US$49.5 billion to address racial inequality (Jan, McGregor, and Hoyer 2021).

Youth at the Vanguard

Undi18, a youth movement in Malaysia, relied extensively on TikTok, Instagram, and Twitter to drive a successful campaign to lower the minimum voting age from twenty-one to eighteen years old in the country's constitution (Ding 2021). The movement is now conducting campaigns to promote 50 percent women's representation in Parliament and politics, institutionalize financing for forest conservation in the constitution, and provide a platform for youth participation in energy and electricity policy.

It is not unusual for leading activists within a movement to quickly capture the public's attention, particularly during a time of crisis or unrest. Energized, tech-savvy youth are often among the public faces of movements as shown by Swedish teen climate crusader Greta Thunberg, Indigenous human rights activist and environmentalist Nira Alicia Garcia of the United States, and Angeline Makore, who advocates for the rights of women and girls in Zimbabwe. But one need not be young to play a prominent role in a social movement, as highlighted by the indefatigable Nina Baginskaya, a seventy-four-year-old geologist who inspired fellow Belarussians—including those much younger than herself—to stand up to their country's dictator, Alexander Lukashenko.

Futurist Erica Orange believes that "one of the major emerging trends is a rising public urgency surrounding climate change—one that is spreading quickly and globally." She notes, "more socially conscious people, particularly millennials and Gen Zers, are joining grassroots movements and rallying around environmental and political causes" (quoted in Patton 2020). Greta Thunberg proves the point made by Orange. The Swedish climate activist invited fellow students around the world to band together and demand immediate action by government leaders to reduce greenhouse-gas emissions. On September 20, 2019, students in more than 160 countries participated in about 2,500 events that brought together four million people demanding urgent action to protect the world against the negative impacts of climate change.

Pandemic-era campaigning for a reduction in greenhouse-gas emissions and greater environmental sustainability generated unprecedented momentum. Environmental, social, and governance (ESG) criteria have become increasingly mainstreamed in business operations. The number of shareholder proposals on board diversity, climate change, worker safety, political activity, and other issues has soared in the past few years. In the first two quarters of 2020, 590 companies reported that they have aligned the trajectory of their emissions with the Paris Agreement on climate change, more than in any prior full year. Financial institutions, corporations, and governments have issued more than US$100 billion in green bonds annually since 2017 and doubled that to US$200 billion in 2019. The figure rose to US$243 billion in 2020 and totaled US$248 billion in just the first six months of 2021 (Bullard 2021). Investments in healthier, animal-friendly, and sustainable food options soared, as plant-based products became more common and research on cultured meat intensified.

Tools of the Trade Adapted Under Lockdown

Social movements utilize a range of approaches to bring about policy change, including consumer purchasing power, pressure on companies, lobbying politicians, and public information campaigns. Fundraising efforts increasingly involve internet crowdsourcing of contributions. A guide[2] to climate justice actions and mobilizations was developed to make advocacy safe during Covid-19 times by performing activities from home.

Examples of "quarantine action" included users posting large numbers of photos with people featuring a common theme or image, banging on pots and pans outside windows (*cacerolazo*), painting a message and sharing it on social media, displaying window and door signs, drawing chalk outlines outside targeted offices (where in-person protests were curtailed by social-distancing rules), holding livestream rallies, and participating in a social-media barrage. Although use of these campaign tools was particularly intensive when people's movement was restricted due to public health concerns, they remain part of the arsenal for post-pandemic advocacy and campaigning.

Despite the constraints posed by the pandemic, social movements were very active in the first months of the pandemic when lockdowns were widespread. Activists devoted a good deal of their energy to protests (even given health risks), defending the rights of workers, providing mutual aid and solidarity, monitoring policy-makers, and offering popular education. Mutual aid groups in Europe relied extensively on social media for organizing, but they found that posters, leaflets, and conversations were vital to reach those not online (Pleyers 2020).

Tech workers have been using tools designed for workplace collaboration, personal communication, and entertainment to conduct union organizing in a sector not known for labor activism. Discord, Slack, Facebook Groups, Reddit, and Signal are among the apps and platforms being used by gig workers and employees of tech firms to advance their rights and interests (Lawrence and Kramer 2021). Some activists employ more edgy, controversial, or legally dubious online methods to advance their political, religious, or social aims.

An example is hacktivism, which is a category of nonviolent digital activity where the motive is not mainly personal financial gain. Sometimes hacktivists practice doxing—the public disclosure of personal, confidential, and/or incriminating information to bring attention to perceived misdeeds or societal threat posed by the individual or group targeted. For example, internet sleuths known as the Deep State Dogs employed to publicly expose (dox) participants in the attack on the U.S. Capitol in January 2021. Many of those exposed for illegal actions lost their jobs and were charged with crimes by law enforcement agencies.

Operation Death Eaters, an initiative linked with Anonymous, works to dox high-profile child predators and traffickers. According to independent journalist Thor Benson, Operation Death Eaters does not employ hacking to find information on the perpetrators exposed. Instead, it generates sources, solicits help from the general public, and utilizes legal means to secure information, including court records, media reports, and primary sources to identify pedophiles and those engaged in sex trafficking. Those working with Operation Death Eaters are creating a database to document corruption and collusion related to abuse of children (Benson 2015). While doxing is used to expose those committing crimes, it can also be used maliciously, putting lives and careers at risk. Even when driven by good intentions, doxing can lead to vigilantism rather than the pursuit of justice under rule of law.

Other forms of hacktivism include distributed denial-of-service (DDoS), a tactic to overload systems and crash a website; virtual sit-ins, whereby individual users repeatedly load web pages to overwhelm a site until it crashes; website redirects, where a hacktivist changes the address of a website so that visitors are redirected to a different site supported by the hacktivist; and geo-bombing, which exposes the Google Earth location where YouTube videos are taken; and defacement, which involves attacking the integrity of a website by altering its appearance. In the wake of the murder of George Floyd by a Minneapolis police officer, the decentralized activist collective Anonymous allegedly launched a DDoS attack on the official website of the Minneapolis Police Department to bring attention to what it claimed was multiple cases of wrongful death by law enforcement in the state of Minnesota (Spangler 2020).

Ultimately, what makes a social movement successful is the influence it has on public policy-making and governance in general. What factors contribute to a social movement that generates impact on policy? Political scientist Hahrie Han, director of the SNF Agora Institute at Johns Hopkins University, has studied collective action in the United States and how movements become powerful. Key ingredients include leaders who are problem solvers and strategists who recognize people as the source of power. Bringing people together to learn, share, negotiate, and cooperate are keys to success. Based on her research, Han concluded that successful local movements have been able to achieve their goals because their leaders were accountable to their members. Maintaining the important human-centric element identified by Han in geographically broader campaigns with strong technological components (and virtual reality components) will challenge future movements seeking sustained impact over time.

Looking past the pandemic, tech-enabled social movements may not come to "govern" in a traditional sense, but their views could begin to carry more weight—and more quickly—than in the past given today's shorter news cycles and the cyber speed with which they can organize and influence large populations. Unlike in Martin Luther King's time, today's activists can reach very large audiences at the press of a key on a computer board. The type of online advocacy will evolve and increasingly enter the metaverse as more and more people, particularly from Generations Z and Alpha, are spending more time in virtual spaces.

Threats to Social Movements

The adept use of technology by youth-infused social movements holds promise for the future influence of these movements. At the same time, retrograde forces have also proved quite capable of utilizing technology, including informal networks promulgating xenophobic and racist ideas, spreading disinformation due to ignorance or anti-democratic aims, and seeking to generate revenues from illegal and nefarious activities. Social movements are particularly vulnerable to cyberattacks, as they are not established organizations with well-resourced IT departments that can mitigate risks. Social movements bring together a disparate group of people, not all of whom are attuned to the serious risks posed by cybercrime. Among those specific risks are phishing, which typically involves deceiving an email recipient into providing sensitive data which can be used to access accounts and files leading to the theft of identity or funds.

Other cyber threats to social movements include trojan horse attacks, where malware downloads onto a computer disguised as a legitimate program, and ransomware, another type of malware used for extortion. Attackers using ransomware typically threaten to publish a victim's personal data or block access unless some payment is made. Amnesty International, the global human rights organization, has reported on increasingly sophisticated techniques to infiltrate the email accounts of human rights defenders in the Middle East and North Africa. Typical tactics include asking users to reset the password on their Google accounts, tricking users into authorizing apps which purpose to secure their Outlook accounts, and abusing legitimate authentication process apps to infiltrate their accounts (Amnesty International 2020).

Social movements and their objectives can also be threatened by the spread of fake news that begins as disinformation—a claim invented for a specific purpose, often a malicious one. Such information may be circulated on social media by persons who find that the disinformation matches their own beliefs and therefore accept it as fact due to confirmation bias. Sharing may start in trusted networks, such as groups on messaging apps or social-media pages. The web of contacts grows as fake news is passed between different trusted networks. Sometimes bots and trolls push fake news onto many social-media timelines. If the disinformation catches the eye of social-media account holders who have large followings, they may share it with their online audience, greatly expanding the number of people exposed to falsehoods.[3] It should be noted that hacktivist approaches used by some members of social movements can also be used against them by their opponents.

Governments, particularly those with an authoritarian bent, will also seek to prevent mobilization of social movements that could threaten their rule. They will seek to undermine social movements through some of the tools above: blocking interest access; online censorship (deleting content, websites, and accounts); or other forms of state repression (arrest, torture, imprisonment, etc.). During the pandemic, many governments not only imposed restrictions on movement to limit the spread of the virus but also tightened other controls on the population and enhanced surveillance.

In February 2021, the Human Rights Watch (HRW) reported that governments worldwide used the Covid-19 pandemic to justify violating the exercise of free speech and peaceful assembly (HRW 2021). Among those targeted are journalists, bloggers, and others posting online, opposition figures and activists, protesters, academics, health-care workers, students, lawyers, cartoonists, and artists. Unfortunately, according to Freedom House, 2020 marked the fifteenth consecutive year of decline in global freedom. Echoing the HRW's findings, Freedom House found that as the pandemic spread, governments across the democratic spectrum repeatedly resorted to excessive surveillance, discriminatory restrictions on freedoms like movement and assembly, and arbitrary or violent enforcement of such restrictions by police and nonstate actors (Freedom House 2021). It should be noted, however, that social movements tend to enjoy more space for peaceful action in democratic states.

In the context of shrinking space for civil society action in many developing countries and undemocratic states, social movements are circumventing government restrictions by clever use of social media and modern technologies. For example, Iran's government routinely filters tens of thousands of websites, including news sites and social-media networks, but Iranians frequently access banned sites through virtual private networks (VPNs) and other anti-filtering tools (Esfandiari 2019). The country's youthful population has not succumbed to repression. Young people are actively using apps and communication platforms to share news and to report information that remains otherwise unreported or is manipulated by the state media and expressing dissent in subtle and not-so-subtle ways (Amini 2020).

Victoria Carty, a professor of sociology, explains how the use of technology by witnesses and protestors upended the societal power balance in authoritarian states during the Arab Spring. The Arab Spring uprisings showed that with the advent of new media platforms, authoritarian forms of government, which had for decades violently suppressed their citizens' exercise of free speech and peaceful assembly with impunity, were now subject to scrutiny from the outside world. Mojos (mobile journalists) circulated their atrocities worldwide and in real time throughout cyberspace, and the mainstream media eventually disseminated those images. This, in turn, put pressure on the governments and military to use more caution (at least in some cases) when dealing with the protest events. The circulation of the documented, unprovoked violence created sympathy for opposition groups and helped with recruitment efforts, allowing the protesters to alter power relations, as they were able to take command of the narrative and hold the police, military, and government accountable for their actions (Carty 2015).

While recognizing the unfortunate trend of democratic backsliding among governments around the world, at least one positive initiative in the other direction warrants attention. In 2014, the government of Estonia created the Citizen Initiative Portal (Rahvaalgatus) to enable members of the public to write proposals to the Parliament on how to amend existing regulations or improve society. If the proposal collects signatures from at least 1,000 Estonian citizens aged sixteen and above, the Parliament is obliged to discuss the proposal with the authors and give an official answer within six months. Since the portal was launched, several citizen proposals have become law following parliamentary action.[4]

Social Movements of Tomorrow

In a report analyzing global trends to the year 2040, the U.S. National Intelligence Council (NIC) assessed that the forces of globalization, such as greater mobility, urbanization, and connectivity, are increasing awareness and prominence of a broad array of constituencies that transcend national boundaries and are making it easier for people to organize around common interests and values (NIC 2021). These identities are playing greater roles within and between countries as groups advocate for recognition and certain objectives.

The NIC cited the example of the global coalition lobbying for gay rights, including through the organization of online campaigns and public events even in socially conservative countries, such as Iran. Between 2013 and 2019, the percentage of people indicating that homosexuality should be accepted in society increased in twenty-one of twenty-seven geographically diverse countries, according to the Pew Research Center, and thirty countries have legalized same-sex marriage since 1989. More recently, since the first outbreak of Covid-19, Costa Rica, various Mexican states, Northern Ireland, and Switzerland have also legalized gay marriage.

The trends report observed that "populations in every [global] region are increasingly equipped with the tools, capacity, and incentive to agitate for their preferred social and political goals and to place more demands on their governments to find solutions." Covid-19 stimulated a greater sense of urgency in tackling threats to the environment and, in turn, to humankind. Movements addressing nature in some way, including protection of biodiversity, environmental protection, and climate mitigation, are sure to remain potent forces for some time.

Similarly, the ongoing battle for accountability, transparency, probity, and responsiveness in government will never cease. Local and national movements will continue to act on these and related issues of civil liberties and human rights. Campaigns conducted to check the power of tech giants will also persist, even as the activists targeting such corporations will continue to rely extensively on their platforms, software, and apps.

What are some of the other areas where significant tech-enabled social movements might emerge or become much larger than their present-day version?

One possibility is *inequality*. Prior to Covid-19, inequality was growing in parts of the world. The difference in pay between workers and corporate chiefs had multiplied many times. The pandemic highlighted the existing gap between the haves and have-nots. High-income countries enjoyed much greater access to vaccines than low-income countries. Vulnerable, marginalized, and poor people tended to be more severely impacted by the crisis than the population as a whole (Kharas and Dooley 2021). Researchers at the Brookings Institution estimate that, by 2030, some 588 million people could still be living in extreme poverty, a figure that is fifty million higher than estimates made before Covid-19 made its appearance.

Another related concern that could stimulate widespread advocacy is *social protection*. The pandemic stretched social safety nets around the world. Authorities responded with new and expanded programs to, among other things, address the loss of jobs and income and the health dimensions of the crisis. Many of these programs were by design short term in nature. But allowing them to expire has not been without controversy. Coalitions have formed to advocate for greater spending on social protection and making temporary programs, or some version of them, more permanent. In this context, the possible adoption of a universal basic income is receiving greater attention.

The third area for potential action is *work–life balance*. As conditions improved in many countries in 2021, and employers began to ask their employees to return to work, many resisted. Having come to appreciate various silver linings of the pandemic, such as more time with family, and to contemplate their values and long-term goals, many in the labor force balked at going back to their places of employment.

In the United States, many quit (or lost) their jobs, and large numbers withdrew from the labor force altogether, contributing to a phenomenon that became known as the Great Resignation. One can anticipate increasing calls for the right to be left alone by one's boss after hours, opportunities to continue working remotely, and a four-day workweek. In many countries, people moved out of big cities to reduce living costs and seek a better quality of life. For example, Canada's two largest cities—Toronto and Montréal—witnessed record-breaking population losses to neighboring areas between July 1, 2019, and July 1, 2020 (Statistics Canada 2021).

Yet another subject that could give rise to activism is *privacy*. During Covid-19, individual privacy continued to deteriorate as governments adopted policies that demanded information and compliance from citizens for health and hygiene protocols. In addition, people spent more time on the internet and, in the process, surrendered more of their personal privacy to multinational corporations controlling social-media platforms and search engines. Expansion in the use of facial recognition technology has also raised alarm bells. Patience may begin to wear thin among a larger share of the population, which could mobilize to reassert control over decision-making.

Social movements have played a critical role in driving change in the world, pressing those in power to address problems confronting humanity. Young people are often among the drivers of such movements, and simultaneously are among those in society most adept at using new technologies. They will continue to harness new and emerging technologies to overcome frequent efforts to suppress their messages and calls for reform. Notwithstanding global democratic backsliding, tech-savvy social movements will remain a powerful force in forging a more civil, inclusive, and sustainable world, and in compelling changes in laws, rules, and practices to achieve that world. Online activism is here to stay.

Key Discussion Areas

- The occurrences of mistrust on government globally.
- The growth in technology use by various social movements.
- The use of tech to negate social movements.
- How technology will be adopted in the social movements of the future.

Notes

1 Elaine Thomas, Asian Development Bank, in email to the author dated October 24, 2021.
2 "Climate Justice Actions and Mobilizations—Action Planning for COVID Safety," Google doc, March 2021, https://docs.google.com/document/d/1C6c0Rz8b4c-NW2gIP23xtL-JiSWUKtnqJt7jj9zhXOg/edit (unattributed authorship).
3 "How False Information Spreads," *BBC*, www.bbc.co.uk/bitesize/articles/zcr8r2p (accessed February 24, 2023).
4 The portal is described in English on the Estonian government's website: https://kogu.ee/en/citizen-initiative-portal/ (accessed February 24, 2023).

References

Amini, Roshanak. 2020. "Knowledge Is Power: Virtual Forms of Everyday Resistance and Grassroots Broadcasting in Iran." *Interface*, May 8, 2020, www.interfacejournal.net/wp-content/uploads/2020/05/Amini.pdf (accessed February 24, 2023).

Amnesty International. 2020. "Fresh Wave of Phishing Attacks Targeting Journalists and Human Rights Activists in MENA." August 21, 2019, www.amnesty.org/en/latest/press-release/2019/08/fresh-wave-of-phishing-attacks-targeting-journalists-and-human-rights-activists-in-mena/ (accessed February 24, 2023).

Benson, Thor. 2015. "Getting to Know Operation Death Eaters." *Medium*, April 24, 2015, https://medium.com/@thorbenson/getting-to-know-operation-death-eaters-64b37c294f01 (accessed February 24, 2023).

Bullard, Nathanial. 2021. "The Corporate Climate: Climate Pledges Are as High as an Elephant's Eye." *Bloomberg*, July 8, 2021, www.bloomberg.com/news/articles/2021-07-08/the-corporate-climate-pledges-are-as-high-as-an-elephant-s-eye (accessed February 24, 2023).

Carty Victoria. 2015. *Social Movements and New Technology*. Milton Park, UK: Taylor and Francis, https://pdf.zlibcdn.com/dtoken/e4c0f5fbf114edc14acd1ece10d33da8/Social_Movements_and_New_Technology_by_Victoria_Ca_3703760_(z-lib.org).pdf (accessed February 24, 2023).

Ding, Emily. 2021. "In Malaysia, Young People Find Their Voice Amid a Pandemic." *Al Jazeera*, September 28, 2021, www.aljazeera.com/news/2021/9/28/youths-are-on-the-frontlines-of-political-activism-in-malaysia (accessed February 24, 2023).

Édes, Bart, and John Garrison. 2021. "COVID-19 Has Boosted Civil Society Participation in Global Meetings Despite Technical Glitches." Observer Research Foundation, January 28, 2021, www.orfonline.org/expert-speak/covid-19-has-boosted-civil-society-participation-in-international-meetings-despite-technical-glitches (accessed February 24, 2023).

Engler, Paul. 2020. "Coronavirus Is a Historic Trigger Event: Now Is the Time for a Social Movement to Rise." *Yes! Magazine*, April 6, 2020, www.yesmagazine.org/social-justice/2020/04/06/coronavirus-community-collective-response (accessed February 24, 2023).

Esfandiari, Golnaz. "Iran's Social-Media Struggles Laid Bare by Telegram and Cleric's Viral Moment." *Radio Free Europe/Radio Liberty*, April 13, 2019, www.rferl.org/a/iran-social-media-struggles-telegram-cleric-s-viral-moment/29879014.html (accessed February 24, 2023).

Foa, Roberto. 2020. "Faith in Democracy: Millennials Are the Most Disillusioned Generation 'in Living Memory'." Bennett Institute for Public Policy, University of Cambridge, October 19, 2020, www.bennettinstitute.cam.ac.uk/news/faith-democracy-millennials-are-most-disillusioned/ (accessed February 24, 2023).

Freedom House. 2021. *Freedom in the World in 2021: Democracy Under Siege*. Washington, DC, https://freedomhouse.org/report/freedom-world/2021/democracy-under-siege (accessed February 24, 2023).

Data Reportal. 2022. "Digital 2022, July Global Statshot Report." July 21, 2022, https://datareportal.com/reports/digital-2022-july-global-statshot (accessed February 24, 2023).

Human Rights Watch. 2021. "Covid-19 Triggers Wave of Free Speech Abuse." February 11, 2021, www.hrw.org/news/2021/02/11/covid-19-triggers-wave-free-speech-abuse (accessed February 24, 2023).

Jan, Tracy, Jena McGregor, and Meghan Hoyer. 2021. "Corporate America's $50 Billion Promise." *Washington Post*, August 23, 2021, www.washingtonpost.com/business/interactive/2021/george-floyd-corporate-america-racial-justice (accessed February 24, 2023).

Kharas, Homi, and Meagan Dooley. 2021. "Long-Run Impacts of Covid-19 on Extreme Poverty." Brookings Institution, June 2, 2021, www.brookings.edu/blog/future-development/2021/06/02/long-run-impacts-of-covid-19-on-extreme-poverty (accessed February 24, 2023).

Kothari, Ashish. 2020. "Corona Can't Save the Planet, but We Can, If We Learn from Ordinary People." *Interface*, April 17, 2020, www.interfacejournal.net/wp-content/uploads/2020/04/Kothari.pdf (accessed February 24, 2023).

Lawrence, Lizzy, and Anna Kramer. 2021. "How Slack and Discord Became Tools for Worker Revolt." *Protocol*, October 13, 2021, www.protocol.com/workplace/slack-discord-worker-protest-tools (accessed February 24, 2023).

National Intelligence Council. 2021. *Global Trends 2040: A More Contested World*. Washington, DC: National Intelligence Council.

Patton, Z. 2020. "Here's What Government Will Look Like in 2030." *Government Technology*, November 18, 2020, www.govtech.com/magazines/gt-special-issue-nov-2020-heres-what-government-will-look-like-in-2030.html (accessed February 24, 2023).

Pew Research Center. 2022. "Public Trust in Government 1958–2022." June 6, 2022, www.pewresearch.org/politics/2022/06/06/public-trust-in-government-1958-2022 (accessed February 24, 2023).

Pleyers, Geoffrey. 2020. "The Pandemic Is a Battlefield: Social Movements in the Covid-19 Lockdown." *Journal of Civil Society* 16(4): 295–312.

Spangler, Todd. 2020. "Did Hacktivist Group Anonymous Take Down Minneapolis PD Website?" *Variety*, May 31, 2020.

Statistics Canada. 2021. "Canada's Population Estimates: Subprovincial Areas, July 1, 2020." January 14, 2021, https://www150.statcan.gc.ca/n1/daily-quotidien/210114/dq210114a-eng.htm?HPA=1 (accessed February 24, 2023).

Van Laer, Jeroen, and Peter Van Aelst. 2009. "Cyber-Protest and Civil Society: The Internet and Action Repertoires in Social Movements." In *Handbook of Internet Crime*, edited by Yvonne Jewkes and Majid Yar. Milton Park, UK: Routledge.

4

CAN DIGITAL INNOVATIONS BE A GAME CHANGER FOR ENHANCED OPENNESS, ACCOUNTABILITY, AND RESPONSIVENESS IN INTERNATIONAL DEVELOPMENT?

Björn-Sören Gigler and Katherine H. Mann

Introduction

Open government, innovations, and disruptive technologies are today's hype words. Many experts are discussing the transformational potential of open government programs and new technologies to enhance accountability from governments and international donor agencies. However, the discussion generally focuses on the potential rather than the realized impact of openness facilitated by new technologies on improved governance and socioeconomic development.

An open development approach is emerging; however, its theoretical underpinnings and the empirical evidence of its impact on development outcomes are lacking. How do we define this new paradigm? What is truly open and collaborative, or to what extent can the openness agenda strengthen existing governance and the social accountability process and result in meaningful changes in the relationship between citizens, governments, and donor agencies? How does this new approach help to deliver and enhance the quality of public services? Which entities should drive this process: governments, donors, or civil society? What role does technological innovations play in such a new development approach? Ultimately, a key question emerges: Is open development a new paradigm or is it just old wine in new glasses?

The main objective of this chapter is to contribute to this discussion by (i) developing a theoretical framework for open development, (ii) investigating the role digital innovations can play in shortening the route to accountability, and (iii) presenting case studies that apply the approach in praxis. To address these questions, this chapter will first provide a short literature review on transparency, technology, and accountability. Second, it develops

DOI: 10.4324/9781003316077-6

an open development framework—the principles, the components, and the stages of the model—applying the public sector literature about co-produced governments to international development.

Then, this chapter examines the "how to" factors of accountability reforms and the enabling factors and barriers of implementing an open development approach. This chapter will analyze the role of technology as a facilitator for policy reforms toward a more open, collaborative, and inclusive development approach. Adopting the open development framework, this chapter analyzes several case studies of digital innovations programs, such as Mapping for Results, Open Aid Partnership, and citizen-feedback programs enabled by digital technologies, to investigate the on the ground impact of the paradigm. Finally, this chapter concludes with some early lessons learned and the challenges and obstacles these open development programs are facing in practice.

Open Development: A New Development Paradigm?

The main hypothesis of the open development approach is that enhanced openness and accountability empower citizens to better hold governments accountable and thus improve the delivery and quality of public services. The poor disproportionately depend on public services compared to other income groups. The World Development Report, *Making Services Work for Poor People*, emphasized citizen's well-being and that poor people in particular are critically dependent on governments' performance; they are particularly vulnerable to governmental inefficiency and the abuse of public office (World Bank 2004). The poor depend on governments for services; however, the government's lack of accountability in delivering effective and quality services continues. Ultimately, improving service delivery and the quality of accountability is critical to addressing poverty (Joshi 2013; Joshi and Moore 2004).

Open development is based on a political commitment to openness and accountability and goes beyond the mere provision of open data sets to collective and collaborative governance (Pradhan and Odugbemi 2011; Busan Partnership Agreement 2011). The initial step is to enhance transparency by opening up government data and improve citizen's access to information. To enhance the accountability of governments, it is however necessary to go beyond the first step and strengthen a two-way flow of information exchange between governments and citizens, as well as to increase the participation of citizens in the public policy-making processes. Such a process creates a "networked" society and a space for horizontal collaboration through this development (Smith, Elder, and Emdon 2011). Transparency is, however, only the initial step toward accountability, transplanting obscured and opaque processes to public scrutiny. Too often, there is an assumption that transparency produces accountability. Enhanced transparency does not necessarily lead to improved accountability (Kuriyan et al. 2011).

At the same time, improved openness facilitated through digital innovations can reduce the distance between governments and citizens, creating multiple information flows that translate into shortening the path to accountability (Wittemyer et al. 2014). Openness however is often contentious depending on the type of legal requirements. Furthermore, open data often conflicts with intellectual property rights and the free commercial access and reuse of the data (Strandburg et al. 2014).

At the center of this new approach stands the issue on how to address the struggle for accountability and how to respond to increased demand for more voice and participation in development for citizens. Jonathan Fox (2014) asserts the importance of bringing supply and demand sides together: "Social accountability strategies try to improve institutional performance by bolstering both citizen engagement and the public responsiveness of states and corporations" (p. 7). For evaluation purposes, there often exists a disconnect between top-down and bottom-up initiatives. Bottom-up monitoring lacks strength. At the same time, growing research indicates local elite capture of top-down initiatives.

The main objective of open development is to leverage digital innovations to broaden and shorten the route of accountability for international donor agencies (Anstey 2011). In the end, how new is this concept? In the 1990s, the development literature argued that development programs improved greatly with local and contextual embedded participation and civic engagement and that local voices are key (Chambers 1995, 1998; Gaventa and McGee 2013; Holland and Blackburn 1998; Hickey and Mohan 2004). If these concepts existed in the 1990s, is open development a true paradigm shift? To create meaningful change and sustainable impact, digital innovations and participation should be used in tandem. It is, furthermore, key to place people and not digital technologies at the center of transformational programs (Gigler 2015, 2021). Such a human-centered approach is citizen-centered, highly iterative, and adaptive to the specific needs of people and stresses that digital technologies need to be placed at the services of human development (Raftree 2012; Hanna 2012).

At the same time, open development enabled by digital innovations faces multiple challenges. The process does not occur in a vacuum. What are the major barriers to this process? Can this openness bridge the accountability gap among stakeholders? Ultimately, who will benefit from this openness, or will it further exclude marginalized groups? Can this openness lead to more effective and inclusive development? Essentially, how do these concepts and themes link with actual development results?

Innovative digital technologies should not be the drivers for sustainable development and determine the way people have to use them, but rather act as an enabler for change. A critical aspect is hereby to uphold the highest possible standards in terms of digital citizen rights, protecting their privacy, ensuring data protection, and protecting people from cybersecurity threats. Cases of privacy and data protection and violations of digital platforms have placed the topic of data protection and privacy at the center of the public debate (World Bank 2021). It is therefore critical to assess both the opportunities but also the risks of digital technologies. Digital Innovations are not a panacea, nor can they enable the rapid economic leap-frogging of developing countries. There are key factors, including economic, social, and cultural factors, that influence whether or not digital technologies, in fact, can have a positive impact on development programs.

The following section lays out an open development framework that brings both the demand and supply side of enhanced governance and accountability together. Furthermore, it investigates to what extent digital innovations can serve as a link between the social accountability programs that aim to enhance citizen participation in decision-making processes and accountability and governance reforms initiated by government and international donor agencies. The use of digital innovations cannot be seen in a void as local socioeconomic conditions are critical for assessing their impact. Open development approaches need to be embedded into a much broader political economy context of government/donor reforms, social movements, citizen's movements, and civic engagement.

Toward an Open Development Framework

Open Development Principles

Enabled through free, open, and easy access to data and information, open development aims to empower all stakeholders in the development process to participate meaningfully in development programs. The open development model is guided by the following principles: (i) the free, open, and easy access to government data and information is a global public good; (ii) human-centered citizens are active agents of development (Gigler 2021); (iii) it is based on distributive and decentralized community networks; (iv) it is enabled through digital technology; (v) it leverages multistakeholder coalitions for change, including coalitions within the government, between governments and donors, civil society and citizens, and with the private sector; and (vi) it has an iterative and adaptive approach that incorporates near real-time citizen feedback in project design and implementation (Bovaird 2007).

Accompanying the guiding principles are the framework's central components and actors: transparency, participation, collaboration, and empowerment.

Supply Side: Free, Open, and Easy Access to Development Data and Information

As shown in Figure 4.1, the major actors of the emerging open development approach come from both the supply and demand side of accountability processes. As shown on the left

Figure 4.1 Bridging the Gap Between the Supply and Demand Sides of Accountability

Source: Adapted from Gigler and Bailur (2014).

side of Figure 4.1, on the supply side are the institutional processes of governments and donor reforms.

Open data programs play a critical role in enhancing the transparency of both governments and international donor agencies. The emphasis of these programs is to enable citizens and the public in general to have free, open, and easy access to key development data and information. A key aspect of open data initiatives is that the use of data should not be restricted in any means and that users are empowered both to access and reuse the obtained data for both commercial and noncommercial uses without any legal restrictions. An example of a far-reaching reform in terms of opening up development data is the World Bank's Open Data Initiative (data.worldbank.org), where the World Bank made 7,000 international development indicators available to the public. It allows users access to a wide range of information, such as project data and indicators. The indicators are free and available in a user-friendly format to download, analyze, and reuse without any restrictions (World Bank Group 2012).

A key step for opening up the development process, however, is to move beyond the supply side of open-governance programs and the simple release of open data to programs that are based on user-centered design principles and that empower citizens to have easily accessible and comprehensible data. Open data programs should be informed by real information and data needs of civil society and citizens rather than being developed in a top-down fashion and in isolation (Barder 2009, 2011a). Experiences indicate that significant institutional and cultural change is necessary so that these initiatives have a larger impact on institutional reform. First, so that these programs can be scaled up and mainstreamed into donor financing operations. In the long term, these programs should not only be reactive to accountability demands from the outside but should also be part of much more comprehensive accountability and governance reforms within governments and international donors. These initiatives have the potential to become part of a much-broader institutional change process toward a citizen-centered development approach.

Demand Side: Strengthened Social Accountability Mechanisms

Simultaneously, it is critical to strengthen the demand side of accountability processes through civil voice and participation in the international development processes. With right to information laws and civil society-led programs, citizens are making more requests to engage with data, to participate in political decision-making processes, and to act on the information provided. Citizens are not passive recipients and consumers of data and development information, but they play an increasingly critical role in making their voices heard and leading the rise of citizen-generated data.

For open development to be successful, it is critical to strengthen both the capacity of civil society and citizen groups to access, process, and evaluate open data and the capacity of donor agencies and government institutions to liberate data and effectively respond to requests and feedback from citizens (Gigler, Bailur, and Anand 2014). A key challenge within this process is how to strengthen the data and informational capabilities of citizens, particularly of poor communities, to translate the improved access to information into concrete steps to enhance their economic and social well-being (Gigler 2015). Civil society organizations play a central role in this process: they can act as infomediaries facilitating improved access to information for citizens and enhancing their capabilities to process and act upon the information and data obtained. Furthermore, donor agencies should support governments to strengthen their technical capacity within key institutions to effectively respond to citizen feedback. Governments and donors alike should establish clear internal business processes across different ministries or departments so that they are able to engage in a meaningful way in a dialogue with citizens. Thus, the demand side and the supply side of open development programs cannot be separated from each other but need to be strengthened simultaneously.

Linking the Demand Side With the Supply Side Through Digital Innovation

Digital innovations have the potential to connect the demand and supply sides of social accountability and governance reforms with each other. New digital technologies can, under certain conditions, be leveraged to become key enablers of institutional change as well as strengthen the capacity of citizens and civic groups to make their voices heard in policy debates. On the supply side, digital innovations have the potential to be disruptive inside government institutions or international donors and amplify existing reforms toward enhanced openness, transparency, and responsiveness. Many disruptive technologies, in particular, that originate from the open-source movement have an intrinsic open and collaborative design. For instance, an open blockchain-based system is characterized by having no central node; rather, platforms are based on a truly open, distributive, and decentralized system, whereby each element can facilitate certain aspects of a project. Therefore, these open-source technologies contribute toward a flat, open, and more democratic structure. For instance, the Open Street Map community has demonstrated the power of such a distributive and collaborative networking in the development of interactive maps in response to natural disasters, such as crisis mapping in Chile, Haiti, Pakistan, and many other places.

These digital innovations demonstrated that it is possible to open up the development process. Citizens become active producers of development data instead of passive recipients of official development information and statistics. The above-mentioned experiences from the crisis mapping and Open Street Maps have demonstrated that they can lead to a generative process of open collaboration between volunteer technical communities and development experts within international donor agencies. Such an approach, based on citizen-generated data and crowdsourcing, implies an important cultural change toward a genuine partnership among civil society, the private sector, grassroots groups, international donors, and governments. Critical to applying crowdsourcing approaches to international development is the recognition that knowledge and experiences are vastly distributed among all stakeholders and not concentrated inside donor agencies alone (Bott, Gigler, and Young 2014).

However, significant challenges remain for applying such an approach at the local level, depending on the distinct sociopolitical context and enabling environment in each developing country. Often, digital technologies only play a minor role in determining whether open-governance initiatives succeed in a certain context; however, regulatory, political, social, and cultural aspects represent important barriers to determining whether development processes can in fact become more open, democratic, and inclusive. To advance in this open development agenda, it is critical to engage into more systematic and long-term social accountability processes and to strengthen multistakeholder coalitions that support more systematic reforms. Civil society organizations play a central role as critical "infomediaries" between governments, international donors, and citizens and thus can facilitate improved dialogues between policy-makers and citizens (Gigler 2015). Furthermore, they can play a critical role in strengthening the capacity of poor communities to access and use development information and data. Innovative start-ups play a key role in developing civic tech solutions, such as apps or open access platforms and data visualizations, that empower a broad range of users. The accountability loop can only be closed if all actors collaborate and contribute their individual expertise within a more collaborative and prolonged process of governance reforms.

Moving Beyond Openness to Collaborative Governance

The framework lays out the main aspects of the open development approach, but how would a process toward opening up development occur? The first and critical step is the political commitment of key policy-makers to the core principles of openness, transparency, and accountability. Alongside the opening up of development information and data, a culture and institutional change toward more collaborative governance needs to take place within governments and donor agencies. In particular, there needs to be a change of incentives for policy-makers, government officials, and development experts to support collaborative development approaches (Ostrom 1996; Mitlin 2008; Needham 2008). Such an approach needs to combine both a high-level political commitment from the top and the support of technical experts to support the implementation of concrete open development programs. In short, it is essential that policy-makers gradually recognize that collaborative governance models can be effective mechanisms to address development challenges (Gigler, Bailur, and Anand 2014).

The second step is the recognition that citizen-generated and crowdsourced data can be a powerful tool in decision-making. Through triangulation of official and crowdsourced data, policy-makers and donors improve the capacity of government and donor agencies to make well-informed policy decisions. Crowdsourced data also offers a reality check or independent evaluation from the local level. For instance, crowdsourced data can function as an independent verification source to gauge the satisfaction of the service being provided to beneficiaries. In particular, this type of data generated by community-based monitoring programs can help identify the quality of services and projects. Going beyond simple access to the data, it brings citizen satisfaction into the implementation and adaptation of programs.

For such a process to work, governments and donors have to be proactive in listening and engaging with citizens and to recognize the important value citizen-generated data has for making decisions. In a third step, it is critical to form multistakeholder coalitions in order to gain the necessary support for the reforms within and outside of government and donors. Governments are not homogeneous entities; and it is key to identify reform-minded champions within key institutions, who can provide the necessary political support for the reforms (Fung and Wright 2003). Coalitions within government or within donors, as well as coalitions with other external actors (such as the private sector and civil society), align incentives and overlap with the interests of individual actors and the common objectives of the coalition. Within the coalitions, the champions need to be strengthened (Pradhan 2014).

Finally, with the free flow of data, there can be better decision-making across internal departments and ministries. These internal and external coalitions can be leveraged to assist and strengthen internal reforms. At the same time, enabling factors provide the context for institutional change. On the supply side, there are both internal and external drivers of change and movement toward this co-produced, open development model.

Institutional change takes time and will require a long and sustained cultural shift toward this open development model. Another enabling factor on the government's side is a crisis of legitimacy characterized by protests from citizen movements demanding greater voice and influence. Governance reforms tend to be a reaction to those instances. Many of these initiatives develop in response to increased civil society pressure and movements. Many developing countries face a severe crisis of legitimacy and are gradually embracing open and accountable governments to address the demands from citizens and civic movements. The open development approach aims to bring the supply and demand side of social accountability mechanisms together in an integrated approach and to bridge the accountability gap between citizens and governments. Enhanced by multiple data flows, it supports decentralized decision-making.

For governments, this indicates that there is a greater flow between national and local governments. In such a decentralized network, solutions can originate from any part of the network. Such an open, decentralized approach allows anyone to offer creative solutions to development problems. Citizens from donor countries demand more transparency and accountability from development aid. With scarce resources for development aid, these citizens pressure for development effectiveness (Knack 2001; Winters 2010). From both sides, civil society organizations hold donor agencies accountable. Various participatory mechanisms, including citizen scorecards, participatory budgeting, and redress tools, strengthen the demand side for good governance—for governments and donors. However, the initiatives run parallel rather than in conjunction. Programs exist at the grassroots level and at the donor/government levels, yet there is little coordination between them. Furthermore, it is essential to strengthen citizen capacities for enabling effective demand-side mechanisms of social accountability.

Digital Innovations as an Enabling Factor?

Digital innovations play an integral role in cementing the various elements of open development. With technology, the knowledge about development is more open, available, and horizontal. It connects the various stakeholders and enables effective two-way connections and responsiveness. However, digital technologies face many constraints and important risks, such as the use of data, which needs to be well managed to protect citizen privacy and ensure the highest possible data protection standards. Thus, to what extent can digital technology be transformational for governance? Digital technologies, when used for the right purposes, can trigger and accelerate the process of institutional reform and change. They can strengthen citizen voices and the overall demand side of the equation. Crowdsourcing enabled through innovative technologies allows policy-makers, citizens, and the general public to access information in almost real time (Gigler 2011c).

Digital technologies can also enhance the display of government data. Many governments simply present data intended for an expert audience rather than general consumption. Mapping and data visualization have the potential to democratize data (Barder 2011b). Examples include geocoding projects to see exactly where donor agencies are funding projects and local citizen-feedback programs. In this digestible format, the data is much more accessible to a broader audience, particularly in places with low literacy rates and limited formal education access. Technology lowers the costs, it has become ubiquitous, and it can harness real-time data. Finally, a vast amount of data can be collected and sorted rapidly. For donors, digital innovation can play a central role in the traceability of development assistance down the chain of project delivery, from the donor funds to direct project implementation (aidinfo 2010). Digital Innovations, such as artificial intelligence and blockchain, can also support programs to better "follow the money" and empower citizens to track the use of funds. Another way to strengthen the traceability of aid is to provide donor country citizens the ability to view the allocation of aid while at the same time allowing recipient country citizens to follow the financial allocation and operational implementation of that aid (Barder 2011a). While the use of technology clearly enables the open development paradigm to be applied, there remains the need for more stringent evaluations that assess the impact that digital technologies have on enhancing the openness, effectiveness, and inclusiveness of development programs.

Open Development in Practice

The following section provides several case studies that leverage digital innovation for enhanced transparency and accountability of international development programs. Specifically, it investigates in more depth the following three innovative programs: (i) Mapping for Results, (ii) the Open Aid Partnership, and (iii) digitally enabled citizen-feedback mechanisms.

Mapping for Results

How can a citizen become involved in a project if people are not aware of the project? With the great advances in GPS and mapping technology, understanding the geospatial location of a project has advanced in leaps and bounds. Mapping for Results leveraged the rapid increased access to technology available, in particular the ubiquitous cell phone. Mapping technology allows for a fast, coordinated response among volunteers, nongovernmental organizations (NGOs), and citizens with a rapid turnover time and builds on the interconnection of geography and aid (Gigler 2010; Dodds and Xu 2012). Likewise, crisis mapping initiatives allow local communities to spatially understand and create a detailed map of communities experiencing natural disaster (Shkabatur 2014b).

The Mapping for Results program of the World Bank was developed in partnership with AidData. It geographically locates World Bank–financed projects on an interactive map that overlays project locations with detailed subnational poverty and human-development indicators.[1] This allows users to carry out detailed analysis on the relationship between the location of the projects and poverty indicators, thus assessing whether projects are located in high-poverty areas (Gigler 2011a). Initially, the Mapping for Results program mapped over 36,000 locations of active World Bank–financed projects in over 140 countries. The project has three strategic goals: (i) report the location of World Bank–financed projects through spatial and geographic visualization; (ii) strengthen transparency and accountability to improve the impact of aid flows; and (iii) strengthen stakeholders at multiple levels (Gigler 2011a). With projects mapped out at the national at the subnational levels, users can use indicators, such as high rates of poverty or health needs, to determine if the projects are indeed addressing the needs of the country.

To assess the effectiveness of the World Bank's projects and development aid, the platform includes a section on project results where users can find more detailed information on the project's key development objectives. Ultimately, this tool allows users an amplified and in-depth analysis into World Bank financing via an easily understandable and empowering interactive platform. The initiative, however, is not without its challenges. In the effort to have precise and accurate maps and pinpoint project locations, there were issues with data verification and logistics. A key challenge was to ensure data accuracy, due to manual task of geocoding, which was very time-consuming and required specialized geospatial skills. Within eighteen months, this innovative program managed to scale up its activities from four pilot countries (Bolivia, Haiti, Kenya, and the Philippines) to geo-code all World Bank–financed projects in the Africa region and eventually reached a global scale. A critical step for ensuring its sustainability was a policy change of World Bank operational guidelines, which made it mandatory for all teams to provide the geo-location of the projects they were financing within the World Bank's operations portal (Gigler, Tanner, and Kiess 2011).

However, while the initiative has made an important contribution in terms of enhancing the transparency of World Bank–financed programs, the meaningful use, analysis, and policy conclusions from the inter active maps require the continuous effort of policy-makers to invest in technology, people, and innovations. The program has nevertheless made an important contribution toward enhancing the accountability of international donors and showcasing the transformative power of open-geospatial data, interactive mapping, and data visualizations.

Open Aid Partnership

The Open Aid Partnership (OAP), launched by the World Bank in partnership with seven bilateral donors in 2011, also aims to enhance development effectiveness by leveraging interactive mapping and open-geospatial data. The OAP has supported several partners countries (e.g., Bolivia, Kenya, Malawi, and Nepal) in the development of a comprehensive Open Aid Map. The Open Aid Map geocodes all aid projects in a county, leading to easy visualization. The OAP information is publicly available and allows developing countries to better analyze financial and results data of donor-financed programs, as well as allows donor agencies to view project concentrations within the developing country. The OAP aims to enhance coordination of programs for donor agencies that are implementing projects in numerous sectors and across countries (Gigler 2011b).

Mapping projects can limit the risk of overlapping projects and minimize the administrative burden to governments, as well as permit citizen feedback and empowerment. Ultimately, this could improve the transparency, decision-making, and development effectiveness of international development. A cogent example is Malawi, which has received aid for over fifty years but still lags in socioeconomic development. In 2008, the Ministry of Finance adopted the Aid Management Platform, a tool to track incoming aid flows (Development Gateway 2010). However, the program did not capture all the information necessary for the Ministry of Finance to make fully informed decisions on projects, nor be fully transparent with the donor agencies. In 2011, Malawi joined the OAP to demonstrate its commitment to aid transparency. The program mapped US$3.7 billion of official development assistance, from thirty-seven donors active in Malawi. This project, however, was an isolated pilot program and was not incorporated into the country's aid management system. Important data constraints continued to exist, in particular with reporting requirements. Reporting continues to be late, as it takes time to precisely locate a project. For the program to have a more sustained impact on the country, the government needs to have greater ownership for its management by defining and steering the actual use and adoption of technologies within institutions. The level of institutional technology adoption will determine the extent to which governments will make full use of the available data for policy-making. For donor agencies, there needs to be greater agency coordination, so they can better focus their financing decisions based on local context and stronger development results.

Digitally Enabled Citizen Engagement

The power of digital technologies can be leveraged for citizen engagement, enabling more direct, easier, and near real-time citizen feedback (Fung 2013; Gigler and Bailur 2014). A first case study is the Check My School Initiative in the Philippines, which is a digitally enabled community-monitoring platform in the education sector. The citizen-feedback platform leverages SMS, mobile phones, and mapping to create better accountability among citizens, providers, and the government. Citizens leveraged the crowdsourcing capabilities of the service to check on the quality of roofs or toilets of their local elementary schools. Based on the citizen feedback received, the Ministry of Education responded with inspections and improvements. The initiative presented clear incentives for the government to act and respond to citizens.

Check My School's data covered over 44,000 local schools in the country, although the data from the Department of Education did not include GPS coordinates. The project did encounter issues with low internet access, capabilities, and technical issues. After the first year of the project, there were several lessons learned including the need to build capacity and create a sustained and constructive dialogue between local schools and government policy-makers, and need for technology effectiveness. Overall, the project saw both successes, such as strengthened collaboration between local schools and National Ministry of Education, and challenges, including the limited use of the data due to low digital capabilities (Shkabatur 2014a).

Another example of participatory digital technology is the governance program, ICT4Gov, which implemented a flagship project in the Democratic Republic of Congo. It incorporates civic tech with participatory budgeting. With the Congo's history of poor institutions, corruption, and violence, citizens have little trust in government institutions. In 2006, the Congo's national government decentralized governance authority to the local level, including managing the local budget. In 2009, the government launched the ICT4Gov program in the province of South Kivu. The program leveraged the use of mobile phone technology to enhance the reach of traditional community meetings. Coupling the use of SMS with in-person meetings and community assemblies, the project encourages greater engagement and knowledge of the budget process and allocation. In the assemblies, citizens vote on potential projects, learn about the decisions made, and offer feedback on the projects. Key sectors such as education and health have seen improvements since the project's implementation. Moreover, the improved levels of local tax collection suggest citizens can see where and how their taxes are spent.

On the other hand, the Maji Matone Project in Tanzania is an example of unsuccessful implementation of digital technology. In 2009, the civil society organization Daraja began the Raising the Water Pressure/Maji Matone Project to solicit citizen feedback on access to water in their rural communities. The project chose to use mobile phones and SMS to gather water users' feedback and information on levels of water availability through an easily comprehensible format that would allow citizens to upload this information via SMS messages, thus providing local government with real-time citizen feedback. However, citizens did not use the SMS system as expected. After six months, the program received only fifty-three messages rather than the expected 3,000. With the information received, local governments were able to repair numerous water access points, but overall the program was deemed unsuccessful. The project attributes its failure to the lack of consideration for gender issues. While women are the primary household water fetchers, most don't have access to mobile phones and/or connectivity. In addition, the incentive for citizens to participate was low, since they were not confident that the feedback provided would improve water access in their communities. The citizens thus had low expectations and a lack of trust in their government's ability to deliver results, based on years of failed promises. Furthermore, even though the messages were anonymous, many users feared that providing critical feedback might result in government reprisals (Daraja 2013).

Another citizen-feedback mechanism, the OnTrack Platform, was implemented by the World Bank's Innovation in Governance Team in 2014/2015 (Innovations in Governance Team 2014). The platform "supported short message service (SMS) and Web-based feedback loops between citizens, civil society organizations, and government implementing agencies involved World Bank-funded community development projects." Thus, the aim was for stakeholders to monitor these projects and provide feedback to government on their effective implementation. Several countries, including Bolivia, Kenya, Nepal, Indonesia, and Zambia, participated in the program (Gigler and Bailur 2014).

In Bolivia, the platform worked with two major projects, the Rural Alliance Project (PAR) and the slum upgrading program Barrios de Verdad (PBCV), both of which are financed by the World Bank. For PAR, the OnTrack platform was integrated into its information system. PAR aims to improve the situation of rural farmers and their access to markets. For this to occur, the farmers needed improved access to technology, strengthened farmer organizations, and improved economic and political relationships with the local government agencies. With OnTrack, farmers were able to provide feedback through their cell phones. The PBCV, for its part, has improved community-based infrastructure programs in poor communities of La Paz. By utilizing OnTrack, a direct communication link between citizens and the mayor's office was established.

In Nepal, the OnTrack platform has worked in conjunction with the national community-driven Poverty Alleviation Fund (PAF), which is financed by the World Bank and aims to enhance the living conditions of the poorest communities. The PAF has empowered citizens to develop and manage their own projects. The program has worked in the forty poorest districts in Nepal before it was expanded to a national scale. The organization utilizes a participatory approach between local government and civil society. This approach has encouraged local citizens to form their own organizations within their communities. PAF encompasses several platforms for feedback and monitoring purposes. An interactive platform as well as an SMS service, OnTrack enables further engagement among citizens, officials, and project groups. The platform includes space for feedback and suggestions. Similarly, it has the option to publish results and information in real time. The program has encountered several key challenges in its implementation phase, such as how to transfer the technology platform and the related technology know-how to local government institutions.

In Bolivia, for instance, this shortcoming was addressed when the PAR project transferred the entire platform to a local technology provider and the government initiated a process to fully integrate a citizen-feedback platform into its existing project management platform. Another key challenge the program addressed is the lack of incentives for citizens to provide continuous feedback using a digitally enabled platform. The program empowered citizens to directly report problems with the implementation of the project at the community level. The transparency and the focus on enhanced traceability of delivery of works and services significantly contributed to enhancing the responsiveness of local program officials. The central project management unit closely monitored the citizen feedback obtained and required local implementing offices to provide a frequent report on how the reported problems/complaints were addressed. This led to a mechanism of gradually "closing the feedback loop" and thus providing citizens the incentives to use the system and to provide feedback. In most countries, the programs lacked a clear strategy on how to leverage technology for continuous citizen engagement. In Nepal and Zambia, the program encountered real restrictions in terms of the capacity of citizens to provide feedback by cell phone. The pilot initiatives in rural areas of Nepal demonstrated that the illiteracy rate, particular of rural women, was so high that the use of SMS was not feasible. To address these challenges, the program made important adjustments and introduced a voice-based feedback system, which also enabled rural communities with very high illiteracy rates to provide feedback. The program also encountered important cultural barriers in rural communities. For the majority of the rural poor and marginalized groups, the entire concept of providing feedback with or without technology to government agencies was unknown and people frequently expressed a sense of general mistrust in the government. Thus, social and cultural factors have represented major obstacles for the successful implementation of the program in particular among the most marginalized communities.

While the OnTrack program generated citizen feedback, demonstrating the value of citizen-generated data to monitor the quality of government programs, it failed by not integrating the feedback system into existing government project management processes. This is a frequent problem with citizen-feedback programs. While they are able to establish digital mechanisms that allow citizens to provide feedback on government services received, they do not strengthen the capacity of government institutions to effectively respond to that feedback.

Lessons Learned From Digitally Enabled Citizen Engagement Programs

From the who to the how, there are many ways to improve citizen-feedback initiatives. To begin with, these initiatives should have clearly stated objectives. An absence of clarity results in unrealistic expectations and a lack of understanding about the objectives of generating feedback. With an explicit purpose and defined objective, it is easier for all stakeholders to understand the aims of the feedback program. This definition will help the program implementers design the optimal feedback mechanism to pursue the stated goals. Moreover, the collected feedback should go beyond the success or failure of a project into more ambitious goals by leveraging technology solutions for a broader reform process. Therefore.

> these initiatives should therefore include long-term policy reform that aims to build citizen capacity to engage and government capacity to provide effective services . . .

> also strive to transform feedback into citizen empowerment and to reform how projects are implemented in the future.
>
> *(Gigler and Bailur 2014, 42)*

Thus, the collection of feedback should have both short-term impact on the project outputs and long-term amplified impact on development outcomes.

Projects should not be designed around emerging technologies. Rather, these digital technologies should be embedded into, and respond to, the needs of projects. They should also take fully into account the local socioeconomic context and existing human capabilities. Using the latest technology may not be appropriate for every project and the technology employed should fit the political, socioeconomic, and cultural context. The technology should also be utilized with enough flexibility so changes can be made for better integration with the local context. Technology, both new and old, should be incorporated to create a hybrid platform of citizen engagement (Gigler and Bailur 2014, 43). Furthermore, technology does not replace the role of civil society organizations (CSOs) in the feedback loop; rather, it enhances its role as an intermediary and infomediary (Galtung 2013).

More traditional, non-tech solutions still bring important value to this feedback process and, in conjunction with digital technologies, can aggregate and form a more complete picture of the situation. Technology can greatly expand the participation and inclusiveness of feedback loops by using varied channels and modes of communication. It is also important to have a more complete assessment of who the stakeholders are and the roles they play. The definition of stakeholders goes beyond the immediate beneficiaries of a project but includes all groups potentially affected by it, even if indirectly. The feedback mechanisms should be able to include feedback from all groups, including those who are members of the community. Furthermore, CSOs can help identify the needs of the local context and enhance communication with stakeholders. At no point should stakeholders lack access to or be excluded from the process. As with engagement in general, it should not be considered an add-on or ad hoc approach, but rather be systematically and frequently applied. Similarly, enhancements should be made to improve and adapt to changing dynamics throughout the process (Gigler, Bailur, and Anand 2014).

Finally, it comes down to strengthening all stakeholders on both the supply and demand sides of the equation. Merely having a platform available for citizen feedback does not guarantee use by the intended beneficiaries. Technology should be accompanied by campaigns to ensure both the citizens' willingness and capabilities to use the feedback mechanism. Thus, citizens will understand what the platform is, how to use it, why they should use it, and determine whether providing feedback is safe. Not only should citizen feedback be increased, but government's capability of acting on the feedback received should be as well. Along the way, this process should be transparent, and there should also be clarity and understanding of the aims and goals of the development project. Moreover, it should enhance two-way communication, help manage expectations, and outline standards and responsibilities for both stakeholders and project implementers. Ultimately, the aim is to close the feedback loop and move beyond feedback alone. As these case studies demonstrate, the use of technology does not inevitably ensure the success of a project or initiative. Other factors—from the local context to access—need to be considered (Gigler, Bailur, and Anand 2014).

Challenges and Obstacles

Even with rapid changes in technology and the new approaches these technologies offer, these case studies demonstrate continued constraints and obstacles to the full execution of this model. These challenges do not originate with the technology itself but the conditions and environment around the technology, such as legal constraints on the extended use of the technology or trust issues between the parties that arise at the local level. Delineations between transparency and accountability are uncertain and vague. Several factors constrain and diminish the impact of digital technologies in bridging the gap among citizens, governments, and donors (Adam and Fazekas 2018; McGee 2013). Institutionally, without mainstreaming digital innovations, they may merely remain the latest fad without being incorporated for future uses. However, governments are beginning to see the value of these initiatives. For donor agencies, there is still much to learn about the legal access to data and the rights to use data for all uses without providing an unfair advantage to large tech companies or undermining citizen's privacy and data protection.

Legal Challenges

Licensing agreements are a central obstacle to the free and public use of data. Learning from experience, donor agencies understand that these arrangements can obstruct data's full potential (see, e.g., iRevolution 2022). Most multinational technology companies have very complicated licensing arrangements that often represent real obstacles for the free use and reuse of data, even in the context of programs that support humanitarian development (World Bank 2021). In contrast, most NGOs and other CSOs use the creative commons license agreement, which is a type of license in which only attribution is a necessary qualification for using the data. Essentially, it is a license for a public good as exemplified by open-source programs, such as Open Street Mapping which uses an Open Data Commons Database License (Open Street Map 2022). The issue of privacy, and the lack of privacy, is a concern when there is an extensive amount of data. The providers of mobile services act as entry points for the internet and will want to protect their share. Lastly, there is a possibility for censorship and special filtering of content (Smith, Elder, and Emdon 2011).

Trust

Trust or a lack of trust on both sides of the equation could also dampen program effectiveness. If citizens have little trust in their governments, then they are reluctant to use feedback mechanisms. A concrete example of this failure is Daraja's Maji Matone Project in Tanzania, in which citizens did not comprehensively use the system due to lack of trust in government. Limited trust and unequal access to mobile technology hampered the possible success of the project. Citizens were disheartened by years of low expectations and did not have the incentives nor the trust to participate (Daraja 2013).

Institutional Mainstreaming and Sustainability

For open development to constitute a real impact, it needs institutional mainstreaming. The hype of today's potential needs to be tomorrow's sustained change and cultural development. Institutions should see this new transparency paradigm as part of the institutional fabric rather than an ad hoc choice for the moment. With institutional mainstreaming being a long-term process, the embedding of digital technologies must be a sustained process. These case studies assist in understanding how donor agencies can advance to implementation and understand the enabling factors to make this happen. Both the demand and the supply side of the equation need to be simultaneously strengthened. The local socioeconomic context is critical to the relative success of a feedback mechanism and use of an open development model. In terms of the demand and supply equation, the citizen demand or "pull" side should be stronger as citizens have vested interest in improved services. A disconnect often exists between initiatives from the supply or "push" side of the equation and local grassroots initiatives. Civil society plays a critical role in raising awareness and mobilizing citizens. At the same time, community monitoring for accountability may not be connect to larger global initiatives. Much of the new open development agenda still lacks integration into programs and projects on the ground.

Conclusion

Development writ large and the open development framework are ultimately about people. Technology has the power and potential to magnify and extend the connections among people, but ultimately the opportunities for development depend on the people themselves. Citizens are more than voters—they can improve services and development through feedback and pressure on governments and donor agencies (Lieberman, Posner, and Tsai 2013). People are the central actors within development; technologies are only a mechanism to further and enhance this interconnected pool of actors. Research needs to develop a nuanced and analytical approach to unpack and evaluate the open development initiatives.

Until now, there is no established or rigorous methodology to compare the various feedback initiatives. With an analytical framework in place, we could fully compare these initiatives and analyze their impact. The paradigm is however still theoretically underdeveloped, and we are still missing the empirical data and evidence that demonstrate the central role open-governance approaches can play in enhancing the effectiveness, responsiveness, and inclusiveness of donor-financed programs.

Open development and open government programs are often not yet fully mainstreamed into the core programs of international donor agencies and national governments. It is critical to move beyond promoting openness and enhanced accountability for their own sake to providing more evidence that open-governance programs have an important positive impact on enhancing development outcomes on the ground. The hope is that this chapter will contribute to the debate on methodology and that the suggested model contributes to establishing a better theoretical foundation for the emerging open development approach.

Key Discussion Areas

- Methods of increasing transparency and accountability in development.
- How digital innovations enhance development outcomes and inclusion.
- Emergence of the open development paradigm and its approaches.

Note

1 World Bank Maps, https://maps.worldbank.org/ (accessed February 24, 2023).

References

Adam, Isabelle, and Mihály Fazekas. 2018. "Are Emerging Technologies Helping Win the Fight Against Corruption in Developing Countries?" Pathways for Prosperity Commission Background Paper Series 21, https://pathwayscommission.bsg.ox.ac.uk/sites/default/files/2019-02/ict-corruption-24feb19_final.pdf (accessed February 24, 2023).

aidinfo. 2010."Show Me the Money: IATI and Aid Traceability." Briefing Paper 1, March 8, 2021, azureedge.net, http://aidinfo.org/files/Show%20me%20the%20money%20-%20IATI%20and%20aid%20traceability.pdf.

Anstey, Caroline. 2011. "New Technology Can Democratize Development." *The Guardian*, November 29, 2011.

Barder, Owen. 2009. "Beyond Planning: Markets and Networks for Better Aid." Working Paper 185, Center for Global Development, Washington, DC.

———. 2011a. "Eight Lessons from Three Years Working on Transparency." *Blog*, February 22, 2011.

———. 2011b. "Ten Steps for Meaningful Aid Transparency." *Blog*, April 7, 2011, www.owen.org/blog/4486 (accessed February 24, 2023).

Bott, Maja, Bjorn-Soren Gigler, and Gregor Young. 2014. "The Role of Crowdsourcing for Better Governance in Fragile State Contexts." In *Closing the Feedback Loop*, edited by Bjorn-Soren Gigler and Savita Bailur. Washington, DC: World Bank.

Bovaird, Tim. 2007. "Beyond Engagement and Participation: User and Community Co-Production of Public Services." *Public Administration Review* 67(5): 846–60.

Busan Partnership Agreement. 2011. "Busan Partnership for Effective Development Cooperation." Fourth High Level Forum on Aid Effectiveness, Republic of Korea, Busan, www.oecd.org/dac/effectiveness/49650173.pdf (accessed February 24, 2023).

Chambers, Robert. 1995. "Poverty and Livelihoods: Whose Reality Counts?" *Environment and Urbanization* 7(1): 173–204.

———. 1998. "Beyond 'Whose Reality Counts?': New Methods We Do Not Need." *Cultures, Organizations and Societies* 4: 279–301.

Daraja. 2013. *Politics, Technology and Change. Learning From the Failure of the Maji Matone Programme*. Njombe: Daraja Development Ltd.

Development Gateway. 2010. "The Experience of the Aid Management Platform Program," https://developmentgateway.org/expertise/aid-management/ (accessed February 24, 2023).

Dodds, Elizabeth, and Qiyang Xu. 2012. *The Importance of Geography for Aid Effectiveness*. Washington, DC: The World Bank Innovation Practice.

Fox, Jonathan. 2014. "Social Accountability: What Does the Evidence Say?" Working Paper No. 1, Global Partnership for Social Accountability, Washington, DC.

Fung, Archon. 2013. "The Fix-Rate: Integrity Action's New Transparency and Accountability Impact Metric." Sunlight Foundation, May 16, 2013. Accessed November 16, 2014.

Fung, Archon, and Erik Olin Wright. 2003. "Thinking About Empowered Participatory Governance." In *Deepening Democracy: Institutional Innovations in Empowered Participatory Governance. The Real Utopias Project IV*, edited by A. Fung and E. Wright. London: Verso.

Galtung, Fredrik. 2013. "The Fix-Rate: A Key Metric for Transparency and Accountability." Integrity Action Working Paper No. 2, www.globalgiving.org/pfil/24168/projdoc.pdf (accessed February 24, 2023).

Gaventa, John, and Rosemary McGee. 2013. "The Impact of Transparency and Accountability Initiatives." *Development Policy Review* 31: s3–28, https://doi.org/10.1111/dpr.12017.

Gigler, Bjorn-Soren. 2010. *Geography and Aid*. Washington, DC: World Bank, March 31, 2010.

———. 2011a. "Mapping for Results". *World Bank Blog*, October 6, 2011, http://blogs.worldbank.org/developmenttalk/mapping-for-results (accessed February 24, 2023).

———. 2011b. "Innovations for Enhanced Aid Harmonization and Coordination: A Case Study of Nepal. 4th High Level Forum on Aid Effectiveness." World Bank Institute, October 11, 2011, www.slideshare.net/SorenGigler/kdi-workshop-on-aid-effectivness (accessed February 24, 2023).

———. 2011c. *Can Technology Be Transformational? Opening Up Development Through Technology*. Washington, DC: World Bank, December 23, 2011.
———. 2015. *Development as Freedom in a Digital Age*. Washington, DC: World Bank.
———. 2021. "Putting People First in the Digital Transformation." *Blog*, March 22, 2022, www.linkedin.com/pulse/putting-people-first-digital-transformation-bjorn-soren-gigler-phd-/ (accessed February 24, 2023).

Gigler, Bjorn-Soren, and Savita Bailur, eds. 2014. *Closing the Feedback Loop: Can Technology Amplify Citizen Voices?* Washington, DC: World Bank.

Gigler, Bjorn-Soren, Savita Bailur, and Nicole Anand. 2014. *The Loch Ness Model: Can ICTs Bridge the "Accountability Gap"?* Washington, DC: World Bank.

Gigler, Bjorn-Soren S., R. Bedford Tanner III, and Johannes Kiess. 2011. *Enhanced Social Accountability Through Open Access to Data: Geomapping World Bank Projects*. Washington, DC: World Bank.

Hanna, Nagy K. 2012. "Open, Smart and Inclusive Development: ICT for Transforming North Africa." African Development Bank Economic Brief, www.afdb.org/fileadmin/uploads/afdb/Documents/Publications/Brochure%20Open%20Smart%20Anglais.pdf (accessed February 24, 2023).

Hickey, Sam, and Giles Mohan, eds. 2004. *Participation—from Tyranny to Transformation? Exploring New Approaches to Participation in Development*. Manchester: University of Manchester.

Holland, Jeremy, and James Blackburn. 1998. *Whose Voice? Participatory Research and Policy Change*. London: Intermediate Technology Publications.

Innovations in Governance Team. 2014. *Project Document: OnTrack: ICT Enabled Citizen Feedback Loop*. Washington, DC: World Bank.

iRevolution. 2022. "Google Inc + World Bank = Empowering Citizen Cartographers?" https://irevolutions.org/2012/01/20/google-inc-world-bank-empowering-citizen-cartographers/

Joshi, Anuradha. 2013. "Do They Work? Assessing the Impact of Transparency and Accountability Initiatives in Service Delivery." *Development Policy Review* 31(S1): s29–48.

Joshi, Anuradha, and Mick Moore. 2004. "Institutionalized Co-Production: Unorthodox Public Service Delivery in Challenging Environments." *Journal of Development Studies* 40(4): 39–40, https://doi.org/10.1080/00220380410001673184.

Knack, Stephen. 2001. "Aid Dependence and the Quality of Governance: Cross-Country Empirical Tests." *Southern Economic Journal* 68(2): 310–29.

Kuriyan, Renee, Savita Bailur, Bjorn-Soren Gigler, and Kyung Ryual Parks, eds. 2011. *Technologies for Transparency and Accountability: Implications for ICT Policy and Implementation*. Washington, DC: World Bank, Open Development Technology Alliance.

Lieberman, Evan, L., Daniel Posner, and Lily Tsai, eds. 2013. "Does Information Lead to More Active Citizenship? Evidence From an Education Intervention in Rural Kenya." MIT Political Science Department Research Working Paper No. 2013-2, https://papers.ssrn.com/sol3/papers.cfm?abstract_id=2228900 (accessed February 24, 2023).

McGee, Rosemary. 2013. "Aid Transparency and Accountability: 'Build It and They'll Come'?" *Development Policy Review* 31(S1): s107–24.

Mitlin, Diana. 2008. "With and Beyond the State—Co-Production as a Route to Political Influence, Power and Transformation for Grassroots Organizations." *Environment and Urbanization* 20(2): 339–60.

Needham, Catherine. 2008. "Realising the Potential of Co-Production: Negotiating Improvements in Public Services." *Social Policy and Society* 7(2): 221–31, https://doi.org/10.1017/S1474746407004174.

Open Street Map. 2022. "Copyright and License." January 19, 2022, www.openstreetmap.org/copyright (accessed February 24, 2023).

Ostrom, Elenor. 1996. "Crossing the Great Divide: Coproduction, Synergy, and Development." *World Development* 6: 1073–88.

Pradhan, Sanjay. 2014. "Foreword." In *Closing the Feedback Loop: Can Technology Bridge the Accountability Gap?*, edited by S. Gigler and S. Bailur. Washington, DC: World Bank.

Pradhan, Sanjay, and Sina Odugbemi. 2011. *The Contours and Possibilities of Open Development, Development Outreach*. Washington, DC: World Bank, https://openknowledge.worldbank.org/handle/10986/6110 (accessed February 24, 2023).

Raftree, Linda. 2012. "ICTD 2012: Does Openness Enhance Development?" Open ICT for Development, updated March 20, 2012, http://openict4d.wikidot.com/ictd-2012:does-openness-enhance-development (accessed February 24, 2023).

Shkabatur, Jennifer. 2014a. "Check My School: A Case Study on Citizens' Monitoring of the Education Sector in the Philippines." In *Closing the Feedback Loop: Can Technology Bridge the Accountability Gap?*, edited by S. Gigler and S. Bailur. Washington, DC: World Bank.

———. 2014b. *Interactive Community Mapping: Between Empowerment and Effectiveness*. Washington, DC: The World Bank.

Smith, Matthew, Laurent Elder, and Heloise Emdon. 2011. "Open Development: A New Theory for ICT4D." *Information Technologies & International Development* 7(1): iii–ix.

Strandburg, Katherine Jo, Solon Barocas, Helen Nissenbaum, Alessandro Acquisti, Paul Ohm, Victoria Stodden, and Steve Koonin, eds. 2014. *Privacy, Big Data, and the Public Good: Frameworks for Engagement*. Cambridge: Cambridge University Press.

Winters, Matthew. 2010. "Accountability, Participation and Foreign Aid Effectiveness." *International Studies Review* 12(12): 218–43.

Wittemyer, Rene, Savita Bailur, Nicole Anand, Kyung Ryul Park, and Bjorn-Soren Gigler, eds. 2014. *New Routes to Governance: A Review of Cases in Participation, Transparency, and Accountability*. Washington, DC: World Bank.

World Bank. 2004. *World Development Report 2004: Making Services Work for Poor People*. New York: Oxford University Press.

———. 2021. *World Development Report 2021: Data for Better Lives*. Washington, DC: World Bank.

World Bank Group, ed. 2012. *World Development Indicators 2012*. Washington, DC: World Bank.

5
GLOBAL ENVIRONMENTAL AND CLIMATE CHANGE GOVERNANCE

John Redwood III

Introduction

Global environmental problems—such as climate change, ozone depletion, biodiversity loss, land degradation and desertification, growing water scarcity and pollution, overfishing, and ocean pollution with plastics—require global solutions, which in turn require improved global environmental governance. In short, they require solutions that are transboundary or worldwide in nature, which require coordinated actions both within and across countries. Many of these issues, moreover, are both increasingly urgent and interrelated, as the United Nations Environment Programme (UNEP) has recently argued in a flagship publication titled *Making Peace With Nature* (UNEP 2021c).

This chapter will survey the main elements of global environmental and climate change governance at present. It will briefly describe the evolution of the most relevant events and institutions in this regard, then focus on the central roles of UNEP and the Conventions adopted at the Rio Earth Summit in 1992, particularly the one on climate change considering the critical importance and urgency of the need to address its ever more serious impacts, together with other multilateral environmental agreements (MEAs). Finally, it will point to some of the ways in which global environmental governance and climate change governance have fallen short to date.

Evolution of Global Environmental and Climate Change Governance Events and Institutions

Global environmental governance arrangements began with the UN Conference on the Human Environment held in Stockholm in June 1972. Among other results, this conference led to the establishment of UNEP and the decision to locate its headquarters in Nairobi, Kenya, immediately thereafter.[1] In the same decade, many countries around the world established Ministries of Environment or similar entities and promulgated environmental legislation, such as the Environmental Protection Agency and the Clean Air Act by the United States in 1970, soon followed by the Clean Water Act in 1972. Many other countries, including developing ones, created environment ministries or agencies and legislation shortly thereafter.

DOI: 10.4324/9781003316077-7

Since its inception, UNEP has served as the global authority that sets the environmental agenda and promotes the coherent implementation of the environmental dimension of sustainable development within the UN system. It is an authoritative advocate for the global environment. The concept of sustainable development with its economic, environmental, and social dimensions was itself formally officialized through another key UN initiative, the World Commission on Environment and Development (WCED)—also known as the Brundtland Commission, after its chairperson, Gro Harlem Brundtland, the former prime minister of Norway—established by the General Assembly in December 1983. Its report, *Our Common Future*, was published in 1987.[2]

The next major international event was the UN Conference on the Environment and Development (UNCED), also known as the Rio Earth Summit, held in Rio de Janeiro in June 1992. Numerous international agencies, including the World Bank,[3] provided specific inputs for this international meeting attended by many world leaders. The meeting endorsed the so-called Agenda 21, which constituted a comprehensive action plan to be implemented globally, nationally, and locally by organizations of the UN system, governments, and major groups in all areas where human activities impact the environment. It also issued the Rio Declaration on Environment and Development and the Statement of Principles for the Sustainable Management of Forests, which were adopted by more than 178 national governments. Soon thereafter, the Commission on Sustainable Development was established in December 1992 to ensure effective follow-up of UNCED and to monitor and report on environmental agreements at the local, national, regional, and international levels. It was likewise agreed that a five-year review of the progress achieved would be made by the UN General Assembly in a special session in New York in June 1997. The full implementation of Agenda 21, a program for further implementation of Agenda 21, and national commitments to the Rio principles were reaffirmed at the World Summit on Sustainable Development (WSSD), held in Johannesburg ten years later in August–September 2002.[4]

The most important outcomes of the Rio Earth Summit from a global environmental governance perspective, however, are arguably the Conventions on Biological Diversity and Climate Change. Work on the UN Convention on Biological Diversity (CBD) began in November 1988 when UNEP convened an ad hoc group of experts on this subject; a draft of the convention was adopted in Nairobi in May 1992. It was opened for signature at UNCED and entered into force in December 1993 after having been signed by 168 countries. The first meeting of the Conference of the Parties (COP), the governance body for each of the environmental conventions, of the CBD was held in the Bahamas in December 1994. The most recent one (COP 15) was held in two parts (October 2021 and April–May 2022) in Kunming, China. The UN Framework Convention on Climate Change (UNFCCC) was signed by 154 nations at UNCED and entered into force in March 1994. Its first COP was held in Berlin in March–April 1995 and the most recent one (COP 26) in Glasgow in November 2021.

The UN Convention to Combat Desertification (UNCCD) was subsequently established in June 1994 and entered into force in December 1996 and is the sole legally binding international agreement linking environment and development to sustainable land management. According to its website:

> [A]s the dynamics of land, climate, and biodiversity are intimately connected, the UNCCD collaborates closely with the other two Rio conventions, CDB and UNFCCC, to meet these complex challenges with an integrated approach and the best possible use of natural resources.

Its first COP was held in Rome in September–October 1997 and the most recent one in Abidjan, Côte D'Ivoire, in May 2022.

Even before the Rio Earth Summit, however, an international mechanism, the Montreal Protocol on Substances that Deplete the Ozone Layer (hereafter "the Montreal Protocol"), had been established to address the global ozone depletion crisis. The protocol, which was the landmark multilateral environmental agreement (MEA), was adopted in September 1987 and is, to date, the only UN treaty that has been ratified by all 198 UN member states. The purpose of the protocol is to regulate the production and consumption of nearly one hundred man-made chemicals that are ozone depleting substances (ODS). When released into the atmosphere, ODS damage the protective atmospheric ozone layer.[5] The parties of the protocol are assisted by the Ozone Secretariat located at UNEP headquarters in Nairobi. In addition, the Multilateral Fund for the Implementation of the Montreal Protocol (hereafter "the Multilateral Fund") was established in 1991 under Article 10 of the treaty with the objective of providing financial and technical assistance to developing country parties to help them comply with the protocol's control measures. This fund, whose secretariat is based in Montreal and is also assisted by UNEP, has four implementing agencies—UNEP, the UN Development Programme (UNDP), the UN Industrial Development Organisation (UNIDO), and the World Bank.

A second important global environmental funding mechanism, the Global Environment Facility (GEF), was created just prior to UNCED and formally established as a US$1 billion pilot program at the World Bank in October of that year. The facility's purpose is to assist developing countries in protection of the global environment and the promotion of environmentally sustainable development by providing new and additional grants and concessional resources to cover the incremental or additional costs associated with transforming a project with national benefits into one with global environmental benefits. At UNCED, it was decided to restructure the GEF and remove it from the World Bank (although its secretariat continued to be co-located at Bank Headquarters in Washington, DC). The Bank, together with UNDP and UNEP, was one of its first implementing agencies, and since 1994, at the completion of the pilot phase, the Bank has also continued to serve as the trustee of the GEF Trust Fund. As part of the restructuring, moreover, the GEF was entrusted to become the financial mechanism for both the CBD and UNFCCC, and in partnership with the Montreal Protocol, the GEF began to finance projects in parallel to the Multilateral Fund to enable the Russian Federation and nations in Eastern Europe and Central Asia (that would not otherwise have been eligible) to phase out their use of ozone depleting chemicals.

The GEF is governed by an assembly composed of all 184 member countries that meets every three to four years at the ministerial level to review general policies and review and evaluate its operations and a council that consists of thirty-two members appointed by the constituencies of the member countries (one from developed countries, sixteen from developing countries, and two from economies in transition), which meets twice annually and approves the operational work program, making decisions by consensus. The secretariat reports directly to the council and assembly and ensures that their decisions are translated into concrete actions by the certified implementing agencies. There is also a six-member Scientific and Technical Advisory Panel that provides the GEF with advice on policies, operational strategies, programs, and projects and is supported by a global network of experts, institutions, and an independent evaluation office that reports directly to the council.

The number of implementing agencies for GEF-funded projects has expanded gradually over time to eighteen and now also incorporates the World Bank Group's International Finance Corporation (IFC), which handles its operations with the private sector, and includes numerous other multilateral organizations, international nongovernmental organizations, and others.[6] It subsequently became the financial mechanism for UNCED, as well as for other key MEAs such as the Stockholm Convention on Persistent Organic Pollutants (2001) and most recently the Minamata Convention on Mercury (2013), whose secretariats are hosted or administered by UNEP.[7] The GEF's work focuses on six main areas: biodiversity, climate change mitigation and adaptation,[8] chemicals and waste including persistent organic pollutants,[9] international waters, land degradation, and sustainable forest management.[10]

Two other important intergovernmental bodies should also be mentioned in this context: the Intergovernmental Panel for Climate Change (IPCC) and the Intergovernmental Science-Policy Platform for Biodiversity and Ecosystem Services (IPBES). The IPPC was established by the UN General Assembly in December 1988 with the initial task of preparing a comprehensive review and recommendations with respect to the state of knowledge of the science of climate change, its social and economic impacts, and potential responses to be included in what was to later become the UNFCCC. From the beginning, it has been jointly overseen by UNEP and the UN World Meteorological Organization. Since its establishment, the IPCC has completed five assessment cycles and published its results. IPCC's sixth assessment reports were finalized in 2022[11] in time for the first global "stocktake" of progress to date under the Paris Climate Agreement (see the section on the Rio Conventions below), which will conclude in 2023.[12] The IPCC was awarded the Nobel Peace Prize in 2007.

The IPBES was created by ninety-four governments in Panama City in April 2012. While it is not a UN body per se, at the request of the IPBES plenary and with the authorization of the UNEP Governing Council[13] in 2013, UNEP also provided secretariat services to it, with the secretariat located in Bonn. Its purpose is to strengthen the science–policy interface for biodiversity and ecosystem services for the conservation and sustainable use of biodiversity, long-term human well-being, and sustainable development. As in the case of the IPCC, its work can be broadly characterized as involving four complementary areas: assessments,[14] policy support, knowledge generation and capacity building, and communications and outreach.

The final major international institution of high significance that plays a major role in global environmental governance is the Green Climate Fund (GCF), whose governing instrument was approved by COP 17 of the UNFCCC in Durban, South Africa, in December 2011. First proposed in December 2009, it is now the main financing mechanism for the UNFCCC, complementing the GEF, and, according to its website, is now "the world's largest climate fund, mandated to support developing countries raise and realize their Nationally Determined Contributions (NDCs) ambitions [under the Paris Climate Agreement of December 2015] towards low-emissions, climate-resilient pathways." Headquartered in Seoul, South Korea, the GCF became fully operational in November 2015 after the conversion of more than 50 percent of the funding pledges received during its 2014 initial resource mobilization efforts. It presently operates through a network of more than 200 multinational and national accredited entities and delivery partners in both the public and private sectors that work directly with developing countries for project design and implementation both for climate change mitigation and adaptation and for associated capacity building. It aims for a 50:50 balance between mitigation—that is, preventing or reducing the emission of GHGs—and adaptation—or adjusting to current and future effects of climate change—and a floor of the adaptation allocation for particularly vulnerable nations, including least developed countries and small island developing states.

The most recent international meeting of greatest relevance was the UN Conference on Sustainable Development, also known as "Rio+20," hosted by Brazil in Rio de Janeiro in June 2012. The conference resulted in a nonbinding resolution subsequently issued by the UN General Assembly titled *The Future We Want*, which stated, among other things, that the participants pledged to "renew our commitment to sustainable development and to ensuring the promotion of an economically, socially and environmentally sustainable future for our planet and for present and future generations" (UN General Assembly 2012). It also reaffirmed their commitment to the principles of the 1992 Rio Declaration on Environment and Declaration and Agenda 21 and to their full implementation as well as to that of the subsequent agreements adopted at Rio+10 and WSSD and reinforced the importance of and need to further strengthen the mechanisms and institutions already in place, including the three conventions, their financing mechanisms, and UNEP. Roughly three years later, the United Nations also adopted the 2030 Agenda for Sustainable Development (UN General Assembly 2015) which features the seventeen Sustainable Development Goals (SDGs) and associated indicators and targets, many of which have environmental aspects, including one specifically for climate action,[15] succeeding the earlier Millennium Development Goals.[16]

UNEP's Role in Global Environmental Governance

The United Nations, together with the major conventions, other MEAs, intergovernmental panels, and selected global funds (i.e., the GEF and GCF), has been central to global environmental and climate change governance starting in the 1970s and extending to the present day. UNEP has been a key element in these institutions and treaties and bears a more detailed examination in relation to its role and activities in terms of global environmental governance. Furthermore, its mandate has evolved and become more comprehensive over time with increasing responsibilities for environmental coordination within the UN system and more generally, the assessment of the world environmental situation, and environmental policy development and assistance. These responsibilities, which had been in place since UNEP's establishment in 1972, were further clarified and expanded by its Governing Council's declaration regarding its role and mandate in 1997, which, among other things, required it to

- further the development of coherent interlinkages among existing international environmental conventions and strengthen its role in the coordination of environmental activities in the UN system in the field of environment, based on its comparative advantage and scientific and technical expertise;
- provide early warning information on environmental threats and serve as an effective link between the scientific community and policy-makers at the national and international levels;

- catalyze and provide international cooperation based on the best scientific and technical capabilities available, further the development of international environmental law aiming at sustainable development and advance the implementation of agreed international norms and policies to monitor and foster compliance with environmental principles and international agreements.[17]

The most recent official statement regarding UNEP's role is contained in the Rio+20 outcome declaration in 2012, which includes the participants' commitment to enhance its voice and coordination mandate within the UN system by strengthening its "engagement in key United Nations Coordination bodies and empowering UNEP to lead efforts to formulate United Nations system-wide strategies on the environment." They also supported the enhancement of UNEP's capacity to

> disseminate and share evidence-based environmental information and raise public awareness on critical environmental as well as emerging environmental issues [and] promote a strong science-policy interface, building on existing international instruments, assessments, panels and information networks, including the Global Environmental Outlook, as one of the processes aimed at bringing together information and assessment to support informed decision making.

In addition, the participants endorsed UNEP's role to

> provide capacity-building to countries as well as to support and facilitate access to technology [and to] progressively provide consolidated headquarters function in Nairobi, as well as strengthen its regional presence, in order to assist countries, upon request, in the implementation of their national environmental policies, collaborating closely with other relevant entities of the United Nations system.
>
> *(UN General Assembly 2012, para. 88)*

This ever-broadening mandate is clearly reflected in UNEP's post-Rio+20 and 2030 Sustainable Development Agenda Medium-Term Strategies (MTSs), including the ones for 2018–2021 and 2022–2025, the latter having been officially approved by UNEA in a virtual meeting in February 2022. In both of these strategic documents, as well as their predecessor for 2014–2017, environmental governance has been one of UNEP's declared strategic priorities and subprograms. However, the most recent MTS, whose implementation began on January 1, 2022, clearly situates environmental governance together with the science–policy interface as the "foundational" subprograms for its three "thematic" ones, climate action, nature action, and pollution action—in short, the principal means to these ends—further supported by two "enabling" ones, financial and economic transformation and digital transformation,[18] the latter recognizing the rising importance of digital communications in today's world (see Box 5.1).

The new strategy pledges closer coordination between UNEP's activities and those of the MEAs for which it hosts the secretariat and/or provides other administrative and technical support. It also commits to continue to apply the UN Development System reforms for effective implementation of the 2030 Sustainable Development Agenda and the SDG formally mandated by the UN General Assembly in May 2018.

Box 5.1 The Importance of Digital Transformation in Global Environmental Governance Going Forward

Together with the need for greatly increased financial and economic support to address the three global existential crises of climate change, biodiversity loss, ecosystem degradation, and pollution, UNEP acknowledges the increasingly important enabling role of the digital transformation. Its new Medium-Term Strategy for 2022–2025 affirms, for example, that "digitalization is sweeping the planet—changing our economy, society, institutions and even our humanity." However, it also recognizes that "this does not always happen in an equitable, inclusive, and sustainable manner." In response, it proposes that its new Digital Transformations Subprogram will focus on the following actions and interventions:

Supporting and scaling up environmental change through an effectively governed and inclusive data architecture and digital ecosystem for the planet.

Catalyzing a transformative use of environmental digital public goods to amplify and accelerate progress towards global climate, biodiversity, and pollution goals and targets.

Strengthening environmental digital literacy and e-governance capacities of diverse stakeholders to engage in the environmental dimensions of digital transformation, with an emphasis on the Global South.

Improving institutional efficiency and impact through a digitally enabled UNEP.

Furthermore, it views digital transformation as an "enabler" by, among other things, allowing UNEP to (i) contribute to climate stability by accelerating the adoption of low-carbon behaviors and products by consumers and citizens; (ii) amplify the adoption of clean technologies and digitalized circular approaches toward a pollution-free planet; (iii) accelerate the science–policy interface through increased influence, uptake, and impact of digital public goods produced by scientific analysis on environmental priorities; and (iv) strengthen global and national capacity to digitalize environmental governance and collective action.

Source: UNEP, Medium-Term Strategy for 2022–2025.

UNEP's latest MTS defines environmental governance as "the institutional and legal architecture needed to make environmental goals and commitments a reality." Its Environmental Governance Subprogram thus seeks to support "coherent decision-making towards more effective legal and institutional frameworks that underpin the achievement of internationally agreed goals for climate, biodiversity, and pollution in the context of the 2030 Agenda." As such, it intends to focus on the following six areas:

- strengthening the transformative role of the Environment Assembly (UNEA) as the highest global environmental decision-making body to deliver on the environmental dimension of the 2030 Agenda for Sustainable Development;
- amplifying impact across the global environmental agenda through enhanced cooperation with the MEAs;

- supporting countries in identifying integrated approaches to the three dimensions of sustainable development, including the incorporation of environmental considerations into sustainable development planning;
- supporting countries in building relevant capacity in environmental law and contributing to the environmental dimension of the 2030 agenda through the Program for the Development and Periodic Review of Environmental Law (Montevideo Program)[19];
- leading the UN system and supporting national governments, at their request, in the development and implementation of environmental rule of law;
- advancing human rights obligations relating to the enjoyment of a safe, clean, healthy, and sustainable environment.

(UNEP, MTS for 2022–2025)

In addition to UNEP's significance for global environmental governance by serving as the secretariat of UNEA, hosting and/or helping to administer the MEAs, and overseeing the intergovernmental panel on climate change (IPCC) and biodiversity and ecosystem services (IPBES), it is important to highlight its coordinating responsibility with respect to the environment within the broader UN development system. This is mainly through its increasingly important role as the chair of the UN Environmental Management Group (EMG). The EMG, whose membership consists of fifty-one specialized UN agencies, including the secretariats of the MEAs, was established as a system-wide coordination body in 2001. With a secretariat located in Geneva, its purpose is to identify issues on the international environmental agenda that warrant cross-agency cooperation and to find ways to engage their collective capacity to generate coherent management responses to these challenges. It works through technical meetings, issue management groups, and task forces and can invite representatives of intergovernmental bodies, civil society, and international nongovernmental organizations to contribute to its activities.

The Role of the UN Rio Conventions and the MEAs in Global Environmental Governance

While, unlike the CBD, UNEP does not house the secretariats of the UNFCCC or the UNCCD, it nonetheless seeks to align its priorities and coordinate closely with their activities. All three of these conventions, moreover, are themselves an essential part of global environmental governance, and UNEP also actively promotes the synergies among them, as highlighted both in its most recent MTS and in the *Making Peace With Nature* report that provides the scientific and technical underpinnings for this new corporate strategy (UNEP 2021c). Each of these conventions, moreover, have their own separate protocols and/or other instruments agreed by their parties to implement the actions and attempt to achieve the objectives and principles upon which they are based.

Space limitations do not permit a discussion of each of these important conventions and other multilateral environmental agreements, but two protocols and the Aichi Biodiversity Targets under the Biodiversity Convention should nonetheless be briefly mentioned. The Cartagena Protocol on Biosafety is an international agreement that was adopted under the CBD in January 2000 and entered into force in mid-September 2003 with 173 parties to it as of the present. It aims to ensure the safe handling, transport, and use of living modified organisms resulting from modern technology that may have adverse effects on biodiversity, also considering risks to human health. The Nagoya Protocol on Access to Genetic

Resources and the Fair and Equitable Sharing of Benefits Arising from Their Utilization entered into force in mid-October 2014 and has resulted in establishment of an Access and Benefit Sharing Clearing House to offer opportunities for connecting providers and users of genetic resources and traditional knowledge. The goals of the twenty Aichi targets, which were established as part of the Strategic Plan for Biodiversity for 2011–2020 under the CDB, in turn, were to (i) address the underlying causes of biodiversity loss by mainstreaming biodiversity across government and society; (ii) reduce the direct pressure on biodiversity and promote sustainable use; (iii) improve the status of biodiversity by safeguarding ecosystems, species, and genetic diversity; (iv) enhance the benefits from biodiversity and ecosystem services; and (v) enhance implementation through participatory planning, knowledge management, and capacity building. A revised strategic plan and associated targets for the present decade are under preparation for discussion and adoption at the next CBD COP which, as noted above, will occur in complementary sessions, the first of which took place virtually in October 2021 and the second occurred in Montreal in October 2022.

While the Desertification Convention does not have specific protocols, it does emphasize several key priority areas and instruments, including protecting arid and semi-arid parts of the world, increasing land degradation and water scarcity by combating drought, and promoting sustainable land and water resource management. The other MEAs, as suggested above, concentrate on preventing or reducing ozone layer depletion and the production, consumption, and trade of hazardous chemicals and other dangerous pollutants, as well as protecting endangered species and other wildlife, including by regulating their international commerce. While all these agreements merit examination in detail, the rest of this section will focus specifically on the Climate Change Convention.

The UNFCCC launched the Kyoto Protocol and, more recently, enacted the Paris Climate Agreement, which was endorsed by the participants in COP 21 in December 2015. The Kyoto Protocol was adopted at COP 8 in December 1997 but due to a complex ratification process only entered into force in mid-February 2005. At present, there are 192 parties to it, as it sought to operationalize the UNFCCC by committing thirty-seven industrialized countries and economies in transition to limit and reduce GHG emissions in accordance with agreed individual targets. The protocol only bound developed countries during its first commitment period (2008–2012) under the principle of common but differentiated responsibilities for emissions reduction, because it acknowledged that they were historically the source of the high level of such emissions at the time it was adopted.[20] While developed countries were expected to reduce their own domestic emissions, flexible arrangements were established under the protocol that allowed them to meet part of their targets through market-based mechanisms involving the purchase of emission reductions in developing countries, specifically, through international emissions trading, the Clean Development Mechanism (CDM)[21] and Joint Implementation (JI).[22]

An Adaptation Fund (AF)[23] was also created to finance climate change adaptation programs and projects in developing countries that were parties to the Protocol, such that it, like the Convention more generally, was designed to facilitate the development and use of technologies that could help boost their climate resilience.

The Paris Climate Agreement is the successor to the Kyoto Protocol. This binding agreement was adopted by 196 parties at COP 21 on December 12, 2015. It entered into force on November 4, 2016. It has the goal of limiting global average temperature to well below 2°C and preferably to no more than 1.5°C compared to pre-industrial levels. It seeks to reach this target through the limitation of GHG emissions as soon as possible to achieve a climate-neutral planet by 2050. It operates on a five-year cycle of increasingly ambitious GHG reduction interventions, and countries were required to submit their revised climate action plans, known as Nationally Determined Contributions (NDCs), to UNFCCC by 2020.[24] Countries were also requested, but not obliged, to prepare and submit long-term strategies (LTSs) for low GHG emissions development and climate resilience to situate their short-term NDCs into a logical sequential framework for these purposes. The agreement also required "making finance flows consistent with a pathway toward low greenhouse-gas emissions and climate-resilient development" and indicated that "support shall be provided to developing country Parties" for its implementation.[25]

The UNFCCC has established both financial and technology mechanisms for climate change, recognizing that both, together with capacity building, are necessary inputs to enable countries, particularly lower- and middle-income ones, to achieve its objective and the targets of the Paris Agreement. Both short- and long-term climate finance, including by the private sector,[26] are important for climate change mitigation and adaptation/resilience-building purposes, with the above-mentioned GEF, GCF, and AF all intended to contribute to this aim. The UNFCCC's financial mechanism, more specifically, consisted of the Global Environment Facility, since the convention entered into force in 1994, but at COP 16, in 2010, the parties established the Green Climate Fund and in 2011 also designated it as an operating entity of the financial mechanism. In addition to providing guidance to the GEF and GCF, the parties established two special funds—the Special Climate Change Fund (SCCF)[27] and the Least Developed Countries Fund (LDCF)[28]—and at the Paris COP agreed that the GEF, GDF, AF, SCCF, and LCDF should all serve the Paris Agreement. The climate technology development and transfer mechanisms under the UNFCCC are briefly described in Box 5.2.

Box 5.2 The Technology Mechanism Under the UN Climate Change Convention

The Technology Mechanism of the UNFCCC supports country efforts to accelerate and enhance their actions to address climate change and seeks to develop and transfer technologies that can effectively reduce GHG emissions and build resilience to its adverse impacts. For this purpose, the 2010 COP in Buenos Aires in December 2004 formally established this mechanism, which consists of two complementary bodies, the Technology Executive Committee (TEC) and the Climate Technology Centre and Network (CTCN), which is jointly hosted by the UN Industrial Development Organization (UNIDO) and UNEP.

The TEC is the policy arm of the mechanism and consists of twenty technology experts from both developed and developing countries which meet several times each year. Since its inception, the TEC has focused on the following areas of climate technology development and transfer: (i) climate technology financing; (ii) enabling environments and barriers; (iii) national innovation systems; (iv) technology research, development, and demonstration; (v) adaptation and mitigation technologies; (vi) technology needs assessments; (vii) technology roadmaps; and (viii) strategic and emerging issues. In addition to the CTCN, it works closely with other UNFCCC entities, including the GEF, GCF, AF, and key technology stakeholders to catalyze climate technology action.

In addition to UNEP, through its Climate Division, and UNIDO, the CTCN is supported by eleven partner institutions with expertise in climate technologies. The center facilitates a network of national, regional, sectoral, and international technology centers, networks, organizations, and private sector entities, and provides free technical assistance to developing countries on climate technology issues. The Climate Technology Network provides access to a large global community of climate technology users, national decision-makers, and financiers under the Technology Mechanism and consists of academic, civil society, finance, private sector, public sector, and research entities, as well as over 130 national focal points or designated entities. The CTCN also serves as a library of climate technology information and tools, which is organized by geographic region and sector and made available through an open-source data base. It likewise provides training and support to strengthen developing country capacity to identify climate technology options, make technological choices, and operate, maintain, and adapt technologies.

Source: UNFCCC 2015.

As partially reflected in its co-hosting of the Climate Technology Centre and Network (CTCN),[29] UNEP plays an important role in support of the UNFCCC in relation to climate change. This is likewise reflected in two of its keynote annual publications, the *Emissions Gap* and *Adaptation Gap* reports, which provide updated information on global climate mitigation and adaptation challenges and international responses to them, respectively. The latest of the former reports, for example, observes, among other things, that

> the emissions gap remains large: compared to previous unconditional NDCs, the new pledges for 2030 reduce projected 2030 emissions by only 7.5 per cent, whereas 30 per cent is needed for 2°C and 55 per cent is needed for 1.5°C.
>
> *(UNEP 2021b)*

The most recent *Adaptation Gap Report*, in turn, finds that "while nations have advanced in planning, huge gaps remain in finance for developing countries and bringing adaptation projects to the stage where they bring real protection against climate impacts such as droughts, floods and sea-level rise" and argues that "public and private finance for adaptation must be stepped up urgently, along with faster implementation." It likewise states that "nature-based solutions—locally appropriate actions that address societal challenges, such as climate change, and provide human well-being and biodiversity benefits by protecting, sustainably managing and restoring natural or modified ecosystems—must also become a priority" (UNEP 2021a).

Multilateral organizations in addition to UNEP, including other UN entities and the multilateral development banks, also play a role in global environmental and climate change interventions and finance. A recent study carried out on behalf of the Multilateral Organization Performance Assessment Network (MOPAN) based at the Organization of Economic Cooperation and Development (OECD) examined the response of twelve of the most important multilateral organizations to the Paris Climate Agreement—specifically the International Monetary Fund, the World Bank, IFC, the African, Asian, and Inter-American Development Banks, European Investment Bank, International Fund for Agricultural Development, UNDP, UNEP, and the GEF and GCF. It found that these multilateral organizations have all substantially raised their financial support and activities for climate change over the past five years and are now focusing increasingly on adaptation as well as mitigation. However, the study also argues that much more needs to be done in the years ahead, not only by them but particularly by both national governments and the private sector. Observing that the countries are in the "driver's seat" with respect to the global response to climate change, this report, finally, puts forward six main lessons, which are among the many that can be drawn from multilateral organization experience to date and that are discussed throughout this and other recent reports:

- the lack of "whole of government" NDCs and LTSs hinders progress on the climate change agenda;
- the focus on measuring climate finance may distract from thinking about climate as part of broader development;
- achieving Paris goals cannot happen without a massive scale up of private sector-led investment in climate change;
- transformational technology is key for moving toward a carbon-neutral world, but the required research and development is outside the mandate of the multilateral organizations;
- well-designed partnerships are important, and their coordination and consolidation are essential;
- reducing support to fossil fuels comes with challenges in the transition that need to be recognized.[30]

Where and How Global Environmental and Climate Change Governance Presently Fall Short

As the sections above indicate, substantial institutional arrangements and instruments exist to promote the required improved global environmental and climate change governance. To date, however, the only real success story has been with respect to the efforts to curb ozone depletion, from which important lessons can be drawn (see, e.g., Miller, Zaelke, and Anderson 2021). In contrast, the efforts to combat climate change, biodiversity loss, land degradation, and pollution are far from being as effective as is required as UNEP's latest reports, as well as its recent *Making Peace With Nature* and other flagship documents have clearly pointed out in the case of climate. Much greater investments and interventions, by both governments and private sector entities, are clearly needed. The risks to the planet, its inhabitants, and ecosystems, as well as the future of coming generations—should the needed financing and actions not be forthcoming—are stark.[31] The importance and urgency of such measures cannot be overstressed. Yet despite all the increasingly dire warnings, global efforts thus far have clearly been inadequate.

One key reason for this is that there is a difference between international commitments, both on the part of national governments and that of the private sector, and actual actions on the ground. Pledges and commitments are necessary, but not sufficient.

Furthermore, even these commitments are presently falling way short, as the recent UNEP *Emissions Gap* report clearly shows with respect to climate change mitigation, the same also being the case with respect to adaptation, to which even less attention has been given to date. The story with respect to biodiversity loss, ecosystem degradation, and associated conservation and protection needs is similar, as is that with respect to land degradation and rising water scarcity, particularly but not only, in the semi-arid parts of the world.[32]

Thus, there is a real risk of "too little, too late" to avoid the potentially disastrous consequences of an inadequate global response to these planetary crises, as UNEP appropriately now refers to them. In addition, despite formal government pledges, such as achieving "carbon neutrality" by 2050, some of their actions continue to be clearly contradictory. Several of those that currently are significant users and/or producers of coal, including China and India, and other fossil fuels as energy sources plan to continue to rely on them at least over the next decade.[33] Other nations whose GHG emissions come largely from deforestation and rural land use change also continue to pursue policies and investments that are clearly contributing to their acceleration rather than restriction, as is the present case of Brazil, for example. In short, not everyone is clearly on board in practice, regardless of their stated intentions.

Further complicating this situation, moreover, is the fact highlighted in the MOPAN (2021) report that the countries are in the "driver's seat"—that is, their individual and collective actions are critical for meeting the global environmental challenges, including those posed by increasing global warming. Moreover, no global "policeman" exists to ensure that countries and their governments meet their declared commitments within the promised time frame or even at all. In practice, short-run economic incentives and energy supply limitations continue to override both short- and long-term environmental, including climate mitigation, and social considerations and priorities. Other persisting key constraints relating to the availability of finance—especially of concessional finance for developing countries from industrialized ones—technology, and institutional capacity must be also addressed. In the case of climate change, adaptation efforts and investments need to be placed on a more equal footing with mitigation ones, including through greater application of and support for nature-based solutions, than has been the case until now, while biodiversity conservation and pollution prevention and abatement activities likewise need greatly increased attention and assistance. The essential links between better global environmental and climate change governance and both poverty reduction and sustainable development are nevertheless increasingly apparent.

It must be concluded, therefore, that existing global environmental and climate change governance and associated mechanisms and instruments urgently require considerable strengthening if they are to be as effective as is now needed. Deeds must be consistent with words and pledges need to represent true commitments, especially in the likelihood that further issues and problems, now unseen and/or unexpected, will arise in the future, as the recent Covid-19 pandemic has clearly shown. As recent books by both experts and non-specialists have optimistically claimed, it is not too late for this to still be possible, and the long-term costs of not properly facing these challenges will undoubtedly be much greater than doing so now. Those costs will fall mainly on our children, grandchildren, and later generations.[34] But as Sir Nicholas Stern (2015) already asked more than half a decade ago, *why are we waiting*? The clock is ticking.

Key Discussion Areas

- The main elements of global environmental and climate change governance
- Various events and institutions leading to the evolution of climate change governance
- Shortcomings in global environmental and climate change governance

Notes

1 See, for example, Ivanova 2021 on both the history of the UN conference and the creation and subsequent evolving mandate and activities of UNEP, which have focused on ozone depletion, marine pollution, desertification, chemicals and hazardous waste, climate change, biodiversity, and forests.

2 WCED 1987. According to this report, the Commission's mandate was to (i) propose long-term environmental strategies for achieving sustainable development by 2000; (ii) recommend ways concern for the environment could be translated into greater cooperation among developing countries and between countries at different stages of economic and social development and lead to the achievement of common and mutually supportive objectives that take account of the interrelationships between people, resources, environment, and development; (iii) consider ways and means by which the international community can deal more effectively with environmental concerns; and (iv) to help define shared perceptions of long-term environmental issues and the appropriate efforts needed to deal successfully with the problems of protecting and enhancing the environment, a long-term agenda for action during the coming decades, and aspirational goals for the world community.

3 This refers specifically to the Bank's World Development Report (WDR) for 1992 (World Bank 1992). The WDR is the Bank's annual flagship publication, dedicated to a specific development topic, first issued in 1978, and continuing to the present.

4 Important inputs were also prepared for this conference, including an advance draft of the World Bank's WDR for 2003 (World Bank 2003). UNEP's third *Global Environmental Outlook* (GEO-3), a periodic comprehensive series that surveys the status of global environmental challenges and responses initiated in 1995, was also issued in 2002 as an input for the WSSD.

5 According to the Montreal Protocol website, it phases down consumption and production of different ODS in a stepwise manner, with different timetables for developed and developing countries. Under it, all parties have specific responsibilities related to the phase out of different groups of ODS, control of ODS trade, annual reporting data, national licensing systems to control ODS imports and exports, and other matters. Developing and developed countries have equal but differentiated responsibilities, but both groups have binding, time-targeted, and measurable commitments.

6 The other current authorized GEF implementing agencies are the African, Asian, and Inter-American Development Banks, the European Bank for Reconstruction and Development, the UN Food and Agriculture Organization (FAO), UNIDO, the International Fund for Agricultural Development, the Development Bank of Latin America, the Development Bank of Southern Africa, the West African Development Bank, Conservation International, the International Union for the Conservation of Nature, the World Wildlife Fund–US, the Brazilian Biodiversity Fund, and the Foreign Economic Cooperation Office, Ministry of Environmental Protection of China.

7 The MEAs also include the Basel Convention on the Control of Transboundary Movements of Hazardous Wastes and Their Disposal, the Rotterdam Convention on the Prior Informed Consent Procedure for Certain Hazardous Chemicals and Pesticides in International Trade, the Convention on International Trade in Endangered Species, the Convention on the Conservation of Migratory Species, and the Vienna Convention for the Protection of the Ozone Layer and the Montreal Protocol—whose secretariats it houses together with those for the CBD and the MLF—as well as those for the Regional Seas Program—UNEP's most important mechanism for conservation of the marine and coastal environment—among others.

8 Climate change mitigation can be defined as reducing or avoiding greenhouse-gas (GHG) emissions through actions in the areas of renewable energy, energy efficiency, sustainable transport, and management of land use, land use change, and forestry. Climate change adaptation aims at helping countries, especially lower- and middle-income ones, become climate resilient by promoting immediate and longer-term adaptation measures in development policies, plans, programs, projects, and actions.

9 The persistent organic pollutants consist of pesticides, industrial chemicals, and unwanted by-products of industrial processes that share the following characteristics: (i) persistence (i.e., they resist degradation in air, water, and sediments); (ii) bioaccumulation (i.e., they accumulate in living tissues at concentrations higher than those in the surrounding environment); and (iii) long-range transport (i.e., they can travel great distances from the source of release through the air, water, and migratory animals, often contaminating areas thousands of kilometers from any known source).

10 This also applies to REDD+ with REDD referring to Reducing Emissions from Deforestation and Forest Degradation (see www.fao.org/redd/en/, accessed February 24, 2023). It refers to a UN collaborative program jointly established and managed by FAO, UNDP, and UNEP launched in 2008. Its coverage was later expanded—hence REDD+—to also include forest conservation, sustainable forest management, and the enhancement of forest (carbon) stocks, which can play an important role in both mitigation and adaptation.

11 See IPCC 2022. These reports, like their predecessors, include a summary for policymakers. The fifth assessment report was finalized in 2013 and 2014. The IPCC has also produced a range of Methodology Reports, Special Reports, and Technical Papers in response to requests for information on specific scientific and technical matters from the UNFCCC, governments, and international organizations.

12 The global stocktake is a process for assessing implementation of the Paris Agreement in order to determine the world's collective progress toward meeting the purpose of the agreement and its long-term goals. The first stocktake got underway at the UN Climate Change Conference in Glasgow November 2022 (COP26) and will conclude at COP28 in 2023. Each stocktake is a two-year process that happens every five years.

13 The Governing Council, composed of all 194 member states, was renamed the United Nations Environment Assembly (UNEA) in 2014.

14 See, for example, IPBES 2019. As with other global environmental reports including those by IPCC and UNEP, it also contains a summary for policymakers.

15 United Nations General Assembly 2015. SDG 17 is stated more specifically (pg. 14/35) as "take urgent action to combat climate change and its impact" with a footnote stating: "acknowledging that the United Nations Framework Convention on Climate Change is the primary international, intergovernmental forum for negotiating the global response to climate change."

16 The eight Millennium Development Goals, including number 7, "to ensure environmental sustainability," had been set for 2015 following adoption of the UN Millennium Declaration in September 2000.

17 UNEP Governing Council, *Nairobi Declaration on the Role and Mandate of the United Nations Environment Programme*, Nairobi: UNEP, February 7, 1997, as summarized in Ivanova 2021, 58–59.

18 UNEP 2021b, 16. Compared with the previous MTS, the Digital Transformations subprogram was new and replaced the previous Resilience to Disasters and Conflicts subprogram, whose actions were integrated into other ones, while the Financial and Economic Transformations one replaced the former Resource Economy subprogram and the Science-Policy one replaced the former Environment under Review one, although the functions of the latter two remained essentially the same.

19 Since 1982, UNEP has conducted its environmental law activities based on sequential ten-year Montevideo Programs, the first one having been officially established in the city after which it is named. In March 2019, UNEA adopted the fifth such intergovernmental program aimed at promoting and implementing environmental rule of law for the period of January 2020 through December 2029, and for which UNEP continues to provide the Secretariat through its Law Division. The Program's specific objectives include: (i) support the development of adequate and effective environmental legislation and legal frameworks at all levels to address environmental issues;

(ii) strengthen the effective implementation of environmental law at the national level; (iii) support enhanced capacity building for increased effectiveness of environmental law for all stakeholders at all levels; and (iv) promote the role of environmental law in the context of effective environmental governance.

20 A Doha Amendment was adopted for a second commitment period for 2013–2020 at COP 18 in December 2012 but only entered into force in December 2020, having essentially been replaced by the Paris Agreement.

21 The CDM allowed a country with an emissions reduction or limitation target under the protocol (also known as Annex B parties) to implement emissions reduction projects in developing countries and, thereby, to earn certified emission reduction credits that could be counted toward meeting its Kyoto target.

22 JI allowed an Annex B party to earn emission reduction units from an emissions reduction or limitation project in another Annex B country that could also be counted toward meeting its Kyoto target.

23 The AF, established in 2001, is overseen by an Adaptation Fund Board and was financed with a share of the proceeds from the CDM. Effective January 2019, it was decided that it would no longer serve the Kyoto Protocol but instead the Paris Agreement under the CMA (Conference of the Parties to the Paris Agreement, which meets annually at the same time as the COP for the UNFCCC) for all matters related to this Agreement.

24 Initial NDCs, known as INDCs, or Intended Nationally Determined Contributions, were submitted by most parties prior to COP 21 and converted into full NDCs shortly after the Paris Agreement was adopted.

25 United Nations 2015, Article 2 (c), pg. 2, and Article 5, pg. 3.

26 Climate finance thus can be defined as local, national, and transnational financing from both public and private sources that seek to support climate mitigation and adaptation actions. It is important for mitigation because large-scale investments are required to substantially reduce GHG emissions and for adaptation because of the need for countries, particularly the most vulnerable ones, to adapt to rising climate change impacts on both rural and urban areas.

27 The SCCF was created under the UNFCCC in 2001 to finance projects related to adaptation, technology transfer and capacity building, energy, transport, industry, agriculture, forestry, waste management, and economic diversification and to complement other funding mechanisms for implementation of the Convention.

28 The LDCF was established at COP 11 in Montreal in December 2005 for the GEF to help the least developed countries prepare and implement National Adaptation Programmes of Action (NAPAs), which provide a process for such countries to identify and carry out priority activities that respond to their urgent and immediate needs to adapt to climate change, with support from UNDP.

29 For information on the specific activities of the CTCN, see its annual progress reports, including the one for 2018 that covers five years of its activities, and the most recent one, for 2020, published jointly by UNEP and UNIDO.

30 MOPAN 2021. These other reports include, first and foremost, the twelve *Emissions Gap* and five *Adaptation Gap* reports issued by UNEP since 2010 and 2014, respectively. See also the UNEP *Making Peace with Nature* report (2021d) and its most recent Global Environmental Outlook–GEO 6 that bears the title *Healthy Planet, Healthy People* (Nairobi 2019) and its annual or biannual *Frontiers: Emerging Issues of Environmental Concern* reports that began in 2016 for examples of other very informative documents that address current global environmental governance challenges and responses more generally.

31 As one example of what might happen should climate change not be adequately mitigated, in addition to the sources mentioned above, see the World Bank reports, *Turning Down the Heat: Why a 4 Degree World Must Be Avoided* (2012) and *Development and Climate Change* (2010), which considers the important links between these two concerns as well as that between biodiversity and ecosystem services and climate change.

32 The case of Brazil at present clearly illustrates this. Not only have droughts increased in their frequency and severity in the semi-arid northeast where they have historically recurred on a periodic basis, but they are now adversely affecting other parts of the country, including the humid

tropical Amazon rainforest, the Pantanal, which is the world's largest wetland, and even the water supply for the major metropolitan and urban areas in the southeast, such as São Paulo, which are increasingly facing supply shortages and the potential need for rationing and thus the need for greater government intervention at the federal, state, and municipal levels throughout much of the country. See, for example, De Nys, Engle, and Magalhães 2017.

33 The invasion of Ukraine by Russia in February 2022 and its aftermath has also led numerous European countries dependent on Russian oil and gas, including Germany, to rely to a greater extent on coal than originally planned for the immediate future as well as to take greater energy saving measures and rethink its previous position regarding the use of nuclear energy.

34 In addition to many of the sources cited above, see, for example, Gates 2021; Nordhaus 2015, 2021.

References

De Nys, Erwin, Nathan L. Engle, and Antonio Rocha Magalhães, eds. 2017. *Drought in Brazil: Proactive Management and Policy*. New York: Routledge and CRC Press.

Gates, Bill. 2021. *How to Avoid a Climate Disaster: The Solutions We Have and the Breakthroughs We Need*. New York: Alfred A. Knopf.

Intergovernmental Panel for Climate Change. 2022a. "Climate Change 2022: Impacts, Adaptation, and Vulnerability," https://www.ipcc.ch/report/ar6/wg2/.

———. 2022b. "Mitigation of Climate Change," https://www.ipcc.ch/report/sixth-assessment-report-working-group-3/.

Ivanova, Maria. 2021. *The Untold Story of the World's Leading Environmental Institution: UNEP at Fifty*. Cambridge, MA: MIT Press.

Miller, Alan, Durwood Zaelke, and Stephen O. Anderson. 2021. *Cut Super Climate Pollutants Now: The Ozone Treaty's Urgent Lessons for Speeding Up Action*. Winchester, UK and Washington, DC: Changemaker Books.

Multilateral Organization Performance Assessment Network. 2021. *Lessons in Multilateral Effectiveness: Pulling Together the Multilateral Response to Climate Change*. Paris: MOPAN, July 2021, www.mopanonline.org/analysis/items/MOPAN_MLE_Climate_Change_July2021_web.pdf (accessed February 24, 2023).

Nordhaus, William D. 2015. *The Climate Casino: Risk, Uncertainty, and Economics for a Warming World*. New Haven, CT: Yale University Press.

———. 2021. *The Spirit of Green: The Economics of Collisions and Contagions in a Crowded World*. Princeton: Princeton University Press.

Stern, Nicholas. 2015. *Why Are We Waiting: The Logic, Urgency, and Promise of Tackling Climate Change*. Cambridge, MA: MIT Press.

UN Environmental Programme. 2021a. *Adaptation Gap Report 2021*. Nairobi: UNEP.

———. 2021b. *The Heat Is on: A World of Climate Promises Not Yet Delivered, Emissions Gap Report 2021*. Nairobi: UNEP, 2021, https://knowledge.unccd.int/publications/emissions-gap-report-2021-heat-world-climate-promises-not-yet-delivered (accessed February 24, 2023).

———. 2021c. *Making Peace with Nature: A Scientific Blueprint to Tackle the Climate, Biodiversity and Pollution Emergencies*. Nairobi: UNEP, February 18, 2021, www.unep.org/gan/resources/report/making-peace-nature-scientific-blueprint-tackle-climate-biodiversity-and-pollution (accessed February 24, 2023).

UN General Assembly. 2012. *The Future We Want*. Resolution 66/288. New York: UNGA, July 27, 2012.

———. 2015. *Transforming Our World: The 2030 Agenda for Sustainable Development: Sustainable Development Knowledge Platform*. Resolution 70/1. New York, September 25, 2015, https://sustainabledevelopment.un.org/Post2015/Transformingourworld (accessed February 24, 2023).

UNFCCC. 2015. "Technology Mechanism: Enhancing Climate Technology Development and Transfer," https://unfccc.int/ttclear/misc_/StaticFiles/gnwoerk_static/TEM/0e7cc25f3f9843ccb98399df4d47e219/174ad939936746b6bfad76e30a324e78.pdf.

United Nations. 2015. "The Paris Agreement," www.un.org/en/climatechange/paris-agreement (accessed February 24, 2023).

World Bank. 1992. *World Development Report 1992: Development and the Environment*. New York: Oxford University Press. Open Knowledge Repository, https://openknowledge.worldbank.org/handle/10986/5975 (accessed February 24, 2023).
———. 2003. *World Development Report 2003: Sustainable Development in a Dynamic World—Transforming Institutions, Growth, and Quality of Life*. Washington, DC: World Bank. Open Knowledge Repository, https://openknowledge.worldbank.org/handle/10986/5985 (accessed February 24, 2023).
World Commitment on Environment and Development. 1987. *Our Common Future*. Oxford: Oxford University Press.

PART 2

Corporate Governance

Corporate governance has always been a societal issue. Since the dawn of modern corporations, ownership and professional management have been separate. The formation of the Managing Director system established the role of a professional responsible to an independent board appointed by the corporation's owners—and eventually by institutional investors.

As family owners fled from Europe during the world wars in the twentieth century, corporate governance grew out of necessity into an agency system, where management was delegated to professional, paid agents. In addition, the migration of entrepreneurs and wealthy families to the United States and the former British colonies propelled the need for the agency system.

Fast forward to the second half of the twentieth century, corporate governance became a pressing issue when conglomerates such as R. J. R. Nabisco and Coca-Cola became targets of takeovers by private equity companies, particularly KKR's takeover of R. J. Reynolds. Many companies added significant penalties known as poison pills and supported their state governments. For example, the state of Indiana prevented Eli Lilly, a large pharmaceutical company, from multiple hostile takeovers. This was followed by the Enron and WorldCom scandals in the United States and Satyam Corporation in India, which led to legislative reforms and the establishment of the U.S. Sarbanes-Oxley act in 2004. The act led to new guidelines for disclosure of not just conflict of interest but also conflict of commitment. It also established checks and balances between a corporation's CEO and its CFO. Finally, it encouraged separation between the chairman of the board and the CEO of the corporation.

Corporate governance is now transforming not as much by policy and compliance but by digital technology. Technology is likely to alter the DNA of a corporation, whether it is institutionally, or family owned, and the digital transformation of corporations will have fundamental and enduring changes in governance. In addition to the internet, Enterprise Resource Planning (ERP) e-commerce, the next generation of technologies, such as cloud computing, blockchain, and artificial intelligence, are key to our understanding of the future of corporate governance.

In "The Future of Corporate Governance in the Digital Age" Jagdish N. Sheth documents just how—as the Industrial Age transformed production through automation, quality control, and standardization—the Digital Age will transform corporate governance.

DOI: 10.4324/9781003316077-8

Governance will become less hierarchical and more distributed, and it will be less compliance driven and more self-regulated. The rise of contract work will bring about greater flexibility and autonomy for the workforce. Also, the corporate boss mentality will give way to a style of leadership modeled after coaching and mentoring. Finally, managing social media will become more important than managing the mass media, and participating in shaping public policy will be as critical as managing public relations.

In a thought-provoking chapter titled "Grief—the Emotion HR Must Address," Abhijit Bhaduri points out that most corporations know how to celebrate success and achievement but do not know how to manage grief. Grief is an invisible emotion; employees are told and trained not to bring personal grief to the office or the factory. Bhaduri articulates and identifies different types of grief: grief of loss, humiliation, loneliness, office politics, loss of income and savings, and even loss of opportunity. In short, grief is everywhere at all times. Unresolved grief finds unhealthy outlets. So, what can the Human Resources Department of the company do? Bhaduri suggests that we need to eliminate myths—that grief is a personal matter or a sign of weakness, or that time heals everything, for example—about grief to make way for change and innovation. Bhaduri debunks the myth that emotions do not belong in the workplace.

In "Digital Marketing Development and Governance: The China Model," Yan Han describes the evolution of governance in China as the country has advanced rapidly in digital technology. More than one billion people in China are digitally connected, and their daily life is all around the smart phone. A key message of this chapter is that government policy on digital transformation is as important as market processes. Investment by the government in digital as well as physical infrastructure and a policy of embracing digital technologies such as the internet, cloud computing, e-commerce, online payments, and social media are as important as private sector marketing.

One of the assets of the corporation is its brand name. It reflects its reputation and attracts consumers, employees, and suppliers. It also motivates the community and the public at large to nurture and support it in times of crisis. Finally, it has economic value in the marketplace. In "A Conceptual Framework of Brand Co-Governance in the Digital Age," Altaf Merchant, Varsha Jain, and Parth Salunke discuss how the digital world has changed brand governance into a framework of co-governance between the company and its customers. Therefore, in addition to brand attributes and brand engagement managed by the company, user motivation, activity, and values form equally important components of co-governance. Social-media brand platforms and user marketing influencers are key to understanding how brands are managed in the marketplace. The authors present a conceptual framework for how brand co-governance mediated by digital platforms generate brand experience in the marketplace.

Finally, in "Corporate Board Governance in a Digital World," Vijay Viswanathan argues that we need a twenty-first-century notion of corporate governance as a result of both ad hoc events, such as the pandemic and climate change, and the rise of diversity, equity, and inclusion principles in the composition of corporate boards. Of course, the biggest impact on the new corporate governance model is the spectacular growth of social media and the need for greater transparency, and the trust and reputation of the corporation and its Board members.

Agency theory has been a useful corporate governance concept for the last century, but it needs to evolve into a concept of stewardship theory. Implementing stewardship theory will require changes in corporate board composition as well as changes in the internal metrics for both the management and the board members.

6
THE FUTURE OF CORPORATE GOVERNANCE IN THE DIGITAL AGE

Jagdish N. Sheth

Introduction

This chapter is about the impact of technology on the management and governance of institutions, such as education, businesses, faith, government agencies, and nongovernmental organizations (NGOs). Typically, the study of governance is focused on the areas of measurement and transparency, particularly the measurement of outcomes and the transparency of processes. This chapter, however, will focus on the democratization of information that is taking place through social media. But more importantly, it will focus on how technology will impact governance over time.

The title of this chapter is "The Future of Corporate Governance in the Digital Age." The impact of technology during the Industrial Age, the Infrastructure Age, the Communications Age, and the Digital Age will be discussed. Each one has had a significant impact, and the consequences, as well as the future governance of institutions.

During the Industrial Age, or Industry 1.0, the Industrial Revolution changed the way products and services were made. The largest impact was on production: most products and services shifted away from custom-made to mass production. As a result, the costs of production fell, making new products more affordable and in turn improving the standard of living. Estimates by the Federal Reserve show that in Great Britain in 1760, the population and average income levels increased tremendously. Gross domestic product (GDP), which was relatively fixed for thousands of years, grew significantly as well. Deirdre McCloskey, an economic historian, argued that industrialization was "certainly the most important event in the history of humanity since the domestication of animals and plants" and "perhaps the most important since the invention of language." The assembly line, which was not limited to the automobile sector, became the key principle of industrialization. Marginal productivity skyrocketed after the evolution of improved capital products like the steam engine and the use of the assembly line. Food also became more plentiful, which encouraged population growth and curbed malnutrition. Efficiency left more time for education, and average real incomes increased significantly (Investopedia Team 2021). Moreover, Frederick Taylor's theory of scientific management influenced management's

DOI: 10.4324/9781003316077-9

procedures and policies and the way humans interacted with machines (Taylor 1911). Core tenets of Taylorism, which is used by many firms to maximize efficiency today, include worker specialization and closely monitoring employee productivity.

More recently, there has been a focus on total quality management (TQM). The goal of this process is to increase both the efficiency and effectiveness of production, known as the economy of production. Research shows that TQM has positively impacted employee participation, morale, and customer satisfaction and is associated with increased profitability (Kumar et al. 2009).

Other methods developed during the Industrial Age are Six Sigma and the lean method. The objective of Six Sigma is to limit variation and defect levels in production using statistical analysis; the goal of lean methodology is to minimize waste and provide the highest value to customers with minimal investment (Purdue University 2021). Both methods have proven effective in a number of different fields. For instance, pilot programs that used lean methodology at Intermountain Healthcare had a significant reduction in turnaround time for pathologist reports. At the same firm, lean methodology also reduced the pharmacy's IV backlog and the time required to conduct patient glucose checks (Schweikhart and Dembe 2009).

In the Infrastructure Age, or Industry 2.0, railways, highways, and trucks changed the way products and services were distributed. All of these infrastructure technologies created labor mobility as well as product mobility. Today, an expert can go where the customers are and vice versa. After the invention of locomotives, weeklong journeys could be accomplished in a matter of days. Moreover, the cost of transporting people, goods, and raw materials fell significantly, and transportation could take place in all weather and seasons (Harvard Business School Historical Collections, n.d.).

The global supply chain became an enormous part of this evolution: today shipping routes are worldwide, and railways and highways are connected between nations. Therefore, understanding logistics and warehousing became key to effective management. This is the power of distribution, and hence, the primary focus is not just the economy of production, but also how technology impacts the economy of *distribution*. In the Infrastructure Age, because shipping, railways, and highways became available and were often integrated, freight began to travel.

The Communication Age, or Industry 3.0, came about with the invention of the telephone, television, computers, and—of course—the internet and mobile phones. There was also a rise in credit card usage and e-commerce during this phase. Online ordering is replacing in person retail store shopping, becoming a first preference rather than a second preference. This switch in how people purchased goods was accelerated by the Covid-19 pandemic; there was a move from physical first to digital first because people were not allowed to shop in stores. Americans spent US$791.7 billion on e-commerce in 2020, a jump of 32.4 percent from 2019 (Palmer 2021). In the process, institutions' bureaucracy or policies and procedures, known as the economy of transactions, began to change.

The Digital Age, or Industry 4.0, has had the most dramatic impact on institutions, because institutions are not only the *creators* of knowledge but also the *archivers* of knowledge. They are in many ways the knowledge custodians. Data, now a vital tool in our everyday lives, is the new oil (*Economist* 2017). It is valuable across all fields of industry: Harvard Medical School, for instance, highlighted research showing the value that machine learning brings to the medical sciences. The automated diagnostic methods were accurate about 92 percent of the time, and human pathologists were accurate about 96 percent of the time. However, when used together, the results rose to about 99.5 percent accuracy and errors were reduced significantly (Prescott 2016).

There are several components of the Digital Age economy beyond the internet, including storage, data centers, artificial intelligence, data mining, and business analytics. Insights or institutional insights change the way experiences are personalized. In this case, the value added by the institution goes toward user, buyer, and payer experiences.

The user experience and the sharing economy become the main thrust of the Digital Age. Today, social media is used in a way that nobody had imagined at the turn of the last century. In 2020, WhatsApp reached a staggering *two billion* active users (Feiner 2020), and Facebook over 2.89 billion *monthly* users across its family of applications, which includes WhatsApp and Instagram (Rodriguez 2020). Think about the power of social media and companies' access to information—and misinformation—twenty-four hours a day, 365 days a year. Social media has had an enormous impact on the way faith, religion, higher education, businesses, government institutions, and NGOs are governed. Social media transcends all jurisdictions and behaves like an independent nation—a "Facebook Nation" has emerged, with implications for governance and management.

Management is all about governance. As a result of accelerating technological changes, governance will shift from its current hierarchical, seniority-based pyramid structure to a more distributed governance. Today, governance and management can be done equally by both the remote spokes and the hub, with no need for centralized corporate headquarters or a central campus at universities. Today, universities and colleges can operate with multiple campuses simultaneously and divide the work accordingly. It is already happening at scientific laboratories where research and development are accomplished by shifting the work from one location to another. Data processing and credit card companies move their business process outsourcing (BPO) based on the time zones. Outsourcing call center operations and payroll has been used by many companies, but BPO is now expanding to more senior levels in financial operations and human resources (Thacker 2021).

Governance is also shifting away from external compliance and toward self-governance. People have always behaved because there have been laws that make them behave. They behave because there are codes of conduct which make people behave and because there is a manual outlining the do's and the don'ts for employees, contractors, and third-party suppliers. Self-governance was created because of increased access to information and reduced costs.

The governance mechanism will change from externally imposed to self-governance. Figure 6.1 highlights how hierarchical governance will give way to distributed governance, and external governance will shift to self-governance. What are the consequences or the new contours of governance as society moves forward? There will be eight significant shifts that are likely to change in the way institutions, especially business institutions, are governed (see Figure 6.2). However, I believe that this will be true among almost *all* institutions.

Enhanced Value of Human Capital

Technology, which displaces human beings, has never devalued them. If anything, technology has enhanced human value and human capital. Over the past 200 years, technological developments have increased wages tenfold (Bessen 2015). Artificial intelligence and similar technologies will improve educational opportunities, reduce disease, and even

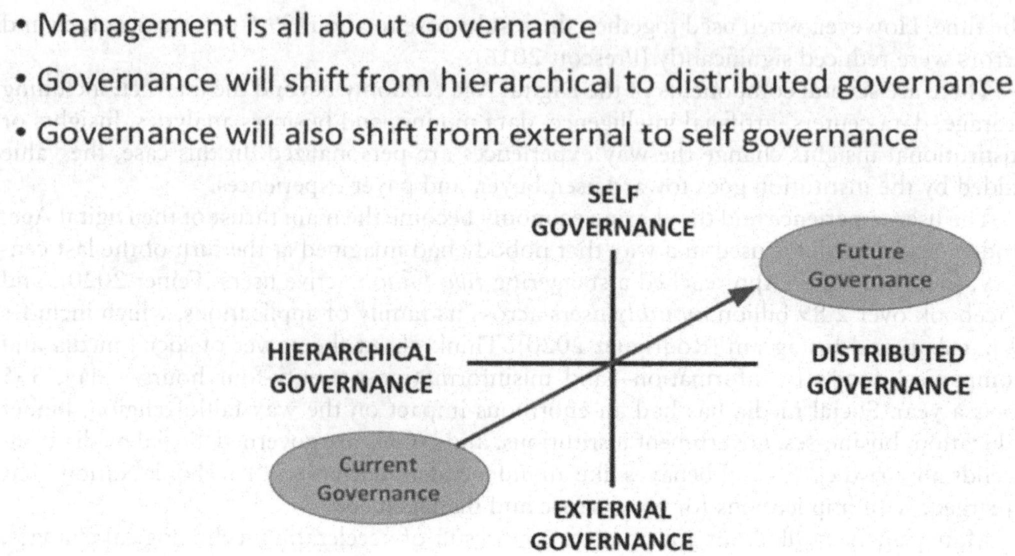

Figure 6.1 Fundamental Shift in Governance

Source: Author.

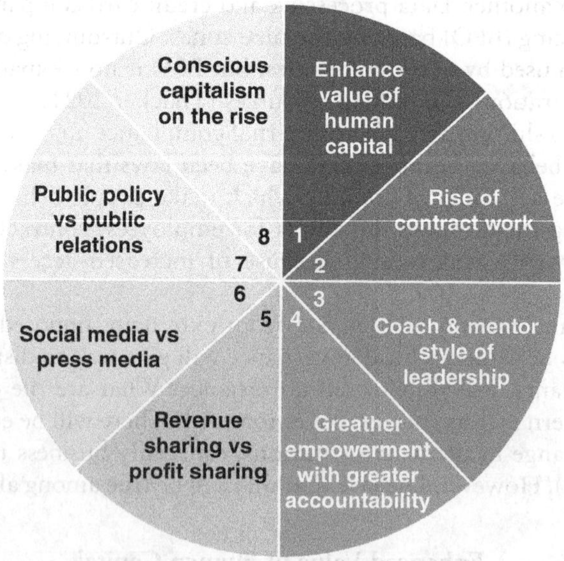

Figure 6.2 Consequences of the Shift in Governance

Source: Author.

eliminate global poverty (Anderson and Rainie 2018). Technology also *creates* new job opportunities. One-third of new employment opportunities that emerged in the United States between 1992 and 2017 did not previously exist or were underdeveloped, including hardware manufacturing, information technology (IT), and application development. In some cases, technology and automation reduce employment, but the gains offset the losses. A 2011 study by McKinsey showed that the internet not only led to the loss of 500,000 jobs in France over fifteen years but also led to the creation of 1.2 million *new jobs*. This represents a net of 700,000 jobs created, or 2.4 jobs generated for every job lost. Technology has also cultivated socially impactful entrepreneurship. Google's Internet Saathi, or "Friends of the Internet," program teaches rural Indian women how to use the internet so that they can provide services to locals using various technological devices. This work includes distribution for telecommunications products, including phones and SIM cards, data collection for research firms, and financial service roles (Manyika 2017).

A particular consequence of this technological change is wage inequality. Agriculture is the lowest-paid industry, followed by factory workers, white-collar clerical workers, and ultimately, blue-collar and white-collar professionals. Even during the pandemic, when farmworkers were deemed "essential workers," they earned only US$14.62 per hour on average in 2020, much less than some of the lowest-paid workers in the United States (Costa 2021). The gap between white-collar professional wages and salaries calculated hourly versus those for factory workers is increasing more and more because technology enables white-collar workers in many cases but replaces blue-collar workers.

Agricultural working conditions are quite brutal. U.S. farmers, especially immigrants, have very little protection. They were omitted from the Fair Labor Standards Act of 1938 and the National Labor Relations Act from 1935. Moreover, they experience high levels of sexual harassment and assault, wage theft, and severe injuries. Many workers are also killed on the job and exposed to dangerous chemicals. The H-2A visa program is often a vessel for exploitation for migrants because it tethers employment and immigration status but does not easily lead to permanent citizenship. Daniel Costa, the director of immigration law and policy research at the Economic Policy Institute, argues that the "structure of the program" enables this activity "often with impunity." Costa also highlighted the lack of "labor law enforcement," which perpetuates worker abuse in the agricultural industry. Inspections held by the U.S. Department of Labor fell dramatically over numerous decades because of low funding and understaffing, exacerbating worker plight. Costa adds that as "agricultural employer, there's only around a 1% chance that you'll be investigated for anything in any given year," and because of this, employers can "get away" with mistreating workers (Sainato 2021).

As society shifts from agricultural labor to factory labor, life improves. There are policies and procedures to ensure that workers' health and safety is managed properly. More importantly, as people move from factory workers to knowledge workers, the wages earned per hour increase dramatically. Knowledge workers, such as data scientists, lawyers, and software engineers, earn about US$50,000 more than construction workers or truck drivers (Minerva Wealth Advisory 2017). College-educated workers have experienced increased pay for decades, while the wages for those without degrees have "stagnated" or "lost ground." Salaries for entry-level investment banking analysts reached six figures in 2021, and dozens of corporate law firm associates received salary increases after firms like Milbank LLP, a prestigious international law firm, raised new lawyer salaries in the summer of 2021 from US$190,000 to US$200,000 (Weber 2021).

Factory workers depend on technology, but unfortunately, this technology is more mechanical and industrial. Today, one cannot be an automobile mechanic if she does not understand computers, and the wages are higher for more sophisticated and smarter technicians enabled by technology. As people move from technicians to managers, the same thing occurs. With all the technology available, they can do a much better job and the wages will rise in the process.

Rise of Contract Work

There will be a rise in contract work as well. Recent research showed that about 20 percent of jobs in the United States are done by workers under a contract; by 2028, freelancers and contractors may comprise *half* of the total American workforce (Noguchi 2018). A new style of leadership must emerge to manage this change. This trend has become more apparent during the pandemic. Today, many employees are asked to return to offices but they refuse because they prefer the flexibility and convenience of remote work. In fact, almost 50 percent of U.S. workers said that they would take up to a 5 percent pay cut to continue working remotely at least part time after the pandemic (Collins 2021). In another study, 70 percent of those surveyed said that they would give up benefits including health insurance, retirement accounts, and paid time off if it allowed them to continue working remotely (Bero 2021).

This trend also occurs among white-collar workers, especially IT professionals. Surprisingly, more hours are put in, and more productivity comes out, but they are willing to take a pay cut because they prefer autonomy and flexibility. In fact, studies show that productivity in the U.S. economy will rise by 5 percent in the post-pandemic world (Curran 2021). Other research showed that workers' productivity at home was 7 percent higher than expected, and 40 percent of workers said that they were more productive working remotely than they were in the office (Stropoli 2021). Clearly, autonomy and self-governance are more important today than employee benefits. This is why institutions must learn to provide more and more mechanisms and technology for self-governance. Governance has become widely distributed across its users.

Coach and Mentor Style of Leadership

The management style also has to change. Organizational leaders cannot behave like they did during the Industrial Age, where command, control, and communication strategies were used. With this method, there is no collective agreement or wisdom that comes about. The purpose of an institution is to unlock the potential of its stakeholders, and this cannot be done if there is a boss. In fact, today, the word "boss" has negative connotations. There must be new leadership that is similar to athletic coaching. The player is more important and receives more publicity and celebrity status than the coach. Many times, people do not know who coached Olympic gymnastics or other large teams—coaches work behind the scenes, as opposed to the current model where companies' senior leaders are visible. This is an invisible way of managing through mentoring, creating value, and unlocking potential.

Greater Empowerment With Greater Accountability

There will also be greater empowerment to people at the periphery or the bottom of the pyramid, but with greater *accountability*. With more distributed governance, there is also more empowerment at those endpoints. The more empowerment there is, the more accountability will be required. The person in charge or even the machine in charge is given the authorization to execute tasks, but this comes with greater accountability. If people are empowered, they have to be held accountable. Otherwise, power corrupts them. The more frontline workers are empowered at any institution, the more accountability measures must be in place, and it should be clear whether people are abusing their power. In relation to Frontline workers—reversing the pyramid—where workers are at the top and management is at the bottom, becomes very important under this theory.

In fact, employees are already becoming empowered. According to the Bureau of Labor Statistics (BLS), a record shows that 4.4 million people quit their jobs in September 2021. At the end of November, there were 10.6 million job openings and 6.9 million unemployed individuals, or the equivalent of 1.5 jobs for each unemployed person (Kamal 2022). Based on federal data that extends to 2000, in March 2021, there was a record level of open job positions, and workers "voluntarily" left their employment at a "rate that matches a historic high" (Irwin 2021). According to Burning Glass Technologies, an analytics company with data on job trends, the number of job listings that said "no experience necessary" jumped by two-thirds since 2019, and the number of postings offering starting bonuses doubled. Moreover, according to the Federal Reserve Bank of New York, the reservation wage, or the minimum wage that workers demand, rose by 19 percent, or an equivalent of almost US$10,000, for people *without* college degrees in March 2021 compared to November 2019. Furthermore, an April 2021 survey of human resources executives from large firms showed that 49 percent of organizations with primarily blue-collar workers struggled to retain employees, a leap from 30 percent prior to the pandemic. Karen Fichuk, an executive of a large staffing firm called Randstad North America, weighed in on the issue: "Companies are going to have to work harder to attract and retain talent." She also noted that "it's a bit of a historic moment for the American labor force" (Irwin 2021).

Younger generations also do not want to work for companies that do not share their values, whether those are gender equality, antiracism, or sustainability. Cheryl D'Cruz-Young, a recruitment officer with Korn Ferry, a U.S. consulting company, spoke about the issue, saying "It's a new world out there," and people "will not work with companies they don't agree with." In a Deloitte study of 23,000 people from forty-five countries, nearly 50 percent of those ages eighteen to twenty-five and 44 percent of those between twenty-six and thirty-eight, said that they chose their workplace because of "personal ethics." In the youngest age group, climate change was the primary concern, ranked higher than education and unemployment. According to Kathy Alsegaf, a global sustainability leader at Deloitte, young people "are really passionate about climate change, and they're taking action." She added that there is a "new sense of purpose, and jobs have to align with that." Data corroborates this. In 2020, for instance, there was the largest growth in the number of recent MBA and bachelor's degree holders who entered the environmental and renewable energy fields. In the same year, there was the most significant *decline* in graduates entering oil and gas. Moreover, almost one-third of Americans between the ages of eighteen and twenty-four said that they fought for climate change in 2021, which included donating to charitable organizations, volunteering, protesting, or reaching out to elected officials (Kantor 2021).

Revenue Sharing Versus Profit Sharing

There will also be a shift in terms of reward systems. The formula for sharing in the creation of value may be less and less anchored to profit sharing and more and more anchored to revenue sharing, which may look like a slight change, but it is still very significant. Organizations will move from salary and basic compensation and will not be anchored to profit sharing because profit setting is messy. A good accounting firm can have great gross margins diluted down to nothing in order to avoid income taxes. It is all man-made. Revenue is a more understood measure and tax authorities agree on this. Uber, for example, has this model with its drivers, who are independent contractors. The driver is like an employee or a pseudo-employee. Individuals have autonomy and are totally empowered, but they share in the revenue per ride. Airbnb also uses a similar formula.

Social Media Versus Press Media

Next, social media is becoming more important than press media. A staggering number of Americans use social media as a news source. A survey of U.S. adults found that 48 percent said that they use social media for news "often" or "sometimes." Moreover, Twitter is used by 23 percent of U.S. adults, and 55 percent of users use it for news regularly. Furthermore, users of ten social-media websites were also asked if they "regularly" get news from listed social-media sites, and 31 percent of adults said that they regularly consume news from Facebook (Walker and Matsa 2021). There is nobody who edits and talks about what is right or wrong. It is just a dissemination of information, and most information is created not by the press or media but by individual users. It is a massive tsunami of information which will shape public opinion and the way public policies are debated. There are laws on paper, but social media will begin to transcend those laws. While nations have laws about due process, for instance, social media does not. Recently, Trump was banned from Twitter, and little could be done to reverse this. Social media is really just a large, swift crowd-based judgment without a jury and a judge, and it must be understood by all institutions for future governance. The #MeToo Movement was a clear example of the judge and jury mechanism at work. Powerful men across a number of industries were dethroned because of sexual misconduct allegations including Les Moonves of CBS, actor Kevin Spacey, and the notorious film producer Harvey Weinstein. *Jeopardy!* host Mike Richards also stepped down as host of the show after sexist comments he made on a podcast a decade prior emerged and spread on social media (Nierman 2021).

Public Policy Versus Privacy Relations

More and more, institutions are also learning that public relations and external affairs are not enough—they must shift focus from public relations to public policy. How can one engage themselves as an institution early in the process of economic, social, and political reforms, and actually have a full understanding of the public policy mindset, as opposed to a public relations mindset? This will require a new breed executives and board members. There must be a chief policy officer rather than an external affairs or public relations officer. This is a very key position because the more policies and laws are shaped, the more compliant institutions will become. Otherwise, companies will always rely on gray markets and will create offshore profit centers and subsidiaries to avoid regulations and taxes.

Conscious Capitalism on the Rise

Lastly, there will be a rise in conscious capitalism (Sisodia, Wolfe, and Sheth 2007). Conscious capitalism reflects the idea that businesses will do well by doing good for their employees and the communities impacted by their policies. How can business create value, not only for their shareholders but also for their stakeholders? More and more companies believe that they need to implement governance to create *shared* value instead of *shareholder* value. In fact, they have begun to understand that creating value for all corporations' stakeholders—including customers, suppliers, investors, employees, and the larger community—is essential. Pella Corporation, one of the largest window and door manufacturing companies in the U.S., made a commitment to invest US$30 million in the rural town of Pella, Iowa, where its headquarters are located, as a means of attracting talent (Scott 2021). Costco has also become well known for its high minimum-wage pay to its workers, positive work environment, and employees that stay in their roles for years (Business Insider 2021). As more companies move their headquarters from small towns where they were formed to capital markets, they will be under pressure and by analysts, press media, and financial media to narrow down their focus to one stakeholder: shareholders and investors.

However, firms must focus on *stakeholders* instead. The UN Sustainable Development Goals identifies focusing on people, planet, and prosperity, also known as the triple bottom line, as an important initiative. The people, planet, and prosperity framework becomes a three-dimensional measurement tool for corporate governance as opposed to profits only. For instance, many companies have begun implementing equitable hiring rules, and some, such as Salesforce, give employees paid volunteer time off. Harvard Business School Professor Rebecca Henderson weighed in on why the triple bottom line is an important initiative: "In many situations, it's possible to do the right thing and make money at the same time." She added that "there's good reason to believe that solving the world's problems presents trillions of dollars worth of economic opportunity" and said that a "shared purpose can make firms both more productive and more innovative." The general public has also become receptive to environmental initiatives. Research showed that forty-eight of U.S. consumers are willing to change their consumption practices to reduce environmental degradation, and in 2018, there was US$128.5 billion in sales of "sustainable, fast-moving consumer goods" (Miller 2020).

This shift is stronger than expected, especially under the environmental, social, and governance (ESG) umbrella. Companies with strong ESG performance often perform better financially than those that do not, and many investors now consider ESG when making investment decisions (Miller 2020). Worldwide sustainable investment skyrocketed to US$30 trillion in 2019, a jump of 68 percent since 2014. ESG capital is growing significantly because leaders like BlackRock CEO Larry Fink are promoting the idea that one must look not only at a corporation's financial returns but also what the firm is doing for society and the environment. Given that BlackRock is the largest asset manager in the world, handling over US$10 trillion in assets, Fink's words are influential. In 2020, he said that climate change would be a "defining factor" for how BlackRock evaluated companies; in a matter of weeks, blue-chip companies declared that they would be carbon-negative or carbon-neutral. In his 2021 annual letter to the chief executives of companies that BlackRock invests in, he emphasized the importance of firms' moral responsibilities during the pandemic, but he noted that the "fair pursuit of profit is still what animates markets," adding that BlackRock focuses on "sustainability not because we're environmentalists, but because we are capitalists and fiduciaries to our clients." Fink makes it clear that ESG is not a trend, but rather it is a necessary tool for any company that wants to be profitable in the long term (Sorkin and Merced 2022).

Other large firms across a variety of industries have embraced ESG, including Alphabet, Microsoft, Bank of America (Rosenbaum 2022), Walmart, and Unilever. In fact, Walmart created the "Project Gigaton" to prevent the release of one gigaton of greenhouse gasses by 2030. This had a trickle-down effect, similar to Fink's influence, because Walmart requires its suppliers to comply with sustainability initiatives in order to continue business with them.

Interest in ESG has grown so significantly that MBA courses have been developed to cater to demand. Just recently, popular MBA classes included those relating to mergers, securities, and game theory. However, today some of the most in-demand classes are those covering impact investing, climate finance, and social entrepreneurship. Todd Cort, the co-director of the Environment and Business Center at the Yale School of Management and a lecturer at the school, has described the "explosion of interest from students" in recent years (Gross 2021). Wharton, for instance, now provides fifty graduate and undergraduate courses on social impact. Furthermore, the Duke University Fuqua Business School now has a class in its core curriculum called "Business and Common Purpose," and at Harvard Business school, 600 students enrolled in second-year elective courses covering social enterprise in 2020, more than doubling from 251 in 2012.

Higher education institutions are also making efforts to become more sustainable. Schools have upgraded their facilities to lower water and energy use, implemented more substantial composting and recycling programs, bought electric vehicles, and invested in clean, renewable energy, and sold fossil-fuel assets. Arizona State created a sustainability department in 2006, and universities like Columbia, Stanford, and Loyola University Chicago recently created departments centered around environmental issues. While a devotion to climate-related problems is essential in and of itself, it is also in these schools' financial interests to do so. Research showed that 75 percent of participants thought that "having information about a college's commitment to the environment would contribute to their decision about whether to apply to or attend the school," up from 66 percent in 2020 (Ho 2021).

Conclusion

Every technology influences and alters the contours of management. The Industrial Age altered the contour of production, and the Infrastructure Age altered the contour of distribution. Moreover, the Communication Age altered the contour of commerce, and, in the Digital Age, technologies including artificial intelligence, blockchain, and social media will change the contours of governance. Governance will shift from a hierarchical to a distributed governance model and from external compliance to self-governance.

The implications for the future of management are enormous. Human capital will command a premium, and contract work will become the new norm. The rise of conscious capitalism will also expand the responsibility of corporations from creating shareholder value to creating stakeholder value. What is the organization doing for the community? What is it doing for customers? What is it doing for suppliers and, of course, investors? One must have a balanced stakeholder scorecard.

Successful leaders will be those who embrace a coach- and mentor-style leadership instead of the traditional boss style of leadership and management. Again, the shift from hierarchical to a more distributed governance, and from compliance or a power-based governance to more and more self-governance, is inevitable. Over time, there will be a significant democratization of governance, and the traditional pyramid, with a small, consolidated group of leaders on the top, will be inverted.

Key Discussion Areas

- The role of technology in governance.
- The Knowledge Age versus the Industrial Age.
- Governance shifting from a hierarchical to a distributed structure.
- The shift from external governance to self-governance.
- Frontline workers' increased autonomy and empowerment.

References

Anderson, Janna, and Lee Rainie. 2018. "Artificial Intelligence and the Future of Humans." Pew Research Center, December 10, 2018, www.pewresearch.org/internet/2018/12/10/artificial-intelligence-and-the-future-of-humans/ (accessed March 25, 2023).

Bero, Tariro. 2021. "Employees Are Accepting Pay Cuts to Keep Working from Home: They Shouldn't." *The Guardian*, September 27, 2021, www.theguardian.com/commentisfree/2021/sep/27/employee-pay-cuts-work-from-home (accessed March 25, 2023).

Bessen, James. 2015. "How Technology Has Affected Wages for the Last 200 Years." *Harvard Business Review*, April 29, 20215, https://hbr.org/2015/04/how-technology-has-affected-wages-for-the-last-200-years (accessed March 25, 2023).

Business Insider. 2021. "Costco Is Raising Its Minimum Wage to $17 an Hour as the War for Workers Continues." October 29, 2021, www.businessinsider.com/costco-raising-wages-to-17-an-hour-2021-10 (accessed March 25, 2023).

Collins, Terry. 2021. "Work Remote after COVID? Nearly 50% of US Workers Would Take a Pay Cut for It, Survey Says." *USA Today*, November 11, 2021, www.usatoday.com/story/money/2021/11/11/workplace-survey-remote-pay-cut-covid/6367601001/ (accessed March 25, 2023).

Costa, Daniel. 2021. "The Farmworker Wage Gap Continued in 2020: Farmworkers and H-2A Workers Earned Very Low Wages During the Pandemic, Even Compared with Other Low-Wage Workers." *Working Economics Blog*, July 20, 2021, www.epi.org/blog/the-farmworker-wage-gap-continued-in-2020-farmworkers-and-h-2a-workers-earned-very-low-wages-during-the-pandemic-even-compared-with-other-low-wage-workers/ (accessed March 25, 2023).

Curran, Enda. 2021. "Work from Home to Lift Productivity by 5% in Post-Pandemic U.S." *Bloomberg*, April 22, 2021, www.bloomberg.com/news/articles/2021-04-22/yes-working-from-home-makes-you-more-productive-study-finds (accessed March 25, 2023).

Economist. 2017. "The World's Most Valuable Resource Is No Longer Oil, but Data." May 6, 2017, www.economist.com/leaders/2017/05/06/the-worlds-most-valuable-resource-is-no-longer-oil-but-data (accessed March 25, 2023).

Feiner, Lauren. 2020. "Facebook's WhatsApp Hits 2 Billion User Milestone." *CNBC*, February 12, 2020, www.cnbc.com/2020/02/12/facebooks-whatsapp-hits-2-billion-user-milestone.html (accessed March 25, 2023).

Gross, Jenny. 2021. "Business Schools Respond to a Flood of Interest in E.S.G." *New York Times*, November 13, 2021, www.nytimes.com/2021/11/13/business/dealbook/business-schools-esg.html (accessed March 25, 2023).
Harvard Business School Historical Collections. n.d. "The Railroads: The First Big Business," retrieved December 6, 2021, www.library.hbs.edu/hc/railroads/first-big-business.html (accessed March 25, 2023).
Ho, K. Karen. 2021. "The Climate Crisis Should Be Pushing Colleges and Universities to Do More to Be Sustainable, Experts Say. Student Recruitment Depends on It." *Business Insider*, October 28, 2021, www.businessinsider.com/climate-crisis-colleges-and-universities-sustainability-greenhouse-gas-2021-10 (accessed March 25, 2023).
Investopedia Team. 2021. "Is Industrialization Good for the Economy?" *Investopedia*, December 21, 2021, www.investopedia.com/ask/answers/033115/industrialization-good-economy.asp (accessed March 25, 2023).
Irwin, Neil. 2021. "Workers Are Gaining Leverage Over Employers Right Before Our Eyes." *New York Times*, June 5, 2021, www.nytimes.com/2021/06/05/upshot/jobs-rising-wages.html? (accessed March 25, 2023).
Kamal, Ruchir. 2022. "Quitting Is Just Half the Story: The Truth behind the 'Great Resignation'." *The Guardian*, January 4, 2022, www.theguardian.com/business/2022/jan/04/great-resignation-quitting-us-unemployment-economy (accessed March 25, 2023).
Kantor, Arielle. 2021. "The Thunberg Generation Demands Jobs That Mirror Green Values." *Bloomberg*, December 9, 2021, www.bloomberg.com/news/articles/2021-12-09/students-young-workers-insist-on-jobs-with-green-values-deloitte-finds (accessed March 25, 2023).
Kumar, Vinod, Fabrice Choisne, David de Grosbois, and Uma Kumar. 2009. "Impact of TQM on Company's Performance." *International Journal of Quality & Reliability Management* 26(1): 23–37, https://doi.org/10.1108/02656710910924152 (accessed March 25, 2023).
Manyika, James. 2017. "Technology, Jobs, and the Future of Work." McKinsey & Company, May 24, 2017, www.mckinsey.com/featured-insights/employment-and-growth/technology-jobs-and-the-future-of-work (accessed March 25, 2023).
Miller, Karen. 2020. "The Triple Bottom Line: What It Is and Why It's Important." *Business Insights*, December 8, 2020, https://online.hbs.edu/blog/post/what-is-the-triple-bottom-line (accessed March 25, 2023).
Minerva Wealth Advisory. 2017. "How Much Do Knowledge Workers Make?" Minerva Wealth Advisory, January 14, 2017, www.minervawealth.com/blog/ideas/2017/1/14/how-much-do-knowledge-workers-make (accessed March 25, 2023).
Nierman, Ethan. 2021. "Be Careful: Cancel Culture Is Here to Stay." *Forbes*, October 5, 2021, www.forbes.com/sites/theyec/2021/10/05/be-careful-cancel-culture-is-here-to-stay/?sh=48d766392ac7 (accessed March 25, 2023).
Noguchi, Yuki. 2018. "Freelanced: The Rise of the Contract Workforce." *NPR*, January 22, 2018, www.npr.org/2018/01/22/578825135/rise-of-the-contract-workers-work-is-different-now (accessed March 25, 2023).
Palmer, Alexis. 2021. "Groceries and Sporting Goods Were Big Gainers in the Covid E-Commerce Boom of 2020." *CNBC*, February 19, 2021, www.cnbc.com/2021/02/19/e-commerce-surged-during-covid-groceries-sporting-goods-top-gainers-.html (accessed March 25, 2023).
Prescott, Bonnie. 2016. "Artificial Intelligence Approach Improves Accuracy in Breast Cancer Diagnosis." Harvard Medical School, June 22, 2016, https://hms.harvard.edu/news/better-together (accessed March 25, 2023).
Purdue University. 2021. "Six Sigma vs Lean Six Sigma: What's the Difference?" *Six Sigma Blog*, June 7, 2021, www.purdue.edu/leansixsigmaonline/blog/six-sigma-vs-lean-six-sigma (accessed March 25, 2023).
Rodriguez, Salvador. 2020. "Facebook Stock Falls After Showing 51% Rise in Expenses." *CNBC*, January 29, 2020, www.cnbc.com/2020/01/29/facebook-fb-earnings-q4-2019.html (accessed March 25, 2023).
Rosenbaum, Eric. 2022. "These Are the Top 100 ESG Stocks in America: The 2022 JUST 100 Ranking." *CNBC*, January 11, 2022, www.cnbc.com/2022/01/11/these-are-the-top-100-esg-stocks-in-america-the-2022-just-100.html (accessed March 25, 2023).

Sainato, Michael. 2021. "'A Lot of Abuse for Little Pay': How US Farming Profits from Exploitation and Brutality." *The Guardian*, December 25, 2021, www.theguardian.com/us-news/2021/dec/25/us-farms-made-200m-human-smuggling-labor-trafficking-operation (accessed March 25, 2023).

Schweikhart, Sharon A., and Amy E. Dembe. 2009. "The Applicability of Lean and Six Sigma Techniques to Clinical and Translational Research." *Journal of Investigative Medicine* 57(7): 748–55, https://doi.org/10.2310/JIM.0b013e3181b91b3a (accessed March 25, 2023).

Scott, Charity. 2021. "Pella, Iowa, Needs Workers: They Prefer Robots." *Wall Street Journal*, July 23, 2021, www.wsj.com/articles/labor-shortage-unemployment-pella-iowa-11659364081 (accessed March 25, 2023).

Sisodia, Rajendra S., David B. Wolfe, and Jagdish N. Sheth. 2007. *Firms of Endearment: How World-Class Companies Profit from Passion and Purpose*. Upper Saddle River, NJ: Ft Press.

Sorkin, Andrew Ross, and Michael J. de la Merced. 2022. "It's Not 'Woke' for Businesses to Think Beyond Profit, BlackRock Chief Says." *New York Times*, January 17, 2022, www.nytimes.com/2022/01/17/business/dealbook/larry-fink-blackrock-letter.html (accessed March 25, 2023).

Stropoli, Ray. 2021. "Are We Really More Productive Working from Home?" *Chicago Booth Review*, August 18, 2021, www.chicagobooth.edu/review/are-we-really-more-productive-working-home (accessed March 25, 2023).

Taylor, Frederick Winslow. 1911. *The Principles of Scientific Management*. New York: Harper.

Thacker, Matt. 2021. "The Business Process Outsourcing Trend: How BPO Benefits Businesses of All Sizes." *Forbes*, January 8, 2021, www.forbes.com/sites/forbesbusinessdevelopmentcouncil/2021/01/08/the-business-process-outsourcing-trend-how-bpo-benefits-businesses-of-all-sizes/?sh=743bef032f49 (accessed March 25, 2023).

Walker, Michael, and Katerina Eva Matsa. 2021. "News Consumption Across Social Media in 2021." Pew Research Center, September 20, 2021, www.pewresearch.org/journalism/2021/09/20/news-consumption-across-social-media-in-2021 (accessed March 25, 2023).

Weber, Lauren. 2021. "In Hot Job Market, Salaries Start to Swell for White-Collar Workers." *Wall Street Journal*, December 26, 2021, www.wsj.com/articles/in-hot-job-market-salaries-start-to-swell-for-white-collar-workers-11640514607 (accessed March 25, 2023).

7

CORPORATE BOARD GOVERNANCE IN A DIGITAL WORLD

Vijay Viswanathan

Introduction

If the first couple of decades of the twenty-first century hold any indication of the challenges that businesses will face in the coming years, corporate boards and senior executives have their work cut out. We have endured unprecedented changes due to the Covid-19 health crisis, environmental disasters, ongoing wars, and many other external shocks.

At the same time, we have witnessed remarkable technological innovations and the emergence of radically innovative business models. From an information technology perspective, computing horsepower and data management capabilities today are generations ahead of those that existed even at the turn of the last century. Big Tech companies like Google, Amazon, Apple, Meta, and Netflix have changed our behaviors pertaining to information search, decision-making, and consumption. And concurrently, a ceaseless entry of new operators uses technology in novel ways to create and serve new markets. In the process, the traditional confines and boundaries of a marketplace have been all but erased. Globalization has enabled easier access to capital and talent, dramatically lowering the cost of entry for new players. The concept of a market as an enclosed bazaar with buyers and sellers has been replaced with digital platforms and open ecosystems that serve a wide variety of customers and varying needs that go well beyond the core product offering.

While many of these innovations enable new business models and novel customer experiences, they also raise important questions for digital governance and ethics. Rapid digitization has brought to fore important issues regarding privacy and transparency. There is an urgent need to clearly address long ignored issues around diversity, equity, and inclusion. As more women and underrepresented communities enter and participate in the market and lead businesses, it is important they have a seat at the table and influence businesses' decision-making processes. At the core, businesses must realize that new strategies have to be crafted to balance profit and purpose, rather than following business models developed after the Industrial Revolution and World War II. These old models, rooted in neoliberalism, are no longer relevant in today's rapidly changing user-/consumer-driven digital marketplace.

DOI: 10.4324/9781003316077-10

Unfortunately, corporate governance (CG) is often in the news for the wrong reasons. This is because contemporary CG models and processes are unable to tackle the issues that they were primarily set up for. As Subramanian (2015) points out, the issues of non-disclosure, conflict of interest, deficiency in board composition, and reliance on irrelevant metrics should alarm shareholders and stakeholders alike. Increasingly, stakeholder activism has emerged as a voice advocating for CG models that ensure that the basic tenets of governance are fulfilled, and the future of communities is secured in a fair, equitable, and transparent manner.

The concept of Corporate Governance (CG) can be traced to the early periods of the twentieth century (Berle and Means 1932; Vinten 2001), but it emerged as an active area of interest for practitioners and academics only in the last few decades of the twentieth century. With globalization driven in part by public corporations, CG continues to attract interest today from a range of constituents all around the world. Extant studies on CG have focused to a large extent on firm governance—which ensures the separation of ownership and control—and specifically on for-profit corporations. The underlying assumption is that the corporate board of the corporation bears the responsibility of corporate governance. The focus of this chapter is to highlight contemporary issues that necessitate fresh thinking around the concept of CG and its implications for contemporary businesses and society. We first provide a brief overview of different corporate governance models and delve deeper into board governance. We then focus on emerging issues that senior executives and board directors should focus on, such as digital and data governance, sustainability, and DEI. We conclude by suggesting metrics that capture the effectiveness of CG.

Corporate Governance Models From the Twentieth Century

CG has its roots in the work of Berle and Means (1932), who proposed that corporate governance should be the responsibility of a board of directors. This theory advocated for a clear line of separation between the ownership and decision-making bodies of a corporation, consistent to alleviate issues that arise from the principal-agent problem. Milton Friedman's (1970) CG model, the bedrock of many U.S. corporations, states, in no unclear terms, that the sole reason for corporations to exist is to maximize profits and shareholder wealth for public interest, employee livelihood, economic welfare, and societal impact. Since then, different theories have been developed to highlight the need for CG (Letza, Sun, and Kirkbride 2004) given the risks of the myopic market model, with its focus on short-term market returns as the way to maximize shareholder wealth (Charkham 1994; Sykes 1994), the abuse of power by executives to further their selfish interests (Hutton 1995; Kay and Gilbertson 1995), and the absence of stakeholders' involvement (Freeman 1984; Blair 1995).

Most theories share broad consensus for the separation of powers and the need for independent oversight but differ significantly in how. Businesses in the United States and the United Kingdom have adopted CG models that differ from their counterparts in continental Europe. In the former regions, CG is primarily the responsibility of a one-tiered board structure composed of nonexecutive directors elected by shareholders. There is one noteworthy difference in CG between the United States and the United Kingdom: in the United Kingdom, CEO duality—serving as the CEO and the president or chairperson of the board—is forbidden, while in the United States, it is not. Businesses in continental Europe have a two-tiered board structure, where, in addition to the board of management composed of senior executives, there is also a supervisory board. The role of the supervisory board is to oversee the board of management and have regular discussions on the company's business strategy and the status of its implementation. The continental European model of CG holds a firmer perspective of separation between ownership and control based on stakeholder theory (Freeman 1984). In addition to shareholder interests, the interests of various internal and external stakeholders, such as employees, customers, suppliers, management itself, government, political, environmental and social groups, and society at large, hold more weight than in the U.S.–UK models (Ahmad and Omar 2016).

Corporate Governance in the Twenty-First Century

In the first decade of this century, the concept of CG gradually began to change and expanded to include aspects beyond maximizing shareholder wealth. A widely used contemporary definition of CG provided by the World Bank (2016) states:

> Corporate Governance (CG) concerns the system by which companies are directed and controlled. It is about having companies, owners and regulators become more accountable, efficient, and transparent, which in turn builds trust and confidence. Well-governed companies carry lower financial and non-financial risks and generate higher shareholder returns. They also have better access to external finance and reduce systemic risks due to corporate crises and financial scandals. Reliable financial reporting, timely disclosures, better boards, and accountable management also facilitate development of stronger capital markets. They improve a country's ability to mobilize, allocate and monitor investments and help foster jobs and economic growth. Better supervision and monitoring can detect corporate inefficiencies and minimize vulnerability to financial crises.

The Organization for Economic Cooperation and Development (OECD) defines *good* CG as something that "helps to build an environment of trust, transparency and accountability necessary for fostering long-term investment, financial stability and business integrity, thereby supporting stronger growth and more inclusive societies" (OECD, n.d.).

Both definitions emphasize financial stability and inclusive growth, issues that are at the intersection of business and society. With global institutions like the World Bank and OECD moving forward with a broader view of CG, corporations too are following suit. The Business Roundtable (2019), an association of CEOs of companies that operate in the United States, released a statement that takes a broader view of CG and includes multiple stakeholders such as customers, employees, suppliers, and the communities in which they work. In many ways, this statement is closer to stakeholder theory and to the continental European model of CG. This statement also signals a significant shift from the Friedman (1970) model. At the same time, it is important to realize that this change in the perspective of CG is, in fact, endogenous. Specifically, these changes are a response to decades-long conversations on sustainability, transparency, and fairness, and subsequent stakeholder activism.

While companies are grappling with these issues, new challenges continue to emerge. For instance, the recent Covid-19 pandemic has highlighted the inability of companies to respond quickly and be financially stable. The economies of several countries contracted, putting at risk the entire livelihoods of daily workers and marginalized communities. It is fair to say that in this world of acute disruptions, no model of CG governance from the previous century has truly met its intended goal. What is of even more concern is that these shocks are perhaps not one-offs, and we might witness similar shocks in the years to come. Businesses should expect to face a wide variety of challenges that will pose significant threats to their mission, their strategies, and the impact they have on various stakeholders. Corporations must reconsider their raison d'etre and find the appropriate governance structure and processes to succeed and create a lasting impact.

Corporate Governance and Macroeconomic Shocks

As stated earlier, businesses now are exposed to a range of sudden unexpected shocks that could result in significant changes to not only their business operations but even their business model. Examples include biological shocks and natural disasters that impact global–local business contexts, extant demand and supply chains, and consequently disrupt how businesses fundamentally operate. The world is still recovering from the Covid-19 pandemic, when supply chains from Asia to the Western world were completely disrupted, resulting in huge economic losses for corporations and a shortage of essential products and services for customers.

Climate change is another example of a shock that falls in this realm. Changing weather patterns are causing significant disruptions in the lives of populations around the world. Consequently, policy-makers are urgently looking for solutions to ensure that future generations can continue to inhabit this planet. While addressing climate change may seem to be a social issue, it is only a matter of time before more stringent policies and laws are enacted that would necessitate a dramatic change in existing business models and strategies. Yet there are only a few companies that are proactively driving change. A possible reason for this inertia could be that managers who care more about their short-term interests have less of an incentive to respond immediately to changes in the environment that impact the medium- and long-term outcomes of the company. However, this is exactly why CG exists, and members of the corporate board must do more to focus on the long-term interests of stakeholders and society.

In other words, the orientation of CG must shift from one that is focused solely on reactive regulatory compliance to one that also proactively drives change to ensure the future financial stability of the corporation—and in the process unlocks value for all stakeholders. Baron (2016) makes a strong pitch for firms to deliberately consider nonmarket strategies—that is, the choice of actions that affect outcomes in the nonmarket environment—in conjunction with a market strategy to affect outcomes in the market environment. Examples of nonmarket strategies in public politics include lobbying, participation in regulatory campaigns, and forming coalitions to collectively address an issue. While certain nonmarket strategies can be used to fend off competition, other strategies can be used to highlight the broader purpose of a business and proactively engage specific stakeholders with certain social preferences (e.g., environmental or social justice issues). Certain nonmarket strategies can even create long-term value by positioning the firm to deal with challenges that may arise in the future. In this context, a particularly interesting form of nonmarket strategy is self-regulation. For instance, when faced with calls for change from activists, companies can choose whether they need to self-regulate and forestall the activist campaign. An alternative nonmarket strategy would be to collaborate with a cooperative activist who has bargaining power and shield the business from confrontational activists to support "soft advocacy."

Advocacy campaigns for regulation of hate speech on social media, and company/brand strategies to support these advocacy campaigns or not, are good examples. The choice of nonmarket strategies can play an important role in shaping public opinion and perception of the company's corporate social responsibility (CSR) initiatives. Corporate boards must, therefore, guide their businesses on utilizing appropriate nonmarket strategies in a fair and ethical manner to enhance the reputation, trust, and legitimacy of the corporation, even as they coordinate with legislators and stakeholders to respond to important social issues and create markets for the future.

Corporate Governance and Digitization

With increasing digitization across the globe, the speed, scale, and scope of information flow have grown exponentially in the last two decades. Statista (2021) reports that in just one minute, 5.7 million searches are made on Google and twelve million messages are sent on iMessage. People are changing the way they seek information, make decisions, and even experience certain products and services. For instance, while the need for music or vacations has not changed, the way we experience them today with Spotify or Airbnb is remarkably different from the way they were experienced at the turn of the century. We have also seen digitization disrupting legacy supply chains. Product development cycles have gotten shorter, and companies now have numerous platforms to get in front of customers and achieve scale. Companies that lead digital transformation in their respective industries are ones that have moved from *doing* digital (e.g., having a mobile app) to *being* digital (e.g., digital enterprise). And some are going further ahead by influencing their partners and stakeholders to create completely new digital ecosystems and platforms.

In contrast to macro-shocks that cause sudden regime shifts, the consistent nature of innovation around digitization is bound to cause constant shifts or chronic disruptions. The marketplaces and platforms that exist today will either cease to exist or live in combination with new platforms that offer completely different and immersive experiences. Companies can look back just a decade ago to recall the fall of reputed brands and corporations with the increasing adoption of e-commerce marketplaces. Technology companies such as Myspace, Netscape, Blackberry, Nokia, and AOL failed to keep pace with emerging marketplaces. These firms were left far behind by their superior rivals and underscore the fact that being a technology company is no guarantee of success. Instead, a critical driver of success is envisioning the marketplace of the future, proactively engaging various stakeholders and building digital capabilities to provide customers a wonderful user experience.

Digitization requires a corporate board comprising of individuals who have a twenty-first-century mindset and who truly understand what it means to be digital. Already, digital platforms are being integrated with virtual/augmented/mixed-reality technologies to create marketplaces of the future. Some companies are leading the way in developing next-generation marketplaces fueled by Web 3.0 and 4.0 (digital and AI worlds), non-fungible tokens (NFTs), and the metaverse (Rosen 2019). It is now common to see bots using artificial intelligence (AI) to deliver novel and personalized experiences for customers (Mitra 2015). While these may seem like exciting opportunities for managers, they also come with certain challenges. Companies have to ensure that AI-driven services are unbiased and do not put the reputation of the company at risk. Uber's surge pricing in times of natural calamities or terrorist attacks is a prime example of an algorithm going awry. As machines collect more data about individuals, there is a greater need for corporations to ensure transparency, security, and fairness in their dealings with customers. To ensure the financial stability of a company and ensure the rights of all stakeholders, CG in a digital economy requires people who understand the constant shifts that come with digitization and, consequently, the opportunities and challenges that come with it.

Boardrooms and Stewards

If there is one area of corporate governance that needs a fresh perspective, it is the way boards are constituted. Personal networks and homophily, especially by gender, are the norm when new board members are recruited. Retired CEOs and executives are too often rewarded with a position in a board, thus reinforcing biases that may already exist due to the lack of diversity. Deloitte's (2015) report on women in the boardroom provides a critical review on the lack of diversity in boardrooms across the world. The study finds that the number of women serving in boardrooms around the world has not seen a significant increase. Less than 5 percent of boardrooms have a woman as the chair. The benefits of more equitable representation go beyond ethical considerations: evidence exists that increasing greater representation for women on corporate boards is associated with a decreasing probability of fraud (Capezio and Mavisakalyan 2016). Dezsö and Ross (2012) find that greater representation of women in top management improves firm performance, especially when the firm is focused on innovation, a critical area of focus in the digital economy. Daily, Certo, and Dalton (1999) provide three other important reasons for greater diversity in the boardroom: first, women account for a large proportion of purchases. They have a strong understanding of the marketplace and would, hence, be able to provide a wide range of strategic options to the corporation. Second, greater diversity would send a powerful signal within the organization, promoting greater opportunities for women in key executive positions. Finally, including women and underrepresented groups in boardrooms is positively associated with stock returns. Daily and Dalton point out that those who incorrectly believe that qualified women do not exist, in fact, tend to create obstacles and a nonconducive organizational environment for women. It is perhaps for the same reason why minority groups are often underrepresented and are hence devoid of a strong voice in the boardrooms to influence change for their communities.

Irrespective of the CG model, U.S. or European, meaningful change is unlikely to take place without equitable representation of different stakeholders. While there has been tremendous focus on metrics that evaluate the effectiveness of different CG models, there is perhaps a more dire need for internally focused metrics that capture the equity, diversity, and inclusion of different boardrooms and their constituent members. Unless this information is captured and used in a systematic way, studies that evaluate the effectiveness of CG models on firm and stock performance are perhaps misleading, as they have omitted an important variable from the analysis. It is only when firms have fair and equitable representation in the boardroom that the rights of all stakeholders as mentioned in contemporary definitions of CG are ensured.

In addition to changing the ways in which boardrooms are constituted, there is also perhaps a need to understand how executives (or managers) perform their tasks. Agency theory (Simon 1957) takes a strong view that executives are self-serving and extrinsically motivated. In their quest to maximize their own utility, they fail to prioritize the long-term interests of the owners (principals). As noted earlier in this chapter, agency theory and its variants have for long formed the theoretical bedrock for most CG models. However, "stewardship theory," proposed by Argyris (1973, 253) built on the work of McGregor (1960) and Maslow (1970), takes a contrary view. The theory suggests that humans, when embedded in organizations that provide opportunities for growth, achievement, affiliation, and self-actualization, are motivated to work on behalf of the organization. Davis, Schoorman, and Donaldson (2018) hypothesize that individuals who are motivated by higher-order needs and intrinsic factors are more likely to become stewards than those motivated by economic needs and extrinsic factors. Stewardship theory can have a significant effect in shifting the focus of CG from monitor and control under agency theory to one where employees understand and identify with the greater purpose of the organization, and engage in self-leadership. Incidentally, this is consistent with the arguments made earlier that corporations must clearly identify their raison d'etre and then share their purpose clearly and broadly with all stakeholders. This approach will hopefully mitigate the issues that arise when there is a mismatch between the stated purpose of the firm (e.g., benefit all stakeholders) and a CG model that focuses on monitoring and controlling executives rather than motivating them to strive for a greater purpose and higher-order goals.

Conclusion

Companies today face a gamut of challenges ranging from disruptions that necessitate an entire change in business models and operations to chronic disruptions, especially those enabled by increasing digitization. From a sustainability point of view, climate change and related stakeholder activism are forcing companies to redesign their supply chains and operations such that sustainable processes are embedded in the value chain rather than bolted on as an afterthought. With increasing digitization, markets, as are traditionally understood, are disappearing and being replaced by platforms and virtual marketplaces with porous and flexible boundaries. To respond to these dynamic shifts, companies must rethink not only their CG models but even how boardrooms are constituted. Equitable representation of various stakeholders and greater diversity are critical if companies truly want to balance profit with purpose. Rather than viewing employees as self-serving agents that need constant monitoring, boardrooms must communicate the purpose of the organization and provide the right environment for employees to strive for higher-order goals consistent with the stated purpose for economic, environmental, and societal impact. Metrics that capture the nature and characteristics of boardrooms are essential to truly measure the influence of CG on firm performance. Table 7.1 summarizes the change in perspective that is needed if we are to move from CG models of the twentieth century to ones that are pertinent for the digital economy of the twenty-first century and beyond.

Key Discussion Areas

- The role of external environmental factors in corporate governance.
- Corporate governance and its various models.
- Climate change and its impact on corporate governance.
- Constant shifts or chronic disruptions due to digitization.
- The need for change in boardroom governance.

Table 7.1 Corporate Governance in the Digital World

	Primary goal of CG of the twentieth century	*Evolving goal of CG for the twenty-first century*
Firm opportunity	Profit maximization	Inclusive growth
Corporate governance value	Shareholder interest	Interests of all stakeholders directly and indirectly affected by the firm
Orientation of governance	Compliance, monitoring, and control of executives	Collectively achieve a higher-order purpose
Organization of boardroom	Close network, inequitable representation for women and other stakeholders	Equitable representation for women and important stakeholders
Skill sets of board members	Industry expertise	Expertise in digital, sustainable operations, nonmarket strategies, and business model transformation
Metrics	Effectiveness in influencing firm results	In addition, metrics that capture representation and inclusiveness in the boardroom

Source: Author.

References

Ahmad, S., and R. Omar. 2016. "Basic Corporate Governance Models: A Systematic Review." *International Journal of Law and Management* 58(1): 73–107.

Argyris, C. 1973. "Organization Man: Rational and Self-Actualizing." *Public Administration Review* 33(4): 354–57.

Baron, D. P. 2016. "Strategy Beyond Markets: A Step Back and a Look Forward." *Strategy Beyond Markets* 34: 1–54.

Berle, A. A., and G. G. C. Means. 1932/1968. *The Modern Corporation and Private Property*. New York: Harcourt, Brace and World.

Blair, M. M. 1995. *Ownership and Control: Rethinking Corporate Governance for the Twenty-First Century*. Washington, DC: Brookings Institution.

Business Roundtable. 2019. "Statement on the Purpose of a Corporation." August 19, 2019, updated May 2022, https://s3.amazonaws.com/brt.org/May-2022BRTStatementonthePurposeofaCorporationwithSignatures.pdf (accessed July 1, 2023).

Capezio, A., and A. Mavisakalyan. 2016. "Women in the Boardroom and Fraud: Evidence from Australia." *Australian Journal of Management* 41(4): 719–34.

Charkham, J. P. 1994. *I Keeping Good Company: A Study of Corporate Governance in Five Countries*. Oxford University Press.

Daily, C. M., S. T. Certo, and D. R. Dalton. 1999. "A Decade of Corporate Women: Some Progress in the Boardroom, none in the Executive Suite." *Strategic Management Journal* 20(1): 93–100.

Davis, J. H., F. D. Schoorman, and L. Donaldson. 2018. "Toward a Stewardship Theory of Management." *Academy of Management Review* 22(1): 20–47.

Deloitte. 2015. "Women in the Boardroom." Deloitte South Africa, June 22, 2015, https://www2.deloitte.com/za/en/pages/risk/articles/women-in-the-boardroom.html (accessed July 1, 2023).

Dezsö, C. L., and D. G. Ross. 2012. "Does Female Representation in Top Management Improve Firm Performance? A Panel Data Investigation." *Strategic Management Journal* 33(9): 1072–89.

Freeman, R. E. 1984. *Strategic Management: A Stake-Holder Approach*. Boston: Pitman.

Friedman, M. 1970. "The Social Responsibility of a Business Is to Increase Its Profits." *New York Times Magazine*, May 13, 1970.
Hutton, W. 1995. *The State We're in*. London: Jonathan Cape.
Kay, J., and A. Silberston. 1995. "Corporate Governance." *National Institute Economic Review* 84(August): 84–97.
Letza, S., X. Sun, and J. Kirkbride. 2004. "Shareholding Versus Stakeholding: A Critical Review of Corporate Governance." *Corporate Governance: An International Review* 12(3): 242–62.
Maslow, A. H. 1970. "New Introduction: Religions, Values, and Peak-Experiences." *Journal of Transpersonal Psychology* 2(2): 83–90.
McGregor, D. 1960. "Theory X and Theory Y." *Organization Theory* 358(374): 5.
Mitra, S. 2015. "From E-Commerce to Web 3.0: Let the Bots Do the Shopping." *WIRED*, August 7, 2015, www.wired.com/insights/2014/09/e-commerce-to-web-3-0/ (accessed July 1, 2023).
Organisation for Economic Co-operation and Development. n.d. "Corporate Governance," www.oecd.org/corporate/ (accessed August 2, 2022).
Rosen, L. 2019. "How Web 3.0 Will Change How We Are Sold to and How We Shop." *21st Century Tech Blog*, January 10, 2019, www.21stcentech.com/web-3-0-change-sold-shop/ (accessed August 2, 2022).
Simon, H. A. 1957. *Models of Man: Social and Rational*. New York: John Wiley and Sons, Inc.
Statista. 2021. "Media Usage in an Internet Minute." September 2021, www.statista.com/statistics/195140/new-user-generated-content-uploaded-by-users-per-minute/ (accessed August 2, 2022).
Subramanian, G. 2015. "Corporate Governance 2.0." *Harvard Business Review* 93(3): 17.
Sykes, A. 1994. "Proposals for Internationally Competitive Corporate Governance in Britain and America." *Corporate Governance* 2: 187–95.
Vinten, G. 2001. "Corporate Governance and the Sons of Cadbury." *Corporate Governance: The International Journal of Business in Society* 1(4): 4–8.
World Bank. 2016. "Corporate Governance." February 24, 2016, www.worldbank.org/en/topic/financialsector/brief/corporate-governance.

8
DIGITAL BRAND GOVERNANCE

Sukaran Thakur

Introduction

"The internet is just a fad" was a common statement made back in the early days of the development of the World Wide Web. The prophesized "bubble" surely got the last laugh. Today a world wherein the internet has not found its roots in every single aspect of daily life would be unimaginable. We wake up to smart assistants ringing alarms that took into account the fact that we set an alarm at 7 a.m. every morning and so offered to make it a weekly occurrence. Our sleepy hands reach out to smartphones to scroll through densely packed information in almost hypnotically good user interfaces; sure enough, with 4.39 billion unique users of the internet, and 3.48 billion users of social media, there's a plethora of information (Kemp 2019). We might receive breakfast from a service provider that we ordered on the web, tracking the movement of the delivery professional using GPS technology all turned into a cute animation of a bike rummaging through the streets. We invest money using the internet, we buy physicals (even a car!) using the internet; and if the next prophesized "bubble" is to have its way, we might soon never look at financial transactions the same way with the advent of cryptocurrencies (DeVries 2016).

Even art—one of the most nuanced markers of the development of a society—has now taken the evolutionary route of non-fungible tokens (NFTs) and thereby gone "all digital" (Wang et al. 2021). This interoperability in common parlance between "internet" and "digital" might be misinformed but does serve as a marker of the times, wherein the all-pervasiveness of this ecosystem has made terms of usage defunct faster than ever in linguistic history. Considering the sheer expansiveness of this concept (for it would be unfair to term this as just "technology"), organizations and governments have struggled to find the appropriate way to both govern and un-govern this space.

At the most fundamental level, digital governance consists of three predominant areas: digital strategy, digital policy, and digital standards (Welchman 2015), (Figure 8.1). However, digital governance must be evaluated and understood from three different lenses, since the lack of definition can make it easy to confuse between them. At the onset is the evolution of media in the digital sphere as "social media" and hence one lens of digital governance is the way organizations must govern their *digital* presence. This digital governance

DOI: 10.4324/9781003316077-11

Figure 8.1 The Three Areas of Digital Governance
Source: Icons from TheNounProject.com.

also expands into the various other aspects that now are a part of "being digital," including information technology (IT) services, human resources practices and systems for remote working, supply chain management and management information systems as well as e-commerce sales channels. The second perspective is that of digitization of governance, wherein we look at how legacy organizations and national or state governments bring in elements of digitization (both of processes and communication channels) into the way they manage governing their jurisdictions. The last lens is the highly controversial emerging space of the governance of the digital world, premised around the fact that many digital-first organizations/companies are now larger than various countries in economic power and social influence, and operate with little or no international jurisdiction. Finding effective, sustainable, and responsible ways of governing these companies is an important and emerging area of discussion (O'Hara and Hall 2018).

Speaking Digitally

If we are to be exact, digital would essentially be anything that uses discrete digits instead of a continuous stream (which we call analogue). How this idea of discrete digits, most notably the binary code, has changed the world is nothing short of magic. But true exploration of the potential of discrete digits lies in what we did with our ability to codify information and share it through digital means. The World Wide Web and corresponding technologies were created for the purpose of information sharing and quickly adapted to becoming as close to the idea of human communication as possible. With Instant Messaging (IM) being the earliest forays into creating virtual personas and communicating over short text and rich-media messages, the eventual creation of social networking websites was the biggest turning point in this evolutionary path of digital communication. Sites like the now-defunct Hi5 and Orkut established what are now some of the ground rules for all digital social interactions—the idea of a profile to create a digital persona and having the ability to communicate, in ways that are both a monologue (the profile description and bio) as well as a dialogue (with "walls" and "scraps" as well as integrated IM technologies). Today with over 3.6 billion people using social media (Digital Users Report 2020)

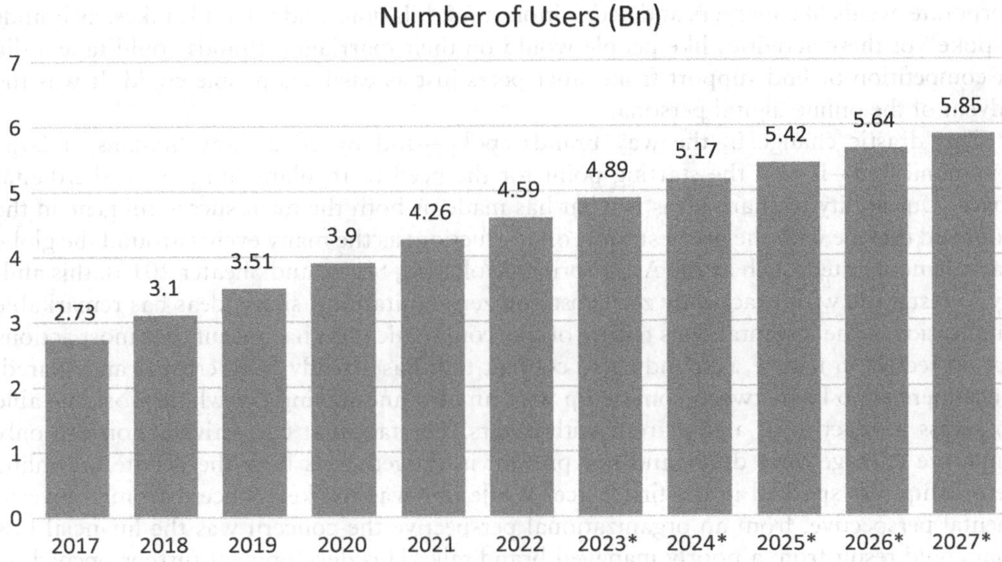

Figure 8.2 Number of Social Network Users Worldwide from 2017 to 2027
Source: Published by Stacy Jo Dixon, Aug 29, 2023 (Statista).

(See Figure 8.2), it is safe to say that social media has evolved into becoming an integral part of everyday life.

In the early days of social media, the focus was individual centric and at max expanded to allowing multiple users to congregate into groups wherein they could hold discussions on common topics. Organizations and companies, though legally their own "persons," did not participate on these networks. One of the more successful executions of this corporate identity on social media was the concept of "pages" on Facebook. A "page" was similar to "profiles" in the sense that it allowed for a display picture (most often a logo for companies and brands) and for individuals to "follow" these accounts to get regular updates that might be posted by the brand. It didn't take too long, however, for the social media giants as well as organizations and brands to realize that brands behaved suspiciously a lot like people did. The ability to have a dialogue, in which people would write a post or comment on a digital post created by the brand and the brand had a choice to respond, accelerated this realization. In the history of marketing, this might have been the very first time that a brand could speak to individual users (outside of courtrooms!). And while, of course, behind the screen the words were typed by an individual, their identity would almost never be revealed, thereby allowing users to interact with the brands they loved, not just the sales teams of these brands. This fundamentally altered how brands spoke, communicated, and personified themselves.

The digital space allowed brands to become more flamboyant with their personalities. Features like "friends-of-brands," which until then had stayed hidden in dust-covered brand-books, became mainstream as brands took to "speaking" to other brands as well. The advent of Twitter and other microblogging platforms took this one step further: brand accounts and personal accounts were for all effects and purposes identical. Serious corporate events like mergers and acquisitions took hilarious and relatable takes, as brands "spoke" of these activities like people would on their marriages. Brands could take a dig at competition or find support from other peers just as easily as people could. It was the advent of the online digital persona.

This drastic change in the way brands spoke—and by effect how humans at large communicated—is also the starting point for the need to regulate and govern the digital space. Our ability to share ideas is what has made us both the most successful gene in the pool and the one with the greatest tools of destruction; as the many events around the globe have demonstrated, such as the Arab Spring (Wolfsfeld, Segev, and Sheafer 2013), this ability to instantly, with practically zero cost and zero limitations, share ideas has remarkable implications. The instantaneous nature of this communication has meant that most actions are corrective in nature, responding to content that has already been created and shared, since there is no lag between coming up with an idea and having the whole world be able to access it, react to it, and share it with others. The fact that corrective action can only minimize damage once done, and not prevent it altogether, is how the debate on online censorship was sparked in the first place. While this was the key concern from a governmental perspective, from an organizational perspective the concern was the financial loss that could result from a poorly managed brand talk. This development further opened up the avenue of digital governance of communication.

For an organization, this communication could stem from both a branded channel of voice (like a brand page or social media account) and from prolific brand custodians. Afterall, a number of CEOs and high-ranking officials of organizations have substantial following, and their digital presence has an automatic impact on the brand's online presence. What a brand should or shouldn't say online would find its home in general brand governance principles. Just like in the space of Above the Line (ATL)[1] or Below the Line (BTL)[2] communication, digital communication too is governed by the general principles of the value system of the brand. An additional challenge is created by the fact that digital is both personal and decentralized and therefore, mass-communication in parallel, something that is not the case with ATL or BTL. In any case, the weight of deciding what the brand could "say" digitally rested on the shoulders of the brand managers (Marland, Lewis, and Flanagan 2017).

The other team on the line of defense is the corporate communications team, which need to establish ground rules for engagement of employees on digital platforms. These platforms instantly gave every single employee the same outreach power that was earlier reserved for top public relations–approved executives. This ability to share an insider perspective of an organization with a global audience has not only opened up a whole new era of transparency (and whistleblowing) that has resulted in a more trusted ecosystem from a consumer perspective, but also raised a number of governance concerns resulting from the sheer difficulty of governing this space from an organizational perspective (Marcum and Young 2019).

Corporate Digital Confusions

Digital has seen an unanticipated evolution (unless you take into account Moore's law that claims that processors will get twice as fast and half as expensive every two years). It is pivotal at this point to clarify that when we say digital we aren't just talking about social media fads (or "trends" as they are now known in common parlance) but also the kind of technology available at our disposal and how well integrated it is with the physical world, such that the word "phygital" is now found in MBA curricula across the world. For organizations that operate as a living and breathing organism of gigantic proportions, senior management found itself grappling with a world that evolved and changed fast and ruthlessly. Add to it the extremely blurred lines between services that can help and the ones that can be used with mala fide intent. Sure enough, cloud storage allows multiple people to work on the same document from different locations with the same ease as that confidential document can be replicated and shared (possibly to a competitor).

The earliest form of digital governance came in the form of cybersecurity (Dunleavy and Margetts 2015). Today's senior management would definitely remember the early days of presentations by a budding IT Department that would teach, often through animated videos, the perils of inserting an unknown pen-drive into the USB socket of a company laptop, resulting in data-locks, ransomware or just plain good-old destruction of data. This sense of fear was indeed the early driver of digital governance, wherein digital only meant information technology of any kind, and the governance was limited to ensuring the data stayed safe and secure. This rapidly changed with the advent of cheaper internet, since that opened up unexpectedly large geographies to becoming unified markets. Suddenly, a commercial enterprise with one office in one city could service consumers sitting thousands of miles away via e-commerce. For a substantial period of time, e-commerce was another sales channel usually grouped with institutional sales. No one could have seen the massive impact e-commerce would have on the development of sales channels and organizations as a whole.

An interesting parallel that can be drawn here is that of the sales channel of modern trade as compared to general trade, which is how Indian Fast-Moving Consumer Goods' companies distinguish between organized and largely-unorganized retail stores. Modern trade, therefore, is the organized arm of retail with branded stores, a digitized billing system and usually standardized warehousing and supply-chain. General Trade, also called Mom & Pop stores are unorganized, unbranded and usually run at a smaller scale. At the beginning of the liberalization years, about three decades ago, modern trade was an elusive and small scoped avenue of making retail sales, limited to a few key players who had limited outreach. Until 2003 to 2004, modern trade was treated like a novelty with limited scope and hence a specialized set of people who would engage with these retail partners on the side; today no sales professional could look at such trade as a novelty that could be an optional sales channel. Modern trade is deeply integrated into the way organizations, especially the FMCG space, operate in India. E-Commerce is going through the same kind of transformation, wherein everyone from publishing houses for books, FMCG giants for their instant-noodles, and consumer goods companies for their white goods are finding footing.

However, what started as being IT or Tech-Support, a minor sales channel, has rapidly expanded to becoming an all-pervasive and integrated space. As L'Oréal India CDO Anil Chilla describes, "Digital strategy is not separated from business strategy anymore." The separation between online and offline doesn't exist in the planning sense anymore, wherein rapid evolution means that all aspects of the brand, product, and go-to-market strategy contain digital as an inherent component and not as a secondary or a supplementary aspect to the strategy. This also means that digital is no longer an option or a choice but instead a necessary aspect that has led all persons in an organization to be digital natives, thereby being digital first in their specific areas of responsibility.

The Disappearing Chief Officer

The evolution of IT and e-commerce into an all-encompassing digital sphere in an organization, where everyone must have the requisite skill sets and an understanding of the digital world from the perspective of their own area of expertise, means that there is a need for someone to act as the common thread that keeps all the different players aligned to a cohesive and singular digital strategy. This role has seen its own share of evolution and has today led to a position on the board table with a chief officer role; however, if history has set any precedence, this seems like a role set to go over another round of evolution soon.

A CDO's role is best defined as being that of animating and driving the digital strategy and correspondingly the digital governance of an organization. However, with everyone from the CEO to ground staff needing to be digitally equipped and educated, the CDO is not one who tells others what should be done but instead an advisor in terms of what the business can do across sales, media, technology, internal processes, supply chain and communications.

This domain expertise becomes further important in an economy where data is the next gold/oil. This data is digital. Exporting market intelligence out of behavioral data is nothing new, but what used to be a mass-activity wherein personas were developed for an entire cohort has now become an extremely personalized and micro-targeted activity wherein the personality of each person can be used as the basis of serving a communication specific to them. This ability of finding the right message for the right person heavily depends on the organization's ability to capture the right data—most of which comes digitally—and then having the right systems, processes, and technologies to use this data effectively. A CDO's understanding of machine learning, artificial intelligence, and big data are pivotal to getting the edge. When an organization like Tesla announces that they are going to accept cryptocurrency as valid payment for their products (BBC 2022), the presence of a digital domain–expert helps the organization tap into rapidly emerging opportunities and find these first mover advantages.

However, a single person may not be able to drive a digital-first approach in an organization anymore. The need of the hour is to run digital strategy at a company level, and all business owners need to understand the importance and scope of what digital can achieve. The current role of the CDO might be a temporary phenomenon, leading swiftly to evolving roles for someone who can act as an anchor to the many new technologies and variations that appear in the digital ecosystem and someone who can craft the guardrails within which the organization can govern its digital presence, as well as the presence of digital within its systems and processes.

Company-level digital strategy needs a certain decentralizing of control, since each function of the organization would need to operate using different norms for using digital technology and digital avenues. At the same time, a fine balance would need to be established between the freedom that decentralization brings and the cost benefits as well as process unification benefits that emerge because of a system of global-contracts that create a unified approach to digital governance. A number of contracts and partnerships, especially those around finance, IT, consumer data, privacy, storage, and protection, are critical in nature and benefit from being governed centrally. A central governance policy for data privacy for consumers would benefit from global best practices, a thorough reading of all avenues of risk and risk management, and the communicative benefit of having a central policy that can be shared with all stakeholders.

Post-Pandemic

The business-wide benefits of digitization are not unknown to senior management, but bringing about change is always an arduous process. Transforming the way financial transactions are monitored or how supply chain efficiency is maximized can cause ripple effects within the organization, though hardly visible from the outside. At the same time, transforming communication and sales practices and making them digital first or at least digital supplemented cause the same ripple effects and are also visible and therefore under scrutiny by consumers and competition alike. However, the lines between internal and external visibility of digital transformation have started blurring in the post-pandemic world.

The rapid evolution associated with digitization of business processes was accelerated due to the Covid-19 pandemic, which saw the first peacetime lockdown of such a large scale—a lockdown that resulted in both companies and consumers evolving to embrace digital avenues of buying and selling to keep in line with social-distancing norms. This also brought to the forefront the ways of working in organizations, since peers were all suddenly on a level playing field in terms of the physical assets available to the business. All organizations were operating connected via the internet, using virtual conferencing, suddenly the presence of towering offices, a large team present for a meeting and other such visual markers of size and scale became invisible. The way organizations embraced remote work in terms of providing flexibility, work-from-home policies, and employee benefits were also widely spoken of and acted like a billboard of the employer practices of the organization.

Challenges in terms of governing the remote-work space abounded. Fundamental practices such as clocking-in and clocking-out or attending meetings and discussions actively need a sense of trust as well as stakeholder-friendly policies and governance norms to be easy to accept. A number of organizations began imposing mandatory use of cameras during meetings (to ensure active participation by the employees), which was met with heavy criticism. The blurry lines between personal and professional space in terms of time of response necessitated rules and governance norms that would prevent employee fatigue and support mental health concerns. These rules and norms evolved almost like a moral code for corporations, or at the least in the form of accountability. This accountability started with a sense of continuity for the consumer experience but quickly was aligned to the accountability to the employees and stakeholders to allow for a healthy work environment.

On the external front too, a number of legacy events such as product launches and press-conferences had to be moved to the online space, needing organizations to reevaluate their digital presence and recalibrate their formats to fit in this new way of communication and execution. This recalibration led many organizations, including government agencies to look at having digital guidelines for the very first time. In parallel, from a consumer's perspective, brands suddenly occupied a more human-like appeal since they all relocated to a personal space, the home.

Digital Brand Governance

Because digital can mean so many different things depending on the industry as well as the practitioner talking about it, it becomes important to establish all that is included in the scope of the definition of digital. While from a business and organizational perspective digital could mean IT or e-commerce or even data, for FMCG and consumer durables digital is usually the front end of the business and would therefore include influencers, partnerships, collaborations, media platforms, social advertisements, consumer data, and even customer relationship management.

As Marshall McLuhan said, the medium is the message. The same is true for the many digital avenues available to brand managers and marketeers. While the messaging that is selected would be governed by the brand book and brand guardrails, or the campaign direction as envisioned by the creative agency working on the same, the selection of the medium that will be used for this communication needs a nuanced understanding of the digital ecosystem. An interesting case study emerged in this space with the advent of TikTok, which is consumed by a markedly different demography in the West than it was (before being banned) in India. The social media platform became popular at the same time as Reliance Jio made the cheapest mobile data plan in the world, available to the masses in India; this parallel popularization meant that the largest demographic segment of TikTok came from the hinterlands of India. The barrage of content being created on the platform was met with divided opinions on the usefulness of such a platform; from a purely brand perspective, it was a clearly demarcated social media avenue that would help the brands reach out to specific audiences. However, brands also had to be sensitive to how they would appear when their presence on such a social media platform becomes widely known.

Governance of digital presence of brands raises the question of trust within the teams and structures put in place for approvals. For most organizations, the brand team works with full-service creative agencies that develop the ad content and then with media-buying agencies that work on securing the best deals for the best placement to take that message to the largest audience possible. The advent of digital also brought forward a new breed of agencies, known, unimaginatively, as digital agencies. These were experts in taking content online, running ads on digital platforms, wherein mass advertising was customizable in its outreach and technical expertise in aspects like programmatic media bought a micro-personalization experience to the end consumer. The mantle of digital brand presence on the shoulders of one single partner did simplify things (from the time of a duo of creative agency and media buyer); one of the most important pillars of digital communication is speed, and speed in terms of multiple partners and creative work is largely based on how long the cycle of creative brief, content creation, feedback, and approvals takes.

But the constantly reducing attention span of the digital consumer means that this cycle needs to keep getting shorter and shorter for it to be able to "catch-the-bus" before a trend or a fad is replaced by another one. This act of staying updated can sometimes mean that the process of briefing, content creation, and approval might all need to happen at one end of the partnership and be executed in minutes instead of days. In the midst of a power outage at the 2013 Super Bowl at the Mercedes Benz Superdome in New Orleans, Oreo Cookie tweeted a single tweet that created more of a buzz than the many million-dollar ads that were showcased at the event. The tweet from Oreo (Figure 8.3) is often cited as the perfect example of moment marketing that can be achieved when robust guardrails are in place that allow the agency to work with confidence and independence. The softer side of this is also the kind of trust that exists in the governance norms created and the ability of the partners to adhere to it, such that the creation of a digital communication piece might or might not need, in the strictest sense, further approvals.

Speaking of marketing without speaking of sales channels and their interdependence would be a half-baked discussion of what digital brand governance can entail. While the pandemic made e-commerce the fastest growing sales channel of the last few years, prior to the pandemic many forward-looking companies were already experimenting with

Figure 8.3 Oreo Moment Marketing: 2013 Super Bowl Tweet

Source: Retrieved from https://twitter.com/Oreo/status/298246571718483968.

"omnichannel" marketing, a connected system of sales that allows all inventory to be available across retail, home delivery, and multi-brand outlets. Such a system created a number of governance concerns, especially around the way data would move between the various stakeholders. However, on-ground implementation brought new, more human-centric problems; concerns around sales incentives, and attribution of the sale, which might not appear entirely obvious at a top-level strategy, ended up becoming some of the most challenging aspects of implementing this connected sales channel. Digital governance working in the vacuum of how processes, systems, and policies impact general human psychology motivators and disruptors would succeed on paper, but fail on the day of execution and implementation. For example, for an apparel retail brand where the sales-staff is incentivized on "who" makes the sale, should a sale that was conducted online, but due to omnichannel, is being executed in the store, be attributed to a sales-staff in store? And if not, then how should the store be compensated for its dwindling inventory of high through-put articles which might have helped the store-staff in achieving their sales-targets? While for a company, a sale may by just that, a sale; the on-ground reality of how multiple stakeholders treat each commercial transaction is far from such simplifications.

This human psychology angle was also brought to the forefront when e-commerce started growing as a medium of buying items that are traditionally considered luxury goods. How does one bring two opposing codes together in a single experience? Luxury is premised on obscuring the price of a product and creating a sensory experience, whereas e-commerce pays an inordinate amount of focus on getting the best deal and offering the widest variety on the same platform. This contrast in codes meant a whole new aspect of immediacy, transparency, and access had to be accounted for in a brand's guardrails; whole new segments on digital brand governance needed to be incorporated in documentation.

Digital Transformation and Governance

The process of creating digital governance norms and outlines can be explored using the many challenges that organizations face when they begin the process of digital transformation. As is evident by now, there is hardly a strict start or stop to this transformation, as various aspects of the organization will phase in these transformations over a period of time and pace. Therefore, organizations find themselves constantly in a state of evolution and evaluation.

Such large-scale changes need a modernization of technologies, processes, and operations that must be achieved through a controlled and phased approach. Information migration between old systems and new technologies have both technical challenges as well as real world challenges. As many business owners discover when legacy data is opened up and put through scrutiny while migrating, data quality in organizations has been an area of concern for a long time, especially if data is gathered through nonautomated and non-standardized systems. It is therefore of importance to set up data governance norms, which should explain not only how data is collected, but who oversees the quality of it and who all have access to the data for operation and execution.

Such transitions need to be executed across the organization. Since each organization operates in its own unique ways, the first few transitions and transformations can serve as learning ground for the remaining business units. These early adopters would help create standardized processes and systems for hand-overs. Having a unified platform off which the team members would work either in parallel (with both old and new systems until the new systems take over entirely) or in serial (where old systems are phased out slowly as new systems are brought in) can further ensure that there is an organization-wide alignment.

Finance and the supply chain are often areas where old legacy hardware and software lingers the longest. For example, Windows XP, an operating system developed in 2003, is still used in as many as 50 percent of all ATMs across the world. This lethargy in transitioning is often triggered by the complexities and interdependence of legacy software, thereby necessitating audit processes before governance norms can be put into place to investigate all intermediate dependencies to be able to upgrade systems. All such governance norms must be driven by analytical decision-making to ensure high efficiency in the resultant systems. Since the sensitivity of such systems make them slow to change, it becomes extremely important to have real-time visibility of the operations, as well as to find ways to automate tasks to reduce human dependency. Here too, governance norms can only be brought into full effect in two stages, the first being around the transition phase when the norms would centre around finding effective ways of monitoring the transition and finding best practices for the transition, and the second being around the final norms that would govern the new systems and ensure their sustainable use, as well as ensure they are upgraded regularly to avoid a large-scale and sudden transition in the future.

Monitoring Progress

As organizations work toward implementing digital governance systems and processes, it is crucial to monitor the progress being made. As discussed, there is rarely a beginning or a clear end to this process—a constant review must be undertaken that can measure the progress being made across quarters. Further, as discussed, digital strategy is now an inherent part of business strategy and is almost inseparable from the general business practices; digital strategy therefore should be evaluated and monitored using what are traditional business markers, most important the return on investment and the linkage to incentives.

To foster a sense of a digital-first company and not just a digital-first CDO/Digital Team, it is important to link a percentage of the incentives of the organization's leaders to digital initiatives and the kind of progress made on these initiatives. While a number of organizations connect top management bonuses and incentives to either bottom line or share-prices, it is critical from a corporate governance perspective as well to focus on digital investments that might have a longer gestation period in terms of innovation deployment. For more in-action initiatives, Commercial Spends need to be monitored from a perspective of return on investment. Collectively, these two markers can be used by the shareholders to monitor the digital-readiness of the organization.

Further, investments made in exploring new technologies and being well prepared for future developments need to be rewarded. The percentage of the annual technology budget that is spent on digital initiatives that are connected to emerging technology areas or are experimental in nature can be monitored as an indicator of the business's digital inclination. Since the pace of reaching the execution stage for such initiatives needs to be fast, it is also important to monitor the time to market of such digital initiatives and to identify the roadblocks and elements that are leading to delays.

Finally, as noted before, every single member of the organization needs to bring a digital-first outlook and thereby incorporate it in the activities they do. The organization needs to find best practices to govern such organization-wide digital-first behavior. This, in early days, can be achieved by having dedicated resources that comprise the digital team, which would function in conjunction with other business units to ensure that general principles and norms are adhered to and therefore act as supporting crew on this journey. The percentage of top technical talent that is attracted, promoted, and retained in this process is a good marker of the quality of digital thought in an organization.

Governing a Digital World

In a world where information is power, social media giants and other tech-giants possess both the means and the desire to influence consumer perceptions, often driven by the information made available to them. Consider the possibility that all users of a particular demography are shown a different route from point A to point B on a map app while the other demography are shown a different route, on ground. That experience could colour a user's perception of the traffic flow in a part of the city or influence their reading of the demography of the population of that geography. This power of influencing how one feels by virtue of what one experiences and see has been at the heart of a number of debates around how these new giants should be governed.

This idea of governing isn't entirely external; it is also present in internal governance, wherein platforms constantly seek to become more fair and more transparent in the interest of attracting larger audiences. Consider the success of TikTok, which is often attributed to the machine-learning algorithm that addressed the problems that early user-content platforms had faced. With Twitter and Pinterest, the onboarding process spends time on understanding the consumer so as to decide what to show the users in their standard feed. With YouTube, the early users and content creators amassed the largest followership, which meant every new content creator had to fight an uphill battle against these. TikTok solved this with their internal policies, which put the focus not on who you follow but on what you like; thereby giving a solution to both the problems. The result was a content stream that felt raw and unfiltered, but most important authentic.

This pursuit of authenticity has been at the heart of a number of scandals involving tech giants, with a lot of concerns around privacy, fake-news and monopolistic practices. However, a combination of these concerns and the kind of scale that these organizations operate on meant that such scandals have all but left a minor dent on the functioning of these organizations. In the recent past, WhatsApp invoked a change in its privacy policy which led to widespread criticism. In mid 2021 they updated their Terms of Service for the business-offering (now used across the globe by brands to send messages to their consumer—WhatsApp for Business), but in the process they highlighted how, for years, they had had a term in their policy that shared WhatsApp data with the parent company: Meta. While this data was supposed to be only the contact number, device information and usage patterns, consumers started questioning if their messages were being read as well; and while WhatsApp did end up making media spends to talk about the concept of privacy and encryption and reinforcing that they had end-to-end encryption for their communications, the entire debate died down almost as soon as it started and did not damage the long-term use of the app. Similarly, the U.S. election and the scandal around Cambridge-Analytica did spark a number of debates on how social media giants and other digital-first organizations collect information and protect the data and the interest of the consumers; however, the long-term impact on the usage of the such social media services has been minimal. These scandals also highlighted the need for the governance of the kind of content that is pushed out to people via such digital outlets. The power of being able to customize the "newsfeed" to each user can be used to show people messages and posts that are aligned to their own interests, to the point that they are not shown any content that might challenge their status-quo and therefore cause a moment of discontent. Even when we look at the more recent concerns around Tik-Tok, it was not only the allegations that the parent company ByteDance was sharing data with Chinese Government Officials, that led to the ban in North America (Both USA & Canada banned the app within days of each other), but also how the algorithmic solution to curating content meant that Tik-Tok could further specific political agendas or other view-points that might be detrimental to security or generally have an adverse impact on societal functioning.

Regulatory efforts need to adapt quickly to this rapidly evolving ecosystem. The General Data Protection Regulation, which came into force under the European Union, was built with the intent of protecting consumer data, but the pace at which the technologies used to accumulate such information change has led to many arguing that the regulation has instead given tech giants direct access to users and to a large amount of first-party data. The General Data Protection Regulation, in this view, has only been good for these companies. India too saw a change in the way social media giants operated: tech companies needed to set up systems to allow for removal of content on the request of government agencies and appoint relevant officers (a chief compliance officer) to act as point-of-contact. Such rules require these websites to be able to identify the first originator of any content and thereby have sparked debates on whether such a data tagging and collection move would help with ensuring a more responsible content creation and consumption ecosystem, or if it would challenge privacy norms.

The Last Word

Digital is no longer a sole aspect of business or an additional tool for organizations to be wary of—it is now an inherent component of how businesses function, and in general, how we consume information, make transactions, and work. In such a hyper-connected and quickly evolving ecosystem, individuals, organizations, brands, and government agencies need to be able to find ways to lead transformation and standardization and find a balance between centralized and decentralized governance norms that can help organizations find the most efficient way of navigating the digital space.

Digital governance activities can be divided into basics/essential decisions centered around investment, resource prioritization, and defining standards and policies for each business unit, or innovation decisions centered around technology selection, new rules and standard development, and forward-looking activities. A focus on both essential and innovation decisions would allow organizations to build their current capabilities as well as create a sustainable digital-oriented organization.

Key Discussion Areas

- Defining digital governance.
- The emergence of digital governance and its various forms.
- The role of digital transformation in the changes within governance.
- The use of "digital" in implementing better governance strategies for corporate and government bodies.

Notes

1 Above The Line: Mass Advertising that reaches across audiences and cannot be targeted specifically to our consumer base. This includes the likes of TV Ads & Newspaper Ads

2 Below The Line: Targeted Advertising that is categorically targeted at a smaller section of the audience and accordingly can be measured for impact in a more precise manner.

References

BBC. 2022. "Tesla Starts Accepting Once-Joke Cryptocurrency Dogecoin." January 15, 2022, https://www.bbc.com/news/business-60001144.

DeVries, P. D. 2016. *An Analysis of Cryptocurrency, Bitcoin, and the Future.* Houston: University of Houston.

Digital Users Report. 2020. Statista.

Dunleavy, P., and H. Margetts. 2015. "Design Principles for Essentially Digital Governance." Paper presented at the American Political Science Association,.

Kemp, Simon. 2019. "Global Digital Overview." *Datareportal*, January 31, 2019, https://datareportal.com/reports/digital-2019-global-digital-overview.

Marcum, D. T., and J. Young. 2019. "Blowing the Whistle in the Digital Age: Are You Really Anonymous? The Perils and Pitfalls of Anonymity in Whistleblowing Law." *DePaul Business and Commercial Law Journal* 1(17), https://via.library.depaul.edu/cgi/viewcontent.cgi?article=1378&context=bclj.

Marland, A., J. P. Lewis, and T. Flanagan. 2017. "Governance in the Age of Digital Media and Branding." *Governance* 30(1): 125–41, https://www.researchgate.net/publication/299355424_Governance_in_the_Age_of_Digital_Media_and_Branding

O'Hara, K., and W. Hall. 2018. "Four Internets: The Geopolitics of Digital Governance." Center for International Governance Innovation, CIGI Paper No. 206, https://www.cigionline.org/publications/four-internets-geopolitics-digital-governance.

Wang, Q., R. Li, Q. Wang, and S. Chen. 2021. "Non-Fungible Token (NFT): Overview, Evaluation, Opportunities and Challenges." University of Cornell, May 16, 2021, https://doi.org/10.48550/arXiv.2105.07447.

Welchman, Lisa. 2015. *Managing Chaos: Digital Governance by Design*. New York: Rosenfeld.

Wolfsfeld, G., E. Segev, and T. Sheafer. 2013. "Social Media and the Arab Spring: Politics Comes First." *International Journal of Press/Politics*, January 16, 2013, https://doi.org/10.1177/1940161212471716.

9

GRIEF

The Emotion Human Resources Must Address

Abhijit Bhaduri

Introduction: Literature Review

In 2003, John James and Russel Friedman evaluated the monetary cost of unresolved grief using the Grief Index. The index accounted for drops in performance and productivity as a result of the personal as well as professional losses born by workers in the United States. The resulting figure was a staggering US$75 billion a year for U.S. companies.

In 2013, R. Davey, C. Fearon, and H. McLaughlin published a paper analyzing the role of organizational grief in understanding employee reactions to redundancy, managing change, and personal development in the UK public sector. The study used the Kübler-Ross grief cycle to study employee reactions to organizational change. The cycle for understanding organizational grief (see Figure 9.1) can be summarized as follows:

- Equilibrium to immobilization: the impact on receiving job or position redundancy information can lead to a passive paralyzing emotional and behavioral state.
- Denial to anger represents an indirect emotional response such as denial behavior and employee avoidance regarding redundant information. Over the period, the employee may demonstrate an angry demeanor and frustration directed toward family, friends, colleagues, or the organization itself.
- Bargaining to depression (and eventually resignation): attempting to haggle or fight back against the unavoidable consequence of a new personal, social, or organizational reality.
- Testing to acceptance: exhibiting susceptibility to new practical job/career choices, and the reemergence of the employee to learn fresh strategies and coping mechanisms for acclimating to personal and organizational change.

The subjects of the study were senior managers and executives in a leading UK public sector agency earmarked for closure in 2012. A sample of directors and senior managers of the public sector organization participated in a series of semi-structured interviews.

Through the data collected from the interviews, it was evident by the senior manager that the extended Kübler-Ross organizational grief cycle was existent in an almost simultaneous, backward, and forward manner, with some employers moving further forward

DOI: 10.4324/9781003316077-12

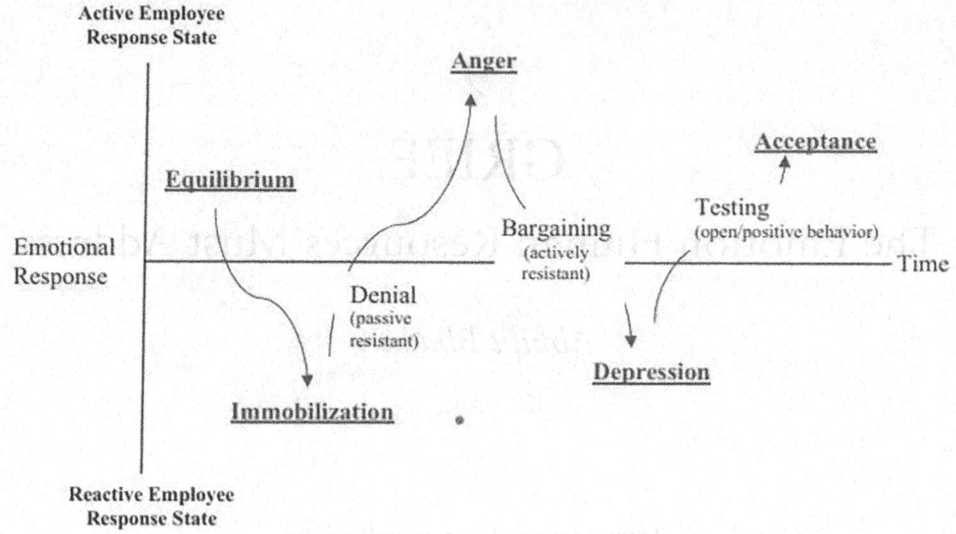

Source: Adapted from Kübler-Ross (1969)

Figure 9.1 The Kübler-Ross Grief Cycle

Source: Adapted from Kübler-Ross 1969.

compared to others. She termed this as "cycling" and refers to a tactic for individuals to avoid comprehending the events of change, leading to reexperiencing the stages of "denial to anger" as well as "bargaining to depression." Human resource (HR) managers must be aware of such cycling and employees must anticipate some recurring negative emotions before breaking through to a more open and accepting place.

Elisabeth Kübler-Ross and David Kessler (2014) explore the concept of grief and how it can be experienced through the five stages of loss, which are denial, anger, bargaining, depression, and acceptance.

A systematic literature review by Khai Wah Khaw, Alhamzah Alnoor, Hadi AL-Abrrow, Victor Tiberius, Yuvaraj Ganesan, and Nadia A. Atshan published in Current Psychology in 2021 highlighted the need to understand the reactions of the employees. The review categorizes them into micro- and macro-reactions. It analyzes the essential characteristics of the emerging field of change reactions along research issues and challenges, benefits of (even negative) reactions, managerial implications, and proposes future research opportunities. The authors suggest that a successful implementation of a change depends on how individuals interact with organizational change.

In the 1950s, psychologist Harry Levinson helped transform U.S. corporate thinking about the workplace by demonstrating a link between job conditions and mental health with contributions to psychoanalytic theory to the management of organizations and famously stated "all change involves loss and loss must be mourned" (Levinson 1965). Mc Kinsey (2020) published a report on organizational grief management, included in the report, George Kohlrieser (1995) asserts to have observed firsthand how the harmful impact of unresolved grief influenced "nearly a third of the 7,000-plus executives" he worked with. According to him the damage exceeded both physical and mental boundaries, resulting in poor management of the organization, along with other impacts on employees' personal lives.

The New Normal: Post-Pandemic Grief in the Workplaces

This pandemic has embarrassed every futurist. Just ask the next one, how many of their predictions about 2020 have come true. I have never seen so much uncertainty about the future. This uncertainty impacts business and jobs. "When will things go back to 'normal'—by that I mean how life was in December 2019," said the head of the largest executive search firm in India. He spoke to me in a confidential personal interview and said that he was worried that mental health issues arising from this pandemic would outweigh any skill-related challenge leaders have ever faced before.

At the start of the Covid-19 pandemic, decisions that would have taken days and weeks were all taken in minutes and hours. Every decision had the risk of becoming a precedent that leaders could possibly regret in the future. No one had the luxury of time to deliberate. Leaders around the world had to choose between reducing salaries and laying off employees. Over two years later, the situation has not changed. Everyone is experiencing moments for which there is no road map. There are missed moments that will never come back. When people say that this is the "new normal," they are reassuring themselves that the churn and destruction is behind us. In our hearts we know that the familiar world we once knew is no more. The coronavirus pandemic has led to a collective loss of normalcy. That discomfort we are feeling is grief (Berinato 2020).

Independent of the pandemic, individual sources of grief take no reprieve when we go about our jobs. A surgeon lost his wife in a freak accident. He survived and was torn apart by survivor's guilt. What bruised him was the behavior of the colleagues as he returned to work. A fellow surgeon said:

> Back at work, a shock of a different kind awaits. Expecting to be greeted by an outpouring of sympathy at his loss, he walks into silence. People go past him and look sideways. They make an off-color joke. Or they work with him and say nothing. His raw grief craves acknowledgment. He knows that nothing will bring her back, but a simple recognition of his loss might just pull him through the day. After all, a sorrow shared is a sorrow divided.
>
> *(Srivastava 2019)*

Grief is an invisible emotion in the workplace because we have long been told that emotions are to be left behind at home when we step into the office. The pandemic toppled that assumption. For many of us, we no longer had to step into an office to be able to go to work. We lived in a bubble that is a curious mix of home and workplace. It was precisely this setting that let me study the same emotion at close quarters.

Grief Is an Enemy We Fight Alone—Especially at Work

When we lose a loved one, we grieve. We need to acknowledge the need for closure without which it is hard to move on. A happy past can remain a memory, not a burden. But death is not the only loss that we experience. Missing out on personal milestones because of commitments at work is a common experience. The lockdowns and quarantines have accelerated these losses for everyone. We have attended funerals, weddings, and birthdays on video. More businesses have shut down in a year than ever before. There are record levels of unemployment in every country.

Suppressing emotions like grief can take a toll on a person's mental health. It's important to remember that everyone grieves differently and that it's okay to seek support from friends, family, or a therapist during difficult times. In most cultural setting expressing grief is still not accepted mainstream behavior. Yet the workplace itself has enough triggers and scenarios where grief is the natural outcome.

Grief is a natural human response to loss, and it can manifest in many ways. It is both a universal and personal experience, and individual experiences of grief vary and are influenced by the nature of the loss

Here are some that I have come across in my work with the clients.

Grief Triggered by Humiliation

> The grief arising out of loss of status and privilege is a meal eaten alone, says the unwritten code.

The corporate world is rife with triggers for grief. Take, for example, the aftermath of a merger or acquisition. Once a big fish in a small pond suddenly find itself swimming in a vast ocean, dwarfed by larger creatures. Consider the case of a family-run pharmaceutical company, once a market leader, that was acquired by a global giant. When the patriarch passed away, his sons sold the business, and the senior leaders of the company were relegated to middle management positions in the multinational firm. Stripped of their privilege and status, they were left to mourn their loss in silence.

In the workplace, there is an unspoken rule that discussing loss of status and privilege is taboo. To do so invites ridicule and scorn. The grief that arises from such losses must be borne alone, according to the unwritten code of conduct. And yet, loss of identity is an all-too-common source of grief in the corporate world. Reorganizations, changes in reporting relationships, and moves to different employers can all trigger feelings of loss and disorientation. These events occur with alarming regularity, yet they often go unnoticed and unacknowledged.

In short, the world of work can be a harsh and unforgiving place, where grief is often met with indifference or even hostility. It is up to everyone to find their own way through these difficult times, seeking support from friends, family, or professionals as needed.

Grief of Loneliness

When I started my consulting work in the United States, my first client was the CEO of a large handset manufacturer. He called me to his office and said:

> I want you to simply listen as I talk to myself. I am not looking for any advice or sympathy or suggestions, I just want to be heard. I cannot share the stress that I carry in my head with anyone else. I can't trust my colleagues to do that. The board will think of replacing me if they feel I am not in control and I don't want to burden my family with all these issues. I am paying you to simply listen.

While it is true that the relationship evolved over time, it was the need to be heard that was an overwhelming aspect of the engagement at the start. We all know that it is lonely at the top. Creating opportunities for senior leaders to acknowledge and share that loneliness is not common practice. The ability to be heard without prejudice is a freedom that the most privileged lack.

The change in organizational structure and reporting relationship very often triggers feelings of isolation when the manager's behavior is not viewed to be inclusive. It leaves people feeling uninvolved and devalued. At the workplace, we often have to balance the need to compete with the need to collaborate. While relationships are built when we collaborate with her peers and colleagues, the organization usually rewards the employee who competes to win. As the pyramid narrows at the top, the winner leaves behind a trail of broken relationships, which are reminders that winning often has a steep price to pay. But in the life of an organization, it is impossible to get away from being a competitor to every peer and sometimes even to one's team members. Competing for credit that paves the way for a future role or opportunity can be blamed for much of the office politics.

Grief of Being a Victim of Office Politics

As a human resources professional with three decades of experience across multiple organizations, I have seen countless cases of people being promised a promotion or a better increment or much awaited career opportunity that never came through. Many leaders have had to acknowledge that office politics shaped the choice of high-potential employees more than objective assessments. Vindictive bosses who ignore the meritorious worker—who does not protest—are as hurtful as the weak boss who rejects his team member's interest to leave us feeling that it is a price we must pay for being employed.

When somebody is hired from another organization, they have to ensure that they do not trigger animosity and opposition in the new office. When the new hire suggests an innovative solution, those who can read between the lines often look out for glances exchanged among others present in the meeting. Motives are ascribed to every move of the new hire. Corporate onboarding programs often aim to bring clarity about the task and the organization's structure and processes but fail to help the individual navigate office politics.

The seeds of grief are often built into an organization announcement.

If a new department is carved out of the existing organization, it can trigger huge resistance among the impacted departments who see it as a loss of opportunity for themselves. If the new department is added to the existing organization, the older employees view the newly formed department as an unnecessary appendage, making them feel unwanted.

Organizational Mechanisms: Employee Identity and Business Culture

Employers often do not be kind to employees who try to unionize. This leads the employees to questioning what they stand for—their identity. When an employer gets called out for an illegal practice, the employees feel that their identity is lost (Bhaduri 2021). Tom Peters, a management thinker, wrote about his conflicting emotions of pride and embarrassment when his former employer McKinsey was ordered to pay damages in the opioid settlement case (Peters 2021b).

He wrote on his blog:

> It is a culture and values and morals issue that runs to the core of the way McKinsey does business. It will in no way be solved with process change and a lecture or two. It requires deep reflection about "who we are and what we believe"—as human beings far more than "professionals." (In my angrier moments, of which there are many, I almost think McKinsey should consider shutting its doors and closing down.).
>
> *(Peters 2021a)*

When people have to question what values they stand for, their identity is being questioned. When Rajat Gupta was sent to prison for his role in insider trading, several McKinsey employees (current and former) were deeply embarrassed—so deeply is one's identity linked to one's employers.

People experience grief when the boss chooses to fawn over a new hire and ignore the people who have stood by him or her over the past. If paying attention and noticing generate the feeling of being valued, looking through and ignoring someone can cause grief. Like many other forms of grief, it is left unacknowledged. Even the grief arising out of being ignored is ignored.

Grief of Loss of Income and Savings

The pandemic has taken a toll on the millions who have been rendered unemployed. Small business owners have had to close businesses that their families have nurtured over a few generations. Restaurant owners have had their lifetime of savings wiped out as businesses came to a grinding halt.

As news about job losses flood the media, people grieve the loss of security. They worry about an uncertain future. The plan someone may have had for their future may have had to be abandoned during the pandemic. I met this family where the employer's plans to downsize operations in India have been cropping up in the newspaper, but no communication was made to the employee. The employers have had to let go of employees who have been with them for years. The guilt of having to let go of people who have been loyal weighs heavy on them. Taking a decision that puts several families in positions of vulnerability needs to be acknowledged. Small business owners talk about the guilt they have experienced as they sit down for a meal at the table with their family weighs heavy. But they are helpless.

A report by Save the Children (2020) showed results from parents and children from forty-six countries, including India, who were surveyed to identify their needs to help fill the gaps. The report showed that children are deeply impacted by the pandemic. Among migrants, 91 percent of households reported loss of income and 60 percent of households reported that they had no money to pay for food, which led to insecurity and domestic violence. Around 11 percent of children in the general group and 17 percent children in the migrants' group reported violence at home during the pandemic. One in ten children would not return to school once the institutions reopened.

The poorest of the poor have been the worst affected. In India, the lockdown triggered the greatest migration of families from urban areas back to their villages. Almost eighty million migrant workers in India—largely contract labor and people working in the unorganized sector—have been among those impacted by the shrinking opportunities for employment. The effect of this migration is yet to be documented fully (Khanna 2020).

Loss of Opportunity

The pandemic has morphed many work-related opportunities. Students who were looking forward to their first day in office have had to make believe that changing the Zoom background with the picture of an office was the best that could happen. Internship plans have been abandoned or diluted.

College students have mourned the loss of opportunities to network with peers and get mentored by professors. Expatriate assignments have been cut short. Projects and training programs have been replaced by the endless tedium of online lectures. Online education is efficient. But it seems to be a poor substitute for the college experience. Freshmen seeking to enter college feel cheated about losing out on a life event. 2020 was a year when everything from finding jobs to being on-boarded or even let go were done over video calls. It has left an unspoken sense of loss that people grieve.

What is common to each of these scenarios is that we are expected to deal with this in private. Workplaces are built around logic and not emotions, which deems the conventional wisdom that makes us put away any emotional upheaval that gets triggered by events such as these.

Unresolved Grief Finds Unhealthy Outlets

Disenfranchised grief, also known as hidden grief or sorrow, refers to any grief that goes unacknowledged or unvalidated by social norms (Shah 2020; Raypole 2020).

Someone grieving the loss of a relationship may not have the opportunity to talk about a sense of loss surrounding the relationship. LGBTQ+ people must often deal with the loss of their relationships alone. Losing a pet can be as devastating for someone as the loss of a family member. The loss of a coach or professor or mentor can be cause for grief but may not have the social permission to be adequately expressed and addressed. When people immigrate to another country, they grieve. People grieve the loss of freedom or mobility or health or loss of physical and mental faculties through the process of aging.

Grief is often expressed through substance abuse. Grief can be expressed through substance abuse. The Covid-19 pandemic has been described as a "shadow pandemic" of grief, trauma, and economic and social dislocation. This has led to an increase in the incidence of mood and anxiety disorders and substance misuse, all of which put people at greater risk for prolonged grief.

In England, there has been a 27 percent rise in people dying while in treatment for drug and alcohol addiction during the pandemic. In addition, as was the case in India, grief can manifest in domestic violence.

> During the first four phases of the COVID-19-related lockdown, Indian women filed more domestic violence complaints than recorded in a similar period in the last 10 years. But even this unusual spurt is only the tip of the iceberg as 86% women who experience domestic violence do not seek help in India.
>
> *(Radhakrishnan and Singaravelu 2020)*

Grief is often suppressed or denied. The emotions do not go away. It shows up in feelings such as anger, guilt, regret, and shame. It hampers the ability of the individual to function effectively at work.

Why Do Employers Look Away When Employees Grieve?

As part of my research, I spoke to several HR leaders of organizations to understand how they viewed the issues around grief. It unearthed some myths and opportunities that organizations need to address before they can provide the guardrails to address grief and its fallouts.

Myth 1: Grief Is Only Triggered by Death of a Loved One

1. Death is a significant event that can create sharp changes in our lives and relationships. However, it is not the only cause of grief. Grief is a natural response to loss and change, and it can be triggered by a wide range of events and experiences. By building an understanding of the true meaning of grief, employers can better understand when and how to support their employees.
2. Grief is not just about resisting change but about processing and coming to terms with it. It is a complex and deeply personal emotion that can manifest in many different ways. For example, employees may grieve the loss of a way of life or the loss of human contact, as their employer's business becomes more automated. These forms of grief may not be as visible as the grief caused by the death of a loved one, but they are no less real or significant.
3. It is important for employers to recognize that grief can have many causes and to create a supportive environment where employees feel safe expressing their emotions and seeking help when needed. By doing so, they can help their employees navigate difficult times and build resilience in the face of change.

Myth 2: Grief Is a Personal Matter. You Grieve Alone

1. Grief is a complex and deeply personal emotion that can be triggered by a wide range of events and experiences. While the death of a loved one is a common cause of grief, it is by no means the only one. In the workplace, employees may experience grief due to a variety of scenarios, such as the loss of a job, changes in responsibilities or work relationships, or personal struggles outside of work. If an employer only recognizes death as a cause of grief, they may overlook the many other factors that can contribute to an employee's emotional well-being.
2. The language of emotions is often not readily used in the workplace, and this can make it difficult for employees to express their feelings and seek support. When an employee is grieving, they may feel the need to keep their emotions private, especially if they do not feel that their workplace is a safe and supportive environment. This can lead to feelings of isolation and can exacerbate the grieving process.
3. It is important for employers to recognize that grief can have many causes and to create a workplace culture that supports employees in expressing their emotions and seeking help when needed. By doing so, they can help to foster a more compassionate and understanding work environment, where employees feel valued and supported through difficult times.

Myth 3: If We Step In, We May Set Expectations That Are More Than What We Can Handle

According to the Center for Complicated Grief (n.d.), acute grief

> occurs in the initial period after a loss. It almost always includes strong feelings of yearning, longing and sadness along with anxiety, bitterness, anger, remorse, guilt and/or shame. Thoughts are mostly focused on the person who died, and it can be difficult to concentrate on anything else. Acute grief dominates a person's life.

Dealing with someone who is still raw from the emotion of dealing with a deep loss leaves most people helpless. The same response appears in organizations when an employee experiences grief arising out of bereavement—paid time-off from work for the death of a relative. This is not legally mandated in India, and it is left to the discretion of the employer to offer time off as they deem fit. Family members are usually defined as parents, grandparents, siblings, spouse, children, and in-laws. Relationships that cause grief could well be the ones not covered by this definition of "family." The death of a distant cousin could be just as harsh emotionally as someone who is described as the family member eligible for a medical benefit. Emotions are harder to classify in these boxes. So, organizations avoid stepping into grey zones.

Myth 4: Time Heals Everything

1. It is a common belief that time heals everything, including grief and loss. However, this is not always the case. While it is true that human beings are remarkably resilient and can often pick up the threads of their lives after experiencing loss, the sense of loss does not always disappear completely. There may still be bad days when the feelings of grief and sadness are overwhelming.
2. Over time, the intensity of these feelings may diminish, and the loss may no longer leave us feeling numb and shocked. However, grief is not something that simply goes away with time. Instead, it becomes integrated into our lives, and we learn to make space for both happy and sad days.
3. In other words, time does not necessarily heal all wounds. Rather, it is the process of acknowledging and working through our grief that helps us to heal and move forward. This process is different for everyone and can take varying amounts of time. It is important to be patient with ourselves and others as we navigate the complex emotions of grief and loss.

Myth 5: Tears Are a Sign of Weakness

In the workplace, shedding tears is often frowned upon, even though it happens often. People cry in washrooms or behind closed doors. Crying in one-to-one settings is seen to be more acceptable than in group settings. But regardless of where they happen, tears still happen. Crying in public because of mild feedback about the work done does not evoke sympathy among most peers. Demanding bosses who leave their subordinates teary eyed frequently are described in less than flattering terms. Tearful individuals are perceived as more in need of help, as more friendly, and observers feel more connected to them. We feel naturally compelled to console someone who cries. One study found that, overall, criers were judged as less competent than non-criers—and the loss of perceived competence was greater for men than women (van de Ven, Meijs, and Vingerhoets 2017).

Myth 6: Don't Ask, Don't Tell

Since most businesses expect grief to be limited to the death of a loved one, they believe that there is nothing the organization can do to soften the blow. Bereavement is understood to trigger grief, but the vast majority of pain is not acknowledged. The grief that arises out of the scenarios we have described above is not even acknowledged in the workplace.

There is an unwritten cultural code in every organization that tells us what kind of situations can be raised at the workplace and what kinds must be dealt with alone. It can be difficult for employees to ask for help with emotional issues in the workplace for a variety of reasons. Unlike asking for a painkiller for a toothache, which is a common and easily understood physical ailment, emotional issues can be complex and deeply personal. There may be a fear of being judged or stigmatized for seeking help or concerns about confidentiality and privacy.

Additionally, the workplace culture may not be supportive of discussing emotional well-being, and employees may not feel comfortable opening up to their colleagues or superiors. All of these factors can make it challenging for employees to seek the support they need for emotional issues. It is important for workplaces to create an environment where employees feel safe and supported in seeking help for their emotional well-being.

Myth 7: Emotions Don't Belong in the Workplace

The traditional belief has been that the workplace operates on logic. Making a "business case" means having to pull together a slew of data points and benchmarks to justify the recommendation being made. Employees are expected to leave their emotions at home.

This is ironic because business leaders want to hire people who are "passionate," which requires someone acknowledging their emotion, the very humanness that is frowned upon in the workplace. Businesses work hard to design great customer experiences. An experience that generates positive emotional engagement must build an emotional connection with the customer or employee.

During the pandemic, the office as a place we assemble in to do our work has disappeared. The office has since then moved into our homes—the very place where we used to leave our emotions when we left for our daily commute.

What Can HR Do?

If we do not recognize our own grief, we cannot recognize it in others. Leaders must learn to recognize and address emotions just as comfortably as they deal with logics and data.

One of the chief human resource officers I spoke to mentioned that grief was an emotion that "is too intense for the organization to address." She confessed that she found it overwhelming to deal with grief of others and talked about her own experience of dealing with the death of an older sibling. "I never got over the guilt that my younger sibling had died in a car crash, while I lived."

If we do not recognize our own grief, we cannot recognize it in others. Leaders must learn to recognize and address emotions just as comfortably as they deal with logic and data. Empathy helps us understand what the other person is going through. When our own feeling of grief has not been addressed fully, connecting with someone else's grief triggers our own emotions that have been put aside or left unresolved. It could be that HR professionals would have to recognize the broader ambit of events that trigger grief to understand that there are several scenarios in the workplace that trigger grief.

Wipro's Ombuds Policy

The Ombuds Policy was introduced by the Wipro, an Indian multinational IT corporation, in 2003 to enable employees and other individuals associated with the company to not overlook any concern but instead raise it at an early stage and in the right manner, without fear of retaliation, victimization, subsequent discrimination, or disadvantage at the workplace (Wipro 2021).

Through Wipro's *Mitr* (translates to "friend") initiative, trained counselors in the company are available to assist employees in need. This program has been in place since 2004 and provides a case study for other organizations who want to help their employers in the grieving process. Wipro makes sure that every site has at least one trained Mitr counselor. Wipro's Employee Assistance Program (EAP) partner and internal and external experts provide five days of training over two weekends to volunteers. Typically, 40 percent of the cases that come in are handled by MITR counselors, and the more serious cases are handled by EAP partner professionals (Arogya World 2017).

Five Ideas HR Can Implement

Teach the Organization to Recognize Grief

Build a broader understanding of grief as an emotion that is more than what we experience only when we lose a loved one. Talking about the many workplace situations that can trigger feelings of loss can be a good starting point. Doing so combats the stigma and helplessness that is currently associated with grief. Once people recognize grief, they will be sensitized to its presence as a subtext in the organization. Instead of making us weak, learning to deal with grief can be empowering.

Build Psychological Safety

Create a culture of empathy and understanding. Make it socially acceptable to talk about grief. Can the team members trust you with their unshared emotions and vulnerability? Trust allows us to accept that others will be supportive when we take moderate risks. Psychological safety is the belief that others will not judge us when we take a risk.

Check-In on Team Members

The office was a great leveler. Everyone put on their "professional face" and came to a shared location. Ever since people started working from home, their workplace is very different. There are single parents or people with responsibilities of elder care. Some of the team members may be sharing a small room with many others over months. Understanding the personal context of team members helps to understand the team members at a meaningful level. It is not transactional. Asking team members to describe how they are feeling is a powerful way for leaders to build trust (UN OMBUDSMAN and Mediation Services, n.d.).

Talk About Your Own Grief

When a leader shares their own feelings of loss or grief, they legitimize the opportunity for others to talk about their own emotions. Linking it to the impact it has had on work makes the organization recognize that unresolved grief impacts the effectiveness and productivity of the employee.

Teach Leaders to Engage at an Emotional Level

Building a human connection often begins by giving someone undivided attention. At the entry-level, a person's analytical thinking and other cognitive skills differentiate them from their peers; at the leadership level, it is the ability to build relationships through deeper emotional connections that differentiates. These are skills that can be taught. It is no different from learning a new language.

We have to stop making our workplaces antiseptic and clinical. We have to infuse the human element in them. Acknowledging the range of emotions that we experience is the first step toward that. It is only after that we can equip leaders with skills and the language needed to deal with grief in the workplace. When leaders learn to recognize grief, they can be in a position to create processes and policies to address them.

Conclusion

As we conclude this chapter, it is important to emphasize the role of HR in building a culture of openness and psychological safety in the workplace. Grief is a natural and universal human experience, one that can be triggered by many different events and circumstances. It is an emotion that demands to be felt and expressed, and it is essential that companies create an environment where employees feel safe to do so. HR can prioritize building a culture of openness and psychological safety by taking practical steps such as

- encouraging open communication and active listening among team members;
- providing training and resources for managers to support their team members through difficult times;
- implementing policies and procedures that promote work–life balance and mental health;
- creating a supportive network of resources for employees who are experiencing grief or other emotional challenges.

By taking these steps, HR can help to foster a healthy and compassionate workplace culture where employees feel supported and valued. Leaders must learn to listen and understand, rather than simply rationalizing or dismissing the emotions of their employees. By addressing the root causes of grief and providing support for those who need it, companies can create a more resilient and supportive workplace for all. So let us embrace our emotions, even the difficult ones, and work together to create a brighter future for ourselves and those around us.

Key Discussion Areas

- An insight into the minds of someone grieving and their need for acknowledgment.
- Types of grief experienced in personal as well as professional lives and the approaches to deal with them.
- Myths accepted as a norm by organizations and HR professionals in relation to an employees' grief.
- Recommendations for HR professionals to help their employees through their grief.

References

Arogya World. 2017. "Tackling Mental Health in the Workplace, Case Study: WIPRO's MITR Program." September 2017, http://arogyaworld.org/wp-content/uploads/2017/10/AW_MITR-CaseStudy_Final.pdf (accessed November 1, 2022).

Berinato, Scott. 2020. "That Discomfort You're Feeling Is Grief." *Harvard Business Review*, March 23, 2020, https://hbr.org/2020/03/that-discomfort-youre-feeling-is-grief (accessed November 1, 2022).

Bhaduri, A. 2021. "Unionization of Tech Talent—Is It Inevitable?" *LinkedIn*, January 12, 2021, www.linkedin.com/pulse/unionisation-tech-talent-inevitable-abhijit-bhaduri/ (accessed August 1, 2023).

Center for Prolonged Grief. n.d. "CG Is a Form of Grief That Takes Hold of a Person's Mind and Won't Let Go." Columbia School of Social Work, https://complicatedgrief.columbia.edu/for-the-public/complicated-grief-public/overview/ (accessed November 1, 2022).

Davey, R., C. Fearon, and H. McLaughlin. 2013. "Organizational Grief: an Emotional Perspective on Understanding Employee Reactions to Job Redundancy." *Development and Learning in Organizations: An International Journal* 27(2): 5–8, https://doi.org/10.1108/14777281311302012.

James, John, and Russel Friedman. 2003. "Grief Index: The Hidden Annual Costs of Grief in America's Workplace." Grief Recovery Institute, Educational Foundation Inc., Sherman Oaks, CA.

Khanna, Anoop. 2020. "Impact of Migration of Labour Force Due to Global COVID-19 Pandemic with Reference to India." *Journal of Health Management* 22(2), https://doi.org/10.1177/0972063420935542.

Kohlrieser, G. 1995. "Unresolved Grief: A Hidden Source of Pain and Failure in the Workplace." In *The 1995 Annual: Developing Human Resources*, edited by J. W. Jones. San Diego, CA: Pfeiffer & Company.

Kübler-Ross, E. 1969. *On Death and Dying*. London: Routledge.

Kübler-Ross, E., and D. Kessler. 2014. *On Grief and Grieving: Finding the Meaning of Grief Through the Five Stages of Loss*. New York: Scribner.

Levinson, Harry. 1965. "Reciprocation: The Relationship between Man and Organization." *Administrative Science Quarterly* 9(4): 370–90.

Peters, Tom. 2021a. "McKinsey Final Thoughts." *Tom Peters Blog*, February 17, 2021, https://tompeters.com/2021/02/mckinsey-final-thoughts/.

———. 2021b. "McKinsey's Work on Opioid Sales Represents a New Low." *Financial Times*, February 21, 2021, www.ft.com/content/82e98478-f099-44ac-b014-3f9b15fe6bc6.

Radhakrishnan, Vignesh, and Naresh Singaravelu. 2020. "Domestic Violence Complaints at a 10-Year High During COVID-19 Lockdown." *Hindu*, June 24, 2020, www.thehindu.com/data/data-domestic-violence-complaints-at-a-10-year-high-during-covid-19-lockdown/article31885001.ece.

Raypole, Crystal. 2020. "Disenfranchised Grief: When No One Seems to Understand Your Loss." *Healthline*, March 30, 2020, www.healthline.com/health/mental-health/disenfranchised-grief.

Shah, Farukh. 2020. "A Generation at Stake: Protecting India's Children from the Impact of COVID-19." Save the Children, www.savethechildren.in/pdfs/A%20GENERATION%20AT%20STAKE_REPORT_FINAL_3.pdf.

Smet, Aaron D. 2020. "Your Organization Is Grieving—Here's How You Can Help." McKinsey & Company, September 17, 2020, www.mckinsey.com/business-functions/people-and-organizational-performance/our-insights/your-organization-is-grieving-heres-how-you-can-help.

Srivastava, Ranjana. 2019. "How Did We Miss Our Colleague's Grief?" *The Guardian*, November 19, 2019, www.theguardian.com/commentisfree/2019/nov/20/i-didnt-know-of-my-colleagues-tragic-loss-but-my-workplace-ignored-his-grief.

UN OMBUDSMAN and Mediation Services. n.d. "Tips for Working Well During the COVID-19 Pandemic," www.un.org/en/ombudsman/assets/pdf/tips.pdf (accessed November 1, 2022).

van de Ven, Niels, Maartje H. J. Meijs, and Ad Vingerhoets. 2017. "What Emotional Tears Convey: Tearful Individuals Seen as Warmer, but Also as Less Competent." *British Journal of Social Psychology* 56: 146–60, https://doi.org/10.1111/bjso.12162.

Wipro. 2021. "Global Company Policy: Ombuds Policy." May 2021, www.wipro.com/content/dam/nexus/en/investor/corporate-governance/policies-and-guidelines/wipros-ombuds-process/ombuds-policy.pdf.

10

A CONCEPTUAL FRAMEWORK OF BRAND CO-GOVERNANCE IN THE DIGITAL AGE

Altaf Merchant, Varsha Jain, and Parth Salunke

Introduction

In the earlier era of traditional media, consumers accepted a brand's messages through various promotions and advertising tactics on platforms such as magazines, newspapers, and television. With the emergence of web 2.0, the communication of a brand's messages extended to various digital platforms, including social-media networking sites, blogging, and many others (Scott 2017). In the Digital Age of "platformization," brands and users actively interact on digital platforms. Issues of trustworthiness often plagued the information shared through traditional media among consumers. Digital platforms enable the interaction between brands and users (consumers) and mitigate such trust issues (Hoffman and Novak 2012; Akar and Topçu 2011; Wang 2015).

Moreover, social-media platforms connect billions of people and enable the exchange of information between brands and users. Thus, the platform and the users play an active role and act as initiators and recipients of the data (Hanna, Rohm, and Crittenden 2011). The platform users enable positive and negative evaluations or word of mouth for a brand (Wang 2015). These interactions are not limited between brands and users but extend to brand-to-brand and user-to-user interactions. Furthermore, brands and users receive various drawbacks, such as trolling, cyberbullying, flaming, and many others, leading to negative consequences for the brand image. Sometimes, these adverse effects are not limited to brands but also impact users, who can be more seriously affected in terms of their mental well-being. Thus, this form of misbehavior extended between users and brands during their interactions on various platforms (Demsar et al. 2021) outlines the dark side of the Digital Age.

Despite such negative consequences, most of the marketing, consumer behavior, branding, and governance literature centers around digital and social-media benefits. Brand governance is studied in the context of, for example, small- and medium-sized enterprises (SMEs) (Renton and Richard 2019), market reputation (Kambara 2010), online brand community (Cooper, Stavros, and Dobele 2018), and governance practices in sports organizations (Taks et al. 2019). However, these studies ignore various dark sides, including conflicts, revenge, brand attacks, and other destructive behaviors leading to risk for both users and brands (Demsar et al. 2021). The risk to users is individualistic and hampers the

DOI: 10.4324/9781003316077-13

person, and the risk to the brand is more comprehensive. Because these risks affect all the stakeholders, a seamless brand experience needs a critical understanding of the governance between and among brand and user interactions.

Digital interactions take place in three forms: (1) from one brand to another brand, (2) from one user to another user, and (3) between the brand and the user. These interactions are not limited to a specific country; thus, localized marketplace evidence is expanded across the globe. For example, the car giants Mercedes and Jaguar trolled each other in the United States market when Mercedes demonstrated the use of chickens to present the excellent body control of the cars. Jaguar reacted with catty instinct and was floated across social-media channels (Ray 2015). These interactions are not only limited to brand to brand, but they also excite the user and lead to further conflicts and brand attacks worldwide in the form of user reactions.

Furthermore, some users on digital platforms develop fake IDs and attack brands, which tarnishes the brand image and the experience on the online platform. In one hilarious but troubling example, a famous comedian created a fake ID named "Customer Support" and interacted with users on various official Facebook pages of brands (Baliunaite and Caunt 2019). Even Trolling and other misbehaviors occur on online brand community pages and disrupt the brand's and the user's engagement (Dineva and Breitsohl 2021). The interaction occurs among users simultaneously, leading to conflicts and cyberbullying, negatively impacting brands and post engagements (Dineva et al. 2022). Therefore, it is essential to govern these co-created interactions to avoid several drawbacks.

Thus, this chapter introduces the new construct of brand co-governance to enable a seamless brand experience in the digital space and avoid various conflicting situations. Brand co-governance can be defined as the governing ability to rethink strategically, monitor, maintain, and control the co-created interactions among brands and users to avoid negative consequences that would affect stakeholders in the Digital Age, moderated by regulators. Furthermore, this chapter proposes a conceptual model for brand co-governance with some antecedents such as brand-centric and user-centric variables, moderators, mediators, and outcomes for managing the dark side of these interactions on digital platforms. Figure 10.1 represents the conceptual model.

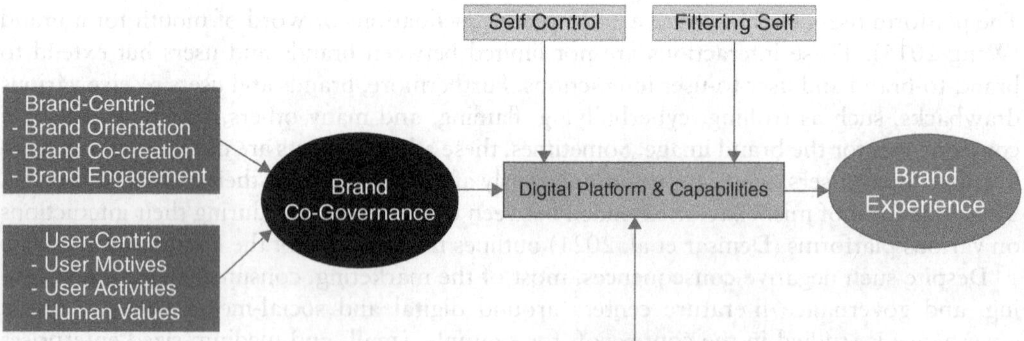

Figure 10.1 Brand Co-Governance Model in the Digital Age
Source: Authors.

Antecedents

The conceptual model proposes brand-centric and user-centric variables as antecedents in the brand co-governance model.

The literature investigation found brand-centric variables such as brand orientation, cocreation, and brand engagement parameters. The user-centric variables include user motives, user activities, and human values.

Brand-Centric Variables

As we discussed, various brands actively channel and communicate their messages, including the interaction of brands and users, in the digital space through platforms such as social media, which can lead to positive or negative impacts on branding and brand values. Brands must govern accordingly to enhance their interactions and brand experiences. Therefore, the brand co-governance model proposed three brand-centric antecedents, which are explained below.

Brand Orientation

Brand orientation enunciates the formation of higher brand values, structures, and norms for effective brand management practices. Brand orientation is a valuable measurement of brand management capabilities (Wong and Merrilees 2005). Higher brand orientation leads to high brand-valuable assets and excellent brand management practices (Gromark and Melin 2011). The brand orientation is often derived from the brand's values and structures, leading to the formation of brand artifacts such as tag lines, mission, vision, price, or strategy canvas, and affects market performance. Therefore, the organization needs to develop high brand values and efficacious artifacts for a brand. Brand orientation influences the firm growth (Reijonen et al. 2012), brand equity (M'zungu, Merrilees, and Miller 2010), and survival of the firm (Urde 1994). Researchers have argued that social-media platforms in the Digital Age can improve the firm's performance with proper brand orientation and influence the organization's marketing practices (Kane 2015). In addition, the digital medium's flow of communication is multidirectional, with users sharing feedback in a space with no geographical boundaries (Odoom and Mensah 2018). Most organizations depend on digital platforms and their capabilities to disseminate their brand messages. For instance, the LEGO brand allows the users or their brand fans to share all the activities performed with LEGO and protect their brand according to their brand values (Renton and Richard 2019). Therefore, to amplify the brand performance and experience in the Digital Age, organizations should focus on developing a brand orientation (Singh and Sonnenburg 2012), keeping in mind the needs and requirements of users.

Brand Cocreation

Scholars initially developed the concept of brand cocreation with a vested interest in value cocreation (viz. joint value creation efforts by both the brand and users). Values are explicitly created through social interactions, and the ability to co-create impacts brand values. Users in the Digital Age influence brands and their online communities, and various brand values are empowered by user activities online (Naylor, Lamberton, and

West 2012). Digital platforms influence the social interactions between/among brands and users and help organizations increase their sales and brand values (Gensler et al. 2013). Thus, cocreating brand values enhance the user–brand relationship and experiences. Values are created by the platform's active users in a continuous process wherein organizations share control over their brand with the stakeholders to increase the brand value (Muniz, Albert, and Schau 2005). Brand cocreation is defined as creating values through networked relations and social interactions (Merz, He, and Vargo 2009). It is also argued that these interactions and networks co-create brand values through the design and features of digital platforms (Merz, He, and Vargo 2009). Cocreation occurs in social media, for instance, through activities such as posting reviews, comments, and sharing individual experiences. User participation on various digital platforms, such as brand communities, can positively or negatively impact the brand's image and reputation (Veloutsou and Moutinho 2009).

Recently, memes have been flourishing on social media, co-created by users and brands on the platform, though they sometimes derail into drawbacks for the brand. For example, the Indian beauty brand Nykaa faced a disadvantage in a brand promotion campaign around the Hindu festival of Navratri that posted condom ads with a Navratri tag. Users responded by creating memes and demanding an apology from the brand for insulting the Hindu festival (Ganguly 2015). Brands must avoid negative consequences by being active in digital channels, managing PR, social listening, using chatbots, and integrating data across departments, if needed, through artificial intelligence. For instance, a Kentucky Fried Chicken (KFC) outlet in the United Kingdom ran out of chicken, and the users escalated the issue on social media. The brand immediately managed the content and public relations by apologizing to the users on social-media platforms for their problems in supply-chain management through an apology letter. By being proactive, KFC avoided or de-escalated any backlash, and some users even responded with "Apologies Accepted KFC."

Brand Engagement

In the last decade, the engagement concept has received much attention in the marketing literature (Brodie et al. 2011). Brand engagement is about developing a consumer attachment to a brand, which can be emotional or rational. Thus, engagement contributes toward involving users, leading to an interaction between a brand and user in the digital space. However, this interaction can lead to negative consequences and hamper the brand experience. Therefore, it is proposed as the antecedent. For instance, there are various online brand communities, and their digital stories help to develop relationships. Without the motive of engagement, interactions will not occur, and there is no need for co-governance.

Thus, brands engage users in the digital space effectively through their posts and in online brand communities, forums, blogs, and networking sites, which evokes several touchpoints for developing effective relationships (Cooper, Stavros, and Dobele 2018). Social-media platforms such as Facebook, Instagram, and Twitter are critical tools for advertising or disseminating brands' messages, as they reach users and evoke engagement (Anghelcev 2013). The ability of brands to engage impacts and influences user behavior through their involvement in brand communication (Gómez, Lopez, and Molina 2019) and facilitates connecting the platform's users and the brand. The engagement is not limited to brand and user;

in social media, several other competitive brands will also engage with a particular brand post. For instance, the Indian food brand Zomato updated its logo several times, which could be disastrous for a well-renowned brand. In response, Amazon tweeted, "Loved all your logos updated in last six months, was #AurDikhao (*show more*) logos was brief to your designer" (Ray 2015). Amazon did this mockingly, but this initiated engagement of users and other brands, leading to several levers of engagement among brands and users on the digital platform. In addition, brands often take stands on societal issues and undertake brand engagement credits, but interactions are fragile as they may harm the brand and lead to criticism (Monks 2020). For example, e-commerce giant Flipkart received backlash for a comment to a customer query about the failed services of delivering to Nagaland. Their customer support responded by saying, "it's outside India" (Mittal 2020). Here, though it is part of India, customer support mockingly started the conversation. The response led to several layers of interactions as customer support messages offended the consumers' feelings. Thus, brand engagement is introduced as an antecedent that enforces interaction between brands and users.

User-Centric Variables

Users are active generators of information in the digital space. Not all users are actively engaged in their interactions on digital platforms; some are passive lurkers (Shao 2009). During interactions, users sometimes receive drawbacks such as trolling, cyberbullying, or sharing their perspectives on a particular brand. Thus, understanding user-centric antecedents is essential.

User Motives

In the digital space, users on a digital platform interact with their insights, opinions, and motives (Heinonen 2011) for the brand's product or service. Scholars investigate users' motives from the lens of the uses and gratification approach that outlines the motives behind the usage of a certain kind of digital media and several consequences based on their motives (Shao 2009; Park, Kee, and Valenzuela 2009; Blumler and Katz 1974). The user in digital space enunciates three primary motives: information, entertainment, and social (Stafford, Stafford, and Schkade 2004). Other motives, in addition to three primary motives, such as community development, self-expression, and self-actualization (Shao 2009), are often ignored in research. User motives can be categorized into two main groups: rational and emotional. The earlier example of the comedian posing as Customer support for various brands stated that he did the stunt for his entertainment and humor. His motive was to let people realize not to take life so seriously. But user motives, which lead to interactions, can also make the user experience the dark side of the Digital Age. Hence, it should be governed effectively as these negative comments can disturb mental and physical well-being. For instance, a user on social media uploaded a video of a customer in a KFC store asking an employee to play a regional song, wherein the request was refused. The demand led to an outrage on social media for not playing regional music with a campaign of #RejectKFC (Bhushan 2021). Here, the user's motive for uploading the video is the self-expression of thought for a particular brand. However, he may have received drawbacks regarding mockery and trolling from consumers. Thus, user motives are important antecedents.

User Activities

The activities of users are broadly divided between active and passive users. Shao (2009) proposed three significant actions of users in the digital space: (1) consuming information and entertainment-related aspects, (2) participating in social interactions, and (3) producing their own set of self-expression and actualization. Here, consumption means synthesizing the content or a message, and participation means cocreation through comments, reviews, and sharing of information within the network. Production means developing one's content, popularly known as user-generated content. The research on the activities of the user determines the dichotomy, which includes their posting for interactions (Contributions) and simply lurking in the digital space (Consumption) (Cooper, Stavros, and Dobele 2018). At the same time, all three significant activities may depend on users' perceptions of specific content, their interest in a particular brand, and the consequences of these activities. Users may not always have positive feedback or activities. For instance, in 2017, renowned actress Priyanka Chopra (a famous Hollywood and Bollywood star) posted her Met Gala look and received several adverse reactions from trolls for her attire and looks (Contractor 2017), which also led to negative setbacks for the designer brand. However, there were not only adverse reactions; some users also engaged with positive responses, and many users also appreciated her look. Thus, it is introduced as the antecedent, as user activities on social-media platforms will decide the drawbacks and positive outlook.

Human Values

Every individual has a set of values that motivate their behavioral actions toward their desirable goals (Chen et al. 2014), and human values influence individuals' actions (Besley 2008). The theory of human values (Schwartz 1992) presents a framework that captures all the potential human values and plays a pivotal role in participation and social behavior on digital platforms. There are ten human values, and they are subdivided into four quadrants and two dimensions. The first dimension enunciates "openness to change versus conservation," wherein one details the independence of the thought process and the other resistance toward any change. The second dimension represents self-enhancement versus self-transcendence; here, the latter details the concern for other users, and the former details one's interest. According to Schwartz, "values are desirable and trans-situational goals dependent on the principles of people's lives." These human values are tested in several cross-cultures and are associated with several behaviors (Bardi and Schwartz 2003) and consumer decisions (Gurnert and Juhl 1995).

Interestingly, there is a strong correlation between human values and user usage of words in social-media space (Chen et al. 2014). For instance, users with openness to change will be more independent in sharing their views or opinions on a social-media platform. Thus, these human values are associated with online behaviors and potentially present the ideals in their interaction (Kalimeri et al. 2019). Human values differ from user to user, which guides their behavior in the digital space.

Mediators for Effective Brand Co-Governance

Digital Platforms and Capabilities

Digital platforms consist of ecosystems of autonomous actors and agents who co-create values through interactions (Hein et al. 2020). These digital platforms work from sociotechnical perspectives, as it involves the users, brand, and platforms technology interface for interaction. Here, it is essential to know how the governance on these platforms is required for a seamless experience. Each platform has different capabilities regarding features, ease of use, and privacy guidelines. For example, Facebook facilitates interaction through community pages, event walls, icons for likes, and stringent policies. These platforms help to have networks and affinity space among users or fans of a particular brand, which generates and exchanges information. Capabilities generally enable brands and users to meet their needs and desires (Rauniar et al. 2013). Digital platforms and their capabilities expose users and brands to interactions between/among them in multiple ways. Not all the members of digital platforms partake in digital personal relationships, such as friends or acquaintances within their network (Rauniar et al. 2013; Lampe, Ellison, and Steinfield 2006), but they share their views or opinions and develop interactions in the digital space. Sometimes, a brand's views differ or even stand against someone's ethical values, norms, or beliefs, resulting in conflict and potential misbehavior, tarnishing the brand's image, or impacting the user's state of mind.

Moderators for Brand Co-Governance Strategies

This chapter proposes two moderators, self-control and filtering self, for effective governance between/among brands and users.

Self-Control

As discussed, brands and users interact on various digital platforms in enormous ways, but they need to make these interactions more pleasurable in experience and avoid drawbacks.

Self-control is a potential moderator for maintaining such pleasant experiences. This does not mean that a user or a brand should not stand for injustice or social change. One must stand but through a polite and optimistic perspective. In the Digital Age, it needs to be co-governed by both brands and users. But here, brands can play a significant role and control the situations of conflicts among the users or between their competitive brands. In general, excessive or impulsive behavior enunciates a lack of self-control (Strack and Deutsch 2004; Verplanken et al. 2005). It leads to a spontaneous response to any situation, but it may not always be harmful behavior. However, this behavior can affect the brand image or well-being of the user (Zahrai et al. 2020). Therefore, one should consciously maintain self-control to avoid such problematic behaviors for brands and users. Maintaining self-control requires a high level of mental cognition or various functions of brands and users (Howlett, Kees, and Kemp 2008). A high level of self-control can lead to many satisfactory outcomes and help avoid numerous negative consequences (Hoffmann, Leonard, and Adrian 2017). For instance, brands should take a neutral position in the Digital Age to prevent users and other competitive brands (Bhushan 2021). However, in certain situations, this strategy may not work effectively, but when taking one perspective, brands should be confident and ready to face the consequences and further manage them. Brands should strategically rethink their stand on societal issues and regional matters in their brand communication. It can tarnish the brand's image, or the message can be perceived the other way around. Thus, brands should first check the cultural sensitivities of their promotional campaign or any other notices. Second, anything that goes out of the brand's digital handle can lead to negative consequences, and hence, the brand should self-control for some time and, if required, respond with factual data. Third, the brand should avoid escalating comments among the users and remain neutral. Fourth, brands should monitor and track all users' negative sentiments and not repeat them in the future (Bosmia 2022). This self-control mechanism applies to brands but is also more critical for the users. They face several user-to-user conflicts, share personal data, and can be the victims of trolling from other users in the digital space. Based on negative sentiments, these interactions can negatively impact engagement (Dineva et al. 2022). Users sharing their opinions and thoughts also face several drawbacks, such as trolling and cyberbullying, that affect their mental well-being. However, they should consciously pause and consider their perspectives before adding them to digital media. Thus, brands and users should govern themselves through self-control to inculcate pleasant experiences to avoid negative sentiments.

Filtering Self

In the complex sociotechnical-based interactions of the Digital Age, it is essential to select the proper behavior to avoid negative sentiments. Filtering is one such conceptualization that focuses on various exclusion and inclusion parameters in the Digital Age on varied interaction platforms (Kini, Pathak-Shelat, and Jain 2022). Users and brands portray themselves differently on various digital platforms; thus, in the online setting, filtering is also influenced by self-presentation theory (Boyd 2008). This theory means that one consciously or unconsciously controls their impressions form by others. Filtering self in the digital space should be contextual and depend on the individual user's culture, markets, and so on, or brand. This can lead to behavioral modifications (Szabla and Blommaert 2020) among/between brands and users. For instance, a brand can receive more negative setbacks in a culturally sensitive country such as India, while the same may not be true in the United States. Therefore, before taking any brand communication, PepsiCo continually reviews cultural sensitives within each brand environment (Bhushan 2021). Besides brands, users on various digital platforms share their unfiltered opinions, which may be a complaint or praise about a brand. The brand Tata-Tanishq faced backlash for promoting interfaith baby showers in their advertisement. Here, those users who liked the advertisement and presented their positive opinions also received backlash from other users in the digital space. Brands should take active steps in filtering several user-to-user conflicts because brands are a part of users' opinions and narratives (Jain et al. 2020). Thus, avoiding negative consequences requires screening from brand and user perspectives as part of co-created governance.

Regulators

Regulators play a vital role on digital platforms by monitoring misbehavior. Policy-makers of a specific country and platform policies serve as regulators for effective governance in the Digital Age. For instance, the frightening riot at the U.S. capitol was an example of violence predicted to be instigated on social-media platforms. Looking at the same riot, Twitter and Facebook banned Trump for promoting violence. At the same time, brands such as Apple and Google regulated their alternative social-media platform and stopped their services (Cusumano, Gawer, and Yoffie 2021). In some instances, platform policies could not govern misbehavior on the platform. Major social-media regulators argue that managing and enforcing specific policies are difficult because it is tricky to differentiate hate from satire and commentary. While sometimes, misbehavior on the platform is subjective and may be biased toward political views. Thus, the regulators of such platforms claim that the onus for moderating the digital space should not be on them but should require the government (policymakers) of the specific country to govern it (Siripurapu and Merrow 2021). Yet countries regulate the digital space differently, as they vary in the consensus of what constitutes harmful content and misbehavior (Pillalamarri and Stanley 2021). For example, the United States and China govern digital content differently, with China having some of the strictest internet regulations in the world. China stringently monitors, filters, and removes any content not in compliance with its policies; brands face the risk of fines or the revocation of media licenses (Pillalmarri and Stanley 2021). Thus, brands and users should follow the guidelines of the regulators. However, they can't solely rely on government or platform policies to govern the content in the Digital Age. Brands and users should self-regulate by monitoring the norms and policies of the platforms and specific countries to avoid inevitable conflicts at a later stage.

Outcome

Brand Experiences

The outcome of the brand co-governance model with specific antecedents, mediators, and moderators for governing the co-created interactions is compelling brand experiences in the digital space. This experience-centricity focuses on reasonable brand control through effective brand management in branding literature (Merrilees 2017). Today, every brand focuses on co-creation with users on a digital platform; hence, their focus should be greater control of these interactions to provide better experiences. Such incidents lead to brand loyalty (Brakus, Schmitt, and Zarantonello 2009), customer satisfaction (Court et al. 2009), customer–brand engagement (Merrilees, Miller, and Shao 2016), and value creation (Helkkula, Kelleher, and Pihlström2012). This conceptual model of brand co-governance focusing on experiences proposes three significant types of experiences on social media following Merrilees' (2017) classification of brand experiences: on-brand experiences, amber experiences, and off-brand experiences. On-brand experiences are usually positive, amber experiences are neutral, and off-brand experiences are generally negative. Concerning brand co-governance, interactions between/among brands and users, if managed effectively through self-control and filtering by both brands and users, will lead to on-brand experiences. If unfiltered exchanges are elevated and lead to negative consequences, they will lead to off-brand experiences. However, there will be certain situations where these interactions are slightly elevated toward negative connotations. Still, the brand and users are not much affected, which may lead to amber experiences. For example, KFC faced a backlash with #RejectKFC on social media for not playing regional songs in their restaurant. As discussed, with adequate brand self-control and filtering strategies, the brand said that it would integrate regional sensibilities into its restaurants (Bhushan 2021). After the backlash, the brand tried to convert its off-brand experiences in the digital space toward on-brand experiences. Thus, these co-created interactions can be better governed in certain situations before receiving negative consequences.

Discussion and Conclusion

The Digital Age fosters several negative consequences or dark sides in the environment (Demsar et al. 2021), and studies on these areas are minimal. It inculcates drawbacks in the co-created interaction between brands and users, and these consequences portray serious and long-run effects, including damaging a brand's image or reputation. At the same time, many serious consequences can occur concerning the user's mental well-being. Based on the marketplace evidence in the examples presented in this chapter, brand co-governance is a convincing framework for avoiding such dark sides of the Digital Age. Although the brand co-governance model outlines the governance areas with some moderators, it is impossible to govern all content in the Digital Age. Some things, such as user-to-user conflicts, may be beyond the brand's control. In several cases, brands also have to follow specific countries' regulations, and failing to do so can become a matter of disobeying law and order. This chapter proposes a few brand- and user-centric antecedents, mediators such as digital platforms and capabilities, moderators for governance such as self-control and filtering self, and regulators taking a view of brands and users. Finally, it proposes brand experiences with an experience-centric approach as an outcome of the brand co-governance model.

However, there needs to be meticulous studies to examine brand co-governance to avoid digital backlash. Academic scholars can test this conceptual model through exploratory studies, examining more moderators and mediators. Practitioners can develop governance strategies for better user experiences in the digital space. The industry practitioners managing various brands can create rules and guidelines based on this conceptual framework. Overall, this chapter provides a framework for the brand co-governance model, which is crucial in the Digital Age.

Key Discussion Areas

- Conceptualizing brand co-governance and its framework.
- Governing digital content and proposing user- and brand-centric variables in the framework.
- Interactions on digital media and its dark side.

References

Akar, Erkan, and Birol Topçu. 2011. "An Examination of the Factors Influencing Consumers' Attitudes toward Social Media Marketing." *Journal of Internet Commerce* 10(1): 35–67.

Anghelcev, George. 2013. "Unintended Effects of Incentivizing Consumers to Recommend a Favorite Brand." *Journal of Marketing Communications* 21(3): 210–23.

Baliunaite, Ilona, and James Caunt. 2019. "30 Hilarious Times This Guy With a Name 'Customer Support' Trolled Clueless Customers." *Boredpanda*, www.boredpanda.com/customer-support-guy-different-companies-logos-facebook-profile/ (accessed April 15, 2022).

Bardi, Anat, and Shalom H. Schwartz. 2003. "Values and Behavior: Strength and Structure of Relations." *Personality and Social Psychology Bulletin* 29(10): 1207–20.

Besley, John. 2008. "Media Use and Human Values." *Journalism & Mass Communication Quarterly* 85(2): 311–30.

Bhushan, Ratna. 2021. "Big Brands Put Localising on Fast Track amid Social Media Backlash." *Economic Times*, November 1, 2021, https://economictimes.indiatimes.com/industry/services/advertising/big-brands-put-localising-on-fast-track-amid-social-media-backlash/articleshow/87448714.cms (accessed April 15, 2022).

Blumler, Jay, and Elihu Katz. 1974. *The Uses of Mass Communication: Current Perspectives on Gratification Research*. Thousand Oaks, CA: Sage Publications.

Bosmia, Tanvi. 2022. "Tackling Trolling: How Trolling Affects Brands." *Business Insider*, February 4, 2022, www.businessinsider.in/advertising/ad-agencies/article/tackling-trolling-how-trolling-affects brands/articleshow/89339397.cms#:~:text=%20Tackling%20trolling%3A%20How%20trolling%20affects%20brands%20,all%20communication%20that%20goes%20out%20from . . . %20More%20 (accessed April 13, 2022).
Boyd, Danah. 2008. "Why Youth Heart Social Network Sites: The Role of Networked Publics in Teenage Social Life." In *Youth, Identity, and Digital Media*, edited by D. Buckingham. Cambridge, MA: MIT Press.
Brakus, J. Josko, Bernd H. Schmitt, and Lia Zarantonello. 2009. "Brand Experience: What Is It? How Is It Measured? Does It Affect Loyalty?" *Journal of Marketing* 73(3): 52–68.
Brodie, Roderick J., Linda D. Hollebeek, Biljana Jurić, and Ana Ilić. 2011. "Customer Engagement: Conceptual Domain, Foundational Propositions and Implications for Research." *Journal of Service Research* 14(3): 252–71.
Chen, Jilin, Gary Hsieh, Jalal U. Mahmud, and Jeffery Nichols. 2014. "Understanding Individuals' Personal Values from Social Media Word Use." *Proceedings of the 17th ACM Conference on Computer Supported Cooperative Work and Social Computing* 405–14.
Contractor, Shreya. 2017. "6 Times Bollywood Celebrities Got Trolled on Social Media." *Be Beautiful*, May 17, 2017, www.bebeautiful.in/lifestyle/art-and-culture/6-times-bollywood-celebrities-got-trolled-on-social-media (accessed April 18, 2022).
Cooper, Tony, Constantino Stavros, and Angela R. Dobele. 2018. "The Levers of Engagement: An Exploration of Governance in an Online Brand Community." *Journal of Brand Management* 26(3): 240–54.
Court, David, Dave Elzinga, Susan Mulder, and Ole Vetvik. 2009. "The Consumer Decision Journey." *McKinsey Quarterly*, June 1, 2009, www.mckinsey.com/business-functions/growth-marketing-and-sales/our-insights/the-consumer-decision-journey (accessed April 28, 2022).
Cusumano, Michael A., Annabelle Gawer, and David B. Yoffie. 2021. "Social Media Companies Should Self-Regulate. Now." *Harvard Business Review*, January 15, 2021, https://hbr.org/2021/01/social-media-companies-should-self-regulate-now (accessed April 28, 2022).
Demsar, Vlad, Jan Brace-Govan, Gavin Jack, and Sean Sands. 2021. "The Social Phenomenon of Trolling: Understanding the Discourse and Social Practices of Online Provocation." *Journal of Marketing Management* 37(11–12): 1058–90.
Dineva, Denista, and Jan Breitsohl. 2021. "Managing Trolling in Online Communities: An Organizational Perspective." *Internet Research* 32(1): 292–311.
Dineva, Denista, Jan Breitsohl, Brian Garrod, and Philip Megicks. 2022. "Consumer Responses to Conflict-Management Strategies on Non-Profit Social Media Fan Pages." *Journal of Interactive Marketing* 52: 118–36.
Ganguly, Sohini. 2015. "2021 Throwback: When Brands Fought the Twitter Rage." *Brandequity*, updated December 15, 2021, https://brandequity.economictimes.indiatimes.com/news/digital/2021-throwback-when-brands-fought-the-twitter-rage/88290108 (accessed April 15, 2022).
Gensler, Sonja, Franziska Völckner, Yuping Liu-Thompkins, and Caroline Wiertz. 2013. "Managing Brands in the Social Media Environment." *Journal of Interactive Marketing* 27(4): 242–56.
Gómez, Carmen Lopez, and Arturo Molina. 2019. "An Integrated Model of Social Media Brand Engagement." *Computers in Human Behavior* 96: 196–206.
Gromark, Johan, and Frans Melin. 2011. "The Underlying Dimensions of Brand Orientation and Its Impact on Financial Performance." *Journal of Brand Management* 18(6): 394–410.
Gurnert, Suzzane, and Hans Juhl. 1995. "Values, Environmental Attitudes and Buying of Organic Foods." *Journal of Economic Psychology* 16: 39–62.
Hanna, Richard, Andrew Rohm, and Victoria L. Crittenden. 2011. "We're All Connected: The Power of the Social Media Ecosystem." *Business Horizons* 54(3): 265–73.
Hein, Andreas, Maximilan Schreieck, Tobias Riasanow, David Soto, Setzke Manuel, Wiesche, Markus Böhm, and Helmut Krcmar. 2020. "Digital Platform Ecosystems." *Electronic Markets* 30: 87–98.
Heinonen, Kristina. 2011. "Consumer Activity in Social Media: Managerial Approaches to Consumers' Social Media Behavior." *Journal of Consumer Behaviour* 10(6): 356–64.
Helkkula, Anu, Carol Kelleher, and Minna Pihlström. 2012. "Characterizing Value as an Experience." *Journal of Service Research* 15(1): 59–75.

Hoffman, Donna L., and Thomas P. Novak. 2012. "Toward a Deeper Understanding of Social Media." *Journal of Interactive Marketing* 26(2): 69–70.
Hoffmann, Wilhelm, Reinecke Leonard, and Meier Adrian. 2017. "Of Sweet Temptations and Bitter Aftertaste: Self-Control as the Moderator of Effects of Media Use on Well-Being." In *The Routledge Handbook of Media Use and Well-Being*, edited L. Reinecke and M. B. Oliver. Milton Park, UK: Routledge.
Howlett, Elizabeth, Jeremy Kees, and Elyria Kemp. 2008. "The Role of Self-Regulation, Future Orientation, and Financial Knowledge in Long-Term Financial Decisions. *Journal of Consumer Affairs* 42(2): 223–42.
Jain, Varsha, Russel W. Belk, Aupama Ambika, and Manisha Pathak-Shelat. 2020. "Narratives Selves in the Digital World: An Empirical Investigation." *Journal of Consumer Behaviour* 20(2): 368–80.
Kalimeri, Kyriaki, Mariano G. Beiró, Matteo Delfino, Robert Raleigh, and Ciro Cattuto. 2019. "Predicting Demographics, Moral Foundations, and Human Values from Digital Behaviours." *Computers in Human Behavior* 92: 428–45.
Kambara, Kenneth M. 2010. "Managing Brand Instability and Capital Market Reputation: Implications for Brand Governance and Marketing Strategy." *Journal of Brand Management* 17(8): 568–78.
Kane, Gerald C. 2015. "Enterprise Social Media: Current Capabilities and Future Possibilities." *MIS Quarterly Executive* 14(1): 1–16.
Kini, Sesha, Manisha Pathak-Shelat, and Varsha Jain. 2022. "Conceptualizing 'Filter-ing': Affordances, Context Collapse, and the Social Self Online." *International Journal of Communication* 16: 1573–93.
Lampe, Cliff, Nicole Ellison, and Charles Steinfield. 2006. "A Face(book) in the Crowd: Social Searching vs. Social Browsing." *Proceedings of Conference on Computer Supported Cooperative Work-2006, Alberta, Canada* 167–70.
Merrilees, Bill. 2017. "Experience-Centric Branding: Challenges and Advancing a New Mantra for Corporate Brand Governance." *Journal of Brand Management* 24(1): 1–13.
Merrilees, Bill, Dale Miller, and Wei Shao. 2016. "Mall Brand Meaning: An Experiential Branding Perspective." *Journal of Product & Brand Management* 25(3): 262–73.
Merz, Michael A., Yi He, and Stephen L. Vargo. 2009. "The Evolving Brand Logic: A Service-Dominant Logic Perspective." *Journal of the Academy of Marketing Science* 37(3): 328–44.
Mittal, Apoorva. 2020. "Brands Put in Strict Internal Guidelines to Avoid Social Media Backlash." *Economic Times*, October 24, 2020, https://economictimes.indiatimes.com/tech/technology/brands-put-in-strict-internal-guidelines-to-avoid-social-media-backlash/articleshow/78835975.cms (accessed April 20, 2022).
Monks, Emma. 2020. "The Rise of Negative Comments on Brand-Owned Social Media Ads." *Crisp*, September 29, 2020, www.crispthinking.com/blog/negative-comments-social-media-ads (accessed April 18, 2022).
Muniz Jr, Albert M., and Hope J. Schau. 2005. "Religiosity in the Abandoned Apple Newton Brand Community." *Journal of Consumer Research* 31(4): 737–47.
M'zungu, Simon D. M., Bill Merrilees, and Dale Miller. 2010. "Brand Management to Protect Brand Equity: A Conceptual Model." *Journal of Brand Management* 17(8): 605–17.
Naylor, Rebbecca Walker, Cait P. Lamberton, and Patricia M. West. 2012. "Beyond the 'Like' Button: The Impact of Mere Virtual Presence on Brand Evaluations and Purchase Intentions in Social Media Settings." *Journal of Marketing* 76(6): 105–20.
Odoom, Raphael, and Priscilla Mensah. 2018. "Brand Orientation and Brand Performance in SMEs: The Moderating Effects of Social Media and Innovation Capabilities." *Management Research Review* 42(1): 155–71.
Park, Namsu, Kerk F. Kee, and Sebastian Valenzuela. 2009. "Being Immersed in Social Networking Environment: Facebook Groups, Uses and Gratifications, and Social Outcomes." *Cyberpsychology & Behavior* 12(6): 729–33.
Pillalmarri, Akhilesh, and Stanley Cody. 2021. "Online Content Regulation: An International Comparison." Gearge Washington University Law School International Law and Policy Brief, December 8, 2021, https://studentbriefs.law.gwu.edu/ilpb/2021/12/08/online-content-regulation-an-international-comparison/ (accessed April 27, 2022).

Rauniar, Rupak, Greg Rawski, Ben Johnson, and Jie Yang. 2013. "Social Media User Satisfaction—Theory Development and Research Findings." *Journal of Internet Commerce* 12(2): 195–224.
Ray, Souvik. 2015. "12 Epic Brand Trolling Instances That Left Us All Laughing for Days." *India Times*, September 10, 2015, www.indiatimes.com/news/weird/12-epic-brand-trolling-instances-that-left-us-all-laughing-for-days-244878.html (accessed April 18, 2022).
Reijonen, Helen, Tommi Laukkanen, Raija Komppula, and Sasu Tuominen. 2012. "Are Growing SMEs More Market-Oriented and Brand-Oriented?" *Journal of Small Business Management* 50(4): 699–716.
Renton, Michelle, and James E. Richard. 2019. "Exploring Brand Governance in SMEs: Does Socialisation Provide a Means to Value Creation?" *Journal of Brand Management* 26(4): 461–72.
Schwartz, Shalom, H. 1992. "Universals in the Content and Structure of Values: Theoretical Advances and Empirical Tests in 20 Countries." *Advances in Experimental Social Psychology* 25: 1–65.
Scott, David M. 2017. *The New Rules of Marketing and PR: How to Use Social Media, Online Video, Mobile Applications, Blogs, Newsjacking, and Viral Marketing to Reach Buyers Directly*. New York: John Wiley & Sons.
Shao, Guoson. 2009. "Understanding the Appeal of User-Generated Media: A Uses and Gratification Perspective." *Internet Research* 19(1): 7–25.
Singh, Sangeeta, and Stephan Sonnenburg. 2012. "Brand Performances in Social Media." *Journal of Interactive Marketing* 26(4): 189–97.
Siripurapu, Anshu, and Will Merrow. 2021. "How Countries Regulate Online Speech." Council on Foreign Relations, February 9, 2021, www.cfr.org/in-brief/social-media-and-online-speech-how-should-countries-regulate-tech-giants (accessed April 27, 2022).
Stafford, Thomas F., Marla Stafford, and Lawrence L. Schkade. 2004. "Determining Uses and Gratifications for the Internet." *Decision Sciences* 35(2): 259–88.
Strack, Fritz, and Roland Deutsch. 2004. "Reflective and Impulsive Determinants of Social Behavior." *Personality and Social Psychology Review* 8(3): 220–47.
Szabla, Malgorzata, and Jan Blommaert. 2020. "Does Context Really Collapse in Social Media Interaction?" *Applied Linguistics Review* 11(2): 251–79.
Taks, Marijke, Benoit Seguin, Michael L. Naraine, Ashley Thompson, Milena M. Parent, and Russell Hoye. 2019. "Brand Governance Practices in Canadian National Sport Organizations: An Exploratory Study." *European Sport Management Quarterly* 20(1): 10–29.
Urde, Mats. 1994. "Brand Orientation: A Strategy for Survival." *Journal of Consumer Marketing* 11(3): 18–32.
Veloutsou, Cleopatra, and Luiz Moutinho. 2009. "Brand Relationships Through Brand Reputation and Brand Tribalism." *Journal of Business Research* 62(3): 314–22.
Verplanken, Bas, Astrid G. Herabadi, Judith A. Perry, and David H. Silvera. 2005. "Consumer Style and Health: The Role of Impulsive Buying in Unhealthy Eating." *Psychology & Health* 20(4): 429–41.
Wang, Wanyi. 2015. "The Power of Social Media: A Case of Kentucky Fried Chicken in China." *BRandBa.se*, January 26, 2015, www.brandba.se/blog/2014/8/19/the-power-of-social-media-a-case-of-kentucky-fried-chicken-in-china (accessed April 18, 2022).
Wong, Yin H., and Bill Merrilees. 2005. "A Brand Orientation Typology for SMEs: A Case Research Approach." *Journal of Product & Brand Management* 14(3): 155–62.

11
DIGITAL MARKETING DEVELOPMENT AND GOVERNANCE
The China Model

Yan Han

An Overview of Digital Development in China

China maintains an overall lead in the digital track (European Center for Digital Competitiveness 2021). The country presents different models in the digital platform distribution and the business practice of digital marketing.

A large scale of internet users and a steady internet penetration rate are prerequisites for digital governance. According to the China Internet Network Information Center (CNNIC), as of June 2021, the total number of Chinese internet users exceeded 1.011 billion, of which 99.6 percent of internet users primarily use mobile phones to access the Internet. The number of rural internet users reached 297 million in the year 2021, accounting for 29.4 percent of total users (China Internet Network Information Center 2021). This foundation and growth have also promoted the highest level of marketing digitization. The revenue of Chinese companies in digital advertising reached 75.33 billion U.S. dollars, accounting for 22.6 percent of the global digital advertising budget (see Figure 11.1). The proportion of digital advertising (in relation to traditional advertising) reached 71.6 percent, surpassing the United Kingdom (66.4 percent) and the United States (54.2 percent). As a result, China is the country with the highest advertising digitization rate in the world (Cramer-Flood 2020).

Explicit Fundamental Factors

Among the many driving factors for Chinese companies' digital marketing actions, five important factors have structured the external fundamental conditions and made China the innovation base for global digital marketing. These five factors are highly influential—user scale, advanced technology, the diversified platform, the synchronously developing logistics service system, and government policy support. The following sections capture digital economy, markets, platforms, and customer engagement.

DOI: 10.4324/9781003316077-14

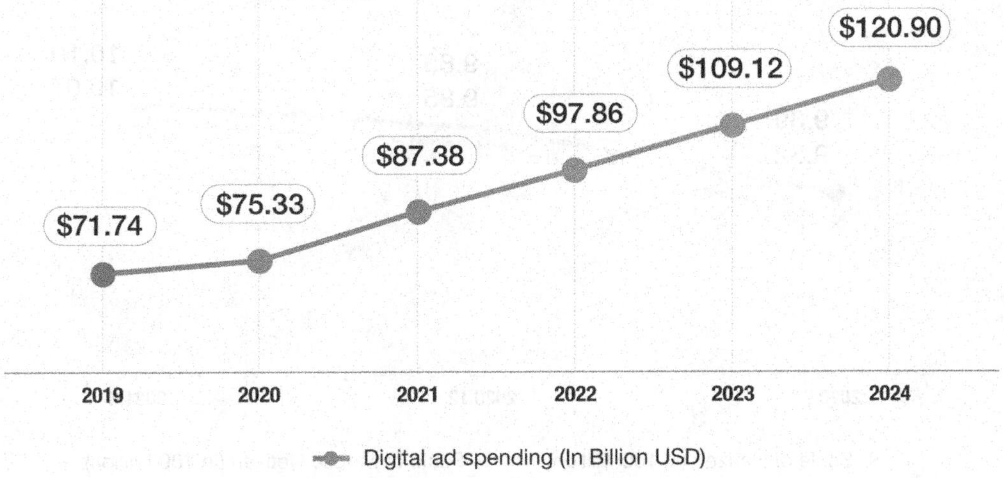

Figure 11.1 China Marketing Advertisement Revenues for 2019–2024

Source: Adapted from eMarketer China Digital Advertisement Spending 2019, 2020.[1,2]

Digitalized Consumer

The large-scale and grassroots massive netizens have formed the habit of digital payment. Such a market base has brought different goals for Chinese enterprises to achieve unique digitalization and create different development paths for digital marketing.

China is the leader in digital payments across the world. It made an estimated US$2.49 trillion in transaction value in digital commerce and mobile payments in 2020, out of a total of US$5.4 trillion in the global market (Statista 2021). As of June 2021, the number of online payment users in China has reached 872 million, accounting for 86.3 percent of all Internet users. Chinese online shopping users account for 80.3 percent of all internet users. The national e-commerce transaction volume reached 37.21 trillion yuan.

More importantly, an inclusive digital system has been established, making farming entrepreneurship and rural consumption possible. In rural areas, internet connectivity is even greater than in large cities. Rural online retail sales have also reached 1.79 trillion yuan (China Internet Network Information Center 2021).

Technology Empowerment

China's high-speed iterative technological situation has brought new transforming tools and spaces for digital marketing to build up—particularly leading communication technology and mobile payment technology; the world's largest communication network; and the three leading positions in the fields of scale, number of standards, and application innovations in 5G commercial development. These opportunities have made Chinese technology companies increasingly realize the importance of joint developments (public and private

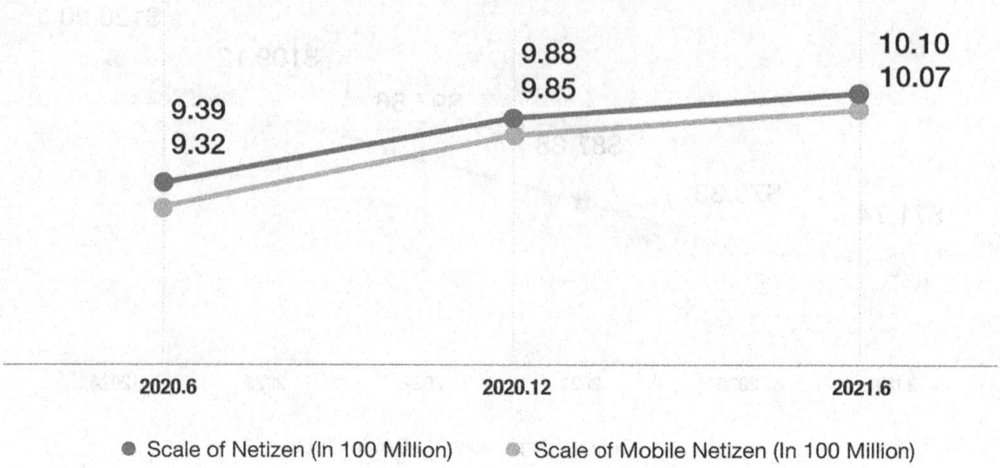

Figure 11.2 China Netizen Scale and Internet Popularity Rate for the Year 2021
Source: Adapted from China Internet Development Statistics Report 2021.

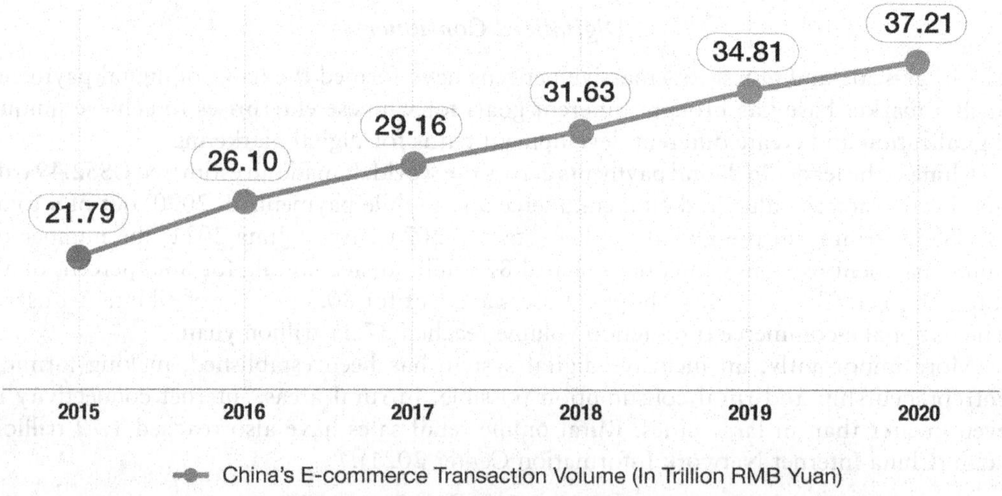

Figure 11.3 China's E-Commerce Transaction Volume and Growth Rate for 2015–2020
Source: Adapted from China Internet Development Report by Internet Society of China.

sector collaborations), depth of technological innovation, and unique business models in the Internet ecosystem. Government policies and investments have contributed to this accelerated business growth and technology developments.

China's fiber-optic broadband users accounted for 94 percent of total internet users by the end of April 2021 (China Internet Network Information Center 2021), fixed broadband speed for end-to-end user experience reached 51.2 Mbps, and mobile network speed ranked fourth among 139 countries and regions globally (Ministry of Industry and Information Technology of China 2021). As of May 2021, China has the highest number of 5G standard-essential patents in the world. Various digital payment platforms are undertaking high-frequency payment services. The national nonbank payment institutions had processed 827.297 billion online payments for 294.56 trillion yuan, and banks processed 235.225 billion electronic payments for 2711.81 trillion yuan (Internet Society of China 2021).

Diversified Platform

The digital platform business models in China have been developing new models through critical assimilation of old ones. China has seen multiple digital platforms specializing in content, social media, entertainment, games, E-commerce, and diversified platform economy closely related to people's lives and work. These diversified platforms provide more direct business methods for the marketing industry to engage with companies and even government-led plans and programs, assisting the enterprise's digital development in terms of foundation and support for execution. At the same time, diversified platforms have also increased the challenges of precision marketing in digital marketing and made consumers' attention more fragmented.

Tertiary Sector Empowerment: Delivery Systems to Support E-Commerce

Another critical factor is the overall gradation of China's industrial structure. "The operation of E-commerce has increased business efficiency, and the deep integration of various new information technologies with the real economy enables the industry to upgrade" (China Internet Network Information Center 2021). The successful development of the tertiary sector constitutes an essential fundamental condition for digitization. The courier service network covers 98 percent of townships in the country. The total amount of China's logistics in 2020 has reached 300.1 trillion yuan (CFLP: China Federation of Logistics and Purchasing 2021).

Institutional Engagement

The guidance and support of the government have improved the underlying logic of Chinese enterprises' marketing. "Digital is the core for marketing" has become common knowledge for almost all companies. The government measures include encouraging the development of science and technology, emphasizing conversion of research achievements, cultivating talents in universities and nonprofit scientific research institutes, and increasingly opening and proactively embracing the digital industry practitioners following international technological rules and regulations.

The "E-commerce Law of the People's Republic of China" was officially implemented on January 1, 2019. It establishes and improves a legal system that adapts to digital development and strengthens rules and regulations regarding market entry, market order, platform management, consumer services standard, technological innovation, intellectual property protection, and safety protection.

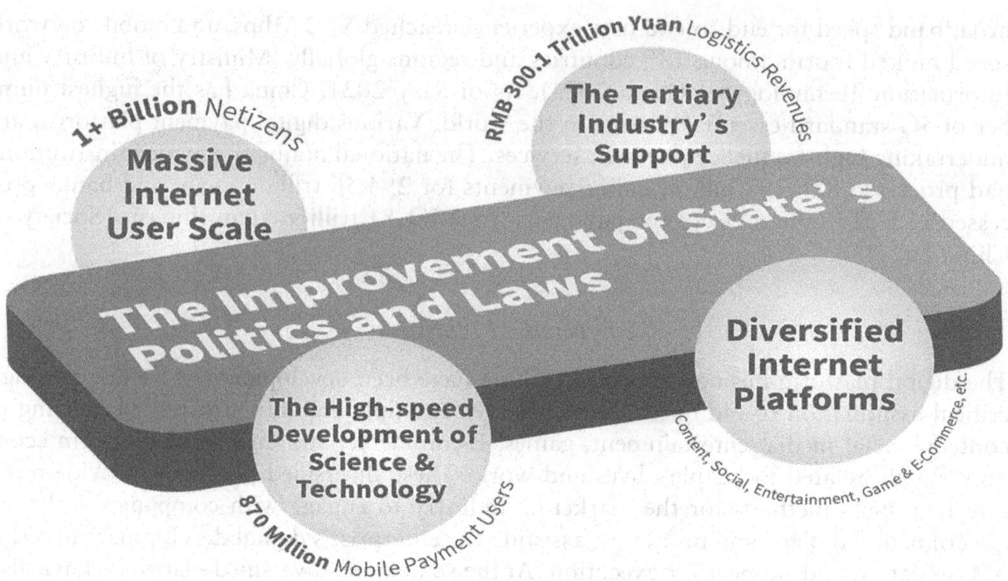

Figure 11.4 The Main Driving Factors of Digital Marketing in China
Source: The Author.

With the considerable internet user scale, the rapid development of technology, diversified Internet platforms, advanced logistics, tertiary industry empowerment, and supportive intuitional environment, these factors give birth to a robust foundation for digital governance and digital marketing in China.

Implicit Influencing Factors

Digital marketing in China also has hidden factors that distinguish it from other regions in the world. They play an increasingly prominent role in the process of digital marketing transformation, just like those explicit factors.

"Internet of Everything"

In the past four decades, the two paths have achieved obvious results. They are the physical infrastructure development path and the virtual technology based platform economy path.

The establishment of an interconnected cloud networking environment led by 5G/6G telecommunication technology has profoundly changed the Chinese consumer's faith in the digital futures and spiritual outlook, and economic perspective with all the digital channels. The simultaneous construction of the physical network also promotes the development of digitalization in the physical space, where high-speed realizations of communications are synchronized.

At the end of 2019, China's total highway mileage reached 5,198,100 kilometers and expressway mileage reached 723,100 kilometers, ranking first in the world (Ministry of

Transport of the People's Republic of China 2020). In the past ten years, high-speed rail has covered more than 95 percent of cities with a population of more than one million, expressway covered more than 98 percent of cities with a population of more than 200,000, and civil airports have covered more than 92 percent of prefecture-level cities (National Development and Reform Commission 2022).

A country as big as China operates like a well-coordinated and efficient organization—this organizational power successfully enables the digital development of Chinese enterprises. As of 2020, China's administrative divisions include 34 provincial-level administrative divisions, 333 prefecture-level administrative divisions, 2,844 county-level administrative divisions, and 38,741 township-level administrative divisions (Statistical Bulletin of China's Civil Affairs Development 2020). National to local governance planning accelerates digital economy transformations.

Internet Thinking

Since the 2010s, the Chinese consumer has become smarter because of the popularization of information and the internet—the result is accelerated digital intelligence and adaptation. Management and operation thinking continue to be iterative. From implementing national policies to selling goods, Chinese people are digitizing everything they do with new ideas and knowledge derived from an immersive digital environment. The concept of "Internet thinking" initiated by Xiaomi in 2011 has opened ideological enlightenment for Chinese enterprise's digital marketing at both industry and social levels (Statistical Bulletin of China's Civil Affairs Development 2020). These alignments are positively influencing China's digital marketing. But at the same time, it also makes Chinese marketing practitioners face a faster iterative environment and more intense challenges. China is leading digital transformation and customer engagement.

The Digital Environment Highlights the Importance of Marketing as the Core Engine for Growth

China is the second biggest country in terms of Facebook revenue after the United States, which already delivered US$24.1 billion in advertising sales in 2018.

Chinese companies pay much more attention to marketing than ever, and they attach a great importance to marketing actions in the digital environment. The consumption increase brought about by the rise of family and individual incomes in China has made traditional marketing methods unable to meet the consumption habits of contemporary consumers who re digital natives. The traditional and digital marketing combination, which reflects "complementing-each-other" approach brings quick responses to digital marketing challenges and valuable opportunities to enterprises who wish to truly explore and practice the marketing essences.

Popularization of Online Payment Habit

Chinese people's digital literacy and lifestyle, particularly living habits in the digital economic environment, as reflected in their welcoming attitude toward new technologies and marketing models, have also cultivated dynamic soils for promoting digital marketing. According to the China Union Pay, 98 percent of Chinese respondents chose mobile

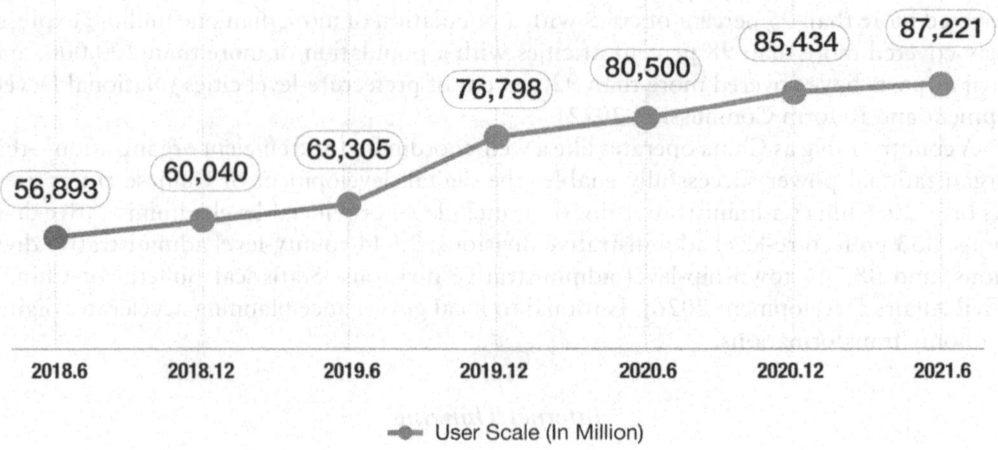

Figure 11.5 China Mobile Payment User Scale and Rate of Utilization
Source: Adapted from China Internet Development Statistics Report.

payment as the most preferred payment method (Paper 2021). China's mobile-paying users in 2020 have reached 854 million, and the usage penetration rate is as high as 85 percent (China Internet Network Information Center 2021). Consumers can use online payment to conduct transactions in daily life with an ordinary street vendor in any fifth-tier city in China, which has broken the segmentation of online and offline behaviors. China has a total of 870 million mobile payment users, with a usage penetration rate as high as 86.3 percent (Paper 2021). Alibaba and Tencent actively participate in the movement away from cash and to mobile payments by encouraging digital platform usages. More than 20 million users make purchases every day through WeChat Pay, and 200,000 people sign up for the service every day (CGAP 2019).

"Fast Culture"

An essential foundation to support economic growth is the "fast" adaptation culture that is universally agreed from the country level in general to the industrial level and leads to consumer consents. Significant items, such as infrastructure development, including highway and railway networks, large energy projects, science and technology base, alongside modest items such as city rebuilding and small items such as daily commuting and courier service, are rapidly developing. The characteristics of such fast development have put forward even more rapid development requirements and expectations for all enterprises in China. Digitization has become an inevitable product of "fast and rapidly evolving culture," economic growth, and business management, and the in-depth development of Chinese enterprise's marketing has further affected consumers' digital life experience.

China's Digital Marketing Model (APP Model)

Chinese companies have formed distinctive digital features in response to China's digital development, which we refer to as "China's digital marketing model." The model stems from integrated marketing communications (Schultz, Tannenbaum, and Robert 1992). Integrated marketing involves leaving a lasting impression on the consumer by repeating the same message from different channels. China's three-orientation model goes one step further and drives consumer behavior from market-oriented *all-area marketing*, traffic-oriented *platform marketing*, and *user-oriented private-domain marketing* (APP model). Rather than building branding, the focus at the center of the marketing technology chain is to achieve sales (conversion from marketing to purchase for increased sales). For consumers, from the first marketing touchpoint to the final purchase—through customer journey—transformation and behavior change are the focus of the chain. Branding leading to sales is the natural consequence of the digital marketing chain. It is more focused on systematic marketing impact. However, this model essentially follows Drucker's fundamental theory of marketing (purpose of products/services marketing is to create the consumer through innovations and customer engagement), but with a different purpose. Consumer orientation does not serve the purpose of fitting consumers' needs with the product (Woodside, Wilson, and Milner 1992). It is neither accomplishing and balancing organizational effectiveness from digital marketing strategies nor achieving the previously set corporate objectives. While "European organizations confer great importance to the interaction with its audience, American organizations tolerate a greater degree of one-way communication" (Matosas-López 2021), China's model focuses on different interests and is opposed to the concept of "permission marketing" (Godin 1999), in which the sales process follows consumers' permission. Today, instead of focusing on perceived usefulness and ease of use, digital marketing approaches are significantly correlated to building and promoting ideation systems' use for creativity in organizations—theorized by Davis (1989); the information technology plays a role in reaching an entry point to a vast ecosystem of both offline and online goods and services for customer-centric marketing and sales (CGAP 2019).

The integration of urban and rural internet infrastructure, fierce competition among digital platforms, sales- and conversion-driven corporate marketing investment, and users' content-driven consumption preferences have jointly created a digital marketing model for Chinese companies. In summary, this model (APP model) has several characteristics:

- market-oriented digital all-area marketing;
- traffic-oriented digital Platform marketing;
- user-oriented digital private-domain marketing.

Market-Oriented Digital All-Area Marketing

Chinese companies combine business scenarios, social scenarios, and big data scenarios to conduct scene-based marketing. The outcome is integrating users' fragmented resources, enabling buyers and sellers to establish mutual trust more quickly and create instant demand so that sales conversion becomes rapid, thus improving market efficiency. Take live broadcasts, for example; it takes real-time communication and interactive explanations to realize sales and purchases. (Such business also exists in traditional people relations, but the cost is high, and communication is insufficient.) As for scene-based marketing, the video presentation format, the 4G/5G high-speed and low-cost network environment, the synchronous changes of consumer groups, and new forms of digitalization are evolving and emerging under the blessing of technology and marketing methods, which integrate online and offline experiences to form a complicated systematic "combinatorial evolution" (Arthur 2014). Arthur argues that, once these technologies interact with each other and make combinations of multiple technologies, they generate new needs for users, thus propelling innovation. This process leads to the emergence of newer forms of technology and moves the economy itself forward. If the economy is an arrangement of a "set of activities and behaviors and flows of goods and services," it is mediated by the prevailing technology. Hence, "technology determines the structure of the economy and thereby much of the world that emerges from this, but which technologies fall into place is not determined in advance." This definition well explains the development process in China.

Such an exploration manifests prominently in the following aspects. First, it creates closed-loop scenarios through digital marketing using short video, live broadcast, and e-commerce platforms, allowing users to always stay in the marketing scenarios constructed by themselves. Second, it chooses different IP event scenes connected to break the limitations of different touchpoints. Such e-commerce IP events include Alibaba's Double 11 (November 11) Shopping Festival, Alibaba's Taobao Maker Festival, and TikTok's Wonderful Shopping Festival. Third is the cross-screen scene migration. In China, more and more smart TV brands enable short videos to be shared from personal mobile phones' small screens to home TV's big screen, thus migrating the mobile scene of short video marketing to the home living room scene.

Traffic-Oriented Digital and Multi-Platform Marketing

The digitization of Chinese companies involves a multi-platform market pattern, with traffic scattered across various platforms. It shows a different model compared with other giants' dominance in other markets. Google and Facebook's advertising revenue accounts for 60 percent of the total global market (Cramer-Flood 2020). Almost 70 percent of digital ad spending goes to Google, Facebook, and Amazon (Sterling 2021). In China, however, the major internet platforms are relatively balanced. In 2019, Alibaba, JD.com, and Pinduoduo accounted for only 40 percent of the total advertising revenue in China, and the combined data of Tencent, Baidu, and Bytedance was only 35 percent. Various large platforms compete with their own digital advantage to attract traffic. These traffic platforms operate almost all businesses that can reach users, including e-commerce, social media, games, music, maps, news, and electronic payments gateways. They all have their own typical characteristics and specific target groups, thus forming a flourishing, diversified, and balanced situation. The market has different players with different entrances: Tencent is a social and game traffic platform; Alibaba's focus is on e-commerce traffic; Baidu's core functionality is as a search engine, news, and video platform; Sina is considered as a news and social topic platform; NetEase is news and game focused platform; Bytedance is a short video platform; Meituan is a life services platform; Bilibili is a comic and animation, cartoon, and game content community platform; Xiaohongshu is a lifestyle platform; and Kwai is a short video platform. In June 2021, the number of online video users (including short videos) in China reached 944 million, accounting for 93.4 percent of the total netizens. Among them, short video users accounted for 87.8 percent of the total netizens (China Internet Network Information Center 2021).

Chinese companies pay significant attention to the conversion rate in digital marketing. Revenue can measure sales made through marketing activity in diversified platforms, attracting traffic, promoting conversion, and marketing investment. The market-oriented "sales results to promote the brand" model is revenue-first strategy, followed by brand building throughout the digital marketing process. It's an entirely different approach compared with other market mix with digital raise and traditional marketing method to brand-cantered marketing. Take TikTok as an example: The total GMV (total merchandise volume) of

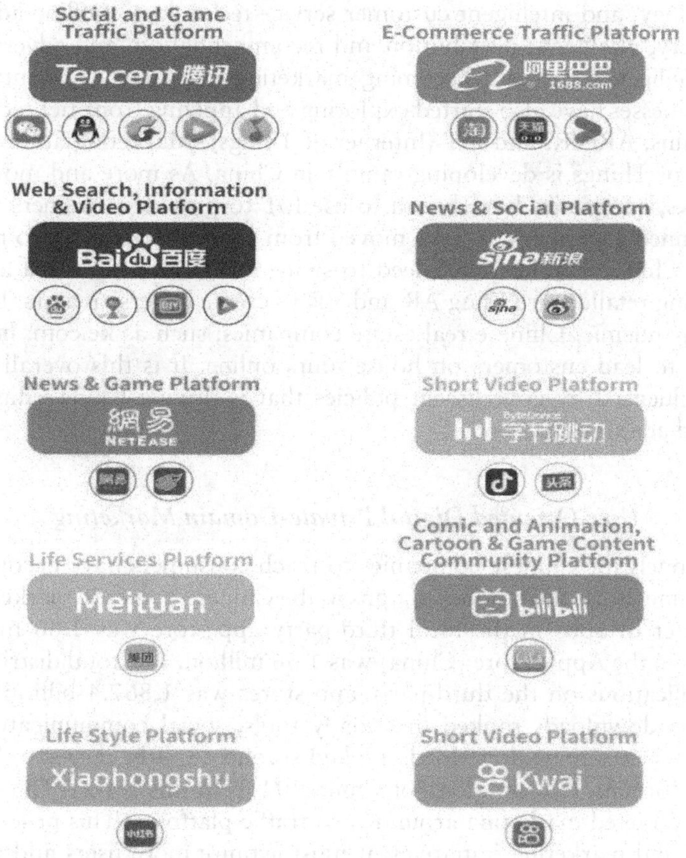

Figure 11.6 Traffic Oriented Digital Platform Marketing
Source: Summaries by Author.

TikTok in 2020 exceeded 500 billion yuan, which was three times the GMV of 2019 with just over hundred billion yuan sold through the TikTok page. The other 300 billion yuan of transactions were led from live broadcast rooms and short videos to other e-commerce platforms such as JD.com and Taobao.com to complete transactions (Late Post 2021).

Brands create user-interested content on TikTok in the form of short videos and live broadcasts, which stimulate the potential demands of consumers. Such needs may instantly convert into sales orders and come back to the e-commerce platform. The new content formats inspire new consuming experiences, opening an all-new traffic growth avenue for brands. On this new traffic growth model, creating enchanting content has become the essential marketing capability for brands.

One noteworthy point about enterprise digitalization in China is that Chinese enterprises do not develop independently or employ the CRM or ERP-based digitalization system as the core model. In particular, the small- and medium-sized enterprises (SMEs) intend to choose mature digital transformation solutions such as Alibaba Uni Marketing Solution.

At the same time, more and more companies are beginning to realize the importance of owning marketing technology. Companies have started to widely use data centers, content labeling technology, and intelligent customer service technology. Offline advertising, programmed delivery, intelligent distribution and recommendation, and advertising powered by artificial intelligence (AI) are becoming marketing technologies of interest to China enterprises. Businesses have also started exploring and applying front-tier technologies such as AI, blockchains, AR/VR, and IoT (Internet of Things). Marketing automation brought by the Internet of Things is developing rapidly in China. As more and more devices connect to networks, companies have begun to use IoT to provide customers with enhanced services. Unmanned supermarkets have moved from concept to reality. To ride most high-speed trains in China, travelers only need to swipe an ID card to board and disembark. Alibaba's clothing retailers are using AR and VR to create buyers' avatars. During the current Covid-19 pandemic, Chinese real-estate companies, such as ke.com, have been using VR technology to lead customers on house tours online. It is this overall cross-industry convergence influenced by government policies that is driving China's digital marketing innovations and adaptation.

User-Oriented Digital Private-Domain Marketing

The digital channels for Chinese companies to reach consumers have become highly fragmented. As of June 2021, the number of apps in the Chinese domestic market was 3.02 million. The number of apps in the local third-party app store was 1.66 million, and the number of apps in the Apple Store (China) was 1.36 million. The total distribution amount of on-shelf applications on the third-party app stores was 1,867.4 billion times. Among them, game app downloads ranked first; daily tools, social communication, music and video, and life services apps downloads ranked second to fifth, respectively (Ministry of Industry and Information Technology of China 2021). In this reality, Chinese companies must carry out targeted marketing around each traffic platform. This poses a challenge to a company's digital marketing initiatives: it must acquire more users and traffic on these different-target platforms. Digital marketing costs are very high, and the cost of acquiring and retaining customers is increasing at an average annual rate of 20 percent. During the ongoing pandemic, almost all brands have stepped up efforts to approach consumers digitally, increasing the cost further (McKinsey 2020).

In China, where traffic is becoming more and more expensive, it has become popular for companies to build their own private-domain traffic platforms. The so-called enterprise private-domain traffic platform refers to a communication platform that companies can fully control and reach consumers without paying third-party platforms. Currently, the largest sources of private-domain traffic for Chinese companies are the mini-programs, official corporate accounts, and live broadcast accounts built by various platforms. At the same time, over 1,000 service providers help build private-domain traffic platforms for companies as well. Together with companies, they are making an ever-flourishing ecosystem of enterprise private-domain traffic platforms.

Private-domain traffic has become an essential asset for brands to influence consumers. The high penetration rate from private domains presents strong user stickiness, high reputation, and high transaction frequency. These characteristics have driven enterprises to come up with the will and actions for user operation.

Marketing firms and practitioners need to be exceptionally good at finding a highly effective balance between users, platforms, and companies for the tripartite benefits to be coupled, and effective operational decisions can be provided for companies. This is also the most important indicator to determine whether a marketing firm has truly entered the forefront of digital marketing concepts and whether it can truly bring sustainable business values to the enterprise. Though there are many netizens, it is still essential for enterprises to carefully analyze and identify target customers among the public-domain traffic, explore profiling, and repeatedly mining private-domain traffic.

Governance Model for Marketing Digitalization

Compared with European and American enterprises, Chinese firms started digital governance relatively late. They concentrated on presenting the platform-centric governance model, which promoted digital governance and systematic governance through digital marketing governance.

Platform-Driven Mode

Most SMEs have not adopted other countries' software governance models to develop industry standards and business systems, but, instead, they rely on the digital ecology of platform companies for digital governance. This model has low investment, high flexibility, and higher efficiency. At the same time, companies began with marketing digitalization, pursuing the goal of quick realization and quick results, which promoted the company's digital governance. For most Chinese small- and medium-sized enterprises, marketing digital governance is urgently needed. Take the designer menswear brand Cabbeen Apparel: in 2019, through Alibaba's Dingding platform, the company successfully transformed from process-driven to data-driven, from internal collaboration to industrial collaboration, and initially realized the company's marketing digitization governance. Dingding's platform breaks down the digital governance of enterprises into five online modules: organizational, communication, collaboration, business, and Economy. Behind these five modules is the digital base of Alibaba Cloud's business. The integrated DingTalk platform of Dingding can help enterprises carry out digital transformation in an all-around way.

"Reverse Path" Digital Governance

For enterprises that strive to complete digital governance, the first step before marketing digitalization should be to achieve three more important digital transformations: organizational, management, and business alignments. Although the maturity of marketing must be brought out by the maturity of the enterprise or the operation, the Chinese model has chosen a reverse path—first, complete the marketing maturity and then promote the enterprise's digitization.

The marketing digitization of Chinese companies—whether it is a company that relies on a platform to digitize itself, a platform-based company that provides solutions for corporate marketing digitization, or a large-scale company that builds its own professional technical team and integrates platform resources to digitize itself—has the ultimate goal to establish a corporate marketing digital brain; that is, to make rapid marketing-related decisions and agile marketing actions in an increasingly digital market. Chinese enterprises' future-oriented marketing digital brain governance model is to return to the origin of marketing through the collaboration between the left and right brains (see Table 11.1): to deliver the right products and information to the right consumers at the right time and place.

Table 11.1 Chinese Enterprises' Future-Oriented Marketing Digital Brain Governance Model

Left Brain (hardware system)	*Right Brain (software system)*
Business data, media data, e-commerce data	Media coverage, social-media comments, user reviews
Data processing	Content generation/creation
Data middle platform	Business middle platform
Data analysis and research	Content production and distribution
Data traffic platform	KOL, KOC content production docking
LBS location-based service-oriented marketing	Physical on-site store display and management
Data operation: e-commerce platform, search engine, social media, and short video platform	Content operation: official website, APP, mini program, the official account
Database operation center	Content Creative center
Input: more data	Output: more content

Source: By Author.

Digital Marketing Intelligence Center

Although many Chinese firms depend on the platforms built by internet companies for digital governance, forming their own technical team to scale up integration has also become popular. The ultimate direction is to build up a digital marketing intelligence center so that this "brain" can generate rapid marketing-related decisions and agile marketing actions in the increasingly digital market.

Cabbeen Apparel, for example, builds data platforms based on the technology of the intelligent data assistant to provide timely data trend analysis, realize the man-machine dialogue and narrative, and push data for business analysis. Data analysis can improve the aging level twenty-four times (from four hours to now five to ten minutes), satisfying the infinite space analysis perspective and continuous precipitation algorithm. Taking the tracking of popular goods as an example: the data center can realize the second-level responses. Popular goods tracking has increased the comprehensive visual presentation of twenty-two indicators (including cycle, moving pin, shop, sold out) and data supporting the evaluation indicators of popular goods. In the middle stage of business, Cabbeen Apparel overturns the previous construction of traditional ERP—Enterprise Resource Planning. It puts forward five services: coding service, attribute service, file service, status service, and policy service. Relying on the underlying architecture of Ali Cloud, the business center takes Dingding as a collaborative platform to build nine centers of membership, order, marketing, content, users, channels, goods, design, and inventory, reshaping the entire business chain process. It also involves more than one hundred applications in the middle of the business, covering

- the upstream of the industrial chain of fabric, textile, printing, and dyeing;
- middle of the chain enterprises like design, research and development, ordering, procurement, production, sales, logistics;
- the downstream of the industrial chain of the business and retail stores.

The four-wheeler drivers of dress marketing in digital governance strategy, through data intelligence market changes and timely decisions—push products, designers, fabric suppliers, garment suppliers (for ecological synergy, carving dress build awareness—feedback—decision—production), and listed "nail" cloud of the supply chain, increase the "small

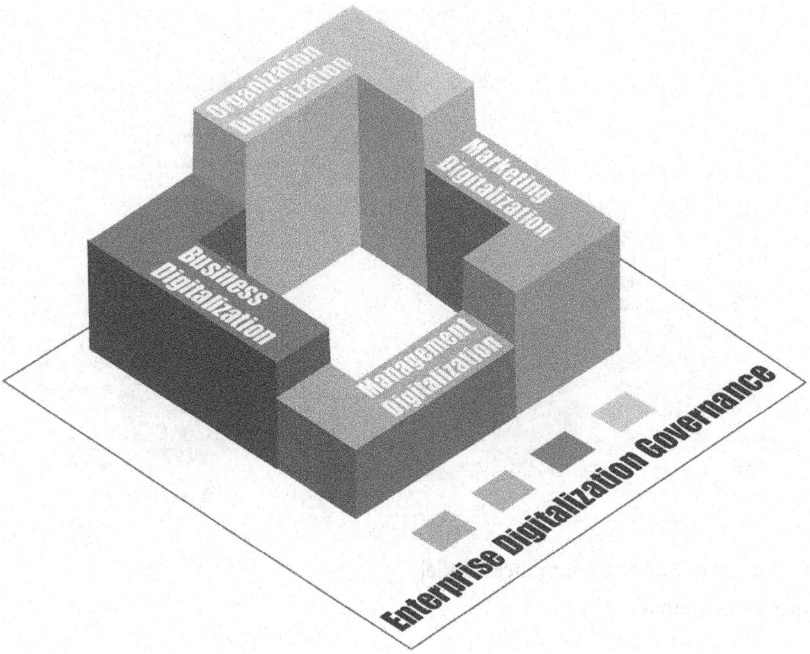

Figure 11.7 Four Elements of Enterprise Digital Governance

Source: Summaries by Author.

single quick" flexibly. Since 2020, Cabbeen Apparel has continued to launch "personalized killer products" to lead the market trend. The capital market has recognized the digital marketing management of Cabbeen Apparel.

Systematic Governance

China's reverse path model is a result of the joint actions of China's marketing industry, Chinese companies, and China's national conditions. From a longer-term perspective, the success of Chinese corporate marketing digital governance still depends on whether the company can establish a governance mechanism for organization, management, and business digitalization. The digitalization of Chinese enterprises in marketing and business has already begun, but the digitalization of organizations and management is not the focus of Chinese enterprises at this stage. The digitization process of Chinese companies currently focuses on business digitization—that is, the ability to acquire customers through digitization (effective marketing).

Triangular Paradigm

Digital governance requires a "proprietary economics" (Hong 2021) mentality where companies lead proprietary investment and trading for direct gains. Most companies—particularly internet companies such as Alibaba—follow a triangular paradigm for digital governance that involves the system, organization, and culture.

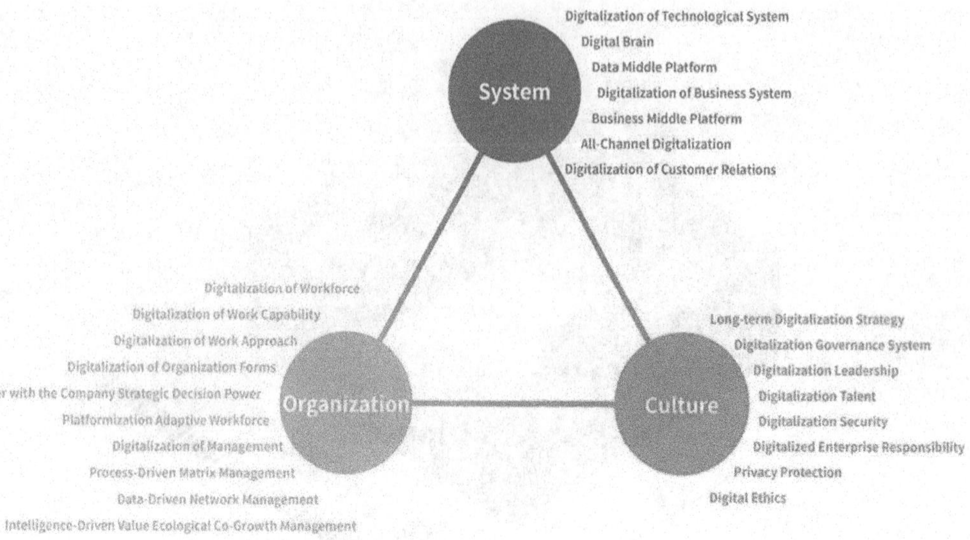

Figure 11.8 Chinese Digital Governance Model
Source: Summaries by Author.

Challenge

Although the digital marketing management of Chinese companies has developed rapidly, the marketing digitalization governance of Chinese companies is still in its infancy. Chinese companies must complete digital marketing management; establish a digital governance mechanism for organization, management, and business as a whole; and carry out digital transformation around three sides of the triangular paradigm. However, they are currently facing the challenge of a shortage of talents, system incompatibility (enterprises and enterprises; platforms and platforms), and higher regulatory requirements, including requirements for privacy and digital asset ownership.

Talent Challenge

A survey from the China Advertising Association shows that the extreme scarcity of digital talent is currently the biggest challenge for Chinese companies (Baijiahao.Baidu.com 2020).

The increasing requirements from all brands for conversion rates will lead to a single pursuit of real-time results. At the same time, digital marketing's lack of industry standards will affect the overall ecological development.

Tendency to Fragment

The fragmentation of the market is another challenge. The fragmentation is twofold: separation between enterprises and separation between platforms.

On the one hand, the digital channels for Chinese companies to reach consumers have become granular. In this reality, Chinese companies must carry out targeted digital marketing around each traffic platform. Such fragmentation will only continue to increase the marketing cost of the enterprise and directly harm the user's value acquisition. Expectations for the tremendous growth brought about by digital marketing may lead to overinvestment in marketing by enterprises, which may adversely affect the healthy development of enterprises. What kind of impact this tendency has on the enterprise itself and the economic environment requires further observation and research.

Regulatory Supervision

In recent years, China has revised the "Anti-Unfair Competition Law" twice, promoted the promulgation of the "E-Commerce Law," accelerated the revision of the "Anti-Monopoly Law," and formulated the nine rules and regulations, including "Interim Regulations on the Review of Concentration of Undertakings Measures for the Supervision and Administration of Online Transactions." It also issued six guidelines including the "Guidelines for Anti-monopoly in the Field of Platform Economy" and "Guidelines for Anti-monopoly Compliance for Business Operators." These laws, regulations, rules, and guidelines indicated that China has built up a basic legal system to monitor competition, covering online and offline. In August 2021, China issued the "Regulations on the Recommendation of Algorithms for Internet Information Services (Draft for Comment)" (Internet Information Office of the People's Republic of China 2021), which stipulated a series of codes of conduct for algorithm recommendation service providers. These regulations included instructions that using algorithms to manipulate user accounts must not use algorithms to shield information, over-recommendations, among others.

The Chinese government's supervision of large-scale internet-technology companies will also have a long-term impact on Chinese companies' marketing digitalization. For most Chinese companies, the government's anti-monopoly measures have allowed them to choose different platforms to do digital marketing rather than only one. In the past, these internet platform companies took advantage of their strong market position to enforce companies onto one platform for marketing. On the other hand, the Chinese government's supervision of algorithmic recommendation services imposes restrictions on companies in the digital marketing process. Precision marketing and personalized marketing will have to face certain challenges.

In addition, just like global companies, Chinese companies face more challenges in their use of user data in the digital marketing process. As a landmark event, Chinese companies also face increasingly stringent regulations on user data privacy and user data security.

Conclusion

In the last few decades, the rapid rise of the internet and information technologies has rapidly changed the Chinese business environment, making it one of the most powerful in the world. China's digital marketing model and digital governance emerged differently from that of other nations based on government supported resource endowment strategy and the totality of digitalization in the country.

Chinese enterprises' organizations, management, and businesses are in a process of digitization. They are accelerating their internal digital transformation, and the growth of such digitalization is irreversible. This trend will profoundly change the ecological structure of China's internet and further strengthen the relationship between digital users and enterprises. As a result, the overall level of China's marketing industry will continue to evolve. At the same time, Chinese companies need a broader vision and technology application empowerment. Through the promotion of the digital marketing industry, the overall digital management of the company will develop in a higher level and more comprehensive direction.

Key Discussion Areas

- An overview of digital development in China.
- Influential factors for Chinese consumers.
- Identifying the digital marketing scenario in China.

Notes

1 www.insiderintelligence.com/content/china-digital-ad-spending-update-q2-2020#page-report.
2 The Economist, "FinTech Report 2021—Digital Payments," May 3, 2021, https://baijiahao.baidu.com/s?id=1698716995315924935&wfr=spider&for=pc.

References

Arthur, W. B. 2014. *Complexity and the Economy*. New York: Oxford University Press.

Baijiahao.Baidu.com. 2020. "Analysis of the Market Status and Development Prospects of China's Digital Marketing Industry in 2020 Digital Marketing Has Become the Mainstream Marketing Method." December 8, 2020, https://baijiahao.baidu.com/s?id=1685480958230462855&wfr=spider&for=pc.

Balloch, Caleb et al. 2020. *China Consumer Insight Quarterly*. McKinsey, www.mckinsey.com.cn/wp-content/uploads/2020/11/%E6%B6%88%E8%B4%B9%E8%80%85%E5%AD%A3%E5%88%8A-2020_%E4%B8%AD%E6%96%871126_s.pdf.

CFLP: China Federation of Logistics and Purchasing. "Logistics Operation Data for 2020." *Baijiahao.Baidu.com*, February 23, 2021, https://baijiahao.baidu.com/s?id=1692449218825796284&wfr=spider&for=pc.

CGAP. 2019. "China: A Digital Payments Revolution." September 25, 2019, www.cgap.org/research/publication/china-digital-payments-revolution.

China Internet Development Statistics Report, http://www.cac.gov.cn/files/pdf/cnnic/CNNIC41.pdf?eqid=e4e39b8a0017a43a0000000664396ab2&eqid=f5beb16500003fb600000003645b3d56&eqid=852ee0d80001848f00000003649010f8.

China Internet Network Information Center. 2021. "Statistical Report on China's Internet Development Status," http://www.cac.gov.cn/files/pdf/cnnic/CNNIC41.pdf?eqid=e4e39b8a0017a43a0000000664396ab2&eqid=f5beb16500003fb600000003645b3d56&eqid=852ee0d80001848f00000003649010f8; www.cnnic.net.cn/hlwfzyj/hlwxzbg/hlwtjbg/202109/P020210915523670981527.pdf.

Cramer-Flood, E. 2020. "China Digital Ad Spending Update Q2 2020." *Insider Intelligence*, June 29, 2020, www.emarketer.com/content/china-digital-ad-spending-update-q2-2020#page-report.

Davis, F. D. 1989. "Perceived Usefulness, Perceived Ease of Use, and User Acceptance of Information Technology. *MIS Quarterly* 13(3): 319–40, https://doi.org/10.2307/249008.

The Economist. 2021. "FinTech Report 2021 –Digital Payments." May 3, 2021, https://baijiahao.baidu.com/s?id=1698716995315924935&wfr=spider&for=pc.

European Center for Digital Competitiveness. 2021. "Statistical Report on Internet Development in China," https://digital-competitiveness.eu/digitalriser/.

Godin, S. 1999. *Permission Marketing: Turning Strangers into Friends and Friends into Customers*. New York: Simon and Schuster.
Hong, Z. 2021. *Propriety Economics*. Hong Kong: City University of Hong Kong.
Internet Information Office of the People's Republic of China. 2021. "Provisions of the Cyberspace Administration of China on the Administration of Algorithmic Recommendations for Internet Information Services (Draft for Solicitation of Comments)." August 27, 2021, www.cac.gov.cn/2021-08/27/c_1631652502874117.htm.
Internet Society of China. 2021. "China Internet Development Report 2021." July 25, 2021, www.199it.com/archives/1277142.html.
Late Post. 2021. "Douyin E-Commerce Company's Annual GMV Exceeds 500 Billion Yuan in 2020, More Than Three Times the Same as in 2019." February 4, 2021, www.chinaz.com/news/1222461.shtml.
Matosas-López, L. 2021. "The Management of Digital Marketing Strategies in Social Network Services: A Comparison Between American and European Organizations." *Journal of Open Innovation: Technology, Market, And Complexity* 7(1): 65.
Ministry of Industry and Information Technology of China. 2021. "Operation of Internet and Related Service Industries in the First Half of 2021." July 29, 2021, www.miit.gov.cn/gxsj/tjfx/hlw/art/2021/art_d4f14614cf174ac89f50f253900c450f.html.
Ministry of Transport of the People's Republic of China. 2020. "China Live Broadcast E-Commerce Industry Research Report." *iResearch*, www.mot.gov.cn/jiaotonggaikuang/ (accessed September 10, 2021).
National Development and Reform Commission. 2022, https://www.ndrc.gov.cn/fggz/fzzlgh/gjjzxgh/202203/t20220325_1320208.html?eqid=aeea6b0c0006f25f00000003646daf76.
Paper. 2021. "China UnionPay Releases 2020 Mobile Payment Security Survey Report." February 2, 2021, https://m.thepaper.cn/baijiahao_11030087.
Schultz, D. E., S. I. Tannenbaum, and F. L. Robert. 1992. *Integrated Marketing Communications: Putting It Together & Marketing It Work*. Chicago: NTC Business Books.
Statistical Bulletin of China's Civil Affairs Development. "Ministry of Civil Affairs of the People's Republic of China." 2020, http://images3.mca.gov.cn/www2017/file/202109/1631265147970.pdf.
Sterling, G. 2021. "Almost 70% of Digital Ad Spending Going to Google, Facebook, Amazon, Says Analyst Firm." *Martech*, June 17, 2019, https://martech.org/almost-70-of-digital-ad-spending-going-to-google-facebook-amazon-says-analyst-firm/.
Woodside, A. G., E. J. Wilson, and P. Milner. 1992. "Buying and Marketing CPA Services." *Industrial Marketing Management* 21(3): 265–72.

PART 3

Education Governance Reform

When online learning became a necessity during the Covid-19 pandemic, one would have thought that there would be a widespread yearning to return to face-to-face education—yet a study included in this part has found that the overwhelming majority wanted prerecorded lectures and online learning to continue in some form even after returning to normalcy. Over three years into the pandemic, educators and administrators are still trying to figure out the right balance between online and on-the-ground learning. To strike that balance, new frameworks for education governance are required, especially as we explore hybrid existence, work environments, and learning ecosystems.

The chapter by Diana Laurillard focuses on how digital innovations enhance teaching and learning and further the UN Sustainable Development Goals (SDGs). The author proposes using her previously developed Conversational Framework, whereby teachers and learners enhance each other's concepts and practices through teaching and learning—allowing greater flexibility in organizing classes, broadening the reach of educators, increasing inclusivity, and enhancing teaching productivity. In addition, educational bodies are encouraged to provide professional training to teachers to better leverage digital tools. The author calls for creating large-scale communities of teachers and learners working together to create an "ecology of knowledge." A particular emphasis is on creating professional development programs for people in developing countries.

Indian companies are the global leaders in education technology, offering models for education governance reform. The chapter by Ronnie Screwvala, Mayank Kumar, and Phalgun Kompalli focuses on the experiences of one of the most important EdTech players in India—upGrad. Unlike some other players in this domain, upGrad focuses primarily on working professionals. The company's strategy is geared toward providing lifelong learning across the entire value chain, offering degrees, study abroad programs, job-linked programs, Executive Masters, and Doctoral Programs through partnerships with leading universities. The sector is of immense importance to countries worldwide, especially developing countries, including India and China, attempting to dramatically increase gross enrollment ratios. The authors point out that e-learning improves employee productivity, boosts engagement, increases knowledge retention rates, and requires less employee time to

DOI: 10.4324/9781003316077-15

learn and conduct assigned tasks and work. They conclude stating "the way forward will be a skills economy, not an information economy."

The chapter by Joshua A. Muskin argues that "the systematic modernization of education is rife with risks, built-in shortcomings, and existential contradictions." As a result, the goal of educators and university administrators should be to "cultivate and capitalize on the creativity and initiative of teachers to yield consistently high and equitable quality." Identifying that education governance across the world has fallen short, Muskin stresses that governance should strive for "heterogeneity not homogeneity." He argues that teachers should metaphorically teach on roads and not on rails. On rails, the destination and the pace are predetermined. On roads, there is much more freedom to choose one's way and pace. Muskin argues that their role of governance at the top should be to define what "quality looks like across the many domains for each teacher school and community."

In their chapter, Shailendra Raj Mehta, Preeti Shroff-Mehta, and Ashutosh Dutt describe a new pedagogical model developed by MICA—The School of Ideas in the summer of 2020 based on flexible online learning—the 30/45 + 36/6 MICA Model. Earlier, in its postgraduate diploma (MBA) program, MICA had a class size of sixty students and a class time of seventy-five minutes. Continuing with this model online created numerous problems—digital fatigue, lack of control, and the inability of the instructor to see the entire class at once. After two months of experimentation, the new model emerged: every faculty member summarized the class's key concepts in a prerecorded thirty-minute video sent to every student. The class time was reduced to forty-five minutes, and the number of students to thirty-six. Class time was spent answering questions and solving problems. Since the repetitive part of the class—covering the theories and concepts—was recorded ahead of time, the faculty task became much more dynamic and refreshing, since they could go deeper into the material than in the traditional learning model. Even though the number of sections and sessions increased, the total time commitment of the faculty in terms of in-class teaching remained the same. Data about the new system's effectiveness was collected from the faculty and the students, who preferred the new approach to the old.

Beheruz N. Sethna, the president of a major public university in the United States, shares the lessons learned from his distinguished academic career in his chapter. His advice was "hire 'wonderful people,' then on good days, get out of their way and let them do what they do best, and on very good days, actually help them do what they do best." His primary recommendation is that universities should follow the Hippocratic oath—"first, do no harm"—by protecting its essence and character, autonomy and academic freedom, and respect for staff and students, and preserving a culture of trust and respect.

In "Political Culture and Educational Governance: Covid-19 and the Limits of Decentralization in Israeli Education," Gad Yair looks at Covid's impact on different segments of the Israeli higher-education sector. The author points out that, historically, the Israeli education system was highly centralized, since it closely reflected the policy of "nation building after independence." Starting in the 1980s and 1990s, decentralization gained momentum, and the responsibility for the "nuts and bolts" of education was devolved to local authorities. As a result of such autonomy, two groups—the Israeli Palestinian and the ultra-Orthodox communities—deemphasized the teaching of subjects such as English, mathematics, history, and citizenship and thus did not adequately prepare the students for the modern world. Covid-19 exacerbated these divisions, as the new education Minister gave school principals at the local level control over when to open and shut down schools.

Yair laments the failure of both—centralization and decentralization, writing that "while Israel is a formal democracy, it has yet to inculcate a democratic habitus amongst its citizenship." In this sense, the pandemic exposed the deep fissures in Israeli society, which are bound to make their presence felt in other domains.

Ellen Hazelkorn and Andrew Gibson in their chapter examine the international organizations, networks, and associations (IONAs) that govern global higher education, research, and development (HERD). They point out that global collaboration—global research platforms that result in programs such as the Human Genome Project or the development of Covid-19 vaccines—"doesn't just happen." It needs cooperation and governance across IONAs. This governance can take both hard and soft forms. University alliances across borders are also critical. Two approaches have been developed to understand the global governance of higher education: the functional institutional approach and the conflict theory approach. The authors lay out the differences between these two approaches and discuss significant trends that have brought global higher education institutions together, culminating in comparability that has led to the development of global rankings. The authors conclude by saying that everyone, including "individuals, disciplines, institutions, and communities," has a major role to play and that we need to "broaden our conceptual frameworks" to analyze this fascinating domain.

These unique chapter's contributions seek to highlight/examine various educational governance frameworks and problems. They highlight that collaboration is not just about between international organizations, global networks, and different institutions, but it's also between teachers and leaners, or teachers and administrators, or across different disciplines and borders; also, that teaching is a "design science" (requires creativity in addition to more traditional ideas of reasoning/education), and this informs the development of new teaching models. Also, how online learning can expand who has access to education and how technology can be used to reduce education inequalities; and finally, by exploring centralization/decentralization, the authors explore how education reform combat hierarchical notions of prestige and authority.

12

THE ROLE OF GOVERNANCE IN OPENING UP DIGITAL INNOVATION IN TEACHING AND LEARNING

Diana Laurillard

Introduction

The Covid-19 pandemic has awoken leaders' interest in what digital transformation can do for every aspect of university governance. Teaching will not escape scrutiny. The future potential of international collaborations, digital transformations, multi-stakeholder access, citizen inclusion, societal equity, and global sustainability explored across a range of professional contexts in this book is equally relevant to the academic community, which has well-established international collaborations for scientific research and student mobility. Universities have had to carry out major digital transformations over the last few years and must now address their ambitious vision and mission statements, of opening up to being more inclusive, improving equity and equality, and contributing to global sustainability. University governance in the form of councils and governing boards provides the best chance of multistakeholder access to higher education (HE) decision-making, but is that sufficient for universities to be appropriately adaptive to such a rapidly changing world?

University leadership should celebrate the resilience and dedication of its academic staff in rising to the challenge and managing to serve their students as well as they have in the past few years. One UK study showed that over 80 percent of students wanted the university to retain the main elements of online learning: recorded lectures and online tests, materials, tutorials, seminars, and discussion forums. However, only 55 percent felt that the mix of in-person and online teaching had been of sufficiently good quality (McVitty, Jackson, and Hutchens 2021).

Fully online sessions were not good enough: students wanted not only to return to campus sessions but also to retain the flexibility of digital learning methods. The expectation of more of both kinds of teaching now creates a considerable challenge for a university's ongoing education strategy. Who can provide this kind of leadership? The academics who learned so much? But there was not enough time for them to be fully effective. Or the leaders and managers? But they had no such learning opportunity to discover the joys and challenges of online teaching.

DOI: 10.4324/9781003316077-16

Blended and online teaching and learning are terms used with great facility now but with little understanding. Online methods combine communication technologies with digital tools and resources that can be both synchronous and asynchronous between individuals, groups, and classes of both teachers and students. The combinatorial mix of possibilities is enormous. The conventional methods of campus and home-based learning through materials, labs and studios, and print resources, for individuals, groups, and classes of both teachers and students, are already a rich mix. Blended learning combines all of these with online and digital methods. It took many centuries to improve but it failed to perfect conventional teaching methods. Suddenly, teachers were asked to master the blend within weeks.

What does this mean for university governance? To what extent do our current models of governance work for this radically new global environment for HE? This chapter uses recent research findings to propose how university governance might adapt to running an institution that must work through these transformational changes.

A different relationship is required between the academic teaching community and university governance—one that will enable and not constrain the innovation needed.

First, the academic community must consider why it would benefit the university and its students to extend the proportion of blended and online learning a university offers. For its students, there are considerable benefits in the greater flexibility such learning would give them, but that is worthless if online methods are not done well enough to improve their learning experience and outcomes. Next, we must consider the dependencies for the intended outcomes, and what this would mean for the responsibilities that university managers and governance must take to ensure a successful change of strategy.

For the university, a planned embrace of online learning as a strategic direction opens up a range of intriguing ways to fulfill the ambitious missions and values we proclaim. To take just two aims, from top UK universities:

> [W]orld-class research and education . . . which benefit society on a local, regional, national and global scale . . . committed to equality of opportunity, to engendering inclusivity.
>
> *(University of Oxford vision)*

> [E]ngaged with the wider world and committed to changing it for the better . . . for the long-term benefit of humanity.
>
> *(University College London [UCL] mission)*

A new focus on digital learning could help the academic community achieve the UN Sustainable Development Goals (SDGs), a collection of global ambitions for changing the world for the better. Universities already contribute to the SDGs, primarily through research and to a lesser extent through curriculum decisions, as they educate the future professional workforce and citizens of everywhere. The global challenges faced by the SDGs are a worthwhile focus for research projects, clearly framing the work toward "the global public good" in teaching (Marginson 2011) and more actively fulfilling those ambitious mission and value statements.

Possible Futures for Blended and Online Learning

Universities had already been equipped with the necessary communication technologies to face the switch to online teaching forced by the pandemic, but academics did not have the foundational preparation that would have been necessary for the proper implementation of such tools in effective teaching methods.

Many teachers across the further and higher education sector made incredible efforts to improve their online teaching practice or use the flexibility of digital methods to help their students through the rigors of lockdown. Some institutions were already on this path and adapted readily to the new demands of lockdown, but many teachers had to rely on the deep knowledge of their small central educational technology units, their librarians' tech-savvy agility, or the colleagues who had always been digital champions (Smith and Traxler 2022). Within this wholly inadequate environment for pedagogic innovation, however, a large enough proportion of the academic community quickly learned how to make use of a limited range of digital tools and resources, to the extent that most students now want more blended learning, not less. They just want them to be of better quality (McVitty, Jackson, and Hutchens 2021).

How Blended and Online Learning Can Benefit Students

Any study of learning through technology must begin with an understanding of what counts as high-quality learning, and what it takes to learn. To answer this question, I developed the Conversational Framework, which aims to preempt the power of technologies to lead innovation, rather than serve the pedagogical analysis of what students need (Laurillard 2002).

What It Takes to Learn and Teach

The research studies on which the Conversational Framework is based have been carried out with students at all levels, so the framework applies to any sector and any subject and is applicable to face-to-face, online, and blended learning.

The framework expresses a simple distillation of the main theories of teaching and learning and represents the teaching-learning process as a series of exchanges between a learner and a teacher and the learning environment and between a learner and their peers, at the two levels of concepts and practices, all acting on the internal developing relationship between the learner's own concepts and practices, as shown in Figure 12.1. The exchanges are two way, indicating that as much as learners are influenced by teacher concepts, teachers are also influenced by learners' articulations of their own concepts and may change the way they present ideas as a result. Each learner's concepts and practices are also influenced by social interaction with their peers, with the learning environment itself (conventional or digital), and with the practice outputs of their peers, as in collaborative projects or peer review, for example.

The framework differentiates between teachers and learners by giving teachers the responsibility to design the learning environment itself. This privileges the development of the concepts they have instantiated in the reading list, or the digital simulation, but the learner may be encouraged to investigate alternative teacher concepts from other authorities or use their informal experience as an alternative learning environment. To develop their concepts and practices, a continual exchange enables them to reflect on and adapt both concepts and practices within the learner's internal conversation (Laurillard 2008, 2012). The repeated cycles of cognitive activity motivate the development and redevelopment of the learner's concepts and practices and the relationships between the two.

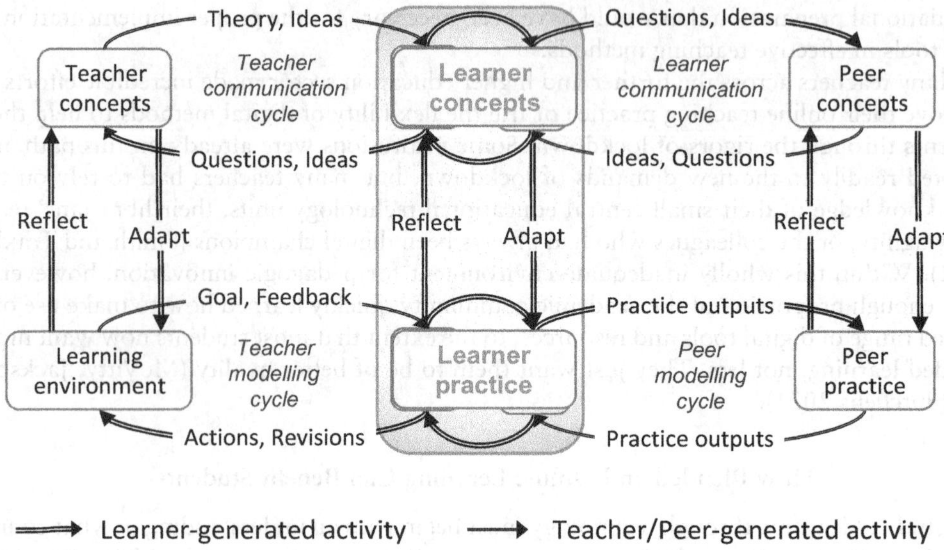

Figure 12.1 The Conversational Framework, Showing the Cognitive Interactions Between the Teacher and the Learner, and Between the Learner and Their Peers, at the Levels of Concept and Practice

Source: Author.

The teacher's concepts and practices are also privileged within the education system, of course, because they define the curriculum and set and grade the formal assessments. It is therefore the teacher's responsibility to design these exchanges as teaching-learning activities that are aligned with the intended learning outcomes and the assessment of them. Teaching is a highly complex design process—neither simply an art nor narrowly a science. Education enables the learner to achieve their potential for concepts and practices of which they have no deep understanding at the beginning. Teaching can therefore be conceptualized as a design science, akin to engineering or architecture, which builds on the empirical work of the learning sciences and employs the creative arts of the performer and guide, but which must also learn from interacting with the learning it generates to improve its own outcomes (Laurillard 2012). The essence of a design science is the continual iterative process: in this case, the learner generates new ideas and behaviors in response to inputs from teachers and peers, then modulates them as they study further. Similarly, the teacher generates concepts and a practice learning environment but also modulates their teaching in response to what students say and do. Both types of actors have a responsibility to adapt in light of the experience. This feature of adaptive learning in the Conversational Framework is essential if we are to discover how best to deploy digital methods in teaching and learning.

The representation of the teaching and learning process as continual exchanges of concepts and practices describes what it takes to learn, and therefore what it takes to teach. It instantiates the responsibilities of the teacher alongside the actions needed from the students. Simon Marginson argues, "Self-formation is a condition of higher education, its central process, and its most important outcome" (Marginson 2023). It is the responsibility of the teaching community to provide the opportunities and resources to help students develop in this way. Self-formation, like self-regulation or student agency (Biesta and Tedder 2007), does not absolve teachers of the responsibility for creating the environment and the cognitive and social transactions in which their students' personal development can flourish. The value of the framework comes in using it to test the pedagogic value of the new digital methods being developed against their intended outcomes, in any educational context.

University and college managers and governance bodies have never tried to dictate pedagogic methods to academics and will not want to engage in the details of them, but it is important that they have a general sense of what difference digital methods can make. One early cross-sector government strategy in the United Kingdom proposed four principal ways in which digital methods could have a differential effect (Department for Education and Skills 2005):

- Supported learning: transforming the activities and exchanges in the teaching-learning process (in both campus and online contexts).
- Flexible reach: opening up an accessible collaborative system (choice about where, when, and how to study for students unable to study on campus).
- Inclusive provision: connecting with all types of student groups (cognitive, behavioral, social, and cultural).
- Teaching productivity: improving efficiency and effectiveness (in terms of outcomes achieved for teacher and learner time).

These four features capture the main ways in which digital methods can improve the experience and outcomes of learning.

Supported Learning

Supported learning focuses on the interactive nature of digital methods. The computer is primarily a sit-forward medium, unlike the book or television which are sit-back media (Livingstone, Bober, and Helsper 2005). With reading and watching, we do not expect to interact but to follow the narrative offered. With digital devices, on the other hand, we do expect to interact, to respond to requests, or to command a response. This is what makes them so valuable for supported learning—independent learning beyond the class—usually asynchronous and online, where the learner is not necessarily in the company of the teacher. Instead, the teacher has planned a learning design for an intended student learning outcome—a sequence of teaching-learning activities, where each activity is aligned with one of the learning types in the Conversational Framework; has an intended duration of some minutes; is studied as an individual, group, or class, with or without the teacher; and is online or not, using a digital environment, tool, or resource (Laurillard et al. 2013). A brief illustrative example of the difference between a conventional campus-based and a wholly online session clarifies the value of such an approach.

A learning design for a campus-based session, say for a week of study on a course with an expected total of ten hours study by the learner, might include

> [t]wo one-hour lectures, a one-hour tutorial in a group of five, three hours of reading, and four hours to produce a short essay according to a rubric.

The numbers are important. This offers a total of two hours watching, one hour of teacher discussion in a small group and seven hours of "self-regulated" learning with brief guidance.

In some countries, universities usually have a small central teaching support unit responsible for supporting academics using digital methods for teaching; in the pandemic, they were called upon to develop emergency online resources and guidance to help the academics struggling to catch up with what online methods could do. The quality of this kind of support was highly variable across universities. Having little prior experience of online learning, and having to switch urgently to its unfamiliar context, individual academics were inevitably making a lot of mistakes, and learning through discovery—for example, forty-five-minute online lectures were not an effective method. Any central EdTech unit would advise on this, but these resources were far too few to meet the need. Ideally, they would have recommended something different.

Using the Conversational Framework, a wholly online version of the above campus session might become:

> One hour as five ten-minute videos watched at home, each with a two-minute quiz, a thirty-minute class discussion online, a thirty-minute online small group tutorial, a thirty-minute exercise to analyse a practical video, three hours of reading, a thirty-minute exercise to find information on a website, two hours to produce a rough draft of the essay using the rubric, thirty minutes asynchronously online to peer review in pairs and improve their draft, and one and a half hours to produce the final version of the essay.

This design guides students through ten hours of a broader mix of watching, practicing, discussing, analyzing, reading, investigating, practicing, and producing—that is, more supported active learning.

There is arguably less value to the student in the online version, because they have only a thirty-minute class discussion with the teacher and a thirty-minute peer review, instead of one hour with a tutor in a small group. However, there is clearly improved value in the online version, because they are supported through the hours they are not with the teacher, instead of relying so much on their assumed ability in self-regulated learning. This version is a rich mix of study methods, more active on their part, as represented in the Conversational Framework, helping to build their sense of agency, and with greater potential to engage them in deep critical thinking (Biesta and Tedder 2007). That is the significant contribution digital methods can make to the quality of student learning.

Flexible Reach

Global HE has a responsibility to make tertiary education accessible to a much-wider range of student groups that is currently feasible, given the mainly location-based provision and the per-student cost of tuition. For the hard-to-reach groups who cannot attend or afford to be on campus (part-time students, people who are not mobile, adults with caring responsibilities, refugees and displaced persons, women prevented from studying, students in low-income countries), poor access cuts off their chance of higher education, no matter how well qualified they are.

Online access to courses and programs can overcome the limits of campus attendance in three ways, by offering

- mainly online courses with occasional attendance requirements to help those with limited ability to attend campus;
- wholly online courses and programs, opening up access for all students who cannot be on campus;
- dual mode programs, in which one year (or semester) requires attendance and other years can be wholly online, making study in an expensive distant location more affordable for many.

Universities have the technology to manage programs of all three kinds as part of their mainstream provision, but the academic learning design and administrative support and logistics involved would require a major shift in skills and workloads for the majority of staff.

Teachers in all sectors have been experimenting with digital methods since the early 2000s, as their personal digital literacy has improved, and they have become aware of what their institution's virtual learning environment can offer. Ministries of Education began to develop new e-learning strategies, although the main effect was to fund the IT industry to develop technological infrastructure and digital resources. These are undoubtedly the *sine qua non* for digital methods, but without the professional development of the teachers, which have nowhere near the same funding nor the time allowance teachers need (Almekhlafi and Al Meqdadi 2010; Kopcha 2012), new kinds of pedagogy and therefore innovative programs of study cannot develop.

Most universities have not prepared for any radical adoption of digital methods, neither for their own professional development nor for the management systems needed (Johnson et al. 2019). This of course affects the feasibility of any rapid move toward more online learning.

Inclusive Provision

Inclusive education promises access to students of all ages and backgrounds, focusing especially on countering the divisiveness of gender, race, and social and cultural differences.[1] Digital methods are some of the strategic tools for greater equality, diversity, and inclusion, and tend not to have the effect of guiding policies and actions except in using accessible and anonymous provision of information, advice, and guidance to students and staff. They allow flexible reach for disadvantaged groups, but they do not change whether the curriculum is designed to include them.

Digital capabilities have a critical impact, however, on ensuring that students are supported with assistive technology tools and resources for physical and cognitive disabilities, such as visual, hearing, or physical disabilities, and learning disabilities such as dyslexia and dyscalculia. A recent systematic study showed that a good assistive technology policy transforms students' ability to engage academically and to study more efficiently (McNicholl et al. 2019). It also makes the significant point that advances in technology are bringing assistive technology features into mainstream devices such as iPads, opening up the potential for full integration of these technologies to enable more diverse social interactions for all students.

Education leaders, therefore, must maintain a policy for inclusion that adapts to technology advances and provides professional development for all staff in the skills and responsibilities they need to fulfill the promise of accessibility for all.

Teaching Productivity

The above three features of digital technologies all carry implications of increased teacher workload: to improve the quality and outcomes of student learning, to increase access to HE for hard-to-reach groups, and to achieve accessibility for students with disabilities. These are not just nice-to-have emergent properties of the general increase in digital methods. They are ways of fulfilling the stated missions and ambitions of tertiary education that can release the learning potential of millions of young adults who are currently unable to achieve their ambitions. But how feasible is the significant increase in workload?

A 2007 review of the approaches to estimating the costs of new technology methods showed that there is no consistency in valuing new technology methods across institutions in terms of costs measured and no consistency in the parameters to be used for comparing the costs of new technology with the costs of traditional methods within an institution (Laurillard 2007), and that did not change in ten years (Kenny and Fluck 2017). The view persists that digital methods will be cheaper due to economies of scale (the fall in unit costs as numbers of students increase) when the initial fixed costs are recovered. However, in practice, technologies and design styles are changing over time, so the initial investment has to be continually updated and cannot necessarily be amortized over many course reruns to achieve the imagined economies of scale (Munro 2018).

An alternative way to achieve economies of scale is to increase student numbers on wholly online courses where the physical estate imposes no limitations. However, doing so creates further analytical complexities, because a large part of the teaching on any tertiary course is the per-student variable cost of teaching (small groups, one-on-one consultations, and assessment of individual work) on the academic side and the per-student variable costs on the administration side where they are not automated.

Modeling the teaching costs and learning benefits of moving to online is therefore an essential undertaking if an institution is to make this a mainstream activity (Kasch, van Rosmalem, and Kalz 2017; Kennedy et al. 2015) and not one that is small enough in impact to be brushed under the carpet of expediency. Many academic departments wishing to innovate choose to run online courses and programs independent of an institutional strategy and thus bear the costs of scaling up on their own—that is, academics work overtime to create and run the course. Without good recruitment campaigns, this strategy will often result in the scale being insufficient to provide any economies.

Economies of scope (sharing resources) are always feasible in the provision of institutional IT systems, for example (Morris 2008), but they can also be achieved for digital teaching resources, because they can be shared and adapted much more easily than conventional resources. They could be publicly available free and open educational resources such as videos, tests, software, and digital tools, or techniques that support access to knowledge and can be embedded within or adapted to local teaching contexts (Organisation for Economic Co-operation and Development 2016; Van Damme and Van der Wende 2018). One such example is the UCL *Learning Designer* tool enabling teachers to articulate and share their learning designs, which work as a kind of starter kit for rethinking the way to teach to a particular type of learning outcome.[2] Academics will not typically adopt someone else's teaching resource, but they will consider adapting one, and digital resources usually make that possible, thereby helping to create economies of scope (Laurillard et al. 2018; Morris 2008).

For an institution to move toward online courses and programs as a mainstream offering, therefore, the underlying teaching costs and learning benefits must be understood for the different combinations of teaching resources, and learning and assessment activities, for different cohort sizes. In the online version above, for example, the teacher has only one half-an-hour class but does not have to find tutors for the small groups. On the other hand, they need more preparation time to record the video lecture sections and quizzes than for the lectures, as well as to find the practical video, find the website they want to recommend, and set up the peer-review process. Existing teaching workload estimates will not represent these details and will not be adapted to modeling the relative return on smaller or larger cohorts.

Some combinations of digital methods have the potential to return good value in terms of both student achievement and the economies of scale that generate enough income to balance the true cost. Without careful modeling and planning by both academics and administrators, the risk is high that both parts will fail.

How Governance Can Balance the Learning Benefits and Teaching Costs of Blended and Online Learning

Educational leadership had not prepared well to exploit the potential of digital methods already available for the benefit of all students, and in the context of the pandemic, emergency had to rely on exceptional commitment and resilience by academic teachers to respond adequately. The two main failings are (1) to organize sufficient professional development in digital methods for both teaching and administrative staff and (2) to scrutinize, understand, and reform the business modeling used for the teaching costs and learning benefits of our academic programs of study. Without these moves in place, the response was ad hoc and inefficient, and it was unable to achieve what students really needed. Governing bodies might therefore now take more responsibility for ensuring two priority policy developments. The first is addressed to the governing body of the institution.

1. *Institutional governance bodies to negotiate and ensure teacher professional development to engage their teaching staff across all disciplines in effective innovation in digital pedagogy.*

Teacher time in all sectors is highly pressured with demands for specific student outcomes and the ever-increasing bureaucratic load to provide evidence of quality and achievements, which squeezes the teaching-learning time to a minimum. Too little space exists for personal development of any kind, and until more recently, digital methods were rarely a priority (Almekhlafi and Al Meqdadi 2010).

What is worse: the move to respond to the need for more blended and online provision is impacting the academic teaching community at a time when it needs to be in the process of reconceptualizing itself. The deployment of academic teaching time rests entirely on the academic staff, which results inevitably in a significantly increased workload of more than fifty hours per week despite the current reliance on teaching assistants, and despite the comforting teaching resource tariffs produced by administrators as expected time allocations for teaching activities. Only 10 percent of academics in an Australian study agreed that 37.5 hours per week was sufficient to perform their academic work (Kenny and Fluck 2017). In the context of these long working hours, teacher professional development (TPD) in digital methods will still not take priority for academics unless it is made a priority by education leaders and management.

The focus, however, must be on assuring effective pedagogy and student outcomes, not merely on the process of TPD or the reward of professional recognition, which is seen as having limited value by most academics. Without the follow-through to understanding the value for students, these measures become just another proxy for quality required by bureaucratic evidence-gathering. Instead, if participation is voluntary, with time allowed, and part of an authentic institutional vision for how to achieve high-quality learning experiences for students, then participants value the process and continue to participate in development as part of their teaching commitment (Spowart et al. 2019).

The key points are to

- provide flexible support to individuals and course teams through central educational technology teams;
- plan to expand the capacity of Educational Technology teams as they are invariably small and over-stretched;
- negotiate with the academic community the vision for a commitment to the value of blended learning and to the time needed for teaching professional development in the context of the move to mainstreaming online learning.

The second policy priority is addressed more to the leaders and managers.

2. *Institutional leaders and managers to learn from academics and departmental planners building a better understanding of how teaching costs and learning benefits balance in different ways when deploying both conventional and online methods.*

For teachers addressing the shortcomings of blended learning means a radical shift forward in the distribution of their teaching workload. For face-to-face methods when the teacher is present and can adjust their teaching to student responses, a forty-five-minute lecture is thought to be reasonable, but it does not transfer easily to the student learning independently at home.

Asynchronous online forms of learning require significantly more preparation than simply recording the lecture. The student trying to learn in their home study environment will need frequent breaks, preferably to test their understanding of the points being made or the correct interpretation of new concepts, graphs, tables, or diagrams. The lecturer will prepare, for example, quizzes, scheduled small group discussions, and interactive exercises interspersed with their presentations and explanations, and it will provide digital tools to help students' engagement and understanding. Creating these opportunities takes more time than conventional methods, not just because they are relatively unfamiliar but also because, with asynchronous online methods now available, academics are often doing more to support self-regulated study time, which is a significant and important benefit to the students.

The standard approach to costing teaching is a top-down model that divides the available budget for teaching among the programs and courses to be taught, to arrive at standard tariffs for preparing and supporting a small selection of the main teaching activities of module/unit planning, lectures, tutorials, labs, student consultations, and student assessments. Such estimating, however, does not differentiate between conventional and online methods. A recent cross-university study in Australia sought to analyze teachers' own estimates of time needed to prepare for these activities, the durations of classes being assumed as fixed (Kenny and Fluck 2017). In general, across all universities and subjects, participants estimated that online methods took between 5 percent and 25 percent more time than the campus version. However, the analysis of how to cost academic time to prepare and support the different types of teaching and learning activities, for both campus and online learning, is complex and still poorly understood (Kenny and Fluck 2017). The study supports the idea that this type of time-based approach is optimal, as long as it identifies the appropriate range of teaching activities. Although there are considerable differences in estimates across individuals according to their experience and subject area, the median values derived are thought to serve as a reasonable standard.

However, while being an important advance on the even narrower definitions found in current university workload estimates, there are several problems with this method:

- The range of activities surveyed is based primarily on the conventional types of teaching activity and is too narrow to account for new digital pedagogies such as asynchronous group work (Koszalka, Pavlov, and Wu 2021), or videos enriched with interactive activities, using in-video quizzes, web content, and video aggregation (Kleftodimos, Lappas, and Evangelidis 2020).
- Standardizing tariffs for preparing teaching-learning activities assumes that the tariffs are static over time, whereas the combinatorial possibilities enabled by blended learning defy any attempt at standardization.
- The group size for each activity is assumed to be either one for student consultation and feedback or the whole class, whereas the number and size of small groups can greatly affect the teacher support time needed.

University managers have traditionally avoided any realistic approach to the analysis of teaching workload (Bates 2001). Over the last two decades, the prevailing assumptions about workload continued, as more digital methods were gradually adopted, so the true costs of teaching were never brought to light. For this reason, IOE, UCL's Faculty of Education and Society, developed a new type of modeling tool to help with understanding the reality of how teaching time is used: the Course Resource Appraisal Modeller (Kennedy et al. 2015).

The modeler puts the planning and estimation of teacher time directly into the hands of the academic, who states the parameters for their module/unit over three runs in terms of cohort size, fee income for teaching, total study hours, and teaching cost per hour. They then define each type of teaching-learning activity used, and for each one decide its total student study time, the teacher hours needed to prepare and support it, and its learning benefits in terms of type of learning (e.g., reading, practical, assessed output), teacher presence or not, online or not, group size (1 or N or whole class), and type of feedback from peer, computer, or teacher. In this way, the individual teacher can model their own ways of organizing and designing the learning activities for their students. The program provides them with feedback on the main learning benefits they have designed against the total teacher hours. They can also compare the fee income for the teaching against its cost

(Kennedy et al. 2015; Laurillard 2007). These parameters meet all the measures proposed from research (Kenny and Fluck 2017) and counter the problems noted above by enabling flexible estimates of standard and innovative activities, and the analysis of the effects of group size. The course team can then scrutinize the relationship between teaching hours and the benefits to students for a range of different cohort sizes. It helps with balancing the fixed development costs and variable student costs against the fee income for teaching, to be sure that it is realistic if numbers are increasing or is affordable if numbers are reducing.

For institutional use, such a tool could support the gradual development of viable designs at module level or course level for other courses to follow or adapt, and so help to develop a reasonable range for standard estimates, but *derived from teacher practice* within the institution, not by fiat.

With the sudden forced acceleration of experimenting with online learning due to the pandemic crisis, the academic teaching community has learned a lot about blended learning design and the attendant workload, but it has not been open to leaders and managers to have had such a learning opportunity. This means that only the teaching community in HE is likely to understand both the costs and the benefits of online learning, and the leadership must be open to listening to and learning from that experience.

Achieving the SDGs

Tertiary institutions will now be considering a strategy for developing online learning programs as part of their mainstream offer. No doubt, many will decide that it is not worth the investment and will continue simply by upgrading their capabilities for blended learning for their on-campus students.

Those universities and colleges that identify with a global perspective in their mission statements and values have learned that online learning methods are now feasible and will presumably want to contribute to the opportunities for creating a collaborative global response to the UN SDG challenges. That must surely include the mission to educate the world. SDG4 identified 260 million children out of school before the pandemic, leading to the aim of 65 million new teachers by 2030 to achieve universal basic education. Progress over the last six years toward this aim is moving very slowly, due to a range of location-specific reasons such as disabilities, conflict, climate change, gender, and difficulties with the journey to school.[3] Many of these issues can be overcome by internet access. Sadly, progress has worsened, since the pandemic left some 1.6 billion children and young people out of school. Meanwhile the progress of access to digital devices has been improving at a much faster rate, even for the developing world, which from 2010 to 2014 accounted for 82 percent of new internet users across the world. The conclusion of the 2014 UN Broadband Commission was that connected devices could be the solution for out-of-school children.[4]

A further reason for lack of progress toward universal education is the lack of teachers—25.8 million primary teachers are needed by 2030—and worse: "Only 85 percent of primary school teachers globally have been properly trained–in sub-Saharan Africa it's just 64 percent (and only 50 percent of secondary teachers)" (Reliefweb 2023).

Tertiary institutions are responsible for training teachers, both initially and in-service, so institutions could make a major contribution to SDG4 by developing the means to train teachers on a large scale to meet the huge demands for *trained* teachers, not just new teachers, as explicitly stated within the SDG4 goal to "Ensure inclusive and quality education for all and promote lifelong learning." We do have the technologies for educating on such a large scale but deploying them is problematic.

Improving Progress to Inclusive and Quality Education

Major large-scale platforms for online learning, such as Coursera, EdX, Xuetangx, and FutureLearn, offer massive open online courses (MOOCs) with the hope that they "show that open higher education has the potential of partly compensating for the inequalities in higher education provision" (Van Damme and Van der Wende 2018). However, such courses offer insufficient educational support for students at any level. The large-scale format of MOOCs cannot incur the per-student variable costs needed for personalized guidance and feedback in the education of students at any level because the standard model does not generate sufficient income. The initial training of teachers is at the postgraduate level, so it needs both online and campus-based elements. MOOCs make excellent supplements to existing institution-based courses, and this has been shown to work well for embedding such courses on blended learning within Post Graduate Certificate of Education courses, for example, but they have not yet changed the model for high-quality student education.

By contrast, these platforms are ideal for professional development, because professionals, unlike students, usually do not expect to receive personalized guidance and feedback, so it is sufficient to provide just the fixed-cost design elements of videos, quizzes, digital tool activities, peer reviews, and open discussions, which means that they can operate affordably on the large scale, having only the fixed costs of design and development.

The use of MOOC platforms, therefore, makes global reach affordable for the professional development of practicing teachers. Whether this is a desirable solution to educating the world's teachers is a separate issue. These platforms are part of an unequal world system that sources most of these technologies and courses from the United States and Europe and therefore contributes to diminishing the potential for agency across the rest of the world (Marginson and Xu 2021). In countries where the cultural and logistical issues in education can be very different from the Western viewpoint, they may prefer to determine, for example, their own curricula for professional development. Would it be feasible to counter this loss of agency by using such a platform for a more open approach to a course for professionals?

Because so much new knowledge on blended and online learning must be developed, given the rapid changes in technologies on offer and the paucity of research on digital pedagogy, the teaching community needs to collaborate on this discovery process, not just to attend a course that can offer only what we know so far. At UCL, therefore, we set out to use the course platform to organize instead a massive open online *collaboration* (CoMOOC) (Kennedy et al. 2022). In this way, we can listen to and learn from all the teachers who participate, wherever they are in the world. An initial step in this direction has been a course on Blended and Online Learning Design, which is promising, because it explicitly sets out to engage every participant "as a member of the whole teaching community, all of us working together to build new knowledge about teaching online."[5] The course is for teachers and trainers in all subjects, in all countries, and from primary to professional levels, because it is about developing pedagogies.

Methods of teaching have always been invariant across subject areas and levels of education: we all use teacher presentations, class discussions, small group teaching, one-on-one teaching, workshops, projects, marked assignments, etc. As we develop different methods for running these online, it is reasonable to share the ideas with teachers in other subjects and sectors, and this applies even more to the diverse types of digital pedagogy now possible. The idea of "signature pedagogies" foregrounds techniques associated with particular types of professional teaching, such as case dialogues for law, clinical rounds for medicine, and the design studio for engineering (Shulman 2005), suggesting that they are particular to the discipline. It is clear why these professional areas should have developed such pedagogies, and they may well be identified as the signature of a professional culture. But as Lee Shulman argues, they need to adapt over time to changing conditions, such as new technologies, and most importantly, they do not need to remain tied to a particular profession. Just as all disciplines and sectors borrowed from the first medical lectures in Bologna, teachers in any context may adapt an idea from any other sector or discipline, bringing the case dialogue method to a poetry class in primary school or the design studio method to an economics class in secondary school. It is reasonable and highly productive for the course to invite participants to share their ideas across both subjects and levels of education.

By orchestrating professional collaboration on innovation in these online platforms, universities can give academics the means to support new and effective methodologies and practices.

Opening Up To New Sources of Knowledge

In addition to its openness to teaching contexts, a course organized as a collaborative community of teachers must have several distinctive features.

- The videos include case studies of teachers using blended methods in a range of contexts and locations.
- Quizzes are designed to invite a shared understanding, but also to elicit a discussion and critique of the theory and cases presented in the videos.
- A digital design tool enables participants to articulate and share their learning designs.
- Discussions at each step invite participants to challenge the concepts and methods offered, and to share their own concerns and solutions.
- The design tool enables participants to take part in peer-review activities, swapping designs or adaptations for critical review.
- Some participants make their final version public for others to use.
- Some designs are recommended to the course team for review and publication as a "curated" design.
- Alumni are invited to join later runs as mentors, alongside the educators in the discussions, passing on their own experiences of trying out the designs they took from the previous run.

This is community knowledge development, enabling an "ecology of knowledge"—that is, "deriving from the practical contributions to the desired action" (Santos 2009) of how best to teach through digital methods. The CoMOOC works by demonstrating digital methods in current practice and documenting new ideas from participants as shareable and adaptable digital assets that take the form of learning designs—that is, the "artisanship of practices" (Santos 2009) that contributes to an ecology of knowledges, rather than an imposed and static knowledge of a particular form of course design in the transmission of knowledge. The CoMOOC process could eventually come close to emulating the process of knowledge development in science and scholarship, which creates shareable and adaptable digital assets in the form of journal papers, but perhaps without so much of the Eurocentrism that currently dominates science (Marginson and Xu 2021). When teachers are able to explore and test the practices found in the course with their own learners, they then report back to further enrich the ecology of knowledge within the course.

This is relevant to the argument in this chapter insofar as the course does succeed in reaching teachers in the developing world and in engaging them in sharing learning designs. At the time of writing, after six runs, the Blended and Online Learning Design course has enrolled over 15,000 teachers, from all sectors, with 39 percent from low- and middle-income countries (LMICs). The reach is low in total, because the course has had no recruitment campaign, but it is promising in the proportion of teachers it attracts from LMICs.[6] The peer-review process has collected 1,600 designs (11 percent of the participants) with 1,900 reviews, leading to a public collection of seventy-five designs, seventeen of them now curated (i.e., the design has been reviewed by the course team). The model therefore succeeds in reaching teachers from all parts of the world and in engaging a good proportion of them in the quite hard work of generating and reviewing learning designs for digital methods. It is at a very early stage, but the signs are promising for this more global collaborative approach to developing and teaching community knowledge of how to teach online.

In this way, the CoMOOC model could make a significant contribution to reducing inequalities in teacher professional development by scaling up the value and reach of tertiary professional development activities. For teachers in developing countries, the model greatly increases their agency for contributing to new pedagogic knowledge in a Western-dominated online culture. It has already been the key to developing an emergency MOOC in Arabic on the Edraak platform to respond to teachers' needs during the pandemic.[7] Here, the prior engagement with research partners in Lebanon enabled a cross-cultural team to support teachers participating from across the Middle East and North Africa region in sharing problems and solutions in their sudden enforced move to online learning (Kennedy et al. 2022).

Universities contribute to all the SDGs through research toward an understanding of what can be done and how to do it in each area; they can also contribute to the education of professionals in those areas, by making their research findings and methods accessible, not just to scientists, but in the form of professional development collaborations for the end users of their research, such as the current UCL FutureLearn course on Sustainable Energy Access for Communities (Kennedy and Moussaoui 2021). Another example is an emergency MOOC created during the Ebola crisis that attracted over 12,000 participants, 69 percent of whom were health professionals and the top ten countries of origin for the participants included five countries with cases of Ebola, including over 300 from Sierra Leone,[8] again demonstrating the feasibility of reaching the intended target audience (Laurillard and Kennedy 2019). Global participants have the opportunity to question and experiment with what is on offer and give feedback on its relevance and viability for their own diverse contexts. For the research team, there is the value of a direct link to their peers and end users of the research, and the knowledge they bring to the issue, giving voice to their endogenous capabilities—*if* they use a CoMOOC approach and not the more typical instructional form. In that sense, universities might begin to move from the one-way public understanding of science to a two-way "understanding of science *by* the public" and "redefine the public good through open discussion *with* the public" (Hazelkorn and Gibson 2017, 17, italics in original).

This new approach to large-scale digital pedagogy applies not just to teachers but also to anyone wishing to achieve a wide understanding of their work and real-world practice contributions from their peers.

How Governance Can Promote the Use of Digital Methods to Achieve the Institutional Mission

How can governance ensure that the opportunities now being discovered in the use of new digital tools and skills will be used to achieve the institution's stated mission? Whether the model of institutional governance is state-centered, market-oriented, or academic self-governance (Dobbins, Knill, and Vogtle 2011), in each case management, quality controls and institutional support are relatively weak with respect to engagement with digital methods in teaching. A governing body does not normally expect to engage with this detail of teaching methods. The previous section proposed two main ways in which a governing body could overcome this by setting the agenda for internal TPD and encouraging the debates and actions needed for new business modeling for blended and online courses. Tackling the institutional mission should be closer to the governing body's brief.

Given the ambition of tertiary institutions to make it their mission to contribute to the making of a better world, the SDGs provide a valuable framework, embracing everything they engage in through both teaching and research. It is inevitable that their governance bodies will want to contribute to the way the institution responds to these opportunities. This suggests a further two policy priorities, the first for the governance body.

3. *Institutional governance to promote the provision of large-scale professional development as a priority for contributing to the SDGs.*

Large-scale online professional development is not a strong feature of university and college education portfolios and is even declining in the United Kingdom (Winterbotham et al. 2020). Institutional virtual learning environments are not usually equipped to run courses on a very large scale, so MOOC platforms provide a valuable partnership, as they offer most of the functionality needed, and where specialist digital tools are necessary, they can be linked in from the off-platform sites.

The business model is important to consider, and fees should be set according to gross domestic product of the location of the participant rather than a flat fee. It is an unusual aim for the education industry. However, this ethical principle for advancing global professional development would appear to match the mission statements and Grand Challenge goals that universities aspire to. Motivation can be high for professionals who know that they need to update their professional credentials or develop specific vocational skills, and in many professional areas and especially in LMICs, this is enhanced by access to a certificate of attendance on a professional development course. MOOCs are usually free at the point of use, but provide the certificate only via an upgrade fee—hence the importance of variable pricing by country. With a sufficient motivational offer to achieve high numbers, and especially if the institution invests in recruitment campaigns for such courses, it should be possible to at least break even. It would be a move into the relative unknown for many institutions, a move that would need to be made strategically. If successful, it would be a significant advance on achieving some of the most ambitious aims and mission statements in the sector.

The final policy priority again comes back to what university leaders might consider.

4. *Institutional leaders to build an adaptive network model of communication and change to enable governance to be rapidly responsive to new and developing knowledges among teachers and researchers.*

With the right model, the governing board can help the institution work toward its mission statements, by listening to academic teachers, researchers, and professional staff, and supporting a move toward more strategically oriented professional development. One of the earliest moves to change the nature of university governance was the Australian move to "the managed university" in 1988 (Croucher et al. 2020), which conceptualized it as more like a business than a traditional collegiate academic culture. A UK think tank later argued that an adaptive network rather than a top-down hierarchical model would be a more efficient way to achieve change, because it functions with no central direction or control, but rather a series of feedback linkages between groups, where governance shapes diverse sets of activities "to enable 'disciplined innovation', where the discipline is a relentless quest to create new manifestations of public value" (Bentley and Wilsdon 2003, 26). At the same time, however, the Lambert Report delivered a critique of the pre-1992 universities in the United Kingdom as being "run as communities of scholars. Their management and governance arrangements were participatory: senates and councils were large and conservative" (Lambert 2003, 93). The report noted, with approval, the recent progress in some universities in making governance and management structures more dynamic and capable of rapid decision-making through delegation to academic and administrative managers and recommended that others should follow. The more managerialist top-down hierarchy became the way forward. It proved to be very problematic. In Australia, the next thirty years were remarkable for the "demonstrable ineffectiveness" of the changes (Croucher et al. 2020). For the United Kingdom, Mike Shattock's later analysis of the effects of governance reform pointed out that it generated the emergence of a more complicit managerial system and a tacit acceptance of limitations on institutional freedoms that over time would stifle institutional innovation (Shattock 2008). And so it has done. One clear example is that digital innovations have been small-scale and nonstrategic over the last twenty years, resulting in an energetic but ultimately inadequate response to the pandemic crisis. A participatory community is not sufficient for a disciplined innovation process, but neither is a tight management structure. The orchestration of exchange and feedback to modify actions is a critical part of any dynamic learning process, just as it is for the individual student in terms of the Conversational Framework for their personal learning process. An adaptive network model across the whole institution has a greater chance of being rapidly adaptive to change through effective innovation. A recent report from the UNESCO-supported Global University Network for Innovation on the social commitment of universities recommends that "Institutions in a world in transition need governance mechanisms for an effective shared mission that takes into account how to serve both local and global needs and demands, through real engagement at all levels" (Grau et al. 2017, 45).

The same report concludes that the SDGs "are a good starting point for establishing concrete global objectives for HEIs" (Grau et al. 2017, 498). It proposes specific responsibilities for action, including "Building capacities for SDG policies, planning and management" (499)—that is, that every institution has a strategic approach to delivering the professional development needed at every level, in every sector.

At the level of global change, it is difficult to see how any form of global governance could help. Dirk Van Damme and Marijk Van der Wende argue that although several mechanisms of global governance of higher education exist, such as global professional bodies, international organizations, and accrediting bodies, none of them "can be analysed as some kind of global governance capable of addressing the main global challenges" (Van Damme and Van der Wende 2018). Universities that already see themselves as global institutions responding to global challenges are likely to be in a better position to adapt to supporting effective global change.

Universities have an important role to play, being seen as a line of defense against the adverse pressures of globalization, which has not delivered improving equality but quite the opposite (Van Damme and Van der Wende 2018). An article by David Leonhardt (2017) shows a diagram of the exponential growth in inequality worldwide, but this diagram shows the level of inequality up to 2014 only. After the Covid-19 pandemic, the same diagram will need a log-scale to represent the corresponding shocking increase in the fortunes of the very few very wealthy.

The mission to create a better world becomes harder as globalization and the concentration of power worsen inequalities. It is important to keep sight of the mission and of what the institution might do to achieve it. Governance bodies have a defining role to play in both. An open adaptive network and an institutional version of the CoMOOC, for example, would enable them to contribute more to those ambitious mission statements and respond with commensurate action.

Conclusion

This chapter has considered two main issues that will affect the development of a tertiary institution, and how the governance body could support and enhance its response. The innovation forced on the sector by the effects of the pandemic has foregrounded the value and potential of digital methods in ways that could improve (i) the quality and inclusiveness of the education we provide and (ii) our ability to achieve the ambitions in our mission statements. In both cases, digital methods of human communication can be shown to bring new methodologies for innovation sharing and knowledge development that are more inclusive for both the students we teach and the professionals we develop.

The analysis for improving our education builds on several underlying concepts to power the forward development of the way we use digital technologies and counter the more instrumental and commercial approaches that these technologies naturally enable. The concepts of student agency, self-formation, supported learning, flexible reach, inclusivity, teacher productivity, and teaching as a design science all help to establish a perspective to guide the use of digital technology to benefit students. The attendant roles for a governing body are to ensure teacher professional development in digital pedagogy and to learn how to ensure the optimal deployment of both conventional and online methods.

For institutional development, the global mission statements provide a focus for an effective global role, and the analysis builds on the concepts of large-scale professional collaborative development for effective innovation, across both teaching and research, and an adaptive network for building new knowledge.

The fundamental approach is to establish a different relationship between the academic teaching and learning communities and university governance that will enable and not constrain the innovation needed.

Key Discussion Areas

- Benefits of digital and blended learning in education.
- The role of governance in promoting blended and digital learning at the institutional level.
- Challenges faced by educational institutes in implementing digital and blended learning.

Notes

1 Universities UK, Equality, Diversity and Inclusion, www.universitiesuk.ac.uk/topics/equality-diversity-and-inclusion (accessed April 7, 2023).
2 UCL Knowledge Lab, Learning Designer, www.ucl.ac.uk/learning-designer/ (accessed April 7, 2023).
3 Reliefweb, "20 Reasons Why, in 2020, There Are Still 260m Children Out of School," February 7, 2020, https://reliefweb.int/report/world/20-reasons-why-2020-there-are-still-260m-children-out-school (accessed April 7, 2023).
4 UNESCO, "Mobile Technology the Key to Bringing 'Education to All', Says UN Broadband Commission," https://en.unesco.org/news/mobile-technology-key-bringing-education-all-says-broadband-commission (accessed April 7, 2023).
5 FutureLearn, "UCL, Blended and Online Learning Design," www.futurelearn.com/courses/blended-and-online-learning-design (accessed April 7, 2023).
6 Lower Middle-Income Countries (per capita GNI $1,006–$3,955 in 2016).
7 www.edraak.org/en/search/?query=Teaching+Online%3A+Be+Ready+Now%21.
8 Open Study at LSHTM, Ebola in Context OER, https://open.lshtm.ac.uk/course/view.php?id=8 (accessed April 7, 2023).

References

Almekhlafi, A., and F. Al Meqdadi. 2010. "Teachers' Perceptions of Technology Integration in the United Arab Emirates School Classrooms." *Educational Technology & Society* 13(1): 165–75.
Bates, A. W. 2001. "National Strategies for E-learning in Post-Secondary Education and Training." UNESCO IIEEP, www.unesco.org/iiep (accessed April 7, 2023).
Bentley, T., and J. Wilsdon. 2003. *The Adaptive State*. London: Demos.
Biesta, G., and M. Tedder. 2007. "Agency and Learning in the Lifecourse: Towards an Ecological Perspective." *Studies in the Education of Adults* 39(2): 132–49.
Croucher, G., W. Wen, H. Coates, and L. Goedegebuure. 2020. "Framing Research into University Governance and Leadership: Formative Insights from a Case Study of Australian Higher Education." *Educational Management Administration & Leadership* 48(2): 248–69, https://doi.org/10.1177/1741143219893101 (accessed April 7, 2023).
Department for Education and Skills. 2005. "Harnessing Technology: Transforming Learning and Children's Services." The Stationery Office, https://webarchive.nationalarchives.gov.uk/ukgwa/20121103055537mp_/www.education.gov.uk/publications/eOrderingDownload/1437-2005PDF-EN-01.pdf (accessed April 7, 2023).
Dobbins, M., C. Knill, and E. M. Vogtle. 2011. "An Analytical Framework for the Cross-Country Comparison of Higher Education Governance." *Higher Education* 62: 665–83.
Grau, F., J. Goddard, B. Hall, E. Hazelkorn, and R. Tandon. 2017. *Higher Education in the World 6: Towards a Socially Responsible University: Balancing the Global with the Local.* Global University Network for Innovation, www.researchgate.net/publication/314840823 (accessed April 7, 2023).
Hazelkorn, E., and A. Gibson. 2017. "Public Goods and Public Policy: What Is Public Good, and Who and What Decides?" Working Paper No. 18, Centre for Global Higher Education, UCL Institute of Education, London.

Johnson, N., T. Bates, T. Donovan, and J. Seaman. 2019. *Tracking Online Education in Canadian Universities and Colleges: National Survey of Online and Digital Learning 2019 National Report*. Canadian Digital Learning Research Association, www.cdlra-acrfl.ca/wp-content/uploads/2020/07/2019_national_en.pdf (accessed April 7, 2023).

Kasch, J., P. van Rosmalem, and M. Kalz. 2017. "A Framework Towards Educational Scalability of Open Online Courses." *Journal of Universal Computer Science* 23(9): 845–67.

Kennedy, E., and R. El Moussaoui. 2021. "Exploring Energy Access for Communities Worldwide." *Procol Lebanon*, May 10, 2021, www.relief-centre.org/blog/from-nigeria-to-lebanon-exploring-energy-access-for-communities-worldwide (accessed April 7, 2023).

Kennedy, E., D. Laurillard, B. Horan, and P. Charlton. 2015. "Making Meaningful Decisions About Time, Workload and Pedagogy in the Digital Age: The Course Resource Appraisal Model." *Distance Education* 36(2): 177–95.

Kennedy, E., C. Masuda, R. El Moussaoui, E. Chase, and D. Laurillard. 2022. "Creating Value from Co-Designing CoMOOCs with Teachers in Challenging Environments." *London Review of Education* 20(1): 43–56, https://doi.org/10.14324/LRE.20.1.45 (accessed April 7, 2023).

Kenny, J., and A. Fluck. 2017. "Towards a Methodology to Determine Standard Time Allocations for Academic Work." *Journal of Higher Education Policy and Management* 39(5): 503–23, https://doi.org/10.1080/1360080X.2017.1354773 (accessed April 7, 2023).

Kleftodimos, A., G. Lappas, and G. Evangelidis. 2020. "Edutainment and Practice in Video-Based Learning: Enriching Educational Videos with Interactive Activities and Games." *International Journal of Entertainment Technology and Management* 1(1): 5–33.

Kopcha, T. 2012. "Teachers' Perceptions of the Barriers to Technology Integration and Practices with Technology under Situated Professional Development." *Computers and Education* 59: 1109–21.

Koszalka, T., Y. Pavlov, and Y. Wu. 2021. "The Informed Use of Pre-Work Activities in Collaborative Asynchronous Online Discussions: The Exploration of Idea Exchange, Content Focus, and Deep Learning." *Computers and Education* 161, https://doi.org/10.1016/j.compedu.2020.104067 (accessed April 7, 2023).

Lambert, R. 2003. *Lambert Review of Business—University Collaboration Final Report*. Norwich: HMSO.

Laurillard, D. 2002. *Rethinking University Teaching: A Conversational Framework for the Effective Use of Learning Technologies*, 2nd ed. London: RoutledgeFalmer.

———. 2007. "Modelling Benefits-Oriented Costs for Technology Enhanced Learning." *Higher Education* 54: 21–39, www.springerlink.com/content/c176t337h7381n51/.

———. 2008. "The Teacher as Action Researcher: Using Technology to Capture Pedagogic Form." *Studies in Higher Education* 33(2): 139–54.

———. 2012. *Teaching as a Design Science: Building Pedagogical Patterns for Learning and Technology*. New York and London: Routledge.

Laurillard, D., P. Charlton, B. Craft, D. Dimakopoulos, D. Ljubojevic, G. Magoulas, Elizabeth Masterman, Roser Pujadas, Edgar A. Whitley, and Kim Whittlestone. 2013. "A Constructionist Learning Environment for Teachers to Model Learning Designs." *Journal of Computer Assisted Learning* 29(1): 15–30, https://doi.org/10.1111/j.1365-2729.2011.00458.x (accessed April 7, 2023).

Laurillard, D., and E. Kennedy. 2019. "The Role of Higher Education in Upscaling Global Professional Development through Open, Online Collaboration." In *The Future of Higher Education*, edited by C. Callender, W. Locke, and S. Marginson. London: Bloomsbury.

Laurillard, D., E. Kennedy, P. Charlton, J. Wild, and D. Dimakopoulos. 2018. "Using Technology to Develop Teachers as Designers of TEL: Evaluating the Learning Designer." *British Journal of Educational Technology* 49(6), https://doi.org/10.1111/bjet.12697 (accessed April 7, 2023).

Leonhardt, D. 2017. "Our Broken Economy, in One Simple Chart." *New York Times*, August 7, 2017, www.nytimes.com/interactive/2017/08/07/opinion/leonhardt-income-inequality.html?smid=pl-share (accessed April 7, 2023).

Livingstone, S., M. Bober, and E. Helsper. 2005. "Active Participation or Just More Information? Young People's Take Up of Opportunities to Act and Interact on the Internet." *Information, Communication, and Society* 8(3): 287–314, http://eprints.lse.ac.uk/1014 (accessed April 7, 2023).

Marginson, S. 2011. "Higher Education and Public Good." *Higher Education Quarterly* 65(4): 411–33, https://doi.org/10.1111/j.1468-2273.2011.00496.x (accessed April 7, 2023).

———. 2023. "Higher Education as Student Self-Formation." In *Assessing the Contributions of Higher Education: Knowledge for a Disordered World*, edited by S. Marginson, B. Cantwell, D. Platonova, and A. Smolentseva. Cheltenham, UK: Edward Elgar Publishing.

Marginson, S., and X. Xu. 2021. "Moving Beyond Centre-Periphery Science: Towards an Ecology of Knowledge." Working Paper No. 63, Centre for Global Higher Education, Department of Education, University of Oxford, Oxford, www.researchcghe.org/publications/.

McNicholl, A., H. Casey, D. Desmond, and P. Gallagher. 2019. "The Impact of Assistive Technology Use for Students with Disabilities in Higher Education: A Systematic Review." *Disability and Rehabilitation: Assistive Technology* 16(2): 130–43, https://doi.org/10.1080/17483107.2019.1642395 (accessed April 7, 2023).

McVitty, D., A. Jackson, and B. Hutchens. 2021. "Students' Experiences of Study during Covid-19 and Hopes for Future Learning and Teaching." Pearson/Wonkhe, February 2021, https://wonkhe.com/wp-content/wonkhe-uploads/2021/02/Wonkhe-Pearson-expectation-gap-II--2021.pdf (accessed April 7, 2023).

Morris, D. 2008. "Economies of Scale and Scope in E-learning." *Studies in Higher Education* 33(3): 331–43, www.informaworld.com/smpp/content~db=all~content=a793532873.

Munro, M. 2018. "The Complicity of Digital Technologies in the Marketisation of UK Higher Education: Exploring the Implications of a Critical Discourse Analysis of Thirteen National Digital Teaching and Learning Strategies." *International Journal of Educational Technology in Higher Education* 15(11): 1–20, https://doi.org/10.1186/s41239-018-0093-2 (accessed April 7, 2023).

Organisation for Economic Co-operation and Development. 2016. *Innovating Education and Educating for Innovation: The Power of Digital Technologies and Skills*. Paris: Paris: September 26, 2016, https://doi.org/10.1787/9789264265097-en (accessed April 7, 2023).

Santos, B. 2009. "A Non-Occidentalist West? Learned Ignorance and Ecology of Knowledge." *Theory Culture Society* 26(7–8): 103–25, https://doi.org/10.1177/0263276409348079 (accessed April 7, 2023).

Shattock, M. 2008. "The Change from Private to Public Governance of British Higher Education: Its Consequences for Higher Education Policy Making 1980–2006." *Higher Education Quarterly* 62(3): 181–203, https://doi.org/10.1111/j.1468-2273.2008.00392.x (accessed April 7, 2023).

Shulman, L. S. 2005. "Signature Pedagogies in the Professions." *Daedalus* 134(3): 52–59.

Smith, M., and J. Traxler, eds. 2022. *Digital Learning in Higher Education: Covid-19 and Beyond*. Cheltenham, UK: Edward Elgar Publishing Ltd.

Spowart, L., J. Winter, R. Turner, P. Burden, K. Botham, R. Muneer, Hendrik van der Sluis, and Isabel Huet. 2019. " 'Left with a Title but Nothing Else': The Challenges of Embedding Professional Recognition Schemes for Teachers within Higher Education Institutions." *Higher Education Research & Development* 38(6): 1299–312.

Van Damme, D., and M. Van der Wende. 2018. "Global Higher Education Governance." In *Handbook on the Politics of Higher Education*, edited by B. Cantwell, H. Coates, and R. King. Cheltenham, UK: Edward Elgar Publishing.

Winterbotham, M., G. Kik, S. Selner, R. Menys, S. Stroud, and S. Whittaker. 2020. *Employer Skills Survey 2019: Training and Workforce Development*. London: Department for Education, https://assets.publishing.service.gov.uk/government/uploads/system/uploads/attachment_data/file/955172/Employer_skills_survey_2019_research_report.pdf (accessed April 7, 2023).

13
ED-TECH REVOLUTION POST COVID-19

Mayank Kumar, Ronnie Screwvala, and Phalgun Kompalli

Introduction

A robust education system determines the competence of the working population for generations. India is the second most populated country in the world after China and is projected to surpass it by 2023, according to the United Nations. Interestingly, around 66 percent of the total population (more than 808 million) is below the age of thirty-five. Nearly 40 percent of the Indian population is between the ages of thirteen and thirty-five.

Hence, having an education system that is geared to improve the competency of the nation and build a socially aware and wholesome society is essential. Competent educational governance helps channelize human qualities and skills in a complementary way.

According to a World Bank report, in low- and middle-income countries, "learning poverty" (the ability to understand and read a simple story by the age of ten) stands at 53 percent.[1] In contrast, is the learning poverty rate is 80 percent on average for the poorest countries in the world. The Coronavirus disease (Covid-19) pandemic and lockdowns have further dented this ability and pushed many countries back by almost two years in their fight for literacy and education. More than 180 countries mandated temporary school closures, *leaving roughly 1.6 billion children and youth out of school* at the height of lockdowns, affecting approximately 85 percent of children worldwide.

The answer to this backward push in reach and access to education by all is e-learning. Technology plays an essential role in helping deliver instruction to students who fall outside the gambit of traditional schools. To bridge the inequalities in the deliverance of education, accelerate learning, reduce learning poverty, and help develop essential vocational skills along with the three R's of education—reading, writing, and arithmetic—countries across the world need to leverage the power of technology.

A proper utilization of technology for effective e-learning must focus on building the following:

- Digital infrastructure: Wi-Fi penetration, mobile and other digital device access, and building appropriate software (apps and tools).

DOI: 10.4324/9781003316077-17

- Human infrastructure: Skilled teachers, student skills, and parental support.
- Teaching infrastructure: Building an appropriate curriculum customized to the needs of the socioeconomic structure, industries, etc.
- Logistics and appropriated administration of the same: To deploy and maintain the technology infrastructure.

Countries should adopt and adapt their education systems to match twenty-first-century needs and competencies. As pointed out above, along with affordable connectivity, infrastructure, and access to devices and tech and curriculum architecture, governments need to collaborate with external partners and float training programs and accreditation of skills in both students and teachers.

It is undeniable that digital formats, e-learning and ed-tech, are already an integral part of education and will continue to be in the post Covid-19 world. Adopting and extending a digital mindset will address the evergreen issues of reach, equity, and quality in imparting education.

Reports indicate that using the best e-learning software tools can increase productivity by 30 percent. Not just that, e-learning boosts employee engagement by 18 percent, and it typically requires up to 60 percent less employee time (SHIFT eLearning). Most importantly, e-learning has better knowledge retention rates (up to 60 percent) compared with face-to-face training. These and other benefits are too important to ignore.

As a result of the pandemic, there has been a 16 percent increase in virtual learning and a 16 percent decrease in instructor-led training. Sixty-two businesses affected by the pandemic are also spending more on training (Shift eLearning n.d.).

The e-learning industry has benefited greatly from the changing learning habits of the world. A multigenerational workforce requires constant upgradation of skills, for which e-learning and ed-tech are great resources.

Education Management Information Systems (EMIS 2.0)

For better reach, equity, and quality, countries need to focus on developing Education Management Information Systems (EMIS 2.0) to support more effective use of data.

Traditional Modes of Imparting Education

The present formal education system in India follows nearly 200-year-old methodologies of rote memorization of information. The schools are based on derivative and mechanistic models, and the focus is on absorbing information rather than developing original thinking and imagination.

Education should not be just geared toward getting a degree and passing exams to get a job. It should be about gaining knowledge and developing a critical mindset and the ability to think logically and rationally. The main goal should be a wholesome view of the world, along with a practical application of skills and information gained.

Proper education is the integral education in which all dimensions of the growing child—physical, mental, psychic, and spiritual—are addressed. A free and natural growth, into oneself and not an imitation of others, is the foundation. It is not a static endeavor.

Industry-Ready Students

By assessing the capabilities of their students and aligning their qualifications to industry requirements, higher educational institutions are seeking to make their students industry-ready. We can achieve this by integrating research and innovation into the core of education and making it affordable for everyone across the nation. Therefore, it is beyond time to do away with traditional rote-learning methods, which concentrate on memorizing rather than gaining a deeper understanding of a subject. Several education institutes, schools, and universities have already moved their processes online to impart a holistic education that encompasses the needs of industries and aspirants both.

With these initiatives, education is expected to undergo a major transformation in the coming years, as the Indian government leaves no stone unturned to implement the most advanced technologies and is eager to transform the country's digital landscape. With the lessons learned during the pandemic, a growing number of educational institutions are moving fully online to accommodate students. Online learning is seen as a viable option for future disasters and natural scenarios, where any disruption in the learning process can be handled by online education and e-learning methods.

Educational Governance

Educational governance plays a crucial role in determining the direction of education policies. Sound academic governance provides a definite structure for governments to achieve set educational goals through the best application of available resources and their authenticity.

Educational governance needs to overcome obstacles such as

- the traditional education system;
- scarcity of funds;
- overpopulation;
- low technological know-how among educational organizations;
- low ratio of opportunities against employment;
- incompetency in skill sets and shortage in teaching staff
- the need for better engagement and motivation for studies;
- community and parental involvement;
- the lack of a better system of determining skill levels (examination systems).

Educational governance also plays a vital role in providing strategic development policies for hiring educational authorities, teachers, and faculties based on their merit; dispersing educational and study material to all the institutions equally; and providing financial aid.

Most importantly, it is crucial to set new policies and benchmarks by analyzing the country's educational institutions.

Ways to Improve the Infrastructure of Educational Governance in India

For India, the shift in focus from physical teaching to digital will greatly ease the pressure on the already stretched physical infrastructure in India. But one cannot ignore the fact that a large part of rural India may be left out of this digital shift.

With the increase of digital technologies in education, the marginalized population residing in rural India, especially underprivileged women and children, are at a disadvantage.

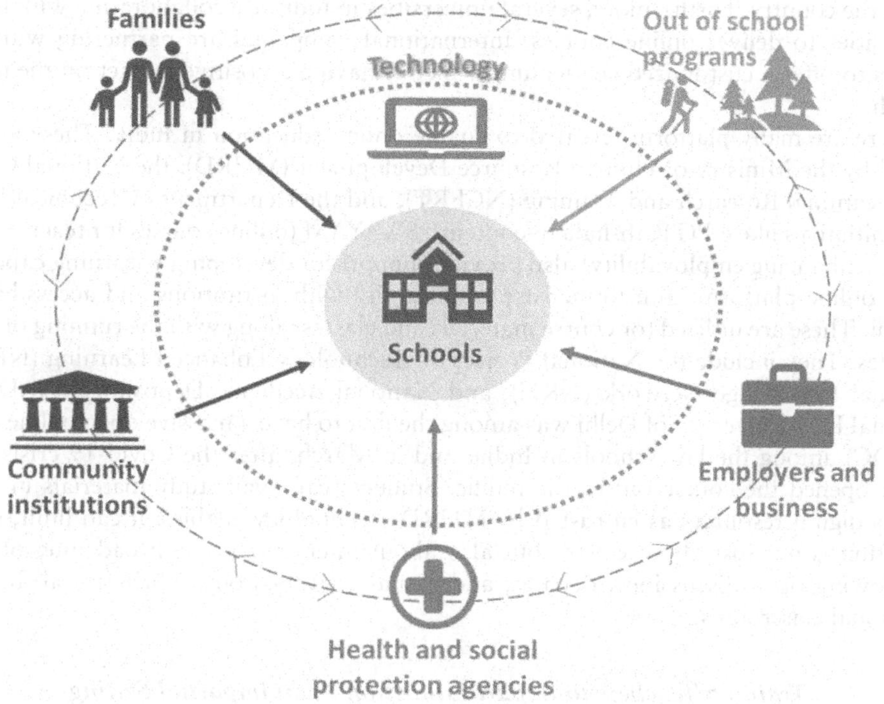

Figure 13.1 Powered-up schools from 2020 report—Beyond reopening schools: How education can emerge stronger than before COVID-19

Source: Emiliana Vegas and Rebecca Winthrop, "Beyond Reopening Schools: How Education Can Emerge Stronger than before COVID-19," Brookings, September 8, 2020, www.brookings.edu/articles/beyond-reopening-schools-how-education-can-emerge-stronger-than-before-covid-19/ (accessed November 1, 2023).

One reason for the estimated nine million students lacking connectivity is the high monthly cost of Internet access. Many free and low-cost resources are available for qualified families, however, and some providers are creating flexible payment options.

Incentives

A viable solution is incentivizing service providers to extend low-cost services in these areas, especially those that provide broadband connectivity for education. A convergence of all digital assets for better dissemination of information is another way. Homes having a television or a phone can be used for digital learning. Even a community-owned television can be provided for the remotest and most marginalized sections. In some rural areas, wireline service is completely unavailable; a mobile hotspot option might be a solution for students in areas with weak cell service.

Government Programs

The Indian government has announced programs, such as DIKSHA and SHAGUN, for undergraduate and postgraduate students. Such programs are gaining immense popularity across the country. Furthermore, several universities in India are collaborating with foreign universities to deliver online courses. International companies are partnering with local players to offer a customized curriculum, which is having a positive impact on the market growth.

There are many platforms created to enable online education in India. These are supported by the Ministry of Human Resource Development (MHRD), the National Council of Educational Research and Training (NCERT), and the Department of Technical Education. Initiatives like e-PG Pathshala (e-content), SWAYAM (online courses for teachers), and NEAT (enhancing employability) also provide support for developing e-learning capacities. Other online platforms aim to increase connectivity with institutions and accessibility to content. These are utilized for course materials and classes, along with the running of online modules. They include the National Project on Technology Enhanced Learning (NPTEL), National Knowledge Network (NKN), and National Acedemic Depository (NAD). The National Law University of Delhi was among the first to have a massive open online course (MOOC) among the law schools in India; and in March, after the Covid-19 crisis broke out, it opened the course out to the public. Students can avail study materials in law as well as digital resources as entrusted by MHRD. Technology enables; it can limit, too, as education is not just about classes but also about interactions, the broadening of ideas, free-flowing open discussions, debates, and casual conversations, which are all better in traditional classrooms.

Training Teachers to Impart Education in an Impartial Setting

Curriculum content and pedagogy will need to be revised to adapt to digital learning models. The quality of teachers and the role of teachers is minimized. That is not to say that a teacher becomes redundant, but rather, he or she is a valuable addition to the delivered content and curriculum. There are now a variety of online videos available to students offering instruction on a variety of topics at a variety of skill levels, and students can participate in real-time video sessions with tutors who live across the state (or even across the world).

Live Interactions

Most importantly, the classroom learning that happens in a live setting, including learning cues and peer interactions, needs to be better incorporated into an online context. Such classroom learning can be done through a mixed model that combines some physical exchanges and meetings with digital learning. A detailed plan with inputs from all invested players, such as teachers, students, government officials, and tech experts, must be chalked out for holistic learning.

Engagement, Motivation, and Overseeing

While education technologies often provide more control, they also reduce parent oversight, which may be detrimental to students who are less motivated or do not receive structured educational support from their parents. Additionally, the technologies could be less effective at engaging reluctant learners than a dynamic and charismatic teacher.

Furthermore, learning is intrinsically social. Strategies that do not involve direct interpersonal interactions are unlikely to influence certain skills. Tutors with high intelligence might be able to help students master certain math concepts but might not be able to train them to analyze literary works critically or discuss the ethics of new legislation.

The importance of good educational governance helps raise the profile of education services, deliverables, and performance that contribute to the entire package of policies, programs, procedures, and implementation. A remarkable amount of work can be drawn out based on the design and principles of a sound education system.

Turning From a Teacher-Centric Mindset to a Student-Centric One

In our approach to education, we have always been teacher-centric (mostly one way). It is finally time for us to move away from physical classrooms focused on teachers and onto digital classrooms concentrating on students. In this way, we can cultivate and develop the quality of self-learning behavior in our students. This will boost greater creativity, stimulate curiosity, and broaden their horizons.

Distanced Geographically but Connected Digitally

Students can connect for learning anywhere and anytime, with a community approach in the digital world. The communities will engage students while providing a place to develop their potential and keep them engaged.

Pedagogy Is Key, but Technology and Content Are Enablers

Access to technology is not a problem. In addition, teaching materials are available. The content is available to educators, since they have been teaching in the physical classroom. Pedagogy is the missing link. For the digital glass room, the pedagogies of a physical classroom may not be suitable. Interaction, gamification, visual richness, and hands-on capability are the key practices for a new digitally focused pedagogy. The effectiveness of learning is dramatically enhanced in this way.

A strong and inclusive public education system is crucial to the short- and long-term recovery of society, and digital learning presents an opportunity to leapfrog toward powered-up schools.

Democratic Education and Ed-Tech

Democratic education is an expression of the concept of choice and control. As a result of the rise of the internet and digitization, education has become more democratic. The internet and virtual platforms have helped foster the rise of a global market of courses and programs that have allowed millions of people in the world to widen their field of action and expand their professional opportunities.

The future calls for a convivial pedagogy that supports the creation of creative, learner-driven curricula, in which open, well-informed, and continuous debate is the fundamental methodology. Educating for better equity, ethical treatment, and enjoyable results can now become a much more practical and enjoyable experience (and a lot less competitive, test-oriented, and world-work-dominated activity). We explore and welcome these possibilities, plus others, associated with the groundbreaking "Education embodied in digitization" reality.

Moreover, as artificial intelligence technology advances, teachers can tailor their instruction according to student needs, providing additional support to those who may have knowledge and skills beyond their grade level. A student's weaknesses can not only be assessed with "intelligent" tutoring, but they also need to be studied as to why mistakes are being made. The technologies could benefit academically underprepared students by improving their ability to reach students from afar.

Although technologies such as virtual instruction and intelligent tutoring have a lot of potential, their failure is almost certain unless the challenges associated with their implementation are understood and addressed. The effectiveness of digital learning for disadvantaged students has yet to be proven at scale.

In some cases, it is better to think of technologies as complementary—for example, when they are implemented well, they require skilled teachers or students with a high level of previous knowledge and abilities. For technologies to benefit traditionally underserved populations, they must be accompanied by additional resources such as high-quality educational content, requisite tech-enabled infrastructure, and scholarships for pursuing them with top universities.

As the worlds of online learning and computer-aided instruction have become more convergent in recent years, blended learning and personalized learning are often referred to as the new paradigms. Educationists have a chance to embrace the new model and make it work. With the cloud, data bandwidth, storage technologies, compute power, analytics, data management methods, and so on, there is a new world of opportunity in the digital world that no one could have imagined a few years ago.

Innovation in education is defined as new ideas or technologies in the current context, if not the world. Our research suggests that the innovations that can help leapfrog education are those that offer a wider menu of options for delivering learning, including

1. following a pedagogy that provides creative, analytical, and receptive methods of teaching-learning;
2. adding new methods of recognizing learning to traditional methods;
3. ingesting a diversity of people and places in school to facilitate learning;
4. embracing technology and data in a way that allows for real-time adaptation rather than simply replacing analog methods.

Resources for Implementing Ed-Tech

Many educational institutes have turned into ed-tech start-ups and created apps for students to access notes and their curriculum and give mock tests to prepare for exams. It allows them to continue their studies uninterrupted.

Providers of education can develop interactive learning platforms for their students that allow them to access video, audio, and image study material as well as text and PDF content that is relevant to their studies. Enhancement of student experience via digital transformation may include

using a mobile application or a web application to enable students to register;
offering a wide range of online learning options;
tracking student progress and enforcing intervention protocols with technology;
enabling the ability to organize classes online.

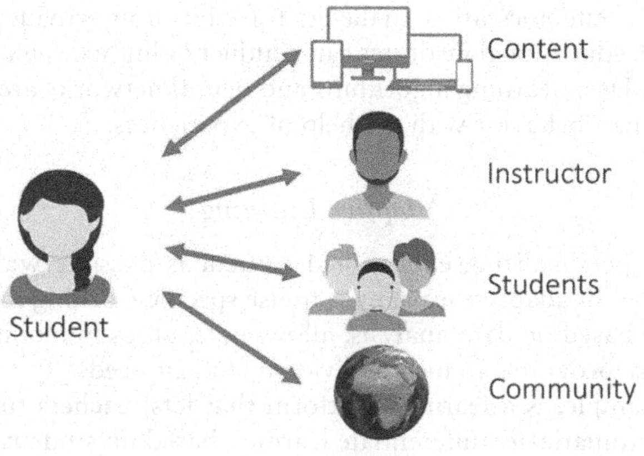

Figure 13.2 Types of Interactions

Source: Jered Borup, Charles R. Graham, Cecil Short, and Joan Kang Shin, "Designing the New Normal: Enable, Engage, Elevate, and Extend Student Learning," Educase Review, January 11, 2022, https://er.educause.edu/articles/2022/1/designing-the-new-normal-enable-engage-elevate-and-extend-student-learning#fnr5 (accessed November 1, 2023).

Alongside that, it also includes

transformation of the campus environment;
transformation in the learning methodology;
transformation of the teaching method.

Using AR/VR to Enhance Learning

In an ever-evolving world, education must embrace new technologies to stay current. The next step in the evolution of the learning system is augmented and virtual reality.

You can create an interactive and virtual environment for your students using virtual reality and augmented reality. In addition to incorporating an interactive visual-audio factor, these technologies can explain complicated concepts. For example, Elements 4D is an AR app that lets students combine various elements to study chemistry in action. With DAQRI's 4D app, the elements of four-dimensional design become a living reality.

Smart Class

Whether educators are teaching online or in person, the digital whiteboard will help engage students with interactive methods. Teachers can use more than two colors on a digital whiteboard when teaching. They can use different colored shapes like circles, rectangles, or stars instead to explain complicated concepts more quickly and interactively.

Online Assessments Powered by AI

Education has become more automated as a result of the transition from pen-and-paper to an online and automated platform. However, administering tests and assessments and determining learning outcomes are a challenge for education providers. With the help of artificial intelligence, educational institutes can conduct online examinations using computers and the internet. Deep learning algorithms and neural networks are used in AI to make machines mimic human behavior with the help of experiences.

Adaptive Learning

Innovating ways of personalizing educational content is possible with adaptive learning technologies. The goal of adaptive learning is to use specific teaching tools to manage interaction with learners based on data analysis, allowing faculties to monitor students' performance and customize programs to meet individual student needs.

Quizalize, for example, is a learning platform that lets teachers turn boring tests into games. Platforms automatically differentiate learning based on student performance.

AI and Chatbots

Institutions are adopting chatbots to meet student expectations while maximizing faculty time. Using AI-enabled chatbots, instructors can analyze students' responses and provide them with learning content based on their choices. Chatbots can also convert lectures into a series of messages that look like real-time conversations to teach students.

Blockchain will become a major part of ed-tech. Using blockchain, ed-tech platforms can connect learners, practitioners, and teachers to deliver automatically their needs including secure documentation such as admission, attendance, payment, and grade records.

When carefully designed and thoughtfully applied, technology can accelerate, amplify, and expand the impact of effective teaching practices. However, to be transformative, educators need to have the knowledge and skills to take full advantage of technology-rich learning environments. Technology can help learning, move beyond the classroom, and take advantage of learning opportunities available in museums, libraries, and other out-of-school settings.

Advantages of Developing a Digital Education Strategy

Tracking of Student Performance

A real-time look at a student's progress is a major benefit of digital transformation in education. Teachers and parents can track the development of students by recording the information in their work using technology. For example, manuals or creative works could be compared at intervals with material already digitally recorded, which would help identify who needs improvement and who needs attention.

Analyzing Data to Improve Results

Analytics can be used by schools to monitor and improve results. By using technology in the classroom, students can better understand what individual children and schools need. Understanding how a student missed a term will make the course easier to take. We can diagnose these shortcomings through technology much easier and more reliably than teachers could in a thirty-plus student classroom.

Collaborative Learning

Digital learning forces collaboration. Learning platforms facilitate teachers in creating and managing groups. Collaborative creative environments, such as Google Docs, Twiddla, and Edmodo, make it easier for coauthors to collaborate on papers and presentations. Interactive instruments like these are already used in organizations.

Providing E-Services

After e-governance was implemented, services like admittance, grading, and results were improved. Feedback, information for documents, requesting certificates, issuing ID cards, and employment applications all became streamlined. Colleges now receive timely alerts via SMS/email.

Private–Public Participation

Most e-government projects involve private agencies as part of a public–private partnership (PPP) for a variety of tasks. A few of these tasks include designing and developing application software, populating data and content in the regional language, procuring and installing network and computer systems, and deploying software and delivering services.

E-Learning Trends and Scope

E-learning is a more cost-effective solution than brick-and-mortar teaching systems, and it keeps up with the continually changing prerequisites for quality education. As a result, it finds extensive application across various sectors like agriculture, health care, education, and training.

The education industry has witnessed significant developments and investments in terms of the rising number of pre-schools, K-12, and a burgeoning number of colleges and universities, which has led to growing number of school enrolments. The *ed-tech and smart classroom market size* was pegged at US$88.82 billion in 2021. The market is estimated to rise from US$101.64 billion in 2022 to US$319.65 billion by 2029 at a 17.8 percent compound annual growth rate (CAGR) during the forecast period. Fortune Business Insights has deep-dived these inputs in its latest research report titled “EdTech and Smart Classroom Market, 2022–2029.”[2]

upGrad

The ed-tech unicorn upGrad was started in 2015, and it is now Asia’s largest higher ed-tech company. According to upGrad, 80 percent of those joining the workforce are generally unable to find a job, and with its keen understanding of the market and skill dynamics, upGrad is best placed to offer the right blend of knowledge coupled with hands-on skills to make learner’s employable or enhance their employability skills.

upGrad offers a wide range of online programs and has collaborations with several top universities in the country, including IIIT-Bangalore, MICA Ahmedabad, Duke CE, Deakin University, Liverpool John Moores University, Golden Gate University, San Francisco, NMIMS Global Access, IMT Ghaziabad, Jindal Global Business School,

Table 13.1 Report (Forture Business Insights, n.d.) Scope and Segmentation

Report coverage	*Details*
Forecast period	2022–2029
Forecast period 2022–2029 CAGR	17.8 percent
2029 value projection	US$319.65 billion
Base year	2021
Ed-tech and smart classroom market size in 2021	US$88.82 billion
Historical data for	2018–2020
No. of pages	160
Segments covered	Instructional aid, smart classroom hardware, educational tool, end user, and geography
Ed-Tech and smart classroom market growth drivers	End users emphasize mobile learning to overcome coronavirus challenges
	Mobile learning to be sought-after with rising trend for online learning programs
	Interactive whiteboards to gain traction from the e-learning trend
	Learning management tools to be trendier due to demand for AI-enabled capabilities

Source: Authors.

BIMTECH, and IIM Kozhikode. The upGrad courses cover general education subjects like arts, education, law, and health and psychology, as well as some of the most trending business and technology subjects like data science, machine learning, artificial intelligence, blockchain, cybersecurity, software and technology, marketing, and management.

With unique human interaction provided by mentors and coaches, upGrad learners have maintained the greatest levels of curriculum engagement, claiming an effective program completion rate of over 80 percent, compared to other MOOCs, for which it is still less than 10 percent. Such one-on-one mentoring interactions have strengthened our students' sense of community and upGrad's position as the world leader in lifelong learning. The global ed-tech company now has over three million learners spread over hundred countries, as well as a strong enterprise business with hundred clients globally.

upGrad hosts offline events like BaseCamp for students, so they can interact with their peers.

In order to help students effectively, many education-based applications have been launched. upGrad was honored with the "Best Education Brand" in 2018 and has also bagged the title of Education Company of the Year by Techcircle in February 2022, thereby strengthening its stature as the trusted Lifelong Learning partner.

Headquartered in Mumbai (India), upGrad is present across over thirty locations including Africa, the United States, and Southeast Asia. It was co-founded by Ronnie Screwvala,

Mayank Kumar, and Phalgun Kompalli, and it has proved to become a robust capital-efficient business model, thereby outlasting its peers within the ed-tech ecosystem.

The company prioritizes career outcomes and uses TAP to monitor progress.

(i) Transition signifies a learner's growth in the form of a job role switching *outside/within the current organization.*

(ii) Acceleration may entail internal lateral growth and promotion or may raise *inside the organization and same industry.*

(iii) *Learners' professional confidence emphasizes the long-term investments in learning and development to become future-ready/domain authorities professional.*

Multiple upGrad learners have broken the annual CTC threshold of INR 1 crore+ (USD 1.3 million) during FY22 while also receiving the highest salary hike of 329 percent during Q4 in the same fiscal year. Based on the results reviewed by a leading Big Four firm, 83 percent of learners experience positive career growth. The upGrad talent pool has received salary hikes of INR 1,000+ crores (US$133+ million) to date which establishes the credibility and mettle of the online higher education segment in India.

Business Model of upGrad

In order to reach a bright future together, upGrad runs on an effective business model that holds a two-way approach between the students and the educators. With this, upGrad functions as a link between the educational institutions and the candidates to give each the best chance of success. With the upGrad app and the website, educational institutions can offer courses on various subjects at reasonable prices.

Candidate's wishing to enroll in the offered courses must complete the essential eligibility criteria fixed by the institution while registering with upGrad. Afterwards, the candidate must pay the course fees. It is possible to pay the entire fee at once or in installments to upGrad. Also, upGrad employs professional guides to enroll professional candidates. The two-way business approach helps upGrad accomplish its ultimate goals and provides an easy way for companies to hire potential employees.

upGrad created a LifeLongLearning portfolio that spans the entire value chain, offering degree, study abroad, and job-linked programs for college students while also providing short-form, executive, master, and doctoral programs through partnerships with top universities and the Ivy League for the global workforce. The goal is to meet a learner's educational needs between the ages of eighteen and fifty-five while simultaneously offering them end-to-end placement support through specialized career development services like one-on-one mentoring with industry leaders, resume building, mock interview preperations, and LinkedIn profile assessment, thus allowing upGrad learners to obtain the greatest possible career outcomes.

How Is upGrad Positively Impacting Its Key Stakeholders

Here are a few marquee innovations brought to life by the global higher ed-tech company, which has strengthened its stature as a leader among its key stakeholders like learners, universities, recruiters, and investors.

(1) Outcome-focused career engine

- With a nonselective approach, upGrad learners come from different walks of life with different skill sets, competencies, and career aspirations. A dedicated mentor team guides them thoroughly to map their abilities and aspirations in a way that accelerates maximum career outcomes for them.
- upGrad has made a generation aware of the importance of upskilling and what the New Age job market requires. upGrad raised US$185 million of external fundraise after being Founders funded for the first six years. This scaled up the valuation to US$1.2 billion, thus making upGrad one of the most-valued ed-tech unicorns in Asia in 2021. Mostly recently, the brand raised a fresh round of US$210 million in an external fundraiser, thereby scaling company's overall valuation to further scale its operations across domestic and international regions.

(2) Integrated lifelong-learning tech platform

- Interactive learning: The experience is made interactive through a combination of synchronous and asynchronous learning, including industry-focused assignments, quizzes, games, and group projects. The ratio of live to recorded lectures is 30 percent to 70 percent.
- Learning through community: For each cohort, upGrad is establishing a dedicated community with a new discussion forum in an effort to encourage students to submit more inquiries and ask questions without holding back while proving studying online is no longer a solitary or private process.
- Deep personalization for inquiry resolution using AI and NLP chatbots: upGrad is placing a lot of faith in cutting-edge technology to pinpoint and close the skills gap within the program, including gamification of the learning experience, audio learning assistants, simulation-based learning, AI-based virtual mentors, facial recognition for engagement monitoring, and automated proctoring.

(3) Industry-relevant and outcome-based curriculum

- upGrad is dedicated to advancing the careers of working professionals and learners by preparing them for next-generation job roles that will demand a distinct set of industry-relevant skills.
- In the fast-paced moving world, upGrad realized the very core foundation of growth is upskilling with industry-ready programs which can help learners enhance their professional competencies through dedicated projects, on-ground floor experiences, industry mentoring, and career sessions. It's packaged with live or recorded lectures, real-time discussion forums, proctored exams, industry-driven projects, masterclasses, bootcamps, on-campus immersion opportunities, capstone projects, and end-to-end career support to enhance a learner's LifeLongLearning journey.
- The modern curriculum and blended learning model are created specifically to meet the preferences and needs of each learner as per their career ambition. Professionals might acquire the necessary information, abilities, and ability to handle any situation with the aid of this cutting-edge curriculum, industry-based examples, and a dissertation.

(4) Deep personalization

- A unified job stream is a one-stop-shop to see job listings from upGrad's hiring partners and third-party recruiter jobs, plus curated jobs from across the internet.

- A unified job stream is also a central tracker to provide seamless tracking of learner's job applications, both on upGrad platform and any other platforms via a chrome extension and self-logger.
- Personalized job recommendations: The brand believes in human interventions to interact with each learner and encourage maximum engagement with the curriculum for driving higher program completion. On collecting over 100,000 data points from learners since the time of onboarding to learning, upGrad understands every individual's needs and their professional aspirations to make the learning journey more personal and immersive. With the help of technology, the tool is used to provide personalized job recommendations to a learner, thus helping them achieve desired career outcomes. Through such engagements, upGrad has been scaling the idea of personalization and community growth.
- Community building: In order to assist learners to interact with business leaders and develop a stronger sense of community, upGrad has been organizing offline mentor and mentee meet-ups. Such post-program services that foster networking with industry leaders also help in strengthening a learner's trust in the brand as their trusted LifeLongLearning partner.

(5) upGrad live

- This dates back to 2020 when upGrad had announced access to its proprietary tech platform, upGrad Live, to all colleges, universities, Government Bodies, and NGOs to not let the pandemic-induced disruptions impact the education flow. The platform has been enabling offline educational institutes to seamlessly replicate the classroom in the virtual space. It's more like a digital campus that upGrad has built for universities to let them reach every corner of India without letting universities fall prey to offline-accessibility challenges.

(6) Coaching and mentorship

- upGrad has built a powerful panel of over 5,500 mentors and career coaches who are working with large corporates, national or international universities, or MNCs, and they are deeply connected within the ecosystem. Divided evenly to take charge of content creation, delivery, and alumni support, these industry leaders actively engage with our learners, use their professional experiences and trivia to enhance the subject foundation, and also help them with placement support for maximum career acceleration. Seventy percent of the overall learning experience is designed and delivered through industry experts that make use of graphics, animations, edits, and simulations for making the learning process more engaging and immersive.

(7) Job-enabled upGrad-branded courses is a new learning model from upGrad
The company creates the largest upskilling program portfolio to allow first-time job seekers and working professionals enhance their skills for getting employable. The thrust is based on five key offerings and opportunities:

- Eighty percent of those joining the workforce find it impossible to crack a job. The upGrad course portfolio is committed to make them employable with the right skill sets.
- Hiring costs for corporations are soaring, which saves time and cost for both employer and employee.

- upGrad works with over 3,700 companies around the world for their training needs, and this value proposition dovetails very well.
- upGrad understands the employee needs with its more than three million learner base over the last seven years, and therefore, it is best positioned to identify all the training elements that go into these courses.
- The programs are mostly online and partly blended, with a few offline centers coming up in major cities, thereby allowing upGrad to take this opportunity to scale and drive massive employment within the country.

Conclusion

E-learning is a more cost-effective solution than brick-and-mortar teaching systems, and it keeps us with the continually changing prerequisites for quality education. As a result, it finds extensive application across various sectors like agriculture, health care, and education. The way forward will be a skills economy, not an information economy. This is where the education system needs to prepare children with skilllsets that are trained to handle situations objectively rather than informatively.

Peer-learning environment and access for adult learning have vast potential with ed-tech. For these systemic changes in learning and teaching to occur, education leaders need to create a shared vision for how technology can best meet the needs of all learners and to develop a plan that translates the vision into action.

Technology-enabled assessments require a robust infrastructure, including high-speed connectivity and devices that are available to teachers and students when they need them. Digital learning content and other resources as well as professional development for educators and education leaders are also mandatory.

Ed-tech's core objective is to create educational programs and courses that meet the needs of the changing period. The job market in India is seen to outgrow traditional job roles. In the next five years, 40 percent of Indian employees will need reskilling, and 60 percent will need upskilling to stay relevant, according to job data analyzed by Monster.com.

In the realm of ed-tech, students can take advantage of innovative solutions beyond classroom learning to create tailor-made curricula and learn in ways tailored to their individual needs. By combining theoretical concepts with experiments, case studies, and assignments, ed-tech solutions and programs are designed to help students improve their skills, critical thinking, and creativity.

Words of Wisdom

In the context of schools and digitalization, transformations could manifest as new ways of teaching and learning, communicating, and organizing work. A painful, yet productive, comprehensive transformation taking place in an inert system with strong norms and visions is, however, a rare phenomenon in schools.

By conceptualizing digitalization as developing in smaller steps, it is possible to analyze a gradual digitalization, even though it might not result in a complete school transformation. As part of the digital transformation process, we must know how teachers, school leaders, and educational technologists understand and implement digitalization, the implementation of digital learning, and changes to new educational and technological infrastructures within schools. It is envisioned that, in turn, this will contribute to an understanding of different levels of learning and thus how to transform the school.

Acknowledgments

We'd like to extend our thanks and gratitude to the teams that put this book together, for their hours of extensive research and overall great partnership—Preeti Shroff-Mehta, Sukruti Phatak, Grishma Trivedi (grishma.trivedi@micamail.in), Devika Menon (devika-menon@micamail.in) and Suhair Killiyath (suhairkilliyath@micamail.in) (MICA), Sohini Sen, Anwesha Ray, and Neha Prasad (upGrad), and Komal Lath and Shweta Mehrotra (Tute Consult), Gurshabad—Bridging Language Gaps . . . Globally and Reema Morendha (Researcher) and Adfactors PR (supported research).

Key Discussion Areas

- Overview of education governance.
- Digital education strategy and its advantages in EdTech.
- upGrad and its impact on digital education.

Notes

1 World Bank, "70% of 10-Year-Olds Now in Learning Poverty, Unable to Read and Understand a Simple Text," press release, June 23, 2022, www.worldbank.org/en/news/press-release/2022/06/23/70-of-10-year-olds-now-in-learning-poverty-unable-to-read-and-understand-a-simple-text (accessed November 1, 2023).

2 Fortune Business Insights, "EdTech and Smart Classroom Market Size, Share & COVID-19 Impact Analysis, By Instructional Aid (Smart Classroom and Mobile Learning), By Smart Classroom Hardware (Interactive Projectors, Interactive Whiteboards, and Others) By Educational Tool (Admission Automation Tools, Administration Tools, Learning Management Tools, Alumni Management Tools, Placement Management Tools, Library Management Tools, and Others), By End-user (Higher Education, K-12, and Kindergarten), and Regional Forecast, 2023–2030," Fortunebusinessinsights.com/enquiry/request-sample-pdf/edtech-and-smart-classroom-market-104662 (accessed November 1, 2023).

References

Forture Business Insights, n.d. Fortunebusinessinsights.com/enquiry/request-sample-pdf/edtech-and-smart-classroom-market-104662 (accessed November 1, 2023).

Shift eLearning. n.d. "15 Facts and Stats That Reveal the Power of eLearning." https://www.shiftelearning.com/blog/bid/301248/15-facts-and-stats-that-reveal-the-power-of-elearning

14

GOVERNING FOR SELF-GOVERNANCE IN EDUCATION

Joshua A. Muskin

Introduction

In the vast majority of countries, well-established formal governance structures operate to define and deliver education, evaluate and certify learning, and distribute the rewards of attainment broadly and fairly, or so most systems claim (Sleeter and Carmona 2017). Whether highly centralized to a national or regional level or assigned to decentralized local governmental authorities, decision-making in education, with few exceptions, occurs as a highly top-down system (Tsai and Beverton 2007). The nearly universal, if often tacit, premise is that ensuring sameness across the myriad dimensions of education delivery will yield sameness in the quality of instruction and learning and then, ultimately, in equitable access to the economic, social, and other rewards of schooling. At least this calculation seems to be universal when one looks at how most education systems operate (Maisuria 2005). Yet when looking at outcomes, few can argue sincerely that equality in the delivery of schooling across a system consistently yields results of equal quality and effect. Rather, inequality of both delivery and results is rampant (Wiseman 2008).

Uneven outcomes may result for one of a few essential reasons (Savage 2016). One, a system may fail to achieve uniform quality due to poor design, an inefficient allocation of resources, the ineffectual dissemination and use of strategies, shoddy supervision, or various other operational shortcomings. Two, the broader context might interfere. Enrolment, attendance, and performance in school may suffer in different locations because children there are malnourished or suffer from other health problems, cultural bias, or other factors. They may be victims of violence at home or in the community. Perhaps their communities lack access to basic infrastructure such as water, sanitation, and electricity, among many other circumstances. Lastly, education results are doomed to be uneven when schools and teachers do not deliver the standard program with equal skill, creativity, or commitment. Across the world, it commonly falls to the system to study these failures, regardless of where they reside, and then to solve them. When they do this, the tendency is to design or find solutions that are uniform and then to introduce these as uniform practice. Where this does not occur, systems encourage bespoke solutions to shared and unique challenges—think Finland and New Zealand. Excellence prevails (Barber and Mourshed 2007).

DOI: 10.4324/9781003316077-18

The core assertion of this chapter is that the systemic homogenization of education is rife with risks, built-in shortcomings, and existential contradictions that are doomed to yield vastly uneven results. Indeed, one need not look far to discover that the logic of homogeneity fails almost everywhere. This is equally true whether speaking of education content, instructional methods, learning assessment, and even desired learning outcomes. Following a brief review of the literature, this chapter provides a more exhaustive list of the fundamental education domains that systems typically govern centrally, in a top-down fashion. It then outlines the many reasons why each classroom and school are unique and, therefore, grossly ill-suited to one-size-fits-all solutions. Positing that the essence of quality and equity across the key governance domains rests within heterogeneous, not homogeneous, approaches, this chapter proposes what local governance might look like and offers concrete illustrative strategies by which central authorities might foster such governance at the classroom, school, and community levels to create the most promising foundation for achieving quality and fairness in teaching, learning, and education outcomes across all settings.

Literature Review

The literature on school governance[1] covers a broad range of topics. Some of these are more functional, focused on the administrative operations and oversight of a school or school system—what one might call the machinery of education. Other topics are more concerned by the respective actors who are charged with the operation and efficacy of a school or system—the "mechanics." Looking functionally at the education machinery and the mechanics who keep it humming, the sector falls essentially across three dimensions, characterized here as the political, technical, and operational. *Politically*, governance structures provide the system's lodestar, defining the aspirations and expectations that society assigns to schools while establishing the essential policies, standards, and resource parameters for attaining these ends. At the same time, they oversee and hold accountable the operational and technical structures and personnel, monitoring and enforcing their adherence to established policy and standards, their use of resources, and progress toward the stated aspirations. This is essentially true whether a system's authority resides at a national, regional/state, or local district level, or even sits with some board structure of a single private school or network of schools (see, e.g., UK Department for Education 2015).

A system's *technical* mechanics control areas such as curriculum and textbooks, personnel management, teacher training, planning and budgeting, testing, monitoring and evaluation, facilities management, and special needs and inclusion. They are usually assigned by level and domain of education: pre-primary and primary; secondary; technical and vocational; nonformal and adult; and tertiary. The *operational* dimension is where teachers and school leaders use the many inputs and apply the system's standards to deliver the curriculum to students in the classroom. It is also where local education agents, such as inspectors, supervise, and monitor, support the teachers and schools, all in the service of student learning.

The common hierarchical form of governance described here draws considerable scrutiny in the research literature. As suggested in the introduction, of particular interest in this chapter are those studies that challenge the top-down nature of education systems. This literature appears to critique education governance primarily from two distinct angles. The first concerns primarily what teachers teach in the classroom and how they teach it.

The second treats more generally the notions of autonomy and authority in education decision-making. In both instances, a core argument is that teachers and other school-level educators and administrators know best. Jelmer Evers and René Kneyber (2016) take a somewhat revolutionary approach to this perspective in their edited volume, *Flip the System*. Here, they assert:

> Teachers should instead act on an assumption of being equal, refusing and interrupting the working of powers in the educational system and laying claim to positions and discretional space that they have not previously been entitled to. To initiate this process, it is not simply a question of the government telling teachers to emancipate. It is rather a question of teachers initiating this process themselves.

The most obvious aspect of education from which teachers can emancipate themselves is the delivery of the curriculum, or what and how they teach. They *can* free themselves in delivering the curriculum because they are alone with it and with their students day in and day out.[2] They *should* lead its delivery because they are uniquely situated to know how best to align the official curriculum to their students' particular foundational knowledge, learning styles, abilities, interests, and lives. Rather than stay constrained by content that will be on the test, as Christine Sleeter and Judith Flores Carmona (2017) and Daniel Alvunger (2018) propose, teachers must have the freedom, or agency, to choose not just the modes of their instruction but also the subjects. Teachers are *not*, Evers and Kneyber (2016, 3) remind us, "trained monkeys" for whom it is "simply a question of finding the right stick to beat . . . or the right brand of peanuts to make him do the desired dance in front of the audience." Teachers bring rich professional and personal lives to the classroom, serving to inform their teaching practices. They navigate both the institutional and broader social structures that envelope their classrooms, exercising their rhetorical agency. They engage in dialogic interaction with each other, administrators, their students, and others to strengthen their overall decision-making and performance (Trippestad 2015; Lai, Li, and Gong 2016; Alvunger 2018).

Gert Biesta and Michael Tedder (2007) and Tom Are Trippestad (2015, 10) explain that agents such as teachers can use this kind of dynamic and symbiotic relationship both to shape and be shaped by rhetorical culture and communicative practices within their professional communities. Such rhetorical agency is guided by multiple discourses and communicative practices that allow for a range of actions. While discourses can be authoritative, they can also be transgressive and paradoxical. Yet this range of possibilities can give a teacher the capacity to explore these dimensions and strategically apply the discourse they may deem appropriate. This encourages creativity while maintaining an overarching curricular structure. "To be a rhetorical agent as a teacher," Trippestad explains, "means to have the ability and capacity to influence others." This gives the teacher a chance to step outside the "box" of a rigid course to build lessons around the students' areas of interest and thereby increase their sense of accountability and participation.

As rhetorical agents, teachers need open "spaces" in which to operate, whether these constitute the concrete space of the classroom or the virtual spaces of the curriculum, the instructional methods they use to deliver the curriculum, and the ways they assess their students' learning. Looking at the classroom space alone, Alvunger (2018, 479) proposes three types that allow teachers to exercise agency: a collective space, an individual space, and an interactive space. In all three, true discourse and meaning-making come from students and teachers', not the curriculum's, deriving sense from a combination of individual and collective experiences, inferences, and reasoning. This explanation gains further significance and intentionality when teachers link within one lesson content from multiple subjects, providing students (and the teacher) "room to act and create" within a contextually relevant reality. They don't just learn as an abstract academic exercise to pass a test (Alvunger 2018, 494) but rather to cultivate knowledge that will serve them in their future lives and livelihoods as well as in their future studies. In this regard, they are channeling the mantra of UNESCO's (1996) Delors Report: learning to Know, to Do, to Be, and to Be Together.)

Scholars who have studied culturally diverse educational institutions such as international schools believe that cross-cultural values, intercultural interdependence, and the integration of ethnic cultures in the curriculum can encourage rhetorical agency among teachers and instructors as a way to create a dispersed yet culturally conscious education system *and students* (Tan 2016; Alvunger 2018). They take into account the local, global, and social positions that both teachers and students occupy to use interactive approaches that facilitate, for example, the integration of ethnic experiences and linguistic diversity.

Many scholars point to the globally recognized success of Finland's and New Zealand's education systems, attributing their results to the their investment in teacher quality and, critically, to the supreme degree of agency that they accord their teachers. Luis Crouch (2015) explains that Finland prioritizes teacher training, and teachers are trusted to take charge of the design of their courses and the methods of instruction they use to teach these. Undergirding this confidence are the teacher recruitment, training, support, and other strategies the two systems operate to ensure and continue to grow the professional capacity of all teachers, as outlined in the landmark 2007 McKinsey study, *How the World's Best Performing Schools Come Out on Top*. Both countries exemplify the success of teacher leadership programs, where the focus lies on securing the quality of the teaching and learning experience by balancing what Muskin (2018) refers to as teachers' intrinsic and extrinsic capacity. Teachers need both knowledge and skills—intrinsic capacity—and the training, support, and conditions to capitalize what they know—extrinsic capacity. In *Flip the System*, Evers and Kneyber's (2016, 73) appeal is that all systems emulate this degree of "teacher professionalism." Sometimes, he argues

> the government will shift some control over to the profession by separating the "how" and the "what." Governments decide "what" teachers should achieve, and they are then "free" to decide how to achieve it. But even that is, to me, extremely contentious. Governments should support a profession but should leave the "how" and the "what" to them.

Broader appeals for autonomy and authority in education decision-making sometimes refer to such explicit areas as school management and community relations. These tend to be much more vague than those who advocate for emancipation in the classroom, though they are not necessarily less earnest or, for that matter, relevant.

Current education systems largely employ broad and comprehensive standardization practices. These operate under the belief that systematic practices will maintain the generalized quality and equity of teaching and learning (Sleeter and Carmona 2017). The top-down generality and homogeneity are meant to ensure standardization; however, the guidelines are often interpreted as the process itself. These practices have been attributed to the notion of a "factory system" designed to produce universally consistent learning outcomes (Schroeder 2011, 883). The then president of the American Federation of Teachers, Al Shanker, referred to such a system in his speech, "The Revolution That is Overdue: From Information Factory to Learning and Teaching in Restructuring Schools," to highlight the need to reform the American education system (May 18, 1989, University of Wisconsin). While standardization is said to have evolved as a result of nineteenth- and twentieth-century utilitarian attitudes, it also served certain egalitarian purposes. Sleeter and Carmona (2017, 4) believe that "standardization is a consequence of standard setting when attempts to improve student learning become bureaucratized and curriculum is defined in detail in terms of what is measurable and is established at state or national levels." However, no matter how standardized the system is, the thesis of this chapter, to repeat, is that this will result in uncertain outcomes. Sleeter and Carmona suggest that this may trace to macro-factors such as course design, training, and administrative bodies as well as to micro-factors such as varying degrees of student commitment and participation due to health, socioeconomic background, and access to resources.

Sleeter (2017) argues further that students who are socially disadvantaged are at greater risk of not learning critical thinking at the cost of higher test scores. While standardized tests can help evaluate a student's academic progress, they are not an adequate marker of a student's capabilities (Schroeder 2011, 882). These abilities comprise most notably students' ability to use what they have learned from the curriculum in practical settings, such as for life and livelihood purposes. Summoning Delors (1996) again, system education standards are often even further removed from the life skills, or twenty-first-century skills, that employers and all of society value with rapidly growing urgency.

Various scholars have also proposed the need for teacher agency in choosing modes and subjects of instruction without being delimited by a standardized evaluation system and measures (Sleeter and Carmona 2017; Alvunger 2018). Much like students, teachers and other educators occupy positions in society beyond the classroom that influence their professional lives and teaching practices and, therefore, the criteria and means by which they appraise these. Scholars believe that a system can encourage a teacher's decision-making in the process of instruction and education by according her/him rhetorical agency and dialogical interaction in all aspects of teaching, including assessment (Trippestad 2015; Lai, Li, and Gong 2016; Alvunger 2018).

While teacher agency in the design and delivery of courses, classroom management, and learning assessment comes with clear advantages and remains the advocacy focus of this chapter, there are certainly drawbacks. Mark Priestley and colleagues (2012) are not alone in arguing in the literature that context matters, often greatly. Certain conditions, such as subject matter, course design, and teacher capabilities and subjectivities, can produce "situations of possibility and constraint" (191). Another limitation is that of language. Systems often expect teachers to use a metropolitan or other national language that is completely foreign to their students and in which teachers themselves may be illiterate or even barely conversant. Teachers are often ill-equipped to deploy their agency or summon their initiative and creativity in the classroom for many other reasons as well, often linked to both their intrinsic and extrinsic capacities (Muskin 2018). Overcrowded curricula, low teaching skill and poor content knowledge, rare and overly conceptual training, absent, superficial, or draconian supervision and support, a penury of pedagogic provisions, shortened school calendars, punitive, irrelevant assessment regimes, hostile classroom climates, and many other constrictive factors leave many teachers ill-equipped and unconfident to exercise agency effectively in the classroom (Muskin 2022).

Erecting an elaborate scaffold—for example, with scripted lessons (Davidson 2015)—to counteract these weaknesses may seem the only or best option an education system has, particularly in middle- and low-income countries where systems are often urged in this direction by international partners. Yet this is little more than a short-term solution, as it is truly only a distant second-best choice. As asserted in the introduction, imposing homogeneity in education delivery will result in neither consistently high quality nor equitable teaching and learning. So, when opting for a uniform scaffold approach to address persistent and pervasive system shortfalls, any system must promptly plan and enact steps to dismantle the scaffolding across its schools as quickly as reasonable, accommodating, of course, the fact that some teachers will be ready to exert their independence more quickly than others. The balance of this chapter is devoted to discussing why and how bottom-up governance offers a key to loosening the systemic homogenization of teachers and teaching, beginning with an overview of what governance in education actually governs.

What School Governance Is Governing

In looking at school governance, an obvious starting point is to articulate precisely what decisions, actions, and resources systems are in fact governing. While others may group these differently, they fall essentially across the following nine domains. The first three are, arguably, the most significant, driven more by political considerations and influenced by sociocultural pressures than by technical analysis and evidence. The remaining domains may also bend to politics, but they are more subject to technocratic decision-making.

1. *Education vision and mission:* School is the crucible in which a nation, region, district, or other jurisdiction shapes its youth to create the society it desires. Here is where patriotic allegiance is forged, where future workers gain the knowledge and skills that will drive economic growth, and where children learn their relationship with and responsibility toward the environment. It is where citizens are fostered to maintain social norms and/or cultivate new ones and where they find their group or groups, situating themselves in relation to other groups, in their community, across the nation, and across nations. A vision may aspire to equity, social cohesion and justice, and a green future just as it may promote ethnic or cultural superiority, territorial integrity, and economic domination. It may be imposed by a ruler, a ruling class, or some other de jure or de facto authority, result from a political process, or emerge from some popular consultation. As such, a jurisdiction's education vision and mission can shift, sometimes suddenly. Whatever the vision, all other domains must be shaped and operate in its service.
2. *Curriculum and textbooks:* The most visible and concrete manifestation of a jurisdiction's vision and mission is the curriculum and the textbooks that serve as the curriculum's main "vehicle." Together, these are where the knowledge, skills, and even attitudes that will serve the vision and mission are captured as content, activities, examples, applications, and other learning elements. In some instances, a curriculum may be neutral and free of a vision-driven agenda—or at least it may seem or be claimed to be so. Certainly, learning basic mathematics involves universally legitimate skills. But as curriculum developers decide what children are adding and subtracting, they may insert various biases, whether implicit or explicit and unwittingly or purposefully. This can be relatively benign, such as favoring metropolitan math problems—for example, the time it takes to cover X miles in a train traveling at Y kilometers per hour—over rural

problems—for example, traveling by camel from one oasis to another or on foot through the mountains. Conversely, it can also be patently and perversely patriotic, such as this word problem from the infamous mathematics lessons from pre-9/11 Afghanistan:

A Kalashnikov bullet travels at 800 meters per second. A mujahed has the forehead of a Russian in his sights 3,200 meters away. How many seconds will it take the bullet to hit the Russian's forehead?

(Dehghanpisheh 2001)[3]

This is also where a jurisdiction decides to teach whether a certain group comprises praiseworthy patriots or recalcitrant rebels or how to teach about past civil or ethnic conflict, its original contact with foreign and Indigenous peoples, and the nature and impacts of technological and economic "progress." Does the curriculum include the arts, religion, race studies, financial literacy, vocational skills, home economics, or other such courses? All such decisions speak directly to the system's vision and mission for schooling.

As a curriculum is intended for all schools across a system, the aim is to imbue all students with the same fundamental knowledge, skills, attitudes, and beliefs. Clearly, different students perceive their lessons differently, bringing to their studies different histories, status, and prospects as related to what they are learning. In the United States, for example, Native American children certainly bring a different understanding to lessons about the "discovery" of America than do the children of European immigrants to the country.

3. *Standardized tests:* Education systems conduct standardized assessments of learning at fixed points along the academic ladder to signal each student's mastery of the official curriculum. In other words, standardized tests are instrumental in answering the question, "In which ways is a student best and least well suited to contribute to the overall vision and mission for which society is educating her or him?" In most systems, the results determine the nature of a student's future education opportunities and, as a consequence, of her or his professional and social trajectory. Certainly, children and their parents may have adequate agency to thwart or influence the fate set by one's test scores. One such strategy is the evening test-taking preparation in which numerous South Korean parents invest to raise their children's chances of entering the best universities, what Mark Bray refers to as "shadow education" (2014). In most instances, though, the choice between an academic or vocational-technical track or abrupt entry into the workforce, studies in the physical sciences, social sciences, or humanities, and university, polytechnic training, or employment are fixed, determined by a student's standardized test results.

   As with the curriculum and vision, however, the fact that a test is standardized does not mean that it is just, equitable, or even unerringly accurate in measuring learning or, especially, potential. As illustrated above, determining a student's knowledge by asking questions that are contextually familiar to some but not to others risks falsifying the true knowledge and potential of the two groups. One version of this bias is the long-standing criticism that the Standardized Aptitude Test (SAT) in the United States favors white males over other groups (Chada 2022; Jaschik 2010; Dickson 2019). As a standardized or homogeneous, test, there is little to no attempt to measure students' knowledge and aptitudes that derive from their home context and that best suit them to thrive and contribute there. Lastly, standardized tests are patently inept at measuring the sorts of personal competencies, also known as twenty-first century, that are essential to move communities, nations, regions, and the world forward. Just a few of these competencies include critical thinking, creativity, perseverance, collaboration, and emotional intelligence. Their cultivation by education systems is critical whether talking about the Sustainable Development Goals, climate change, the Fourth Industrial Age, the culture wars, or whatever future for which society must prepare its children and youth.

4. *Infrastructure and instructional resources:* An education system also governs decisions concerning infrastructure and instructional resources. These include their very nature, such as what they look like, the materials used, what to furnish and what not to provide, and other basic characteristics as well as their quality, and how much, when, and where to distribute them. Again, it is not uncommon for systems to standardize these assets. In this way, one can walk into a third grade classroom or secondary school science laboratory in one context and find a very similar looking set of classrooms, even when these appear in vastly different contexts. There are compelling justifications for this sort of homogeneity. Core to these is to ensure that children and communities with different socioeconomic profiles have equal access to quality learning. But again, the planning for sameness neither truly achieves consistent sameness nor does it necessarily yield same or even similar results.

   Such discrepancy traces to many factors. For one, equal investments in its schools by a jurisdiction are commonly calculated by using a per capita formula. It is not surprising that such an approach will often result in very different education settings. This can happen because the cost and availability of materials may be higher in one location, such as remote communities, or because parents or the community are able to bring additional funds to the school and classroom. Another factor is the environment. Quite simply, the same classroom design and materials may create extremely different learning conditions when located in a city, in a mountainous region that is vulnerable to extreme cold, and in a desert. It certainly wouldn't accommodate a nomadic pastoralist community. Lastly, the capacities of the teachers and administrators assigned to use these assets can vary greatly and affect the learning that results. If teachers are ill-trained and rarely supported to use the various learning materials that their system provides to them, even the best equipped science laboratory or primary classroom will not produce consistent learning outcomes. Unfortunately, the schools where this scenario prevails are predictably most prevalent in schools situated in remote, poor, ethnically or racially marginalized, or other disregarded communities.

5. *Pedagogy:* In many education systems, the lessons teachers design and the methods they use to deliver these are also subjected to top-down governance. Uniform pedagogy results from several sorts of direction and interaction that teachers encounter. These include the concepts and techniques they acquire at teacher training colleges and that they must be able to demonstrate to be certified. They are codified in the curricula, textbooks, teachers' manuals, and other instructional materials that teachers must use precisely, faithfully, and completely. (At least this is what teachers believe, even though I have yet to meet a curriculum designer who says that this is what is officially intended.) At its extreme, this takes shape as fully scripted lessons, which dictate such aspects as the examples, exercises, assessment questions and methods, and the pacing every teacher must use. This conjures the memory of a through-the-looking-glass-like direction from one scripted lesson in which the lesson guide literally instructs the teacher to "raise your right arm now." Many school leaders and inspectors also seem to have missed the memo

from curriculum designers that the curriculum is a flexible guide, not a rigid recipe. Whether with in-service training or classroom observations, their tendency is to enforce pedagogic orthodoxy across all teachers. They do this by asking such questions as, "Are you on the right lesson?" "Are you using the prescribed instructional method correctly?" and "Does your lesson plan conform fully to the curriculum?" Lastly, teachers stick to convention because that is what their senior colleagues tell them is necessary to stay secure in the profession.

Once again, the expectation that teachers will adhere slavishly to a single version of pedagogy and yield learning outcomes of a consistent nature and quality is ludicrous. Even if the prescribed pedagogy varies by subject and the learners' grade level, sticking with what the central governing structures say "works" and therefore must prevail in all instruction will not lead to uniformly solid results in the classroom. This is true neither across learning contexts nor, as any teacher would confirm, even with the same learners in the same classroom. Whether simply to combat the boredom that excessive repetition inevitably wreaks or to recognize that students' energy, attention, concentration, and other levels ebb and flow over the course of a day, a week, and a year, virtually any teacher will affirm that pedagogic variety is essential. There is no one "what works" in teaching.

6. *Teachers and teacher training:* Related closely to pedagogy is the teacher. This is the person most directly responsible for translating instructional methods, and indeed virtually all education investments, into learning. Education systems may aspire to heterogeneity in the personal characteristics of its teaching corps, seeking diversity by sex, ethnicity, geography, interests, and so on. But once in the circle, the custom in most systems seems to be to fit all into a mold of homogeneity. The form of the mold is forged by the few fundamental parameters described above. Irrespective of the personal attributes and unique assets a teacher may bring to the classroom, the opportunity to capitalize on these is commonly circumscribed by the official curriculum, the high-stakes tests that will determine most students' future education, livelihood, and life prospects, the resources they have available, and the pedagogy the system trains and enforces them to use.

These molding strategies begin with the selection process: who are the candidates that society tends to attract, or rather to channel, to the teaching profession? In many education systems, particularly in developing country contexts, most who enter the teaching profession do so because their secondary school academic results do not qualify them for other, more prestigious and lucrative professions. In other words, many, and arguably most, come to the role with minimal motivation or academic acumen—not a great start. Once in a teacher training college, future teachers work to hone their knowledge of the content they will be teaching and acquire the pedagogy they will use to transmit this knowledge to their students. Upon certification, off to the classroom they go. Here, their supervisors and experienced colleagues routinely tell them to forget what they learned in class and indoctrinate them to the survival skills of the true classroom, usually a chalk-and-talk, or drill-and-kill, delivery of the entire textbook. The occasional in-service training and inspection visits they receive cement the pedagogic orthodoxy further, as does the code of conduct to which they must commit and adhere. For those who settle into the mold successfully, the reward is advancement along the official career path.

Returning again to the core argument of this chapter, it is clear that cookie-cutter versions of a teacher and teaching will not produce uniform quality in learning? There is no single ideal avatar, or "who works," of the ideal educator. Consider the following question, which I have asked educators and education leaders in scores of workshops I have led over the past few decades: "Looking back over the entirety of your personal academic career, how many of your teachers truly exhibited excellence and had a significant and enduring impact on your life?" There has yet to be a teacher, teacher trainer, or education official, at whatever level who has required a second hand to respond to this question. Furthermore, the teacher whom one educator might place in a personal pantheon of pedagogues may actually feature in another former classmate's nightmares. The teachers these educators recall were usually the "rebels," those instructors who brought creativity, context, and inspiration to the curriculum, texts, and assessments, who varied their pedagogy, who challenged their supervisors, and who used the available resources in innovative ways while adding their own.

7. *Parental and community engagement:* Systems often also define narrowly and uniformly the role that parents and the community play in their children's learning. This starts with the requirement to send their children to school, usually to a government-authorized school. There may even be penalties associated with not doing so. The expectation is, further, that parents will ensure their children's regular school attendance and provide conditions and attention at home to enable their children's academic success. However, following up with parents or guardians at home is rarely something a system includes among a school's or teacher's responsibilities.

   Many systems do create structures within a school for parents and the broader community to monitor and, hopefully, support their children's education. These often go by the names of "Parent-Teachers Association," to which "Students" is sometimes added or, "School Management Committee." Some systems accommodate both. Unsurprisingly, the scope of influence these structures have tends also to be limited and standard, with very little opportunity to influence instruction directly. Rather, parents' roles in a school seem to focus mostly on fundraising, the maintenance and improvement of school facilities, student attendance, and issues of security and discipline.

   The assignment to parents of responsibilities for their children's schooling and school, all of which link uniformly to their economic status, level of literacy and education, and management capabilities, would seem, again, to result in vastly nonuniform outcomes.

8. *Funding:* The considerable diversity of communities' assets across a system are compounded by the common capita funding formula—often referred to as "capitation granting"—used to allocate resources for the creation and operation of schools. Systems often embrace a uniform cost-per-student formula to indicate equity, allowing them to say that they are valuing all children equally and giving them an equal opportunity to learn. Yet again, however, centralized governance fails, since homogeneous funding formulas clearly do not produce homogeneous quality in the delivery or outcomes of schooling. This happens for at least four reasons. One, the same system may have different governing structures, each of which may have a different wealth profile. This could leave the overall governance of education with widely differing capitation quotients across different sub-populations, anchoring qualitative discrepancies in terms of infrastructure and instructional assets, teachers' qualifications, capacity, and commitment, parental support both at home and in the school, school management, and pedagogic supervision, and more. Two, as mentioned above, costs for basic education materials may be greater in poorer and more remote areas. The cost of transportation explains much of this difference, but other factors may pertain, too. For example, teachers may require incentives or additional allowances to accept a remote posting. Three, more remote and poorer

regions are often less densely populated, so the capitation calculation leaves them with less funding with which to provide infrastructure and educators for the same number of classes. Last, these same populations are less able to compensate for the deficiencies of the government education system by mobilizing additional resources to invest further in their school or by providing alternative learning opportunities to their children.

9. *Complementary services and programs:* Finally, the same logic differentiates the effectiveness of top-down governance of education in communities when looking at the range of other factors that affect students' ability to learn. Whether addressing peripheral enabling factors within the school, for example with extracurricular programs or health services, or outside, at the community level, the provision of services and other opportunities using a standardized formula can overlook vastly nonstandard needs. This analysis pertains to addressing such dimensions as students' health and nutrition, equity and inclusion, psychosocial health, and security, among others. A one-size-fits-all approach is doomed to fall short, if not fail entirely, unless it is designed to consider deeply and strategically the prevailing sociocultural norms, economic profile, peace and security situation, and climatic vulnerability, among many other factors.[4]

It is the combination of these many domains and the multiple synergies that operate across them that weigh most heavily on the quality of education and learning across a system. Navigating this complexity can be guided by governance structures at the top of a system, but truly managing the myriad points of intersection must reside with local level governance.

The Risks of Homogenizing Education

At its essence, the aim of this chapter is to distinguish between viewing a factor as a goal and as a strategy. At this time in global history, most societies expect that a core goal of a central governing structure is to provide equality of opportunity and at least a basic standard of living to all citizens—at least most espouse this. While many may doubt the sincerity of such claims, even they view pursuit of the goal as a core responsibility. This is true regardless the form of government or the nature of the economic system a jurisdiction operates.

To repeat from the introduction to this chapter, it is also universally accepted that the institution of education is vital to achieving this ideal. Arguably, no society can legitimately claim strategies that mirror completely its education goal, operating a system that yields full equality of opportunity and the attainment of basic living standards for all. As Walker et al. (2019, 5) assert:

> While schooling remains segregated by class, wealth, ethnicity, gender or other signifiers of privilege and exclusion, this cements inequality. Segregated patterns of schooling build segregated communities, driving a wedge between the haves and the have-nots, right at the start of life.

As indicated earlier, commonality that sets apart those systems that analysts frequently claim to come close, such as Finland and New Zealand, is the liberty they provide to teachers and schools to make their own decisions about most of the nine factors above. The intention here is not to study these two systems to analyze how they do this. The aim instead is to explore the nature of bottom-up governance more conceptually. This begins with understanding why the homogenization of education so routinely fails to produce the desired outcomes, whether for learning and learners or for society. The explanation is simple, though it embodies vast complexities that surpass the scope of the current analysis, suited for a book, not a chapter.

Basically, homogenization fails because every school and, indeed, every classroom is unique. Just like planting the same crops in different soils will result in harvests of different quantities and qualities, so too will the same education inputs produce different learning in different settings. This uniqueness emerges from the many different factors that characterize a classroom and fall most easily across two basic domains: personal traits and contextual factors. In turn, these pertain to the two key classroom actors: the teacher and students. The uniqueness these features create in a classroom grows exponentially when considering the myriad ways in which they intersect and interact.

Beginning with *personal traits*, teachers and students alike are distinct both individually and as groups in many ways. They are stronger and weaker in different academic subjects, whether due to natural aptitude, previous learning, personal motivation, or other reasons. They harbor a variety of individual talents, interests, experiences, and networks that might inspire or equip them better to teach or study one academic area or another. They also bring different personalities and personal competencies that will influence how they interact with each other, with different teaching and learning methods, with the learning content, and in the overall management of the classroom.

Looking at *contextual factors*, both sets of classroom actors and the overall school harbor and are affected by unique combinations of characteristics that define their families, their family heritage, and their communities. Perhaps, most distinct are family assets. These extend beyond simple family income to include material wealth, landholdings, knowledge, ancestral status, personal networks, and more. Such factors often reflect the socioeconomic features that characterize a locale and might, for example, distinguish a pastoralist from an agricultural society or a rural from an urban setting. They concern more than simply the wealth of an area, referring as well to sociocultural norms, technological expertise, access to markets and services, and more. "Culture and education are complex phenomena, and their causal relationship is of a 'chicken or the egg' character" (Giorgetti et al. 2017, 1). Local culture also often influences education, affecting such decisions as who enrolls and for how many years. This frequently affect girls and children with disabilities especially. Culture can also instigate community actions around who can teach, who can attend class, the delivery of certain aspects of the curriculum, and other aspects of a school's operation. Lastly, the nature of a school's and each classroom's facilities and resources can differ widely, despite a system's intentions and the equal capitation funding calculation. The local natural environment can similarly vary vastly, visible in the terrain, temperatures, weather, and other climatic conditions as well as in the man-made infrastructure and efforts taken to control these conditions; for example, building bridges to cross roaring streams during the rainy season, heating classrooms during cold winters, or shortening instructional hours when temperatures become oppressive.

This analysis clearly extends beyond Howard Gardner's (2006, 8–18) identification of different learning individual styles, characterizing nine types of student intelligence: verbal-linguistic, logical-mathematical, spatial-visual, bodily kinesthetic, musical, interpersonal, intrapersonal, naturalist, or existential. For one, it considers the factors that might influence a teacher's preferred or most natural instructional style. At the same time, it considers how the mix of styles and many other characteristics, including assets as well as deficits, that students and teachers bring together in a classroom interact and can be manipulated to enhance or, conversely, to impede both individual and collective learning. Lastly, it considers the many extraneous but still highly influential factors that are so critical in determining the nature and quality of teaching and learning.

The conceit that an education system can govern in a homogeneous way for all of this intrinsic and rich diversity that characterizes each and every classroom and school must be recognized by system operators and their partners alike as a core culprit in the recurring failure of education. This does not mean that all top-down governance is bad. To the contrary, there are several aspects for which one can argue it is valuable, and even necessary. One of these is to govern for heterogeneity, not homogeneity. In other words, systems must create policy, practice, and capacity that promotes effective bottom-up governance as a complement to top-down governance. Similar to how Woolcock describes a mutually reinforcing top-down and bottom-up dynamic for civil society (see Muskin, Kamime, and Adlaoui 2011, 130), a system can simultaneously circumscribe and unleash autonomy at the classroom and school levels by embedding clear policies, responsibilities, practices, and capacity within these local structures. In this way, a system cultivates the synergies and linkages that will move the strategic attainment of equality and opportunity closer to the goal.

How to do this is taken up in the next section.

Governing From the Bottom-Up

It may be appropriate at this point to assert that it is not the intention to argue here for education governance by anarchy. Classroom and school-level governance does not mean giving teachers, local administrators, students, and parents total autonomy to decide why, what, how, where, with what, and when they teach and learn, nor how they measure and certify what they have taught and learned. It does mean, however, giving them considerable discretionary authority over all these factors, allowing them to adapt each of the nine governance domains above to address the heterogeneous characteristics that make each learning context unique. This means both mitigating any challenges and capitalizing on the prevailing assets of a population, school, and locale.

Metaphorically, the aim is to place teachers and schools on roads, not rails, in the delivery of education. On rails, learning must occur at a precise pace, in a precise way, and cover a precise body of content to arrive at a narrowly defined common place at the same time. Any disruptions to the journey put the whole education enterprise at risk. On roads, the ultimate destination is known and shared by all classes, but it may be defined more vaguely and generically to allow for precise, more effective and relevant interpretation. Roads provide ample opportunity to alter the pace and the route. A class may slow down to accommodate students' need to spend more time on a topic to absorb it fully, benefiting from a review of earlier fundamental concepts, greater practice, richer feedback, or remedial instruction. A teacher may slow down a lesson to take time to enrich students' learning of a topic by exploring it more fulsomely. Conversely, a class may speed up. A teacher may decide to do this when students have mastered a concept or skill more quickly or because they agree that a lesson is redundant or simply irrelevant, uninteresting, and neither useful nor necessary to achieve the core learning objective. Both slowing down and speeding up might involve a full academic detour. A teacher and class may stretch out, speed up, or skip a lesson or module to take a "side street" or, at risk of abusing the metaphor, go off-road or disembark to discover something far outside the prescribed lesson. While putatively outside the formal curriculum, such diversions may strengthen even more students' attainment of the core competencies from the academic topics as well as their critical thinking, learning, and many other competencies.

The shift from rails to roads has significance for all nine of the core governance domains described above. Putting teachers, local education authorities, and communities "behind the wheel" to steer schools and classes to better outcomes because teaching and learning are more relevant requires a combination of skill, opportunity, and resources. It also benefits from an unequivocal expression that this is what the system expects and concrete descriptions of what local agency in education looks like in practice. Following are illustrative strategies of local agency for each of the nine governance domains.

1. *Education vision and mission:* Schools mobilize parents, teachers, administrators, local leaders, and other members, and even students to adapt the system-wide vision and mission to the local context. They may start by determining the degree to which the official version pertains to the priorities and circumstances of their local context and population and then decide how to embrace those elements that align and to accommodate those that do not. Schools and communities may also articulate additional or alternative elements of an education vision and mission that reflect priorities and circumstances that are specific to their locale, aiming to ready their children for the future they expect and/or desire for them. These may feature, for example, sociocultural elements—such as a pastoralist lifestyle—or economic dimensions—such as commerce or trades—that characterize a place.
2. *Curriculum and textbooks:* On the road, teachers are using the official curriculum selectively and flexibly. They rely on it to identify the core learning competencies their students must master and as a source of additional content and exercises. But they do this in service of creating their own syllabi and lessons. For the bulk of what they teach, they draw on knowledge, techniques, resources, activities, and other elements from the local context—economic, sociocultural, natural, technological, and so on—to provide the content, examples, exercises, projects, and other strategies with which to direct students' learning. They call on experts from the local community to help make learning relevant, practical, and stimulating. As students progress to higher grades, the balance of content, exercises, and so on provided by the official curriculum and texts and derived from the local context may gradually shift from the local to the system level, but local content and skills will always be included. Moving from the bottom to higher up the education governance structure, teachers and local education agents are providing contextualized lesson plans and content to central curriculum designers to incorporate into texts and other materials the system produces. This sharing brings greater richness to the official curriculum while it can also help to legitimize a system's more far-flung and marginalized locales.
3. *Standardized tests:* Exercising their agency in testing, teachers and local education agents produce questions to assess localized knowledge and contextualized applications of core learning objectives to include as sections in localized versions of the official standardized assessments. As with localized lessons, the central testing authority may in turn select interesting locally generated assessment items to include among the standardized test questions that all students must answer.

4. *Infrastructure and instructional resources:* Driving this domain, local education authorities and others design and construct or renovate education facilities to meet the system's minimum standards while incorporating elements that suit the particular environmental, sociocultural, and other features of the local context. In turn, local education authorities present plans and budgets to central authorities to request additional funding to cover exceptional costs related to extraordinary environmental, socioeconomic, or other structural needs, aiming for equity in outcomes, not in inputs. From a more academic angle, schools and local education authorities procure, mobilize, and/or create additional instructional resources they may need. These can serve especially to incorporate local knowledge and techniques into the teaching of the official curriculum.
5. *Pedagogy:* In the classroom, teachers exercise their agency by thoughtfully choosing, adapting, and varying the pedagogic methods they use with the purposeful intention of

   - maintaining their students' focus, active engagement, and learning;
   - combining the learning of content with the ability to apply their lessons practically (making learning relevant) and the cultivation of personal competencies;
   - adjusting lesson delivery to the students' particular interests, mood, energy level, needs, and other characteristics, including both those that their students exhibit usually and those that may occur at a particular moment;
   - connecting lessons to other content, including from other subject areas.

   By organizing teachers into communities of practice within a school or across nearby schools, they may engage in permanent action-research related to the choice and use of pedagogy and thereby hone at the same time their skills, performance, and results.
6. *Teachers and teacher training:* Governing education from the bottom-up may include the aggressive recruitment of secondary school graduates and university leavers by local education authorities and, even, schools and communities, encouraging them to serve as teachers in their home communities. (While perhaps most relevant for marginalized areas, the advantages of "home-grown" teachers can pertain universally, especially for primary grades.) Whether drawn home by a sense of obligation or allegiance, because of a dearth of acceptable options elsewhere, or to take advantage of special incentives, these new recruits would receive pre-service teacher training in the areas where they will serve. Alternatively, regional education authorities and teacher training colleges may coordinate to expand the pool of recruits, enlisting motivated local secondary school-leavers to serve as full-time paraprofessional teachers while taking courses part-time to receive official teacher certification. All teachers may benefit from the same education communities of practice mentioned above to lead their collective professional development and collaborate in strengthening the quality and relevance of their instruction and classroom management.
7. *Parental and community engagement:* The strategic involvement of parents and the broader community in the local governance of schooling is widely recognized to be vital and can take many forms. To start, school leaders and local education and other authorities must actively encourage their involvement, mobilizing, training, and supporting parents and key community actors to participate directly in the elaboration and implementation of school improvement plans, focusing on quality, equity, and inclusion in school access, participation, and performance. Schools and education authorities may also enlist local development actors to support the creation and operation of parents'

and guardians' groups (especially mothers) to undertake economic and social initiatives. These might aim simultaneously to (i) improve the financial ability of individual families to support their children's schooling and (ii) tackle social, cultural, and other endemic barriers to all children's success at school. Lastly, school and other local education leaders may train, support, and encourage teachers to enlist local community resource persons to contribute to or assume fully the design and delivery of lessons related to their area of expertise to help students learn about their local context while also strengthening their academic learning by applying their lessons practically.

8. *Funding:* The local governance of funding may begin with schools' joining with parents and other local actors to specify what funds they will need by setting both long-term and short-term school improvement targets and strategies. Their planning and budgeting should feature the key areas of

   - infrastructure and equipment;
   - instructional materials;
   - teachers and teacher professional development, including the operation of education communities of practice;
   - extracurricular activities and programs;
   - special projects and project-based learning.

   Through the local education authority, schools may submit their improvement plans to system-level planners to request the needed funding. Parents and local actors will also likely need to supplement what the central system authorities provide. To do this, they may mobilize local economic and social actors, parents, and other government structures to provide additional financial, material, technical, volunteer, and other in-kind inputs.

9. *Complementary services and programs:* Lastly, schools may incorporate actions with relevant local development partners in the design, implementation, and monitoring and evaluation of their formal improvement plans. Specifically, children's ability to attend and succeed in school depends also on their health and nutrition, their families' economic status, access to water and sanitation, their safety at school and on the way to and from home, and many other development factors. Stated most simply, not all education problems have education solutions. Schools can encourage engagement with both public and private actors across these sectors by including representatives of relevant local development partners in their official School Management Committees. Governing "up," school leaders and local education authorities may lobby with or direct education system leaders to formalize relations with certain other development sectors at the highest levels of government administration to enlist their efforts to promote school success.

As is hopefully evident, the exercise of bottom-up governance across all the domains embodies a few common features. To begin, the perspectives, experiences, capacities, and responsibilities of the full group of local stakeholders are pertinent and must be represented and considered. It is not sufficient simply to designate one local actor to speak on behalf of local interests; rather, a range of voices, from teachers and local education leaders to parents, community leaders, and students, must all be heard and have an influence. Next, for each domain, a specific set of actions and decisions exists that the system reserves for local definition and initiative. Importantly, these actions and decisions are not simply superficial. Rather, they affect strategically and significantly what happens in the school and classroom, who makes it happen, the resources available, and the ultimate results, among other aspects.

Finally, the elevation of local agency across all education governance domains does not mean that system-level governance is no longer germane. It is not the intention to sever schools completely from central authority or influence. For one, as the effects of local agency yield new approaches and improved strategies and outcomes across the domains, there result both lessons and concrete models, methods, and products for the central system authorities to embrace. Thus, connection via a bottom-up pathway is valuable. Two, there are many ways that schools and local education authorities need and benefit from a system's expertise and leadership. A review of these appears in the next section.

Governing Top-Down for Effective Bottom-Up Governance

Whether following or leading, an education system's central authority legitimately retains three main functions. The first is *goal setting*. This involves basically the establishment of universal standards for all schools and students to achieve. These standards feature elements that are truly transversal, avoiding those that explicitly (or implicitly) emphasize priorities, context, or capacities of just one or a few sub-populations over others or that are so generic that they do not pertain satisfactorily to any single population. Rather, they address such things as pedagogic methods, codes of conduct, and critical knowledge and learning competencies that all teachers can adapt and adopt to any school context.

The second function concerns *enabling local agencies*. In this role, central authorities purposefully create "space" for local agencies to shape each education domain to fit local circumstances. This involves decentralized system agents in strategically equipping and explicitly encouraging teachers, schools, and communities to avail their agency by providing them guidance, resources, training, and support to adapt and apply the standards.

The third function is *validation*. In this role, central authorities monitor and evaluate the related actions of all actors responsible for the respective governance domains, concerning both those operating at the front lines of instruction and those who train, supervise, and support them. The aim is to ensure that all actors are fulfilling their respective roles appropriately and achieving the desired learning outcomes and to make adjustments when implementation and results are unsatisfactory. These three central functions pertain to each of the nine governance domains as outlined in the Table 14.1.

In summary, governance from the top yields better education design, delivery, and outcomes by fostering and aligning with governance at the bottom and providing a broad stroke outline of what quality looks like across the many domains for each teacher, school, and community to fill in with the fine details. The ability to do this may vary greatly from school or locale to another, and even from one teacher to the next. Capacity may be tied to personal or collective knowledge, skill, and motivation just as it may be material, defined by the level of access to resources, whether financial, material, or technical, or by the nature and degree of discrete challenges to overcome. Elevating teacher, school, and community agency is not, therefore, simply a status to enact, declaring that "Teachers and schools are now self-governing." Rather, it is a goal to pursue. This means, practically, that systems remain responsible for providing training, support, guidance, resources, and oversight to equip local actors over time to exercise their agency effectively and appropriately with growing competence and confidence and operating with the expectation that all contribute increasingly to this goal.

Table 14.1 Roles to Fulfill the Nine Education Governance Domains

Goal setting	*Enabling local agency*	*Validation*
1. Education vision and mission		
Identify the economic, social, environmental, and other universal elements of the education vision and mission for which the system is preparing all its students, defining these in ways that are truly transversally relevant and applicable.	Acknowledge openly the limits of these universal elements and how they may differ across communities. Express the expectation and provide concrete guidance, training, and support to permit and encourage schools, communities, and broader local jurisdictions to articulate their own education visions and missions that suit their unique contexts.	Incorporate into official monitoring, supervision, and evaluation ways to (i) confirm the universal relevance of system-wide vision and mission elements and their widespread pursuit and (ii) support the articulation of additional elements to formulate locally relevant education visions and missions.
2. Curriculum and textbooks		
Create curricula and textbooks for all levels of education that guide teachers and schools in ensuring that all students acquire the core learning objectives and competencies—cognitive, practical, and personal—they will require to advance through their education and training careers and to move into life and livelihood effectively and with fulfillment.	Ensure that all curricula provide ample space for teachers to improve students' learning by (i) contextualizing lessons with relevant content, skills, and applications; (ii) conducting continuous formative assessment; (iii) incorporating students' personal competencies (see Muskin 2015); and (iv) training, supervising, and supporting teachers to use this space effectively.	Build tactics directly into teacher supervision and monitoring to check (i) that they are drawing fulsomely and effectively on the local context in their lesson design and delivery to guide students in achieving the core learning objectives from the official curriculum and (ii) that pre-service and in-service training and teacher supervision are promoting and supporting this practice.
3. Standardized tests		
Create tests with generic items that permit pupils to demonstrate their degree of mastery of the core competencies for each main subject area and also include questions that permit students to show their understanding by linking standard curricular content to their respective local contexts.	Train and support teachers and local education agents to contextualize their teaching and assessment of the core competencies from the curriculum in ways that also guide students to recognize these in their generic form. Similarly, incorporate into standardized test sections or spaces that allow for items that are unique to sub-areas within a system, whether defined by language, geography, sociocultural, or other factors.	Assess the quality of locally generated test items, providing training and support to local agents to ensure their viability and significance. Also, analyze standardized test results by sub-population and locale to ensure that no built-in bias results from common test items or the overall instrument.

(Continued)

Table 14.1 (Continued)

Goal setting	*Enabling local agency*	*Validation*
4. Infrastructure and instructional resources		
Establish minimum quality standards and quantitative norms for education facilities and instructional resources for all schools, distinct for the different cycles.	Provide technical and financial support to different schools and districts to ensure that each school's facilities and materials are sufficient to achieve the minimum quality standards and adapted to the unique characteristics of the local context, especially to help schools address any particular environmental constraints or socioeconomic disadvantages.	Confirm that plans for facilities—new or renovated—and instructional resources both meet the minimal standards and address a school's unique conditions and that the plans are implemented well.
5. Pedagogy		
Produce and disseminate comprehensive technical descriptions of the many pedagogic methods that the system embraces and guidance for their effective and appropriate use along with the evidence base for selecting these.	Provide guidelines for training and supporting teachers to use the respective pedagogic methods judiciously and effectively. Produce curricula and textbooks that give teachers simultaneously the opportunity and the obligation to select pedagogic methods that are best suited to the content and the context.	Supervise and support teachers to select pedagogic methods judiciously and to use them flexibly, not slavishly.
6. Teachers and teacher training		
Set minimum standards for the qualifications, capacities, and personal qualities required to become a teacher and establish teacher training and certification modalities and incentive structures to attract high-quality candidates with various profiles from all locales that the system covers.	Provide alternate pathways to teacher training and certification, especially to encourage the recruitment of qualified persons from remote and other marginalized areas who will be happy to serve as teachers in these communities, bringing their linguistic skills, sociocultural familiarity, networks, and other appropriate assets to their instruction.	Track the appointment, retention, and career advancement of high-qualified teachers to communities for which they possess appropriate linguistic, sociocultural, and personal assets.

(Continued)

Table 14.1 (Continued)

Goal setting	*Enabling local agency*	*Validation*
7. Parental and community engagement		
Establish or strengthen formal structures for parents and communities to support local schools and schooling, providing guidelines for how these stakeholders can provide not just financial, material, and management support but also contribute to a school's curricular and extracurricular programs while also taking measures at home and in the community to promote students' learning.	Train school directors and local education authorities to actively promote parents' "360-degree support" of their children's schooling—in the classroom, at school, across the community, and at home—and provide guides, case studies, and media coverage to orient, encourage, and appreciate this.	Include parental and community engagement indicators in official education statistics and in the assessment of each school's performance.
8. Funding		
Set and provide funding for schools and districts that do not rely simply on capitation formulas but rather permit them to cover the gap between their current situation and the minimum standards for all budgetary categories—facilities, instructional resources, teachers, supervision, etc.	Provide guidance and support to schools to identify the gaps they face and to develop long-term school improvement targets and short-term school improvement plans and budgets to address these. Establish formal steps for schools to (i) seek central funds to support the plans and (ii) mobilize local financial, material, and in-kind aid to contribute further.	Local education authorities compare school improvement plans and budgets against independent appraisals of key school strategic and funding needs to determine how likely it is that each plan and budget will address a school's true needs. They also appraise each school's implementation of its plan to determine what assistance or further funding may be required. Systems may also measure the local funding and other inputs a school mobilizes.
9. Complementary services and programs		
Articulate the ways by which decisions and actions taken by other sectors—for example, health, women's affairs, economic development, and public works—currently contribute and can contribute further to improving school access, equity, learning, and outcomes, and set related targets for the system and schools to attain.	Establish functional relations with structures from other sectors and define concrete steps for local schools and education authorities to take to mobilize the technical, material, financial, and other support of these structures' local units.	Monitor and report on relationships and initiatives that schools and local education structures plan and undertake with partners from other sectors.

Source: Author.

Conclusion

The crux of this chapter has been to explore how all education systems can make the advantages of school-level governance enjoyed by some outlier schools and systems available to all their schools. How can a system retain authority in the definition of the broad aims of an education system and in the measurement and enforcement of schools' attainment of the associated standards, while enabling and authorizing schools and classrooms to make the necessary decisions to meet these standards, and others that they and their local communities might identify, to achieve optimal learning outcomes for society, communities, and individuals? How does the system put teachers and schools on roads, not rails, permitting sudden stops, acceleration, and detours to avert obstacles and to capitalize on valuable opportunities in order to maximize learning of the curriculum in each classroom? What does governing a system in a way that results in true governance, not just administration, at the school and even the classroom level look like; in other words, when does the *responsibility* to succeed pair with actual *authority* to make the sorts of decisions that are most likely to foster success?

In addressing these questions, this chapter looked critically at how systems can balance centralized and localized governance of the core education components of curriculum and learning objectives, instructional resources, pedagogy, training and professional development, supervision, and learning assessment to achieve greater learning outcomes, both during and after a child's academic career. The aim is to turn current education governance systems on its head, "flipping the system," as Evers and Kneyber say (2016), to shift much of the decision-making and authority to the school and classroom and limit system leadership to more of an oversight and support role. In simplest terms, the hope is to lay a foundation for senior structures within an education system to understand that they, in fact, work for schools and teachers, abandoning the idea that teachers and schools work for the system.

Key Discussion Areas

- The risks of a homogenous curriculum and education system.
- The role of teachers, local education authorities, and communities in steering schools and classes to better outcomes and in defining better what "better" means.
- The main functions of the education system's central authority.

Notes

1 It should be noted that the focus of this chapter is on governance at the primary and secondary education levels, not tertiary.

2 A Belgian colleague once related to me how his son's teacher would teach his lessons at a two-side blackboard, flipping over to the officially sanctioned lesson when he heard the school inspector approach his classroom.

3 "Where 'J' Is for Jihad," *NBC News*, 2022.

4 Australia's School Resource Standards offers one example of how a system's funding formula can take into account distinct conditions and needs of a local context. This approach adds to the "base per student amount. . . . Loadings [that] provide for students with disability, low English proficiency, Aboriginal and Torres Strait Islander students, socio-educational disadvantage, school location and school size" (see www.aph.gov.au/About_Parliament/Parliamentary_departments/Parliamentary_Library/pubs/rp/rp2223/Quick_Guides/FundingForSchools).

References

Alvunger, Daniel. 2018. "Teachers' Curriculum Agency in Teaching a Standards-Based Curriculum." *Curriculum Journal* 29(4): 479–98, https://doi.org/10.1080/09585176.2018.1486721.

Barber, Michael, and Mona Mourshed. 2007. "How the World's Best-Performing School Systems Come Out on Top." McKinsey and Company, updated July 4, 2023, www.mckinsey.com/~/media/mckinsey/industries/public%20and%20social%20sector/our%20insights/how%20the%20worlds%20best%20performing%20school%20systems%20come%20out%20on%20top/how_the_world_s_best-performing_school_systems_come_out_on_top.pdf (accessed July 1, 2023).

Biesta, Gert, and Michael Tedder. 2007. "Agency and Learning in the Lifecourse: Towards an Ecological Perspective." *Studies in the Education of Adults* 39(2).

Bray, Mark. 2014. "The Impact of Shadow Education on Student Academic Achievement: Why the Research Is Inconclusive and What Can Be Done About It." *Asia Pacific Education Review* 15(3): 381–89.

Chada, Sasha. 2022. "Are the SATs Biased? An In-Depth Look—Ivy Scholars." Ivy Scholars, updated July 10, 2023, www.ivyscholars.com/2022/07/27/are-the-sats-biased/#:~:text=The%20SATs%20are%20likely%20biased,point%20in%20a%20few%20years (accessed July 1, 2023).

Crouch, David. 2015. "Highly Trained, Respected and Free: Why Finland's Teachers Are Different." *The Guardian*, June 17, 2015, www.theguardian.com/education/2015/jun/17/highly-trained-respected-and-free-why-finlands-teachers-are-different (accessed July 1, 2023).

Davidson, Marcia. 2015. "Scripted Reading Lessons and Evidence for Their Efficacy." USAID, updated July 4, 2023, https://2012-2017.usaid.gov/sites/default/files/documents/1865/Davidson.pdf (accessed July 1, 2023).

Dehghanpisheh, Babak. 2001. "Where 'J' Is for Jihad." *NBC News*, December 17, 2001, www.nbcnews.com/id/wbna3067359 (accessed July 1, 2023).

Delors, Jacques et al. 1996. *Learning: The Treasure Within*. Paris: UNESCO, updated July 4, 2023, www.google.com/books/edition/Learning/tGXxgar1fCQC?hl=en&gbpv=1&printsec=frontcover (accessed July 1, 2023).

Dickson, E. J. 2019. "The SATs Are Trying to Level the Playing Field—Sort of." *Rolling Stone*, May 16, 2019, www.rollingstone.com/culture/culture-news/sat-adversity-score-racial-discrepancies-836299/ (accessed July 1, 2023).

Evers, Jelmer, and Rene Kneyber. 2016. *Flip the System: Changing Education from the Ground Up*. London: Routledge.

Gardner, Howard. 2006. *Multiple Intelligences: New Horizons*. New York: Basic Books.

Giorgetti, Filiz Meseci, Craig Campbell, and Ali Arslan. 2017. "Culture and Education: Looking Back to Culture Through Education." *Paedagogica Historica* 53: 1–2, 1–6, updated July 4, 2023, https://doi.org/10.1080/00309230.2017.1288752; www.tandfonline.com/doi/full/10.1080/00309230.2017.1288752?scroll=top&needAccess=true&role=tab (accessed July 1, 2023).

Jaschik, Scott. 2010. "New Evidence of Racial Bias on SAT." *Inside Higher Ed*, June 21, 2010, www.insidehighered.com/news/2010/06/21/new-evidence-racial-bias-sat (accessed July 1, 2023).

Lai, C., Z. Li, and Y. Gong. 2016. "Teacher Agency and Professional Learning in Cross-cultural Teaching Contexts: Accounts of Chinese Teachers from International Schools in Hong Kong." *Teaching and Teacher Education* 54: 12–21, https://doi.org/10.1016/j.tate.2015.11.007.

Maisuria, Alpesh. 2005. "The Turbulent Times of Creativity in the National Curriculum." *Policy Futures in Education* 3(2): 141–52.

Muskin, Joshua. 2015. "Student Learning Assessment and the Curriculum: Issues and Implications for Policy, Design and Implementation." UNESCO-IBE, Current and Critical Issues in Curriculum and Learning Series No. 1, updated July 9, 2023, https://unesdoc.unesco.org/ark:/48223/pf0000235489 (accessed July 1, 2023).

———. 2018. "Strengthening Teacher Capacity: What Do We Really Mean?" Learning Portal, International Institute for Educational Planning, https://learningportal.iiep.unesco.org/en/blog/strengthening-teacher-capacity-what-do-we-really-mean (accessed July 1, 2023).

———. 2022. "When Teaching and Learning the Curriculum Clash." UNESCO IIEP Learning Portal, https://learningportal.iiep.unesco.org/en/blog/when-teaching-and-learning-the-curriculum-clash (accessed July 1, 2023).

Muskin, Joshua, Abdelhak Kamime, and Abdellah Adlaoui. 2011. "Empowered to Empower: A Civil Society–Government Partnership to Increase Girls' Junior Secondary School Outcomes in

Morocco." *Research in Comparative and International Education* 6(1): 129–46 (accessed July 1, 2023).

Priestley, Mark, Richard Edwards, Andrea Priestley, and Kate Miller. 2012. "Teacher Agency in Curriculum Making: Agents of Change and Spaces for Manoeuvre." *Curriculum Inquiry* 42(2): 191–214, https://doi.org/10.1111/j.1467-873X.2012.00588.x.

Savage, Glenn C. 2016. "Who's Steering the Ship? National Curriculum Reform and the Re-Shaping of Australian Federalism." *Journal of Education Policy* 31(6): 833–50.

Schroeder, Susan. 2011. "Un-standardizing Curriculum: Multicultural Teaching in the Standards-Based Classroom." *Urban Education* 46(4): 880–87.

Shanker, Albert, 1989. "The Revolution That Is Overdue From Information Factory To Learning and Teaching in Restructuring Schools." Speech delivered to the American Federation of Teachers at the Robert LaFollette Institute of Public Affairs, University of Madison. chrome-extension://efaidnbmnnnibpcajpcglclefindmkaj/https://reuther.wayne.edu/files/64.62.pdf.

Sleeter, Christine, and Judith Flores Carmona. 2017. *Un-Standardizing Curriculum: Multicultural Teaching in the Standards-Based Classroom.* New York: Teachers College Press.

Tan, Charlene. 2016. "Teacher Agency and School-Based Curriculum in China's Non-Elite Schools." *Journal of Educational Change* 17(3): 287–302, https://doi.org/10.1007/s10833-016-9274-8.

Trippestad, Tom Are. 2015. "The Glocal Teacher: The Paradox of Teaching in a Glocalised World." *Policy Futures in Education* 14(1): 9–23, https://doi.org/10.1177/147821031561264.

Tsai, Yao, and S. L. Beverton. 2007. "Top-Down Management: An Effective Tool in Higher Education?" *International Journal of Educational Management* 21(1): 6–16.

UK Department for Education. 2015. "Governance Handbook for Trustees of Academies and Multi-Academy Trusts and Governors of Maintained Schools," https://thehub.bathnes.gov.uk/Article/9104 (accessed July 1, 2023).

Walker, Jo, Caroline Pearce, Kira Boe, and Max Lawson. 2019. "The Power of Education to Fight Inequality." updated July 4, 2023, July 7–10, 2023, www.oxfam.org/en/research/power-education-fight-inequality (accessed July 1, 2023).

Wiseman, Alexander W. 2008. "A Culture of (In)Equality? A Cross-national Study of Gender Parity and Gender Segregation in National School Systems." *Research in Comparative and International Education* 3(2): 179–201.

15

A FLEXIBLE ONLINE LEARNING INNOVATION

30/45 + 36/6 MICA Model

Shailendra Raj Mehta, Preeti Shroff-Mehta, and Ashutosh Dutt

Introduction

This chapter documents and analyzes collaborative online education innovations made by the MICA—The School of Ideas community, involving the faculty, students, and management in response to the Covid-19 pandemic. The model discussed in this chapter was developed after an intense two-month period of interaction and experimentation among nearly all our faculty colleagues. While the three coauthors of this chapter have chosen to document this framework, the credit for the model belongs to the MICA faculty collectively. Any remaining faults in this chapter, however, are entirely ours.

Online education or e-learning has been around since the dawn of the computer age. It has evolved from nascent to mature conceptualization stages, design, pedagogy, processes, technology platforms, and delivery. Before the advent of the internet, and until early 1960s, it was referred to as Computer Based Training. However, the early reviews of e-learning, especially of open educational resources, were disappointing (Atkins, Brown, and Hammond 2007). Another more recent movement, combining artificial intelligence with e-learning, is Massive Open Online Courses (MOOCs). MOOCs have emerged as the new way to reach a large audience with educational materials, but so far, they have failed to maintain learners' attention over the long term. The available literature on MOOCs (Wong et al. 2019) suggests that the jury is still out on their effectiveness. Even though we now understand how effective active learning principles are, the current pedagogical landscape of MOOCs too often allows for passivity, leading to the unsatisfactory performance experienced by many MOOC learners today (Davis et al. 2018). The learners in MOOCs must be self-regulated (Alonso-Mencía et al. 2020), often resulting in unorganized and incomplete learning. This need for self-regulation explains MOOCs' ongoing challenges in moving from targeted and niche models to fully scaled-up capacities for various global stakeholders such as instructors, learners, technology partners, educational institutions, government, and industry.

However, the Covid-19 virus quickened the search for an alternative to the traditional face-to-face learning model. More than a billion students worldwide were affected by the pandemic. Physical schools shut down overnight, while educational technology solutions

DOI: 10.4324/9781003316077-19

mushroomed around the globe. These technology interventions allowed learning to continue uninterrupted for those who could afford it, but children from underprivileged and rural backgrounds were left behind and bore the brunt of the drawbacks from this rapid switch.

While developing these online solutions, the stakeholders' main concern was that teaching quality would quickly degrade in an environment that had no face-to-face contact and where all instruction was conducted online. This chapter describes a model for online teaching and engagement that utilizes the merits of face-to-face teaching and clubs it with the benefits of online education. It has been developed in India at MICA—The School of Ideas, a specialized management school focusing on Strategic Marketing and Communication.

Dilemma

Background

In the core MBA program, MICA traditionally had four sections of about sixty students each. Our standardized classroom duration was seventy-five minutes for direct engagement with the instructor and interactive learning. Toward the end of March 2020, it became clear that we would have to move entirely online, at least for the foreseeable future. Yet how to transport the existing model online was not clear. After a period of intensive deliberations lasting almost two months, and after several iterations and extensive testing, our faculty decided to standardize the online delivery and evolve a standard set of protocols to avoid student confusion and maximize effectiveness.

In our faculty meetings, it quickly became apparent that a class size of sixty was too large for a group to teach effectively with two-way interaction. After experimentation with smaller and larger sizes, we determined the optimal online class size to be around thirty-six students. At this scale, we could manage our deliberations online quite well. This proposal led to a different problem because the workload of the faculty would dramatically increase: a typical professor who taught four sections of a class would have to teach the same material six times. Our faculty members believed that repeating the same material four times is about the limit before the onset of severe boredom.

Online Learning Pedagogy Innovations

After much experimentation, we decided on a teaching model, which we call the 30/45 + 36/6 MICA Model (see Figure 15.1, which captures the model developed at MICA). Classes would begin with a thirty-minute prerecorded video, in which the basic concepts and principles are discussed. This video would be circulated to the students at least a day in advance of the live forty-five-minute session, in which the instructor would discuss the material in an online class of thirty-six students. Students would be required to keep their videos on. The live session would consist of intensive two-way interaction in which questions are asked, opinions solicited, and doubts cleared. Instructors would often break up the class into six breakout sessions of six people each, where more intimate discussions could occur; the professor would virtually circulate among these breakout rooms. The students were not shortchanged, since they would get seventy-five minutes of instruction per class, as they had before the switch to online learning. With this model, both the instructor and the students are fresh, prepared, and ready to engage.

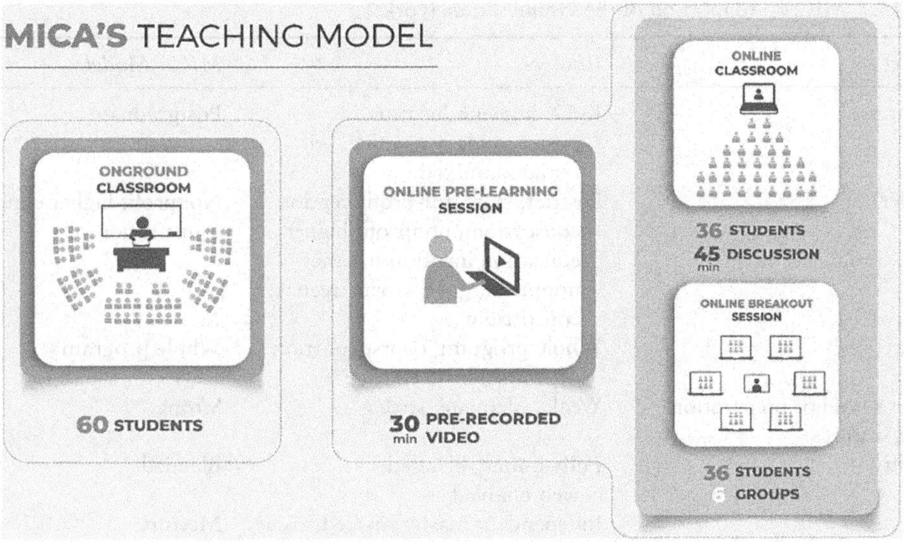

Figure 15.1 MICA's Teaching Model: 30/45 + 36/6 Pedagogy Innovation

Source: Authors.

Technology Platform

We also standardized our delivery on the Zoom platform. We found it far more versatile and more comfortable to use than Microsoft Teams, Google Meet, BlueJeans, or any other platforms. In the classroom discussion portion of a course, the six-by-six grid of student faces featured on the Zoom screen was easily manageable by the professor. The breakout rooms and whiteboards are also comfortable to manage.

Pedagogical Comparisons

Recent surveys of online learning research (see Means, Bakia, and Murphy 2014) indicate that learning outcomes depend on a multiplicity of variables. The first variable is modality, which is whether the learning is online, offline, or mixed. The second variable is pacing—whether learning is student-paced, class-paced, or mixed. The third variable is the student-instructor ratio. The fourth variable is pedagogy, with the choices being expository, practice environment, exploratory, and collaborative. Long agreed-upon principles of pedagogy include interactivity, cooperation, active learning, prompt feedback, effective time management, expectation setting, and respect for diversity (Chickering and Gamson 1987). The fifth variable is the instructor's role online, which ranges from active, minimal, to no involvement. The sixth variable is the student role online, where the choices are listening and reading, solving problems, simulation, and collaboration. The seventh variable is synchrony—that is, whether the communication is synchronous or asynchronous. The eighth variable is online assessments, and if they are present, how they support the students. And finally, the ninth variable is feedback and whether it is automated, provided by peers, or provided by the instructor.

In Table 15.1, we compare the MICA model with the standard MOOC framework components. For this purpose, we use the framework of Barbara Means, Marianne Bakia, and Robert Murphy (2014) to outline various choices.

Table 15.1 MICA's Adaptation of the Online Framework

Context	*Choices*	*MICA Model*
Field of use	K-12, higher education, postsecondary training, self-initiated, mixed	Postgraduate
Provider	District, state, for-profit vendor, consortium, nonprofit higher education institution, other nonprofit, government agency, consortium	Nonprofit higher education institution
Breadth	Whole program, course, portion of course, brief episode	Whole program
Learner's level of preparation	Weak, adequate, strong	Strong
Design features		
Modality	Fully online, blended, web-enabled	Blended
Pacing	Independent mastery-paced, class-paced, mixture	Mixture
Pedagogy	Expository, practice environment, exploratory, collaborative	Collaborative
Online communication synchrony	Asynchronous, synchronous, both	Both: 30/45 model
Intended instructor role online	Active instruction, small presence, none	Active instruction
Intended student role online	Listen and read, complete problems and answer questions, explore simulation and resource, collaborate with peers in building knowledge	All four
Role of online assessments	Determine if student is ready for new content, tell system how to support student, provide student and teacher with information about learning state, calculate student's risk of failure	Tell system how to support student
Source of feedback	Automated, teacher, peers, mixed, none	Teacher and peers
Implementation		
Learning location	School, home, other, mixed	Home
Co-located facilitator	Primary instructor, monitor and facilitator, absent	Absent
Student-instructor ratio		36 and 6 breakout rooms
Level of online student–content interaction	High, medium, low	Medium moving toward high
Level of online student–instructor interaction	High, medium, low	High

(Continued)

Table 15.1 (Continued)

Context	*Choices*	*MICA Model*
Level of online student–student interaction	High, medium, low	Medium
Intended outcomes		
Cognitive	Declarative knowledge, procedural skills, problem-solving, and strategies	All four
Engagement	Primary goal, secondary goal, not explicit goal	Primary goal
Productivity	Course pass rate, graduation rate, time to completion, cost	High on all counts
Learning to learn	Self-regulation, new media skills	High

Source: Authors' adaptation of Framework from Barbara Means, Marianne Bakia, and Robert Murphy (2014).

MICA Online Learning Innovations Model Impact

Two methods of assessment—quantitative and qualitative feedback—were used to evaluate the new system's impact. We now touch upon them in turn.

Quantitative Feedback

To understand the impact of the new model, we surveyed all faculty and students—the community at MICA. All full-time and adjunct faculty members and students of the two-year management program (PGP) were sent a survey (see appendix) in the third week of July 2020. By then, the PGP first year and PGP second-year students had experienced the model for five and three weeks, respectively. It is noteworthy that PGP second-year students had also experienced the on-campus learning model while they were in the first year of the program.

Among the 208 respondents to the survey, 193 were students, and fifteen were faculty members. There were 112 PGP first-year students and eighty-one PGP second-year students.

Close to three out of four respondents (73 percent) rated the MICA model better than other learning models, comparing it to on-campus learning and other models of online learning. The response was equally welcoming from both first- and second-year students with no statistically significant difference between them (at alpha = 0.05). While 78 percent of PGP first-year students found the MICA model better, 68 percent of the PGP second-year students found the model to be better than on-campus learning.

Of the faculty members who responded, 60 percent also found the MICA model better, with 40 percent finding it much better than other models.

A sentiment and emotion related (use of word date analysis using algorithms and machine-learning models) analysis was done on the 207 qualitative responses about the MICA model. The tool used was the bag of words model—it uses word data analysis based on algorithms and machine-learning model. The overall sentiment came out to be highly positive and indicated high level of trust. Some of the select verbatim experiences have been shared in the appendix.

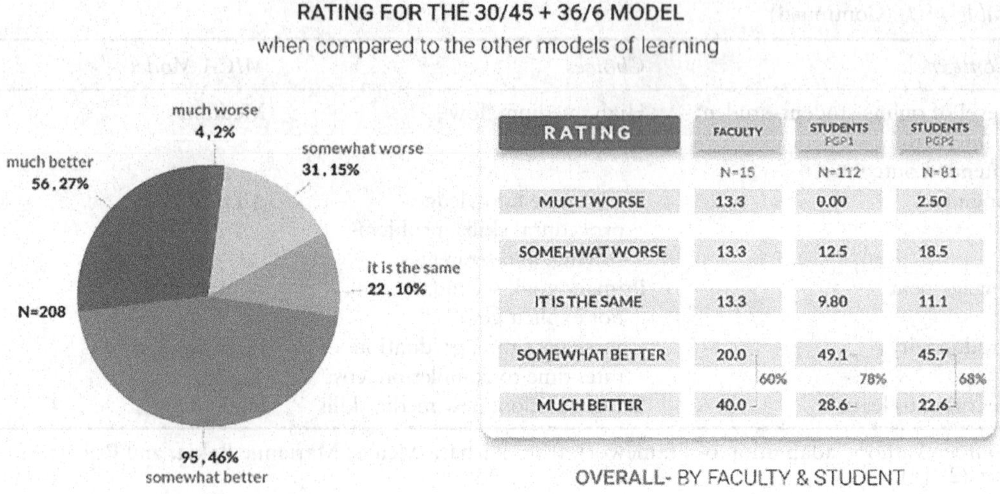

Figure 15.2 The Impact

Source: Authors.

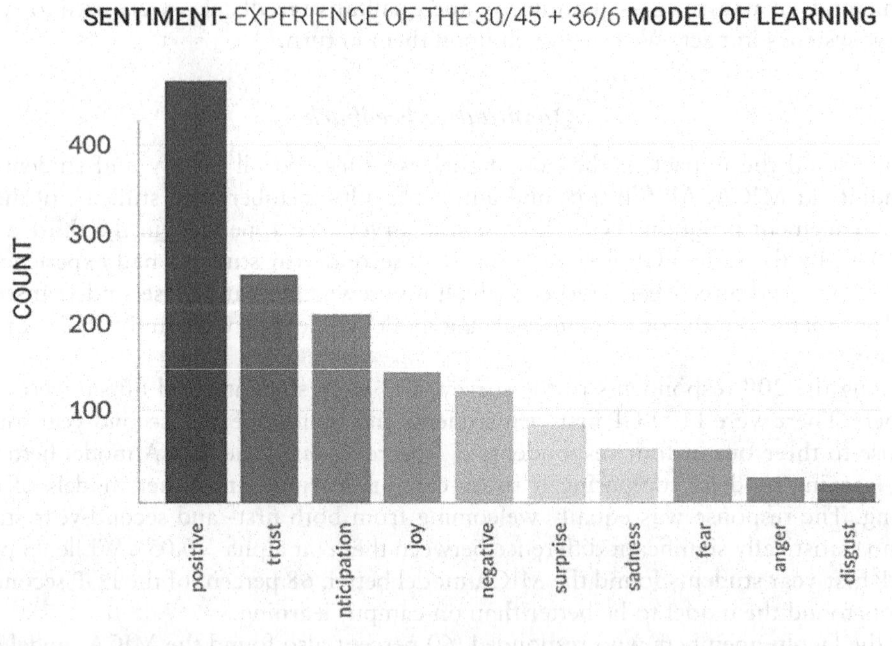

Figure 15.3 Sentiment Analysis

Source: Authors.

We can conclude that there was a significantly positive response to the 30/45 + 36/6 MICA Model. A clear majority of the faculty members and students found it better than other models of learning. While the model does warrant extra effort from faculty members, it allows the students to learn at their own pace and maintains academic rigor by allowing live doubt-clearing discussions with MICA faculty. The next cycle has been smoother for the faculty, as they are able to reuse many of the prerecorded videos.

Qualitative Feedback

We invited elected student representatives to share the student body's experiences in the first few weeks of class. Their verdict was unanimously favorable. The faculty too has discussed their experiences in faculty meetings. These discussions also have been overwhelmingly positive where students pointed to the extra flexibility they had as a benefit or faculty found they were able to engage students in the online format without sacrificing lesson quality. It appears that this model has worked well so far. If this trend continues, we may retain some elements of this model even when face-to-face classes resume.

Limitations and Extensions

For now, we have standardized all MICA classes with the 30/45 + 36/6 MICA Model. Yet we cannot be too sure that we have hit upon the right balance once and for all—there is the potential for what is known as the Hawthorne effect (Adair, Sharpe, and Huynh 1989; McCarney et al. 2007), in which a change is perceived to be better because "special attention" is paid to the participants, or greater salience is attached to a situation. The novelty effect is also a consideration: things are perceived to be better simply because they are new or different (Poppenk, Köhler, and Moscovitch 2010). In the Covid-19 times, when most students sitting at home, bored, and deprived of human contact, any interaction online would be perceived to have additional value. Further evaluations need to be conducted during the remainder of the academic calendar to ascertain the robustness of our results. It is very likely that faculty and students will continue to learn from a hybrid approach (online and in class) in learning pedagogy innovations.

Higher education institutions around the world are undergoing digital transformation leading to deep pedagogical and platform innovations. They are establishing in-house technology platforms and tools, as well as partnering with leading ed-tech providers for cutting-edge program offerings internally (for the existing learner groups), and externally by reaching out to new learner groups keen to upskill and upgrade professional qualifications across multiple disciplines and subject areas.

The future of higher education is hybrid—the intersections of in-person and online learning. MICA has also established partnerships with some of the leading global ed-tech platforms, is participating in government supported technological initiatives, and has established an in-house digital and face-to-face learning quality enhancement studio for supporting faculty teaching innovations.

Appendix

Survey to Assess the Impact of the MICA Model

MICA has moved from an on-campus learning system to an online learning system. We have broken the batch into six smaller sections for all core courses. Each section comprises thirty-six students. The session has been broken into thirty minutes of asynchronous recorded content and forty-five minutes of live discussion. We call this 30/45 + 36/6 MICA Model. We would like to seek your feedback on this innovation.

Email address:

Q1. What is your experience of the 30/45 + 36/6 MICA Model of learning?
Q2. Please share with us some of the positives of the model as compared to on-campus learning or other models of online learning.
Q3. Please tell us how we can improve this model even further.
Q4. Please rate the 30/45 + 36/6 MICA Model when compared to other models of learning.

- Much better
- Somewhat better
- It is the same
- Somewhat worse
- Much worse

Verbatim Experiences Shared by Faculty and Students

Some of the verbatim responses quoted below give a well-rounded view of the MICA model's impact:

By PGP Second-Year Students

I find that the new model has increased the learning curve by a huge margin. The 45 minutes dedicated to discussion is great because it lets us ask questions in a way we didn't when we were on campus. I personally find myself responding and participating more in the online forum than I did in a classroom scenario.

Really great, videos can be reviewed as per need and live sessions provide the clearing of doubts and direct interaction. Lesser students per class also enables better attention. The problem is that due to many subjects, there has been a gradual increase in the screen time. So a day off in a week should be there.

I am really enjoying this method as the online 75 minutes of the class is not tiring now since I can watch the 30 minutes anytime, I want to. Zoom calls of 45 minutes are more interactive and the discussion happens in a guided way as per the pre-recorded videos.

I think this has been a very good experience and the on-campus learning should also follow the same ratio as it gives a chance to interact more and express more.

By PGP First-Year Students

The idea of breaking us into batches was really nice, because it makes it easier for us to interact with the faculty and in making things organized. Also, the breakup of time is also appreciated, because staring at a screen for 75 minutes at a stretch would have been arduous and concentration would have wavered a lot.

The idea of having a pre-recorded video is beneficial because we can choose to learn at our pace plus revisit as and when needed. Some of those videos also run longer than 30 minutes but that's alright, as long as we get the entire live session for discussions. However, at times during the live session the faculty explains what was talked about in the pre-recorded video or introduces new concepts which are relevant, but it leaves us with no time to clear our doubts. We are then asked to fill it in a Google sheet which is a way slower process.

It's been really pleasant so far. It's good that the class has only 36 students—the teachers are able to pay more attention to each student. The 30/45 system has also been good so far. We've received some pre-recorded videos that are beyond 30 minutes and invariably what happens in class is that the same 30+ minute gets discussed with our examples/inputs. The class is used as more of a doubt solving session/classroom discussion forum. This in my opinion works very well in subjects like Quants & accounts because we spend our own time working on the solution and then it gets discussed in the class; but in the other theory subjects, I would like to see a little bit more value addition in the class apart from the pre-class video sent to us.

It has been good but being from a tier 2 city I have had plenty of network issues even after purchasing a Wi-Fi connection but as far as learning is concerned, I am satisfied with the model.

My experience with the 36/6 model was greatly helpful. I felt to some extent each one of us could participate in discussions and the concept of break out rooms by subdividing the class was very good and it reduced the difference between online and off-line class.

By Faculty Members

I have completed 32 sessions including both PGP 1 and PGP 2. I've found that the student preparedness for the class and the quality of conversations have significantly improved compared to the regular classes. I am quite enjoying my sessions as a faculty as well. There have been zero disciplinary issues from the students' side or whatsoever which is never the case with regular classes.

More creative alternatives to the 30-min pre-class video may need to be considered IF there are many sessions by different faculty in a single day. The present model may prove to be tiring for students (from a learning experience point of view) if they have to go through 5–6 videos of 30-min each for 5–6 sessions next day (which may be the case on days having peak load).

I did face issues with the scheduling having just 15 minutes between sessions for PGP1. If this can be increased to 20–25 minutes, it can give us some breathing space before heading to the next session.

Key Discussion Areas

- An insight into a new institution-wide, standardized, interactive, and learner-centric online learning model (for Covid-19 and post Covid-19 learning innovation and application).
- Development and background of the model and its pedagogical comparisons with other models.
- Quantitative and qualitative feedback (original quotes in the appendix) on the surveys conducted for various stakeholders and insights on the limitations of the model.

References

Adair, John G., Donald Sharpe, and Cam-Loi Huynh. 1989. "Hawthorne Control Procedures in Educational Experiments: A Reconsideration of Their Use and Effectiveness." *Review of Educational Research* 59: 215–28.

Alonso-Mencía, M. Elena, Carlos Alario-Hoyos, Jorge Maldonado-Mahauad, Iria Estévez-Ayres, Pérez-Sanagustín, and Carlos Delgado Kloos. 2020. "Self-Regulated Learning in MOOCs: Lessons Learned from a Literature Review." *Educational Review* 72: 319–45.

Atkins, Daniel Ewell, John Seely Brown, and Allen L. Hammond. 2007. "A Review of the Open Educational Resources (OER) Movement: Achievements, Challenges, and New Opportunities." Report to the William and Flora Hewlett Foundation, https://hewlett.org/wp-content/uploads/2016/08/ReviewoftheOERMovement.pdf.

Chickering, Arthur W., and Zelda F. Gamson. 1987. "Seven Principles for Good Practice in Undergraduate Education." *AAHE Bulletin* (March): 3–7.

Davis, Dan, Guanliang Chen, Claudia Hauff, and Geert-Jan Houben. 2018. "Activating Learning at Scale: A Review of Innovations in Online Learning Strategies." *Computers and Education* 125: 327–44.

McCarney, Rob, James Warner, Steve Iliffe, Robbert Van Haselen, Mark Griffin, and Peter Fisher. 2007. "The Hawthorne Effect: A Randomised, Controlled Trial." *BMC Medical Research Methodology* 7: 30.

Means, Barbara, Marianne Bakia, and Robert Murphy. 2014. *Learning Online: What Research Tells Us About Whether, When and How*. New York: Taylor & Francis.

Poppenk, Jordan, Stefan Köhler, and Morris Moscovitch. 2010. "Revisiting the Novelty Effect: When Familiarity, Not Novelty, Enhances Memory." *Journal of Experimental Psychology: Learning, Memory, and Cognition* 36: 1321.

Wong, Jacqueline, Martine Baars, Dan Davis, Tim Van Der Zee, Geert-Jan Houben, and Fred Paas. 2019. "Supporting Self-regulated Learning in Online Learning Environments and MOOCs: A Systematic Review." *International Journal of Human–Computer Interaction* 35: 356–73.

16

CHANGING AND UNCHANGING PRINCIPLES IN AN UNCERTAIN AGE OF UNIVERSITY GOVERNANCE

Autonomy, Accountability, and Innovation

Beheruz N. Sethna

Introduction

Let me start this introduction with a personal story, the relevance of which will soon become clear.[1] Since I stepped away from the position of university president (a role in which I had the honor of serving for nineteen years) and became a full-time faculty member, I have spent part of most summers teaching at *Balgram*, an orphanage school in rural India (regrettably, my participation was paused during the pandemic). *Bal* means child, and *gram* is abode or village, so this is aptly named as an abode for children.

My relationship with *Balgram* started almost fifteen years ago, after someone recommended that I look into giving them a donation. I asked what level of giving they were looking for. They told me that it would take INR. 6,000 to sponsor one child for one year. That amount understandably went up as time went on.

One of the lessons I had learned in my years as the president was that an annual gift, while always welcome, puts the fundraiser in a difficult position if the person declines to give the same amount the following year. Not wanting them to be in the same awkward situation, I gave them ten times that amount, INR. 60,000 and told them to bank the money and spend the interest which was upwards of 10 percent at the time in India. That way, they never had to come back to me, and they had that income stream for the entire duration of the child's education. And, when the child had graduated ("passed out" of school as they say in India), they had that income stream that could be used for another child.

Another thing I had learned as the president was that sometimes donors place so many restrictions on gifts that it becomes difficult to find a good student that meets all their restrictions. So, I placed no restrictions on my gift—neither of gender, religion, or age. I simply told the school to choose a child and let me know.

Gradually, my sponsorship grew to two, three, four, and finally to eight children at *Balgram*. In addition to writing checks (the amount it would take increased over the years) for

DOI: 10.4324/9781003316077-20

their sponsorship, I would take them gifts—always one fun gift like a doll or car and one educational one like a play computer or Scrabble. I would also take smaller gifts for the entire orphanage of about one hundred children.

But, while I was the president, my visits to India were very brief; my visits to *Balgram* were only two or three hours long. I became increasingly dissatisfied with my own contributions. I decided I had to do more and give more than money—I had to give my time. So, after I relinquished the presidential role and became a full-time faculty member, I chose to keep my summers free for *Balgram*.

I teach children at *Balgram* science and encourage them to practice their English with me. Science experiments don't always work perfectly the first time you try them, so they learn perseverance as well, and my reward comes when they get it for the first time. I take pictures of their smiles of enjoyment and accomplishment and share them in real time with them to motivate them to do more. While it is challenging (because of my own limitations and because of unreliable electrical power, though that situation is getting better each year), it is very rewarding as well. One would imagine that the children would deeply resent some nutty professor from America coming and messing up their vacation time—time for goofing off, watching Bollywood movies, and playing games. But, amazingly, they don't. Each morning, they ask me to come back in the afternoon and each afternoon, they want me to come back the next day.

Over the years, I have given more money and, thanks to the beneficence of my Rotary Club and neighboring Rotary Clubs, and of individual donors in my city, I have been able to leverage my funds to help fund major initiatives. One of these major projects was to buy solar heaters for the children.

When I go to teach the children, I go in the summertime. It is very hot, and there is no air conditioning. The water that comes out of the faucets is also uncomfortably warm. So, were it up to me, the *last thing in the world* I would have thought of would be to use the funds on would have been a *heater* of any kind, solar or otherwise.

But I asked the administration what they wanted most, and they said that they needed a solar water heater. I accepted their decision and agreed to contribute my money and raise other funds around their needs. The administration explained that in the wintertime, the temperature dropped significantly, and the water became far too cold for the kids to bathe. There are no showers in the orphanage, and certainly no bathtubs, so the way the children clean themselves is by filling a bucket full of water and washing themselves with that water. When that water in the bucket is very cold, the kids stop washing themselves and that leads to unhygienic conditions with serious health implications. I would never have known or understood the urgent need for heaters had I not had the humility to know that *I do not know* their business, the humility to ask, and the humility to learn. The presence of funds in my pocket does *not* give me any of this.

In fundraising circles, people talk, only partly tongue-in-cheek, of the "Golden Rule"—*not* the Golden Rule we were taught as children to do unto others as you would have them do unto you—"He or she who has the gold makes the rules." While I was the chief fundraiser of the university, I generally lived by that "rule" because those "with the gold" want money to go to their pet projects, but when it came time for me to be the donor to *Balgram*, I declined to do that. I knew that those experts there could make better and more relevant decisions than I could, in terms of the pressing needs of the orphanage.

After all, the fact that I have some money to share does not magically invest in me the knowledge base and expertise as to the running of orphanages or the selection of children who need help. That is not my field; I have not spent one day of my life doing that job, and so I must trust those who have done this for many years.

Now let me go from Lonavala, India, of the 2000s to approximately 450 years earlier in time and approximately 4,000 miles to Italy, and talk of Michelangelo, one of the greatest artists of all time. Artists in those days were supported by patrons; Michelangelo had two primary patrons: Pope Julius II and the Medici family. Think for a moment how the great works of Michelangelo would have turned out if, by virtue of their financial support, either the pope or the Medici family would have had decision power over the Pietà or the David, two of the most awesome and awe-inspiring sculptures of the Western world, or the scenes from Genesis on the ceiling of the Sistine Chapel in Rome or the Last Judgment on the altar wall. Can you visualize the Medici family—by virtue of the fact that *they* had the funds to allocate (or not allocate)—deciding the form of the limbs or the muscular structure of the sculptures, or the Pope insisting on his design for the artwork or the colors used in the Sistine Chapel paintings? It seems reasonable to believe that Michelangelo may have quarreled frequently with his patrons over his work, but at the end of the day, it was the subject-matter expert rather than the patron who prevailed.

The possession of funds did not mean that magically either the Pope or the Medici family had the knowledge base and expertise or abilities as to the enhancement of sculptures or paintings. Had they interfered with Michelangelo's decisions, we would be staring up at a "committee" or "patron" version of the Sistine Chapel today and wondering, "What *were* they thinking?"[2]

So, now I come to one of the main points of this chapter on University Governance—in a word, *autonomy*.

Autonomy and Academic Freedom

Just as the existence of funds in my pocket do not magically endow me to make good decisions as to what projects to undertake or what children to support at an orphanage in rural India, just as the existence of funds in the pockets of the pope or the Medici family did not magically endow them with creative or artistic genius, so too the existence of funds in those entities that fund universities and colleges do not magically endow these funders with academic knowledge and expertise to make academic decisions.

There are limitations to the "Golden Rule" of funding. At *Balgram*, I left the important decisions to the local administrators and experts. The existence of "gold" in my pockets did *not* give me the expertise to question those who had spent their professional lives and careers in school or orphanage management. That is not my field; I have not spent one day of my life doing that job, and so I must trust those who have done this all their lives. And, I emphasize that, had I insisted on funding *my* pet projects (since I was the one with the "gold") rather than something that the orphanage administrators wanted, the children would not have benefited as much as they did. Recollect the solar heater episode which I would never have thought of.

Funding agencies and donors would find it more productive to leave academic decisions and university governance decisions to those who have done it for their entire careers. This is not, by any means, the opinion of the author alone. On May 22, 2021, the Indian Institute of Technology (IIT) Alumni Centre held a webinar (IIT Alumni Centre 2021) that featured Dr. Naushad Forbes, co-chairman of Forbes Marshall, in conversation with Prof. Ashok Misra, former director of IIT—Indian Institute of Technology Bombay (Mumbai), in that excellent webinar—the point was repeatedly made for institutional autonomy as well.

The implications for university governance are that systems need to be built around the principle of institutional autonomy, and funders of institutions or boards should be monitoring progress on major goals and plans, not getting into the details of how universities achieve those goals. Of course, a very important part of leadership is also to serve those you lead—and so leaders should be held responsible for institutional climate as well. Boards should endow the institutions with autonomy, but they are still responsible for holding the leader responsible for the institutional climate, for innovation, and for accountability.

Related to institutional autonomy, perhaps unique to academic institutions, is the concept of faculty autonomy and academic freedom.

The American Association of University Professors (AAUP) 1940 "Statement of Principles on Academic Freedom and Tenure" states:

> Advancing and protecting academic freedom is the AAUP's core mission. Academic freedom is the indispensable requisite for unfettered teaching and research in institutions of higher education. As the academic community's core policy document states, ". . . institutions of higher education are conducted for the common good and not to further the interest of either the individual teacher or the institution as a whole. The common good depends upon the free search for truth and its free exposition.
>
> *(AAUP 1940)*

Through the start of the Covid-19 pandemic and after, while most things changed and will continue to change, there are some guiding principles that should not change. Among these are institutional and faculty autonomy and the concept of academic freedom.

Lest anyone reading this chapter suggest that I am relatively alone in this insistence on autonomy and academic freedom as foundational principles of good governance, or that this is a dream solely of the *American* Association of University Professors, we should be aware that as recently as mid-June of 2021, university leaders from across Europe came together to ratify an [8] agreement made in 1988 in Bologna, Italy, called the *Magna Charta Universitatum*, which established fundamental values of "autonomy and academic freedom." In the past thirty-three years, the number of academic institutions that signed the document increased from 388 to about 900. In June 2021, they signed the new Magna Charta "which expands on the principles outlined in the original document in light of the globalization of higher education that occurred in the decades since the first Magna Charta was signed on Sept. 18, 1988." David Lock, secretary-general of the association, stated, "Note the principles are the same."

> They're all there: the importance of autonomy, the importance of academic freedom, the importance of universities serving society. . . this document says . . . very boldly, "Education is a human right, a public good and should be available to all."

So, while change is inevitable, this chapter makes the bold claim that some principles should not change, such as institutional and faculty autonomy and the concept of academic freedom. A good governance system must respect and revere these unchanging principles.

Innovativeness[3]

Institutions of higher education have been innovative and have been the source of some great inventions.

> There are seemingly countless examples, including Gatorade, invented at the University of Florida; Google, which began at Stanford; web browsers and plasma screens, both created at the University of Illinois; and the drug that became the allergy medicine Allegra, developed at Georgetown University.
>
> *(Redden 2021)*

Other inventions that have changed the world for the better include the first operation in Europe under anesthetic, antiseptic surgery, X-rays, ultrasound, the contraceptive pill, DNA fingerprinting, and the webcam, and many more.

A criticism often levied against universities is that they are too slow, far too slow, to change. Some of this is intentional: well-thought-out changes are more likely to stand the test of time. However, some of this "slowness" is avoidable. A former Fortune 500 CEO (CNBC 2015) I know who later headed a large university system would say that we faculty behave as if time had no value. To a large extent, he was right. But, often, well-thought-out changes take time. For example, unlike a marketing promotion in the corporate world which can be changed promptly if it is not working, a curriculum for a new major represents a significant commitment for a period of several years, when you consider the recruitment of students, admission, a four-year curriculum, and at least a couple of cycles before then next revision, we are looking at decisions which will impact the better part of a decade.

The pandemic of 2020 demonstrated that faculty could act fast, promptly, and effectively. Our lives suddenly changed in mid-March of 2020 and universities around the world went online; within a week or two, faculty who had never taught a single online course in their lives, suddenly had to do so. At my own university, faculty did an amazing job, turning on a dime to convert their face-to-face courses into an online mode, aided very ably by our Center for Teaching and Learning (CTL). When we started planning for the fall semester, concepts, words, and phrases that had not hitherto been part of the lexicon of many of us suddenly became reality. These included Dual Modality Delivery or DMD, split rosters, videos, screencasts, and narrated PowerPoint presentations. There was a sudden need for faculty from all disciplines to learn about the latest technology in video and audio recording, and the limitations of bandwidth.

Our CTL advised faculty to

> build an online course that has face-to-face components (i.e., learner-centered activities like practice, hands-on exercises, working through examples/procedures, discussion, and so on). These in-class components become extensions of online content, videos, and readings, while also allowing for checking student comprehension in real-time and ensuring neural encoding of knowledge learned from online course content. In essence, students will engage with course content and summative assessments online (primarily via CourseDen) with face-to-face sessions being opportunities for students to practice skills and shore up comprehension.[4]

Box 16.1 shows an example of workshops that were used to help faculty with their courses. These continued throughout the 2020–2021 year.

Box 16.1 Examples of Workshops

CTL Workshop Topics During Pandemic-Related Instruction

March and April 2020—twice daily synchronous, drop-in sessions (9:00–11:00 a.m. and 1:00–3:00 p.m.) on any topic

May 2020—two sessions per week with rotating topics from the following list: • Designing a Better Online Course

- Creating Engaging Learning Materials
- Setting Up a CourseDen Gradebook
- Designing Meaningful Online Assessments
- Help with CourseDen Tools

Plus the first online version of the Innovations in Pedagogy Conference (twelve synchronous sessions)

June and July 2020—two sessions per week with rotating topics from the following list:

- Creating Engaging Learning Materials
- Designing Meaningful Online Assessments
- Help With Online Instruction in CourseDen
- Incorporating Live Teaching in Online Classes
- Motivating Online Learners
- Including Collaborative Activities in Your Online Class
- Providing Meaningful Feedback and Streamlining Grading
- Setting Up a CourseDen Gradebook
- Making Our Online Materials Accessible
- Designing a Better Online Course

Plus three summer cohorts of four-part workshop series on teaching online, meeting once a week for a month to discuss strategies for designing courses, planning learning materials and activities, creating community, and offering feedback.

Fall 2020—weekly workshops (two to four per week) with rotating topics from the following list:

- Dual Modality Delivery: Strategies for Enriching In-class Meetings
- Creating Engaging Learning Materials, Activities, and Assessments
- Help with Online Instruction in CourseDen
- Building Community and Motivating Online Learners
- Live Teaching in the Online Environment

- TILTing Your Assignments for Transparency and Equity
- Providing Meaningful Feedback and Streamlining Grading
- Online Peer-Review Training

Spring 2021—weekly workshops (three per week) with rotating topics from the following list:

- Designing Meaningful Assessments
- Creating Engaging Learning Materials, Activities, and Assessments
- Help with Online Instruction in CourseDen
- TILTing Your Assignments for Transparency and Equity
- Building Community and Motivating Online Learners
- Making Your Teaching More Inclusive
- Providing Meaningful Feedback and Streamlining Grading
- Making Your Course Content Accessible
- Designing (or Redesigning) Your Course
- Digital Multimedia Tools for Teaching and Learning
- Developing Students' Creative Thinking Skills
- Online Peer-Review Training

Plus the second online version of the Innovations in Pedagogy Conference (thirty-two synchronous sessions with fifty-six presentations)

Source: Author.

Online help guides were also made available throughout the year. Box 16.2 shows one such example.

Box 16.2 Moving Instruction Online

Moving Instruction Online Effectively—An Advanced Guide For Faculty

Contact CTL
Access CourseDen
Contact UWG Online (Technical Assistance for Faculty & Students)

The purpose of this website is to help UWG faculty with planning and preparing for their fall courses, especially via *CourseDen*, UWG's Learning Management System.

For individual help with best practices for designing and delivering online courses, contact the Center for Teaching & Learning: ctl@westga.edu or 678–839–5289. For technical assistance with CourseDen for students and faculty, contact UWG Online at online@westga.edu or 678–839–6248.

Dual Modality Delivery
Getting Started With CourseDen
Communicating With Students
Ensuring That My Online Content Is Accessible
Presenting Content to Students
Assessing Student Work
Recording and Posting Grades in CourseDen's Gradebook

Source: Author.

The University System of Georgia also did a great job providing faculty and institutions with support for their courses. Box 16.3 shows such an example.

Box 16.3 University System of Georgia Guides for Faculty

USG Guides for Faculty

The following documents have been created to assist all USG faculty in moving online: USG Resource Guide for Transitioning to Remote Instruction (eCampus)

This eCampus guide takes faculty through three alternative pedagogies for moving a course online: putting the course in a learning management system (LMS), developing a course through videoconferencing, and keeping an online course simple for students with low or zero internet access or technology at home.

Guiding Principles for Moving Instruction Online (CC-BY 4.0)

With the assistance of the UGA Center for Teaching and Learning, this open-licensed USG guide explains best practices in online instruction, including communications, content delivery, discussions, assignments, labs, and exams.

Supporting the Motivation of Online Learners—Building Expectancy (UVA Motivate Lab)

As emergency remote learning forced classrooms to transition to online formats, many students have questioned whether they can learn in this new modality. Targeting the question "Do students believe that they can do the task?" this resource from the USG partners at University of Virginia—Motivate Lab provides resources to increase students' motivation and prevent disengagement.

List of Virtual Lab Resources (eCampus)

This is a live Google Doc by eCampus staff listing digital alternatives to in-person laboratory exercises.

> ***Proctored Exam Alternatives Guide (eCampus)***
>
> This eCampus document provides alternatives to giving proctored exams in case proctoring services are overwhelmed due to the crisis.
>
> *Source: USG Guides for Faculty, www.usg.edu/keep_teaching_usg/usg_guides (accessed September 3, 2023).*

While all of these are simply *examples* of pandemic-related innovations, the main point to be made here is that, while it is true that universities do generally move slower and in a more deliberate manner than the corporate world does, when necessary, trust in faculty and support systems *can lead to quick and effective results.* Outside research and resources are welcome. Outside interference with the functioning of universities and colleges and prescriptions as to how universities had to do things would not have been helpful when faculties had just days to gear up for effective instruction at the start of the pandemic.

Accountability

Upholding autonomy and a spirit of innovation does *not* mean that a university, a university president, a university administrator, or a faculty member can do whatever he or she wants. There has to be accountability for fiscal results, for achieving realistic performance measures, for maintaining an environment conducive to faculty and staff giving their best to the students, to the institution, to their professions, to their communities, and to the world in general.

Institutional Accountability and Program Accountability

Universities have to comply with many rules, regulations, and performance measures. For the most part, we all understand that, though from time to time, we recognize the irony in this. For example, many of the same legislators who decry the evils of regulation in general are either unaware or unconcerned that they are being inconsistent in heaping regulations and constraints on universities and colleges. Also, faculty who decry the increase in administrators are either unaware or unconcerned that someone *has* to maintain, analyze, and report this information. A faculty member will not be willing to do these time-consuming activities on the way to class or a research meeting, so it has to be an administrator or staff member. (As a side note, I figure that if I shook up legislators and faculty members in the same paragraph, at least no one could accuse me of playing favorites and having either a liberal or conservative agenda.)

Universities collect, analyze, and report on a lot of data on compliance. These are mandated by their boards and state governments (data on enrollment, graduation rates, etc.), by federal regulatory agencies (such as for financial aid, health and safety) and for accreditation purposes, more fully described below.

The key points about accreditation to be made here are that, in the United States,

- institutions are held to very high standards of academic, student success, and financial accountability. Accreditation is based on review by peer institutions, rather than on review by governmental agencies;
- this drives home the point made earlier that review is most meaningful and relevant when done by individuals who are deeply knowledgeable about universities rather than by individuals who have not spent any significant time doing what universities do.

Accreditation as an Instrument of Accountability

In the United States, there are two types of accreditation: regional and national/professional. Regional[5] accreditation focuses largely on institutional accountability, while national/professional accreditation focuses largely on program accountability.

Regional accreditation is a requirement for survival in the medium or long term and is necessary for being eligible for many federal government programs. When we talk of regional accreditation, it means that the entire college/university and all its programs together are accredited by your regional accrediting agency.

This is important to emphasize, because regional and disciplinary accreditation are peer-reviewed accreditation and reaffirmation. In many other countries, accreditation is conferred and reviewed by governmental agencies. In the United States, the process is a very rigorous one and entirely peer-driven; it includes a continuous improvement process; a tremendous amount of information being collected, analyzed, and reported; personal visits of the accreditation teams (of peers) to the campus during which they check records and speak with every constituency (faculty, staff, students, alumni, community and professional members, etc.); a very detailed report by the accrediting team; modifications to the report based on campus input; a review by the commission on accreditation; and a final decision which may include a follow-up report or visit. In my role as a university president through such periodic reviews (plural) and also having served for five years as a commissioner of the largest such accrediting bodies, I can assure proponents and skeptics alike of the rigor of such a process.

Another type of accreditation is accreditation of a *specific program* (as contrasted with regional accreditation, which accredits the entire institution with all its programs) by a national accrediting agency.

This accreditation is desirable: it is an indicator of quality for graduate schools and for employers, but it does not represent an existential threat in terms of survival of the university or institution.

Strategic Planning

Additionally, and probably more interesting, is that universities use information for data-driven, data-informed decision-making. This enables an institution to be nimble, to turn fast if need be.

Arguably, the most exciting use of such data and information is in the area of strategic planning, because here we are not analyzing data just because we have to report results to stay compliant with state, federal, and accrediting agencies, but because we want to grow, to improve ourselves, to capitalize on our strengths, and to improve on our areas of weakness.

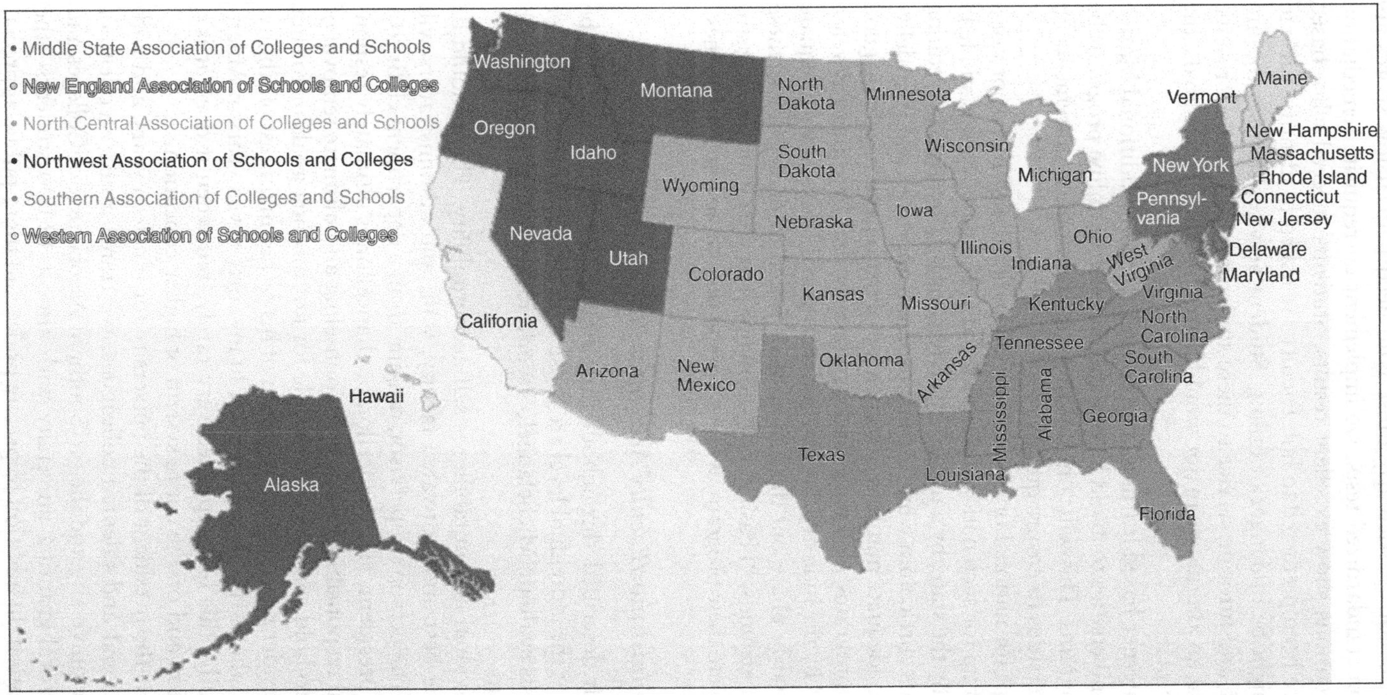

Figure 16.1 CHEA-Recognized Regional Accreditation Associations

Source: "College Accreditation—Regional vs. National Accreditation: A Guide," eLearners, www.elearners.com/colleges/regional-accreditation-vs-national-accreditation/ (accessed September 3, 2023).

Normally, a strategic planning process occurs every five years and is a ground-up and inclusive exercise. At many excellent universities, including my own, we identify groups of students at the time of admission, particularly those who need help. If low scores are identified in high school or on standardized tests, we implement co-requisite remediation to help students. Such interventions show excellent results. Students succeed who, based on entry parameters, may have been predicted to fail. Faculty are asked to identify, early in the semester, students who might be in danger of failing. Student Services staff spring into action and provide counseling and tutoring service to these students, with excellent results. If the student and staff feel that an alternative major would better meet long-term goals, the appropriate advising can take place.

The pandemic leveraged internet-based learning, but it also placed an additional burden on accrediting agencies and universities to avoid having the increase in online programs be a license for lower-quality programs. This will continue to place additional requirements on accrediting agencies and universities to ensure quality.

Programs may choose to opt for national or professional accreditation. Whether or not a program chooses to open itself up for such national scrutiny and accountability, it is still held responsible by the institution, by the state, by a university system, or by a regional accrediting agency for intense scrutiny of its curriculum while earning program approval, and later delivering results in terms of having adequate numbers of students in a major, and providing good educational outcomes. Many programs also have advisory boards that help them develop students who are well regarded by the industry. Programs that are unable to sustain adequate numbers of majors will voluntarily phase out the major, or be asked to do so, unless these majors can be justified on other grounds. "Phasing out" the major refers to giving existing students the opportunity to complete their program, while stopping the admission of new ones.

Administrator/Faculty Accountability

Consistent with the approach described throughout this chapter, the best people to be entrusted with accountability at the individual level are those with the most expertise rather than external entities. Let artists evaluate Michelangelo's work, rather than the people with pots of money who funded him.

The ideal approach to individual accountability is self-accountability. There should be clarity of expectations and the best and motivated faculty, staff, and administrators will ensure that the job gets done. The person's supervisor, ranging from a department chair to a dean, vice president, provost, president, vice chancellor, or chancellor, is ultimately responsible for holding the individual responsible. Progressive counseling and ultimate removal of a person are options. Failure to hold someone responsible for not meeting goals or for not being a good and motivating leader represents abrogation of his or her main responsibility, and an admission of failure on the part of the supervisor. In my forty-seven years in American higher education, thankfully, this has happened very rarely, but when it does, it is a poor reflection on the institution and on the entire system of higher education.

I had the honor of serving as the president of the university for nineteen years, and with the invaluable help of exceptional and talented colleagues, we transformed a college of about 7,500 students to a state university and then to Southern Association of Colleges and Schools (SACS) Level VI doctoral-granting university with almost 12,000 students—the highest level of SACS accreditation. In addition to private praise and more public appreciation shown within the university community, once about every five years I would write a public column in the local newspaper thanking key members of the university community by name, and praising them for their work and specific accomplishments in the preceding five years; I also used that opportunity to thank outstanding members of the external community as well. While the bulk of the column was tailored each time to the details of the immediately preceding period, the headline and ending paragraphs of the column were always the same. The headline was: "Don't look at me—someone else did it!" While this phrase is typically used to deflect blame, I consistently used it to deflect praise that might normally accrue to the president. I then provided details of major projects for which I would be praised or thanked, and clarified that it was my colleague who was the one who did it and deserved the praise.

The last few paragraphs were also the same in each column (they were written about five years apart, so nobody minded):

> Don't look at me-they did it! So, this is my finger-pointing story for today, and I'm sticking with it!
>
> So, if they did all that, what did I do for 19 years anyway?!
>
> On a good day, I got out of the way and let my great colleagues do what they do best—Educational Excellence in a Personal Environment.
>
> On a very good day, I helped them do what they do best. I made a nuisance of myself by raising resources from the University System or the State or from our generous friends.
>
> On a great day, I hired or helped hire these wonderful people from all over this great nation and the world, and create an environment and initiatives that enable talented people to develop innovations-and an environment that applauds creativity and service to our students and other constituencies.
>
> On a really terrific day, I had a good idea myself. Well, I may have thought I had a "good" idea almost every day but it's just that it was a (rare) terrific day when at least one other person in the world agreed that that idea was a good one!
>
> But, it is my colleagues and friends who get the credit for accomplishing most of the great UWG acts that bring so much credit to the institution and so much pleasure to you.

The point of including this letter here in a section on accountability is to emphasize the autonomy thread that has run throughout this chapter: "On a good day, **I got out of the way** and let my great colleagues do what they do best." "On a very good day, **I helped them** do what they do best." "**I hired or help hire** these wonderful people." The point is that a key part of a well-run organization is giving autonomy while holding individuals accountable for results.

In today's climate, we hear stories of the need for faculty accountability. During the past forty-seven years in three different U.S. states (red and blue) and in three very different kinds of universities (private and public, R1, Research-Intensive, R3, college and university, commuter and residential, small and mid-sized), like countless other institutions with which I have had some degree of familiarity, there are methods of evaluating teaching, scholarship, and service, and there are well-established procedures for handling grievances. Unless there is an accusation of sexual or physical attack or specific intimidation, a good system of accountability would suggest that a direct conversation with the faculty member often resolves the situation. And, if it does not, then it appeals go up the chain. Along with my colleagues, we have investigated many complaints; we took every complaint very seriously, and found that there were always two sides to the story. Students and/or parents and sometimes people from outside the university should know that their concerns are treated with respect, but the system of checks and balances and accountability works. An example follows.

A member of the faculty at the University of West Georgia had written a book on a potentially controversial topic. An on-campus lecture (not part of his class) given by the author about the issues addressed in his book, came to the attention of persons in the community. Numerous letters were written to the local newspaper, and we received many telephone calls berating the faculty member. These individuals not only demanded that he should be fired but also suggested that community members cease providing financial support for the university if he was not fired. As it happened, this incident occurred at about the time the major fundraising events of the year were about to take place.

The matter was investigated by his immediate supervisor, the department chair; the faculty member, his students, and others were interviewed. While he did talk of his book and his scholarly defense of his work, he did so outside of his class. His students consistently said that his book was not part of the course, and so there was no question about feeling any pressure to agree or disagree with the views of the author.

We not only refused to consider any demands for his removal, but I personally responded to all those who had filed complaints with a clear defense of the concept of academic freedom in the context of higher education. Although this provoked further sharply critical statements, I did not yield an inch to pressure. Among other things I wrote at that time was a piece that stated:

> Freedom of expression is a fundamental principle of this great country, is guaranteed by the constitution, and is an essential aspect of learning. . . . The very essence of a university is the free exchange of ideas (within the realm of the law, of course). Were we to do otherwise, we would be guilty of violation of the First Amendment, a cardinal principle of the founding of our country, and of higher education in general. Some [of the letters I have received] suggest that free speech is okay only if we happen to agree with the viewpoint expressed—but that is not America.

A couple of additional points need to be made in connection with this case: (1) the professor had offered to debate and discuss the matter with the complainants; no one took him up on the offer; (2) the fundraising events that year were a success with a substantial increase over previous years; and (3) a local pastor made a point of sending a check in support of freedom of speech, even though he did not agree with the findings of the book. What a guy!

We felt that this entire firestorm could have been avoided if those who had a problem with the book had talked with him directly before threatening all kinds of dire action. Yet the system worked. Complaints were taken seriously, the key players were respected and interviewed, and academic freedom was strongly supported.

Summary and Conclusions

The preceding pages have talked of autonomy, innovation, and accountability. These are all important parts of university governance. In this chapter, I have suggested some overarching principles of good governance in higher education.

First, Do No Harm

As an interesting side note, although 'first, do no harm' is attributed to the ancient Greek physician Hippocrates, it isn't a part of the Hippocratic Oath at all.

Governance systems, first and foremost, should preserve and celebrate the essence, the true character of the institution. What makes a university great (and, by "great" I do not mean the most famous or the richest, but what does great good for our students, particularly those who need help the most) is the *character* of the institution—the faculty and staff who are committed to the education of their students. To bring in rules and regulations, which hurt the faculty, staff, and students, is unproductive.

While accountability systems are necessary, if they start changing the fundamental properties of what makes a university tick and thrive, they are unproductive. To use a very simple example, in one university, a professional trip to a neighboring town in the same state to give a talk or attend a meeting did not require a travel authorization in advance. Then, they changed the rules such that every trip even to a nearby location in the same state requires an advance travel authorization and approvals up the chain. This can lead to some faculty either reducing their professional travel or simply paying out of their own pocket; neither of these scenarios being productive, and possibly being in conflict with the "First, do no harm" principle. The purported rationale for the change is because the administration wants to know what the plans are if someone misses class during this trip. In today's world of online videos and assignments, missing class is not usually an issue, and it should be a matter of *trust* that responsible faculty members would not leave their students hanging out for an hour just waiting for the professor to appear. Even granting that it is reasonable that several administrators up the chain need to know how each professor who is on a professional trip is covering each class, the travel authorization form could have easily been required *only* if class is to be missed. This is an example of a counterproductive solution in search of a problem.

The irony is that some of those who would regulate universities to the ground are *the same people* who profess to believe that regulation is damaging.

- They do not favor regulation for business and industry; in fact, it is decried as evil and harmful.
- They favor many, many regulations for universities and colleges, including those on faculty speech (broadly defined).
- Yet they say that higher education should operate "more like a business."
- And, they are oblivious to the inconsistencies in their approaches.

I suggest again the sense of the points made earlier:

- Let artists evaluate Michelangelo's work, rather than people with pots of money who funded him.

  The fact that I have some money to share does not magically invest in me the knowledge base and expertise as to the running of orphanages or the selection of children who need help. That is not my field; I have not spent one day of my life doing that job, and so I must trust those who have done this for many years.

- Draw your own conclusions for implications about university governance.

Governance systems need to be predicated on *trust* and respect.

As a concluding point to this chapter, I refer you to an excellent statement from PEN America (n.d.). It encapsulates the essence of many earlier points made in this chapter. Their Statement of Purpose is a very well-written statement, which is too long to reproduce here but I strongly recommend that an interested reader read it in its entirety. The Mission Statement is as follows:

> The Champions of Higher Education, coordinated by PEN America, affirmatively promote a positive vision of American higher education as an essential guarantor of free expression in a democracy, and defend the autonomy of educational decisions made by colleges and universities against political and legislative incursions.

So, now, to refer to the implied question in the very title of this chapter: What should *not* change in this constantly changing world?

- The essence and the character of the university
- The respect for autonomy and academic freedom
- The respect for the faculty, staff, and students (declining to get into long-drawn-out discussions about the relative importance of these three, I list them in alphabetical order)
- The need for a culture of innovation
- The need for a culture of trust and respect

Good governance and accountability systems need to be driven by these overarching principles, rather than the other way around.

Without these principles, you have a fancy accounting system and nothing else.

Key Discussion Areas

- Discussion around university governance.
- An overview of institutional autonomy and academic freedom.
- Role of institutional accountability and program accountability.

Notes

1 In this article, which is an opinion piece, he is explicitly not speaking on behalf of any institutions with which he is affiliated. These views are personal in nature and do not represent the views of any of these institutions.

2 Much of these arguments are drawn from previous writings of mine:

- "Giving Money and Time to Bring About Change," *HUKTA*, Summer 2015, Atlanta, GA.
- "The Golden Rule . . ., " *Fundamatics*, December 2015, IIT Bombay Alumni Magazine.

3 For this section, the author is indebted to material and information shared by Dr. Rob McRae, which was developed by the UWG faculty and staff. He gratefully acknowledges their contributions. Dr. McRae is currently Assistant Provost at Middle Georgia College.

4 For example, Mays Imad, "Leveraging the Neuroscience of Now," *Inside Higher Ed*, June 2, 2020, www.insidehighered.com/advice/2020/06/03/seven-recommendations-helping-students-thrive-times-trauma, (accessed March 26, 2023); Crystal O. Wong, "Building Relationships: How to Connect from a Distance," *Faculty Focus*, October 14, 2020, www.facultyfocus.com/articles/online-education/building-relationships-how-to-connect-from-a-distance/ (accessed March 26, 2023); Shruti Nagpal, "Raising Student Motivation During the Pandemic," *Faculty Focus*, October 19, 2020, www.facultyfocus.com/articles/effective-teaching-strategies/raising-student-motivation-during-the-pandemic/ (accessed March 26, 2023).

5 Beheruz N. Sethna, "What Does It Mean for a US University to Be 'Acredited'?," *Quora*, www.quora.com/What-does-it-mean-for-a-US-university-to-be-accredited/answer/Beheruz-N-Sethna (accessed March 26, 2023). In the United States, colleges and schools are accredited by Regional Accrediting bodies, as shown in Figure 16.1.

References

American Association of University Professors (AAUP). 1940. "Statement of Principles on Academic Freedom and Tenure, and Advancing Academic Freedom." www.aaup.org/report/1940-statement-principles-academic-freedom-and-tenure (accessed March 26, 2023).

CNBC. 2015. "College Inventions That Shaped the World." June 5, 2015, www.cnbc.com/2015/06/05/college-inventions-that-shaped-the-world.html (accessed March 26, 2023).

"College Accreditation—Regional vs. National Accreditation: A Guide." eLearners, www.elearners.com/colleges/regional-accreditation-vs-national-accreditation/ (accessed September 3, 2023).

IIT Alumni Centre. 2021. "Building Great Universities for India—An IITACB Webinar." Youtube video, May 23, 2021, www.youtube.com/watch?v=IzQ9IdJxaVM&list=PL0zMQ-70IHlX-df3u2Tto6dkKHCRC6iFL&index=3&t=2s (accessed March 26, 2023).

Pen America. n.d. "Champions of Higher Education Statement of Purpose." https://pen.org/champions-statement/ (accessed March 26, 2023).

Redden, Elizabeth. 2021. "A New Magna Charta." *Inside Higher Ed*, June 25, 2021, www.insidehighered.com/news/2021/06/25/new-global-document-reaffirms-values-academic-freedom-and-university-autonomy?utm_source=Inside+Higher+Ed&utm_campaign=8fa21062e5-DNU_2021_COPY_02&utm_medium=email&utm_term=0_1fcbc04421-8fa21062e5-198507589&mc_cid=8fa21062e5&mc_eid=c4f7433554 (accessed March 26, 2023).

17
POLITICAL CULTURE AND EDUCATIONAL GOVERNANCE
Covid-19 and the Limits of Decentralization in Israeli Education

Gad Yair

Introduction

Covid-19 has sent paradoxical waves throughout the Israeli system of education. The initial governmental reaction to the pandemic mandated a full closure that lasted months. However, centralized governance proved to be too far removed and too inefficient in supplying appropriate adaptations to face Covid-19 constructively. Slowly, local educational authorities replaced central decision-making by implementing de facto adaptations. Schools began to offer classes in natural settings, and local authorities took control of activities and health precautions.

Consequently, after months of dealing with the failures of centralized control, a new government recommended that decision-making and responsibility should indeed center on the local government level and even below—the schools themselves. "The Ministry of Education will function as a regulator," announced the ministry, adding that the office would pursue a policy of decentralized governance (Ilan 2021b). If the Ministry of Education should indeed implement this directive, then Covid-19 will have succeeded where decades of debate and attempts at decentralizing Israeli educational governance have previously failed. Will the new policy withstand political temptations to return to centralized control—or will Covid-19 and its variants force governance structures to adapt and readapt for the long haul? These were the long-term questions critical in determining governance reform in the post Covid-19 world.

Though isolated, Israel educational governance is not insulated. In the past few decades, Israel has become more integrated with global educational agendas (Volansky 2020). It takes part in international assessment programs like *PISA and TIMMS*, and it responds to global calls for improvement in STEM (science, technology, engineering, and mathematics) education (Feniger, Livneh, and Yogev 2012). Notwithstanding the 2017 decision by the Donald Trump and Benjamin Netanyahu administrations to divorce from UNESCO, both Israeli politics and the educational administration remain entangled in the cobwebs of global centralized assessments, as well as by centralized national testing programs—primarily the twelfth-grade matriculation exams (Ayalon and Shavit 2004). Surprisingly, the

DOI: 10.4324/9781003316077-21

new government of Naftali Bennett's administration has announced that, in response to the Covid-19 pandemic, it will transform the nuts and bolts of daily life in schools. Exams are to make way for social and emotional learning (SEL), and the variety of matriculation exam topics will be narrowed down (Haddad 2021). Since exams and assessments are a major tool in the centralized governance of education systems (Newman and Chin 2003), Covid-19 may indeed prove to have helped transform the Israeli education system in the long term.

This chapter focuses on the governance of the Israeli system of education. It sets out by describing the historical roots of centralized governance and the policy of nation building after independence (Hanson 1998; Weiler 1990; Hannaway 1993). It then analyzes the structural and hierarchical division of labor between the central and local government, while outlining the prior attempts to move more centralized responsibilities to the local level. Those early efforts were blunted by two forces: first, the global trend toward centralization through the increase in international assessment programs; second, the weakening control of the centralized government vis-à-vis Israeli Palestinian communities and ultra-Orthodox localities. The final sections of this chapter will assess the impact that Covid-19 has had on the balance of power and shared responsibilities of central and local authorities in Israel, first generally, and then in the realm of education. Given the current fluid situation with Covid-19—as it proves stubborn against full amelioration—the final sections must remain tentative. As the pandemic continues to march on, we can only conclude that the pendulum of educational governance—the policy pendulum that swings between centralization and decentralization—is yet to come to a final rest (Volansky 2020). I will conclude by suggesting that the historical moment created by the pandemic has exposed a cultural preference for centralized governance, which, I argue, limits the pressure that Covid-19 exerts toward decentralization.

Historical Roots of Centralized Governance

After declaring independence in 1948, the newly formed Israeli government faced significant challenges (Eisenstadt 1967). Having survived coordinated military attacks by its Arab neighbors, Israel faced unprecedented waves of immigrants (Eisenstadt 1954). The first to arrive were European Holocaust survivors. Polish and Russian survivors arrived along with French speakers and German speakers, and the latter were accompanied by surviving Jews from Greece, Hungary, Romania, and other European countries. The only elements that unified those immigrants were common prayer traditions and a Christian host environment in their country of origin. A few years after the European mass migration, another wave of refugees arrived. This time, the arrivals were Jews deported from Muslim countries—Iran and Iraq from the east and Algeria and Morocco from the west. This wave of arrivals shared a Muslim host environment, the Arabic language, and a common prayer tradition. However, these new arrivals had almost nothing in common with veteran Israelis, or with the earlier European arrivals. Israel thus became a place of multiple languages and a myriad of cultural conventions (Khazzoom 2008).

The huge heterogeneity within the Jewish population of Israel was further complicated by Israeli Palestinians, who became citizens after what is referred to as the catastrophe or Nakba (United Nations)[1] uprooted the majority of the Palestinian population in the 1948 war for Israeli independence. Though most Israeli Palestinians were Muslim and spoke Arabic, Israel also hosted Christian and Druze enclaves and some smaller minorities as well (Mazawi 1995; Sa'ar 2007). Initially, these non-Jewish groups were seen as potentially hostile to the newly formed Israeli state. The government suspected that the Palestinians remained allied with neighboring Muslim countries. Furthermore, their culture, which they shared with the Arab world, practically disconnected them from the Jewish majority. Hence, the Palestinian citizens of Israel shared neither a common language with the Hebrew-speaking majority, nor a cultural affinity with its Western orientation. The new state was thus a cultural, religious, and linguistic mélange.

Given those circumstances, the first prime minister of Israel David Ben-Gurion's government sought to create an Israeli common ground, especially among the influx of Jewish immigrants. The policy took various forms. It created a program for the study of Hebrew as a common language. It abolished the previous ideologically separated para-military groups and created a joint military (the Israeli Defense Forces [IDF]) under a single authority. It supported the creation of new common ideals and national myths, shared holidays, and unified national ceremonies. And it created a common school system with a joint curriculum for the vast majority of the population. Even the Israeli Palestinians shared this common curriculum, although they studied it in Arabic. While Israel has not granted its Palestinian citizens full cultural autonomy, religious autonomy has been permitted—allowing the Palestinians to maintain an independent national identity. Another exception to the unified and centralized educational policies of the government was its "status quo" agreement with the ultra-Orthodox Jews. This small minority was allowed to enjoy full autonomy.[2]

Bearing those exceptions in mind, Israel managed to create a functional society with a common language, curriculum, and holidays and ceremonies. These commonalities formed the foundation of a new culture and a new national identity. But the maintenance of cultural integration hinged on centralized control over schooling. The Israeli Ministry of Education maintained the use of regulations and administrative structures from the pre-state British Mandate, and even centralized its control structure. It also centralized teacher-preparation programs and instituted common matriculation exams. For a few decades, this centralized structure managed to unify Israel and maintain educational control over the vast majority of the Israeli population. But over the years, the minor exceptions made in the early 1950s proved to have long-term consequences. Rising calls for cultural autonomy led to calls for decentralized governance. During the 1990s, the pendulum swinging toward decentralized governance gained momentum.

Thus, the administration of schooling was divided: the central Ministry of Education decided on the curriculum, standards, exams, teacher preparation, and all aspects relating to "the mind and soul." Local educational authorities were left with the responsibility for the nuts and bolts of maintenance and daily operations. Under this traditional division of labor, schools must answer to a dual structure: the centralized ministry on the one hand, and the local authority on the other. As mentioned, during the first decades of Israeli statehood, this division of labor faced few challenges. During the 1980s, however, local authorities pushed for an increase in decentralization. In a first experiment of its kind, the Ministry of Education and the City of Jerusalem agreed to transfer more authority to the local government—with the expectation that this experiment would pave the way for an overall decentralization of education in Israel.

But almost four decades later, the Jerusalem experiment of decentralized educational governance has not expanded to other local governments. Moreover, with the years, some of the responsibilities that had been devolved to the City of Jerusalem were taken back by the central government. Nevertheless, the pendulum began a movement toward greater decentralization of educational decision-making and authority in favor of local governments. A legal precedent allowed parents and local authorities curricular leeway over 25 percent of school hours. Empirical studies of local-authority-level departments of education found, however, that most authorities lacked pedagogical expertise (Hajaj-Berger, Gamliel, and Yair, unpublished working paper 2021). For local authorities to rise to the challenge of decentralization, they first had to be transformed. Hence, with the support of the Ministry of Interior (which oversees local authorities), the council of local authorities created new programs to train local civil servants. It also pushed the Israeli Parliament to put local educational authorities under mandated regulations, which require educational leaders with expertise in educational administration and pedagogy at the helm. The leaders of that movement toward decentralization believed that once the local government was led by knowledgeable administrators, the central government would be more willing to transfer educational responsibilities to the local authorities.

From the 1990s onward, over the next two decades, headway was made in the initiative to professionalize educational administration at the local level. Consequently, the traditional prestige hierarchy between the central Ministry of Education (which was responsible for the brain and soul) and local educational authorities (which were responsible for supplying chalk, cleanup, and security) evaporated. Local educational authorities today employ highly skilled and well-trained individuals. The groundwork for decentralization was now in place.

This groundwork was supported by further efforts on the part of the Ministry of Interior to professionalize and support the independence of cities and local authorities. But the interests of the ministry went deeper than professionalization. The minister, who represented religious political parties and communities, sought to increase the cultural autonomy of ultra-Orthodox localities. Specifically, he sought to increase state funding for religious communities while providing ever-greater educational autonomy and protection from intervention by the secular state. Given the territorial separation between the communities—and given the fact that schooling within ultra-Orthodox communities is mostly independent—the religious parties had a vested interest in increasing cultural and administrative autonomy.

Consequently, from the 1990s onward, the local authorities that serve majority ultra-Orthodox communities enjoyed ever more autonomy. The central government, while providing funding for schooling, had little control over curricula, school composition, or assessment and examination. For ultra-Orthodox cities and local authorities, increased decentralization meant de facto independence. Seven decades after the status quo agreement between Ben-Gurion's government and the ultra-Orthodox parties, the latter, driven by unequal demographic growth, enjoyed unparalleled autonomy, inviting the nickname of "a state within the state."

By the dawn of the twenty-first century, the decades-long efforts of the Ministry of Interior to support the decentralization of education seemed to have been successful. Human capital at the local level had improved significantly. Most local educational authorities had become adept at providing extracurricular programs. And as education became a local affair, mayors and council members grew more interested in education and youth issues (Yair 2005). In 2003, the Israeli government nominated a national commission for the reform of education (the Dovrat Commission). One of its major recommendations was to create broad local educational authorities and to devolve central government responsibilities to those newly decentralized bodies. In 2004, the government adopted the report and stated that it would follow the report's recommendations—but the recommendation to amalgamate local educational authorities never materialized. In contrast, one of the recommendations that was indeed implemented annulled the intent to decentralize education: the creation of a national centralized testing authority (i.e., RAMA). In the subsequent years, the pendulum began to swing back to centralization (Volansky 2020).

The recommendation for the creation of a national testing authority followed the first two waves of PISA, the global international program for assessing youths' preparedness for a global society. Given the poor performance of Israeli students on PISA and other major assessment programs, the Dovrat committee recommended the reform of Israeli education while creating a national independent authority to oversee the effectiveness of the reform efforts. The elected head of the new authority emulated the American Educational Testing Service (ETS). However, the Israeli authority worked through the central administration, and with wide governmental support it managed to create a program of mandatory annual examinations that covers all students in all schools (in specific grade levels each year). Like the mandatory exam in the twelfth grade—the matriculation—the new Meitsav examination program put a stranglehold on prior decentralization efforts, especially at the individual school level. Moreover, the legal standing of the new authority meant that it reported directly to the Minister of Education, bypassing the administration of the ministry while imposing its agenda on professional decision-makers at both the national and the local level. The Israeli education system was now run by a centralized examination authority.

Indeed, since 2005, Israeli elementary and middle schools have been under extreme pressure from the national examination authority, as well as from parents, city mayors, and local council members, to increase student achievement on standardized tests (Feniger, Israeli, and Yehuda 2016). Previous programs to increase the choice and variation in school offerings were sacrificed to the need to attain expected standards. This meant that schools had to narrow their curricular offerings and focus on preparing students for the national examinations. Promises to "make a thousand flowers blossom"—to offer an increased variety of school programs at the local level—were abandoned. PISA overruled Israeli education from the outside, while RAMA centralized it from the inside.

Armed with ever-expanding quantitative evidence, the national authority for examinations proved that the Israeli education system is split into three sectors, with Israeli Palestinian and Jewish ultra-Orthodox schools representing the lowest-achieving sectors. The evidence exposed that the central government only rules 65 percent of the Israeli school system. Whatever achievements that centralization and national reforms could boast, they were taking place only in schools and localities that took part in national efforts. The yearly reports exposed stubborn achievement gaps between the three sectors. They supported a growing realization, especially with regard to ultra-Orthodox schools: they simply do not prepare students for the modern world. They shun the teaching of mathematics, science, history, citizenship, and English—all central areas of the national curriculum—and hence cater for failure. While they generate loyal, religious students, that loyalty is not to Israel but to the ultra-Orthodox state within the state. As for the Israeli Palestinians, their similar insistence on cultural autonomy contributes to their standing at the periphery of Israeli society and the Israeli economy. In short, the centralization achieved by the national examination authority mostly affected secular and national religious schools. It is vital to have certain standardized curriculum and assessment requirements for all schools across the nation.

The effort to overhaul Israeli education through a nationalized system of examinations gave rise to the public realization that Israel runs three practically independent systems of education and that the government has little to say in two of them. In fact, this realization reflects a split in the administrative structure that has given rise to the three branches of Israeli education. In Jerusalem—the locus of the national decentralization experiment and by far the largest city in Israel—the educational authority was split into three branches long before this public realization. It runs a unit serving Palestinian students, another for ultra-Orthodox schools, and a third for the common national or public schools. Jerusalem is not alone. The same split structure runs through the central Ministry of Education with its three administrative and mostly independent organs. In 2015, the president of Israel Reuven Rubi Rivlin provided an apt description of this balkanized system of education, suggesting that Israel is "a Society of Tribes."[3]

The president's critical speech in 2015, which became known as the Four Tribes speech, constituted a rallying cry against the split of Israel into a balkanized territory with three tribes.[4] The Palestinian citizens of Israel live in separate cities and localities, they attend separate schools, and they do not serve in the Israeli military. They do not intermarry with Jewish Israelis, and the two groups share very few contact points. But as the Israeli president pointed out, ultra-Orthodox citizens also grow up in separate communities. They too study in independent schools; they too avoid serving in the military, and they too hardly marry their Jewish non-Orthodox counterparts. This split society is buttressed by political parties that cater to the specific interests of each tribe. Given the socioeconomic dependency of two of the tribes, Israeli politics have evolved to serve tribal rather than common or public interests.

The split tribal society was able to function while the size of the minority tribes was small, explained President Rivlin. But demography changed the status quo. Currently, the Palestinian citizens of Israel constitute 20 percent of its population, and the Ultra-Orthodox 15 percent. In less than a generation, he warned, the division of labor between the three tribes will be unsustainable. The two minority tribes will become the majority, and their economic dependence on secular Jewish citizens—in terms of taxation and military service—will no longer be sustainable. Moreover, instead of a multicultural society, Israel will be better identified as a caste society, or even an Apartheid society. Though commentators often claim that the three tribes choose to live separately, critiques suggest that, like other Apartheid societies, Israel will not be able to sustain this separate and unequal structure.

In his "four tribes" speech, President Rivlin called on leaders from the three tribes to rethink the basic understanding of Israeli society and politics. Should catastrophe strike, he suggested, it will inevitably result in struggle and unprecedented conflict. Five years later, catastrophe indeed struck Israel: Covid-19 has served as a reality check for the government's ability to provide solutions for the two minority tribes. The pandemic forms the context of the return toward decentralization in educational governance.

Covid-19 and the Failure of Centralized Governance

As Covid-19 has made soberingly clear, President Rivlin's characterization of Israeli society as splintered was correct. Centralized and uniform response policies to the pandemic have created a backlash among both Israeli Palestinians and ultra-Orthodox communities. The belief that Israel enjoys a national capacity to respond to wars and terror attacks has now been shattered. In 2020, the government implemented three successive lockdowns and attempted to minimize social gatherings. However, compliance with the centralized policy was unevenly distributed. And major stratification in compliance was soon followed by the uneven social distribution of illness and death. Under those circumstances, the implementation of mandatory policies brought about delegitimization and disenchantment with centralized control. After the third lockdown, the governmental response to Covid-19 decreased the legitimacy of centralized control and gave rise to local adaptations.

During March 2020, when the first cases of Covid-19 appeared, the Israeli government was quick to announce a lockdown. Schools were shut, and religious venues were banned. Muslim and Jewish prayer houses were physically locked, and believers were ordered to pray at home or in open gardens. Decision-makers—politicians and health experts—did not fully appreciate the meaning of those bans and the backlash they would motivate. Recent sociological studies of Covid-19 lockdown policies have shown how religious communities experienced those policies as brutal blows to their way of life (Hajaj-Berger, Gamliel, and Yair 2021). Some respondents claimed that synagogues had only been shut twice in Jewish history: following the Roman destruction of the Second Temple (more than 2,000 years ago) and during the Nazi reign in Europe. For religious Jews, the decision to shut down the synagogues was unimaginable and unacceptable. Similarly, for Palestinian Muslims the lockdown policy provided further painful evidence of Jewish colonization and the destruction of historical Palestine. Either way, the association of Covid-19 policies with those historical cultural traumas provides telling evidence about the attitudes toward Israeli centralized governance during the Covid-19 pandemic.

As the government was losing the battle for legitimacy with respect to the Israeli Palestinian and ultra-Orthodox communities, new cries against the unified response to Covid-19 arose in secular Jewish communities as well. Covid-19 spread quickly and unevenly—mostly in Arab and religious localities. Systematic reports exposed those cities and local authorities who were experiencing highly divergent case numbers. These variations created collective tribal blame campaigns. Localities with low numbers of Covid-19 cases began to adopt local solutions and policies. City mayors and councilors understood that the central government was either too slow or too inaccurate in responding to local variations. Tel Aviv, for example, allowed residents to be vaccinated before the government approved the vaccines for general use. Other local authorities developed independent responses to the evacuation of sick people, the identification and assistance of isolated individuals, and the distribution of food to the needy. As evidence of those decentralized solutions began to be known, the government was pushed to accept a policy of local variations—the "traffic light policy." Localities with minimal Covid-19 cases were categorized as green, and those with significant case numbers as either yellow or red. Decentralized control and decentralized responses were now in the open.

The drive toward a decentralized response to Covid-19 was not ideologically driven. Rather, it was driven by the realization that Covid-19 was socially and geographically distributed, and that attempts at a unified or common governmental response amounted to a loss of resources—and, no less importantly, the loss of governmental legitimacy. But the secret was now in the open: the Israeli government had little control over the two minority tribes: the Israeli Palestinian and Ultra-Orthodox communities. The three tribes society was now evident for everyone to see. Centralized governance was in disrepute. In contrast, assisted by new technologies and community support, mayors and local council members gained autonomy in responding to Covid-19. Localities were now taking the lead in administering and coordinating health services for their residents. The division of labor between the central government and the local authorities shifted once again. Decentralization regained momentum. Educational governance was soon to follow.

Covid-19 and Educational Decentralization From Above

After failing to form a functioning government in three consecutive elections, Netanyahu finally gave in. The new government—a mélange of left-leaning and right-wing parties—nominated a minister of education, Dr. Yifat Shasha-Biton, with a Ph.D. in education and ample experience in governing education from below—from a local-authority position. She was also a provost of a teacher training college. Clearly, she seemed the right person for the post. Shasha-Biton had planned for the role extensively and announced her vision well before being nominated as the minister (Haddad 2021). Then, after the government was finally formed, in June 2021, messages about the ministry's policy for the coming administration began to emerge. In a nutshell, the new policy tilts toward decentralization. The minister builds on the government's new liberal policy with regard to Covid-19. The government offers free vaccination and testing, but it is the responsibility of individuals and local authorities to avail themselves of those opportunities. There are no lockdowns, nor a uniform response across the country. The new government practically decentralized the entire response to the pandemic.

The new educational administration appears to be following suit. The Minister of Education announced that her long-term vision is to minimize the centralized control of schooling. Her administration plans to do this by cutting down the number of matriculation exams, for example, and by providing school principals with more pedagogical leeway. Local educational authorities, she announced, will gain greater responsibility. "The government will be responsible for setting standards," the minister announced. "But local educational authorities, school principals and teachers will bear the responsibility to make sure they meet them," she added.

The Covid-19 Delta variant created an immediate obstacle to the implementation of this new policy. The new school year, set to commence on September 1, 2021, was just around the corner. Weeks prior to the occasion, the minister sent a clear message. The central government is too far from localities, and it will be the mayors and school principals who will have to act as street level bureaucrats. The only way for schools to function, per Shasha-Biton, is for local educational authorities and schools to step-in with local adaptations. The government will only mandate school closures and impose distance learning in local authorities that health officials designate as "red," meaning with significant rates of infection. Otherwise, she announced, school principals will be responsible for deciding when to close classrooms, or cohorts, or the entire school. The government only set a national standard: students are to attend school if 70 percent of students are vaccinated. It is the responsibility of teachers and school principals to make sure that this standard is met—and to cater for the complex situations of hybrid learning. While the government's aim was to encourage parents to vaccinate children for in-person schooling, the only way this policy could be implemented was through decentralization.

This educational policy seemed aligned with the experience of the preceding months. On the one hand, the central government proved incapable of making flexible and timely decisions. On the other hand, local authorities proved able to take the initiative and develop local adaptations. Decentralization from the bottom-up was viewed as a panacea.

Paradoxically, however, the government now announced that decentralization would be imposed from above. It made clear that rather than being voluntary and based on local initiative, decentralized responsibility would now be centrally mandated. Parents, teachers, principals, and local educational authorities are to decide the fate of in-person schooling in 2021–2022. The government has stepped aside.

The reaction of educators to this top-down policy was prompt. "We lack the necessary resources to guarantee that 70 percent of the students are vaccinated," declared some. "Parents' pressure on teachers and schools will be simply too much," called others (Ilan 2021a). And yet others criticized the policy for increasing social gaps in students' learning opportunities. But whatever the specifics of those reactions, they exposed a deep cultural code, an expectation for the central government to lead, decide, take control, and otherwise call the shots for the entire country. It seemed that notwithstanding prior calls for decentralization, educators and many local educational authorities were still expecting the central government to take responsibility for decision-making. After the central government began to realize its inability to govern from above, and as it began to push the policy pendulum toward decentralization, it was now the local authorities and school principals who cried out—too fast, too much.

Covid-19, Governance, and Political Culture: Concluding Ruminations

The inability of local authorities to initiate adaptations to respond to Covid-19 reflected historical traditions. The Israeli Palestinians have been accustomed to colonial rulers—whether the Ottoman Empire, the British Mandate, or Israeli control. As for ultra-Orthodox communities, they have never taken responsibility for operations of state and have never adopted codes of sovereignty. Thus, though they often protest state intervention in their communities, the two tribes are fully dependent on external supplies for the infrastructure of daily living, including educational budgets and services.

The dependence of local governments on the central government is one more testimony to the failure of centralization in Israel's divisive social structure. This dependency also suggests that while Israel is a formal democracy, it has yet to inculcate a democratic habitus among its citizenship. Citizen led movements and democratically driven policy reforms are critical in any democracy. Indeed, Israelis regard their government as a superhuman agency that is supposed to save them (Yair 2011). They argue with the state of Israel, they pray for it, and they demand that it serve and secure them. Unlike in other Western democracies, Israelis do not advocate for self-governance and local responsibility. They wait to be ordered and expect the government to govern. Culturally, it seems, they lack the liberal values that drive or motivate local collective action and democracy from below.

The traditional cultural expectation for the central government to govern from above has not been shattered by Covid-19. Though the pandemic exposed the weakness of centralized governance, and although some communities rose to the challenges created by its slow and inaccurate response, most have remained expectant and dependent on centralized governance. Those local variations are bound to increase ecological and social inequalities across the country, especially in education. And given the new policy to decentralize educational decision-making and responsibility, those inequalities are bound to increase.

It will take time to assess whether the new government and the new minister of education succeed in moving the policy pendulum toward greater local responsibility. With few local capabilities and little motivation for self-governance, decentralization from above may amount to irresponsible action by the central government. It might end up in a situation of collective incapacity to act—either from above or from below. While Covid-19 has presented a magnifying glass to observe the movement of the pendulum of governance, it will probably take a longer time to assess whether Israel has indeed changed its political culture (Volansky 2020). Given the stubborn resistance of cultural predispositions, it is doubtful that decentralized governance will constitute the final resting point of the pendulum.

Key Discussion Areas

- The history of educational governance in Israel and the efforts made by various governments to decentralize it.
- The two-decade struggle to implement decentralized governance in Israel.
- The impact of Covid-19 on governance.

Notes

1 United Nations—The Question of Palestine. https://www.un.org/unispal/about-the-nakba/ (accessed April 23, 2024).
2 Three generations later, this exception would constitute one of the major challenges faced by Israeli society.
3 www.idc.ac.il/he/research/ips/pages/4tribes.aspx.
4 The fourth tribe referred to the settler movement.

References

Ayalon, Hannah, and Yossi Shavit. 2004. "Educational Reforms and Inequalities in Israel: The MMI Hypothesis Revisited." *Sociology of Education* 77(2): 103–20.

Eisenstadt, Samuel Noah. 1954. *The Absorption of Immigrants: A Comparative Study based Mainly on the Jewish Community in Palestine and the State of Israel*. London: Routledge & Kegan Paul.

———. 1967. *Israeli Society*. New York: Basic Books.

Feniger, Yariv, Mirit Israeli, and Smadar Yehuda. 2016. "The Power of Numbers: The Adoption and Consequences of National Low-Stakes Standardised Tests in Israel." *Globalisation, Societies and Education* 14(2): 183–202, https://doi.org/10.1080/14767724.2015.1010438.

Feniger, Yariv, Idit Livneh, and Abraham Yogev. 2012. "Globalisation and the Politics of International Tests: The Case of Israel." *Comparative Education* 48(3): 323–35, https://doi.org/10.1080/03050068.2011.622539.

Haddad, Trabalsi. 2021. "'The Revolution Begins': Minister Yifat Shasha-Biton's Plans for the Education System." *YNet*, June 14, 2021, www.ynet.co.il/news/article/HJ6aH11So00 (accessed October 1, 2023).

Hajaj-Berger, Hagar, Tova Gamliel, and Gad Yair. 2021. "Urgent Ethnographies: Studies of Covid-19." Unpublished manuscript.

Hannaway, Jane. 1993. "Political Pressure and Decentralization in Institutional Organizations: The Case of School Districts." *Sociology of Education* 66(3): 147–63.

Hanson, Mark E. 1998. "Strategies of Educational Decentralization: Key Questions and Core Issues." *Journal of Educational Administration* 36(2): 111–28.

Ilan, Shahar. 2021a. "Administrative Independence 'Will Increase Disparities'." *Calcalist*, August 2, 2021, www.calcalist.co.il/local_news/article/skqmfvvkf (accessed October 1, 2023).

———. 2021b. "Yifat Shasha-Biton: The Ministry of Education Should Turn from an Operator to a Regulator." *Calcalist*, August 24, 2021, www.calcalist.co.il/local_news/article/bkrignzbf (accessed October 1, 2023).

Khazzoom, Aziza. 2008. *Shifting Ethnic Boundaries and Inequality in Israel, or: How the Polish Peddler Became a German Intellectual*. Stanford, CA: Stanford University Press.

Mazawi, Andre Elias. 1995. "University Education, Credentialism and Social Stratification Among Palestinian Arabs in Israel." *Higher Education* 29(4): 351–68.

Newman, Katherine S., and Margaret M. Chin. 2003. "High Stakes: Time Poverty, Testing, and the Children of the Working Poor." *Qualitative Sociology* 26(1): 3–34.

Sa'ar, Amalia. 2007. "Contradictory Location: Assessing the Position of Palestinian Women Citizens of Israel." *Journal of Middle East Women's Studies* 3(3): 45–74.

Volansky, Ami. 2020. *Students of Yesterday, Students of Tomorrow: Three Waves of Reform in the World of Education (1918–2018)*. Tel Aviv: Schoken.

Weiler, Hans N. 1990. "Comparative Perspectives on Educational Decentralization: An Exercise in Contradiction?" *Educational Evaluation and Policy Analysis* 26(2): 433–48.

Yair, Gad. 2005. "In a Double Bind: Conflicts Over Education and Mayoral Election Outcomes." *Local Government Studies* 31(2): 167–84.

———. 2011. *The Code of Israeliness: The Ten Commandments for the Twenty First Century*. Jerusalem: Keter (Hebrew).

18
GOVERNING GLOBAL HIGHER EDUCATION AND SCIENCE

IONAs and Ever-Renewing Webs of Interconnection

Ellen Hazelkorn and Andrew Gibson

Forthcoming: in P. Shroff, J. Sheth, J. Garrison and S. Mehta (eds), *The Routledge Handbook of Global and Digital Governance Crossroads* (forthcoming 2024) https://www.routledge.com/The-Routledge-Handbook-of-Global-and-Digital-Governance-Crossroads-Stakeholder-Engagement-and-Democratization/Shroff-Sheth-Garrison-Mehta/p/book/9781032160870

A Changing Higher Education and Research World

Even when the development of a globally connected world is seen as a process which is steadily reforming and advancing, there are often noted staging posts. Immanuel Wallerstein (2006) noted three phases of what he termed the European World Economy, beginning in the sixteenth century with the triangular trade of enslaved people and goods in the Atlantic economy between America, Africa, and Europe and ending with the current phase of modern global capitalism. Marx and Engels described an earlier phase of this process as the replacement of "old local and national seclusion and self-sufficiency [with] . . . intercourse in every direction, universal interdependence of nations. As in material, so also in intellectual production" (Marx and Engels 1948, 124). According to Castells, however, the global economy of today differs qualitatively from these previous world economies (1996, 92). Despite the fact that global integration of peoples and cultures has been occurring over centuries, the process of "globalisation" only came to be "considered by many to be the key social, economic and political development" (Germain 2000) as one of the defining concepts of our time by the late twentieth century.

In today's world, trade and movement of people are not just oblivious to national boundaries but are actively creating many new goods and services, new ways of living and working, and tools for networking and policymaking which further integrate people and nations into an increasingly interconnected and interdependent world. This works both ways, of course, and the world's increasing interconnectedness means that countries, people, or issues which were previously unfamiliar or distant can become immediate and challenging, such as disease (e.g. Covid-19, Ebola, or Zika), migration (e.g. crossing the Mediterranean or from Central America), politico-religious movements (e.g. jihadi extremism), and financial crisis

DOI: 10.4324/9781003316077-22

("Black Monday" on Wall Street in 1929, the 1997 banking crisis in Thailand, collapse of the subprime mortgage market in 2007 in the United States). Indeed, the rapid spread and mutation effects of Covid-19 are a particularly powerful indicator of the extent to which the world is tied together by interests which transcend social, cultural, ethnic, and/or economic boundaries. Similarly, global warming produces significant local effects with knock-on effects for food, health, water, and the eco-system, further highlighting the "we're all in this together" phenomenon. Neo-nationalism, protectionism, and opposition to immigration—alongside various "culture wars" articulations—are angry reactions against this very interconnectedness (Inglehart and Norris 2016).

Higher education, research, and development (HERD) has, along with the rest of society, been transformed by these developments. Its role with respect to talent maximisation and knowledge production and exchange has been central to its mission. As such, its place in a globalised economy is well understood by policymakers and seen as crucial to effecting change in a dynamic and rapidly changing global landscape. Global diffusion of knowledge signifies a changed understanding of the role of knowledge and science for nation states to build national capacity and capability and strengthen global positioning. But higher education and science have always had a significant international aspect, long before the emergence of nation states. As with prior versions of an integrated world economy, one can point to examples from history (Latin as a trans-European language of the academy, mobility of humanist scholars, etc.) to make this point. This aspect of collaboration and cooperation across borders—indeed often before some borders existed—must not be lost sight of. It is in the immediate aftermath of World War II, however, when the United States emerged as the dominant player in the global research landscape, when a new phase of "global" higher education and science became visible.

World War II led to two major developments which helped transform the global science landscape. The Manhattan Project was a US-led research initiative between 1939 and 1946, involving Canada and the United Kingdom, to build the first atomic bomb. In subsequent decades the United States, along with European countries and Japan, dominated science and technology. The first lesson here was the importance of international collaboration in undertaking "big science"—projects requiring multiple partners, institutions, and often countries—which has propelled a "global tendency for convergence" (Adams 2012) and collaboration. Subsequent decades have seen a realignment of research towards networked transnational collaboration responding to global challenges rather than those relating to war (Aebischer 2016). Today, while proximity remains a key enabler, open science systems and digital platforms, along with English as the current lingua franca for science (Montgomery 2013, 82–100), are driving the transformation of science into a global and cooperative enterprise (Marginson 2018, 3).

The second lesson was the US experience of "scientific advancement fully underwritten by the federal government and providing new knowledge to the rest of the world". The concept was promulgated by Vannevar Bush, Head of the US Office of Scientific Research and Development. His 1945 report, *Science: The Endless Frontier*, to President Roosevelt asserted the fundamental relationship between science and the state as key to economic development and sustainability (Montgomery 2013, 74). Science was no longer exclusively the preserve of the academy but became a tool of international competition. This opened the door for science policy and moved "research science . . . from the margins of policy to the normal business of state" (Marginson 2018, 6; Guston 2000). This helps explain why research (often interpreted in Anglophone terms as "scientific research", thus side-lining the humanities and social) is regularly assigned to the purview of ministries of business and/or the economy, as distinct from higher education in many countries. Indicators of investment, especially in the bio-sciences and technology, have become powerful drivers of resource-intensive competition and government policy and international benchmarking and rankings, disregarding the academy's definition of scientific excellence (Hazelkorn 2016, 3). The global nature of higher education is seen today in the transformation of the higher education landscape by global rankings. No doubt, global rankings are a controversial measure of quality, but they do display an underlying epiphenomenon about scientific and academic performance in terms of human and capital investment, which has already occurred.

Competition is not the only story here as rankings would seem to suggest. Examples of cooperation in "big science" (de Solla Price 1963) have come quick and fast and represent one of the primary models of how science is conducted today. Such an intensification of international *collaboration* is well illustrated by the Human Genome Project formally launched in October 1990, which remains the world's largest biological project involving twenty universities and research centres in the United States, the United Kingdom, Japan, France, Germany, and China, setting a model for multilateral collaboration in pursuit of a common good (Callaway 2020; Satti 2020). The UN adoption of the 2030 Agenda for Sustainable Development in 2015 recognised that societal problems are territorially blind and that no country has the knowledge or research capacity or capability to solve such challenges on their own. High levels of collaboration are also evident in the search for a vaccine for Covid-19 which involved many different research teams from around the world, facilitated by early publication and sharing of a machine-readable genome of the novel coronavirus virus by Chinese scientists (Richardson 2020; Xu 2020).

IONAs – Governance as Coordination

International collaboration like this in science—and in education—doesn't just happen. It needs coordination, and *international organisations, networks, and associations* (IONAs) are the effective nodes of coordination and connection in international higher education and global science.[1] While historically the focus was on local and within nation-state activities, governance concerns have necessarily become more complex in the global age and expanded beyond national borders (Hazelkorn and Gibson 2017). While the nineteenth century is credited with the birth of international arrangements, the twentieth century saw significant growth in an *institutionalised* multilateral system (Abbott, Green, and Keohane 2016). The initial Western desire and need for international cooperation in the wake of World War II laid the groundwork for the evolution of multilateralism in the form of membership of international institutions and organisations. The role of multilateral arrangements and international organisations (IOs) as coordinators arose from the complexity of global developments and decision-making (Held and McGrew 2002, 12), since "dynamics of interdependence . . . have consequences that are global in scope" (Rosenau 2002, 72). International institutions are "complexes of rules and norms, identifiable in space and time" (1988, 383), creating what Nye and Keohane term "complex interdependence" (Nye and Keohane 1998, 83). This is true of IOs, but the complexity is compounded when higher education and science are considered as significant non-state actors and institutions enter the equation.

Governance in global HERD can work in different ways. At one extreme of the spectrum of forms of governing, often regarded as "hard governance", decisions might be mandated by constitution or by law. These usually have a binding legal force, with regulations or directives being introduced to provide additional strength to policy decisions or set out guidelines as to implementation. Such instances are limited with regard to global HERD.[2] Instead, governance of international science and higher education operates in broader terms as *coordination* of what is a fragmented, disparate ecosystem of simultaneously competing and collaborating institutions and other commensurate interests.

Understanding governance in these terms proposes a "softer" more voluntary or mutualised form. These might take the form of frameworks or performance systems in higher education or standards and protocols in research and science. Peer power can be hugely effective whether through informal or formal associations, through the influence of "academic tribes" and academic culture (Becher and Trowler 2001) or by reputational authority. Agenda setting is another form of influence which can be found at the international level, along with the creation of "epistemic communities" which work towards and underpin these agendas (Haas 1992).

Governance as coordination can be arranged in myriad ways, ranging from hierarchical structures which impose directives on members on the one hand to co-managing or voluntary arrangements on the other. The European Union, for example, works via a process called the open method of coordination or voluntary cooperation using guidelines, peer learning, and sharing best practice (Gornitzka 2005). To consider just the actors involved, the impulse to coordinate research and science comes from IOs, and nation states, and higher education institutions and research institutes, *and* other interests. The tools by which they seek to do this presents a multifaceted picture, along a continuum of varying degrees of formality: agreements, declarations, networks, alliances, frameworks, memoranda of understanding, benchmarking, and rankings. Any one of these efforts to coordinate science and research alone might be sufficient to create some form of global governance. But combining and compounding all these configurations create a dynamic web of governance which is deeply and necessarily complex rather than merely complicated.

IOs are but one form of governance but so also are networks and associations. Grouping them under one broad term of international organisation cloaks the sheer scale of activity—the number, scope, and relevance of international and multi-lateral organisations, networks, and associations—which has expanded dramatically. Between 1900 and 2000, the number of IOs rose from 37 to over 400 (Telò 2013, 34–35). The OECD says that the number of nongovernmental organisations involved in international policymaking increased from 41 in 1945 to c.4,200 in 2015 (OECD 2016, 8). Indicative of this increase is the number of international treaties which has also expanded (Ikenberry 2003, 536–537; Peterson and Bouchard 2014, 18); according to the UN, c. 339 multilateral treaties were lodged with the Secretary-General as of May 2016 (United Nations 2016). The complexity of the global world has witnessed an upsurge in informal as well as formal frameworks and rules-based systems and processes across many fields of life and dimensions: national, regional, institutional, and/or professional. As

> the world approaches an integrated international economy through international flows of capital, goods, and labour, the more the need for some kind of multilateral regulation of these flows intensifies, further the need for the evolution of a global polity to complement this global economy and global civil society.
>
> *(Gamble 2013, xxxv)*

When thinking of transnational governance, we usually think of a group of multilateral inter-governmental and field-specific organisations (e.g. UN and its extended family of agencies[3] [UNESCO, WHO, WIPO, etc.], OECD, WB, NATO, IMF, WTO) and their prescribed regulatory regimes (Henry et al. 2001).

Governing mechanisms are promoted and sustained by a web of governments, policymakers, and non-state and societal actors using soft law instruments such as guidelines, protocols, benchmarking, and peer learning with varying degrees of delegated authority and powers of representation (Guzzini 2012; Held and McGrew 2002; Marginson 2018, 23). While "governance, particularly at the world level, is no longer predominantly the preserve of national states" (King 2009, 7), neither is it ignorant of nation states, policy, culture, and values, as the recent Covid-19 pandemic attests. It is vital also to distinguish global governance from global government.

To return to a previous point, international cooperation and coordination in science and higher education did not *start* with the state; nor does it end there today. Therefore, it is important not to focus simply on the abovementioned and commonly referenced IOs but also to address networks and associations. Such networks and associations have long been a part of international HERD, and they remain so at national and regional settings (Harrison, Smith, and Kinton 2015), although their activities are not always "legible" to those studying governance as an international or global construct. It is these networks and associations that transcend boundaries and are not necessarily under the purview of the state that distinguishes international higher education and global science. They operate according to different logics and with different goals to those of governmental and intergovernmental organisations:

> Self-organizing networks that span the globe are the most notable feature of science today. These networks constitute an invisible college of researchers who collaborate not because they are told to but because they want to, who work together not because they share a laboratory or even a discipline but because they can offer each other complementary insight, knowledge, or skills.
>
> *(Wagner 2008, 2)*

There has been a burgeoning of transnational networks and frameworks which, typically with the support of nation states and/or IOs, have been responsible and effective for pushing higher education and research towards greater international involvement (Altbach and Knight 2016; Montgomery 2013). They have enabled the sharing of ideas and identification of new solutions. In addition, the growing use of social media, conferencing tools, and open science platforms is contributing hugely to their proliferation—especially since the Covid-19 pandemic.

Unlike IOs, networks and alliances are evolving and dynamic, and while capable of being "strategically planned", they are not centrally coordinated. They seek to amplify and secure HERD interests while learning to compete and collaborate often with academics and researchers previously unknown or less considered. Beneath the headline activities, there is a complex, multi-layered web of alliances, bilateral partnerships, and formal agreements across the full range of activities. They concern quality assurance and accreditation; mutual recognition of academic qualifications and credentials; cross-border student, graduate, and professional mobility; transnational education and cross-border provision; research protocols and RDI activity, including scientific methods and clinical trials, researcher careers, funding and dissemination, and intellectual property. There are formal structures with articles of association or constitution, membership fees, administrative support, and the provision of various services essential to sustain global supply chains for knowledge development and talent mobility.

The global order of the twenty-first century is a complex and competitive space with "new international agreements and arrangements drawn up to manage global interactions" (Altbach 2004, 21). HERD organisations and institutions operate across blurring global, national, and local boundaries pursuing policies and priority-setting that respond to and reflect requirements and demands which may often (appear to) "contradict the internal rationality of bureaucratic or collegial arrangements" (Ordorika and Lloyd 2015, 136) or academic ideals (Readings 1996) while in effect strengthening their role and effectiveness. The formation of transnational networks and alliances operating across boundaries and borders has become particularly significant and influential actors at the global level. Transnational university alliances play an increasing role in strengthening teaching and learning, especially research activities, as well as in advocacy seeking to influence regional and international policy (Vukasovic and Stensaker 2018).

Too often, these common rules and frameworks are portrayed as rules promulgated by a hegemonic order, or simply taken for granted. Instead, they should be acknowledged as being indispensable to enabling and strengthening HERD in a global world. This chapter argues that the shape, role, and importance of this underpinning and buttressing infrastructure should not be overlooked. We argue that IONAs are essential to increasing and sustaining global interconnectedness and interdependency. To understand how this is so, it is worth briefly working through some of the existing theories of international higher education and global science governance.

Theories of Transaction: Perspectives on Global Higher Education and Science

The governance of global HERD has been theorised by two broad schools of thought: (i) functional theories such as institutionalism and global interdependencies and (ii) conflict theories on structures of power.

Functionalist, institutional approaches to the governance of global higher education and science derive from the political science and international relations literature and as such tend to focus on matters of organisation and administration between nation states. It speaks primarily of global governance and regulation in terms of inter-governmental IOs addressing what can be understood as "state failure" and a perceived necessity of institutions enforcing political norms. Nation states are seen as significant policy actors, but their activities are coordinated by IOs as transnational, international, intermediary inter-governmental organisations. IOs are portrayed as helping to negotiate the means by which multiple nations and stakeholders can seek to coordinate, anticipate, and better respond to global tensions and challenges. Rather than individual policy actions, international structures and networks are regarded as mutualising interests out of common interest as well as necessity. In this scenario, IOs are vehicles of multilateralism and international collaboration.

In such approaches, HERD is just one sector like any other, and HEIs are just like firms or corporations. Systemic and policy change recommendations are discussed commonly as logical responses for countries, societies as well as institutions. Compromise and mediation and peer- and bench-learning are contemporary expressions for sharing experiences as to what works, which is a cornerstone of institutionalists' position. Despite different approaches to governance, IOs are seen to share ideological harmony—especially with respect to overall objectives of collaboration but also (neo)liberal values. The main focus is tracing structural "gaps" and how they might be addressed.

In contrast, conflict and structures of power perspectives consider IOs to be hegemonic drivers of globalisation and harmonisation. As inter-governmental organisations, IOs practice both "hard" and "soft" forms of governance in order to overcome "capability gaps" between the nation state and the "global". However, the over-determining roles and rules of IOs reflect the "hegemonic market-oriented logic of governance", which Gramsci and others (Ordorika and Lloyd 2015, 131) suggest act as agents of globalisation that promulgate the liberal order and liberal capitalism (Pratt 2006, 101). For example, pursuance of the modernisation and accountability agendas at a national and institutional level is seen as a challenge and/or threat to traditional academic values and purposes which are nation-bound. As such IOs, purposefully or not, effectively undermine or displace the nation state. While functionalism regards policy sharing or borrowing as relatively unproblematic, if not indeed "efficient" and leading to an end goal of "harmonisation", conflict theory critiques this as evidence of hegemonic or "imperialist" logic (Hartmann 2010). As global outlooks and norms influence and/or overtake thinking, decisions, and processes (Hameiri 2010, 23–24), myriad IOs and "transboundary processes and actors" emerge within an inter-state system (Stephen 2014, 915).

A key difference between the two approaches is that functional institutionalists look primarily at the historical and structural basis for international decision-making, while the latter looks at the "impact of ideas once they become institutionalized" (Verger 2014, 17). They also draw on and emerge from different literatures: the former primarily looks to political science and international relations, international law, international regime theory, political economy, and international economics, while the latter draws on theoretical and critical perspectives in history, sociology, educational studies, geography, and political economy. Accordingly, functional institutionalists typically emphasise rationales and mechanics and focus on matters of finance, trade, environmental, energy, poverty reduction and international development, health, the internet, and migration but rarely say anything about higher education or research. In contrast, conflict theorists present and analyse HERD as the prevailing theoretical construct for their studies. Indeed, the field of higher education studies has by and large viewed the emergence and role of IOs, and correspondingly the myriad international arrangements, as an extension of power relations to a global level. Notably, these two bodies of thought rarely intertwine or draw from each other's perspectives or experiences.

To some extent, both schools of thought exude zero-sum perspectives on how and why global HERD is coordinated. Broadly speaking, they assume that interactions through IOs are transactional (viewing this as either a positive or a negative). The functional intuitionalist view is that international forms of coordination and interaction exist to share information in order to "harmonise" approaches or "borrow" policies. From a conflict perspective, this process is regarded critically as leading to forms of "epistemic governance" (Alasuutari and Qadir 2014) by a top-down external force which pre-determines or narrows policy options. Both stances note the significance of the "three most important" IOs in global HERD (Zapp 2020), namely the OECD, World Bank, and UNESCO—about which most has been written. Both approaches understand and explain the structural position of such IOs from historical perspectives but more often as static elements in what is purported to be a "structure" of global governance in international higher education, research, and development.

A key problem with both perspectives is that the "structure" of globalised higher education governance is a theoretical construct and does not adequately represent the role of IOs in national or institutional settings. Even in the realm of international economic integration, Rodrik (2000, 178) throws cold water on the extent to which "globalization" happened, believing it "remains remarkably limited". A second problem is that the focus on IOs often overlooks the historical, sociological, and disciplinary significance of international networks and associations in higher education. On the rare occasion these networks and associations are considered, their emergence and role are not contextualised, nor is the long history of networked interactions in higher education and science given due attention. Yet these networks and associations are actively building and expanding upon national and regional relationships, thereby illustrating the extent to which collaboration is intrinsic to HERD, as Wagner (Wagner 2008) convincingly argues. A third deficit concerns the limitations of seeing IONA networking as a static (i.e. once off rather than an ongoing process) and narrow understanding of governance as rules and regulations. In other words, seeing HE membership in a network or association as simply a transactional way to address an informational gap or meet another need fails to make sense of HEIs being promiscuous members of multiple and diverse networks and associations simultaneously.

From a macro perspective, neither functionalist institutionalism nor conflict theories can fully account for the fact that there are thousands of IONAs with significance for higher education and research—and their number is mushrooming. If attention was expanded beyond the inter-governmental formulations of IOs, it would facilitate a deeper understanding of these forms of HERD collaboration and coordination. As such, there is a disconnect in understanding how HERD functions due to conceptualising spaces as discrete levels, such that the regional being regarded as one "level", the national another, and global yet another. In addition, fixation on the big three IOs is distortionary both in their effect and in their breadth. Taking a wider lens, over fifty research and higher education training consortia were formed in the United Kingdom in a period of just ten years (Harrison, Smith, and Kinton 2015)—and this represents only a small subset of the IONA landscape.

In contrast to both of these perspectives, this chapter argues that global governance should be understood as coordination rather than as government imposing top-down rules and regulations. The interplay between world society, a global economy, the production and circulation of knowledge goods and talent, and institutional and organisational behaviour and logics reflects and responds to

> the complex, tangled, and interwoven nature of the relevant political relations, which include important horizontal and transversal linkages—indicated in notions such as "network state" or "network polity"—as well as the vertical linkages implied in multilevel governance.
>
> *(Jessop 2012)*

These relationships are expressed in a variety of institutional forms and respond to a dizzying array of interests, which we call international organisation, networks, and associations or IONAs. Relationships may be formal but are frequently informal, non-formal and voluntary, bilateral and multilateral, forms of coordination or exchange. As a totality, IONAs underpin an evolving loosely coupled web which supports and enables international education and global science. They involve not just IOs and nation states but increasingly innumerable coalitions, consortia, and HEIs. The next section illustrates the nature of governance as collaboration in higher education and its implications.

Mapping Webs of Coordination in International Higher Education and Global Science

The nomenclature used by and about IONAs is very broad and includes, inter alia, organisation, association, alliance, consortia, network, league, federation, society, group, and councils (Wächter 2000, 127, 169; Beerkens 2002, 297). They include "assessing, ranking and accreditation bodies; academic associations, scholarly societies and student unions; rectors' conferences; networks of universities and umbrella organisations; global think-tanks etc. in the transnational mediation and circulation of ideas in the global university field" (Reuter, Oberg, and Wijkström 2018). In Europe, many have origins which coincide with the launch of the first large-scale EU programmes in the mid-1980s (Wächter 1999, 130–131). Their objectives include cooperation, sharing resources, student and staff mobility, policy advocacy, and reputation-enhancing activities (Beerkens 2005; Brankovic 2018; Vukasovic and Stensaker 2018)—and the focus of attention may vary between national government or IOs, although the latter's activities are itself a major factor in the growth of such associations.

The Union of International Associations—itself an IO formed after World War I to provide services to and study IOs—maintains information and statistics about these organisations, and its *Yearbook of International Organizations* records IOs from 300 countries and territories; approximately 1,200 new organisations are added annually (Shumate et al. 2019, 27). It lists 1,719 organisations relating to "education" and 2,912 for "research" out of almost 70,000 international nongovernmental organisations and inter-governmental organisations. The UN records 5,161 nongovernmental organisations, of which 90 have "education" officially in the title (Economic and Social Council 2018). Brankovic identifies 185 national and international university associations established since the end of the nineteenth century (Brankovic 2018; Bjørnåvold et al. 2019). A report for the World Bank describes an alphabet soup of 13 international and 48 regional tertiary education networks, promoting networking, facilitating staff/student exchanges, and organising activities of different degrees of formality (Henard 2020). Our own research has identified a list of over 1,000 IONAs with a remit for higher education and research—and this is by no means a full or finished picture. Summarising this, and looking to international HERD as a whole, Wagner's network analysis of global science shows an increasing density of interconnection in what she calls the "new invisible college", with no sign of slowing in this process of integration, communication, and collaboration (Wagner 2008). The key point here is that there is no evidence that this process is slowing down or reducing—quite the contrary.

Aspects of internationality and knowledge exchange have been present since the formative years of universities and have been accelerating in pace with globalisation. Rather than classifying organisations and networks, this chapter focuses on several key characteristics which may help us understand the growth and increasing importance of governance for international higher education and global science. IONAs must be contextualised in the light of six large trends. First, the spirit of internationalisation and scientific exchange has been intrinsic to universities and the spread of and discourse around ideas since the foundation of Bologna University—and long before this in other settings of higher learning, in other cultures and civilisations. Second, since World War II, there has been an ever-closer affinity of higher education with the nation state (see Ruegg 2012, for a variety of perspectives on this). Third, increasing economic and political integration at the global level as well as financial and other supports from multilateral or governmental organisations/agencies have been a critical stimulus for the formation of higher education research and development organisations and networks. Fourth, talent is the essential oil of the global knowledge-based society. It relies absolutely on international graduate and professional mobility, which itself is dependent upon systems and practices that provide mutual recognition of academic qualifications and credentials. Quality assurance and other bilateral arrangements, including mutual recognition of qualifications, are the essential lubricant (e.g., UNESCO 2019). Fifth, accessing and buttressing resources, laboratories, and expertise, especially for research, are a trigger for the formation of and membership in IONAs. In turn, collaborations—especially collaborative publications—have become key indicators of "excellence". Finally, in a global world, international comparability is king—serving as an indicator of geopolitical potency, status, and reputation for countries and for HERD as well as a criterion for IONA membership. Ironically, the absence of "international rules or international institutions, let alone governance" along with internationally agreed data definitions, indicators, and data has enabled commercial rankings to take hold and prosper (Nayyar 2002).

These characteristics speak to different components of the web of governance that IONAs comprise. IOs have much to do with the second, third, and fourth, and to a lesser extent the fifth, characteristics. But this misses the whole picture—most of the organisations and associations doing the actual work are not the IOs but the IONAs. Universities are central players, but they are outnumbered by a vast number of people from across the full expanse of the HERD landscape who officially, unofficially, and voluntarily help to ensure that international higher education and global science works as a coordinated system. Those aspects of governance which IOs address are well understood and theorised in the literature and account for many of the transactional aspects as well as some normative dimensions. However, the role of and participation in networks and associations are much less understood and frequently simply morphed into IOs. Rather, they must be understood in their own light and as entities with their own logics.

Competing Logics of Governance

Networks and associations highlight the significance not just of transaction—as portrayed by IOs—but also of *mutually beneficial collaboration and interaction* and the maintenance and continual re-establishment of connections. This characteristic illustrates why such transnational connections are not simply a one-way or top-down vector, a new form of imperialism whereby countries or HERD are pawns in a geopolitical game (Hartmann 2008). This is not to ignore the fact that higher education and science are used and interpreted as indicators of geopolitical prowess and that "excellence" is used as a geopolitical instrument. But the web of IONAs which holds international HERD together is much more than that—and to suggest we can explain the global landscape by over concentration on three IOs is a reductionist argument.

Another way this point might be made is through reflection on Susan Strange's observation on the four values animating international political economy: security, efficiency, equity, and autonomy. Of these, autonomy is the highest value in the political economy of HERD—overriding the other three values of efficiency (which institutional perspectives prize), equity (which often features as a primary concern of conflict perspectives), and security (which enters the fray only occasionally). This exposes a tension inherent in international higher education and global science—that

> modern science is without doubt an emergent social process that is international in scope and cannot be effectively controlled by governments. And yet it is the taxpayers of different nation-states who are asked to fund this process.
>
> *(Wagner 2008)*

IOs and states, concerned as they are with expenditure, focus on efficiencies—but scientists and their networks are most focused on doing good science, and thus having the autonomy to do so. Using the lens of IONAs helps us to better understand how such competing values and interests overlap and interact. It also allows for a perspective that sees dispute and disagreement as necessary and generative within HERD—and not something that needs to be explained or finessed away into an artificial and premature "consensus".

This chapter aims to show how governance-as-coordination takes place through IONAs. Cross-border interaction is not only about closing gaps of "coverage" in a system of governance; nor is it a tale only of hegemonic power—though it can be these things in part. One of our initial questions was why there are so many IONAs in international higher education and global science, and why many more are established every year. Part of the explanation is that, per Rodrik, globalisation is not complete, and perhaps never will be. It is also not uni-directional and must be reinvigorated and engaged with continually. Networks and associations exemplify the never-to-be-complete aspect of the international governance of HERD—often pulling in another direction to IOs and/or articulating different arguments but very often working complementarily and in partnership, pursuing a common agenda. There is a considerable sharing of expertise across IONAs and with the big-three IOs. This is a much more dynamic landscape which necessitates a process rather than a static view, such that it makes more sense to speak of moving towards governing international higher education and global science rather than achieving aspirational governance.

Because the governance of HERD requires constant renewal, there will continue to be new IONAs. There is no legislation here to settle things once and for all. In the wake of the 2020 pandemic, there were noticeable calls for more multilateralism (Hazelkorn 2020), a "healthier multilateralism" (Satti 2020), a global health security agenda (Jenkins 2020), a viral Manhattan Project (Grove 2020), and a new Marshall Plan (Teferra 2020). Nevertheless, Hirst and Thompson issue a note of caution, suggesting there is no "inherent dynamic that prevails over all countervailing forces" (Hirst and Thompson 2019, 16). This can be understood analytically by saying there is no single logic nor one theory that can capture everything. But there is a call to action—an ongoing need to make cooperation in international higher education and global science happen. This will not happen without active and continued engagement.

The IONA framework allows us all to see that states and inter-governmental actors are not the engines of coordination, and that individuals, disciplines, institutions, and communities have a constitutive role in erecting and maintaining the webbing of global governance. Strengthening global governance along with its myriad multilateral institutions requires reforms which better recognise tensions around global common goods, favouring a more pluralist and "open and social multilateralism" (Badie 2017, 30–32; Keohane 2002;

Marginson 2018)—but the best way to move this forward is to broaden our conceptual frameworks so we can correctly assess what and who are involved.

Notes

1 The terms "international higher education" and "global science" are used interchangeably.
2 There are enforceable guidelines and so on around intellectual property rights and copyright, for example. https://ec.europa.eu/growth/industry/strategy/intellectual-property/enforcement-intellectual-property-rights_en; https://www.wto.org/english/tratop_e/trips_e/ipenforcement_e.htm
3 https://www.un.org/depts/los/Links/UN-links.htm

References

Abbott, K. W., J. F. Green, and R. O. Keohane. 2016. "Organizational Ecology and Institutional Change in Global Governance." *International Organization* 70(2): 247–77, https://doi.org/10.1017/S0020818315000338

Adams, J. 2012. "Collaborations: The Rise of Research Networks." *Nature* 490(7420): 335–36, https://doi.org/10.1038/490335a

Aebischer, P. 2016. "Universities: Increasingly Global Players." In *Perspectives on emerging issues. UNESCO Science Report 2015* (pp. 3–5). UNESCO.

Alasuutari, P., & Qadir, A. 2014. "Epistemic Governance: An Approach to the Politics of Policy-Making." *European Journal of Cultural and Political Sociology* 1(1): 67–84, https://doi.org/10.1080/23254823.2014.887986

Altbach, Philip G. 2004. "Globalisation and the University: Myths and Realities in an Unequal World." *Tertiary Education and Management* 10(1): 3–25, https://doi.org/10.1080/13583883.2004.9967114

Altbach, Philip G., and J. Knight. 2016. "The Internationalization of Higher Education. Motivations and Realities." In *Global Perspectives on Higher Education and Lifelong Learners*, edited by Phillip G. Altbach. John Hopkins University Press. https://doi.org/10.1177/1028315307303542

Badie, B. 2017. "Uncertain Global Governance." In *Still a Western World? Continuity and Change in Global Order*, edited by S. Fabbrini and R. Marchetti, (pp. 23–32). Routledge.

Becher, T., and P. R. Trowler. 2001. *Academic Tribes and Territories. Intellectual enquiry and the Culture of Disciplines*. SRHE & Open University Press. https://doi.org/10.1306/74D70B87-2B21-11D7-8648000102C1865D

Beerkens, E. 2002. "International Inter-Organisational Arrangements in Higher Education: Towards a Typology." *Tertiary Education and Management* 8(4): 297–316. https://doi.org/10.1080/13583883.2002.9967086

———. 2005. "Transnational Actors in the European Higher Education Area: European Opportunities and Institutional Embeddedness." In *Transnational European Union: Towards a Common Political Space?* edited by W. Kaiser and P. Starie, (pp. 170–190). Routledge. https://doi.org/10.4324/9780203016534

Bjørnåvold, J., S. P. Grm, E. Villalba, G. Kostakis, A. Pouliou, A. Rusu, M. Graham, A. Dej, B. Chakroun, K. Ananiadou, and M. Singh. 2019. *Global Inventory of Regional and National Qualifications Frameworks: Vol. II*. Cedefop. https://doi.org/10.2816/841519

Brankovic, J. 2018. "How do Meta-Organizations Affect Extra-Organizational Boundaries? The Case of University Associations." In *Towards Permeable Boundaries of Organizations?* edited by L. Ringel, P. Hiller, and C. Zietsma. Emerald Publishing Limited. https://doi.org/10.1108/S0733-558X20180000057010

Callaway, E. 2020. "China Coronavirus: Labs Worldwide Scramble to Analyse Live Samples." *Nature* 578(7793): 16, https://doi.org/10.1038/d41586-020-00262-7

Castells, M. 1996. *The Rise of the Network Society. The Information Age: Economy, Society and Culture. Volume 1*. Blackwell Publishers. de Solla Price, D. J. 1963. *Little Science, Big Science*. Columbia University Press.

Economic and Social Council. 2018. "List of Non-Governmental Organizations in Consultative Status with the Economic and Social Council as of 1 September 2018." *United Nations*. https://doi.org/10.1163/ej.9789004180048.i-962.115

Gamble, A. 2013. "Foreward." In *Globalisation, Multilateralism, Europe. Towards a Better Global Governance?* Edited by M. Telò, (pp. xxxiii–xxxvi). Ashgate Publishing.

Germain, R. D. 2000. "Globalization in Historical Perspective." In *Globalization and its Critics. Perspectives from Political Economy*, edited by R. D. Germain, (pp. 67–90). Palgrave in association with Political Economy Research Centre, University of Sheffield.

Gornitzka, Å. 2005. Coordinating policies for a "Europe of knowledge". Emerging practices of the "Open Method of Coordination" in education and research. *Working Paper* (Issue 16). Arena. Centre for European Studies, University of Oslo, Norway.

Grove, J. 2020, April. "Would a "Viral Manhattan Project" Help Overcome Covid-19?" *Times Higher Education*.

Guston, D. H. 2000. *Between Politics and Science: Assuring the Integrity and Productivity of Research*. Cambridge University Press.

Guzzini, S. 2012. "The Ambivalent 'Diffusion of Power' in Global Governance." In *International Political Economy meets Foucault*, edited by S. Guzzini and I. B. Neumann, (pp. 1–36). Palgrave Macmillan. https://doi.org/10.1057/9781137283559

Haas, P. M. 1992. "Introduction: Epistemic Communities and International Policy Coordination." *International Organization* 46(1): 1–35, https://www.jstor.org/stable/2706951

Hameiri, S. 2010. *Regulating Statehood: State Building and the Transformation of the Global Order*. Palgrave Macmillan.

Harrison, J., D. P. Smith, and C. Kinton. 2015. "New Institutional Geographies of Higher Education: The Rise of Transregional University Alliances." *Environment and Planning A* 48(5): 910–36, https://doi.org/10.1177/0308518X15619175

Hartmann, E. 2008. "Bologna Goes Global: A New Imperialism in the Making?" *Globalisation, Societies and Education* 6(3): 207–20, https://doi.org/10.1080/14767720802343308

Hartmann, E. 2010. "The United Nations Educational, Scientific and Cultural Organisation: Pawn or Global Player?" *Globalisation, Societies and Education* 8(2): 307–18, https://doi.org/10.1080/14767721003780645

Hazelkorn, E. 2016. "Introduction: The Geopolitics of Rankings." In *Global Rankings and the Geopolitics of Higher Education*, edited by E. Hazelkorn, (pp. 1–20). Routledge, https://doi.org/https://doi.org/10.4324/9781315738550

———. 2020, April. "Time to Strengthen Multilateralism in Higher Education." *University World News*.

Hazelkorn, E., and A. G. Gibson. 2017. "Global Science, National Research, and the Question of University Rankings." *Palgrave Communications* 3(1): 1–21, https://doi.org/10.1057/s41599-017-0011-6

Held, D., and A. McGrew. 2002. "Introduction." In *Governing Globalization: Power, Authority and Global Governance*, edited by D. Held and A. McGrew, (pp. 1–21). Polity Press.

Henard, F. 2020. "Collaborating to Compete." *The Global Landscape of International Tertiary Education Networks*.

Henry, M., B. Lingard, F. Rizvi, and S. Taylor. 2001. *The OECD, Globalisation and Education Policy*. IAU Press/Pergamon/Elsevier.

Hirst, P., and G. Thompson. 2019. "The Future of Globalisation." In *The Handbook of Globalisation*, edited by J. Michie, (3rd ed., pp. 16–31). Edward Elgar Publishing.

Ikenberry, G. J. 2003. "Is American Multilateralism in Decline?" *Perspectives on Politics* 1(3): 533–50, https://doi.org/10.1017/S1537592703000380

Inglehart, R. F., and P. Norris. 2016. "Trump, Brexit, and the Rise of Populism: Economic Have-Nots and Cultural Backlash." No. RWP16–026; Harvard Kennedy School (HKS) Working Paper.

Jenkins, B. 2020, March. "Now is the Time to Revisit the Global Health Security Agenda." *Brookings*.

Jessop, B. 2012. "Obstacles to a World State in the Shadow of the World Market." *Cooperation and Conflict* 47(2): 200–19, https://doi.org/10.1177/0010836712443172

Keohane, R. O. 1988. "International Institutions—Two Approaches." *International Studies Quarterly* 32(4): 379–96.

———. "Governance in a Partially Globalized World." In *Governing Globalization. Power, Authority and Global Governance* (pp. 325–247). Polity Press.
King, R. 2009. *Governing Universities Globally. Organizations, Regulation and Rankings.* Edward Elgar Publishing.
Marginson, S. 2018. "The New Geopolitics of Higher Education." No. 34; Centre for Global Higher Education Working Paper Series, Issue 34.
Marx, K., and F. Engels. 1948. *The Communist Manifesto.* George Allen and Unwin Ltd.
Montgomery, S. L. 2013. *Does Science Need a Global Language?* University of Chicago Press.
Morescalchi, A., F. Pammolli, O. Penner, A. M. Petersen, and M. Riccaboni. 2015. "The Evolution of Networks of Innovators Within and Across Borders: Evidence from Patent Data." *Research Policy* 44(3): 651–68, https://doi.org/10.1016/j.respol.2014.10.015
Nayyar, D. 2002. The Existing System and the Missing Institutions. In *Governing Globalization: Issues and Institutions,* edited by D. Nayyar, (pp. 356–384). Oxford University Press.
Nye Jr, J. S., and R. O. Keohane. 1998. Power and Interdependence in the Information Age. *Foreign Affairs, September/,* 81–94.
OECD. 2016. Megatrends affecting science, technology and innovation. In *OECD Science, Technology and Innovation Outlook 2016* (p. 18). OECD Publishing.
Ordorika, I., and M. Lloyd. 2015. "The State and Contest in Higher Education in the Globalized Era. Critical Perspectives." In *Critical Approaches to the Study of Higher Education. A Practical Introduction,* edited by A. M. Martinez-Alemán, B. Pusser, and E. M. Bensimon, (pp. 130–152). Johns Hopkins University Press.
Peterson, J., and C. Bouchard. 2014. "Making Multilateralism Effective. Modernising Global Governance." In *Multilateralism in the 21st Century. Europe's Quest for Effectiveness,* edited by C. Bouchard, J. Peterson, and N. Tocci, (pp. 13–38). Routledge.
Pratt, D. 2006. "New Public Management, Globalization, and Public Administration Reform." In *Fairness, Globalization, and Public Institutions. East Asia and Beyond,* edited by J. Dator, D. Pratt, and Y. Seo, (pp. 101–112). University of Hawai'i Press.
Readings, B. 1996. *The University in Ruins.* Harvard University Press.
Reuter, M., A. Oberg, and F. Wijkström. 2018. Governing a Transnational Field: Civil Society Organizations as Intermediaries in Global University Governance. *Paper Prepared for the 13th ISTR Conference, July,* 0–28.
Richardson, L. 2020, April. Universities Fill the Void. *Foreign Affairs.*
Rodrik, D. 2000. "How Far Will Economic Integration Go?" *Journal of Economic Perspectives* 14(1): 177–86.
Rosenau, J. N. 2002. "Governance in a New Global Order." In *Governing Globalization. Power, Authority and Global Governance* (pp. 70–86). Polity Press.
Ruegg, W. (Ed.). 2012. *A History of the University in Europe Volume IV: Universities since 1945.* Cambridge University Press.
Santander, S. 2013. "Regional, Interregional and Global Arrangements and Multilateral Organisations." In *Globalisation, Multilateralism, Europe. Towards a Better Global Governance?* edited by M. Telò, (pp. 389–422). Ashgate Publishing.
Satti, S. J. 2020, March. "The Need for Healthier Multilateralism." *The Nation.*
Shumate, M., A. Pilny, K. R. Cooper, and Y. Atouba. (Eds.). 2019. *Yearbook of International Organizations, 2019–2020. Guide to Global Civil Society Networks. Volume 5: Statistics, Visualizations and Patterns.* Union of International Associations and Brill Publishers.
Stephen, M. D. 2014. "Rising Powers, Global Capitalism and Liberal Global Governance: A Historical Materialist Account of the BRICs Challenge." *European Journal of International Relations* 20(4): 912–38, https://doi.org/10.1177/1354066114523655
Subramanian, S. 2020, March. "'It's a Razor's Edge we're Walking': Inside the Race to Develop a Coronavirus Vaccine." *The Guardian.*
Teferra, D. 2020, April. "COVID-19—A Vindictive Messenger for Multilateralism." *University World News.*
Telò, M. 2013. "The Three Historical Epochs of Multilateralism." In *Globalisation, Multilateralism, Europe. Towards a Better Global Governance?* edited by M. Telò, (pp. 33–74). Ashgate Publishing.

UNESCO. (2019). *Global Convention on the Recognition of Qualifications Concerning Higher Education* (Issue September). UNESCO.

United Nations. 2016. "Multilateral Treaties deposited with the Secretary-General, as of 27 May 2016."

Verger, A. 2014. "Why do Policy-makers Adopt Global Education Policies? Toward a Research Framework on the Varying Role of Ideas in Education Reform." *Current Issues in Comparative Education* 16(2): 14–29.

Vukasovic, M., and B. Stensaker. 2018. "University Alliances in the Europe of Knowledge: Positions, Agendas and Practices in Policy Processes." *European Educational Research Journal* 17(3): 349–64, https://doi.org/10.1177/1474904117724572

Wächter, B. 1999. "European Associations in Higher Education." *European Journal for Education Law and Policy* 3(2): 127–31, https://doi.org/10.1023/A:1022996713945

———. 2000. *Handbook of European Associations. A Practical guide to Academic Networks in Europe and Beyond*. Lemmens Verlags- & Mediengesellschaft mbH.

Wagner, C. 2008. *The New Invisible College: Science for Development*. Brookings Institution Press.

Wallerstein, I. 2006. *World-Systems Analysis: An Introduction*. Duke University Press, https://doi.org/10.5860/choice.42-4956

Xu, X. 2020, March. Hunt for Coronavirus Cure is Making Science More Open. *University World News*.

Zapp, M. 2020. "The Authority of Science and the Legitimacy of International Organisations: OECD, UNESCO and World Bank in Global Education Governance." *Compare* 00(00): 1–20, https://doi.org/10.1080/03057925.2019.1702503

PART 4

Digital, Cultural, and Creativity Governance

Over the years, digitization has impacted the world, but no considerable frameworks for governance in a digital world have emerged to address our global reliance on digital and technology platforms and tools. Human, institutional, and societal governance transformation is integral to the digitally enabled world. This fourth part of this handbook is focused on digital, cultural, and creative governance and provides a useful contextual framework along with several examples to substantiate these transformations occurring from global to local levels. The six chapters cover a wide range of topics, including language and communication, artificial intelligence, and data-driven and creative governance. The chapters also focus on the interesting tension of establishing a global framework that is cognizant of variation at the local level.

They all explore the value (whether tangible or intangible) of ethics and virtues, in particular within this concept of trust—whether public trust is likely to be high or low in governance, AI, or the power of language. The key questions raised across chapters are who are we becoming and how do we establish new models, based on active examination and learning, to keep pace with a rapidly changing world.

The first chapter by Drissia Chouit focuses on the unconscious way we communicate—raising awareness of the role that knowledge about language and communication play in the digital world—in order to show the centrality of language and communication in building peace or instigating conflicts. This chapter discusses three major parts of awareness: self-awareness, communication-awareness, and language awareness and linguistic literacy. Tackling relevant issues in social-media communication and information literacy, Chouit examines the role of language in the infodemic stemming from disinformation in the Covid-19 pandemic. This chapter highlights the power of language and communication to bring about a positive change in societies and constructive intercultural relations.

Trust is the focus of the next chapter, by Hyesun Choung, Prabu David, and John S. Seberger. They explore how trust is subject to influences across multiple levels of analysis—ranging from the individual level (intrapersonal and interpersonal) to collective level (institutions and society). This chapter examines how a multi-dimension, multilevel conceptualization of trust predicts support for self-governance of artificial intelligence (AI) by corporations and compares it with support for intervention through government policies

DOI: 10.4324/9781003316077-23

for regulating AI. This chapter emphasizes the importance of training in virtue ethics, calling for ethics-based auditing or internal review processes to build trustworthy AI within the multilevel framework proposed by the authors.

The chapter by Arpan Yagnik, Rodrigo Martínez Romero, and Montserrat Koloffon Rosas introduces the 4P4R model of creative governance, which centers creativity as a comprehensive approach to governance. It involves a process of learning, discovery, and transformation to bring about social and political change. The model is designed and intended to be a "user-ready" model that generates practical, actionable guidance for governance that can be applied as a near-term intervention as well as a strategic long-term approach to bring about outcomes of peace-building, trust-building, and social healing and reconciliation. This chapter concludes by reviewing and devising plans to inspire creative governance across global, glocal, and local levels.

In another chapter, Sandeep Menon examines how to design a good governance model in the Digital Age and what will be the key components of self-driven and decentralized governance in the digital era. He synthesizes various studies on the peer-led governance models with networked governance, multiple-user control, decentralization and chaotic systems, and compares it with the traditional governance model rooted in "hierarchical and centralized control" to rework and reimagine shared governance in a digital world. He establishes various steps through which visualizing and defining new governance systems would be possible based on peer-driven accountability and open-governance approaches. This chapter provides interesting insight into how various governance models could be implemented through peer-to-peer review and social agreements backed up by automation as opposed to traditional, institution-led enforcement models.

Jaya Deshmukh and Alessandro Galtieri in their chapter discuss the ways in which data can be regulated. They call for data to be considered a global common good rather than limiting data to a source of profit for a select few, examining data life cycles, the data players or actors at different stages of the data life cycle, and data infrastructure. This chapter presents various frameworks and models, as well as ethical context, to explain the exploitation of data in detail. It concludes with insights on establishing a data governance framework and the wider implications of using data and data governance to create opportunities, improve governance, empower people, and solve the problems of the public.

The final chapter, by Prabu David, Preeti Shroff-Mehta, and Sanjay Gupta, presents a values-driven framework for leadership and governance—a framework guided by the active examination of who we are becoming. The authors emphasize the cocreation of value with multiple stakeholders in the transition from being to becoming, calling for a value-driven leadership framework for governance. New models of leadership and governance are urgently needed, in particular models that emphasize practical wisdom through the cultivation of technomoral virtues. This chapter concludes with some early lessons learned, including privacy challenges and operational obstacles, that citizen-feedback programs are facing in practice.

19

MEDIA AND INFORMATION LITERACY FOR POST COVID-19 GOVERNANCE

Promoting Peace and Intercultural Dialogue Through Language and Communication

Drissia Chouit

Introduction

Language has a double-edged power in building peace or igniting conflicts. Language and communication form part of every aspect of our daily lives, and the success we achieve in building relations and positive environments is greatly dependent on the way we use language and the way we communicate.

In fact, we are all born with the ability to communicate; language is acquired in the first years of childhood within a particular social and cultural context, inductive of linguistic and communication competence. But the whole process takes place in an unconscious way, and this is why the ability to communicate is taken for granted by most people.

This chapter aims to bring to the consciousness this unconscious knowledge about language and communication to show the centrality of language and communication in building peace or instigating conflicts. This chapter is divided into three parts: self-awareness, communication-awareness, and language awareness and linguistic literacy, which constitutes the main part of this chapter, showing linguistic literacy in action. It tackles the following main points: (1) the weight of words, (2) the not-so-innocent way we name people and events, (3) how different wordings lead to different interpretations, (4) the role of grammar in structuring deep underlying meanings, and (5) the role of language in the disinformation infodemic.

Self-Awareness: Understanding the Self

We can easily notice that in endeavors to solve world problems relating to thorny issues like racism, armed and non-armed conflicts, and extremism in views, attitudes, and actions, the focus is always on "the other": we seek to "understand the other," to understand other cultures and beliefs. These are commendable goals that should be strengthened to become a

DOI: 10.4324/9781003316077-24

way of being and a way of behaving in harmony with others. Yet both communication and action start with the "self"; mutual understanding, therefore, begins with self-awareness.

Self-awareness refers to conscious knowledge about the self: being aware of who we are, how we think, and which beliefs and value-systems we hold. We should, by extension, be self-critical, by analyzing the way we think and how we interpret events and make sense of the world. We should have the ability and openness to question our attitudes and beliefs in order to ensure that they do not bear prejudicial attitudes or beliefs that may be harmful to others.

Emotional intelligence, based on awareness and management of emotions, is the necessary counterbalance of critical thinking, which is based on rationality and logic. As humans are more emotional than rational beings, we should heighten our critical thinking skills, but we should also raise consciousness about our emotions to be aware of what makes us happy and what frightens us, to be aware of the reasons behind our fears and joys, and to be aware of how we act or react when we are under the impact of strong emotions in order to understand which type of emotional individuals we are, which type of personality we have, and, therefore, how we deal with the emotional content to which we are exposed. Equally important is to be aware of how we react to the emotions, views, attitudes, beliefs, and value-systems of others. At this very basic level, open-mindedness stems from having an accepting attitude vis-à-vis different perceptions and cultural values, while close-mindedness is equated with having exclusive views and attitudes.

Therefore, combining emotional intelligence and critical thinking paves the way to self-awareness and self-understanding, which in turn leads to a better understanding of the other. If we have such high-order critical thinking skills, self-awareness, self-control, and self-management, then we have the potential to contribute substantially to peace-building and the construction of positive environments wherever we are. If not, we must take time to reflect on ourselves and to understand ourselves, because if we do not understand ourselves, we cannot understand the other. If we have a flawed way of thinking, we will always evaluate other perspectives in a flawed way. And if we cannot control our emotions and have a positive attitude, we will always conflict with each other. None of these skills and competencies is innate; they should be learned and practiced regularly until they become an integral part of us: a way of being and behaving. The combined roles of education, family, and the media are primordial in this regard.

Communication-Awareness: Understanding the Nature of Communication

Communication-awareness refers to understanding how people communicate—the nature of communication. Understanding the communication process helps us to understand ourselves both as individuals and as social beings.

The Transactional-Perceptual (Trans-Per) Model of Communication (Sereno and Bodaken 1975; Morreale, Spitzberg, and Barge 2007) defines communication as a perceptual system that involves the intersection between internal stimuli that exist within the self (the internal system) and external stimuli that exist in the context of communication (external system).

Thus, personal elements like personality traits and frame of reference—a lifetime of experiences, education, social and cultural belongings, attitudes, perceptions, affiliations, and ideologies—are elements that each individual brings with them to every interaction they may make with another human being. The internal system, therefore, is an integral aspect of building a constructive and collaborative environment for debate, negotiation, and effective intercultural dialogue. Empathy is needed in order to understand others, their feelings, and their concerns.

In addition, when we communicate, we share not only information and viewpoints but also emotions and attitudes. In a way, when we communicate, we want to influence the other by convincing them of the validity of our own viewpoint or, further, by making them change their attitudes and behaviors to better match our own. This subtle but influential characteristic of communication is deeply ingrained in all types of communication. Not being aware of it may lead to easy manipulation.

The ability to deconstruct the message and reconstruct the meaning is a fundamental linguistic skill. Linguistic literacy is essential to understand how we communicate and to make sense of what we are exposed to.

Language Awareness and Linguistic Literacy: Understanding How Language Works and Application of This Knowledge to Various Texts and Contexts

Linguistic Literacy in Action

Language awareness refers to understanding how language works—how language is encoded and decoded both at the discursive level and at the level of encoding social, power, or solidarity relations. It is also about the weight of words that we use in our everyday life, or words to which we are exposed in various communication contexts.

Awareness About the Weight of Words

Being aware that words have an impactful weight helps us to be careful about the words we use and to be attentive to those used by others. Recent efforts have been made to reduce the use of gendered or pejorative language, in an effort to make language more inclusive, demonstrating the power of words: for example, the use of "chairperson" instead of "chairman," the use of "co-cultures" instead of "sub-cultures," and the use of "people with special needs" or "people differently abled" instead of "handicapped." Eliminating language that reinforces social inequalities can be a force of positive change for equitable, just, and culturally inclusive societies, because it disrupts the sociocultural practices that legitimize these social inequalities.

The Way We Name People and Events Is Not Innocent

The way we name people, places, things, and events impacts our perceptions and attitudes, the way we think about those people and places, and the way we treat them. Language can be used to polarize people and nations (Paololucci 2009; Weber 2009), separating them into either good or evil, civilized or uncivilized, ethnically superior or ethnically inferior, human beings or dehumanized animals (Steuter and Wills 2009) or those who are created to rule and those who are created to be ruled. Such biased categorizations and labeling of people and nations instigate defensive attitudes that lead to social unrest, conflicts, and wars (McSweeny 1999). The divisive politics of former president Donald Trump set his supporters against all the others who do not embrace the same ideology. This section aims to shed new light on the phenomenon of Trump.

When Donald Trump was persistently claiming that the "election was stolen from him," the verb "steal" denotes that he won the election, but it was taken from him illegally by "counting millions of people who voted illegally," according to his tweet on November 27, 2020, along with subsequent tweets. That was a lie. Trump knew that he was lying, and he was doing that on purpose to mobilize his followers in the fight to take back their alleged right to determine the outcome of the election. He also knew that his supporters believed him because he had prepared them to accept his allegations and alternative truths. He started his four-year presidential term with attacking the press, making "fake news" the buzzword of 2016 and heightening distrust in the editorial independence and trustworthiness of the press. He ended his term by contesting the polls and augmenting distrust in all democratic institutions. After inculcating disbelief in polls, he scaled up, appealing to their nationalistic sense of belonging: "We fight like hell, and if you don't fight like hell, you're not going to have a country anymore." He addressed his own people as being part of the same family and fighting for a common cause (We, meaning you and I, as opposed to everyone else who didn't vote for him) using the assertive verb form, the present simple, to give instructions: have to "fight like hell." And he used the evidential verb form, present continuous, with the meaning of an evident future happening, to explain why his followers should "fight like hell": "If YOU don't fight like hell," it is evident that "you're not going to have a country anymore" (for the linguistic explanation of tenses, see Chouit and Nfissi 2018). What happened at the U.S. Capitol on January 6, 2021, was the crystallization of obedience to instructions—for Trump's supporters, it was a fight for their nation and their stolen right.

In the trial of those involved in the Capitol riots,

> many of the defendants blamed the commander in chief they followed for the violence that left five dead during the insurrection Jan 6. In court documents, media interviews and through official attorney statements, staunch supporters of Former President Donald Trump who carried out the attempted coup argue they were merely doing what they thought the nation's leader had asked, some citing a cult-like loyalty.
>
> *(Axon and Salman 2020)*

That's it: a *cult-like loyalty* that explains the power that Trump had over his supporters. It is the technique used by extremist groups to have full control over their followers. Clint Broden, attorney, explained how this takes place: "You have to understand the cult mentality. They prey on vulnerable victims and give them a sense of purpose. In this case, Trump convinced his cult followers that they were working to preserve democracy" (cited in Axon and Salman 2021).

Exclusive doctrines are the foundations of extremism: either you are with us, or you are an enemy to fight. How do these doctrines flourish? They first kill judgment independence and critical thinking in their followers and instill in them a culture of dogmatism to the extent that they become the thinking mind and their followers are subjected to them, obeying their orders in an absolute way. Most of the time these followers have low self-esteem, or sometimes they overestimate themselves, thinking that they are better than others. Both categories are antisocial because those who have too low or too high self-esteem either believe that there is no social justice, or they feel threatened in a society that does not give them the opportunity to play an important role. As a result, the extremist leader makes them feel that they are very important people and that they have a sacred role to play in order to redress social justice, to preserve their cultural/religious identities, to protect their rights, to protect national security, or to penalize wrongdoers. These communication strategies raise the self-esteem of followers and give them a sense of belonging to a community that cares about them and shares with them common goals and a common future. The feeling that they have a noble mission to fulfill makes them fully involved in this new community, fully subjected to their leader (Rosenberg and Tiefenthaler 2021) to the extent that they can indulge in violent acts (Geheren and Loo 2021) or killing of people to achieve the goals assigned.

How can they reconcile between a noble mission to the benefit of society and violence or killings of people? How can they set an inner balance between two opposing attitudes at the same time: one advocating good for the country and the other accepting the killing of members of the same country? To understand this, we have to understand both propaganda techniques and conspiracy theories.

Propaganda is "typically one-way communication that is carefully controlled, systematic, sustained, and well organized, often intended to damage an opposing viewpoint" (Baldwin 2005). It is mainly based on "cognitive dissonance" and "rationalization" to accept two opposing courses of action:

> Propaganda relies on two basic psychological principles to achieve its purposes: cognitive dissonance and rationalization. . . . Cognitive dissonance is said to occur when a person simultaneously holds two inconsistent beliefs, such as an aversion to killing versus the need to take up arms to defend one's country. . . . For example, people historically have justified and provided legal sanction for taking life during wartime, even though they condemn and punish it in times of peace.
>
> Propagandists also rely upon what is commonly referred to as *the rationalization trap*. The trap is set by intentionally arousing a person's feelings of cognitive dissonance by threatening his or her sense of self-esteem or security. It is then sprung by offering a single solution to reduce the dissonance. In times of armed conflict, one of the most common methods of reducing dissonance is through dehumanization. For example, most people are reluctant to treat others inhumanely. To overcome this hesitation, a propagandist might portray a particular group of people as so dangerous that to offer them any consideration or humane treatment would be a threat to national security. Dehumanizing a group in this way makes it easier for members of the propagandist's target audience to maltreat members of that group.
>
> *(Baldwin 2005)*

Conspiracy theories push the principle of "rationalization" further, to refute any counter-argument/proof as being part of the conspiracy, which makes conspiracy theorists stick even more to their beliefs and defend them more strongly. McKay Coppins (2020) explains how this applies to Trump followers:

> For many of the president's followers, the past four years have been one long, quasi-religious exercise in suspending disbelief. To adhere to the Church of Trumpism was to reject anything that might challenge its orthodoxies. The news was fake. The polls were fake. The investigations and scandals and fact-checks were fake. It only stood to reason that if Trump lost his bid for reelection, the defeat would be fake as well.

Different Wordings Lead to Different Interpretations

Importantly, different wordings of the same thing lead to different meanings and interpretations and convey different underlying attitudes and beliefs. No two words have exactly the same meaning. Both nuances of meaning and substantial differences in meaning must be taken into account when we use different labeling to refer to some people or to some events. In the January 6 Capitol riot, for instance, the word "terrorism" was used to refer to the actions of American citizens. Shereen Marisol Meraji (2021), the co-host and senior producer of NPR's *Code Switch* podcast, gives many examples in this regard:

> Republican Representative Nancy Mace from South Carolina used the label "domestic terrorist." . . . Melina Abdulla, a Black Lives Matter Organizer and Pan-African studies professor at California State University, Los Angeles, . . . gets even more specific, calling the group "white supremacist terrorists."

House Speaker Nancy Pelosi used three labels: "rioters," "insurrectionists," and "terrorists."

On CBS News's *60 Minutes* on January 18, 2021, one of the experts invited by Bill Whitaker (2021), Oren Segal, who runs the Center on Extremism for the Anti-Defamation League, said that what happened at the Capitol "may have been the most predictable terrorist incident in Modern American history." While other news outlets labeled them "pro-Trump mob" or "Trumpists," the *New York Times* in an article titled "Decoding the Far-Right Symbols at Capitol Riots" (Rosenberg and Tiefenthaler 2021) stated that there were "militia flags and banners of extremist groups." And in *NewsNation*, Judge Deborah M. Fine made it clear that "the events at the Capitol were not a protest. 'This is a riot. This is an insurrection,' she said." (Geheren and Loo 2021)

Giving an exact name to what happened at the Capitol seemed to be difficult at the moment, especially with news coming from diverse sources and diverse lenses and interpretations of the event. This showcases how different wordings lend themselves to different interpretations. In fact, the meaning of "riot" is different from the meaning of "insurrection"; an "insurrection" is not "an act of terrorism," and it is not always the case that an act of terrorism is described to be "the most predictable terrorist incident." Moving in the scale from "riot" to "terrorism," transiting by "insurrection" gives different levels in the tenacity of the violent acts committed. But all these wordings have in common the strong condemnation of the violent acts that took place at the Capitol. Besides, calling them "pro-Trump mob" makes explicit the link between those involved in the violent acts and then-President Trump. Referring to them as "true Trump believers" or "Trumpists" stresses more this link. This shows how different wordings referring to the same event can lead to different interpretations and impact how we perceive events and make sense of the world. It also shows the importance of linguistic literacy in making sense of what we are exposed to.

The Role of Grammar in Structuring Deep Underlying Meanings

Other examples of the importance of linguistic literacy include the use of grammatical forms to structure deep underlying meanings (Chouit 1997, 2014, 2021b). See, for example, the difference between "war in Iraq," "war on Iraq," and "Iraq war," where the difference in meaning lies in the use of prepositions *in* or *on*, or the absence of a preposition, using a compound noun. The preposition *in* indicates the geographical location of the war:

Iraq, with no precision of those involved in the war, while preposition *on* indicates that Iraq was subject to an invasion from foreign forces. The compound noun "Iraq war" refers to presupposed information about what happened in Iraq (Paololucci 2009): an invasion that happened on baseless claims.

The careful use of language is a powerful yet subtle tool in organized disinformation, used to manipulate public opinion and behaviors. The Iraq War was called "Operation *Iraqi Freedom*" by the George W. Bush Administration (Bush Doctrine 2005; Estes 2005; Amoureux 2008; Reese and Seth 2009; Weber 2009). The adjective "Iraqi" and the noun "freedom" were used to construct the belief that the war was meant to help Iraqi people liberate themselves from dictatorship and build democracy, which was a false claim:

> Critics of the administration's policies say that the idea of promoting democracy is simply a way to justify the invasion in the absence of evidence of Iraqi WMD or terrorist connections. They argue that, despite the U.S. call for greater freedom in the Middle East, its allies such as Egypt, Kuwait, and Saudi Arabia are some of the least democratic and most authoritarian states in the region. These critics also challenge the notion that democracy can be forced on a country from outside, and that western-style democracy is the most appropriate form of government for all societies.
>
> *(Haley 2005)*

The first Iraq War was referred to as a "clean war," using "smart bombs" (Beier, 2003) and conducting "surgical operations" (Robins 1996) to construct a favorable public opinion (Kanjirathinkal and Hickey 1992), by making people believe that there were no or minimal civilian or U.S. Army casualties because "smart bombs" attacked military targets with high precision, described to be like a surgical operation. How can a war be "clean"? How can a bomb be "smart"? How can a military operation with heavy military weaponry be like a "surgical" operation? Large audiences believed these stories, because they were proud of the achievements of the American Army in such an unprecedented technological war, depicted worldwide as a war without casualties.

The American media did not verify the accuracy of information before circulating it worldwide and around the clock, relying on embedded journalism that reported only what was allowed for journalists to report, taking thus full control of what happened in the battlefield, what was to be reported, and what was to be screened out (Larson 2001; Kosicki 2002). It was a war of words and images supporting the words that made the Bush Administration win the war in the minds and hearts of their citizens *before* winning it on the battlefield (Exoo 2010).

The Iraq War gives a stunning example of the skillful use of language for dubious purposes to construct and control public opinion, helped by cutting-edge technology and embedded journalism. Such an example of organized disinformation constitutes a threat to democracy, peace, and intercultural dialogue, especially when the media join the political game. The Covid-19 pandemic was not exempt from such disinformation.

The Role of Language in the Infodemic: Disinformation and Covid-19

Let us first clarify that the difference between "misinformation" and "disinformation" is a question of *intentionality*. Misinformation is an *error* involving a deviation from truth or accuracy *by mistake, not intentionally*, which can be caused by ignorance, deficiency of data, imprudence, or inattention. Disinformation, on the other hand, is deliberate *deviation from truth or accuracy with the intention to deceive* and manipulate people for reasons of profit or ideology.

The Covid-19 pandemic saw an unparalleled surge of disinformation (Chouit 2021a) both at the scientific level of the nature, origin, and treatment of the virus and at the level of communication of media about the pandemic.

Nature, Origin, and Treatment of the Virus: Polarization Over Scientific Facts

From the very beginning, scientific facts were countered by science deniers and conspiracy theories: disinformation targeted the pandemic in its essence and origin, denying its existence, by calling it a hoax or speculating about its dubious origins—that it was created in a Chinese Laboratory, caused by American soldiers, created by Bill Gates, caused by 5G—or by showing strong resistance to medical instructions to counter it, starting with doubts about the efficacy of preventive measures, from wearing masks to propagating anti-vaccination stances based on false statements or unverified treatments.

How to Name It: Polarization Over Words

Former president Trump was persistent in calling Covid-19 the "Chinese virus," claiming that it was not racist to do so and that it has no prejudicial consequences on Chinese or Asian Americans: he claimed the name to be just "accurate." Neither the name nor the justifications are accurate. Calling it the "Chinese virus" is both inaccurate and stigmatizing, because when people are associated with diseases, they are subject to discrimination that causes harm and prejudice to them and affects how they are seen by others. Such racially motivated words exacerbate tensions between communities and states and lead to hate crimes against people perceived to be linked to the disease. The term is inaccurate because it does not refer to the pandemic in a scientifically provable way. This is why the World Health Organization gave Covid-19 a purely scientific name: the *co* stands for *corona*, the *vi* for *virus* and the *d* for *disease*. As the director-general of the World Health Organization, Tedros Adhanom Ghebreyesus, said on February 11, 2020, when he disclosed the name of the disease: "Having a name matters to prevent the use of other names that can be inaccurate or stigmatizing" (Lovelace 2020). The language that we use does matter; we should pay particular attention to see to it that its meaning is clear and accurate, with no embedded biased values, as executive director of the World Health Organization Mike Ryan rightly stated:

> Viruses know no borders and they don't care about your ethnicity, the color of your skin or how much money you have in the bank. So it's really important we be careful in the language we use lest it lead to the profiling of individuals associated with the virus.
>
> *(Kopecki 2020)*

Conclusion

All is a matter of language and communication. Media and information literacy is not only a necessity but also a basic human right (Wilson et al. 2011; Nfissi and Chouit 2016) in a world characterized by an explosion of both information and disinformation in various forms and platforms. Linguistic literacy has proved to be of prime importance for understanding underlying meanings and embedded values in messages. Undeniably, language can build peace as well as it can instigate conflicts and tensions. Being aware of the power of language and communication can help us invest this knowledge for positive change in societies and constructive intercultural relations.

Key Discussion Areas

- The pivotal role of media and information literacy in building peace and mutual understanding.
- The significance of linguistic literacy as a key component of media and information literacy.
- Dissemination of information during the Covid-19 pandemic and times of crisis.
- Significance of language and communication for media.
- Aspects of language that aid or obstruct dissemination of information.

References

Amoureux, J. L. 2008. War on Terrorism. In *Encyclopedia of U.S. Campaigns, Elections, and Electoral Behavior*, edited by K. F. Warren. London: Sage.

Axon, R., and J. Salman. 2021. "Trump Blamed for Capitol Riot by Some Who Were Arrested." *USA Today*, February, 10, 2021, www.usatoday.com/in-depth/news/2021/02/10/trump-blamed-capitol-riot-some-who-were-arrested/4361411001/ (Accessed February 10, 2021).

Baldwin, B. M. 2005. "Propaganda." In *Encyclopedia of United States National Security*, edited by Richard J. Samuels. London: Sage.

Beier, J. M. 2003. "Discriminating Tastes: 'Smart' Bombs, Non-Combatants, and Notions of Legitimacy in Warfare." *Security Dialogue* 34(4): 411–25.

Bush Doctrine. 2005. *Encyclopedia of United States National Security*. Edited by R. J. Samuels. London: Sage.

Chouit, D. 1997. *Une nouvelle approche du micro-système THIS/THAT en anglais contemporain*. Collection Grammatica. France: La Tilv Paris, France.

———. 2014. "A Linguistic Approach to Communication Strategies in Media Discourse." In *Proceedings of the International Conference on Media, Culture and Education, Meknes 23–25 November 2010*, edited by D. Chouit. Meknes: Meknes Print Shop.

———. 2021a. "Combining Media-Information Literacy and Ethical Technology for More Inclusive Educational Systems." In *Proceedings ARICON May 2021: Applied Research International Conference, London, May 20–21, 2021*. London: ARICON, https://arintconferences.com/wp-content/uploads/2021/07/ARICON-May-2021-London-.pdf.

———. 2021b. "Grammar as Communication: A Discourse Grammar of Deixis." *Social Sciences, Humanities and Education Journal (SHE Journal)* 2(2): 96–111, http://e-journal.unipma.ac.id/index.php/SHE/article/view/9229. https://doi.org/10.25273/she.v2i2.9229.

Chouit, D., and A. Nfissi. 2018. *Understanding Grammar in Context: A Step-by Step Guide*. Fez: Info-Print.

Coppins, M. 2020. "When the MAGA Bubble Burst." *Atlantic*, November 7, 2020, www.theatlantic.com/politics/archive/2020/11/trump-bannon-election-party/617020/ (Accessed February 13, 2021).

Estes, K. W. 2005. "Iraq War of 2003." In *Encyclopedia of United States National Security*, edited by Richard J. Samuels. London: Sage.

Exoo, C. F. 2010. *The Pen and the Sword: Press, War, and Terror in the 21st Century*. London: Sage.

Geheren, M., and N. Loo. 2021. "Federal Judge Refuses to Release Man Wearing Horns and Face Paint from Custody after Capitol Riot." *NewsNation*, January 16, 2021, www.newsnationnow.com/us-news/dc-riots/federal-judge-refuses-to-release-man-wearing-horns-and-face-paint-from-custody-after-capitol-riot/ (Accessed January 17, 2021).

Haley, J. 2005. "Bush, George W., and National Policy." In *Encyclopedia of United States National Security*, edited by R. J. Samuels. London: Sage.

Kanjirathinkal, M., and J. V. Hickey. 1992. "Media Framing and Myth: The Media's Portrayal of the Gulf War." *Critical Sociology* 19: 103–12.

Kopecki, D. 2020. "WHO Officials Warn US President Trump against Calling Corona Virus 'the Chinese Virus'." *CNBC*, March 18, 2020, www.cnbc.com/2020/03/18/who-officials-warn-us-president-trump-against-calling-coronavirus-the-chinese-virus.html (Accessed April 7, 2020).

Kosicki, G. 2002. "The Media Priming Effect: News Media and Considerations Affecting Political Judgments." In *The Persuasion Handbook: Developments in Theory and Practice*, edited by J. P. Dillard and M. Pfau. London: Sage.

Larson, C. U. 2001. *Persuasion: Reception and Responsibility*. East Windsor, CT: Wadsworth.

Lovelace, B. 2020. "World Health Organization Names the New Corona Virus: COVID-19." *CNBC*, February 11, 2020, www.cnbc.com/2020/02/11/world-health-organization-names-the-new-coronavirus-covid-19.html (Accessed February 13, 2020).

McSweeny, B. 1999. *Security, Identity and Interests: A Sociology of International Relations*. Cambridge: Cambridge University Press.

Meraji, S. M. 2021. "What Does It Mean to Call the Capitol Rioters 'Terrorists'?" *Code Switch*, NPR podcast, January 14, 2021, www.npr.org/sections/codeswitch/2021/01/14/956881738/what-does-it-mean-to-call-the-capitol-rioters-terrorists (Accessed January 14, 2021).

Morreale, S., B. H. Spitzberg, and J. K. Barge. 2007. *Human Communication: Motivation, Knowledge and Skills*. Belmont: Thomson Learning.

Nfissi, A., and D. Chouit. 2016. "A Moroccan Perspective." In Opportunities for Media and Information Literacy in the Middle East and North Africa, edited by M. Abu-Fadil, J. Torrent, and A. Grizzle. Sweden: International Clearing House on Children, Youth and Media, https://milunesco.unaoc.org/wp-content/uploads/MIL-Mena-2016-english.pdf.

Paololucci, P. 2009. "Public Discourse in an Age of Deception: Forging the Iraq War." *Critical Sociology* 35(6): 863–86.

Reese, S. D., and C. L. Seth. 2009. "Framing the War on Terror: The Internationalization of Policy in the US Press." *Journalism* 10(6): 777–97.

Robins, K. 1996. *Into the Image: Culture and Politics in the Field of Vision*. New York: Routledge.

Rosenberg, M., and A. Tiefenthaler. 2021. "Decoding the Far-Right Symbols at the Capitol Riot." *New York Times*, January 13, 2021, www.nytimes.com/2021/01/13/video/extremist-signs--symbols-capitol-riot.html?action=click&module=Top%20Stories&pgtype=Homepage (Accessed January 17, 2021).

Sereno, K., and E. M. Bodaken. 1975. *Trans-Per Understanding Human Communication*. New York: Houghton Mifflin Company.

Steuter, E., and D. Wills. 2009. "Discourses of Dehumanization: Enemy Construction and Canadian Media Complicity in the Framing of the War on Terror." *Global Media Journal—Canadian Edition* 2(2): 7–24.

Weber, F. 2009. "Terrorism." In *Encyclopedia of Time: Science, Philosophy, Theology, and Culture*, edited by H. J. Birx. London: Sage.

Whitaker, B. 2021. "How Did Rioters Breach the U.S. Capitol on January 6?" *60 Minutes*, CBS News, January 18, 2021, www.cbsnews.com/news/60-minutes-united-states-capitol-riots-2021-01-17/?ftag=CNM-00-10aab4e (Accessed January 18, 2021).
Wilson, C., A. Grizzle, R. Tuazon, K. Akyempong, and C. K. Cheung. 2011. *Media and Information Literacy Curriculum for Teachers*. Paris: UNESCO, http://unesdoc.unesco.org/images/0019/001929/192971e.pdf (Accessed June 15, 2011).

20

A MULTILEVEL FRAMEWORK FOR AI GOVERNANCE

Hyesun Choung, Prabu David, and John S. Seberger

Introduction

Artificial intelligence (AI) systems are becoming increasingly adept in their ability to learn, reason, self-correct, and emulate human decisions in various domains (Russell et al. 2016; Turing 1950; Watson 2019). Modern AI systems are driven by machine-learning (ML) techniques to accomplish tasks such as recognizing faces and voices, reading X-rays, screening job applicants, identifying credit card fraud, and enabling law enforcement. Alongside professional and institutional use of ML-driven AI, consumer applications of AI are increasingly ubiquitous in daily personal life—embedded in home devices, smart city management, and autonomous driving systems (Gorwa, Binns, and Katzenbach 2020; Lockey et al. 2021). AI is also used to tackle challenging social problems, including the maintenance of public health (Wahl et al. 2018), social justice (Graham and Hopkins 2021), and public safety (Kankanhalli et al. 2019).

Even though governments, corporations, and individuals benefit from the successes of AI technologies, the detrimental effects of AI are increasingly apparent, including algorithmic biases and challenges to civil liberties, increased surveillance (Whittaker et al. 2018), and the diminution of human agency (Seberger 2021). To realize the potential benefits of AI, it is necessary to address the detrimental effects and risks of AI. Such a process is further complicated by AI's reliance on ML algorithms that have been characterized as a black box, because the inner workings of these algorithms are opaque and not easily explainable (Barredo Arrieta et al. 2020). Though some researchers have developed methods to translate the deep learning inside the black box into formal rules, this area is still nascent (Samek et al. 2019)—hence the legitimately pressing concerns about the lack of transparency and understanding in current AI technologies (Shin and Park 2019). The pervasiveness of AI and the autonomous decisions it renders in many areas of life, compounded by its black-box approach to sensitive data, have created an urgent need for well-defined and human-centered principles of governance that conform to ethics and fundamental human values (Jobin, Ienca, and Vayena 2019). Such principles of governance may mitigate the risks of AI and make it possible to realize AI's full potential.

DOI: 10.4324/9781003316077-25

In the past few years, influential groups and organizations have addressed the need for governance by issuing guidelines and ethical frameworks for the development and deployment of trustworthy AI. These include the Organization for Economic Co-Operation and Development (OECD 2019), the European Commission's High Level Expert Group on Artificial Intelligence (AI HLEG 2019), the Institute of Electrical and Electronics Engineers (IEEE), Microsoft, DeepMind, and Google (Hagendorff 2020; Jobin, Ienca, and Vayena 2019), organizations driven by different motives, ethical imperatives, and missions.

However, in the absence of a mediating governance structure, ethical principles do not automatically translate into practice (Mittelstadt 2019). Given the wide reach of AI across social, cultural, and national borders, governance structures for AI require guiding principles sensitive to the contexts in which they will be deployed. For example, the concept of privacy has widely variable definitions across cultures (Farrall 2008). A codified principle for ethical AI that involves privacy would, therefore, need to be sensitive to such cultural variance. While individual rights and autonomy are foundational in the AI HLEG (2019) ethical guidelines, such Western constructs may not map cleanly or ethically to social contexts where individual rights are subsidiary to the rights of the political party and the state. Despite the complexity of intercultural differences, three groups of dynamically interdependent stakeholders are universally implicated in the concern for ethical AI governance: governments, corporations, and citizens. Any baseline for AI governance, then, necessarily involves these three groups and their interrelationships. We approach such interrelationships through the lens of trust.

A Multilevel Approach to AI Governance for Trust-Enhancing Practices

In the broadest sense, trust is defined as a confident relationship with the unknown (Botsman 2017). As we—users, scholars, designers, and policy-makers—prepare for a future with ubiquitous AI and its unknown dimensions, trust is essential to realizing a future in which the risks associated with machine intelligence are mitigated and its benefits are nurtured. Effective governance is a cornerstone of trust and is necessary to mediate the relationship between humans and AI technologies. A framework for governance of AI can be achieved only by acknowledging the agency of governments, organizations, and citizens, and their interdependencies.

In the following sections, we review governance principles from three perspectives: the transnational/national (i.e., governmental), the organizational (i.e., corporate), and the individual. We provide a detailed review of trust at the individual level from a psychological perspective. This review is followed by an examination of ethical frameworks for governance that have been adopted by the European Union (EU), IEEE, and Big Tech. We conclude by offering a multilevel framework of AI governance that is built on trust and guided by ethics.

International and National Governance

Amid the fierce competition among countries for global leadership in AI (Castro 2019), some efforts toward international consensus building have been undertaken. The International Panel on Artificial Intelligence (IPAI) at the Group of Seven (G7) summit in 2019 aimed to follow the example of the International Panel on Climate Change (IPCC) to support the responsible development of AI "grounded in human rights, inclusion, diversity, and innovation" (Government of Canada 2019). In 2020, the Group of Twenty (G20) countries committed to advance the G20 AI Principles drawn from the OECD's recommendations about AI. These principles seek to foster public trust and confidence in AI by promoting values such as inclusiveness, human-centricity, transparency, robustness, and accountability (Box 2020).

Given AI's potential to improve health, education, agriculture, manufacturing, and energy, countries and international bodies are unsurprisingly eager to develop and adopt AI. At the same time, such eagerness is countered by the perceived threat of machine agency and automated decision-making, as well as the displacement of humans by automation and robots. Such risks associated with AI are perceived differently in different societies relative to dominant political ideology, value-systems, and culture norms. For example, citizens from traditional collectivist cultures, such as China, may be more inclined than citizens from individualist cultures to sacrifice personal data and choose security over privacy (Kostka, Steinacker, and Meckel 2021). Despite the unavoidable cultural and contextual differences, a mix of international principles and policies is urgently needed to build trustworthy and human-centered AI (OECD 2020).

Such efforts are underway. The Beijing Academy of Artificial Intelligence has released a set of principles endorsed by leading Chinese universities and organizations (Beijing Academy of Artificial Intelligence 2019), which includes basic human values such as the good of humanity, diversity and inclusion, and ethics as founding principles. Similar values were highlighted by the European Commission's AI HLEG, including human dignity and autonomy, prevention of harm, fairness, explicability, accountability, privacy, and social and environmental well-being (AI HLEG 2019). Despite the similarities, the differences in political systems in China and the EU will eventually shape the implementation of these values.

In the United States, despite efforts to pass AI governance policies in state legislatures (National Conference of State Legislatures 2021), there have been no major AI-specific legislative successes at the federal or state level. One related legislation, however, is the California Consumer Protection Act (CCPA), which focuses on data privacy and generally emulates the General Data Protection Regulation (GDPR) enacted by the EU (Somers and Boghaert 2018). Though not directly related to AI, the CCPA could have a significant effect on how the data practices of AI technologies become normalized.

In summary, international bodies and nations have proposed key principles of trustworthy AI. Many of these principles are founded on the values of human rights, such as dignity, freedom, and autonomy. Such principles optimistically envisage a future in which human intelligence coexists with artificial intelligence. However, enforcement or the real-world implication of these policies on technology firms, software developers, and data brokers is not clear. As described in the next section, technology firms and oversight bodies have taken it upon themselves to develop individual policies in the tradition of corporate self-governance.

Corporate Self-Governance

AI is designed and deployed by corporations, who have their own role to play in governance. In addition to implementing national policy, industries and corporations can complement government regulations with self-governance. A notable advance is a call to action for ethically aligned design for business created by the IEEE Global Initiative on Ethics of

Autonomous and Intelligent Systems (Chatila and Havens 2019). The IEEE's policy calls for participatory design and attention to ethics throughout the AI development cycle. Such guidance frames AI governance as a sociotechnical necessity that could positively impact humanity by underscoring the importance of trust, transparency, and accountability among corporate leaders.

Similar policies have been adopted by Big Tech companies. Corporations such as Google and Microsoft have developed policies, which are posted on their websites. Google's policy states that the company is optimistic about AI and is sensitive to its potential harm (Google n.d.). Key values that inform Google's position include empowering humanity, uplifting society, and addressing fairness and bias. Concern for privacy and accountability are also mentioned: Google states that it will not use surveillance that violates internationally accepted norms, nor will it pursue weapons or systems intended principally to cause harm. Microsoft similarly emphasizes responsible and trustworthy AI that empowers others and encourages the use of AI for socially responsible outcomes (Microsoft n.d.). The importance of trust is widely discussed in Microsoft's policy. Other companies like Apple, Amazon, and Facebook employ AI in their consumer-facing products and demonstrate a sensitivity to trust in written statements, which is integral to corporate reputation. It appears that Big Tech companies are keenly aware of the importance of trust. Their approach to self-governance hinges on building trust through ethical practices promoted in their AI policies. It remains to be seen, however, how accurately such written statements reflect the real-world practices of such companies.

In the United States, tech corporations exercise significant influence on both technological development and regulatory methods (Cihon, Schuett, and Baum 2021). Although companies formulate their own ethical guidelines or adopt ethically motivated self-commitments, they currently do not have clear standards for practice or internal assessors and are hesitant to create a binding legal framework (Hagendorff 2020). One way to enhance corporate self-governance is to assess and mitigate risk from design to implementation and to institute a certification or accreditation program for AI developers who are trained to anticipate risks (Roski et al. 2021). Certification would also include training in ethics, and some have recommended virtue ethics as a promising approach (Hagendorff 2020), which differs from traditional ethics approaches in that it locates ethics in specific contexts dependent upon traits of individuals rather than universal codes of conduct. Another suggestion is developing and initiating "ethics-based auditing" for organizations and academic researchers who develop or deploy AI (Mökander and Axente 2021).

Through self-governance and ethics in training and evaluation processes, corporations have the power to shape our shared computational futures. However, as in many areas, corporate self-governance can be held more accountable through higher-level policy from governments that emphasize common good over corporate gain. Much like the added accountability that accrues from top-down governmental policies, bottom-up demand from citizens can drive accountability in corporate governance.

AI Literacy and Governance by Citizens

Citizens have a right to trustworthy AI. To empower individuals to claim agency, enhancing citizens' competencies and literacy in AI is essential. User empowerment requires interventions that offer an alternative to the digital resignation—a sociotechnical phenomenon resembling learned helplessness in which users resign themselves to having little agency over how their data is used—that some individuals have grown to accept (Seberger et al. 2021). It begins with providing users a meaningful understanding of a broad set of sociotechnical factors that contribute to and characterize their use of an AI technology. AI literacy has been defined as "a set of competencies that enables individuals to critically evaluate AI technologies; communicate and collaborate effectively with AI; and use AI as a tool online, at home, and in the workplace" (Long and Magerko 2020, 598). Recent efforts to foster AI literacy in the United States include an open learning opportunity for underrepresented students (AI4ALL 2019) and integration of AI programs into K-12 curricula (Zimmerman 2018).

Given the rapid pace at which AI is evolving, however, it is unclear how prior AI literacy campaigns remain relevant to the changing landscape of AI. For example, recently, ChatGPT developed by OpenAI has taken the world by storm because of its natural language processing ability and fluency in writing. While the responses provided by the ChatGPT may sound convincing, until the technology matures, literacy interventions may be required to train citizens to critically evaluate the quality and veracity of responses.

However, AI is a relatively new technology, and the majority of citizens hold optimistic perspectives about AI without a sophisticated knowledge of potential risks (Carrasco et al. 2019). Relying purely on citizen action for an emerging technology whose future is unknown is unrealistic and even unfair. In the long term, such an approach may amount to negligence. While government- and corporate-led efforts to inform and educate the public are essential, an integrated approach that includes citizens, corporations, and government is likely the most responsible and robust approach.

Psychology of Trust

To develop a model of governance for a new and potentially disruptive technology that touches the lives of citizens, trust is essential (Shin 2021; Wu et al. 2011). But the beginning of the twenty-first century has been marked by a significant erosion of trust in institutions and governments (Edelman 2021). The logical response to this crisis of trust is to build systems that instill confidence among citizens from different cultural backgrounds and values systems (Gillath et al. 2021; Thiebes, Lins, and Sunyaev 2020).

Although earlier we defined trust as "a confident relationship with the unknown" (Botsman 2017), here we examine trust in depth as a cornerstone of all relationships. Among individuals, trust is defined as "a psychological state comprising the intention to accept vulnerability based upon positive expectations of the intentions or behavior of another" (Rousseau et al. 1998, 395). Besides vulnerability and positive expectations of one another, trust combines characteristics, intentions, and behaviors (J. D. Lee and See 2004; Mayer, Davis, and Schoorman 1995) and is required to build mutuality and interdependence between parties.

Trust in humans can be defined as an amalgam of one's belief in another's ability, benevolence, and integrity (Mayer, Davis, and Schoorman 1995). Ability refers to skills and competencies to successfully complete a given task. Benevolence pertains to whether the trusted individual or party has positive intentions that are not based purely on self-interest. And integrity points to the sense of morality and justice of the trusted party and is related to attributes such as consistency, predictability, and honesty. If such characteristics are absent, meaningful interpersonal interactions cannot be forged.

Though interpersonal trust has been applied to technology with human-like characteristics (Calhoun et al., 2019; Gillath et al. 2021), some researchers caution that the principles of trust among humans cannot be applied directly to human-to-machine trust (Madhavan and Wiegmann 2007). Researchers have noted that trust in technology is qualitatively different from trust in people (McKnight et al. 2011). The key distinction is that a human is a moral agent, whereas technology lacks volition and moral agency. However, given the extent to which AI technologies manifest the value-system and agency of the designer, this may no longer be a tenable distinction. Beginning with the dimensions of trust in human interaction, McKnight and colleagues (2011) revised the three dimensions of trust in technology as functionality, reliability, and helpfulness. Functionality refers to the capability of the technology, which the authors likened to human ability. Reliability is the consistency of operation, which is analogous to integrity. Helpfulness indicates whether a specific technology is useful to users and maps onto the benevolence dimension of human trust.

But AI is more than just a technology—it is an emergent sociotechnical system that strives for autonomy by replacing tasks and decisions made by humans. In that sense, McKnight's definition and the dimensions of trust in technology need to be adapted to the AI context. Unlike prior information technologies that relied on user input and the execution of rules programmed by humans, AI-driven technologies are capable of learning on their own and exercising functional autonomy, such as making decisions. AI's ostensible "intelligence" can be traced to its contextual awareness, data collection, processing, and decision-making abilities.

The autonomy and decision-making of AI in social domains, such as interpreting language, recognizing faces, or screening job applications, have led experts to sound the alarm on potential risks. Lankton, McKnight, and Tripp (2015) found that, when humanness is embedded or perceived in the technology, a trust-in-humans scale works better than a trust-in-technology scale. And when these technologies are depicted as capable of human qualities, including reasoning and motivations, they can induce high expectations and initial trust (Glikson and Woolley 2020). These findings suggest that trust in the human dimension of technology is a dynamic concept that varies considerably based on the context and the characteristics of the trusted agent. In short, trust in AI includes components of trust in people and components of trust in technology (Choung, David, and Ross 2022b).

Trust in automation (J. D. Lee and See 2004) is another framework relevant to the conceptualization of trust in AI and is anchored on performance, process, and purpose. Performance in automation refers to operational characteristics, including its reliability and ability. Process corresponds to the consistency of behaviors. Purpose describes why the automation was developed and the designers' intent. Table 20.1 summarizes the dimensions of trust in people, technology, and automation.

Table 20.1 Dimensions of Trust

Basis of Trust in People	**Basis of Trust in Technology**	**Basis of Trust in Automation**
Mayer, Davis, and Schoorman (1995)	Lankton, McKnight, and Tripp (2015)	Lee and Moray (1992)
Competence/ability	Functionality	Performance
Integrity	Reliability	Process
Benevolence	Helpfulness	Purpose

Source: Authors.

Multiple approaches to framing trust in technologies have been developed because our propensity to trust machines is interesting in and of itself. Researchers have identified contexts in which humans are more willing to entrust personal information to machines than to other humans, which has been explained as the machine heuristic (Sundar and Kim 2019). This is a robust effect that can be elicited by adding simple interface cues that suggest that the user is interacting with a machine. In turn, these cues are enough to prime machine characteristics such as accuracy, objectivity, neutrality, and unbiasedness. While some of these characteristics may be well deserved, some of this trust may be misplaced because machine-learning algorithms that rely on data that represent human behaviors and practices may be inadvertently perpetuating human biases in AI.

Positive appraisals of machines also extend to algorithmic appreciation (Logg, Minson, and Moore 2019), the belief that algorithms are smarter, more objective, and better decision-makers than humans. The countervailing perception to algorithmic appreciation is algorithmic aversion, the tendency to be critical of algorithms for their reductionism, lack of humanity, and subjective thinking (Dietvorst, Simmons, and Massey 2015, 2018). The psychology of machine heuristics, algorithmic appreciation, and algorithmic aversion justify the need for a better understanding of the relational attributes of trust between humans and machines. As governance policies for AI are designed, one must pay heed to warnings that the human tendency to treat computers as social actors is changing rapidly given our growing experience with computers and AI (Gambino, Fox, and Ratan 2020). We must develop a suitable understanding of trust that is sensitive to the emerging relationships between humans and AI.

Propensity to Trust

In the previous section, we focused on the dimensions of trust. Now, we return to the multilevel conceptualization of governance with individuals, corporations, and governments as stakeholders and the trust propensity at each level. The multilevel conceptualization combined with trust propensities accommodates interdependencies and power differences among the three stakeholder groups, resulting in a governance model that spans from the individual (i.e., intrapersonal and interpersonal) to the collective (i.e., institutions and society) (Fulmer and Dirks 2018). Such a multilevel framework of trust furthers our understanding of the process through which trust evolves and is crystallized over time (Hoff and Bashir 2015).

Trust at the individual level begins as a disposition or a general tendency to trust another person (Mayer, Davis, and Schoorman1995). This is known as propensity of trust and is predictive of initial trustworthiness (Alarcon et al. 2018; Colquitt, Scott, and LePine 2007). Much like the propensity to trust people, propensities to trust corporations, institutions, industries, and governments must be considered when building AI systems that aspire to trustworthiness. For example, an individual with a high trust propensity for other individuals may have a low trust in Facebook and support social-media regulation but support development of AI for social good. A multilevel, multidimensional understanding of trust would allow for a governance design that can be principled and yet flexible to accommodate such nuances and complexity.

Ethics and Trust Lenses in the Multilevel Framework

Corporations (e.g., Google, Microsoft) and national and international bodies (e.g., IEEE, European Commission) have identified ethical values and requirements that include the following themes: privacy protection, fairness, diversity, nondiscrimination and social justice, accountability, robustness, safety, resilience, transparency, explainability, human autonomy, loss of human jobs, need for human oversight, and limiting the use of AI as a weapon in wars (Hagendorff 2020). While there is significant overlap in the values and themes emphasized by different groups, the policy from the European Commission's AI HLEG (2019) offers a framework that is sufficiently nuanced and is an inspiring call to action. The AI HLEG framework rests on four ethical values—human autonomy, prevention of harm, fairness, and explicability. In addition, it underscores the rights of vulnerable members of society and the historically marginalized. The authors recognize the potential benefits and risks of AI and the need for risk mitigation. Drawing from these values and ethical principles, seven requirements are offered (see Table 20.2).

These requirements contribute to the three trust dimensions of people: competence, integrity, and benevolence. These requirements of trust can help to identify possible foundations of trustworthy AI (Choung, David, and Ross 2022a). For example, the competence dimension encompasses aspects of how an AI system functions, taking into consideration aspects such as safety, robustness, accountability, and explainability. The integrity dimension focuses on such human-centered characteristics of trust as fairness, nondiscrimination, privacy, and transparency. In concert, integrity and competence serve as guardrails for the sociotechnical configuration of AI. While these two dimensions may be sufficient to build trustworthy AI in the short term, the future of AI as a cohabitant of the human ecosystem

Table 20.2 Seven Ethics Requirements for Trustworthy AI Proposed by the European Commission's High Level Expert Group on Artificial Intelligence

Ethics requirements for trustworthy AI	*Description*
Human agency and oversight	AI systems should allow people to make informed decisions. There should be a human oversight mechanism through a "human-in-the-loop" approach.
Technical robustness and safety	AI systems should be safe, reliable, and reproducible to minimize unintended harm.
Privacy and data governance	Ensure privacy and data protection, which requires adequate data governance framework.
Transparency	AI systems and business models should be transparent, and the AI systems' decisions should be explainable to the stakeholders. People need to be informed about the systems' capabilities and limitations.
Diversity, nondiscrimination, and fairness	AI systems should be accessible to all, and unfair biases should be avoided. Minimizing algorithmic bias is also important.
Societal and environmental well-being	AI systems should benefit human beings and they should take into account the social impact and environmental consequences.
Accountability	AI mechanisms should be put in place to ensure responsibility and accountability for AI systems and their outcomes.

Source: Authors.

requires enlightened approaches to computing in which machines must be trained to be benevolent. The best part of our humanity is in our willingness to look past individual self-interest and to make commitments and sacrifices for the common good. Creative approaches to nurture such benevolent values like respect for human autonomy, social justice, social and environmental well-being, and compassionate computing are emerging areas that should be considered as an ethical lens for trustworthy AI of the future.

In the multilevel framework we outline in Figure 20.1, each level—governmental, corporate, and individual—serves as a lens through which the impacts of AI on the complex assemblage of people, corporations, and governments are interrogated. More specifically, through such lenses, we might systematically observe and test the effects of different attempts at trustworthiness in AI, ultimately arriving at an understanding of an emergent complex sociotechnical system that has trust as its core. While responsibility of governance will fall heavily on the corporations using and deploying AI, what corporations do will depend on top-down policy-making by governments and bottom-up demands for trustworthy AI by people. In this regard, AI appears as a call to agency even as the functions of AI challenge the agency of end users. The enforcement of governance at the corporate level can be achieved by ethics-based auditing (Mökander and Axente 2021). Although audits create an added layer of bureaucracy, which could slow down innovation, they can take on different forms based on the scope and context of the project. Indeed, when the credo

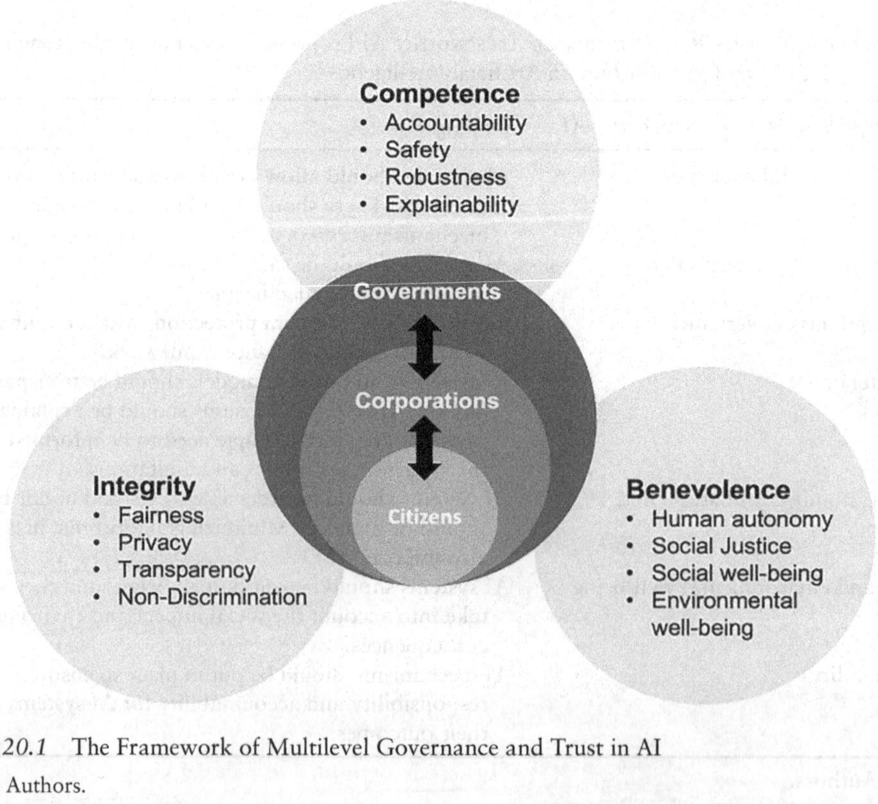

Figure 20.1 The Framework of Multilevel Governance and Trust in AI

Source: Authors.

best defining contemporary techno-solutionism is, "move fast and break things," additional bureaucratic checks may well prove beneficial. Much like universities, which rely on internal review boards to ensure the ethics and integrity of research, corporations could have their internal review boards with different levels of scrutiny, from expedited to full review. Broader scale review boards, such as those like the Food and Drug Administration (FDA), may also be developed to provide external insurance.

Virtue Ethics

The ethics of trustworthy AI can be evaluated in relation to three groups of stakeholders: governments, corporations, and people. The conceptual boundaries of trust for each of the three groups of stakeholders and the interdependencies among them can be assessed using three dimensions of trust: ability, integrity, and benevolence. Such dimensions should be bolstered by engagement with contemporary research on the nature of human trust and trust propensities for machines, humans, and institutions. Trustworthy AI evolves in tandem with the ethics of AI. A framework of ethics that draws from the three widely recognized ethical approaches—deontological, utilitarian, and virtues-based—could further improve our trust in AI.

The deontological approach based on rules and the utilitarian approach based on the cost-benefit calculus of maximizing good and minimizing harm to the largest group of individuals can both inform the development of governance principles. In addition, the virtue-ethics approach (Hagendorff 2020; Vallor 2016) can be a promising addition to nurture the right values in individual developers of AI.

While both the deontological and utilitarian approaches have an important role in macro-level perspectives, virtue ethics, which focuses on the individual, is a burgeoning area that can have an immediate and lasting impact. In other words, top-down ethical principles and actions can serve as extrinsic motivation, and virtue ethics can serve as intrinsic motivation.

Virtue ethics aims to nurture in individuals their own internal compass of values and virtues along with guides to implement them into practice. Virtue ethics inculcates sensibilities like fairness, kindness, compassion, and generosity and examines these virtues in specific contexts relevant to a domain, such as privacy or surveillance. Such investments in training in virtue ethics complemented by ethics-based auditing or internal review processes appear to be promising avenues to build trustworthy AI within the proposed multilevel framework.

Conclusion

AI is an exciting technology with enormous risks and benefits. Until recently, the technology has been developed without sufficient consideration for its social implications. Given the pervasive nature of AI and consequential decisions it makes, governance policies are needed. In this chapter, we have outlined a framework that emphasizes the interdependencies among three stakeholders—governments, corporations, and citizens. Furthermore, we offer competence, integrity, and benevolence dimensions of trust as lenses to examine the interrelationships among the stakeholder groups. We concluded by offering AI ethics as a mechanism to build trust among stakeholders and identify virtue ethics. Along with rule-based ethics, virtue ethics is a promising approach to nurture the right sensibilities required for AI governance.

Key Discussion Areas

- Relevance and acceptance of AI by its key stakeholders
- Governance models for ensuring trustworthy AI
- Offering a multidimensional, multilevel model of trust in AI
- Corporate self-governance and government regulation of AI

References

AI4ALL. 2019. "AI4ALL," https://ai-4-all.org (accessed February 28, 2023).

AI HLEG. 2019. "Ethics Guidelines for Trustworthy AI." *European Commission*, November 8, 2019, https://data.europa.eu/doi/10.2759/346720 (accessed February 28, 2023).

Alarcon, G. M., J. B. Lyons, J. C. Christensen, S. L. Klosterman, M. A. Bowers, T. J. Ryan, S. A. Jessup, and K. T. Wynne. 2018. "The Effect of Propensity to Trust and Perceptions of Trustworthiness on Trust Behaviors in Dyads." *Behavior Research Methods* 50(5): 1906–20, https://doi.org/10.3758/s13428-017-0959-6.

Barredo Arrieta, A., N. Díaz-Rodríguez, J. Del Ser, A. Bennetot, S. Tabik, A. Barbado, S. Garcia, S. Gil-Lopez, D. Molina, R. Benjamins, R. Chatila, and F. Herrera. 2020. "Explainable Artificial Intelligence (XAI): Concepts, Taxonomies, Opportunities, and Challenges toward Responsible AI." *Information Fusion* 58: 82–115, https://doi.org/10.1016/j.inffus.2019.12.012.

Beijing Academy of Artificial Intelligence. 2019. "Beijing AI Principles." *Journalism AI*, May 25, 2019, https://journalismai.com/2019/05/25/beijing-ai-principles-beijing-academy-of-artificial-intelligence-2019/ (accessed February 28, 2023).

Botsman, R. 2017. *Who Can You Trust? How Technology Brought Us Together and Why It Might Drive Us Apart*, 1st ed. New York: Public Affairs.

Box, S. 2020. July 24). "How G20 Countries Are Working to Support Trustworthy AI." *OECD Innovation Blog*, July 24, 2020, https://oecd-innovation-blog.com/2020/07/24/g20-artificial-intelligence-ai-principles-oecd-report (accessed February 28, 2023).

Calhoun, C. S., P. Bobko, J. J. Gallimore, and J. B. Lyons. 2019. "Linking Precursors of Interpersonal Trust to Human-Automation Trust: An Expanded Typology and Exploratory Experiment." *Journal of Trust Research* 9(1): 28–46, https://doi.org/10.1080/21515581.2019.1579730.

Carrasco, M., S. Mills, A. Whybrew, and A. Jura. 2019. "The Citizen's Perspective on the Use of AI in Government." *BCG Digital Government Benchmarking*, March 1, 2019, www.bcg.com/publications/2019/citizen-perspective-use-artificial-intelligence-government-digital-benchmarking (accessed February 28, 2023).

Castro, D. 2019. "Who Is Winning the AI Race: China, the EU or the United States?" *Center for Data Innovation*, August 19, 2019, https://datainnovation.org/2019/08/who-is-winning-the-ai-race-china-the-eu-or-the-united-states (accessed February 28, 2023).

Chatila, R., and J. C. Havens. 2019. "The IEEE Global Initiative on Ethics of Autonomous and Intelligent Systems." In *Robotics and Well-Being*, vol. 95, edited by M. I. Aldinhas Ferreira, J. Silva Sequeira, G. Singh Virk, M. O. Tokhi, and E. E. Kadar. Basel, Switzerland: Springer International, https://doi.org/10.1007/978-3-030-12524-0_2.

Choung, H., P. David, and A. Ross. 2023a. "Trust and Ethics in AI." *AI & Society* 38: 733–45. https://doi.org/10.1007/s00146-022-01473-4.

———. 2023b. "Trust in AI and Its Role in the Acceptance of AI Technologies." *International Journal of Human-Computer Interaction* 39(9): 1727–39. https://doi.org/10.1080/10447318.2022.2050543.

Cihon, P., J. Schuett, and S. D. Baum. 2021. "Corporate Governance of Artificial Intelligence in the Public Interest." *Information* 12(7): 275, https://doi.org/10.3390/info12070275.

Colquitt, J. A., B. A. Scott, and J. A. LePine. 2007. "Trust, Trustworthiness, and Trust Propensity: A Meta-analytic Test of Their Unique Relationships with Risk Taking and Job Performance." *Journal of Applied Psychology* 92(4): 909–27, https://doi.org/10.1037/0021-9010.92.4.909.

Dietvorst, B. J., J. P. Simmons, and C. Massey. 2015. "Algorithm Aversion: People Erroneously Avoid Algorithms after Seeing Them Err." *Journal of Experimental Psychology: General* 144(1): 114–26, https://doi.org/10.1037/xge0000033.

———. 2018. "Overcoming Algorithm Aversion: People Will Use Imperfect Algorithms If They Can (Even Slightly) Modify Them." *Management Science* 64(3): 1155–70, https://doi.org/10.1287/mnsc.2016.2643.

Edelman. 2021. "Edelman Trust Barometer 2021." Annual Edelman Trust Barometer, 58, www.edelman.com/sites/g/files/aatuss191/files/2021-03/2021%20Edelman%20Trust%20Barometer.pdf (accessed February 28, 2023).

Farrall, K. N. 2008. "Global Privacy in Flux: Illuminating Privacy across Cultures in China and the U.S." *International Journal of Communication* 2: 993–1030.

Fulmer, A., and K. Dirks. 2018. "Multilevel Trust: A Theoretical and Practical Imperative." *Journal of Trust Research* 8(2): 137–41, https://doi.org/10.1080/21515581.2018.1531657.

Gambino, A., J. Fox, and R. Ratan. 2020. "Building a Stronger CASA: Extending the Computers Are Social Actors Paradigm." *Human-Machine Communication* 1: 71–86, https://doi.org/10.30658/hmc.1.5.

Gillath, O., T. Ai, M. S. Branicky, S. Keshmiri, R. B. Davison, and R. Spaulding. 2021. "Attachment and Trust in Artificial Intelligence." *Computers in Human Behavior* 115(52): 106607.

Glikson, E., and A. W. Woolley. 2020. "Human Trust in Artificial Intelligence: Review of Empirical Research." *Academy of Management Annals* 14(2): 627–60, https://doi.org/10.5465/annals.2018.0057.

Google. n.d. "AI at Google: Our Principles." *Google AI*, https://ai.google/principles (accessed October 20, 2021).

Gorwa, R., R. Binns, and C. Katzenbach. 2020. "Algorithmic Content Moderation: Technical and Political Challenges in the Automation of Platform Governance." *Big Data & Society* 7(1): 2053951719897945, https://doi.org/10.1177/2053951719897945.

Government of Canada. 2019. "Declaration of the International Panel on Artificial Intelligence." Innovation, Science and Economic Development Canada [Backgrounders], May 16, 2019, www.canada.ca/en/innovation-science-economic-development/news/2019/05/declaration-of-the-international-panel-on-artificial-intelligence.html (accessed February 28, 2023).

Graham, S. S., and H. R. Hopkins. 2021. "AI for Social Justice: New Methodological Horizons in Technical Communication." *Technical Communication Quarterly* 31(1): 89–102, https://doi.org/10.1080/10572252.2021.1955151.

Hagendorff, T. 2020. "The Ethics of AI Ethics: An Evaluation of Guidelines." *Minds and Machines* 30(1): 99–120, https://doi.org/10.1007/s11023-020-09517-8.

Hoff, K. A., and M. Bashir. 2015. "Trust in Automation: Integrating Empirical Evidence on Factors That Influence Trust." *Human Factors: The Journal of the Human Factors and Ergonomics Society* 57(3): 407–34, https://doi.org/10.1177/0018720814547570.

Jobin, A., M. Ienca, and E. Vayena. 2019. "The Global Landscape of AI Ethics Guidelines." *Nature Machine Intelligence* 1(9): 389–99, https://doi.org/10.1038/s42256-019-0088-2.

Kankanhalli, A., Y. Charalabidis, and S. Mellouli. 2019. "IoT and AI for Smart Government: A Research Agenda." *Government Information Quarterly* 36(2): 304–09, https://doi.org/10.1016/j.giq.2019.02.003.

Kostka, G., L. Steinacker, and M. Meckel. 2021. "Between Security and Convenience: Facial Recognition Technology in the Eyes of Citizens in China, Germany, the United Kingdom, and the United States." *Public Understanding of Science* 30(6): 671–90, https://doi.org/10.1177/09636625211001555.

Lankton, N., D. H. McKnight, and J. Tripp. 2015. "Technology, Humanness, and Trust: Rethinking Trust in Technology." *Journal of the Association for Information Systems* 16(10): 880–918, https://doi.org/10.17705/1jais.00411.

Lee, J., and N. Moray. 1992. "Trust, Control Strategies and Allocation of Function in Human-Machine Systems." *Ergonomics* 35(10): 1243–70, https://doi.org/10.1080/00140139208967392.

Lee, J. D., and K. A. See. 2004. "Trust in Automation: Designing for Appropriate Reliance." *Human Factors* 46(1): 50–80, https://doi.org/10.1518/hfes.46.1.50_30392.

Lockey, S., N. Gillespie, D. Holm, and I. A. Someh. 2021. "A Review of Trust in Artificial Intelligence: Challenges, Vulnerabilities and Future Directions." *Hawaii International Conference on System Sciences*, Conference proceedings compilation publication. 5463, https://doi.org/10.24251/HICSS.2021.664.

Logg, J. M., J. A. Minson, and D. A. Moore. 2019. "Algorithm Appreciation: People Prefer Algorithmic to Human Judgment." *Organizational Behavior and Human Decision Processes* 151: 90–103, https://doi.org/10.1016/j.obhdp.2018.12.005.

Long, D., and B. Magerko. 2020. "What Is AI Literacy? Competencies and Design Considerations." *Proceedings of the 2020 CHI Conference on Human Factors in Computing Systems*, April 1–16, https://doi.org/10.1145/3313831.3376727.

Madhavan, P., and D. A. Wiegmann. 2007. "Effects of Information Source, Pedigree, and Reliability on Operator Interaction with Decision Support Systems." *Human Factors: The Journal of the Human Factors and Ergonomics Society* 49(5): 773–85, https://doi.org/10.1518/001872007X230154.

Mayer, R. C., J. H. Davis, and F. D. Schoorman. 1995. "An Integrative Model of Organizational Trust: Past, Present, and Future." *Academy of Management Review* 20(3): 709–34.

Mcknight, D. H., M. Carter, J. B. Thatcher, and P. F. Clay. 2011. "Trust in a Specific Technology: An Investigation of Its Components and Measures." *ACM Transactions on Management Information Systems* 2(2): 1–25, https://doi.org/10.1145/1985347.1985353.

Microsoft. n.d. "Responsible AI Principles from Microsoft." *Microsoft*, www.microsoft.com/en-us/ai/responsible-ai (accessed October 20, 2021).

Mittelstadt, B. 2019. "Principles Alone Cannot Guarantee Ethical AI." *Nature Machine Intelligence* 1(11): 501–07, https://doi.org/10.1038/s42256-019-0114-4.

Mökander, J., and M. Axente. 2021. Ethics-Based Auditing of Automated Decision-Making Systems: Intervention Points and Policy Implications." *AI & SOCIETY*, October 27, 2021, https://doi.org/10.1007/s00146-021-01286-x.

National Conference of State Legislatures (NCSL). 2021. "Legislation Related to Artificial Intelligence." *NCSL*, September 15, 2021, www.ncsl.org/research/telecommunications-and-information-technology/2020-legislation-related-to-artificial-intelligence.aspx (accessed February 28, 2023).

Organization for Economic Co-operation and Development (OECD). 2019. *Artificial Intelligence in Society*. Paris: OECD Publishing, https://doi.org/10.1787/eedfee77-en

———. 2020. "Examples of AI National Policies: Report for the G20 Digital Economy Task Force." Saudi Arabia, www.oecd.org/sti/examples-of-ai-national-policies.pdf (accessed February 28, 2023).

Roski, J., E. J. Maier, K. Vigilante, E. A. Kane, and M. E. Matheny. 2021. "Enhancing Trust in AI through Industry Self-governance." *Journal of the American Medical Informatics Association* 28(7): 1582–90, https://doi.org/10.1093/jamia/ocab065.

Rousseau, D. M., S. B. Sitkin, R. S. Burt, and C. Camerer. 1998. "Not So Different after All: A Cross-discipline View of Trust." *Academy of Management Review* 23(3): 393–404, https://doi.org/10.5465/amr.1998.926617.

Russell, S. J., P. Norvig, E. Davis, and D. Edwards. 2016. *Artificial Intelligence: A Modern Approach*, 3rd ed. London: Pearson.

Samek, W., G. Montavon, A. Vedaldi, L. K. Hansen, and K. R. Müller, eds. 2019. *Explainable AI: Interpreting, Explaining and Visualizing Deep Learning*. Basel, Switzerland: Springer, https://doi.org/10.1007/978-3-030-28954-6.

Seberger, J. S. 2021. "Reconsidering the User in IoT: The Subjectivity of Things." *Personal and Ubiquitous Computing* 25(3): 525–33, https://doi.org/10.1007/s00779-020-01513-0.

Seberger, J. S., M. Llavore, N. N. Wyant, I. Shklovski, and S. Patil. 2021. "Empowering Resignation: There's an App for That." *Proceedings of the 2021 CHI Conference on Human Factors in Computing Systems*, May 7, 2021, 552: 1–18, https://doi.org/10.1145/3411764.3445293.

Shin, D. 2021. "The Effects of Explainability and Causability on Perception, Trust, and Acceptance: Implications for Explainable AI." *International Journal of Human-Computer Studies* 146: 102551, https://doi.org/10.1016/j.ijhcs.2020.102551.

Shin, D., and Y. J. Park. 2019. "Role of Fairness, Accountability, and Transparency in Algorithmic Affordance." *Computers in Human Behavior* 98: 277–84, https://doi.org/10.1016/j.chb.2019.04.019.

Somers, G., and L. Boghaert. 2018. "The California Consumer Privacy Act and the GDPR: Two of a Kind?" *Financier Worldwide*, November 2018, www.financierworldwide.com/the-california-consumer-privacy-act-and-the-gdpr-two-of-a-kind (accessed February 28, 2023).

Sundar, S. S., and J. Kim. 2019. "Machine Heuristic: When We Trust Computers More Than Humans with Our Personal Information." *CHI'19: Proceedings of the 2019 CHI Conference on Human Factors in Computing Systems*, May 2019, 538: 1–9, https://doi.org/10.1145/3290605.3300768.

Thiebes, S., S. Lins, and A. Sunyaev. 2020. "Trustworthy Artificial Intelligence." *Electronic Markets* 31: 447–64, https://doi.org/10.1007/s12525-020-00441-4.

Turing, A. M. 1950. "Computing Machinery and Intelligence." *Mind* 59(236): 433–60, https://doi.org/10.1093/mind/LIX.236.433.

Vallor, S. 2016. *Technology and the Virtues: A Philosophical Guide to Future Worth Wanting*. UK: Oxford University Press, UK.

Wahl, B., A. Cossy-Gantner, S. Germann, and N. R. Schwalbe. 2018. "Artificial Intelligence (AI) and Global Health: How Can AI Contribute to Health in Resource-Poor Settings?" *BMJ Global Health* 3(4): e000798, https://doi.org/10.1136/bmjgh-2018-000798.

Watson, D. 2019. "The Rhetoric and Reality of Anthropomorphism in Artificial Intelligence." *Minds and Machines* 29(3): 417–40, https://doi.org/10.1007/s11023-019-09506-6.

Whittaker, M., K. Crawford, R. Dobbe, G. Fried, E. Kaziunas, V. Mathur, S. Myers West, R. Richardson, J. Schultz and O. Schwartz. 2018. "AI Now Report 2018." *AI Now Institute*, New York University, December 2018, https://ainowinstitute.org/AI_Now_2018_Report.pdf (accessed February 28, 2023).

Wu, K., Y. Zhao, Q. Zhu, X. Tan, and H. Zheng. 2011. "A Meta-analysis of the Impact of Trust on Technology Acceptance Model: Investigation of Moderating Influence of Subject and Context Type." *International Journal of Information Management* 31(6): 572–81, https://doi.org/10.1016/j.ijinfomgt.2011.03.004.

Zimmerman, M. R. 2018. *Teaching AI: Exploring New Frontiers for Learning*. Eugene, OR: International Society for Technology in Education.

21
4P4R MODEL OF CREATIVE GOVERNANCE

Arpan Yagnik, Rodrigo Martínez Romero, and Montserrat Koloffon Rosas

Introduction

The 4P4R model of creative governance marks a stark departure from the Weberian bureaucratic model. It is an orbital model, which includes a 360-degree outlook through the 4Ps and the 4Rs. This model is a synergetic collusion of three frameworks: creativity, spiritual politics, and systems thinking.

This chapter aims to present a model that can be instantly applied in near-term interventions as well as a long-term framework. This chapter focuses on presenting the model, explicating the different orbits and elements from the three different frameworks that make up this model and ends with a Creative Governance Laboratory for readers and leaders to utilize the full model or parts of it as they see fit and be part of cocreating a future that abounds with healing, well-being, and smiles.

Being Kind and Strong: Jacinda and Creative Governance in Action

Jacinda Ardern has been the prime minister of New Zealand since 2017. Her unique approach to governance is based on strength and kindness. Around the world and across history, governance approaches based on strength alone—stemming from constant insecurity and fear—have not yielded humanitarian or progressive outcomes. However, Arden's incorporation of kindness adds a new flavor to modern governance. To be kind despite being strong demonstrates a superior understanding of the rationale for governance and a robust democracy. In her response to the Christchurch mosque shootings, Ardern demonstrated a deep sense of compassion and empathy for the victims and their families, while also taking decisive action to address the underlying causes of the attack (Osseiran 2020). Most recently, Arden resigned from her post in a display of tremendous kindness for her own self, whereas strength would have dictated that she fight to retain her position.

Ardern's innovative approach made a difference during the beginning of the Covid-19 pandemic. The overall management of the coronavirus crisis by mainly male leaders adopting a strength-only based approach has not been stellar.

DOI: 10.4324/9781003316077-26

On the contrary, even though women make up only 7 percent of heads of state, women-led nations seem to be more successful at managing the coronavirus crisis, with the suggestion that "the presence of a female leader may be a signal that a country has more inclusive political institutions and values" (Taub 2020). In this small group of female political leaders, who range from Angela Merkel in Germany, Sanna Marin in Finland, and Tsai Ing-wen in Taiwan, it is Prime Minister Jacinda Ardern of New Zealand, who has been particularly praised for her leadership style and governance during the pandemic. Cami Anderson (2020) and Amanda Taub (2020) analyzed and highlighted diverse elements and characteristics of what is referred to as the female approach to governance and leadership to deal with the threats highlighted. The elements that apparently seem to have made the difference are as follows:

- listens with humility to outside voices and expert knowledge
- considers varied information sources
- caring
- compassionate
- thoughtfulness
- other-directed
- emotionally intelligent
- motherly
- engenders trust
- communicates empathetically
- ability to know what you don't know

By reviewing the list, Ardern's deviation from the strength-only-based approach becomes apparent. The leadership style championed by Ardern weaves integration and solidarity, showing that true strength can emerge from sensible compassion and that the healing of a nation requires listening to the different voices of culturally diverse citizens (Williamson 2020). This approach contrasts with far-right political movements that deny scientifically proven planetary boundaries, encourage social divisionism, and conform to the swaggering ideals of masculinity based on projecting power, acting aggressively, and cowing the nation's enemies into submission (Alexander and Andersen 1993).

Seen from another angle, the leadership perspective of Ardern is related to the concept of spiritual politics (Martínez Romero 2020). This concept can be defined as a dilemma reconciliation process because it refers to a holistic integration between the expansion of a leaders' spiritual intelligence and the development of his/her political intelligence. As a result, the leader can effectively manage public affairs and contribute to the effective solution of social development problems, thrive in the global economy, and respect planetary boundaries, which are defined as safe operating space for humanity with respect to the Earth system, beyond which the world runs the risk of major, potentially irreversible, environmental change (Rockström et al. 2009).

Spiritual politics also refers to a servant-leadership practice focused on three attributes: healing, trust-building, and community development (Greenleaf 1970). This type of leader is committed to developing and enabling others, building a community by reducing his or her self-interest and power drive, and thereby serving others more autonomously (Bunt-Kokhuis and Sultan 2012).

Spiritual politics is also a cross-cultural journey, because context matters (Johns 2006). How dilemmas are manifested and the leadership approaches to deal with and resolve them are culturally determined. Concepts like "politics" or "spirituality" have different meanings according to local contexts and unique historical configurations. To honor, explore, learn from, adapt, respect, and adjust to these different historical interpretations and the configuration of experiences is part of spiritual politics as a cross-cultural journey. As such, the implementation of creative governance practices is inherently culture-specific and contingent upon local contexts, necessitating a nuanced and adaptive approach to cross-cultural realities (Kooiman 2003)

Global Governance and Creative Governance

In the past two decades, the world has witnessed significant changes, such as digital transformations, technology innovations, global warming, and global power shifts. In this context of interlinked global transformations, the Covid-19 pandemic emerged, intensifying most of the preexisting challenges in other issue areas. In view of the multiplicity of large-scale challenges across the board,[1] and in the spirit of requisite variety[2] to increase our level of awareness,[3] in this chapter, we share our view on global governance futures through our creative governance model.

Much progress has been made on an international level to adopt a holistic and truly global Sustainable Development Agenda, which considers the social, economic, and ecological dimensions for improving well-being of individuals and communities. We argue, however, that listing out a number of goals belonging to different issue areas is a good place to start, but still nowhere near any actual problem-solving. Listing out a number of goals and calling for widespread action to reach them may have the counterintuitive effect of worsening the original situation, due to inviting rushed decisions without a foundational understanding of the implications caused by the implemented response. Unfortunately, this is the status quo of global governance practices, and given the looming consequences that await us if these issues remain unresolved, the common conclusion is that we need even more action at an even faster speed.

In general, spiritual leadership is about inner motivation to take action as an individual, and inspiring others to do so as well, while meeting two fundamental needs of both leaders and followers: calling and membership (Fry 2003). The former is related to what provides meaning and purpose to their lives, and the latter to the sense of belonging and connectedness to one another in the workplace community. Admittedly, there is no single definition of spiritual leadership—on the contrary, one could go as far as claiming that every type of spiritual leadership is unique in its own way. However, a common characteristic is that spiritually guided action tends to be characterized by seeking deep understanding, avoiding quick fixes, and instead connecting with the core of the persisting problem in tandem with the human essence. The Management, Spirituality, and Religion Interest Group of the Academy of Management highlight this search for depth in their definition of spirituality, pointing the way to empirical inquiry: "the capacity of the human consciousness to apprehend ultimate meaning and ultimate value symbolically" (Tackney et al. 2017). We find parallels to these principles in some managerial approaches that declare that executives can lead organizational transformation and leaders can govern national change more effectively by articulating a clear statement of the problem to solve before initiating changes (Navarro-Astor, Román-Onsalo, and Infante-Perea 2017).

Our creative governance model is guided by the akin principles of systems thinking and spiritual leadership, offering practitioners a readily available problem-solving tool to approach global governance challenges. In other words, the intention behind it, along with one of the scholarly contributions, is to serve as a generalizable blueprint for policy-making at the most practical level.

A fundamental recognition and stance in our model are that what is usually referred to as *problems* are in fact undesirable *symptoms* produced by the underlying structure of the system. For example, climate change *per se* is not a problem—it is the undesired symptom that arises from a complex collection of interconnected actions and their collective dynamics. This collection of interconnected actions is not the problem themselves either; they are the causes of the undesirable symptoms. The *problem* is, as we see it from our collective vantage point, the existing gap between the current and the desired state of the system.

Going back to our current global governance practices, we can see that listing out goals for sustainable development implies that the current state of the system has been identified as undesirable, and an ideal state of the system has been defined as the goal. We say we are facing, for example, a climate change problem, because the current state does not match the state we have declared as ideal. While differentiating between these elements helps to gain clarity about the issue, none of this is yet engaging in formal problem-solving.

Structured problem-solving practices begin with the development of a problem statement: that is, a logical argument that links the observed data to root causes and, eventually, to a solution (Repenning, Kieffer, and Astor 2017). It is of extreme importance here to not take lightly the task of "linking observing data to root causes." Root causes are the one component in the system structure that, when intervened, guarantees that the undesired symptom will completely disappear, thereby solving the problem. Root causes are therefore at the very center of our model. However, root causes are well hidden in the system structure, and in complex systems, there is usually more than one, which in turn interacts with other system components. Finding the root causes producing the undesired system behavior requires some serious and careful analysis (formally called Root Cause Analysis or RCA) and a deep understanding of the whole system structure.

Global governance challenges are complex challenges. Indeed "the challenges associated with managing the COVID-19 pandemic illustrate the urge with which societies need to learn to deal with complexity" (Dingwerth and Pattberg 2022). When dealing with complex problems, guessing the root causes intuitively is impossible, because they are distant in time and space (2000). When skipping the necessary analysis, the implemented policies are probably not going to fix the problem and may even create unanticipated (side) effects. On the bright side, the payoff of embracing a rigorous root cause analysis before jumping to make decisions (policy) and design solutions, promises big payoffs. When it comes to the complex problems that we are facing, most of the undesired symptoms share the same root causes. This means that by addressing one properly identified root cause, many undesirable symptoms will be corrected simultaneously.

Appraisal of Weber's Theories of Bureaucracy

Max Weber's theories of bureaucracy formed the basis of New Public Management (NPM). While NPM was developed in the 1980s and 1990s, there are certain valuable components that can still be applied today. Processes such as citizen participation, co-production, and managerial orientation evolved with changes such as globalization and global public policy.

Scholars believe that even though society has gone through a complete overhaul, especially on the digital and technological front, public administration has not evolved as much (Kattel, Drechsler, and Karo 2019). Aspects of NPM have been used in updated models of Weberian public administration that scholars such as Christopher Pollitt and Geert Bouckaert describe as the Neo-Weberian State (NWS). Importantly, the NWS starts with the classic Weberian concepts and incorporates those into executing NPM. Weber's ideal type of bureaucracy was characterized by

- hierarchical organization;
- a formalized chain of command;
- division of labor;
- regular assignment of tasks and execution;
- all decisions and powers specified and restricted by regulations;
- officials with expert training in their fields;
- professional growth according to technical qualifications;
- qualifications evaluated by organizational structures and not individuals.

Weber believed in certain preconditions for the emergence of bureaucracy, such as

- an increase in the population being administered and associated public and private spaces;
- along with an increase in the complexity of the administrative tasks, the need for an updated monetary economy that would require efficient administrative systems;
- a culture of democratization and rationalization with an increasing demand for equal rights and opportunities;
- systems of bureaucracy spurred by the development of communication and transportation technologies, which would in turn make efficient administration possible and actionable.

Although Weber himself was not the greatest proponent of bureaucracy, he believed that in line with modernization, bureaucratization would be the most efficient and rational way of organizing human activity. It would be the foundation of exercising rational-legal authority and become an essential practice of governing people in the modern world.

Weber however did believe that bureaucracy would put individual freedoms at risk and that the current trend of increasing rationalization of human life would trap individuals in a cage of bureaucratic, rule-based, rational control. Numerous features of what is known as modern public administration are based on this conception of a classic, hierarchically organized civil service and are called "Weberian civil service" or "Weberian bureaucracy." Some critics argue whether Weberian bureaucracy would positively contribute to economic growth. Another major critique against Weberian public administration has been from the perspective of community action, which involves grassroots and bottom-up decision-making processes. However, contemporary scholars highlight the benefits and the need for coordinated state and center in executing development or mission-oriented innovation policies today (Mazzucato 2017). The coordinated effort also encourages policy-makers to revisit the narratives of policy building for a more effective form of application and global execution.

Spiritual Politics: A New Paradigm

The current levels of crisis and distrust of existing democratic governance models can be seen as an invitation to revisit traditional narratives, disrupt existing thinking, and stimulate creative innovations. Unorthodox approaches are needed—not just for Weberian pubic administration thinking—in order to reform global governance and ensure transformation for societal, institutional, and financial resiliency in the digital era.

Spiritual Politics provides a relatively new unorthodox paradigm to reimagine the world of governance (Martínez Romero 2020). The concept can be seen as an oxymoron. Why even consider the possibility of reconciling such apparently opposing learning territories, such as external public affairs for thriving societies, and internal private quests of meaning and purpose for individual fulfillment? We contend that politics and spirituality possess shared foundational principles and convergent domains of intersectionality and are ultimately united in their aim to facilitate human flourishing, which can be understood as reaching the highest level of human well-being and thriving (Nussbaum 1992).

Spiritual politics is a heart-driven approach to leadership, which endorses the kindness and strength-based approach of Ardern in the integration of masculine and feminine holistic approaches. Spiritual politics encapsulates the creative journey of any changemaker and refers to a type of leadership that emphasizes the importance of human flourishing, empathy, social justice and historical development serving the evolution of societies over time. The concept is dynamic, polysemic, and transdisciplinary. Spiritual politics can be understood as a process to implement demands of justice and correct everything that stands against love. This proposition comes from a direct quote of Dr. Martin Luther King Jr., who used those words in a famous speech that reflected on the relationship between the forces of power and love. He pronounced the following words on August 16, 1967, in Atlanta, Georgia:

> One of the greatest problems of history is that the concepts of love and power are usually contrasted as polar opposites. Love is identified with a resignation of power and power with a denial of love. What is needed is a realization that power without love is reckless and abusive and that love without power is sentimental and anemic. Power at its best is love implementing the demands of justice. Justice at its best is love correcting everything that stands against love.
>
> *(Luther King 1967)*

Spiritual politics is about reconciling seemingly opposing forces and engaging in a holistic approach to governance and social change. As a concept, it invites social actors to embark on a learning journey to speak both the language of love and the language of power: the former is the language of empathy, compassion, and understanding, while the latter is the language of strategy, negotiation, and force (Kahane 2010). By speaking both languages, a leader can build relationships, inspire action, and effect change in ways that respect the dignity of all involved while remaining grounded in practical realities. Martin Luther King Jr.'s ability to speak both the language of love and power was central to his success in advancing the civil rights movement. He recognized the importance of both spiritual and political power, and he was able to use his leadership to inspire and motivate others to action. This is evident in his ability to mobilize people during the Montgomery Bus Boycott, the March on Washington, and the Selma to Montgomery marches. Spiritual politics also involves a transformative journey of self-discovery and inquiry that is grounded in a deep love for fundamental questions about life and meaning (Olalla 2004). As a leadership practice, it is a form of self-directed learning that is focused on exploring the fundamental values and beliefs that shape a leader's perspective on the world. As such, spiritual politics can be a powerful tool for developing wisdom, defined by Julio Olalla as the ability to navigate the complexities of life with insight, compassion, and a deep sense of purpose. From the attributes identified by Larry Spears, who served seventeen years as the president and CEO of the Robert K. Greenleaf Center for Servant-Leadership, spiritual politics is primordially concerned with three attributes: healing, trust-building, and community development (Brewer, Higgins, and Teeney 2010). Servanthood, or placing others before the self, is at the heart of this leadership practice.

As a creative leadership journey, spiritual politics integrates the vertical and horizontal dimensions shown in Figure 21.1. These dimensions represent an ontological movement in which the changemaker as an observer sees different planes of existence (Echeverria 1994)—to look in and look up, as well as a lookout and look at the "us." By finding everlasting sources of power on the vertical dimension (look in and look up, beyond status or any organizational position), transformation can occur at the horizontal area (lookout and look "us"). This horizontal movement marks a transition from accepting current social unequal realities (as is) to shaping the emergence of desirable social outcomes, such as trust-building, peace-building, and social reconciliation (to be). Looking out involves acknowledging political struggles. The realities of structural inequalities are faced and called out. Historical challenges and mindset change resistances in the public arena are identified. Without romanticizing, denying, criticizing, or idealizing social structures or institutions, seeing social realities as they are requires an ethics of deep listening and active acceptance (Moulton 2009). This kind of acceptance involves an act of acknowledging

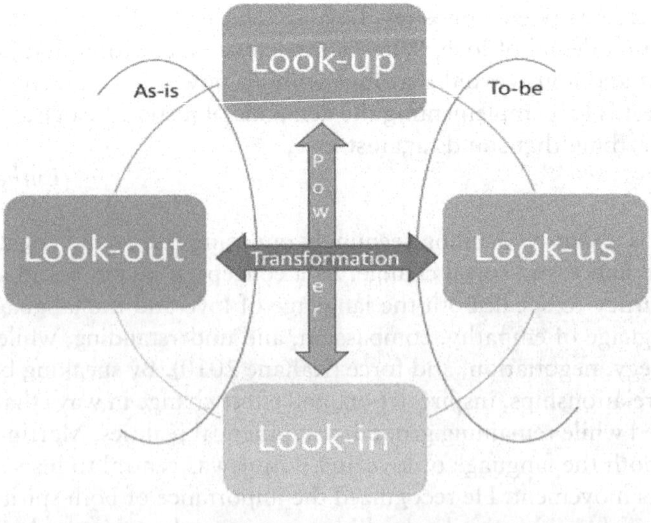

Figure 21.1 Spiritual Politics and Its Dimensions for Exercising Power for Social and Personal Transformation.

Source: Martínez Romero (2020).

and understanding the economic, political, and cultural systems that shape social realities, without assigning value judgments to it. This nonjudgmental acceptance practice does not mean that a leader must approve of or be resigned to a given situation. Rather, it simply means accepting the reality of a situation as it is, without getting caught up in evaluative judgments or interpretations.

Looking in embarks on the endless journey of self-knowledge, self-inquiry, and self-introspection, by finding the strength to look within and embracing fundamental leadership questions—Who am I? What does it truly mean to be human? Hope, courage, empathy, and resilience are seen as human innate capacities, as well as developed emotional assets. Looking up suggests the attitudes of invocation, surrender, faith, and trust. It involves a relationship with the mystery of life, with grace and the omnipresence of the Sacred and Spirit as an intangible life-affirming guiding force. For leaders who might not see themselves as spiritual beings, sources of transcendental motivation can be found in a sense of purpose and meaning, inspiration from role models, or connection with others in order to build meaningful relationships (Van Velsor 2008). This transcendental aspect of reality creates an intersection with the performing social work and can assist leaders in finding the root causes of observed problems. By recognizing the intangible and spiritual aspects of human existence, leaders can gain insight into the underlying root causes of social issues that are often deeply embedded in cultural, historical, and systemic structures (Hodge 2013). This understanding can help leaders approach social problems in a more comprehensive and nuanced way, recognizing the interconnectedness of all aspects of the human experience and seeking to address issues at their source rather than merely treating surface-level symptoms.

Looking at us involves recognizing that social reconciliation is the ultimate purpose of this leadership political practice. Unity, forgiveness, love, justice, and equality become political goals, which imply a change in the political cultures of every nation. This involves a reconciliation process between the individual "I" and the collective "we" in a dynamic dance between the agency of people and systems dynamics.

Spiritual intelligence and political intelligence are two concepts central to the spiritual politics process. To show the richness of these concepts, we present a general discussion mobilizing different definitions that illustrate the complementarity of these bits of intelligence we possess as human beings.

Spiritual Intelligence

For some, spiritual intelligence relates to the intelligence that makes us whole, that gives us our integrity, and with which we can place our lives in a context of broader and richer meaning (Srivastava 2016). For others, this type of intelligence calls for multiple ways of knowing and for the integration of the inner life of mind and spirit with the outer life of work in the world (Vaughan 2002). Spiritual intelligence can be cultivated through questioning, inquiry, and practice. Spiritual intelligence is necessary for discernment in making choices that contribute to psychological well-being and overall healthy human development. Through training and maturity, spiritual intelligence is expressed through wisdom and compassionate action in the world. Robert A. Emmons defines spiritual intelligence as the ability to experience heightened states of consciousness and utilize spiritual resources to solve problems in the sense of using the intelligence that comes from a person's ultimate concern (Emmons 2000). Key behaviors that illustrate this approach to problem-solving are leaders taking the time to listen deeply to the concerns and needs of diverse communities, making decisions that prioritize the well-being of all people rather than just a select few, and working to creating structures that are grounded in principles of justice, fairness, and equity, with a focus on supporting the most vulnerable members of society.

Political Intelligence

According to the Global Public Policy Network (GPPN), political intelligence relates to the leader's capacity to analyze, understand and, ultimately, solve humanity's contemporary challenges through innovative solutions in the pursuit of the common good (GPPN 2020). Political intelligence plays a significant role in the process of addressing the main challenges of contemporary governance, which involves talking about pressing public policy challenges, analyzing policies, critically assessing policy innovations, and evaluating solutions to shape tomorrow's world. Some define political intelligence as a decision-making capacity that enables social actors to further their self-interest in situations that involve rivalry and questions of power. For others, political intelligence is the leadership capacity to interact strategically in a world where government, business, and broader society share power to shape the future in a global economy; as such, political intelligence is about using skills and strategies to maneuver through political minefields to achieve personal and collective goals (Reffo and Wark 2014). Both spiritual and political intelligence are fundamental aspects of our 4P4R model of creative governance.

4P4R Model of Creative Governance

The 4P4R model of creative governance is an orbital model (see Figure 21.2). It is neither linear nor hierarchical. It is incremental and equitable. Table 21.1 lists and provides a brief explanation of every element that constitutes the model. Further explanation will be provided soon after.

Orbit 1

At the core of the 4P4R model of creative governance is the knowledge and intelligence of root causes. Root causes are the known and unknown reasons why we are the way we are and why we are not the way we are. They refer to the essence, the self, and the heart. It is the spirit of creative governance. Root causes are complex, intricate, and nuanced. They are not easy to unravel primarily because of humanity's obsession with simplifying everything using an anthropomorphic framework. However, in this case, we acknowledge the complexity and, instead of simplifying it, we let it remain complex but at the same time also work toward comprehending root causes at the level of complexity that they are by conducting a root cause analysis (RCA).

Root causes can be greed, trauma, fear, survival, or even desires. Root causes can also be expressions of non-identification with ego or ego-transcendence (Klaus and Fernando 2016)—therefore, revealing a shift of identity toward core human qualities that arise from an identification with a non-egoic self, like compassion, love, flow, and a deep sense of unity and interconnection with the whole. The key point here is that this quest to seek the root causes stimulates a departure from the symptom-based mentality and framework. An example of a symptom-based framework of approaching governance and directed change as mentioned earlier is the approach of the Sustainable Development Goals (SDGs).

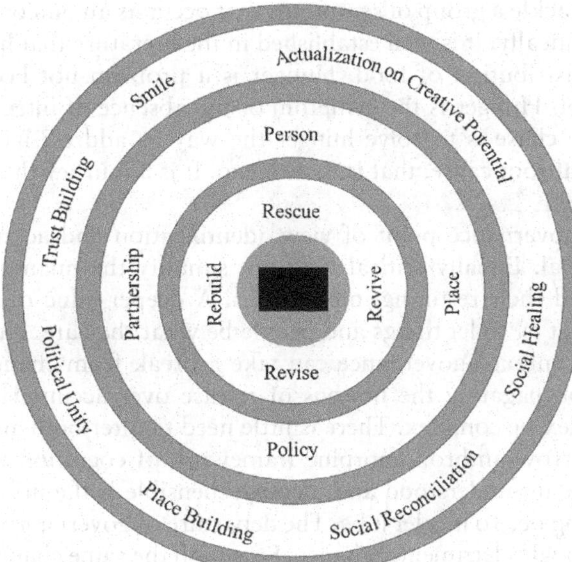

Figure 21.2 4P4R Model of Creative Governance

Source: Authors.

Table 21.1 Elements in the 4P4R Model of Creative Governance

Orbit	*Elements*	*Brief explanation*
1	Root causes	Root cause refers to the essence, self, and heart. It is the spirit of creative governance.
2	Rescue	The process of salvaging wisdom and traditions (WTs), especially ancient ones.
	Revive	Revive WTs through academic, political, and practical conversations.
	Revise	Make WTs pertinent to the times by integrating modern thinking and adapting the work to the governance context.
	Rebuild/ Revitalize	Application and expression of the WTs to reconstruct governance through the elements of the third orbit.
3	Person	Person symbolizes all living entities with a composite of numerous dynamic tangible and intangible nuances. It can take the form of an individual, a family, a community, a group, or a nation.
	Place	Place refers to the symbolic simplification for the inner being as well as the surroundings, such as the ecosystem, the structure of governance, the education system, the tax system, the system of commerce, availability and access to gainful employment, nature and forms of remuneration, work environment, and many more.
	Policy	The policy is the simplified symbol of many tangible and intangible creations of the human mind.
	Partnership	The partnership is the symbolic simplification of alliances with and between people, places, and policies.
4	Outcomes	Actualization of creative potential, smile, social healing, trust-building, peace-building, and social reconciliation.

Source: Authors.

SDGs attempt to tackle a group of symptoms that occur as an outcome of the root causes not being addressed ideally. It is well established in the literature that hunger can be solved through equitable distribution of food. Hunger is a problem not because of the dearth of food on the planet. Hunger is the symptom of the absence of intent to share resources equitably. While the chase is to solve hunger the way to address its sustainability is by addressing a potential root cause, that is, greed, ego. It is a journey that starts with the self and extends to society.

From a creative governance point of view, identification and acknowledgment of the root causes are critical. Equally critical is to not simplify the nuance and complexity of these root causes and their resulting implications. A deeper ethic of acceptance is being propagated here—that is, to let things and people be what they are. Humanity and—more importantly in this context—governance can take a break from changing people, things, and situations, by propagating the notions of release over accumulation. Let simple be simple and let complex be complex. There is little need to alter both and bring them at the same level of the narrow anthropomorphic framework of cognition and comprehension. Tolerance toward the un-understood and incomprehensible is the first step toward letting someone or something be. To just let it be. The departure of governance and humanity from *to be* to *to do* has brought detrimental change. Some call the same change progress, whereas others refer to it as regress. Perhaps, it is time that governance must aim for something else and allow change to be a by-product. And this is what can be achieved through creative governance approaches.

The next section will explain the 4Rs in detail and elaborate on their role in the second orbit. The beauty is that one can pick this model and start using it as a framework at any level or orbit depending on the needs assessment.

Orbit 2

The second orbit consists of 4Rs: Rescue, Revive, Revise, and Rebuild. The 4Rs are the preparatory set of reflective and creative action items in the creative governance approach. After the identification of the root causes, through the 4Rs, we gather support from what is already out there in terms of wisdom and traditions both new and ancient. This allows us to integrate Ancient Wisdom Traditions (AWTs) with modern processes and approaches to stimulate liberating change.

Let us understand the 4Rs with an example of integrating ancient wisdom traditions and contemporary political science followed by the Mexican School of Conscious Politics. This emerging not-for-profit organization proposes to integrate an Open Government approach with the power of AWT. In the state of Oaxaca, Mexico, for example, traditional governance structures, such as *usos y costumbres* (customs and habits), are practiced locally. In these structures, communities are ruled by traditional assemblies, which are in most cases mandatory for community members, and they allow for citizen deliberation on local issues, resource allocation, and elected community representatives. Out of 570 municipalities in Oaxaca, 480 have adopted such traditional governance structures, making it a widespread phenomenon (Magaloni, Díaz-Cayeros, and Ruiz Euler 2019). Creative governance is practiced when the recognition of community deliberation processes within assemblies used as a decision-making mechanism can match transparency, participation, and accountability, the three key principles of Open Government. This effort requires innovation on the part of local and regional authorities in their interaction with citizens and how they manage their administrations. A dialogue between Western and Indigenous views of governance is established. Transparency requires authorities to make it easier for citizens to access information, notably through open data and records management. It should go hand in hand with greater participation of communities and civil society in the public decision-making process, including protection for whistleblowers and ongoing cocreation of action plans. Clear commitments, with objectives, measurable goals, planned activities, execution times, clear managers, and expected results, have to embrace the organic wisdom process of traditions and Indigenous approaches to governance. Technical policy knowledge is as important as supporting the human growth journey of communities and individuals. To achieve this strategy, the Mexican School of Conscious Politics has introduced the creative concept of "technical tequio." *Tequio* comes from the word in Nahuatl "tequitl," which means work or tribute, after a pre-Hispanic tradition of collaboration or service in species and labor from the people of a certain region, to build, preserve, and repair common spaces and goods. Now, it is not understood as a tribute for a dominant group, but for oneself and the community through unpaid community service. Technical tequio is about engaging highly trained professionals that want to contribute to heal social wounds by solving public problems, with specific projects and needs.

AWTs need to be salvaged and rescued from the forgotten and sometimes lost crevices of human intelligence and standardization. The process of salvaging wisdom and traditions that hold value requires empathy for the people that have walked on this planet before us, their intelligence systems, their creative endeavors, and breakthroughs, which could very well be what we now label as AWT. The rescue also requires vulnerability at the ego level and surrender of the same ego to not consider the modern ways to be superior or effective.

Revive is the second step, wherein the rescued WTs, especially AWTs, are acknowledged through academic, political, and practical conversations. After having been languishing for centuries or millennia, many such traditions need revival. The process of the revival includes context-appropriate comprehension of the tradition and apt documentation of the intent and outcomes that emerged from the AWT. The academic conversations bring these back into the public sphere to be picked up by political deliberations for their potential utility in actualizing the desired outcomes. Revival is an important phase, because many AWTs are contextually inappropriate or simply don't have the substance in them to aid in transformation. The analysis assessment and deliberations of such issues are critical before efforts are put into revising them.

Revising is a pivotal aspect because it is unlikely that a form of AWT that was pertinent centuries or millennia ago would also be as applicable today as it was then. All the anachronisms have to be carefully chiseled out and at times even newer add-ons have to be incorporated. Given the astronomical changes in the nature, scope, and scale of societal changes, it is highly unlikely for ancient wisdom or tradition to be optimally effective in the as-is form. Revision allows the relevance of the AWT to remain for utility and amplification and the irrelevant of the AWT to be left out.

Rebuild is the last R. Once an AWT is rescued, revived, and revised, it can be applied in combination with modern technology or practice to rebuild aspects of governance through the 4Ps of the third orbit. In the rebuild, we see the expression of the AWT in its most relevant form based on the societal ecosystem.

In India, the example of Panchayat governance demonstrates the process of going through the 4Rs for rescuing an ancient system, reviving it, revising it to fit in the new structure, and applying it in the rebuilding of the societies and the nation. This system is the village-level system of governance, also known as the Panchayat system. Panchayat is an older tradition of governance of villages found in India where five selected and elected elders or wise people address and resolve much of the conflict that arises in the village. Any new proposal for a change from within also goes through them in an open deliberation process. One of the five is the equivalent of the convenor and chairperson and also plays the role of a tiebreaker in case of a tie. When India became independent this system was revived and revised by making it a part of the formal government structure and giving it authority, autonomy, as well as accountability, which was more of the Weberian bureaucratic in nature. In India, even today we see an amalgamation of the newer and modern styles of governance along with the more ancient and older forms of governance. Every village has a Panchayat, where elections are contested fairly and openly and a majority of local issues and projects are resolved and given a green signal locally. This unique synergy has enabled the People, the Place, the Policy, and the Partnerships to thrive and to take steps closer to the desired outcomes. We will look at the 4Ps in the next section.

Orbit 3

In the third orbit, we introduce the 4Ps, in which creative strategies and creative problem-solving can be seen in action. These 4Ps are People, Place, Policy, and Partnership. Each has a distinct role and significance in a human's life and surrounding environment. Creative governance must equitably and closely align itself with each of the four. None is more important than the other. It is only through the synergy of the four that life can be enriched. The absence of any of the four is likely to create imbalance and disharmony.

Person

Person symbolizes all living entities with a composite of numerous dynamic tangible and intangible nuances. It can take the form of an individual, a family, a community, a group, or a nation. A person is a composite of numerous dynamic tangible and intangible nuances, including all of the person, along with their flairs, whims, and fancies.

Governing a person in creative governance means allowing him or her to be and not persuade him or her toward doing. A person is not necessarily significant by doing. A person just by being is also significant. This is the driving philosophy of creative governance. As Thomas Legrand (2022) explains, this is a politics of being, that walks on two legs—wisdom and science—and recognizes that all living beings have the right to flourish. Doing is symbolic to the many activities a person does including procreation, economic, religious, social, and preference-based activities, and more. Doing can be regulated because there is a larger scope of variance in the activities in doing. But that is not the case in being. Being does not present a larger scope of variance, but there is a scope for variance in the by-products of being.

Place

The place is the symbolic simplification for the inner being, as well as the surroundings, the ecosystem, the structure of governance, the education system, the tax system, the system of commerce, availability and access to gainful employment, nature and forms of remuneration, work environment, and many more. The place can be related to the context defined as "situational opportunities and constraints that affect the occurrence and meaning of organizational behavior as well as functional relationships between variables" (Johns 2006).

The place has a deep impact on the creativity, industriousness, resourcefulness, and resilience of a person. In one such instance, for the past thousands of years of human history, humans have consistently marched toward comfort as a singular goal when it comes to defining and designing spaces. This singular goal has systematically decreased the dynamism in the spaces that we spend most of our time. Our spaces are more and more static, unfazed by the dynamism and change outside. Our ability to regulate the internal environment has a large majority of civilized world living in practically the same static or unchanging environment.

Governance structures also in the hopes of optimization, at times knowingly and at times unknowingly, remove dynamism from the place. Static places and static systems contribute to a reduction in cognitive expression and processing. Fundamentally, we are very good at creating mental shortcuts, otherwise known as heuristics, to effectively navigate the space or the place around us. When living in and with nature, such shortcuts are important, but due to the dynamism of nature, they don't negatively impact the creativity, industriousness, resourcefulness, and resilience of a person.

In creative governance, one must be extremely mindful of the space they are creating. Constant questioning and altering of the space, not with the goal of confusing people or making it more difficult but to moderate and promote dynamism, are critical.

Policy

Policy again is a simplified symbol of many tangible and intangible creations of the human mind. A policy can also be seen as an extension of *sankalpa*, a decision to explore a path to see if it leads to the chosen destination. In public affairs, policy refers to the leader's capacity to analyze, understand, and ultimately solve humanity's contemporary challenges through innovative solutions in the pursuit of the common good (GPPN 2020).

A policy can also be seen as a law, regulation, procedure, administrative action, incentive, or voluntary practice of governments and other institutions. Policy decisions are frequently reflected in resource allocations. Who makes these resource allocations, how are resources allocated, who gets more resources, and who remains deprived of resources?

Typically, a very small number of individuals make decisions affecting thousands and millions of people. A creative governance example would be participatory budgeting where the notion of giving everyone a voice by acknowledging their equal superiority in discerning the good of the community is rescued, revived, and later on revised according to the context and time. Participatory budgeting started in 1989 and is now practiced with different intensities in 7,000 cities around the world.

Partnership

A partnership is the symbolic simplification of alliances with and between people, places, and policies. The United Nations' definition of a multi-stakeholder partnership for the SDGs highlights the

> ongoing collaborative relationship between or among organizations from different stakeholder types aligning their interests around a common vision, combining their complementary resources and competencies and sharing risk, to maximize value creation towards the Sustainable Development Goals and deliver benefit to each of the partners.

An important prerequisite here is the ability to find similarities between the goals and interests of aligning and non-aligning parties. It is easier to identify differences but identifying similarities requires some practice. Partnerships for stewarding the planet and its people away from maladies will require negotiation and a shift toward developing tolerance for partial success at times.

Orbit 4

The last orbit refers to desired outcomes of creative governance. This non-exhaustive list includes the following aspects:

- Actualization of creative potential: The extent to which we are in touch with our creative potential and are afforded an ecosystem where the fearless and uninhibited expression of creative proclivities is encouraged.
- Smiles: The extent to which life is a joyful, creative experience resulting in a smile on people's faces. An indicator of the absence of stress, anxiety, trauma, trouble, and skirmishes.
- Social healing: Process of solving a social development problem seen from a holistic perspective. Inspired by the work of Marianne Willamson, we can define this concept by recognizing that the principles that apply to our personal healing also apply to the healing of communities, societies, and our larger world. By calling on citizens to turn the compassion, love, and courage in their hearts into a powerful political force for social good and transformation, we can transform spiritual activism into social and political activism (Williamson 2000).
- Trust-building: An intangible social dimension that serves as the relational "glue" of different factors to bring people together in safe environments that naturally induce higher levels of collaboration, increased creativity and risk-taking.
- Peace-building: Activity that aims to resolve injustice in nonviolent ways and to transform the cultural and structural conditions that generate deadly or destructive conflict. It revolves around developing constructive personal, group, and political relationships across ethnic, religious, class, national, and racial boundaries. The process includes violence prevention; conflict management, resolution, or transformation; and post-conflict reconciliation or trauma healing before, during, and after any given case of violence (Kroc Institute for Peace Studies 2018).
- Social reconciliation: One of the main purposes of creative governance is a spiritual politics leadership practice, a path where unity, forgiveness, love, justice, and equality are seen as political goals, which requires a change in the political cultures of every nation. This involves reconciliation between the individual "I" and the collective "we," in a dynamic dance between systems and agency.

Summary and Conclusion

Creative governance in bits and pieces has been practiced in many places. But creative governance as a comprehensive approach to governance is still in its nascent stages. One salient example of such governance, the experimental Indian township of Auroville, has used 4Rs to create a place, invent policies, and build partnerships to actualize the outcomes in the fourth orbit: unity, healing, utilizing creative potential, and more.

Based on an epistemology of vulnerability and practice of academic engagement where changemakers, scholars, policy-makers, citizens, and key stakeholders take the personal risk of being emotionally open, honest, and transparent (Brené 2015), creative governance needs to embrace a science of constant cyclical and self-reflective improvement based on testing, failing, learning, improving, and re-entering, as any lean methodology would suggest. This learning mindset should not only be practiced by civil servants and elected officials, who are traditionally associated with the work of politics and governance. Faith leaders, social activists, business managers, social entrepreneurs, engaged scholars, students, and normal and extraordinary citizens—all of us—can actively participate in this journey of learning, discovery, and transformation. This process can strengthen participatory democracies and cleanse our relationship with politics by restoring a more virtuous understanding and practice of our political beingness.

One area of discussion on the creative governance agenda is education. What does it mean to meet the needs of future generations of leaders to be effective in diverse business, social, and political environments? Given the current social tensions of our political landscape, are we educating future leaders to follow Ardern's model and put in practice leadership principles of spiritual politics, creative governance, and systems thinking? As Julio Olalla (2004) observes:

> Our traditional education system is not addressing the breakdowns of what is happening in the world today. In business, in our relationships and in our communities, we need to recover the soul as a domain of learning. We are taught to pursue a life that we will never reach and need to be reminded that "more" does not equal "better."

Recovering wisdom as a core educational value present in ancient and modern governance traditions is fundamental. The education of any political leader and citizen activist needs to include the integration of spiritual intelligence and consciousness development. This educational endeavor highlights the systemic interconnection between elements, like mind, body, language, emotions, culture, history, and spirit at both the individual and community level. As Einstein famously said, one cannot solve the problem at the same level of consciousness as it was created. Therefore, the 4P4R creative governance model can also be used as an educational approach to teach skills to effectively manage public affairs challenges and, at the same time, develop the spiritual intelligence of students who are the present and the future political leaders. Activating the Indigenous footprint we all carry and respecting planetary boundaries seems to be ethical imperatives of our times.

Cross-cultural dynamics also play an important role in creative governance. While concepts like "spiritual politics," "ancient wisdom traditions," "people," "places," "partnerships," or "policies" can mean different things in different contexts. Spirituality can help in this mission. If a person's spirit is defined as the vital principle or animating force traditionally believed to be the intangible, life-affirming force in self and all human beings then spirituality can provide a common universal sense of shared humanity that is key to honor dignity, respect diversity, build trust, heal wounds, liberate creative potential, and allow the flourishing of more genuine smiles.

Creative Governance Laboratory

This section offers you four activities to apply and experiment with creative governance in your respective settings.

Activity I

Find and reconcile your leadership dilemmas:

As a creative governance practice, dilemma reconciliation provides a powerful framework by combining opposites and navigating strategic tensions to create holistic solutions (Trompenaars 2005).

Dilemmas are not necessarily paradoxical, since a paradox assumes that one choice invalidates the other, whereas, in a dilemma, both options may be desirable, necessitating a reconciliation of competing values. In that sense, ethical dilemmas are mutually exclusive though desirable (and/or undesirable) options, which are often the result of conflicting or contradictory values held by individuals or organizations, deciding between which may result in tension and dispute.

In this chapter, we have discussed spiritual politics as a dilemma reconciliation process. This perspective integrates the logic of love and the logic of power. As a paradigm of inquiry can you build upon "through-through" thinking i which is a type of nonlinear thinking that emphasizes interconnectedness and complexity, rather than focusing on the Cartesian logic of either/or or cause-and-effect relationships?

Seen as a form of holistic thinking and practice of creative governance, this approach can foster innovation by discovering new alternatives in a search for continuous learning (Burger and Llerena 2008).

Activity Prompt

What are the current dilemmas you need to reconcile in your governance practices? Do you see opportunities in the search for wholeness when presented with the following dilemmas?

- technical cognition/emotional intuition
- hard skills/human skills
- ancient wisdom traditions/contemporary policy science
- contemplative inner practices/Proactive social engagements

To make sense of this complexity, we used the six-step framework developed by Frons Trompenaars and Charles Hampden-Turner to reconcile dilemmas (see Figure 21.3).

Use the Reconciliation Sheet provided in appendix 2 to follow the six-step dilemma reconciliation process.

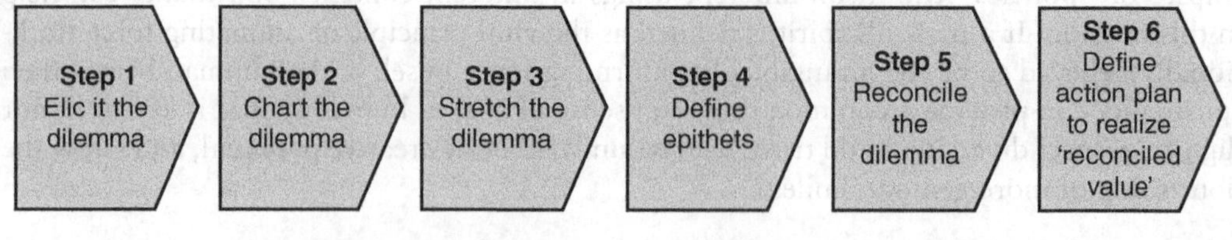

Figure 21.3 Hampden-Turner and Trompenaars Framework to Reconcile Dilemmas
Source: Trompenaars and Hampden-Turner (2004).

Activity II

Explore ancient wisdom traditions from your land and how they are engaged with governance.

The creative governance model includes 4Rs related to ancient wisdom traditions. They represent an invitation to honor Indigenous forms of governance, present in different societies around the globe. As we have seen in Mexico, for example, Ancient Wisdom Traditions are present in community deliberation processes within assemblies and are used as a decision-making mechanism. Traditional governance structures (called *usos y costumbres*, customs and habits) are practiced locally. The social communities are governed by traditional assemblies, which usually are mandatory for community members, and they foster citizen deliberation on local issues, such as resource allocation, or electing community representatives (Magaloni, Díaz-Cayeros, and Ruiz Euler2019).

Activity Prompt

Which alternative forms of governance can you learn from as a changemaker? Can you find Indigenous ancient wisdom traditions in your local culture or other cultures, which you could rescue, revive, revise, and revitalize to meet present and future needs?

Activity III

Challenge the model to enhance it but more importantly make it your own.

The 4P4R model of creative governance is a starting point and by no means a definitive or ultimate way of governance. The essence of creativity is to keep defying the status quo. In the spirit of defying the status quo, it is vital to apply your individual creativity to innovate and enhance or tweak and tinker with the model to make it your own. This chapter introduces an initial framework.

Activity Prompt

Invoke your inner creative being and spend time with the 4P4R model of creative governance with the goal of challenging the inherent weaknesses and eliminating them, and at the same time adding or changing the structure and nature of the model to better fit your individual and local dilemma.

Activity IV

Utilize the 4P4R model of creative governance to assess the presence and extent of creative governance in the following two places.

1) Auroville: https://auroville.org/

   Auroville wants to be a universal town where men and women of all countries are able to live in peace and progressive harmony above all creeds, all politics and all nationalities. The purpose of Auroville is to realize human unity.

2) Próspera: https://prospera.hn/

> Próspera partners with governments like Honduras to promote and operate Economic Development Hubs—similar to Special Economic Zones (SEZs). These hubs are integrated with local communities and have semi-autonomous governance and regulation. With a common law legal framework, familiar and flexible regulations, a bill of rights, low taxation, and protections for the environment, Próspera enables entrepreneurs to solve problems structurally and responsibly for the people of Honduras and the rest of the world.

Acknowledgment

The authors would like to thank Suhair and Devika for their able support and assistance. The authors would also like to express deep gratitude to Pepe García for his invaluable support and encouragement from the Mexican School of Conscious Politics project. For providing the core academic filters of the spiritual politics constructed with trust, courage and generosity, a heartfelt expression of gratitude to Dr. Sylvia van de Bunt and Dr. Fons Trompenaars, co-directors of the Servant-Leadership Centre for Research and Education (SERVUS) at the Free University of Amsterdam. And finally thanks to the Initiatives of Change Creative Leadership Team, who made our (Arpan and Rodrigo's) encounter possible through their outstanding Creative Leadership Conference.

Appendix 1

Table 21A.1 List of Authors/Leaders Who Practice Some Aspects of the 4P4R Model of Creative Governance

Leaders/Authors	*Quotes/Ideas*
Adam Kahane (Kahane 2010)	Spiritual politics, in the words of Adam Kahane, is about learning to speak both the language of love and the language of power. This recognizes the centrality of dialogue and joint commitment to address our most pressing problems—be it a strategic issue inside a company or a societal challenge like poverty, conflict, or climate change.
Marianne Williamson (Williamson 2000, 22)	"The principles which apply to our personal healing also apply to the healing of the larger world. By calling on citizens to turn the compassion in our hearts into a powerful political force for social good, we transform spiritual activism into social activism and in turn we transform our countries into nations seriously invested in the hope of every child and in the potential of every adult." Williamson campaigned for the Democratic nomination in the 2020 United States presidential election and understood that social healing is an integral part of what she calls holistic politics.
Margaret Wheatley (Wheatley 2017)	Wheatley refers to "warriors of the human spirit": they are leaders, activists, citizens, and human beings who want to make a meaningful contribution in this historical time of increasing assaults on the human spirit and all life, with the purpose and intention of serving well. To be effective with their energy and influence, these social actors train to refrain from fear, aggression, and control to embody the best human qualities of generosity, insight, compassion, and love.
Brother Phil Lane Jr (Prophecy eagle, condor and quetzal)	Global Justice and Healing Commission https://m.facebook.com/GlobalJusticeAndHealingCommission/

Source: Authors.

Appendix 2

Trompenaars Hampden-Turner
Culture for Business

Reconciliation Worksheet

1. Describe the Dilemma:
On the one hand ____________________
On the other ____________________
Dilemma holder ____________________

10

3. List Positives for Y-axis:
+ ____________
+ ____________
+ ____________

List Negatives for Y-axis:
- ____________
- ____________
- ____________

1,10
4. ____________ ____________

10,10
5. ____________ ____________

5,5
4. ____________ ____________

10,1
4. ____________ ____________

2. Y-axis label: ____________

0,0 2. X-axis label: ____________ 10

3. List Positives for X-axis:
+ ____________
+ ____________
+ ____________

List Negatives for X-axis:
- ____________
- ____________
- ____________

5. Reconciliation statement:
Through..
....
....
....

1. Identify the dilemma
2. **Chart the dilemma**
a. Be specific by making the dilemma
Defined under 1 more concrete
b. Label the axes reflecting the opposing
positions (positive or neutral)
c. Plot the positions of the actors
3. Stretch the dilemma
Describe the positives and negatives of each side of the dilemma
4. Make epithets
Put epithets (sweet and sour) in each of the
boxes
5. Reconcile the dilemma
Ask how Value X can support Value Y and vice versa
6. Develop action plan

6 Action Plan
1 ____________
2 ____________
3 ____________

Which behaviors support this:
1 ____________
2 ____________
3 ____________

Key Discussion Areas

- An overview of the connections along global governance, creative governance, and spiritual politics.
- 4P4R approach to creative governance.
- Introduction and discussion of the root causes of issues.
- Review and devise plans to inspire creative governance in global, glocal, and local levels.

Notes

1 As captured by the United Nations' 17 Sustainable Development Goals.
2 The notion that a certain amount of diversity in viewpoints and perspectives is required for groups and organizations to address complex problems as they emerge.
3 This relates to the insight that "problems cannot be solved by the level of awareness that created them" (a quote commonly attributed to Albert Einstein, but probably actually introduced by the spiritual teacher Ram Dass. For a review of the possible original source, see https://en.wikiquote.org/wiki/Talk:Albert_Einstein#Unsourced_and_dubious/overly_modern_sources)

References

Alexander, Deborah, and Kristi Andersen. 1993. "Gender as a Factor in the Attribution of Leadership Traits." *Political Research Quarterly* 46(3): 527, https://doi.org/10.2307/448946 (accessed April 5, 2023).

Anderson, Cami. 2020. "Why Do Women Make Such Good Leaders During COVID-19?" *Forbes*, April 19, 2020, www.forbes.com/sites/camianderson1/2020/04/19/why-do-women-make-such-good-leaders-during-covid-19/#7ea90a7b42fc (accessed April 5, 2023).

Brené, Brown. 2015. *Daring Greatly: How the Courage to Be Vulnerable Transforms the Way We Live, Love, Parent, and Lead*. New York: Avery.

Brewer, J. D., G. I. Higgins, and F. Teeney. 2010. "Religion and Peacemaking: A Conceptualization." *Sociology* 44(6): 1019–37.

Bunt-Kokhuis, S. G. M., and Sultan, N. 2012. "Servant-leadership: the Online Way! E-learning where community building is key". *European Journal of Open, Distance and E-Learning*, 1–10, https://old.eurodl.org/?p=archives (accessed April 5, 2023).

Burger-Helmchen, Thierry, and Patrick Llerena. 2008. "A Case Study of a Creative Start-up: Governance, Communities, and Knowledge Management." *Journal of Innovation Economics & Management* 2(2): 125, https://doi.org/10.3917/jie.002.0125 (accessed April 5, 2023).

Dingwerth, K., and P. Pattberg. 2022. "Theorizing Global Governance." In *Handbook on Global Governance and Regionalism* (pp. 21–35). Edward Elgar Publishing Cheltenham, UK.

Echeverria, R. 1994. *Ontología del lenguaje* [Ontology of Language]. Santiago de Chile: Dolmen Ediciones.

Emmons, Robert A. 2000. "Is Spirituality an Intelligence? Motivation, Cognition, and the Psychology of Ultimate Concern." *International Journal for the Psychology of Religion* 10(1): 3–26, https://doi.org/0.1207/s15327582ijpr1001_2 (accessed April 5, 2023).

Fry, L. W. 2003. "Toward a Theory of Spiritual Leadership." *Leadership Quarterly* 14(6): 693–727.

Global Public Policy Network. 2020. "About GPPN," www.gppnetwork.org/about (accessed April 5, 2023).

Greenleaf, Robert K. 1970. *The Servant as Leader*. Westfield, IN: Greenleaf Center for Servant Leadership.

Hodge, D. R. 2013. "Spiritual Assessment in Social Work and Mental Health Practice." *Social Work* 58(3): 233–41.

Johns, Gary. 2006. "The Essential Impact of Context on Organizational Behavior." *Academy of Management Review* 31(2): 386–408, https://doi.org/10.5465/amr.2006.20208687 (accessed April 5, 2023).

Kahane, Adam. 2010. *Power and Love: A Theory and Practice of Social Change*, 1st ed. Oakland, CA: Berrett-Koehler Publishers.

Kattel, R., W. Drechsler, and E. Karo. 2019. "Innovation Bureaucracies: How Agile Stability Creates the Entrepreneurial State. UCL Institute for Innovation and Public Purpose." Working Paper Series (IIPP WP 2019–12). https://www.ucl.ac.uk/bartlett/public-purpose/publications.

Klaus, Lauren, and Mario Fernando. 2016. "Enacting Spiritual Leadership in Business through Ego-Transcendence." *Leadership & Organization Development Journal* 37(1): 71–92, https://doi.org/10.1108/lodj-04-2014-0078 (accessed April 5, 2023).

Kooiman, J. 2003. *Governing as Governance*. Newbury Park, CA: Sage Publications.

Kroc Institute for International Peace Studies. 2018. "What Is Strategic Peacebuilding?" University of Notre Dame, https://kroc.nd.edu/about-us/what-is-peace-studies/what-is-strategic-peacebuilding.

Legrand, Thomas. 2022. *Politics of Being: Wisdom and Science for a New Development Paradigm*. New York: Ocean of Wisdom Press.

Luther King, M. 1967. "Where Do We Go From Here?" Annual Report Delivered at the 11th Convention of SCLC, quote retrieved from https://www.goodreads.com/quotes/731652-one-of-the-greatest-problems-of-history-is-that-the (accessed April 5, 2023).

Magaloni, Beatriz, Alberto Díaz-Cayeros, and Alexander Ruiz Euler. 2019. "Public Good Provision and Traditional Governance in Indigenous Communities in Oaxaca, Mexico." *Comparative Political Studies* 52(12): 1841–80, https://doi.org/10.1177/0010414019857094 (accessed April 5, 2023).

Martínez Romero, R. 2020. "On Meaning and Purpose: A Qualitative Study on Spiritual Politics as a Servant-Leadership Practice, Dilemma Reconciliation Process and Cross-cultural Journey." Unpublished master's thesis manuscript, VU Amsterdam.

Mazzucato, M. 2017. "Mission-Oriented Innovation Policy." UCL Institute for Innovation and Public Purpose Working Paper, 1 University College London, London, UK.

Moulton, J. G. 2009. "Embracing Deep Listening and Active Acceptance in Qualitative Inquiry: A Response to Thompson." *International Journal of Qualitative Studies in Education* 22(3): 305–13.

Navarro-Astor, Elena, Marisa Román-Onsalo, and Margarita Infante-Perea. 2017. "Women's Career Development in the Construction Industry across 15 Years: Main Barriers." *Journal of Engineering, Design and Technology* 15(2): 199–221, https://doi.org/10.1108/jedt-07-2016-0046 (accessed April 5, 2023).

Nussbaum, Martha. 1992. "Human Functioning and Social Justice: In Defense of Aristotelian Essentialism." *Political Theory* 20(2): 202–46.

Olalla, Julio. 2004. *From Knowledge to Wisdom: Essays on the Crisis in Contemporary Learning*. Boulder, CO: Newfield Network.

Osseiran, S. 2020. "Jacinda Ardern: Authentic Leadership and the Politics of Empathy." In *Global Advances in Humanitarian Work Psychology*, edited by J. H. Stryker, C. J. C. Burges, and J. A. Arnetz, (pp. 223–34). Springer International Publishing. https://doi.org/10.1007/978-3-030-37364-9_14

Reffo, G., and V. Wark. 2014. *Leadership PQ: How Political Intelligence Sets Successful Leaders Apart*. London: Kogan Page Publishers.

Repenning, N. P., D. Kieffer, and T. Astor. 2017. *The Most Underrated Skill in Management*. MIT Sloan Management Review Massachusetts, USA.

Rockström, Johan, Will Steffen, Kevin Noone, Åsa Persson, F. Stuart Chapin, Eric Lambin, Timothy M. Lenton, et al. 2009. "Planetary Boundaries: Exploring the Safe Operating Space for Humanity." *Ecology and Society* 14(2), https://doi.org/10.5751/es-03180-140232 (accessed April 5, 2023).

Srivastava, Prem Shankar. 2016. "Spiritual Intelligence: An Overview." *International Journal of Multidisciplinary Research and Development* 3(3): 224–27, www.allsubjectjournal.com/archives/2016/vol3/issue3/3-3-74 (accessed April 5, 2023).

Sterman, J. 2000. *Business Dynamics: Systems Thinking and Modeling for a Complex World*. The McGraw-Hill Companies.

Tackney, C. T., S. Chappell, D. Harris, K. Pavlovich, E. Egel, R. Major, et al. 2017. "Management, Spirituality, and Religion (MSR) Ways and Means: A Paper to Encourage Quality Research." *Journal of Management, Spirituality & Religion* 14(3): 245–54.

Taub, Amanda. 2020. "Why Are Women-Led Nations Doing Better With Covid-19?" *The New York Times,* May 15, 2020, www.nytimes.com/2020/05/15/world/coronavirus-women-leaders.html (accessed April 5, 2023).

Trompenaars, A. 2005. *Building Cross-Cultural Competence: How to Create Wealth from Conflicting Values*. Yale University Press, Connecticut, USA.

Trompenaars, F., and C. Hampden-Turner, C. 2004. *Managing People Across Cultures*. Chichester: Capstone.

Van Velsor, E. 2008. "A Complexity Perspective on Leadership Development." *Complexity Leadership* 1, 333–46.

Vaughan, Frances. 2002. "What Is Spiritual Intelligence?" *Journal of Humanistic Psychology* 42(2): 16–33, https://doi.org/10.1177/0022167802422003 (accessed April 5, 2023).

Wheatley, M. 2017. "Who Do You Choose to Be? An Invitation to the Nobility of Leadership." *Leader to Leader* 85: 37–41.

Williamson, Marianne. 2000. *Healing the Soul of America: Reclaiming Our Voices as Spiritual Citizens*. New York: Simon & Schuster.

22
TECHNOLOGY-ENABLED SELF-GOVERNING MODELS FOR THE DIGITAL WORLD

Sandeep Menon

Introduction

The internet is a strange place. It can be incredibly democratizing, as well as rebelliously anarchist at the same time. This, in turn, has a spiraling effect on all forms of governance in an increasingly digital world. The internet's democratizing power essentially flows from being founded in information disintermediation. For example, today in India, if someone wants to pull up statutory filings, the Profit & Loss, or annual report of any corporate, they no longer need to leg it to the nearest government office, apply in triplicate, and wait for three weeks for a response. It is all now available online at the click of a button. From simple querying to even deep forensic audits, everything can be achieved quickly, by anyone desiring to do so.

Just having ready access to data at such depth is deeply empowering from a governance perspective. On the other hand, the digital world is also constantly challenging regulatory frameworks based on traditional rules that are enforced by an authority, typically the state. For example, the state, through its institutions, has controlled the ability to print money, the right to track its flow around the world, as well as the ability to peg its value relative to other currencies. However, we now see the emergence of mediums such as crypto currencies that are turning this entire monetary paradigm around on its head. It would not be a stretch to call developments like crypto currencies a sociopolitical, anarchist idea emerging from the digital world. One that allows individuals, corporations, and institutions, both legitimate and illegitimate, to move millions across borders without leaving a trace. This emasculates the ability of governments to govern through monetary policy and cocks a snook at almost all traditional financial regulatory mechanisms (De-Filippi and Loveluck 2016).

Paradoxically, the underlying blockchain technology also enables the very opposite functionality of trackability. One of its biggest use cases is e-signing and authentication of digital documents as well as journey tracking of goods and services around the world, using immutable tagging. This allows for robust documentation and contracting as well as voluntary traceability. So a consumer can now see whether their coffee is ethically sourced from environmentally sustainable sources, whether the diamond they are buying is a blood diamond, does baby powder come from factories using child labor and so on. All increasingly important ESG (environmental, social, and governance) factors that are now in the spotlight and affecting the market capitalization of some of the largest corporate entities

DOI: 10.4324/9781003316077-27

around the globe. In this scenario, multi-stakeholders and user-driven digital global governance can facilitate democratization, decentralization, and ethical culture as well as practices that will influence governments, businesses, and the social sector. The key question is: how to regulate and monitor these evolving self-governing communities and networks?

Governance of Digital Platforms and Self-Driven User Communities

The difference comes down to how the technology is implemented. Increasingly, developer communities play a major role in making these technology choices. Because they often implement the technical architecture without any regulatory oversight, the responsibility of implementing governance models also tends to flow to them. This puts them in the position of having to make a difficult choice: either hand over the code and access to state actors or agree to put in place effective self-governance mechanisms themselves. Up until now, they have been staunchly opposed to state actors coming in to enforce the same. But there is a limited window of time available to them before civil society decides they are not able to effectively self-govern and regulation by the state is legally enforced. So far, most digital platforms have been able to stave away this eventuality with varying degrees of success.

In fact, while it may be tempting to look at the internet as the wild west where governance gets diluted, this may not be the reality. Just because digital technologies disrupt existing power structures in the governance world, this may not represent a descent into an anarchist abyss.

What we may instead be witnessing is a reset of how governance is defined and enforced in a digitally led world. It is now enabled by technology and enforced through data transparency and peer-review based self-governance.

From the viewpoint of a traditional regulator who carries the might of the state behind them for enforcement, the internet's way might seem like chaos. But somewhere, there is a method to this madness. The digital world essentially believes in peer and community-led establishment of standards as well as enforcement. It promotes an organic form of governance that happens in a very transparent manner, as opposed to the opaque processes of institutional regulators. It has naturally evolved to follow three clear steps.

1. The community decides what standards are to be maintained and documents the same publicly.
2. Peers agree on how those standards are to be enforced among themselves, in a democratic and transparent manner.
3. Technology kicks in as an enabling, automated force. And data transparency removes the scope for human subjectivity.

Human societies and indeed digital societies are very capable of self-governance. One example of this can be seen in the open-source movement that dominated tech discourse in the early 2000s. Until then, legally enforced software licensing was the norm governing usage rights in the tech world. Traditional thinking was that enterprise grade security and support was critical, R&D costs money, and hence commercial interests needed to be protected through regulatory licensing. Organizations such as Microsoft, Adobe, and Oracle built large revenue focused divisions whose only task was to discover license violations and legally enforce commercial contracts through punitive sanctions. An effective but highly adversarial process that divided users and vendors into opposing camps.

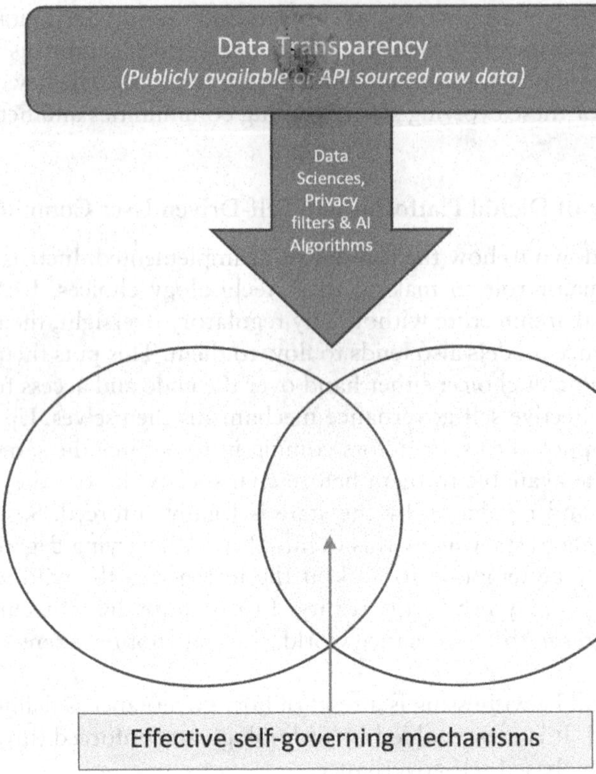

Figure 22.1 Open-Source Model for Effective Self-Governance
Source: Author.

However, the open-source model turned this entire licensing-based regulatory regime around on its head. It enabled a community-led development process where a strong peer group would now crowdsource the R&D through collaborative efforts, ensure peer-review-based governance, plug security leaks by essentially pitting hacker against hacker, and then put in place a revenue model based around support (tied to skills) rather than legal licensing enforced by a corporate entity.

This gave us an early and interesting insight into how various governance models could be implemented through peer-to-peer review and social agreements backed up by automation as opposed to traditional, institution-led enforcement models.

So how does a self-governing model differ from traditional governance models?

The Journey From Traditional to Digital Governance

Traditional models of governance, as defined by the United Nations, are centered around the cornerstones of transparency, responsibility, accountability, participation, and responsiveness.

Overcoming Institutional Control Bias: Governing the Commons

What we see in most traditional models is that they have a bias toward being enforced by institutions.

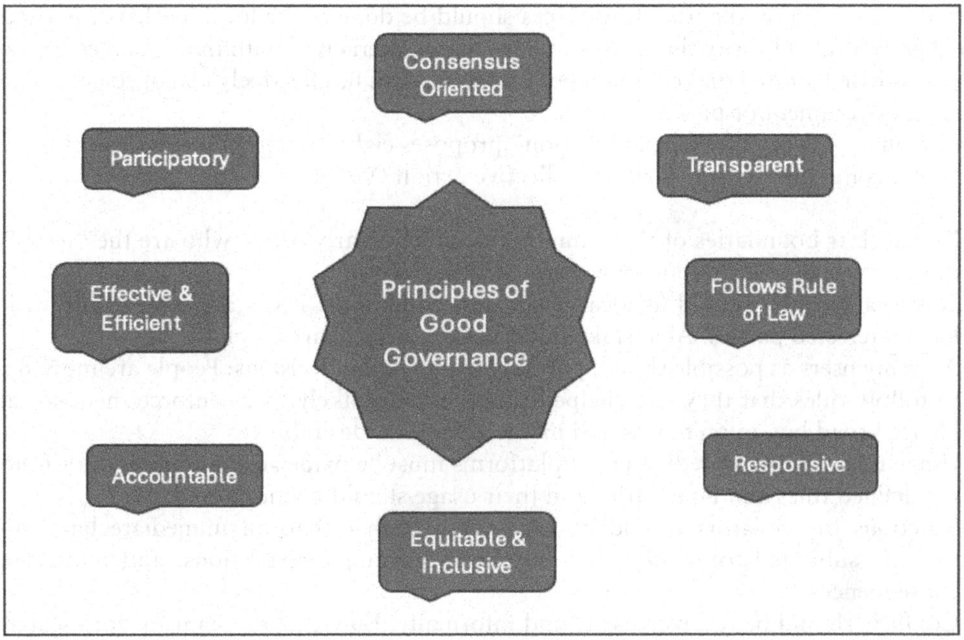

Figure 22.2 Principles of Good Governance
Source: *Governance and development (English)*. Washington, DC: World Bank Group (1992).

They assume that a "government" or some kind of institutional body is in charge, and they define how participants should behave, in order to implement good governance. This typically works well in a structured environment where it is clear who is the owner, or the entity responsible for good governance. It is also prone to abuse, as state actors who decide to go rogue typically have all the reins of power in their hands and can subvert the processes of governance to their own ends. Checks and balances are brought in through institutions and independent watchdogs as well as media but as we have seen in recent times, they can all be managed through the right strategies.

However, as we enter the complex and borderless world of digital interactions, it is often less clear as to who exactly is "in charge" and whose responsibility it is, to make sure that the principles of good governance are followed. For example, who decides what governance policies should be enforced on a content publishing platform based out of Lithuania, or indeed on TikTok that is often suspected to follow different governance practices in different parts of the world. Who will govern internet activity through a VPN that holds no logs and sweeps all traces of internet activity?

It is in this scenario that we are required to examine how alternate, peer-based governance models could work effectively.

Interesting insights into this can be seen in Nobel Laureate prof Elinor Ostrom's work on "Governing the Commons" (Ostrom 2015). If we consider the internet to be a common good that needs to be governed in a manner that everyone benefits from it, then many pieces of the puzzle start falling in place. Prof. Ostrom's theory postulates that local communities are best suited to manage their natural resources as they are the ones that use them, and that all regulation on the use of resources should be done at the local level, as opposed to a higher, central authority that does not have direct interaction with the resources. She successfully demonstrated that common pool resources can be effectively managed collectively, without government or private control.

Ostrom's "Theory of Collective Action" proposes eight principles for successful governance of a common resource through collective action (Williams 2018).

1. Define clear boundaries of the common resource: Clearly define who are the "users" of the various common resources within the digital world.
2. Governance rules should fit local needs and conditions: Rules are best determined by local interested parties. Aka, stakeholders and users of various platforms.
3. As many users as possible should participate in making decisions: People are more likely to follow rules that they have helped create and are likely to co-enforce them socially. Hence broad buy-in on norms and methodologies is desirable.
4. Usage must be monitored: Users of platforms must be made accountable for not following defined rules and boundaries and their usage should be monitored.
5. Sanctions for violators should be graduated: Rather than an immediate ban, violators are subjected to a graduated system of warnings, restrictions, and reputational consequences.
6. Conflicts should be resolved easily and informally: Low-cost mechanisms for escalation and dispute resolution that encourages compliance.
7. Higher-level authorities recognize the established rules of community governance: Governments or other territorial authorities should ideally recognize and back up, or at least not undermine collective action agreements and conflict resolution.
8. Common resource management should follow a bottom-up model: Responsibility for governing the larger digital space should start from users of the smallest platforms and assets and include the entire interconnected system.

Governance for the Digital-First Generation

While many of the above principles can be logically transposed to the digital world, it comes with its own set of needs and challenges. To begin with, we need to decode the difference between "networks" and "communities" in the digital world and define a community in a useful manner.

This is aptly captured in an HBR article by Henry Mintzberg that helps us differentiate between the two (Mitzberg 2015). In summary, he postulates that networks are groups of people who are joined together by common interests but not necessarily shared values. Communities on the other hand, are groups of people who really care about common issues and are willing to function as a whole for the greater good. So, for example, you may be part of a group called "Developments in Artificial Intelligence" on LinkedIn. Initially, it is just an informal network based on shared interests. Information gets exchanged and there are some discussions. Now suppose one of the members was unable to proceed on some seminal work because of an archaic government regulation that prohibits the same. If all the members of the group were to believe this was fundamentally wrong and came together to lobby with the government for a change or revision of this regulation, then it starts to behave like a genuine community that cares for both the sector and the individual member of the community. The impact is fundamentally different.

Effective self-governance mechanisms are best implemented by communities rather than informal networks, and it is important to differentiate between the two.

Step 1: Defining What Drives Digital Communities

If caring is what differentiates a community, then the logical step in identifying digital communities that can effectively self-govern would be to identify the value-system that drives them. Put more simply, what do they genuinely care about?

For example, when it comes to corporate and digital governance, modern digital communities typically care about the following:

- privacy and safeguarding of individual liberties
- data transparency
- diversity and Human values
- environmental safety (climate change, etc.)
- ethical sourcing
- equitable manufacturing processes
- financial probity, anti-corruption, etc.
- shareholder-friendly fiduciary behavior
- sensitive marketing

Can all the above standards be maintained through peer review and a shared incentives-based framework, rather than enforced by punitive state institutions? Yes, it can, however, the foundation needs to be laid through genuine data transparency.

Step 2: Enabling Effective Data Transparency

In order to translate a value-system into digital behavior, it helps to break things down into workflows. Once we ensure that there are little, if no secrets in the process of how we execute any of the defined workflows, then it is relatively easy to lead that toward transparent public reporting and peer-based enforcement of governance standards. These models may turn out to be even more robust than existing models in practice.

For example, a coffee brand may today claim to be "fair trade," but there is really no mechanism for the consumer to verify whether every single consignment comes from such sources. Corporates famously indulge in "show and don't tell" tactics, led by rampant symbolism that may not reflect the inner workings of the organization.

Now consider a scenario where there is blockchain-based tracking and real-time reporting of all procurement systems. Every supply-chain report is automatically logged to a peer-reviewed website without any human intervention in the process. The data is verified by a constantly shifting, volunteer-based group that cannot be influenced as it is never constant, nor predictable. This represents a near unbreakable governance model with no institutional or regulatory overload. On the other hand, higher value and revenue returns are available to the brand as this real-time auditing is constantly online for any consumer to verify, thus building credibility and brand equity.

This is not to say that the role of actors such as financial and regulatory auditors will be diminished. It may just become far more accessible. Today, most audit reports can only be understood by domain experts. Most often, the meaning is lost in translation to the lay man who struggles to understand the financial jargon, let alone be able to conduct anything approaching a deep dive analysis of the audit report. However, when we introduce a peer or AI-based review while throwing the data open to anyone who cares to look, it suddenly becomes far more difficult to couch sensitive information inside layers of jargon.

Technology then has a great role to play in disrupting and improving existing governance models.

Step 3: Use of Technology as an Enabling Factor

The question is, how will it be enabled? That depends on how much control traditional stakeholders such as corporates, institutions as well as the state are willing to cede. We live in a world today that is ensconced in cozy, mutually beneficial relationships between all actors, often at the cost of society at large. Unless there is a fair amount of democratic, consumer and shareholder pressure, change may come about very slowly indeed. However, these same actors may soon have no choice but to embrace digital disruption in governance because we are increasingly transnational in every context. We now need to be held to global standards in a world of buy anywhere, manufacture anywhere, sell anywhere, and live anywhere (including virtual spaces). So governance standards will necessarily need to be set to meet the highest common denominator, irrespective of how lax the regulatory mechanisms of individual countries or societies may be.

Three Fundamental Cornerstones of Peer-Led Governance Models

There are three factors that are critical to success while designing a digital-first, peer-review-based governance model:

1. availability and transparency of data
2. level of automation and the use of AI in associated workflows
3. neutrality and depth of engagement by the human capital that is examining the inferences.

Variable 1: Data Availability and Transparency

Data is the lifeblood of digital governance. It flows through everything and keeps everything ticking. Hence the process of defining what kind of data will be available and to whom, becomes critical in the governance process. Largely, data can be divided into the following pools:

- confidential data that has competitive/security implications and needs to be rigorously guarded.
- public data that is defined to be accessible to all, as per policy.
- internal data that may not be revealed in its raw form but is allowed to be accessed anonymously by AI and automation engines, to draw inferences.

The first two pools of data are relatively easy to handle as their management is a simple matter of gatekeeping versus access. However, the third pool of data is most challenging It requires significant investments into secure data warehousing, mining, masking, and AI. So the question of who will bear the cost of using it and maintaining it for governance

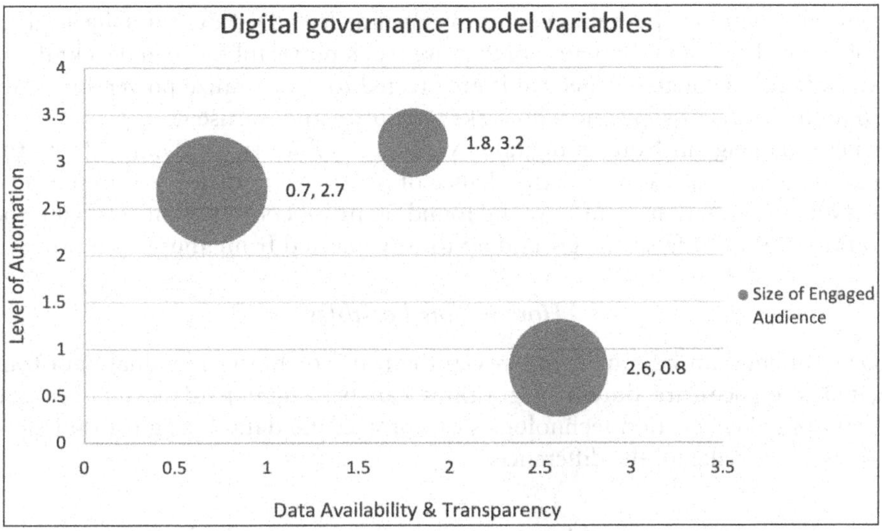

Figure 22.3 The Various Steps of Defining New Digital Governance Systems
Source: Author.

systems comes up. Luckily, increasing deployment of cloud-based automation and AI are driving the costs down significantly. The day may not be far when data streams flowing into cloud-based governance workflows may function pretty much like utilities that are paid for as services, by those who desire to utilize the same. A good example of this is the use of "Adhaar" in India—a central database for identity verification that is accessed seamlessly by all stakeholders and improves the efficiency of KYC verification tremendously.

Of course, such widespread use of data to drive governance comes with its own set of risks around privacy concerns, data leaks, and ethical questions around where the data is coming from, and do the originators have a say around how their data is used. For example, should a poor country that allows children to work from the age of twelve, have to reveal how many teen workers are employed in their garment factories and is it fair for that data to be then used against them by societies who judge this to be wrong? Should the data of an illegal immigrant who works on an assembly line be available to immigration services who serve a subpoena on a data bank to reveal the same? Should data about which people oppose a specific government policy be available to the very governments who are invested into rolling out those policies? If no, then how is the data going to be architected in a manner where certain aspects of it just cannot be accessed, even under duress? How are privacy features going to be baked into the very digital processes that use them, such that it becomes humanly difficult to abuse the same data?

Variable 2: Automation and AI in Making Sense of the Data

Data may be the fuel, but the real engine of governance in a digital world is the increasingly sophisticated array of AI and automation engines that drive a level of intelligence that can surpass the average human mind. We are producing over 2.5 quintillion bytes of data every day, and this is only set to rise exponentially. Such a huge overload of information is pretty much unusable without the right engines to consume it and produce intelligent inferences. The problem is that a superhuman tool that uses such powerful fuel can be a knife that cuts both ways. It can be hugely beneficial if architected to decentralize power, or a dangerous weapon in the hands of someone who seeks to control and misuse it.

The new challenge in front of digital governance architects will be the ability to design these intersections in a way where the chance of abuse is minimized within the very architecture. Not very different from how the founding members of nations thought about the constitution. Designed from the ground up to be protected from abuse by future actors.

How Is This Possible?

Intelligent systems can be taught to "sweep the trail" or burn individual data trails after aggregated inferences are drawn. Algorithms can be taught to depersonalize data, and blockchain-based encryption technologies can protect the data during transmission. Intelligent design can make all the difference.

Variable 3: Depth of Engagement or Participation by User Groups

As seen before, the problem with self-governing peer circles is that human beings tend to voluntarily engage only with what they are interested in and act only when they care. This does not represent a challenge in governance scenarios where they have an individual personal outcome at stake and there are established governance frameworks: for example, monitoring the financial data of a corporate that one is invested into, or how the tenders are being awarded in a contract where public money is being used, etc. However, it becomes less predictable when the community does not clearly see the link to individual outcomes and does not have sufficient experience with crafting self-governing models where effective frameworks do not already exist.

One scenario where this plays out is when governance standards need to be maintained through periods of significant disruption and change. Often, the stakeholders themselves may be changing and the new entrants haven't plugged into a workable governance framework. Let us take the case of delivery workers on food apps who are replacing traditional restaurant workers or maybe Uber drivers who are replacing traditional cab drivers. Both taxi unions and restaurant workers represent extremely regulated and highly governed segments that are getting disrupted by technology. With the entry of new aggregators who consider themselves mere "facilitators," the old regulations are pretty much meaningless as the nature of key stakeholders has changed overnight. A whole new community is forming around the disrupted model and what we see is that initially governance standards tend to drop and become exploitative in the short run. Simply because the new communities of food delivery agents and Uber drivers have not yet had the time to organize, engage with civil society and start influencing the governance of the corporations that employ or facilitate them. Even if the data and the peer-driven models to enforce governance exist theoretically, there simply isn't an organized and effective community that is capable of driving governance.

On the other hand, once the rate of participation becomes high, it becomes easier to avert scenarios where individual actors exploit low maturity communities. In the digital world, the knowledge of this happening comes up quickly to everyone in the peer network. Allowing for quick and flexible framing of usage guidelines that prevents such exploitation.

Good Governance in the Digital Age

The central question is: How does one go about designing good governance models in the Digital Age?

Like everything else in the digitally disrupted world, it would be an error to assume that the technology is just a new channel to access old systems. Instead, all existing governance processes will need to be broken down into granular detail and redesigned from the ground up. This is likely to involve foundational changes.

In short, governance in a digital world cannot just be a front-end "interface" change.

The abiding feature of digitalization is disruption and hence the need to rework and reimagine processes completely. By design, it should not be about enabling new user interfaces to old systems. This will distinguish good from bad in an era of digitally enabled governance systems.

The critical sequential steps in defining the new digital governance system are explored below.

1. Identification of specific workflows within larger governance processes:
   Following the principle of structuring governance frameworks from the bottom-up, it often makes sense to identify the subprocesses or workflows within a governance process. For example, if we were to consider a common scenario where content is uploaded onto publishing platforms such as Instagram and twitter, there could be the following subprocesses at play:
- reliable identification and KYC of the user (aka the registration and login workflow);
- content upload process;
- internal review and publishing mechanism;
- peer-/consumer-review and escalations;
- secondary review and execution of defined actions.

   The stakeholders for each of the workflows may vary, and hence, it becomes important to define the governance policy and steps within each workflow and then tie it up to the larger governance framework.
2. Objectives alignment between owners and stakeholders as to what improvements and automation may be desirable in those workflows:
   In the same example, the following happens:
- Content producers would typically want faster uploads and lesser review lead times in the publishing process.
- Platform owners would value least use of resources and overheads in the internal review process, while allowing content that allows for the most engagement without exposing themselves to legal consequences or a social backlash.
- Consumers would want the ability to quickly flag undesirable content and have their feedback evaluated, based on defined norms.

   In order to bring alignment between all three parties, technology would need to design a highly responsive system that operates seamlessly, with a high degree of neutrality and objectivity. Functioning in a manner that is predictable, consistent, and acceptable to most participants of the community.
3. Breaking down those workflows into individual components and checkpoints, plus identification of stakeholders for every checkpoint:
   As one has seen recently with the allegation of thought policing on platforms such as Twitter, a simple workflow like the internal review and publishing process can quickly

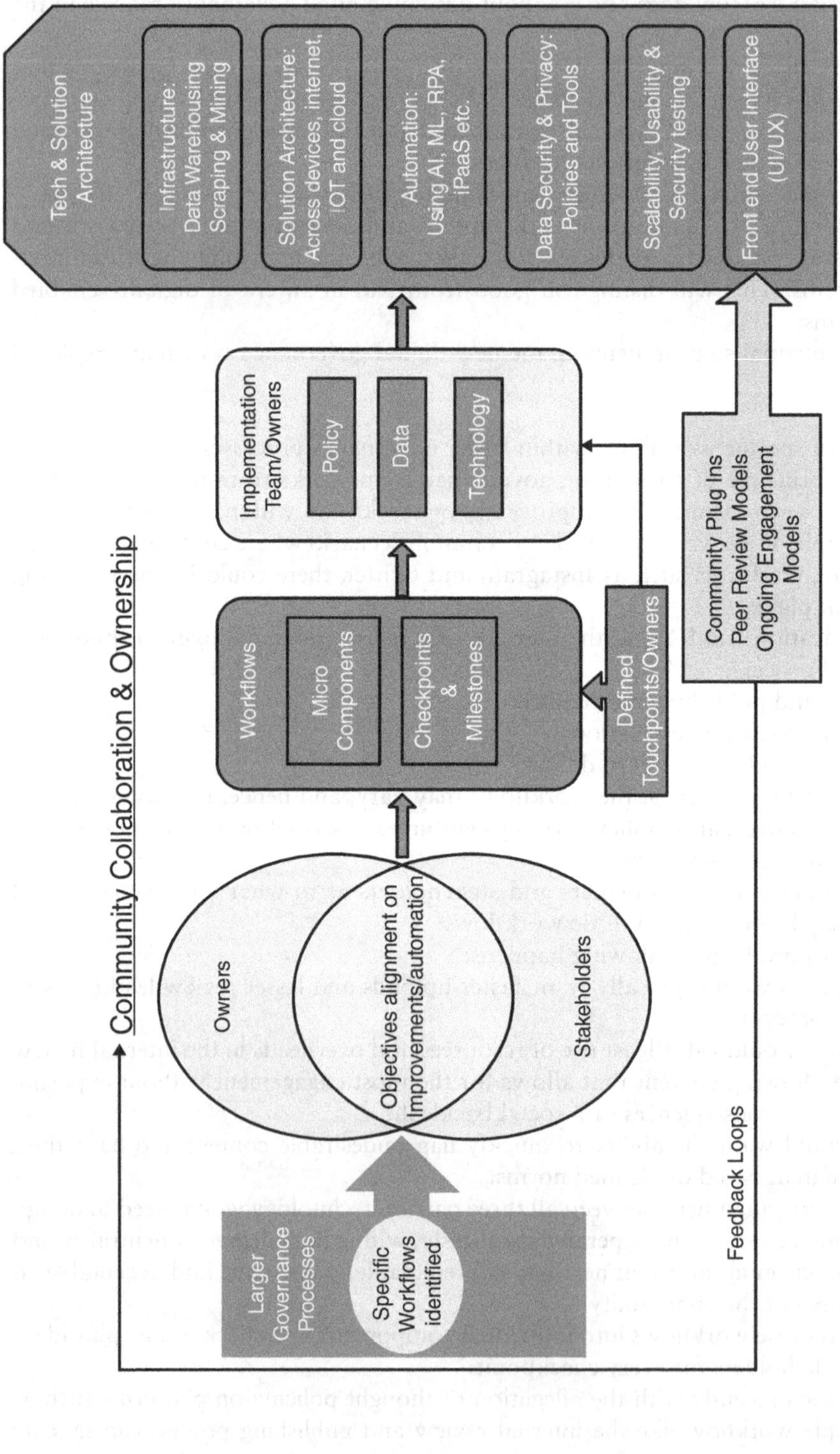

Figure 22.4 Peer-Led Governance Model
Source: Author.

become complex. How much of a say does an internal review team have over what is acceptable? Who defines these norms? Does the content producer get to have a say and furnish his opinion? How does the peer community get to have a say, given that the content may not even get to the peer-review stage? Is there a truly neutral escalation mechanism?

As we have seen in the case of Twitter, trying to simplify this could even lead to stakeholders doing away with internal review mechanisms, which are bound to be subjective and slow execution and engagement down. Unfortunately, we then open ourselves up to a lot of debatable content getting published and widely consumed before peer reviews can flag them. In some cases, this may result in majoritarian excess or deeply divided factions that spew hate at each other. Granular stakeholder identification and graded ownership and responsibility assigned at every level is the only way to get around these complexities.

4. Crafting implementation teams with the right mix of policy, data, and technology owners:

   It is not just enough to know the right governance rules and processes to be followed, but in the digital world one has to ensure that data in usable formats is available for timely decision-making and the technology architecture has been designed to be able to leverage that data, feed it to the right owners and tools, and facilitate the actions that need to be carried out in real time. If a clear alignment between these three areas does not exist, we end up with scenarios where the intention is right, but the execution is flawed.

   For example, we may decide to shorten the internal publishing review process by using an AI engine to check for "offensive" keywords or sentences in proposed content. Or we may use visual data recognition patterns to identify nudity in videos, but that has resulted in situations where images of breastfeeding were deemed offensive and blocked by the AI tool, only to result in a major backlash from the user community that found it permissible. So, the ability to align what the governance policy should be, with effective use of data and technology to facilitate the same, falls on the shoulders of the implementation teams that bring these domains together.

5. Defining the enabling technical architecture by getting the team to examine how every component of the workflow can fit seamlessly into a larger technology workflow:

   The overall technical architecture is really where the rubber hits the road, as it defines how effectively the various processes, tools and stakeholders engage in an efficient manner to ensure effective governance.

- The Data Warehouse forms the foundation of any good technical architecture. We begin by asking questions such as where it will be housed and securely accessed from, what kind of mining tools and what degree of access will be permitted and to whom, what privacy and anonymizing filters will be implemented at the raw data level, and how will the raw data be protected.
- A solution architecture would need to be designed that integrates workflows across devices, internet, IOT and cloud infrastructure, etc.
- Identification of the right set of Automation tools using AI, ML, RPA, iPaaS, and so on, such that human subjectivity is kept to a minimum and efficiency, scalability, and consistency are maintained.
- A cyber security framework that allows for rigorous testing for security vulnerabilities, usability, and scalable architecture. Typically, one that integrates peer review and vulnerability tracking as well as bug fixes into the core philosophy.
- Defined data privacy policies that are encoded into the tech architecture, with no back doors and with automated policies on erasing trails and anonymizing data.

- The front end is usually where user communities engage with and plug into the technology stack. It then becomes very critical to design the User Interfaces (UIs) and User Experience (Ux) in a way that ensures seamless community participation in peer-review models, while promoting a high level of engagement at the same time.
- Finally, the roll out and feedback loops need to be crafted into a virtuous cycle that allows for free exchange of ideas, while trapping bad actors at an early stage.

Conclusion

Designing truly egalitarian self-governing systems that are sustainable, objective, efficient, and safe in the digital space is a highly complex process. They typically work best when designed as intelligent systems that learn, flex, integrate, and improve as they go—in turn, reaching very high levels of efficiency over time. In many ways, this process follows the same philosophy of AI and self-learning systems. Rather than trying to get it perfect the very first time, it makes sense to design the system in a way that it can learn from the gaps and error corrections that come along and can integrate those learnings and keep refining the governance model as the framework matures. The key variable in this equation is constant change regarding what is deemed as acceptable to the community, at different points of time. And that is where it becomes important to plug peer inputs and reviews into the policy layer, which is then brought to life through the technology architecture, into the digital world.

Key Discussion Areas

- Traditional governance to digital governance transformations.
- Peer-to-peer governance.
- Self-driven digital communities and networks.
- Governing the commons and theory of collective action.
- Digital democratization.

References

De Filippi, Primavera, and Benjamin Loveluck. 2016. "The Invisible Politics of Bitcoin: Governance Crisis of a Decentralised Infrastructure." *Internet Policy Review* 5(3), https://doi.org/10.14763/2016.3.427.

Governance and development (English). 1992. Washington, DC: World Bank Group. http://documents.worldbank.org/curated/en/604951468739447676/Governance-and-development

Mitzberg, Henry, 2015. "We Need Both Networks and Communities." *Harvard Business Review online*, https://hbr.org/2015/10/we-need-both-networks-and-communities

Ostrom, Elinor. 2015. *Governing the Commons: The Evolution of Institutions for Collective Action*. Cambridge: Cambridge University Press.

Williams, Jeremy. 2018. "Elinor Ostrom's 8 Rules for Managing the Commons." *Earthbound Report*, January 15, 2018, https://earthbound.report/2018/01/15/elinor-ostroms-8-rules-for-managing-the-commons/ (accessed August 1, 2023).

23

THE CASE FOR DATA AS A NEW COMMON GOOD

The Example of Water

Jaya Deshmukh and Alessandro Galtieri

Introduction: Data as Water

Data is the new rivers of our society. Well-managed water, with thought-through, empathetic water-sharing agreements across countries for lakes and rivers, robustly engineered dams, locks and canals, and environment-friendly rules and regulations, can unlock incredible value for a single citizen and entire nations alike—so too can well-governed data bring abundance and security for everyone.

Data has frequently been dubbed "the new oil." We feel that the analogy is wrong and that data is in fact the new water:

- Oil was created once and can be exploited only once, while data can be used multiple times.
- Data can also be regenerated, taking new forms.
- Data, now more than oil, is vital to the digital economy.
- Value is created in data flows rather than static assets.
- Future wars will be about access and fair exploitation of water and data, not just oil.

At the foundation of this approach is the recognition that data is not just about economic value but also potentially a human right issue and an economic development lever, and that data processing and management entail both positive and negative externalities.

We think that data needs to be recognized as a common good. To further the water analogy: there is already an existing body of rules and precedents about governance of water in international law, as water has been recognized as a common good for centuries. However, this set of rules is based on state-focused laws and precedents, and there is no equivalent coherent private law framework. Some principles exist in most jurisdictions: for instance, you can own a river or a lake, but when the water leaves your land, it is no longer yours. You could build a dam—but then the utility of water decreases, crucially for everyone, including you. The value of water—like data—is due to the fact that it circulates.

Every interaction with actors and different data sets is a chance to make data more valuable, but the difficult part is to identify which part of data adds value, much like how each

DOI: 10.4324/9781003316077-28

individual drop of rain increases a river, but it is difficult to quantify/identify. Our current legal and governance rules have attempted to identify the "owners" of all components of a data set (all the droplets), but this is not a scalable solution and it does not necessarily result in economic value for the owner and certainly not in an increased, optimized use of the data set.

If we were to use the current water management solutions for data, we would identify the relevant actors, pay (or charge) them a fair share, and then agree that data just naturally flows throughout. In this waste management solution process, the role of telecommunications operators (such as Colt) is to ensure data integrity (that the water is drinkable) and transparency (where data comes from and, if requested by the authorities, what the content is).

So, if we see data as water, as a shared resource, the questions become less about ownership and more about economic exploitation and fair use. Alternative models that try to assign ownership of individual data points and track their usage to charge it have been proposed but have all proven unrealistic.

It is therefore important to discuss data "stewardship." Data governance is vital, as the economic exploitation is less relevant than the correct or incorrect use of the resource. To a certain extent, the ownership of the share in a company is less relevant than the good governance of the company: bad governance and stewardship can create economic benefits for some (e.g., the shareholders), but at the same time, they will significantly damage the interest of other larger group of stakeholders (employees, suppliers, local communities), which cannot be seen or remedied just in monetary terms. Managing water well will require good governance structure, culture, processes and accountability for being responsive to all stakeholders and users. This model can be used for data flows as well.

We maintain that the best way to categorize data is as a common good, or common. The economic definition of common is any unregulated-access resource, such as air, rivers, and the sea (and the fish stock it contains). In a legal context, it has held the meaning of being neither private nor public property, but rather held jointly by the members of a community.

Economic theory has long held that common goods cannot be properly managed. The expression "tragedy of the commons" (Hardin 1968) is used to describe a situation in which individual users with open access to a resource, and with no formal rules that govern access and exploitation, will act independently and exclusively according to their own self-interest and, contrary to the common good of all users, will cause depletion of the resource through their uncoordinated action. Overfishing, for example, results in the depletion of fishing stocks.

We now know that this is not true (see Feeny et al. 1990). The stewardship of common resources can sometimes protect and enhance the common resource instead of depleting it. Common grazing land for the livestock, shared water and irrigation systems, health care for all are good example of stewardship. Thus, the stewardship of data commons is a valuable option that deserves serious consideration.

The Data Life Cycle

Data is increasingly generated from billions of internet-connected devices (known as the Internet of Things). It is the record of any kind of transactions, including financial ones, and has exploded in volume in the last decade. This explosion allows for new opportunities to

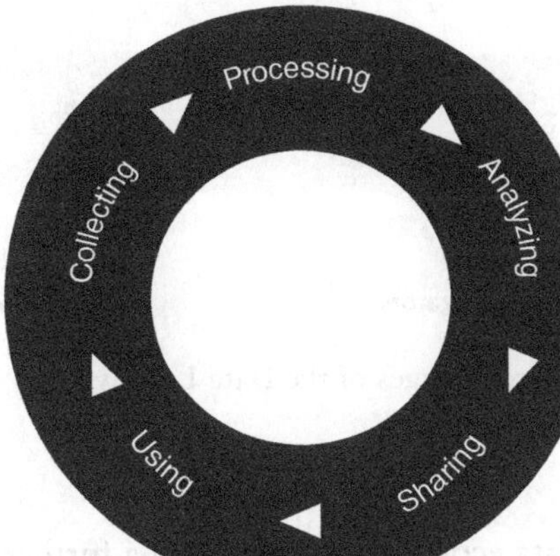

Figure 23.1 Life Cycle of Data

Source: Authors.

utilize data to tackle complex problems but has also created new risks related to privacy, surveillance, and data concentration.

Importantly, data is not itself a simple asset but rather the result of a process known as the data life cycle. This data life cycle is composed of five distinct stages, as shown in Figure 23.1.

- Collecting: The data practitioner gathers data from a wide variety of sources, such as internet-connect devices, but also surveys, censuses, business operations, web-based collections, and other sources.
- Processing: The data practitioner cleans the data to make it usable. Processing can entail removing irrelevant or inaccurate information, reformatting content to be usable by a different system or software, or validating the data.
- Sharing: The data practitioner accesses the collected and processed data with other practitioners with the intent of deriving insights from it. This step is optional and often skipped, but doing so significantly limits the potential utility of data.
- Analyzing: The data practitioner assesses and interprets the data collection with a goal of extracting insights.
- Using: Finally, this data practitioner acts on the insights derived.

All these actions may affect data collected for future processing. All processing therefore needs to be considered with the potential for *data reuse.*

The Data Players

The different stages of the data life cycle can be carried out by a single organization, but this is increasingly unlikely. Typically, a large variety of data actors are involved in the different stages of a single data set (see Figure 23.2)—and then that data set can be combined with other data sets and be the object of further processing.

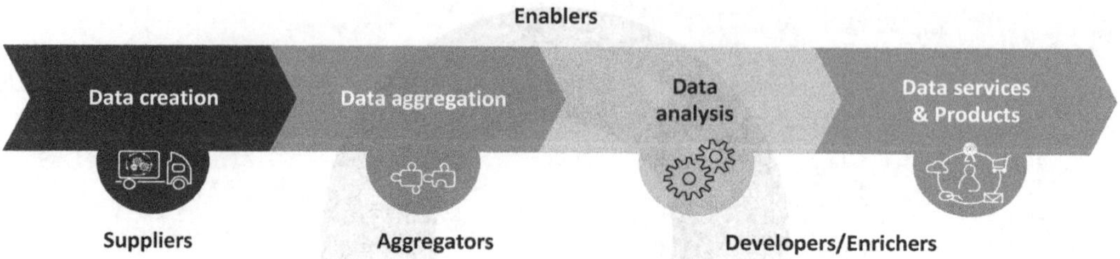

Figure 23.2 Data Actors in Different Stages of the Data Life Cycle
Source: Authors.

The development of the data economy has provided a further stimulus to the emergence of the infomediary sector, in which companies analyze and process information from the public and/or private sector to create value-added products for third parties or the public, thus building a business model around the linkages in the data value chain.

The Data Infrastructure

We can distinguish broadly between soft and hard data infrastructure—both are essential, and access to either is crucial to all data actors and broadly for all of society. Soft data infrastructure consists of

- data assets such as data sets, identifiers, and registers;
- the standards and technologies used to curate and provide access to those data assets;
- the policies that inform the use and management of data assets;
- the organizations that govern the data infrastructure.

Hard data infrastructure consists of the whole of the interconnected networks, cloud solution, public and private data sets, all the accessible data storage platforms/systems/facilities that can be shared. In this ecosystem, network operators have a crucial role to play, as custodians of the data and facilitators of the vital data flows. Increasingly, with the blurred distinction between large, hyper-scale data center facilities and edge computing, as well as the constant data flows from the Internet of Things, it can be maintained that network infrastructure is an integral part of the global cloud.

The challenges, as per the management of water, are clear on

- how to fund data infrastructure as a public good, as it may need large investments;
- how to incentivise investment in shared data and ensure that the benefits are distributed fairly;
- how to compensate the data stewards;
- how to process personal data to gain value from it while respecting data protection rules;
- how to keep options open for potential future uses of data.

If these challenges are not tackled, data might not be accessible to those who need it, due to organizations hoarding all the data they've collected (or purchased). In this scenario, data is treated like oil, which will severely limit the wider value of data. Data concentration

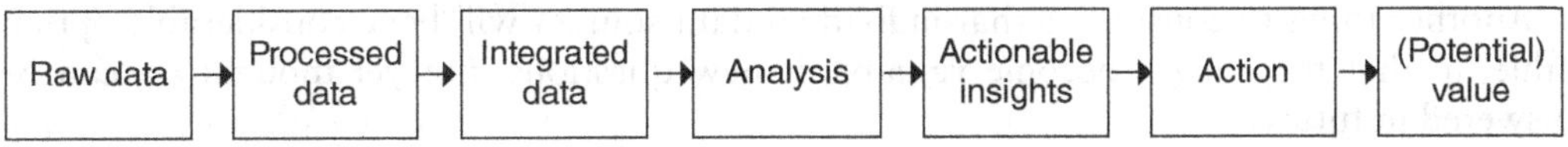

Figure 23.3 Data Flow

Source: Mawer 2015.

has already been found to be harmful to competition and to hinder innovation and growth (HM Treasury 2019). The Open Data Institute (ODI Strategy 2018–2022, theodi.org) identified another scenario related to fragile trust—in where data might not be collected or used to the extent it could be, due to unaddressed concerns about the harm that data might cause people and communities. They call this scenario the "wasteland," where a lack of consideration of ethics, equity, and engagement prevents society exploiting data in ways that could support human flourishing.

The ultimate aim of data collection should therefore be to ensure that there is as much creation of value as possible from data, and that it is shared widely in society. We need to define economic value broadly, from a holistic perspective of value to the whole society, not solely on commercial value to the data actors. In fact, by focusing on data *flows*, the value of data can be captured as shown in Figure 23.3.

The important thing is to concentrate less on who "owns" the content of the boxes, and more on the possibilities for many actors to be allowed to be part of the flows indicated by the arrows—by having access to the data flows.

We make reference to current initiatives in Open Data as examples of this broader vision of data utilization and exploitation, but it is not our intention to argue for that particular model as the only paradigm for the use of data. However, there is a value in exploring such open models, in that they present aspects that replicate some of the resource management solutions that humankind has already successfully deployed for other resources, such as water.

The Economic Value of Data: The Limitations of the Current Approach

The economics of data are still being investigated; for instance, in February 2020, data was evaluated as having a value of €830 billion in the EU alone (European Commission 2020). This is likely to be an underestimation.

First of all, many of the available studies use market valuations or transactions as the basis for estimating the value of data (Nguyen and Paczos 2019). By definition, these valuations exclude externalities (positive and negative) as well as complementarities and other effects. Considering exclusively data markets as a basis for policy leaves a certain amount of value "on the table"—for instance, the additional value that could be derived from enhanced access to enable additional uses, or the additional value from being able to combine different data sets (Coyle et al. 2020).

Also, unlike many conventional goods or assets, many people can use the same data at the same time without it being depleted. So while data is a public good or a common good, it is also a shared—club good when access to it is excluded by technical and/or legal means (to the members of that particular "club"). Data is therefore shared to varying degrees, and the traditional categories of ownership or transaction do not apply to it very easily.

Another thing to consider is that individual data sources will have considerable option value, in that they might become valuable if new questions, not yet thought of, can be answered in future.

Many of the organizations accumulating data have been doing so because of data's potential rather than actual uses. This has led to the huge concentration of, among others, personal data in the hands of a few global tech companies. At least in some countries, this is not lawful—the EU's General Data Protection Regulation (GDPR) legislation rules out the accumulation of individuals' data for anything other than specified purposes for which it has been collected. This approach is respectful of the individuals' rights and is clearly designed to prevent negative externalities for the individuals in the form of data breaches (illegitimate use of such data without consent).

This approach, however, may significantly obstruct innovation; significant innovations usually derive from new questions to the same data set, rather than new answers to old questions. While the GDPR legislation does not formally require individuals' permission to be sought for any new use of their data, many data actors are currently taking an overly cautious approach. The question is therefore how to handle the risks of asking all these owners of reservoirs to allow new, larger data lakes to be created for common (public and private) good. What kind of data policies will be critical for self-regulation? How to protect privacy without taking away access to data?

Some data actors, of course, are not keeping data private only out of caution for possible regulatory consequences—they want to extract maximum economic value from it. One of the concerns about the data economy is that big incumbent tech companies might continue to capture—as private profit—a large proportion of the value being created. Preventing such companies from hoarding/exploiting data to provide value-added services has proven difficult and could be counterproductive.

One way of bringing about a fairer distribution of the economic welfare created by data use would be the direct approach of using competition policy to open the data-driven markets to other providers. This requires rule-makers and regulators to think about who may benefit from different types of data, and about the potential public good that could be generated. Otherwise, in the absence of an appropriate redistributive policy framework, the benefits are likely to be distributed unequally.

There are also other considerations that have been raised (Coyle et al. 2020):

- The value of data is potentially limitless but hard to quantify. Societies that find ways to unlock the value of data and distribute it fairly will be at an advantage.
- None of the current data valuation methods is effective, but that doesn't mean data has no value. The value of data is realized in how it is used, and dependent on context.
- It is restrictive to think about policy just in terms of personal data. A lot of the wider value to society comes from aggregating data.
- We don't know how data might be used in the future, so policy-makers and researchers should avoid creating conditions that might limit its use.

Access to data is crucial to its value. The more accessible data is, the greater is its social worth, subject of course to the risk and investment considerations we mentioned. Restricting access to data limits who can use it to develop a product or service, and who can use it to make decisions. We argue therefore that trustworthy data institutions (such as data trusts) could help increase access to data.

Data access highlights the broader point that the regulatory environment changes market valuations. The market transactions currently observed are not capturing a fundamental reality; rather, the market value of data is endogenous, depending on policy choices. There are likely to be many trade-offs between creating private incentives to invest in collecting and using data and capturing social benefits. The value of data will depend on the societal trade-offs, analogous to those in the domain of intellectual property, in which there is a trade-off between the private incentive to invest in innovation created by the temporary monopoly provided by patent or copyright, and the social benefit of ensuring wide access to innovations as quickly as possible. Investment in Covid-19 vaccine research and dissemination is an example of private incentives for the larger public good.

The Open Data Movement and Its Benefits

A possible model for the future of data is the Open Data framework (see Figure 23.4). There are different definitions of what constitutes a real open data ecosystem—for the purposes of this discussion, we define open data as publicly available data that can be universally and readily accessed, used, and redistributed free of charge. The format is also important: open data must be structured for usability and computability.

It could also be argued that data exists on a spectrum, as shown in Figure 23.5 across public to private spheres.

On a global level, initiatives such as the Open Data Barometer[1] and the OECD Government at a Glance (OECD 2017) assess the impact of Open Data.

The private sector not only reuses Open Data published by the public sector but also generates and collects additional valuable data, which has the potential to become Open Data if it is allowed to "re-flow" back into the public domain. There is growing evidence about the economic value of privately held data, which is of public interest.

Over the past years, while many governments have accelerated their Open Data initiative, the momentum toward private data sharing has increased as well.

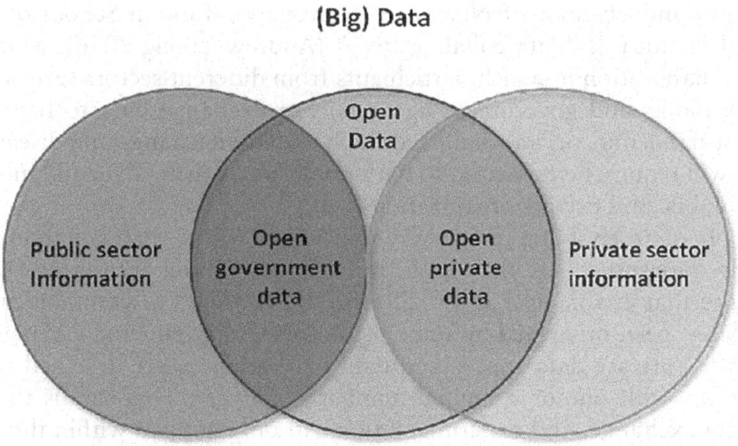

Figure 23.4 Open Data Framework

Source: Authors.

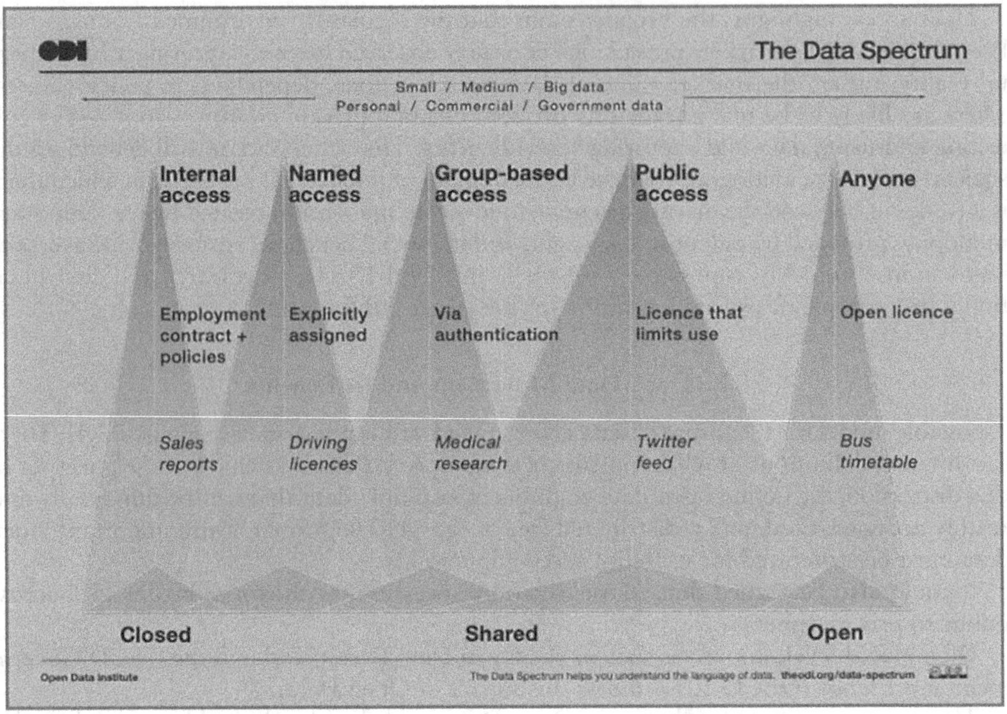

Figure 23.5 The Data Spectrum

Source: Open Data Institute.

Initiatives such as the Open Company Index[2] stimulate companies to open up their data. In the European Union, the Big Data Value Public–Private Partnership[3] and further initiatives look at the potential of privately held real-time data and big data.[4]

The GovLab, and offshoot of New York University's Tandon School of Engineering, had pioneered the idea of "data collaboratives" (Andrew Young 2016), which refers to a new form of collaboration in which participants from different sectors (private companies, research institutions, and government agencies) can exchange data to help solve public problems. Post-pandemic, ocietal challenges such as climate change and disease prevention and response will require better access to both public and private data and more collaboration between public and private organizations.

One example of an enabling technology that would allow such collaboration—whose use is already widespread—is the Application Programming Interfaces (APIs), the set of defined rules that enable and allow different applications to communicate with each other—which has been privileged by some regulators (Borgogno and Colangelo 2018). In contrast to APIs, private data spaces and data marketplaces are designed for individual data transactions with one or a limited number of buyers. This entails that a (limited) amount of data exchange, and experimentation can only happen within those spaces and marketplaces.

As we mentioned above, the high cost of data acquisition has deterred many actors from sharing data and creating a sustainable ecosystem for data reuse. There are a few examples where this has been mandated by public authorities, such as the Payment Services Directive in the European Union, which mandates banks to open their data sets. This has enabled the birth of a large number of new actors and "challenger" banks, arguably generating value for both these private actors, their users/customers, and increasing the efficiency and the transparency of the whole banking system. There are also examples, albeit rarer, of private companies spontaneously sharing their data sets, such as Tesla's strategy for open innovation that includes sharing its patent portfolio (Musk 2014). The European Union has some recommendations to increase data reuse (EuDEco 2018), and to facilitate business-to-government data sharing (European Commission, Directorate-General for Communications Networks, Content and Technology 2021). There are also a number of other data collaboration initiatives, including public–private partnerships.[5]

There is also a potentially transformational value in promoting and using open data in developing economies (Verhulst and Young 2017). A number of examples show that doing so is beneficial across the world, providing a strong case for the social value of data. An effort by the government of Namibia to eradicate malaria with the use of satellite and cell phone data is a salient public health example. Researchers were able to draw maps of environmental factors like vegetation density, population, and rainfall that affect mosquito and parasite populations and the likelihood of transmission and identify areas where citizens were at high-risk. Mobile phone data provided by Namibia's largest telecommunications provider assisted researchers to track human movement—and thus the spread of malaria.[6] This is also discussed well in Part 1 of this handbook that focus on digital transformation in international development.

In the field of education, the "Mejora Tu Escuela" initiative in Mexico, founded by the Mexican Institute for Competitiveness, is an online platform that provides citizens with information about school performance, helping parents choose the best option for their children and providing tools to get involved in their children's schooling. It also provides school administrators, policy-makers, and NGOs with data to identify areas that require improvement. Some of the data used to create the Mejora platform was also instrumental in identifying corruption in the education sector and targeting public outrage regarding "phantom" teachers on school payrolls, unchecked teacher absenteeism, and misappropriated funds, among other issues (Davies et al. 2019).

Open data in itself is of course not a panacea that can solve all problems without political or civic engagement. A case study is the Electricity Supply Monitoring Initiative in India. The poor quality of energy infrastructure in parts of India results in frequent shortages, blackouts, and interruptions. As there is no publicly available data on the energy supply issues, the Electricity Supply Monitoring Initiative (ESMI) was launched in 2014 by the Pune-based nonprofit Prayas Energy Group. ESMI collects information from cities across 200 locations in India through devices installed in key sites to record voltage data, which log this information with a central server (Prayas, Energy Group 2019). This data is then made publicly available through the website watchyourpower.org, where users can monitor their power supply and compare this with other regions. ESMI data shows that rural areas experience four to five times more power disruptions than cities or districts, highlighting important evidence about the Indian power supply. Whether this evidence will create meaningful change remains dependent on an institutional willingness to act on the insights generated.

An initiative called "open development" is designed as a networked and innovative pathway to improving international aid and development efforts. The International

Development Research Centre (IDRC) identifies a number of key elements present in open development work, including

- the power of human cooperation;
- shared ideas and knowledge;
- the ability to reuse, revise and repurpose content;
- increased transparency of processes;
- expanded participation;
- collaborative production.

The central idea behind open development is "harnessing the increased penetration of information and communications technologies to create new organizational forms that improve the lives of people" (Longshore Smith and Reilly 2013). This would include user-driven shared-governance approaches.

The analysis of academic literature also seems to show that open data can contain true opportunities for development involving multiple stakeholders (Hilbert 2015).

In addition, private actors have a role to play in the development of open data sets. Overall, there are several reasons why the private sector should share their data (at least to a certain degree), and they can be grouped into three categories:

- Business development and efficiency
  - to sell data-related services
  - to help supply-chain partners
  - to crowdsource solutions
  - to create a platform for engagement with customers and talent
- Legal and regulatory:
  - to comply with legal or regulatory obligations
  - to demonstrate compliance, for instance regarding sourcing, sustainability, transparency, and anti-corruption measures
- Collaboration and reputation:
  - to support public–private partnerships
  - to support collaborative innovation
  - to build trust and improve reputation

Data Institutions

One model that has been proposed is that of data institutions, which already play significant roles in the data ecosystem in the United Kingdom (see Figure 23.6). Data institutions may

- hold data on behalf of an organization or person, or group of them, and share it with others who want to use it for a particular purpose. UK Biobank,[7] for example, was set up in 2006 to steward genetic data and samples from around half a million people for health research;
- combine or link data from different sources and provide insights and other services back to those that have contributed data; in the maritime sector, HiLo[8] takes data generated

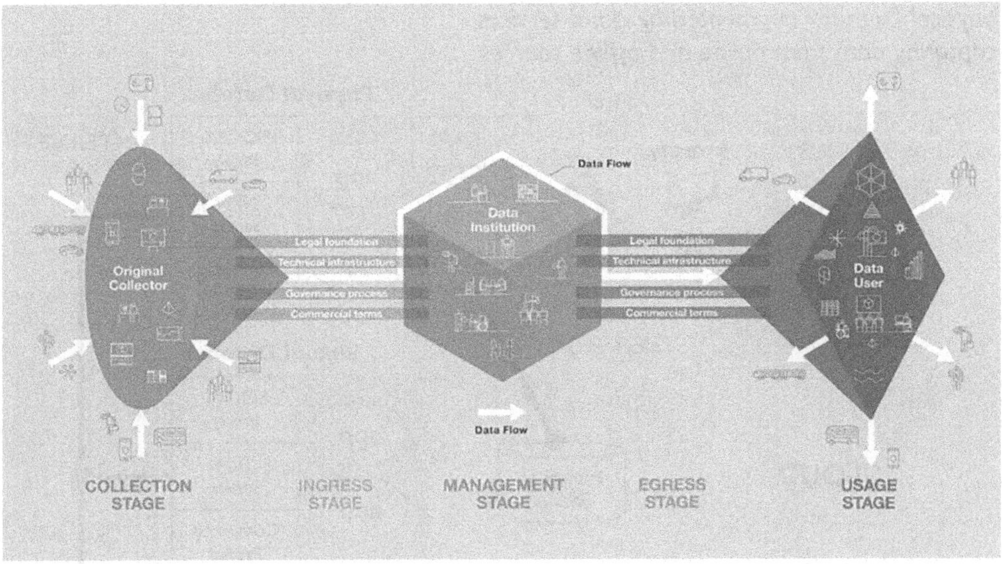

Figure 23.6 Data Institutions

Source: Open Data Institute ("The Role of Data Institutions," available at https://theodi.org/project/rd-data-institutions/, accessed August 1, 2023).

by around 3,500 ships globally to generate risk and safety analyses related to lifeboat accidents, engine room fires, and other incidents;

- create open data sets that anyone can access, use, and share to further a particular mission or cause; OpenCorporates,[9] Open Apparel Registry,[10] and 360Giving[11] each collate and make accessible important open data about companies, factories, and funding, respectively;
- develop and maintain common data infrastructure for a sector or field, such as by registering identifiers or publishing open standards; this is what happened in the UK banking system, with a company, Open Banking Limited[12] established to develop standards and guidelines for open banking.

One example of a centralized model of data institution can also be seen in the case of the Aadhaar card in India. The Aadhaar card contains biometric information and is a twelve-digit unique identity number that can be obtained by residents of India,; it is issued by the Unique Identification Authority of India (UIDAI). The card (similar to social security ID in the United States) has become central to everyday life for many Indian citizens,[13] and UIDAI maintains a very large data set, which potentially could be anonymized and "reused" for policy planning purposes.

Other approaches have also been adopted, either directly sharing data sets, pooling data through portals, or establishing platforms as mediators between providers and users of data. One example was Databox (see Figure 23.7), a project that gave individuals control over the data they provided, including data generated by Internet of Things devices such as smart thermostats and meters. The data was held in a physical device controlled by

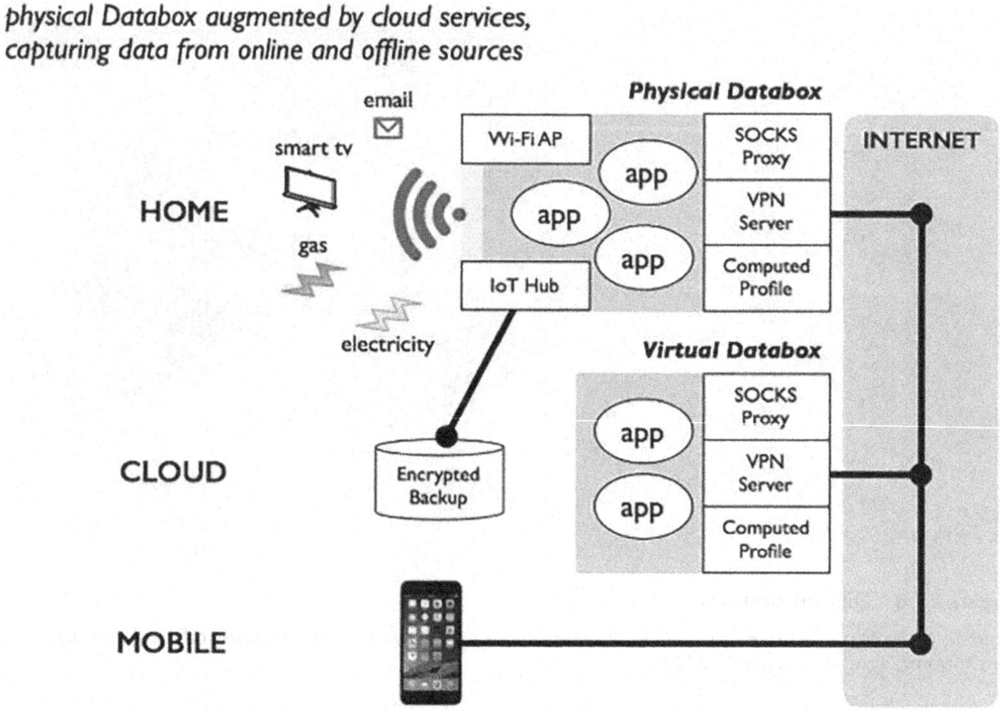

Figure 23.7 Databox
Source: Mortier et al. (2016).

the individual, rather than in the cloud, using "containerization" technology (cloud native application that connects with other technologies, packaging together of software code/ frameworks). This was a successful proof of concept, but it did not succeed commercially.

Another approach in the United Kingdom has been attempted in the energy industry: data sharing has been mandated by the government as part of the rollout of smart meters. The Data Communications Company[14] manages the smart meter infrastructure, including data: meters are linked to the telecommunications network, enabling consumer data to be shared with competing energy suppliers, energy network operators and other authorized parties, such as third-party intermediaries that offer energy saving, switching, or load shifting services.

An alternative approach is Tim Berners-Lee's initiative Solid,[15] which centers on individuals controlling their own data, including terms of access and storage, in a decentralized model. Users store data in one or more "pods" (personal online data stores) hosted by an entity they can select, and they can permit different organizations to access data of different types. Solid's focus is therefore on individuals owning data they generate, and on safeguarding privacy. In other words, it is concerned with reducing negative data externalities from loss of privacy; to capture the potential social value from realizing positive externalities, the services and apps using data need to accumulate access permissions from individual users. This approach, however laudable the intent, does not allow full exploitation of the potential of data through good governance.

Data and Ethics

Whatever the model chosen, these models of data stewardship will have to encompass, at least to a certain degree, a number of data ethics considerations. The Open Data Institute's Data Ethics Canvas provides a useful model to assess all possible ethical and humane aspects of data use (see Figure 23.8). Other guidance of course exists, for instance in the public sector.[16]

Another crucial consideration will be whether the data sets will be used by any form of artificial intelligence, as it is increasingly likely. Such use would entail additional scrutiny. The proposed EU Regulation on Artificial Intelligence,[17] for instance, will provide key regulatory guidelines for strengthening trust.

Establishing a Governance Framework

It is therefore crucial to establish appropriate governance frameworks for this new data world we live in. This, of course, is highly dependent on the approach that societies take on the management of socially and economically valuable resources. The "individualistic" and dispersed approach would be at one end of the scale, while the "wholly communitarian" and centralized approach would be at the other end. Each one or a combination can be applicable as relevant.

As we have seen, some models for the management and exploitation of common resources can be suggested by history already.

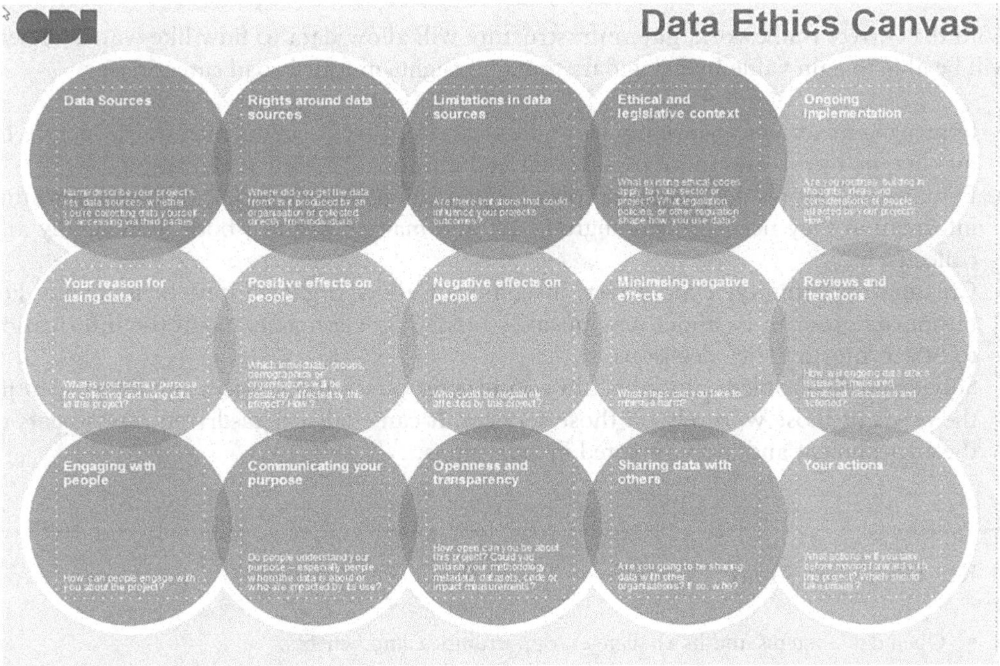

Figure 23.8 Data Ethics Canvas

Source: Open Data Institute.

One example is the "polder model," a method of consensus decision-making originating in the Netherlands. Polders are land reclaimed from the sea and kept dry thanks to a complex system of canals, ditches, and windmills; polders require constant pumping and maintenance of the dykes. Since the process of land reclamation began, without unanimous agreement on shared responsibility for the maintenance system, the polders would have flooded. This meant that all individuals and societies living in the same polder were forced to cooperate and set aside differences for a greater purpose. We need a governance framework for data use as robust and inclusive as the polder mode.

Governance frameworks will create safeguards to mitigate risks of harmful outcomes and also maximize the economic and social use of data. Not all frameworks will be appropriate for all data sets and uses—a collection of aggregate temperatures taken by thermostats in one neighborhood does not require the same safeguards of health records of a whole city.

So, the first step is to determine an appropriate and fit-for-purpose governance model. Then, the model should clarify end-to-end responsibilities: as we have said, data is not static but exists on a cycle. As part of a commitment to responsible data stewardship, data actors can assess and seek to prevent risks across the full data life cycle. This end-to-end data responsibility is essential for preventing harm and ensuring trust.

Finally, governance frameworks should identify the appropriate data licensing model. Data licensing regimes provide a way to secure and promote the reuse of data, can introduce interoperability requirements, and develop specific permissions and conditions around use, redistribution, modification, nondiscrimination, and so on (Support Centre for Data Sharing n.d.).

Conclusion

With the correct framework, data infrastructure will allow data to flow like water. Society will be able to gain value by using data to gain insights in four broad categories:

- Improving governance: Insights from data can improve how organizations operate by making their processes more transparent and improving resource allocations.
- Empowering people and organizations: Insights can empower people by communicating information they need to meaningfully act and make decisions, both individually and collectively.
- Creating opportunity: Data-driven insights can allow organizations to innovate. For businesses, this can be about new business models; governments might use information to better inform policy decisions.
- Solving public problems: Insights can optimize processes and services and better identify the needs of those who rely on those services. It can enable data-driven assessments of the environment and more targeted interventions.

Key Discussion Areas

- Open data systems and its challenges, opportunities, and benefits.
- An overview of data cycle, data players and data institutions.
- Data governance framework and data-related ethical considerations.

Notes

1 opendatabarometer.org (accessed August 1, 2023).
2 http://registries.opencorporates.com/ (accessed August 1, 2023).
3 https://ec.europa.eu/digital-single-market/en/big-data-value-public-privatepartnership (accessed August 1, 2023).
4 European Commission, Digital Europe eIDAS Enablers, https://ec.europa.eu/cefdigital/wiki/display/CEFDIGITAL/Context+Broker (accessed August 1, 2023).
5 Data Collaboratives Explorer is a repository of over 250 data collaboratives initiated around the world with the goal of creating new public value. Data Collaboration for the Common Good is a report from the World Economic Forum outlining value propositions for public–private data partnerships and strategies for maximizing that value.
6 Open Data Watch, "Data Impacts Case Studies: Using Satellite and Cell Phone Data to Eliminate Malaria in Namibia," http://dataimpacts.org/project/malaria/ (accessed August 1, 2023).
7 www.ukbiobank.ac.uk/this (accessed August 1, 2023).
8 https://hilomrm.com/ (accessed August 1, 2023).
9 https://opencorporates.com/ (accessed August 1, 2023).
10 https://info.openapparel.org/ (accessed August 1, 2023).
11 www.threesixtygiving.org/ (accessed August 1, 2023).
12 www.openbanking.org.uk/ (accessed August 1, 2023).
13 For a view on the experience of Indian citizen with the card, see, for instance, https://stateofaadhaar.in (accessed August 1, 2023), which provides the data of a large-scale survey.
14 www.smartdcc.co.uk/ (accessed August 1, 2023).
15 https://solid.mit.edu/ (accessed August 1, 2023).
16 For instance, the UK Data Ethics Framework, guidance from the United Kingdom's government digital service outlining how public sector organizations might appropriately and responsibly use data, available at www.gov.uk/government/publications/data-ethics-framework (accessed August 1, 2023).
17 https://eur-lex.europa.eu/legal-content/EN/TXT/?uri=CELEX%3A52021PC0206 (accessed August 1, 2023).

References

Borgogno, O., and G. Colangelo. 2018. "Data Sharing and Interoperability Through APIs: Insights from European Regulatory Strategy." *SSRN Electronic Journal*, November 21, 2018, https://doi.org/10.2139/ssrn.3288460.

Coyle, Diane, Stephanie Diepeveen, Julie Wdowin, Lawrence Kay, and Jeni Tennison. 2020. "The Value of Data." Bennett Institute for Public Policy, www.bennettinstitute.cam.ac.uk/wp-content/uploads/2020/12/Value_of_data_summary_report_26_.pdf (accessed August 1, 2023).

Data Impacts. n.d. "Phone Records Track Malaria." *Dataimpacts.Org*, https://dataimpacts.org/project/malaria/ (accessed August 1, 2023).

Davies, T., S. Walker, M. Rubinstein, and F. Perini, eds. 2019. *The State of Open Data: Histories and Horizons*. Capetown: African Minds.

EuDEco. 2018. "Report on the Final Model on the European Data Economy," https://eur-lex.europa.eu/content/news/building_EU_data_economy.html (accessed August 1, 2023).

European Commission. 2020. "The European Data Strategy." February 19, 2020, https://ec.europa.eu/commission/presscorner/detail/en/fs_20_283 (accessed August 1, 2023).

European Commission, Directorate-General for Communications Networks, Content and Technology. 2021. "Towards a European Strategy on Business-to-Government Data Sharing for the Public Interest: Final Report Prepared by the High-Level Expert Group on Business-to-Government Data Sharing." *European Union*, February 15, 2021, https://op.europa.eu/en/publication-detail/-/publication/d96edc29-70fd-11eb-9ac9-01aa75ed71a1/language-en (accessed August 1, 2023).

Feeny, D., F. Berkes, B. J. McCay, and J. M. Acheson. 1990. "The Tragedy of the Commons: Twenty-Two Years Later." *Human Ecology* 18(1): 1–19, https://doi.org/10.1007/bf00889070.

Hardin, G. 1968. "The Tragedy of the Commons." *Science* 162(3859): 1243–48, https://doi.org/10.1126/science.162.3859.1243.

Hilbert, M. 2015. "Big Data for Development: A Review of Promises and Challenges." *Development Policy Review* 34(1): 135–74, https://doi.org/10.1111/dpr.12142.

HM Treasury. 2019. "Unlocking Digital Competition, Report of the Digital Competition Expert Panel." *GOV.UK*, March 13, 2019, www.gov.uk/government/publications/unlocking-digital-competition-report-of-the-digital-competition-expert-panel (accessed August 1, 2023).

Longshore Smith, Matthew, and Katherine Reilly. 2013. *Open Development: Networked Innovations in International Development*. Cambridge, MA: MIT Press.

Mawer, C. 2015. "Valuing Data is Hard." *Silicon Valley Data Science*, September 21, 2015, www.svds.com/valuing-data-is-hard/ (accessed August 1, 2023).

Mortier, R., J. Zhao, J. Crowcroft, L. Wang, Q. Li, H. Haddadi, Y. Amar, A. Crabtree, J. Colley, T. Lodge, T. Brown, D. McAuley, and C. Greenhalgh. 2016. "Personal Data Management with the Databox What's Inside the Box?" In *Proceedings of the 2016 ACM Workshop on Cloud-Assisted Networking*. https://doi-org.hult.idm.oclc.org/10.1145/3010079.3010082

Musk, Elon. 2014. "All Our Patent Are Belong To You." *Tesla*, July 27, 2019, www.tesla.com/blog/all-our-patent-are-belong-you (accessed August 1, 2023).

Nguyen, D., and M. Paczos. 2019. "Measuring the Economic Value of Data and Data Flows." Presentation at OECD Working Party on Measurement and Analysis of the Digital Economy, Paris, May 7, 2019, https://doi.org/10.1787/6345995e-en.

OECD. 2017. *Government at a Glance*, https://doi.org/10.1787/22214399.

The Open Data Institute 2023. "Our Strategy 2018–2022." https://theodi.org/documents/88/ODI-Strategy-for-web.pdf (accessed August 1, 2023).

Prayas, Energy Group. 2019. "Minute-Wise Voltage Data Collected in Electricity Supply Monitoring Initiative." *Harvard Dataverse*, https://doi.org/10.7910/DVN/CLLZZM.

Support Centre for Data Sharing. n.d. "Report on Collected Model Contract Terms." *Eudatasharing.Eu*, https://eudatasharing.eu/legal-aspects/report-collected-model-contract-terms (accessed August 1, 2023).

Verhulst, Stefaan G., and Andrew Young. 2017. "Open Data in Developing Economies: Toward Building an Evidence Base on What Works and How." *GovLab*, https://odimpact.org/files/odimpact-developing-economies.pdf (accessed August 1, 2023).

Young, Andrew. 2016. "The GovLab Selected Readings on Data Collaboratives." *GovLab*, June 10, 2016, https://blog.thegovlab.org/post/the-govlab-selected-readings-on-data-collaboratives (accessed August 1, 2023).

24

LEADERSHIP AND GOVERNANCE FOR THE DIGITAL FUTURE

The Role of Virtue Ethics

Prabu David, Preeti Shroff-Mehta, and Sanjay Gupta

Introduction

In the emerging digital economy, a major shift is underway. Technologies that promise to solve humanity's grand challenges also pose existential threats to human autonomy. During this period of societal transformation, we can be observers of change or agents of change. By embracing virtue ethics and examining who we are as human beings, we have the agency to shape what we are becoming (Seberger, Choung, and David In press). Being and becoming are important metaphysical questions among philosophers of ontology. Even as we examine who we are, we must simultaneously engage in the complementary pursuit of who we are becoming. The impermanence of all things and the certainty of change were addressed by the ancient Greek philosopher Heraclitus from the sixth century BCE, who is known for saying, "No man ever steps into the same river twice." When reflecting on the inevitability of change, existential philosophers, notably Nietzsche, have associated it with turbulence and chaos (Nietzsche 1962). To manage the change, we need ethical policies and technomoral virtues at ethical guardrails, which are introduced in this chapter. Specifically, we place stakeholder capitalism and ESG (environmental, social, and governance) within a technomoral framework and offer a values-driven model of governance that rests on cocreation of value.

During this transition from *being* to *becoming*, governments and corporations will need the trust of citizens, customers, users, investors, and advocacy groups. As we race ahead into the Fourth Industrial Revolution (Industry 4.0) characterized by the convergence of technologies such as artificial intelligence, neural interfaces, and genome editing, to capabilities such as advanced robotics, 3-D printing, and the internet of things, fundamental economic and societal shifts are underway (Schwab 2016). In this New Age, there is an urgent need to cultivate virtues and moral theory into our current education and training paradigms to ensure a productive, safe, and harmonious future for the well-being and prosperity of people and the planet. Specifically, a set of virtues that are relevant to innovation and technology, described as "technomoral virtues," can transcend geography, language,

DOI: 10.4324/9781003316077-29

and culture, resulting in principled digital governance that is necessary to achieve a promising and sustainable future for humanity (Vallor 2016).

The promise of a bright digital future depends in part on education, and educators are vested with the responsibility to prepare students for: future success in their careers; developing a thirst for lifelong learning; becoming invested citizens in their communities; and recognizing the importance of stewardship of our planet. While disciplinary knowledge, domain-specific skills, and technology savvy may be threshold requirements for entry into the job market, employers are keenly interested in well-rounded graduates who are curious, creative, collaborative, communicative, and of strong character to lead and govern effectively in an increasingly complex digital economy. In this milieu, what is the role of education and responsibility of educators in preparing tomorrow's digital world leaders whose pursuit of excellence is guided by emotional intelligence, values, ethics, and empathy.

Character is developed in students and employees by nurturing virtues such as integrity, generosity, compassion, and courage (Vallor 2016), and honesty, justice, responsibility, and care (Hagendorff 2022), which are essential for governance in a digital world. We already see a turn toward virtue ethics in ideas such as the cocreation of value (Prahalad and Ramaswamy 2004), stakeholder capitalism (Kelly, Kelly, and Gamble 1997; Schwab 2021), and the ESG (environmental, social, and governance) movement (Bhandari, Ranta, and Salo 2022), which are examined in the following sections. These organizational shifts buttressed by virtue ethics, which are integrated in Figure 24.1, have global significance for human-centered digital transformation. The proposed framework in Figure 24.1 is elaborated in the rest of this chapter.

Cocreation of Value

In an influential article, Prahalad and Ramaswamy (2004) introduced cocreation of value as an alternative to the traditional market economy, which focuses on creating value for

Traditional Model	New Model
Exchange-based transactions	Interaction-based, relational transactions
Focused on creation of value	Focused on co-creation of value
Shareholder capitalism	Stakeholder capitalism
ESG (Environmental, Social, and Governance) principles as an afterthought	GETS (Governance, Environmental, Technology, and Social) principles infused into all facets of the institution
Short-term value extraction (profit)	Long-term value co-creation (prosperity)
Ethics driven primarily by principles	Ethics driven by principles, values, and virtues
Power rests primarily with the organization	Power is shared between the organization and its stakeholders

Figure 24.1 Governance Model for the Digital Future

Source: Authors.

shareholders. Cocreation is a fundamental shift from an exchange-based model of markets to an experience-based model that includes ongoing dialogue and interactions, and ongoing participation of stakeholders, customers, investors, and users. The cocreation approach argues for a new economic model of value based on experiences in which an organization and its *stakeholders* are collaborators actively engaged in principled exchanges and mutually desirable outcomes.

Given the size and impact of trillion-dollar Big Tech corporations that are larger than economies of many countries, more is expected than the products or services they offer. A great product or service at a good price that is readily available is necessary but no longer sufficient. In the current market environment, corporations and their CEOs are expected to offer brand purpose and thought leadership on societal causes and concerns that are directly or indirectly related to their core business mission. Business leaders are expected to meet the expanding expectations of consumers, employees, and other stakeholders to champion environmental and social causes even at the risk of reputational or monetary loss (Arogyaswamy 2020).

Although corporate mission statements are commonplace and expected, the growing number of corporations that offer a purpose statement suggests a shift toward a value-based compact between a firm and its stakeholders. Considering the finding that 72 percent of the respondents believe that a company should have a purpose beyond profit (Gast et al. 2020), it is not surprising that corporations are pursuing social values and an inclusionary approach to value creation. For example, Microsoft (Microsoft n.d.), the second-most valuable company in the world, publicly states that it is putting its mission of empowering "every person and every organization on the planet to achieve more," into action through the following commitment: "We believe that technology is a force for good and are working to foster a sustainable future where everyone has access to the benefits and opportunities created by technology."

Salesforce, the pioneer of customer relationship management (CRM) technology, was founded in 1999 with a vision of profitability and philanthropy as core pillars of the company's DNA. That vision took shape as the "1–1–1 model," which is a promise to return 1 percent of the company's equity, 1 percent of its product, and 1 percent of employees' time back to the community (Salesforce 2020).

In setting up that model, Salesforce also co-founded "Pledge 1%," a new movement to integrate social impact into the core DNA of every company. "Pledge 1% inspires, educates, and empowers all entrepreneurs and companies to leverage their assets to be a force for good." This movement has gathered impressive momentum: since 2014, more than 10,000 companies in over one hundred countries have joined the Pledge 1% movement, generating more than US$1 billion in value through volunteer hours, product, and funding.

While value creation and profitability used to be the singular goal of a corporation and its shareholders, cocreation is a willful effort to share power and information, in turn offering customers and stakeholders a say in the design of products and services and in the creation of greater overall value. Instead of a traditional customer-centric approach that aims to please, cocreation goes the extra mile to engage customers as collaborators in creating experiences (Ramaswamy and Gouillart 2010). This collaborative process of cocreation of value is made increasingly possible through interactive and social media (Ramaswamy and Ozcan 2019), and achieved through dialogue, increased access and transparency, and engagement with customers/investors on risks and benefits associated with social and environmental causes.

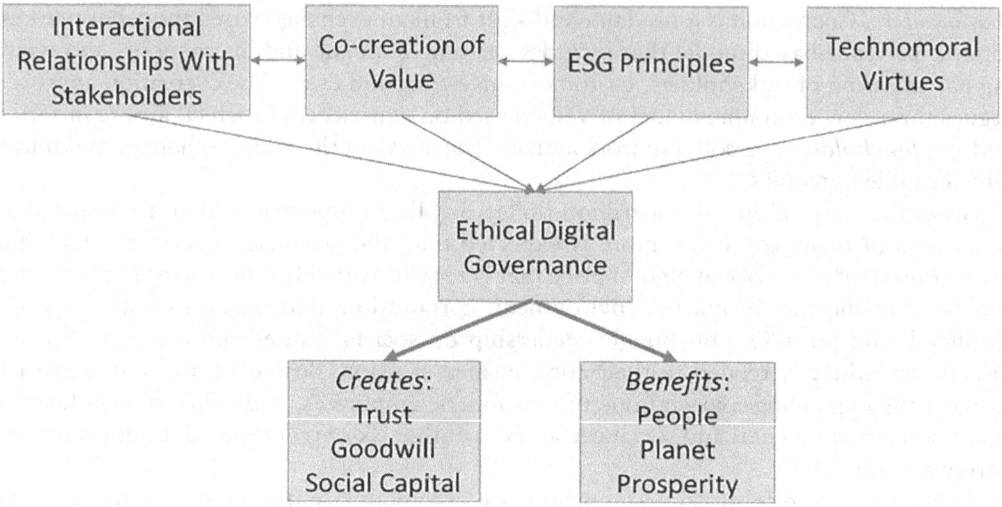

Figure 24.2 Differences Between Traditional and Proposed Models of Governance
Source: Authors.

Customer and Stakeholder Power in a Data-Driven Digital World

The rise in power of customers, employees, and other stakeholders can be attributed to user data and user-generated content that power the information economy and to the affordances of social media. The role of technological innovations in the empowerment of individuals through democratization and decentralization is addressed by authors of other chapters in this book.

Today's customer is informed, networked, empowered, and active. Customers can orchestrate support and present their grievances and demands to a global audience with relative ease, thus exerting pressure even on powerful corporations like Google or Apple with ubiquitous presence and strong name recognition. Such demands are not usually driven by self-interest but by collective concern for environmental outcomes, human rights, or data protection.

The rise of the engaged customer is also fueled by perceptions of a rightful stake in organizations that receive billions of dollars in revenues from the personal data of customers and users. Other chapters in this book highlight data as a common good that is mined through analytics for outcomes that benefit the consumer and the corporation. In the perpetually-on-and-perpetually-connected ecosystem (David 2017), the surveillance economy harvests user data that serve as the backbone of many business models (Nissenbaum 2011; Zuboff 2019). Furthermore, the pervasive presence of Big Tech brands such as Google, Apple, Meta, Amazon, and Netflix, leads to a sense of deep brand familiarity. The interactive and customized experiences these brands offer through machine learning, natural language processing, and chatbots intensify the relationship between the user and the corporation, justifying the demand for the cocreation of value.

The pervasiveness of Big Tech brands in everyday life is complemented by the familiarity with founders and CEOs, who maintain a high profile through their presence in social and traditional media. A notable example is Elon Musk, CEO of Tesla, who has tweeted about once an hour since acquiring Twitter (Schiffer, Newton, and Heath 2023). Furthermore, in an increasingly polarized world in which public trust and satisfaction in government is at historic lows, in a Pew survey, only about two-in-ten Americans expressed trust that Washington can do the right thing about always or most of the time (Pew Research Center 2022). To fill the trust gap created by political leaders, in some instances the public has turned to CEOs for leadership. For example, during the pandemic, CEOs of biotechnology, pharmaceuticals, and technology companies played an important role in calming the public and providing credible information.

Public Sentiment of Corporations and CEOs

The 2021 Edelman Trust Barometer study, based on a sample of 33,000 respondents from twenty-eight countries, offers evidence of the public's expectations of CEOs. Eighty-six percent of the respondents said that they expect CEOs to speak out on public matters, and 68 percent said that CEOs should step in when the government does not fix societal problems. On topics such as job loss created by AI and robotics, wage equity, and climate change, more than two-thirds of the respondents stated that CEOs must get involved in shaping the conversation (Edelman 2021).

Pressured in part by such public opinion and in keeping with the times to be socially responsive, CEOs have offered their perspectives on key social and political topics, such as sustainability and climate change, Black Lives Matter, the war in Ukraine, China's Hong Kong policy, and transgender bathrooms. Responding to such environmental, social, political, cultural, and global issues adds the risk of alienating some stakeholders. At the same time, remaining silent on these important matters could be equally risky, leading to perceptions of disengagement or being out of step with the times.

To meet the expectations of customers, investors, and employees, corporate leaders and corporations are thrust into the spotlight, risking their reputation. Under these challenging circumstances, we believe that leadership and governance cannot be driven exclusively by risk assessments based purely on a monetary cost-benefit calculus but through values, virtue ethics, and a technomoral framework. Before we introduce virtues within a technomoral framework, we examine stakeholder capitalism and ESG (environmental, social, and governance) factors, which serve as a vital link between the cocreation of value and a values-driven model of governance.

Individual and Collective Interests in Stakeholder Capitalism and ESG

Box 24.1 Business Roundtable Redefines the Purpose of a Corporation to Promote "An Economy That Serves All Americans"

On August 19, 2019, 181 CEOs of America's largest corporations overturned a twenty-two-year-old policy statement that defined a corporation's principal purpose as maximizing shareholder return (Business Roundtable n.d.).

In its place, the CEOs of Business Roundtable adopted a new Statement on the Purpose of a Corporation declaring that companies should not only serve their shareholders but also deliver value to their customers, invest in employees, deal fairly with suppliers, and support the communities in which they operate.

Doug McMillon, President and Chief Executive Officer of Walmart and Chairman of Business Roundtable, said at the one-year anniversary of releasing this statement:

> During a time of tremendous challenge, Business Roundtable CEOs have shown what it means to live the principles we announced almost a year ago. Concurrent health, economic and racial crises have made clear how various systems are connected—and that multi-stakeholder capitalism is the answer to addressing our challenges holistically. America's CEOs remain steadfast in our commitment to pursue economic prosperity and expanded opportunity for our employees, customers and the communities we serve.
>
> (Business Roundtable, "One Year Later: Purpose of a Corporation," https://purpose.businessroundtable.org/ [accessed October 1, 2023])

Although we have used the term stakeholders interchangeably to refer to customers and employees in the previous section, it is important to examine what it means to be a stakeholder in an organization. A key difference between a customer and a stakeholder is the balance between self-interest and collective interest. While self-interest explains most of the day-to-day interactions between customers and an organization, collective interest better explains the motives of stakeholders. The commitment to social or environmental causes among stakeholders can trump self-interest and pocketbook concerns. Customers who are willing to pay more for clean energy or sacrifice comfort for reduced energy consumption are not acting entirely out of self-interest but as citizens and stakeholders who expect principled reciprocity from corporations (David 2004). Much like individuals, corporations also operate out of both self-interest and collective interest. While profit-driven shareholder capitalism is akin to self-interest, the current emphasis on ESG signals an organization's commitment to the collective good.

As an alternative to the traditional model of capitalism that is based on value creation for shareholders, stakeholder capitalism points to a different design in which the interests of multiple stakeholders, including customers, employees, and communities, are taken into consideration along with the interests of shareholders (Hemphill, Kelley, and Cullari 2021). Such corporate commitment to social responsibility and the betterment of society is not new and has inspired initiatives such as corporate social responsibility (CSR) (Windsor 2001) and green marketing (Dangelico and Vocalelli 2017). Under CSR, corporations could meet their social responsibility by selectively choosing a particular outcome, such as the fast-food chain Wendy's commitment to foster care adoption and Patagonia's commitment to the environment and sustainability.

Addressing the demands of stakeholders does not mean that businesses ignore their core responsibility of generating enough revenues in the face of fierce competition to pay their workers, meet their debt obligations, satisfy their shareholders, or basically survive. While meeting their core responsibility is a necessary condition for the survival of a business, that is simply not enough to thrive in today's environment with growing stakeholder demands.

In today's social climate, organizations are expected to do more because shareholder capitalism has not sufficiently addressed, or arguably even exacerbated, the gaps in health, wealth, and opportunity (Schwab 2021). Furthermore, a majority (56 percent) of the respondents in an Edelman survey reported that capitalism was doing more harm than good (John 2020). State capitalism, which has transformed the Chinese economy, also has not performed better than traditional shareholder capitalism in addressing social inequities and the well-being of the planet. To address shortcomings of both shareholder and state capitalism, Klaus Schwab, founder and executive chairperson of the World Economic Forum, offered stakeholder capitalism, which involves the cocreation of value with a long-term outlook aimed at addressing the well-being of people, planet, and prosperity (Schwab 2021).

Critics of stakeholder capitalism claim that it is simply "socialism" in disguise and bound to fail. However, many leading voices have countered these claims publicly and with force. For example, a reader of an article on stakeholder capitalism authored by Alan Murray, CEO of Fortune and coauthor of a column Friday Feedback in the magazine, expressed concern that Mr. Murray's support for stakeholder capitalism amounted to "actually advocating for Marxist-socialist-workist-hyper-regulation and control." In response, Mr. Murray stated:

> [W]e should define our terms. Socialism refers to government ownership of the means of production, and as someone who spent most of my career covering Washington, I know better than to have any sympathy for that approach. If it is "woke" to call on business to pay attention to its effects on people, communities, and the environment, then call me "woke." As for "hyper-regulation," I believe the best way to avoid it is for business to do a better job modulating its own behavior.
>
> *(Murray and Meyer 2022)*

Similarly, Larry Fink, CEO of BlackRock Inc., one of the world's largest investment and advisory firms with over US$8.6 trillion under management as of December 31, 2022, stated in his 2022 letter to CEOs:

> Stakeholder capitalism is not about politics. It is not a social or ideological agenda. It is not "woke." *It is capitalism*, driven by mutually beneficial relationships between you and the employees, customers, suppliers, and communities your company relies on to *prosper*. This is the power of capitalism.
>
> *(Fink 2022)*

Stakeholder capitalism requires the recognition of both tangible and intangible value. For example, empowering staff to advance the diversity, equity, and inclusion (DEI) goals of an organization may improve morale and productivity, which are tangible outcomes. Concurrently, an organization's inclusive excellence may create a favorable reputation, in turn contributing to goodwill capital, which is intangible. Although the benefits of goodwill capital may be intangible, a track record of responsible actions may serve as a buffer or insurance when an organization is faced with a crisis.

The Evolving Global Social Contract of Multi-Stakeholder Governance

Governance of a multi-stakeholder system is a challenging task that requires balancing competing interests. Consider the ongoing controversy involving the Walt Disney World

Resort in Orlando, Florida, and Ron DeSantis, Republican governor of Florida and presidential aspirant (Glueck and Robles 2022). When the Florida legislature banned classroom instruction on sexual orientation and gender identity from kindergarten to third grade, former Disney CEO Bob Chapek opted to remain silent. Under intense pressure from some employees and consumers, he expressed concern over the legislation that is widely construed as an assault on LGBT rights. Responding to Disney's statement, Governor DeSantis swiftly signed a law that could limit Disney's control of its vast property in Florida, which could cost the corporation millions of dollars. The controversy has continued to drag on under the leadership of CEO Robert Iger, placing the corporation in the public eye, although the corporation had little to do with the controversy.

Another example of a challenging multi-stakeholder decision is the controversy created by Jack Dorsey, former CEO of Twitter, who banned former President Donald Trump from Twitter following the storming of the U.S. Capitol by pro-Trump supporters on January 6, 2020 (Conger and Isaac 2021). While the ban was lauded by some key stakeholders and Democrats as much-needed action to stop former President Trump's attempts at misinformation and disinformation, it was widely criticized by some Republicans as an overreach by Big Tech. As with Disney, Twitter, too, faced a no-win situation. In both cases, action or inaction could only please one-half of the population and alienate the other.

Handling such sensitive situations requires values, temperance, and wisdom, which make up higher-level virtue ethics (Hagendorff 2022). There is no substitute for practical wisdom because no system of ethics applies uniformly or tidily to such complex situations. Therefore, the values that form practical wisdom must be nurtured in individuals and societies. Furthermore, these values are not immutable. They evolve over time and their effects on stakeholders vary by political affiliation, geography, context, and culture.

It is important to note that unlike a strict code of ethics, virtue ethics is an honor system that can be easily exploited. Numerous examples of blatant ethical failures, such as fraud, misleading information, cover-ups, and poor judgment, have eroded stakeholder trust in corporations and their leaders. In recent years, well-known corporate brands such as Enron, Wells Fargo, Boeing, and BP have suffered from high-profile failures in leadership and governance. Two such recent ethical breaches have involved leading auto manufacturers. For over a decade, Volkswagen was found to have bypassed the U.S. emission standards for their diesel engines by installing software ("defeat device") in their cars to pass the emissions standards within a laboratory test environment even though the emissions exceeded the limit under normal road driving conditions (Gates et al. 2015). In 2017, VW pleaded guilty resulting in financial liabilities of nearly US$22 billion. Recently, the Chrysler unit of Stellantis pleaded guilty to the U.S. Justice Department's charge of violating the Clean Air Act and agreed to pay US$300 million for false and misleading representations about its emissions control systems by using software in its cars that allowed it to circumvent the Federal pollution standards (Goldstein 2022).

Protection of Privacy and Personal Data in the Digital Economy

In the digital economy, ethical failures with broad impact can result from vulnerabilities in software and technology. These failures have resulted in breaches of privacy and data protection, use or misuse of AI, facial recognition and algorithmic bias, and other matters related to social media and information technology. For example, a vulnerability in a third-party Facebook app was exploited by Cambridge Analytica, which harvested personal data from more than 80 million users to develop a digital advertising campaign during the 2016 election for former President Trump, which involved discrediting opposition candidates (Kang and Frenkel 2018). In one of the most egregious data hacks, personal data and identifiers of more than 147 million Americans were stolen from the credit reporting company Equifax, leading to significant backlash and criticism about the company's slow response and lack of transparency (Bernard et al. 2017).

In addition to personal data protection, new technologies demand our vigilance and thoughtful engagement on other aspects. Rapid advances in AI require ethical and trustworthy approaches that take into consideration both functionality and social implications (Floridi et al. 2018). As discussed in other chapters in this handbook, trust is fragile. To instill confidence among stakeholders, trustworthy AI requires corporate robust self-governance, government policies, and user engagement.

For instance, the promise and peril of AI are apparent in face identification, a technology with great potential for authentication and customization of human experience, but with potential algorithmic bias by gender and race (Buolamwini and Gebru 2018) and with grave implications for privacy and ethics. Clearview AI, a facial recognition vendor, has scraped 20 billion facial photos posted on social media and websites to build a facial recognition system that it sells to law enforcement. While Clearview AI's technology helps law enforcement apprehend criminals, improve safety in public spaces, and identify lost children, the widespread deployment of security cameras raises the specter of a dystopian surveillance state predicted by George Orwell (Hill 2020). Facial recognition is fraught with ethical challenges, leading Microsoft, Amazon, and Meta to pause the sale of the technology.

Face recognition is but one of the numerous technologies that deserve careful ethical consideration. Algorithms driven by machine learning are pervasive and influence health care (Parikh, Teeple, and Navathe 2019), prison sentencing (Eckhouse et al. 2019), consumer lending decisions (Hassani 2021), and job application screening (Hunkenschroer and Luetge 2022). For example, fintech firms are using AI-driven algorithms and diverse sets of data to create alternative credit scores for underserved loan applicants who might be turned away from mainstream financial services like a home mortgage. The application of these emerging technologies to maximize benefits to humans and minimize harm to humanity requires technomoral judgment and wisdom, which can be offered through virtue ethics.

The opportunities, failures, and challenges discussed in the above examples underscore the need for corporate culture and governance based on sound values and principles that are founded on virtues such as generosity, courage, compassion, patience, kindness, temperance, and wisdom. Without applying these virtues and values, it would be impossible to develop an ethos of cocreation of value or stakeholder capitalism. Similarly, without integrating technology into the mix of ESG, an adequate model of governance cannot be developed for the digital economy (see chapters in Part 1 for different perspectives).

Opportunities and Threats in a Digital Economy

With the rise of machine agency, humans and technology are moving toward a new future that is both exciting and uncertain. In this future, algorithms will exercise more control over our experiences and influence outcomes in our lives, challenging us to examine "who's in charge here, human or machine?"

As technology gains autonomy, we expect it to demonstrate character and benevolence that we are accustomed to in interpersonal interactions (Lankton, McKnight, and Thatcher 2014). Through better design parameters, training data sets that are adjusted for bias, and rigorous testing and evaluation, the public must demand technology companies and engineers to develop trustworthy and ethical AI. Values that contribute to the integrity dimension of trust in technology share similarities with the values that undergird stakeholder capitalism, such as concern for the people, planet, and prosperity, and a commitment to social and environmental justice. And the benevolence dimension of trust is related to the cocreation of values in which stakeholders are accepted as collaborators and co-owners rather than target markets for value extraction by powerful corporations.

One might argue that the emphasis on integrity and benevolence is naïve in a competitive marketplace, because it might stifle creativity and innovation and weaken the corporation. The underlying assumption of this argument is that creativity and innovation require workarounds and the obfuscation of reality, such as the Silicon Valley mantra of "fake it till you make it." The Theranos saga is an unfortunate example of this line of thinking in which a corporation raised more than US$700 million, resulting in a US$10 billion valuation at its peak, by falsely claiming it had developed a novel blood-testing technology that led to the formal dissolution of the company, criminal fraud conviction of the founders and order to pay US$452 million in restitution (Streitfeld 2022; Bobrowsky 2023). However, such narrow and cynical views of competition are misguided. Creativity indeed can flourish within a framework of values and strengthen an organization in the long run. For example, instead of using creativity to expand mission creep, the same creativity can be used for innovations in privacy protection technology. Trustworthy AI, then, requires new creativity with ethical boundaries to meet corporate social responsibilities and stakeholder expectations.

Ethics of AI: A Global Framework for Human and Stakeholder Rights

With the global reach of the digital economy, the ethics of AI must transcend differences in nationality, culture, and political ideologies. Corporations, governments, professional organizations, and Big Tech corporations have identified values such as fairness, accountability, transparency, explainability, right to privacy, and human autonomy as universal values that must shape the future of AI (Floridi et al. 2018). Although these values may be universal, their instantiation varies by culture, country, and circumstance.

For example, while both the U.S. and Chinese governments may agree that privacy is a fundamental human right, given their political ideology and cultural differences, the two countries differ vastly on the trade-off between privacy and security (Kostka, Steinacker, and Meckel 2021). Acknowledging such differences, the European Commission's High-Level Expert Group on AI (AI HLEG 2019) has offered a comprehensive ethical framework for AI with seven ethical requirements: human agency, technical robustness and safety, privacy and data governance, transparency, nondiscrimination and fairness, social and environmental well-being, and accountability. In summary, these ethical requirements point to the role of human accountability throughout the AI production cycle—from its creation to social implications to ongoing performance review.

Other international and national bodies, including the Group of Seven (G7), Group of Twenty (G20), Beijing Academy of Artificial Intelligence (BAAI), and the Institute of Electrical and Electronics Engineers (IEEE), have issued policies to protect the rights of citizens and users (Hagendorff 2022). Though not directly tied to AI, the General Data Protection

Regulation (GDPR) enacted by the EU and the California Consumer Protection Act (CCPA) provide guidance on personal data protection and privacy.

Noting the importance of trust in AI, corporations such as Google, Microsoft, Meta, Apple, Amazon, and many others have self-governance policies, which are posted on their corporate websites to address stakeholder concerns. Google's commitment to AI includes empowering humanity, uplifting society, and addressing fairness and bias. Google also asserts that it will not pursue weapons related solely to cause harm. Similarly, Microsoft emphasizes its commitment to responsible and trustworthy AI that empowers and is used for socially responsible outcomes.

A review of governance frameworks advanced by regulatory agencies and corporations revealed that AI ethics is influenced by the four key principles of bioethics (Floridi et al. 2018), two of which can be traced to Hippocrates, a physician and philosopher from the fourth century BCE, who advised healers to help and do no harm. In addition to the two Hippocratic principles of beneficence and nonmaleficence, autonomy and justice round out the four principles of bioethics (Beauchamp and Childress 2019).

The thoughtful balancing and application of the four bioethics principles in different contexts, augmented through training, institutional commitment, and mechanisms such as Institutional Review Boards (IRB), contribute to "principlism." Over time, the application of principlism in everyday practice builds confidence in practitioners, leading to nuanced treatment protocols that are revised periodically. Bioethics works because of the Hippocratic oath, rigorous internal review process, and a not-for-profit service ethos. However, AI was not conceived with such noble purposes (Mittelstadt 2019). Efficiency, functionality, innovation, profits, and an arms race mindset have driven the advancement of digital technologies, intertwined with the ideals of connecting humanity and addressing information inequalities.

It is important, therefore, to develop and nurture principles for the digital economy that are akin to the principles of bioethics. In combination with principlism, which is a macro-level, top-down approach, a bottom-up approach of cultivating technomoral virtues among the designers and developers of new technologies is required. Along with training, certification, audits, and regulatory mechanisms (Mittelstadt 2019), which comprise the principlism approach to digital governance, a mindset shift rooted in virtues is needed to achieve a good life in which humans and technology co-exist. To realize this good life, we turn to virtue ethics, specifically technomoral virtues, as a critical requirement of digital governance.

Virtue Ethics as Foundation for a Good Life

Virtue ethics can be traced back to Aristotle and his vision of a "good life," which he described as a life of human flourishing (Koehn 1995). In explaining the good life, Aristotle emphasized eudaimonia, which literally translates to good spirit. The eudemonic realization of a good life is both fulfilling and virtuous and is driven by purpose and meaning. The core assumption is that a person who strives for this good life will naturally approach their work with competence, character, and benevolence, engaging thoughtfully about what we are becoming and thus, as it relates to AI, building trustworthy technologies (Choung, David, and Ross 2022a, 2022b). The critical question is: how to integrate human virtues and digital world ethics in global influences that shape what are we becoming, and how our lives are shaped in the twenty-first century?

Virtue ethics exists along with the deontological and utilitarian approaches, which are dominant traditions in moral philosophy. The deontological, or rule-based, approach advanced by Kant is based on the categorical imperative, a rational moral principle that must be universalizable without exceptions. In brief, Kant posited that an individual's action can be deemed moral only if that action could be accepted universally. For example, although a lie may be harmless or even necessary in one situation, for it to be moral, we must accept lies in all situations. Despite the moral clarity of the categorical imperative, its absolutism limits its usefulness in everyday applications (Arogyaswamy 2020).

An alternative to the Kantian approach is utilitarian ethics advanced by Jeremy Bentham and John Stuart Mill. According to utilitarianism, the moral choice is one that maximizes happiness for most people involved. Built on a cost-benefit calculus to maximize good and minimize harm, utilitarianism focuses on consequences. The challenge with utilitarianism, however, is determining and quantifying good and harm, weighing the trade-offs and living with the consequences of the choice. For example, consider the classic trolley problem, which is highly relevant to scenarios that must be addressed by AI in autonomous vehicles. If a trolley is barreling down a track with the likelihood of killing five people, doing nothing guarantees the death of five individuals. Instead, pulling a lever to divert the train to a different track may result in the death of one person. What is the right moral action?

The utilitarian approach might suggest that you make the active choice of sacrificing one life to save five lives. While that might sound rational in the abstract, imagine being the person who must pull the lever and live with that choice. The Kantian categorical imperative does not offer much clarity either because killing is universally wrong.

Though we may never experience a literal version of the trolley problem, decision-makers routinely contend with variations of the trolley problem when choosing the lesser of two bad outcomes or balancing competing goods. Consider the early days of the Covid-19 pandemic, with overflowing hospitals and limited medical supplies, when doctors and nurses worked overtime under challenging conditions to save as many lives as possible, often having to make trade-off decisions in deploying their limited resources. Relying on practical wisdom acquired through professional training and internalized ethical norms, doctors and nurses made difficult decisions that earned our trust. Their expertise was not driven by grand principles of morality and ethics but through the four practical decision-making principles assimilated and practiced over their professional careers—doing good, minimizing harm, operating with a sense of justice, and respecting human autonomy. How does one nurture such a value-system among programmers, engineers, and technologists who have not sworn to the principlism of the health-care community?

Searching for Practical Wisdom Through Virtue Ethics and Technomoral Virtues

The answer to an ethical framework of governance for the digital economy must include policies and principles and a commitment to virtue ethics. Interestingly, many of the virtues relevant to the future are ones that have withstood the passage of time. The virtues introduced by Socrates and Aristotle in 300 BCE remain relevant in the twenty-first century. Aristotle highlighted virtues of character including trust, compassion, courage, justice, honesty, patience, temperance, and wisdom. All these virtues contribute to practical wisdom, which is a meta-virtue that is crucial to leadership and governance. Aristotle also offered moderation or balance in everything, even in virtues, and offered the golden mean as the ideal.

For example, too little courage is cowardice and too much courage is recklessness. The virtuous person has the internal efficacy to summon the right amount of courage necessary to address a particular situation. Furthermore, Aristotle offered two pathways to cultivate virtues and fine-tune the golden mean—observing and learning from others who are moral exemplars, and through moral habituation. He posited that virtue is a habit. Much like vices are bad habits, virtues are good habits to cultivate through careful observation and practice.

Aristotle's virtue theory does not offer principles or rules. It is a simple moral theory that argues that a virtue can be cultivated, and a good or virtuous person will act virtuously and with practical wisdom to make good decisions that are appropriate for the situation. A good decision is not merely a clever decision but a morally sound one that brings about eudaimonia or flourishing in the individual and others.

Faith traditions also emphasize the nurturing of virtues as a key requirement for a good life. Compassion, generosity, courage, justice, and self-discipline are integral to all faiths. As expressed by the Apostle Paul in the New Testament, Christian virtues known as the fruit of the spirit include love, joy, peace, patience, kindness, goodness, gentleness, and self-control. These virtues share similarities with virtues promoted in other faiths and traditions. By consolidating virtues advocated by Aristotle, Buddha, and Confucius, Vallor (2016) offers the following *technomoral virtues* for shaping the future of technology: honesty, self-control, humility, justice, courage, empathy, care, civility, flexibility, perspective, magnanimity, and technomoral wisdom. The overarching outcome from these technomoral virtues is practical wisdom that can applied to different contexts.

Technomoral virtues in turn lead to technomoral wisdom, which is essential among designers, developers, and brokers of innovative technologies. However, neither technomoral virtue nor wisdom can be cultivated in the abstract or in a void. Wisdom is acquired through experience and engagement with ethical dilemmas about the benefits of technology and potential long-term effects on people and the planet. Furthermore, there is no shortcut for acquiring technomoral virtues. They are acquired over time in community through relationships with others, understanding and managing oneself, engaging in continuous practice, and committing to developing moral character.

Consolidating insights from three traditions—Aristotelean, Buddhist, and Confucian—Vallor (2016) offers seven core elements to cultivate the virtues that are the substance of moral character: moral habituation, relational understanding, reflective self-examination, intentional self-direction or moral development, perceptual attention to moral salience, prudential judgment, and appropriate extension of moral concern. Interestingly, some of the elements offered by Vallor, such as self-awareness, self-regulation, social awareness, and relationship management, are central to emotional intelligence, an influential framework widely used in management and leadership development (Mayer, Roberts, and Barsade 2008).

Vallor's approach is also distinct because of the moral framework within which emotional intelligence is embedded. The moral framework calls attention to perceiving moral issues (such as ESG Sustainability), using practical wisdom in addressing moral issues (environmental destruction), expressing concern and engaging in moral action (purpose-driven business strategy and societal impact), and most importantly, commitment to moral development as an intentional, ongoing process (corporate vision and strategy for addressing climate change). Technomoral virtues have an important role in digital governance on topics such as privacy and data protection, the surveillance state, intrusion into civil liberties, autonomous weapons, machine agency, artificial intelligence, and more. With every advance, technomoral prudence is required to assess the long-term effect on the planet and the type of humanity that we will become.

Concluding Remarks

In this chapter, we have reviewed four related topics that are integral to the future of digital governance: cocreation of value, stakeholder capitalism, ethics, and technomoral virtues. Each topic underscores character development and values that are crucial to corporate culture and citizenship. Although each topic offers separate insights for shaping corporate culture, collectively they converge as an integrated framework for digital governance that supports trustworthy and ethical AI. Given its outsized role, technology deserves a dedicated place within the ESG framework.

Cocreation of value is a mindset shift from instrumental exchange to relational interactions between customers and the corporation. Unlike the traditional focus on the creation of value for shareholders, cocreation is a movement toward collaborative engagement between stakeholders and corporations. Stakeholders expect more from corporations, particularly from Big Tech companies that rely heavily on user-generated data and content. In addition to expectations of environmental and social governance, corporations must attend to ethics and trust in technology to maintain corporate reputation, retain talent, and increase stakeholder capital. The governance of technology will require policies, principles, and virtues to integrate with each other to create the desirable positive outcomes. With ethics serving as guardrails, the cultivation of technomoral virtues will play a catalytic role in animating a future in which humans continue to flourish.

Affordances of technology have continuously altered the course of humanity. Early technology like the spear and the arrow enabled humans to become hunters. The same technology was used to wage war, create division, and establish power hierarchies. Humanity is at the threshold of another technological transformation, also known as the Fourth Industrial Revolution, defined by the emergence of the digitally interconnected economy and sweeping technological advances such as artificial intelligence and pervasive computing that offers both utopian promise and dystopian dread. Using ethics as guardrails and the cultivation of technomoral virtues, we can develop the trust and practical wisdom that will determine who we are and what we become.

Key Discussion Areas

- Cocreation of value and power of stakeholders.
- Rise of stakeholder capitalism.
- Environmental, social, and governance (ESG) principles.
- Technomoral virtues and virtue ethics.
- Ethics in leadership and governance.

References

AI HLEG. 2019. *Ethics Guidelines for Trustworthy AI*. Brussels: European Commission, https://data.europa.eu/doi/10.2759/346720.

Arogyaswamy, Bernard. 2020. "Big Tech and Societal Sustainability: An Ethical Framework." *AI & SOCIETY* 35(4): 829–40, https://doi.org/10.1007/s00146-020-00956-6.

Beauchamp, Tom, and James Childress. 2019. "Principles of Biomedical Ethics: Marking Its Fortieth Anniversary." *The American Journal of Bioethics* 19(11): 9–12, https://doi.org/10.1080/15265161.2019.1665402.

Bernard, Tara Siegel, Tiffany Hsu, Nicole Perlroth, and Ron Lieber. 2017. "Equifax Says Cyberattack May Have Affected 143 Million in the U.S." *The New York Times*, September 7, 2017, www.nytimes.com/2017/09/07/business/equifax-cyberattack.html.

Bhandari, Krishna Raj, Mikko Ranta, and Jari Salo. 2022. "The Resource-based View, Stakeholder Capitalism, ESG, and Sustainable Competitive Advantage: The Firm's Embeddedness into Ecology, Society, and Governance." *Business Strategy and the Environment* 31(4): 1525–37, https://doi.org/10.1002/bse.2967.

Bobrowsky, Meghan. 2023. "Theranos Founder Elizabeth Holmes's Request to Stay Out of Prison Denied." *The Wall Street Journal*, May 16, 2023, www.wsj.com/articles/theranos-founder-elizabeth-holmess-request-to-stay-free-on-bail-denied-52ef7530.

Buolamwini, Joy, and Timnit Gebru. 2018. "Gender Shades: Intersectional Accuracy Disparities in Commercial Gender Classification." In *Proceedings of the 1st Conference on Fairness, Accountability and Transparency*, 77–91. PMLR, https://proceedings.mlr.press/v81/buolamwini18a.html.

Business Roundtable. n.d. "One Year Later: Purpose of a Corporation," https://purpose.businessroundtable.org/ (accessed June 3, 2023).

Choung, Hyesun, Prabu David, and Arun Ross. 2022a. "Trust and Ethics in AI." *AI & SOCIETY*, 13, https://doi.org/10.1007/s00146-022-01473-4.

———. 2022b. "Trust in AI and Its Role in the Acceptance of AI Technologies." *International Journal of Human–Computer Interaction*, 1–13, https://doi.org/10.1080/10447318.2022.2050543.

Conger, Kate, and Mike Isaac. 2021. "Twitter Permanently Bans Trump, Capping Online Revolt." *The New York Times*, January 8, 2021, www.nytimes.com/2021/01/08/technology/twitter-trump-suspended.html.

Dangelico, Rosa Maria, and Daniele Vocalelli. 2017. " 'Green Marketing': An Analysis of Definitions, Strategy Steps, and Tools through a Systematic Review of the Literature." *Journal of Cleaner Production* 165 (November): 1263–79, https://doi.org/10.1016/j.jclepro.2017.07.184.

David, Prabu. 2004. "Extending Symmetry: Toward a Convergence of Professionalism, Practice, and Pragmatics in Public Relations." *Journal of Public Relations Research* 16(2): 185–211, https://doi.org/10.1207/s1532754xjprr1602_3.

Eckhouse, Laurel, Kristian Lum, Cynthia Conti-Cook, and Julie Ciccolini. 2019. "Layers of Bias: A Unified Approach for Understanding Problems With Risk Assessment." *Criminal Justice and Behavior* 46(2): 185–209, https://doi.org/10.1177/0093854818811379.

Edelman. 2021. "Edelman Trust Barometer 2021." Annual Edelman Trust Barometer, www.edelman.com/sites/g/files/aatuss191/files/2021-03/2021%20Edelman%20Trust%20Barometer.pdf.

Fink, Larry. 2022. "The Power of Capitalism," www.blackrock.com/corporate/investor-relations/larry-fink-ceo-letter (accessed June 3, 2023).

Floridi, Luciano, Josh Cowls, Monica Beltrametti, Raja Chatila, Patrice Chazerand, Virginia Dignum, Christoph Luetge, et al. 2018. "AI4People—An Ethical Framework for a Good AI Society: Opportunities, Risks, Principles, and Recommendations." *Minds and Machines* 28(4): 689–707, https://doi.org/10.1007/s11023-018-9482-5.

Gast, A., P. Illanes, N. Probst, B. Schaninger, and B. Simpson. 2020. "Purpose: Shifting from Why to How." April 20, 2020, http://ceros.mckinsey.com/authors-sidebar-mobile.

Gates, Guilbert, Jack Ewing, Karl Russell, and Derek Watkins. 2015. "How Volkswagen's 'Defeat Devices' Worked." *The New York Times*, October 8, 2015, sec. Business, www.nytimes.com/interactive/2015/business/international/vw-diesel-emissions-scandal-explained.html.

Glueck, Katie, and Frances Robles. 2022. "Punishing Disney, DeSantis Signals a Lasting G.O.P. Brawl with Business." *The New York Times*, April 22, 2022, sec. U.S, www.nytimes.com/2022/04/22/us/politics/desantis-disney-florida.html.

Goldstein, Matthew. 2022. "Stellantis to Pay $300 Million to End an Emissions Case." *The New York Times*, June 3, 2022, sec. Business, www.nytimes.com/2022/06/03/business/stellantis-diesel-emissions.html.

Hagendorff, Thilo. 2022. "A Virtue-Based Framework to Support Putting AI Ethics into Practice." *Philosophy & Technology* 35(3): 55, https://doi.org/10.1007/s13347-022-00553-z.

Hassani, Bertrand K. 2021. "Societal Bias Reinforcement through Machine Learning: A Credit Scoring Perspective." *AI and Ethics* 1(3): 239–47, https://doi.org/10.1007/s43681-020-00026-z.

Hemphill, Thomas A., Keith E. Kelley, and Francine Cullari. 2021. "The Ascendancy of Stakeholder Capitalism: What Is Its Meaning for Corporate Governance?" *Journal of General Management* 46(4): 262–73, https://doi.org/10.1177/0306307020982132.

Hill, Kashmir. 2020. "The Secretive Company That Might End Privacy as We Know It." *The New York Times*, January 18, 2020, sec. Technology, www.nytimes.com/2020/01/18/technology/clearview-privacy-facial-recognition.html.

Hunkenschroer, Anna Lena, and Christoph Luetge. 2022. "Ethics of AI-Enabled Recruiting and Selection: A Review and Research Agenda." *Journal of Business Ethics* 178(4): 977–1007, https://doi.org/10.1007/s10551-022-05049-6.

John, M. 2020. "Capitalism Seen Doing 'More Harm Than Good' in Global Survey." *Reuters*, January 20, 2020, sec. Business News, www.reuters.com/article/us-davos-meeting-trust-idUSKBN1ZJ0CW.

Kang, Cecilia, and Sheera Frenkel. 2018. "Facebook Says Cambridge Analytica Harvested Data of Up to 87 Million Users." *The New York Times*, April 4, 2018, sec. Technology, www.nytimes.com/2018/04/04/technology/mark-zuckerberg-testify-congress.html.

Kelly, Gavin, Dominic Kelly, and Andrew Gamble, eds. 1997. *Stakeholder Capitalism*. Houndmills, Basingstoke [England] : New York: Palgrave Macmillan.

Koehn, Daryl. 1995. "A Role for Virtue Ethics in the Analysis of Business Practice." *Business Ethics Quarterly* 5(3): 533–39, https://doi.org/10.2307/3857397.

Kostka, Genia, Léa Steinacker, and Miriam Meckel. 2021. "Between Security and Convenience: Facial Recognition Technology in the Eyes of Citizens in China, Germany, the United Kingdom, and the United States." *Public Understanding of Science* 30(6): 671–90, https://doi.org/10.1177/09636625211001555.

Lankton, Nancy, D. Harrison McKnight, and Jason Bennett Thatcher. 2014. "Incorporating Trust-in-technology into Expectation Disconfirmation Theory." *The Journal of Strategic Information Systems* 23(2): 128–45.

Mayer, John D., Richard D. Roberts, and Sigal G. Barsade. 2008. "Human Abilities: Emotional Intelligence." *Annual Review of Psychology* 59(1): 507–36, https://doi.org/10.1146/annurev.psych.59.103006.093646.

Microsoft. n.d. "What We Value," www.microsoft.com/en-us/about/values (accessed June 3, 2023).

Mittelstadt, Brent. 2019. "Principles Alone Cannot Guarantee Ethical AI." *Nature Machine Intelligence* 1(11): 501–7, https://doi.org/10.1038/s42256-019-0114-4.

Murray, Alan, and David Meyer. 2022. "Friday Feedback: Stakeholder Capitalism vs. Socialism," https://fortune.com/2022/02/18/friday-feedback-stakeholder-capitalism-vs-socialism-ceo-daily/ (accessed June 3, 2023).

Nietzsche, Friedrich Wilhelm. 1962. *Philosophy in the Tragic Age of the Greeks*. Gateway edition. Washington, DC: Regnery.

Nissenbaum, H. 2011. "A Contextual Approach to Privacy Online." *Daedalus* 140(4): 32–48.

Parikh, Ravi B., Stephanie Teeple, and Amol S. Navathe. 2019. "Addressing Bias in Artificial Intelligence in Health Care." *JAMA* 322(24): 2377, https://doi.org/10.1001/jama.2019.18058.

Pew Research Center. 2022. "American's Views of Government: Decades of Distrust, Enduring Support for Its Role," www.pewresearch.org/politics/2022/06/06/americans-views-of-government-decades-of-distrust-enduring-support-for-its-role/ (accessed June 6, 2023).

Prahalad, C. K., and Venkat Ramaswamy. 2004. "Co-Creation Experiences: The Next Practice in Value Creation." *Journal of Interactive Marketing* 18(3): 5–14, https://doi.org/10.1002/dir.20015.

Ramaswamy, Venkat, and Kerimcan Ozcan. 2019. "Digitalized Interactive Platforms: Turning Goods and Services into Retail Co-Creation Experiences." *NIM Marketing Intelligence Review* 11(1): 18–23, https://doi.org/10.2478/nimmir-2019-0003.

Ramaswamy, Venkatram, and Francis J. Gouillart. 2010. *The Power of Co- Creation: Build It with Them to Boost Growth, Productivity, and Profits*. 1st Free Press hardcover ed. New York: Free Press.

Salesforce. 2020. "How Far Can the 1–1–1 Model Go?" www.salesforce.com/news/stories/how-far-can-the-1-1-1-model-go-this-tech-darling-has-a-unique-approach/ (accessed June 3, 2023).

Schiffer, Zoë, Casey Newton, and Alex Heath. 2023. "Tears, Blunders and Chaos: Inside Elon Musk's Twitter." *The Guardian*, January 29, 2023, www.theguardian.com/technology/2023/jan/29/tears-blunders-and-chaos-inside-elon-musk-twitter.

Schwab, Klaus. 2016. *The Fourth Industrial Revolution*. First U.S. edition. New York: Crown Business.

———. 2021. *Stakeholder Capitalism: A Global Economy That Works for Progress, People and Planet*. Hoboken, NJ: Wiley.

Seberger, John S., Hyesun Choung, and Prabu David. In press. "To Imagine More Deeply: Understanding What AI Communicates." In *Research Handbook on AI and Communication*, edited by Seungahn Nah. Northampton, MA: Elgar Publishing.

Streitfeld, David. 2022. "The Epic Rise and Fall of Elizabeth Holmes." *The New York Times*, January 4, 2022, sec. Technology, www.nytimes.com/2022/01/03/technology/elizabeth-holmes-theranos.html.

Vallor, Shannon. 2016. *Technology and the Virtues: A Philosophical Guide to a Future Worth Wanting*. New York, NY: Oxford University Press.

Windsor, Duane. 2001. "The Future of Corporate Social Responsibility." *The International Journal of Organizational Analysis* 9(3): 225–56, https://doi.org/10.1108/eb028934.

Zuboff, Shoshana. 2019. *The Age of Surveillance Capitalism: The Fight for a Human Future at the New Frontier of Power*. London: Profile Books.

PART 5

Health and Environmental Sustainability Governance

This part on health and environmental sustainability governance analyzes the need to strengthen transformational and sustainable governance approaches within the corporate, health, and environmental sectors in light of two concurrent societal crisis, the Covid-19 pandemic and climate change. For over two years, the pandemic has exposed weaknesses in global health systems and is responsible for over six million deaths. Many more health crises and pandemics are likely to impact world population. Global warming is an existential threat to the entire planet, and its effects are intensifying and accelerating. This part also analyzes the impacts of climate change on human health and how intergovernmental health and environmental agencies are undertaking mitigation and adaption efforts to address those impacts. Governments and businesses need to adopt an international governance framework for sustainable development based on the environmental, social, and governance (ESG) sustainability frameworks. Businesses, such as the fashion industry, need to be transparent and accountable not only at the corporate level but also throughout the entire business value chain. Likewise, to better respond to future pandemics and the effects of climate change, governments need to improve health system performance as well as expand universal health coverage in developing countries.

The first chapter by Sarah Angold discusses the international fashion industry's negative contribution to several global problems such as global warming, environmental pollution, and biodiversity loss. The author presents an outline for an international governance framework for sustainable development to mitigate these impacts. This chapter focuses on various fashion case studies and environmental governance structures that exist in the United Kingdom. Angold concludes by reflecting on further regulatory policies needed and recommends policies and practices for achieving effective fit-for-purpose sustainable governance approaches.

The next chapter by Aimée Girdwood and Christina Bartholomew analyzes the role the legal profession can play in promoting more sustainable governance practices in the corporate sector. They argue that business should adopt higher levels of responsible business standards that incorporate and respond to ESG values. This chapter focuses on the role lawyers can play in promoting the adoption and practice of ESG principles by companies. When that client is a business, advice and counsel must reflect the principles of

DOI: 10.4324/9781003316077-30

transformational governance to be in the best interest of the business's long-term, sustainable future.

The third chapter by Preeti Shroff-Mehta, Vijay Viswanathan, Sukaran Thakur, and Parker Lemal-Brown analyzes how legacy and start-up companies are focusing on environmental and social governance sustainability dimensions in different ways. In the past, such companies overwhelmingly concentrated on stock-market performance and profits, but today many are adopting sustainable practices, redefining their global value chains, and taking up green restorative measures. These changes in corporate behavior are also heightened by the challenges posed by the Covid-19 crisis and the negative environmental impact of many companies. This chapter examines the track record and approach of numerous companies to analyze the scope, scale, and sequencing of how they integrate ESG values into their business plans. It compares legacy, technology, and start-up companies to highlight that large legacy companies might struggle more to adapt ESG as a holistic approach, while start-up companies are in a better position to focus on all three components of ESG governance and compliance, and also to emphasize ESG-I (Self-Governance) focused on leadership and self-transformation as the key for ESG theory and practice.

The chapter by K. V. Ramani provides a framework for health systems to operate in crisis times. This chapter details the primary objectives of health systems and presents a framework for their management based on the governance triangle of government, service providers, and beneficiaries. It further analyzes major health policies and their impact on health system performance in the post-pandemic period. This chapter lays the case for how the adoption of universal health coverage (UHC) will ensure a better quality of life and contribute toward economic and social development, particularly in developing countries.

The final chapter by Henry Falk examines the catastrophic environmental, economic, and social impacts of global warming on health, including changing patterns of diseases, mental health, and global medicine. This chapter highlights various initiatives undertaken by intergovernmental and nongovernmental organizations at the global level to mitigate (prevent) and/or adapt (respond) to the many impacts of climate change. This chapter concludes by examining the many steps taken in the United States by national and local governments to adapt health systems to this new reality.

The key reflection questions are futuristic and thought-provoking. In the face of national and multilateral government inaction on climate change (or not enough action), diversity, and inclusion, do individual responsibility and corporate governance step up and fill the gaps? What are the implications of this translation of responsibility? What are national versus global approaches and innovations to problem-solving (Covid-19 vaccine procurement being a good example). Do better resourced countries, who contribute more to climate change, need to help struggling countries who are overwhelmingly feeling the effects? These chapters all point to health as more than just about being free from disease. Rather, they present health in a more holistic sense of mental, physical, and emotional well-being of individuals, communities, and society. How can digital world and human governance frameworks better reflect this holistic idea of health?

25

SUSTAINABLE FUTURES

Developing a Governance Framework for Transition in the Fashion Industry and Beyond

Sarah Angold

The Globe in Crisis

Securing a sustainable future is one of the defining governance problems of the twenty-first century. The world is facing three interrelated environmental crises of climate change, biodiversity collapse, and toxic environmental pollution. In his book *Green Swans*, renowned sustainable development expert John Elkington (2020) talks of "Super Wicked Problems." Time is running out to solve these problems, and those causing them need to contribute to addressing them. Unfortunately, the necessary coordinated governance structure required to address them is weak or nonexistent, and irrational inaction toward these crises undermines any necessary long-term strategy (Levin et al. 2012). The topics of this chapter constitute a series of super wicked problems that pose complex system challenges for a multitude of industries and global governance as a whole.

In August 2021, the Intergovernmental Panel on Climate Change (IPCC) released its latest major climate assessment report (AR6). Its message was blunt: the world is close to breaching the 1.5°C threshold that the international Paris Climate Agreement pledged to avoid, putting unprecedented stress on the natural systems that support life on earth.

At the time of writing, greenhouse-gas emission trends put the world on course for at least 2.7°C of heating above pre-industrial levels. A 2.7°C trajectory was also quoted in the run up to the Conference of the Parties to the UN Framework Convention on Climate Change Summit 26 (COP26) in Glasgow 2021 (UNFCCC Secretariat 2021), demonstrating that in the past eighteen months, despite stark warnings, nothing has changed. In this 2.7°C warming scenario, we can expect to see hundreds of millions of people displaced (Australian Academy of Science 2021) due to flooding, fires and heatwaves, devastating storms, regular disease outbreaks, and widespread famines. The United Nation's special rapporteur on extreme poverty and human rights, Philip Alston, warns of a "climate apartheid" in which only the rich can escape "overheating, hunger and conflict" (BBC News 2019).

The landmark 2019 global assessment report from the UN-Appointed Intergovernmental Science-Policy Platform for Biodiversity and Ecosystem Services (IPBES) outlined the alarming rate at which the diversity and abundance of life on earth is being destroyed (IPBES 2019). The existence of one quarter of all known species is now threatened, as

DOI: 10.4324/9781003316077-31

human activity may already be precipitating a sixth mass extinction event on Earth (Ceballos, Ehrlich, and Dirzo 2017).

Meanwhile, air, water, and soil pollution from chemicals and plastics are undermining the resilience of entire ecosystems and the health of human and animal communities around the world. At the time of writing, the effects of ingesting the microplastic particles and fibers now ubiquitous in air, water, and soil (*New Scientist* 2019) are yet to be determined. However, the World Health Organization (WHO) estimates that 4.2 million deaths are caused worldwide every year by ambient air pollution (WHO 2021). The UK government has consistently failed to meet the EU's air pollution standards, and its air quality plans have been judged in court to be unlawful on three separate occasions. In 2022, a *historic High Court ruling found the UK government's entire climate strategy to be "unlawful"* and "inadequate" and ordered that it should be reworked by the end of March 2023. It also found that parliament and the public were "effectively kept in the dark about a shortfall in meeting a key target to cut emissions."[1] The 2030 Strategic Framework for International Climate and Nature Action, published by the government on March 30, 2023 (HM Government 2023), aims to address the High Court's criticisms. At the time of writing, this legislation is only one month old, making it too early to assess its success.

Poorer communities and nations will experience the adverse effects of climate change and ecological destruction most acutely. Geographical location, weaker health-care and welfare systems, greater direct reliance on local agriculture, and lack of funding or capacity for climate adaptation make many communities in low-income nations, often referred to as the Global South, more vulnerable (Islam and Winkel 2017). The UN Secretary-General António Guterres framed the IPCC report as representing a "code red for humanity" (United Nations 2021).

What Are Sustainability Governance and Sustainable Development Concepts?

Governance can be defined as the various rules of practice and structures of accountability or scrutiny that an individual company or business sector can be subject to, either voluntarily or statutorily, via self-regulation, co-regulation, or direct state regulation and licensing arrangements (Puppis 2010).

At the root of the challenge in establishing sustainability governance is the question of what role the UK government *ought* to be playing. How heavily should the government be legislating versus relying on market forces? Should the goal be incremental change or systemic overhaul? Could Richard Thaler and Cass Sunstein's (2009) "Nudge Theory" encourage change at scale without curbing freedom of choice? Nudge Theory is based upon the idea that by shaping "choice architecture" (e.g., displaying confectionary by the supermarket checkout), one can influence the likelihood that individuals will choose one option over another. A key factor of Nudge Theory is the ability for an individual to maintain freedom of choice and to feel in control of the decisions they make.

While opinion here will partly depend on political leaning, this chapter will draw from a broad range of sources, including interviews with industry leaders and reports from the British Fashion Council and the Centre of Sustainable Fashion to suggest what role the UK government should, and more importantly, *needs* to play in order to enable a sustainable transition.

"Securing the Future—The UK Government Sustainable Development Strategy (2005)"[2] defines the goal of sustainable development as enabling "all people throughout the world to satisfy their basic needs and enjoy a better quality of life, without compromising the quality of life of future generations."

It is only since the industrial revolution—and largely only in the latter half of the twentieth century—that governance practices and structures to manage our impact on the environment have become more formalized. For example, the EU, which today has some of the most progressive environmental policies of any country or group of countries in the world, had no environmental policy, laws, or administration at its outset in the late 1950s (Jordan and Gravey 2021). It was only in the 1970s and 1980s that the first items of EU environmental policy were agreed by the Council of Ministers, following proposals from the European Commission. Indeed, in many ways, environmental governance remains in its infancy.

International Sustainability Governance

At the international level, the United Nations has provided the main forum for dialogue and agreement on environmental governance. The promising early success of the Montreal Protocol on Substances that Deplete the Ozone Layer, adopted in 1987, is still the only UN treaty that has been ratified by every country on the planet.[3] Five years later in 1992, the UN Earth Summit established two major international governance structures for climate and biodiversity: the United Nations Framework Convention on Climate Change (UNFCCC) and the Convention on Biological Diversity.[4] These ongoing multilateral processes have led to global agreements to halt biodiversity decline as per the Aichi Biodiversity Targets adopted in 2010[5] and limit climate heating as per the Paris Climate Agreement from 2015.[6] However, progress has been limited and delivery on the legally binding internationally agreed biodiversity targets has been poor. At the time of writing, nationally determined contributions proposed under the Paris Climate Agreement do not go nearly far enough to limit temperature rises to between 1.5°C and 2°C. In 2015, at the UN Sustainable Development Summit, 193 member states agreed on the 2030 Agenda for Sustainable Development, which lists seventeen Sustainable Development Goals (SDGs) covering social and environmental priorities such as promoting gender equality, access to clean water, sustainable consumption and production, and reducing pollution. Today, the UN SDGs continue to serve as a road map toward the realization of the 2030 UN Agenda. That said, as we pass the timeline's halfway point, and global emissions continue to increase, it is clear that a more robust commitment is required from all stakeholders to ensure that the agenda is achieved "in its entirety, without any areas of underachievement which may ultimately serve to undermine the whole" (Eggenberger 2022).

The World Economic Forum's SDG progress report (Eggenberger 2022) noted that "the greatest steps forward have been achieved through cooperation, rather than isolated efforts," strengthening the case for greater government collaboration with the private sector, academics, and municipalities in "a 'whole-of society' effort to achieve sustainable development."

National Sustainability Governance in the United Kingdom

The United Kingdom boasts some early examples of environmental legislation, such as the Alkali Act (1863) and the Clean Air Act (1956), but it was not until 1970 that the first Department of the Environment was created within the British Government. The UK environmental regulator—the Environment Agency, a nondepartmental public body that reports to the Department for Environment, Food and Rural Affairs—was established in 1996. Parliamentary scrutiny of environmental policies has increased since the 1990s. In 1997, the Environmental Audit Select Committee was established in the House of Commons to scrutinize government and public sector performance in this area.

In the mid-2000s, climate change rose up the UK political agenda, and the growing consensus around the issue led to the UK government introducing the Climate Change Act 2008. This legislation set a legally binding target for the United Kingdom to reduce greenhouse-gas emissions by 80 percent of 1990 levels by 2050 and established a system of five yearly carbon budgets to reduce emissions cumulatively toward that target. The act covers the so-called territorial emissions that occur within the United Kingdom but it does *not* cover the embodied "consumption emissions" associated with the products UK consumers buy if the raw material production and manufacturing occur in other countries. The act established an independent Climate Change Committee (CCC)—an expert panel supported by a full-time secretariat to advise the government on setting carbon budgets and model pathways to reduce emissions across the economy. The CCC is required to produce an annual progress report to Parliament on reducing emissions and a biannual progress report on adapting to climate change. In 2019, the UK Parliament approved the government's proposal to strengthen the target in the Climate Change Act in line with the Paris Climate Agreement goals of 2015. The United Kingdom's legal target is now to reach net-zero greenhouse-gas emissions by 2050.

A raft of new governance measures on sustainability are being enacted in the United Kingdom. Following a recommendation by the Environmental Audit Committee (House of Commons Environmental Audit Committee 2018), the UK Government set out its *Green Finance Strategy* (Department for Business, Energy & Industrial Strategy 2019), which promised to establish new responsibilities for financial regulators to "have regard for the Paris Agreement when carrying out their duties." It also announced the government's intention to make climate-related financial disclosures mandatory for listed companies and large asset owners, through the Task Force on Climate-Related Financial Disclosures (TCFD). The TCFD had been established in 2015 by the international Financial Stability Board (FSB) to develop consistent climate-related financial risk disclosures for use by banks, companies, and investors. The relevant financial regulators in the United Kingdom, the Financial Conduct Authority and the Pensions Regulator, have been implementing this decision since April 6, 2022, from which date over 1,300 of the largest UK-registered companies and financial institutions became required by law to disclose climate-related financial information. Further financial regulation is promised in the UK chancellor's *Greening Finance: A Roadmap to Sustainable Investing*, published in October 2021. The roadmap sets out new Sustainability Disclosure Requirements (SDRs) and includes requirements for all investment products to justify sustainability claims and to disclose the environmental impacts of the activities they finance.

New legislative action in the Environment Act gives the UK government powers to encourage a shift in design practice and enable consumers to make informed purchasing decisions. The law also enables the government to introduce extended producer responsibility (EPR) schemes (detailed below) for specified products or materials,[7] which could encourage the shift from a linear to a circular economy. These powers have yet to be noticeably utilized.

Finally, the Competitions and Markets Authority (CMA) recently launched the Green Claims Code, with new fines for companies that fail to verify sustainability claims. The intention is to clamp down on "greenwashing"—leading people to believe that a company is doing more to protect than it really is—and empower consumers to make more sustainable choices. We will unpack this, along with other specific legislation in relation to fashion, in the following case study.

Fashion Case Study

Fashion in Crisis

The global fashion industry contributes to climate change, biodiversity loss, and river and ocean pollution on an enormous scale.

In February 2019, the UK House of Commons cross-party scrutiny body, the Environmental Audit Committee (EAC), published *Fixing Fashion: Clothing Consumption and Sustainability* (House of Commons Environmental Audit Committee 2019). The report concluded that the way we make, use, and dispose of our clothing is unsustainable. It identified expanding consumption in the UK "fast fashion" industry as a key contributor to climate heating, ocean pollution, and water stress in the Global South. It noted the United Kingdom's textile waste problem as well as concerns about the seemingly disposable nature of clothing that is cheaply produced and purchased, thereby enabling a consumer and media obsession with newness. Fashion's environmental price tag is hefty, particularly in the initial stages of production, whether growing natural fibers or chemically producing synthetic ones. The report concluded that it is vital to keep clothes and fibers in use for longer as part of a circular system of reusing, reselling, upcycling, and recycling.

Textile Waste

In 2022, The Ellen Macarthur Foundation (2022) revealed that, globally, less than 1 percent of clothing is recycled, leading to the equivalent of a truck load of clothing being sent to landfill or burnt every second.

The Waste and Resources Action Programme (WRAP)'s *Textiles Market Situation Report 2019*—featuring figures from 2017 to 2018—was, at the time of writing, the most up-to-date and comprehensive analysis of fashion consumption, waste, and recycling in the United Kingdom. WRAP estimated that UK consumers discarded 1.04 million tons of clothing in 2017 (WRAP 2019). When bed sheets and tablecloths, bags, footwear, and leisure textiles, like sleeping bags, are included, the total is 1.7 million tons of textiles. According to a residual waste survey, UK households put an estimated 336,000 tons of *clothing* into household bins (destined for landfill or incineration rather than upcycling/recycling) in 2017.

Overproduction, overconsumption, and waste were key recurring themes throughout the expert interviews I conducted for this book. Interviewees were asked specific, non-leading questions about the ways in which public governance supported or undermined each interviewee's professional pursuit of a sustainable transition.

In my interview with him, Alan Wheeler, CEO of the UK Textile Recycling Association, explained that recycling can only be part of the solution: "There's just too much production, too much stuff."[8] Rachel Arthur, sustainability consultant for organizations like Google and the UN, agrees: "When you look at science-based targets there is literally only one conclusion: whatever happens, the fashion industry *has* to reduce production."[9]

The Climate Footprint of Fashion

The climate impact of the fashion industry continues to grow as consumers buy more (World Economic Forum 2020). Global Fashion Agenda's *The Pulse 2019 Update* revealed that "the pace of sustainability progress in the fashion industry . . . is not moving fast enough to counterbalance the harmful impact of . . . rapid growth."[10] Boston Consulting Group supported this assertion that sustainable efforts "are being outweighed by the rapid growth of the global fashion economy" (Farra 2019). According to research by consultant firm McKinsey, undertaken in partnership with Global Fashion Agenda, the global fashion sector was responsible for 2.1 billion metric tons of greenhouse-gas (GHG) emissions in 2018, about 4 percent of the global total. "To set that in context, the fashion industry emits about the same quantity of GHGs per year as the entire economies of France, Germany, and the United Kingdom combined" (Berg et al. 2020). The McKinsey report suggested that, given the fashion industry's current pace of decarbonization, emissions will be capped at around 2.1 billion tons per year by 2030, "roughly the same as they are today." This is almost double the level necessary to align with the Paris Agreement goals of limiting temperature rise to 1.5°C.

Approaching the Problem From a Governance Perspective

New and effective governance structures are urgently needed to halt the damage being caused by the industry. The United Kingdom's voluntary industry agreement *Textiles 2030* could—if designed and implemented effectively—provide potential governance models for industries in transition. Indeed, by calling for halving emissions in the next decade, Textiles 2030 sets the most ambitious targets for the fashion industry in the world. However, there is considerable skepticism about the effectiveness of voluntary targets, even when blended with legislative action and financial incentives for sustainability.

A substantial problem for the governance of the fashion industry in a globalized supply and demand system is that of defining the extent of the industry itself and what might constitute suitable points for intervention. We could start with the citizen who purchases an item. How do they make a purchase decision? Do they look at the label or consider the information available online to see where the product was made and its material content? Do they reflect on the reputation of the brand, considering information in the public sphere from campaign groups like Fashion Revolution, media reports, or sustainability influencers on social media? Do they have enough information to make an informed decision as well as a level of financial stability (or privilege) to consider paying a higher price for a product with a better environmental and ethical footprint?

As we move along the supply chain, we see that those involved in designing, commissioning, and buying products at a brand level are also making decisions that could involve and be characterized as governance. Do they ask how the materials are made and by whom? Do the conditions of extraction and manufacture factor into their purchasing decisions? Do they prioritize cost, aesthetics, or sustainable credentials? Are they signatories to any voluntary codes around treatment of workers responsible for manufacture? Do innovative and sustainable fashion enterprises face unfair competition from businesses focused on reducing costs and maximizing profits regardless of potential negative environmental or social implications?

At a factory level, often abroad and in developing countries, the manager who sources fibers and materials and directs garment workers makes further decisions. Do they cut corners and exploit workers to maximize profit? Could they influence the carbon content of the energy their factory employs or are they reliant on their country's particular energy mix? How much agency does each garment worker have in terms of choosing a workplace that uses safe dyes, disposes of chemicals properly, and maintains dangerous machinery with care?

Finally, at the stage we refer to as the bottom of the supply chain, are farming methods organic or regenerative? Are producers paid a fair price for fibers and is land being used for clothing crops at the expense of feeding local populations? Climate change will have a disproportionate impact on the Global South, yet more developed countries are largely responsible for emissions. What do we owe those countries that suffer at our expense? Finally, developed nations have reached their wealthy positions through unrestricted industrialization that created enormous emissions. How can we enable developing countries who are striving to do the same, without the planet paying a hefty environmental price.

At each stage, we are faced with definitional and informational uncertainties to which can be added general problems of deciding on the best strategies for providing sustainable services that span many sectors. For instance, should nuclear energy be included in the mix for generating electrical power sustainably? Here, a lack of integrated policy between international governments, NGOs, investors, financial institutions, and industry creates barriers to consistent policy conducive to action. Public leaders in sustainable development should understand that "sustainability leadership is not about addressing just one or two core areas, it also means embedding sustainable development into an organization so profoundly that it is indistinguishable from mainstream culture" (Bierney et al. 2010). This is the task facing governments globally, and one which many argue has not yet been adequately addressed.

In supply chains stretching out from the United Kingdom, environmental governance has, until recently, relied on the voluntary decisions of consumers, businesses, and producers to "do the right thing." These decisions are often based on very little supply-chain information. This method has proved unsuccessful on many occasions, as evidenced by the limited progress toward a sustainable transition in the fashion industry. Lord Nicholas Stern, leading climate economist and author of the seminal 2006 government study into the costs of climate change, famously asserted that "climate change is a result of the greatest market failure the world has seen." He further noted that "those who damage others by emitting greenhouse gasses generally do not pay" (Benjamin 2021) for this negative impact.

Let's look at how we might characterize climate change as a market failure. First, our current economic model (capitalism) uses a metric of success (GDP) that is not aligned with sustainable goals and relies on global markets to "self-regulate" through the mechanism of price. In other words, changing prices (through demand and supply) are expected to lead to an efficient allocation of resources and the best overall outcome for society, without any governmental intervention.

In his book *Less Is More, How Degrowth Will Save The World* (2021), economic anthropologist Jason Hickel notes that, historically, capitalism has driven empire and slavery. Today, it continues to drive inequality in climate crisis, where wealthy nations exploit the global atmosphere in yet another form of colonialism. UK Minister of Parliament Caroline Lucas goes as far as to assert that "we need a new economic model, which puts people's quality of life and well-being first. That means growing the right things, like thriving communities" rather than just growing GDP (Lucas 2022).

In the case of climate change, the adverse effects of greenhouse gases are "external" to the market (an externality). This means that they are not "priced" or indeed paid for by the producer or individual purchaser. Therefore, there is often only an ethical—rather than an economic—incentive for businesses and consumers to reduce their emissions. As a result, the market fails by over-producing greenhouse gases (among other things). The individual who purchases goods does not pay the "cost" of emissions (through a higher market price), yet enjoys the benefit of the item purchased. Meanwhile, the rest of society endures the environmental and humanitarian fall out and receives no benefit from the product. Individual and political preferences for market intervention remain mixed. However, some experts suggest that adopting the levers of taxation and subsidy for emissions and sustainable practice, respectively, as well as the outright banning of some harmful practices and chemicals is the only way to "level the playing field." This could enable sustainable businesses to be price competitive, thereby addressing the market failure through legal intervention. On the other hand, as consumers increasingly consider sustainable credentials a driver of purchase, and green business opportunities like clean tech expand rapidly, some suggest that the market will readjust in time without intervention. The problem is, given the current level of global emissions, not to mention their upward trajectory, it is difficult to view waiting and seeing as a feasible option if we are to avoid environmental catastrophe.

Some feel that government is "dragging its heels"[11] in designing and implementing strong sustainability governance. In the interviews carried out for this chapter, interviewees identified a number of complex and systemic barriers that are severely limiting progress. These include the absence of standardized sustainability definitions specific to the industry,[12] the challenge of varying and nonbinding corporate governance structures,[13] a lack of political will and consensus on the best strategies,[14] and the need for better frameworks with which to address them,[15] as well as opaque supply chains and the absence of good data upon which to base recommendations.[16] Professor Tim Jackson argues that the lack of government funding to drive policy and innovation research at speed, and scale innovation, is a core challenge (Jackson 2016). The United Kingdom "can't fight climate crisis with austerity," warned Stern in an interview with the *Observer* in 2021, amid claims that the UK Treasury is resistant to increase spending on green programs which are key to enabling progress toward net zero carbon emissions (Savage 2021). Clare Shine, director and CEO at Cambridge Institute for Sustainability Leadership (CISL), notes the challenge of short termism: "human beings are much better at reaction than prevention, even though in every sector the economic data tells us that prevention is much cheaper."[17]

Meanwhile, activist groups like Extinction Rebellion are gaining increasing support outside of their niche roots. In September 2019, global climate strikes saw four million people take to the streets, demonstrating the appetite for government intervention from members of the general public.

Fashion Industry Reports Around the Role of the UK Government

In September 2021, the British Fashion Council's Institute of Positive Fashion released its *Circular Fashion Ecosystem* report with the aim of presenting a blueprint for a circular fashion economy in the United Kingdom. Transitioning from a linear economy (where raw materials are turned into a product that becomes waste at the end of its life) to a circular economy (where products are endlessly rescued, upcycled, recycled, or fully biodegraded) is key to eliminating waste and managing natural resource scarcity on a finite planet (Raworth 2017).

Broadly, the report cited the following three key observations below (among many others) and noted that "the UK government should lead on policy creation, incentive-setting, and investment for developing the required innovations and enabling infrastructure for a circular fashion economy in the UK."

1. Significant research and coordination are needed to maximize collaborative actions. Information accessibility and transparency throughout the ecosystem must be improved.
2. There is more work to be done to educate the consumer on garment care, end of garment life, and recycling.
3. Digital technologies can facilitate and unlock multiple elements of the target state.

(Institute of Positive Fashion 2021)

In my interview with Shailja Dubé, Lead of Institute of Positive Fashion at the British Fashion Council, she elaborated:

> I see the government's responsibility as three-fold: 1, Ensure accessibility to sustainable choices for citizens by creating the right set of business conditions through regulation, tax breaks, and incentives; 2, Invest in upskilling and green jobs and a shift to the circular economy in order to future-proof society and industry; 3, Co-create inclusive solutions through multi-stakeholder initiatives, as collaboration between government, industry, and other actors is key to accelerate positive impact.[18]

More specifically, an interactive diagram (Institute of Positive Fashion, n.d.) highlights what the British Fashion Council regards as the UK government's roles in leading and enabling a sustainable transition in the fashion industry. Suggested "leading" roles include standardizing local-authority textile collection systems, investing in advanced textile sorting, financing emerging technologies for the fashion industry, scaling up recycling, introducing an Extended Producer Responsibility (EPR) scheme, developing feedstock and label standards, modeling industry and innovation hubs, and providing grants and start-up incubation funding. Suggested "enabling" roles include mainstreaming circular design; supporting manufacturing in the United Kingdom; educating for circularity; changing perceptions of recycled content; shifting consumer practices; formalizing skills; boosting recommerce; investing in upskilling for sortation and recycling; modeling economic and material flows; mainstreaming metrics for societal prosperity; and directing investment toward circular performance (Institute of Positive Fashion 2021).

The European Commission's 2019 report *Mapping Sustainable Fashion Opportunities for SME* recognized small and medium-sized enterprises (SMEs, which make up the majority of businesses in the UK fashion sector) as key agents of change requiring support. "With the right support, [SMEs] can lead the transition towards a more sustainable fashion industry" (European Commission 2019). In the Centre for Sustainable Fashion's 2020 report *Rethinking Fashion Design Entrepreneurship: Fostering Sustainable Practices*, Principal Investigator Sandy Black, agrees: "Micro and small independent fashion businesses have functioned as the 'research and development' for the wider fashion industry for many years, while they themselves struggle to survive" (Centre for Sustainable Fashion 2020). Professor Dilys Williams adds:

> [W]e have seen visions, practices and processes undertaken by fashion designer entrepreneurs that might, if recognised, create a zeitgeist in practice and values based on their alternative approaches. . . . Such businesses offer the potential to shift the fashion system from one that contributes to our current ecological and social crisis to one that contributes to prosperity in ecological, social, cultural, and economic terms.

Interviewee's Suggestions Concerning the Role of the UK Government

Definition

While there exists an EU wide taxonomy that defines what can be regarded as "sustainable activities" (European Commission 2020), and the United Kingdom is in the process of developing its own, the absence of comprehensive, industry-specific definitions is problematic.

"Government has not defined what sustainable fashion is," asserts Mary Creagh CBE, former MP, shadow secretary of state for transport, and chair of the Environmental Audit Select Committee.[19] In another interview, the Global CSO of a leading international luxury brand pointed specifically to materials: "The government must provide a definition of sustainable materials." While Condé Nast and the Centre of Sustainable Fashion have attempted to fill this gap with their Sustainable Fashion Glossary,[20] it remains the case that the UK government has not yet standardized definitions for individual industries, leaving a confusing communication landscape in which it is difficult to regulate and hold companies to account.

Bring Cohesion

Recognizing the "interconnected interdependence of sustainability issues" is crucial to driving inclusive global progress,[21] but "trying to find a cohesive governance strategy is a huge integrational challenge when different sectors have been working towards different treaty obligations with different longevities, different sets of vocational codes and training, and different measurement standards."[22] "How do you enable competing interests and resource issues to exist in a collaborative space and create a broad long-term vision to guide action planning?" asks Clare Shine, director and CEO at the Cambridge Institute for Sustainability Leadership. Since bringing cohesion requires oversight and decision-making powers across entire economic systems, the government and supra-governmental organizations like the United Nations are best placed to navigate this challenge.

Regulate Materials

The chief sustainability officer of well-known global fashion brand noted, "Where there is clear [scientific] consensus . . . government should step in to ban materials that are damaging and implement minimum standards internationally to prevent the 'race to bottom',"[23] where unsustainable practices are adopted, because they are the cheapest option. This would help to level the playing field for sustainable brands who find it difficult to be price competitive. However, in some cases, disagreement about which materials are, overall, most sustainable still prevails. "The problem is, we're not comparing like for like" said Abbie Morris, CEO of leading ESG-compliance platform Compare Ethics, "it's apples and pears." Recycled polyester is a case in point. While WRAP suggests that "there is an opportunity to grow the use of recycled polyester to help minimise carbon emissions," campaign group "Changing Markets Foundation" (CMF 2021) is not alone in asserting that we should not be encouraging any material that "cement[s] the industry's reliance on fossil fuels."

In addition to regulating unsustainable materials currently in the market, the UK government also needs to create a trade environment to support the development and uptake of sustainable materials. At present, many new sustainable materials can't compete with "traditional" materials and synthetics (which have been optimized over decades) in terms of quality, durability, performance, and price. As we move into an era with new kinds of sustainable material development, including those that are made from waste streams (like agricultural or food waste) or biofabricated (grown in a lab like alternative proteins), appropriation of materials will become a key consideration alongside overall consumption levels. If we are unwilling, as a society, to buy dramatically fewer clothes, then those items not designed for long-term use must be produced using very little energy and resource, from materials that can easily biodegrade (without chemical intervention) or be repeatedly recycled (without loss of quality/fiber shedding/significant energy use) at end of life. Such materials do not yet exist at the necessary scale, but in the future, it is likely that some combination of reduced consumption and more appropriate use of materials, alongside the growing second-hand, upcycled, and digital fashion (that only exists online for social media and our online avatars), markets will make up a more sustainable fashion landscape. Of course, as the types of materials we use and how they are sourced/created changes fundamentally, the very structure of the way that government regulates materials will need to adapt to address the opportunities and challenges that inevitably arise within new applications of science and technology. Designers must also be encouraged to consider material use at design stage, with disassembly and end of life in mind.

Create a Fair-Trade Environment

Hannah Phang, head of marketing and advocacy at sustainability consultancy Futerra, said that the UK government must "generate a fair system that has accountability for industry."[24] Another interviewee noted the need to "create a marketplace where the circular economy can thrive."[25] Since "Trade deals are driven by cost . . . the government should consider using financial instruments (be it taxation, subsidies, or both) to level the playing field so that it's a race to the top for sustainable materials," and "circular business models like rental and repair" become more attractive to industry and consumer alike. "As long as it pays to be unsustainable, chasing profits will win out over 'doing the right thing' for the majority of businesses, making exploitation and pollution a competitive advantage."[26] Even for businesses that genuinely want to be more sustainable, the conflict of interest between legally binding shareholder agreements (that prioritize the pursuit of profit) and required actions for a sustainable transition puts brands in a difficult position.

Establish International Government Collaboration for a "Just Transition"

Greenpeace defines a just transition as "moving to a more sustainable economy in a way that's fair to everyone—including people working in polluting industries" (Greenpeace 2021), for example garment workers in developing countries. A huge part of this global challenge is figuring out how to support people whose livelihoods would be affected by the transition to a greener future. As new, more sustainable industries pop up to replace those that are outdated, the task of reskilling workforces globally is a mammoth one. Automation may often have a role to play in increasing production efficiency (which can improve environmental sustainability); however, this is likely to reduce the number of jobs for those who are most vulnerable in the supply chain. How do we balance global environmental priorities with humanitarian ones and then regulate for that?

"A just transition is bigger than one government" explains Mary Creagh, noting that "governments must collaborate, and trade unions must be recognized" internationally in order not to leave anyone behind. Of course, these multilateral relationships also bring their challenges. Since climate change affects populations across the globe differently, governments, who have the needs of their own economies and voters at heart, are unlikely to agree on what "fair" looks like.

The fashion industry is not only global, but it also relies upon dozens of other industries like transport and energy in order to operate. Without integrated solutions between industries and across international borders, systems change that benefits the globe remains out of reach.

Enable Tangible Action

As we look set to not meet the reduced carbon emission targets set by the Paris Agreement, there is concern that "setting lofty new goals"[27] will be no more effective at inciting action in the absence of a detailed road map for implementation. "The Government must regulate sustainable initiatives to create structures conducive to action" asserts UN Environment Programme strategist Rachel Arthur. There must be regulatory frameworks and incentives to meet targets and deadlines with those who fail being held to account. "The responsibility for acting upon scientific evidence . . . lies squarely with policy-makers,"[28] agrees Clare Shine. In the Business of Fashion's recent podcast episode "Unpacking Fashions Role in Slowing Global Warming," Michael Sadowski, former vice president of sustainability at Nike, agrees: "industry and consumer co-optation aren't going to pull us through—we need proper government oversight to make this all work, sending signals to industry and consumer [that it is] time for change."

Reconsider Metrics of Success

For many years, the government has measured and reported on annual success in relation to gross domestic product (GDP). This narrow, short-term view of what it means to be successful does not take into account other factors of public good, like "how we make life liveable for people and societies," by fulfilling "basic needs"[29] that lead to happiness and well-being on a healthy planet. Conversely, GDP does include many kinds of economic activities that are deeply negative for society, simply because they generate revenue. For example, GDP increases with every murder because of the associated "work" created. "Fundamentally, societal prosperity needs be part of our Key Performance Indicators for business (KPIs)" explains Shailja Dubé, who added, "Government could implement an evolved set of metrics to measure business 'success' beyond the financial."[30]

Emerging Governance Framework for Fashion in the United Kingdom

The first major cross-industry initiative to reduce environmental impact in the fashion industry was coordinated by the waste charity WRAP and launched in 2012. The Sustainable Clothing Action Plan (SCAP) ran in England, Northern Ireland, and Wales until 2020 and delivered modest reductions in carbon emissions and water use but failed in its targets around waste (targeted 90,000 tons a year, achieved 1,168 tons) (White 2021).

It should be noted that SCAP did lay out some early steps and frameworks for a sustainable transition for fashion, which provided a useful signal to the industry that change was coming. However, in its 2022 report, *License to Greenwash*, the Changing Markets Foundation (CMF) criticized how certification schemes and voluntary initiatives including SCAP facilitated greenwashing in fashion. It found that "most had 'failed to meaningfully uphold high levels of ambition' and were not transparent enough to hold signatories to account."

The voluntary nature of initiatives like SCAP and its successor Textiles 2030 is plagued by a number of inherent problems.

First, signatories, who are not legally tied to any goals that they set themselves, have the "freedom to cherry-pick which interventions to target" (CMF 2022). This means that they can set a low bar (some have set targets that had already been achieved) and ignore categories of analysis where they would come off badly. Since progress is only reported on a collective level, there is no incentive for individual brands to improve, and no negative comeback for brands that fall short. Furthermore, brands could advertise ambitious targets knowing that customers would be none the wiser if they weren't met.

The CMF also noted that some targets were "based on flawed data and assumptions" (CMF 2022). For example, SCAP's footprint calculator tool assumed that the water footprint of polyester fiber production was negligible, whereas the Water Footprint Network's research concluded that "the water footprint of polyester can be as high as 71,000 cubic metres per ton of fibre," in comparison with 10,000 cubic meters per ton for cotton. The calculator recommends that brands replace cotton with polycotton to reduce environmental impact, disregarding the challenges that this blend presents at the end of life (to recycling and biodegradation) as well as its fossil-fuel content.

"This is a critical oversight . . . whereby poor data leads to inaccurate results" (CMF 2022) and the absence of a systems-led approach means that certain negative social and environmental consequences (e.g., water systems that are polluted with toxic dyes) are overlooked altogether.

Finally, it is crucial to note that all positive reductions in CO_2 and water use reported by SCAP were calculated per ton of clothing rather than as an absolute measurement of the brand's impact. Similarly, targets were set (as they have been for Textiles 2030) "per volume of garment sales/aggregate footprint of new products respectively, which allows for infinite growth" (CMF 2022). This means that brands can report on "sustainability improvements," while their overall impact on the environment worsens, because they are producing and selling in ever greater quantities.

According to WRAP's "own honest analysis of its impacts, most of the targets were reached irrespective of the SCAP initiative" (CMF 2022). The CMF concluded that SCAP "facilitated delaying tactics" for fashion brands who were not serious about making sustainable improvements. WRAP responded that its voluntary initiatives were created "in absence of legislation," pointing again to a failure of *government* to assume a leading role in defining and creating a supportive landscape for a sustainable transition in the fashion industry.

Textiles 2030

In April 2021, WRAP launched the successor to the Sustainable Clothing Action Plan. Textiles 2030 will run from 2021 to 2030.[31] In a submission to Parliament, WRAP told the Environmental Audit Committee:

> Textiles 2030 has been designed to take the learnings from SCAP, and to incorporate them in an agreement which has more ambitious targets and which attracts more of the sector to become signatories, in order to respond to some of the key points made in the Committee's "Fixing Fashion" report.[32]

The retailers and brands which have signed up to Textiles 2030 will report annually to WRAP on:

1. the total quantity of textile products placed on the market (in tons);
2. the proportions of different fiber types in the totality of new products sold;
3. the improvement actions taken, measured as a proportion of products by weight.

Meanwhile, manufacturer signatories, reuse organizations, recyclers, and other signatories will supply data each year to help determine the overall life-cycle environmental impacts of textiles. WRAP will then collate the data and report the collective progress of signatories toward the targets. Data for individual signatories will not be published.

WRAP has also unveiled the Textiles 2030 Roadmap, which aims to direct signatory actions under Textiles 2030. This sets out the water and carbon reduction targets and the key milestones (including target dates) that it deems necessary to introduce circular use of textile products and materials at scale.

Analysis of Textiles 2030: Strengths and Weaknesses

Strengths

Textiles 2030 builds on experience from previous WRAP initiatives and provides a Paris Agreement-aligned framework specifically for textiles that sets out plans to halve the industry's climate impact. WRAP recognizes that frameworks around sustainability need to set clear and specific science-based targets. Textiles 2030 has also attracted a wider participation than previous WRAP schemes.[33] The agreement is supported by more than half the UK market at launch, with nearly 60 percent of clothing placed on the market (by sales volume) by UK retailers coming under the agreement. In theory, the collaborative nature of such initiatives supports a learning environment where companies can benefit from each other's research, while simultaneously driving progress through competition in the environmental space—which, if successful, would foster investment and innovation.[34] "Industry must adopt a sharing mentality to drive solutions at speed and scale" notes Hannah Phang of Futerra in the Business of Fashion's podcast on Unpacking Fashion's Role in Slowing Global Warming.[35] It is suggested that schemes like Textiles 2030 could run alongside mandatory government policy. While the potential for legislative and voluntary mechanisms to complement each other in this space is keenly debated, successful implementation could lead to circularity being mainstreamed as a concept in the UK fashion industry. Textiles

2030 also allows civil society to have a clear line of sight around what targets are and aren't being met in aggregate in the textiles industry over the next ten years.[36]

Weaknesses

As a voluntary scheme with 60 percent market participation, the Textiles 2030 framework only covers a proportion of the industry. In some cases, those absent are likely to be brands that are less engaged with a sustainable transition or that wish to avoid scrutiny of their practices. Many industry experts agree with Shailja Dubé that "voluntary schemes are insufficient to achieve a climate positive and inclusive economy."[37]

Textiles 2030 will publish *aggregate* industry targets and results measured as a proportion of relevant products by weight but not the achievements of individual brands. As such, individual participants will not be held accountable for their contributions (or lack thereof).

Textiles 2030 is funded by brands that are themselves decision-makers in target setting, presenting a possible conflict of interest. Financially, it may not be in the immediate financial interest of these brands to set more ambitious goals

Although the delivery timetable is in line with the Paris Agreement, "Much of what is suggested in Textiles 2030 is being done already" argues Paul Foulkes-Arellano, an expert in circularity at Circuthon Consulting. He notes, as an example, "collaborations on footprint measurement tools and evidencing of the impacts of interventions." Since "many brands are already on this journey," 2030 seems like an unambitious timeline for actions that, in many cases, "could be achieved within 2–3 years."[38]

From past precedent, "we know that voluntary agreements aren't met on a whole raft of environmental initiatives, and there are no legal or financial penalties for failing to meet targets" observes Foulkes-Arellano. For example, the targets of the United Kingdom's 2008 voluntary agreement on plastic bag reduction were only met by two retailers—Co-op and M&S (the latter imposed its own additional charge). When government intervened with a plastic bag tax in 2015, there was a truly meaningful reduction in use of more than 95 percent. Notably, the tax sent a clear signal to consumers, who rejected single-use plastic bags in favor of reusable options, despite the tax being only 5 pence per bag.

Textile 2030's co-designers and administrators WRAP decided not to include targets for reducing microfiber pollution, concluding the following:

> More research needs to be done to determine the quantity of textiles-derived microfibers, to enable businesses and governments to focus efforts on the most critical factors for microfiber release into the environment, and the most effective mitigation methods.[39]

This decision leaves a well-known and obviously significant textile industry pollutant completely out of the transition equation.

The landscape detailed above arguably provides fertile ground for greenwashing. In its 2018 survey, the Changing Markets Foundation (CMF) found that two-thirds of UK consumers found it "difficult to know which brands meet higher ethical standards" (Wicker 2020). In 2021, its *Synthetics Anonymous* report assessed brands across the spheres of fast fashion, luxury fashion, and online retailing based on their sustainability claims and found that 59 percent could be classified as "misleading."

By signing up to an agreement with a delivery timeline that may be longer than necessary and that ignores microfiber pollution, carries no penalties, and does not hold to account either privately or publicly, some unscrupulous companies could enjoy the marketing benefits of appearing engaged with the sustainable transition while, in practice, doing little or nothing. The fast fashion sector, which is notorious for driving high volumes of sales at very low cost, carries a particular reputation for greenwashing; however, this practice continues in the luxury sector as well.

The CMF concludes that "as long as progress remains voluntary, sustainability in the textiles sector will remain optional" and called for "strengthened legislation and strong regulation on green claims" (2022).

Competition and Markets Authority (CMA) "Green Claims Code"

The Green Claims Code, published in September 2021, is designed to help businesses comply with UK law around accurate communication. The CMA pledged to carry out a full review of misleading green claims in early 2022 with fines to be levied against offending brands. In particular, firms making green claims "must not omit or hide important information" and "must consider the full life cycle of the product." While this is a cross-industry code, the CMA mentions the fashion and textile industries as particular targets for reform. The code runs alongside a wider awareness campaign that the CMA launched ahead of COP26. The code is a welcome positive pressure, and if enforced effectively, it will hold businesses making misleading sustainability claims (greenwashing) to account, both through fines and fear of reputational damage.

At the time of writing, the Green Claims Code has been a somewhat successful deterrent in making unsubstantiated environmental claims. "Fashion brands aware of the CMA's new powers to enforce fines of up to 10 percent of global turnover, plus court action, and that's scary," explains Abbie Morris, founder of Compare Ethics. While no fines have yet been levied, fashion brands, including Boohoo, Asos, and George at Asda, are publicly under investigation, and there is a "sense of fear" among leading UK brands about the consequences of issuing misleading communications.

However, there remains the ongoing challenge of accessing complex international supply-chain data. While Andrea Coscelli, chief executive of the CMA, explains that the code "has been written for all businesses—from fashion giants and supermarket chains to local shops," there is some concern that "SMEs will be disproportionately affected"[40] because they are unlikely to own the factories they work with or have much influence over or access to information about their practices.

"If we don't get this right, there is a real danger that businesses will just stop talking about their environmental actions," says Morris.

> We have witnessed a period of "Greenhushing" (where businesses refuse to talk about sustainable progress for fear of getting it wrong) over the last few months, and although we now seem to be heading towards a more level playing field, the situation is still really delicate.[41]

Too much uncertainty and a lack of harmonization between the United Kingdom and global counterparts could, in theory, cause brands to stop making sustainability claims altogether. "That is a real reality, one that we all want to avoid," says Morris. "Ensuring the right balance between accelerating progress whilst demanding credible, specific data to back up all claims is essential."

Finally, the code is limited by its inability to address the need for better standardization of terms.[42] For example, the term *circular economy* has great potential to affect consumer choices,[43] yet it's unclear how companies could make verified claims using this language when there is no agreed definition.

Product Environmental Footprint (PEF) Methodology

This EU initiative began trials in 2013 and falls under the Circular Action Plan.[44] Its aim is to provide more comprehensive and robust life-cycle analysis by creating industry and product-specific guidelines and attempting to address nuanced detail around issues like polyester recycling. However, the system is incredibly complex, and an insider interviewed for this chapter reported that maintaining accuracy is a big challenge at this level of specificity.

2018 Resources and Waste Strategy

This strategy, which aimed to "preserve material resources by minimising waste, promoting resource efficiency, and moving towards a circular economy in England" (HM Government 2018) outlined several policy approaches that could be applied to products such as textiles:

- eco-design strategy, which proposes setting minimum resource efficiency standards for certain product types (including textiles), with a parallel requirement to label certain products with their resource efficiency;
- EPR for textiles, which is to "drive greater circularity by making it more attractive financially."

Eco-Design

The intention of eco-design policy is to set effective standards for resource-efficient product design, using powers in the Environment Bill to drive behavioral change in businesses and consumers where encouragement is not sufficient. The Environment Bill enables ministers to set minimum standards for textile products and introduce requirements for improved labeling and consumer information, highlighting durability, repairability, recycled content, and production impacts. Ministers were also exploring the potential for introducing product design requirements around resistance to abrasion, dimensional stability, and color fastness (the resistance of a material to change in any of its color characteristics or transfer its colorants to adjacent materials). In particular, they noted the potential benefits of

- enabling better textile waste collection, with an expectation that this is to be funded through the Textiles EPR;
- identifying how best to support investment and innovation in the textiles reprocessing sector, building on research insights and support from Defra through the Resources Action Fund for textiles reuse and recycling;
- establishing five circular economy research centers, and a central hub to coordinate activity, funded by £30 million allocated through the Engineering and Physical Sciences

Research Council with support from Defra. These centers include the Interdisciplinary Textiles Circularity Centre, based at the Royal College of Art, which aims to lead research on how technological innovation can create renewable material from post-consumer textiles and household waste for use in textiles products.

Extended Producer Responsibility (EPR)

EPR is a policy approach gaining traction around the world as a legal mechanism to make producers take responsibility for the waste and environmental externalities of the products they produce. The key principles of EPR are as follows:

- Producers bear the cost of managing their products at the end of their life, rather than society (taxpayers, charities, etc.) picking up the tab.
- Variable fees can be used to encourage producers to design their products in a more sustainable way, in line with the waste hierarchy. For example, producers may pay a lower fee for products that are easier to reuse, repair, or recycle.
- Schemes are designed and implemented to make it easy for consumers to play their part and ensure more waste is collected for reuse or recycling.

The Department for Environment, Food and Rural Affairs (DEFRA) (2011, 34–36) promised to consult on an EPR proposal for textiles, for discussion with stakeholders by the end of 2022. EPR was to be considered alongside other measures, including

- a ban on landfill and incineration;
- separate collection requirements for textiles;
- greater eco-design and information requirements to drive action on textile waste reduction "higher up the hierarchy."

Extended Producer Responsibility (EPR): Established Examples

France was the first country to establish an EPR system for textiles in 2008, and at the time of writing, Sweden and the Netherlands had recently introduced schemes too. In France, all those who place textiles products in the French market must either collect and process used textiles themselves or contribute to an accredited body that will do this for them. Producers pay fees based on the quantities of garments they place in the market and item sizes. A not-for-profit body ReFashion (originally Eco TLC) is accredited by the French Authorities with devolved producer responsibility for the sector. They have the power to vary or modulate the costs paid by producers (where costs reflect the sustainability of the product, for example, recycled content, durability, recyclability, and end of life disposal cost) to encourage better design and material usage.[45]

Success of EPR in France

The French scheme has been successful at increasing the collection of clothing, home textiles, and footwear. It has expanded sorting capacity and reduced the number of textiles going to landfill or incineration.

So far, it has been less successful in incentivizing companies to introduce eco-design principles.

In 2012, the French EPR introduced "eco-modulated fees" to offer producers a discount for meeting thresholds of post-consumer recycled content, pre-consumer recycled content, and later, from 2019, durability. However, despite ReFashion's recent reports of growth in eco-modulated production, only 2.16 percent of all declared items placed in the market are currently being registered as eco-products.

According to the UK Textiles Recycling Association (TRA), one criticism of the French scheme is that the "very low levies" of less than 1 Euro cent per garment do "not help to incentivise improvements in sustainability further up the supply chain."[46] In evidence to Parliament, the TRA contrasted this with the levels set for chemical taxes in Sweden, "which will really focus the minds of producers who will want to ensure that their products do not attract these high levies."

Introduction of EPR to the United Kingdom

In and of itself, the UK government agreeing to "consultation on EPR is an important market signal"[47] that demonstrates to industry (and to some extent the public) that waste reduction and circularity are on the government's agenda. Survey evidence also suggests that "industry would welcome EPR"[48] to level the playing field between businesses adopting sustainable versus unsustainable practices. When designing an EPR scheme for the United Kingdom, it is helpful to draw upon France's precedent, particularly since these initiatives have a lengthy test and adjust timeline.[49]

Already we can note the risk of designing EPR in a way that does not adequately incentivize eco-design and adjust appropriately. "Government must set standards for eco design," asserts Mary Creagh. Michael Sadowski agrees: "Legislation must require manufacturers to hit sustainability minimums so that brands are forced to step up and co-invest." The need for "extensive economic modeling around EPR"[50] in order to recommend the appropriate levy (most likely much higher than 1 Euro cent) is also recognized. "EPR is essentially subsidising recycling" Creagh continues, and it "must be self-sustaining" in terms of cost—that is, cost of collecting and sorting goods and implementing appropriate (ideally circular) end of life solutions, but also funding "much-needed innovation in recycling processes."[51] However, broader concerns surrounding EPR remain. "Overproduction and underutilization is the elephant in the room in fashion" asserts Creagh. "We need an EPR to make us think twice about volumes." However, while the French EPR demonstrates improved textile collection and reuse and recycling rates, there is no evidence that the scheme has reduced overall consumption. Our waste system is also "vulnerable to fraud and supply-chain dips."[52] Fraud issues are prevalent within the United Kingdom's plastic EPR, and there is concern that, unless policed differently, a textiles EPR would be no different. "There are also some very delicate policy decisions ahead around what size and types of companies are included in EPR."[53] The appropriate way to deal with a product at the end of its useful life varies dramatically, and a one-size-fits-all policy is unlikely to be effective. Finally, the UK Government's original suggestion of introducing the scheme in 2025 is "too far away."[54] Following the British parliament's declaration of a climate *emergency* on May 1, 2019, the suggested speed of implementation of EPR seems inadequate.

Fixing Fashion Recommendations

In its 2019 *Fixing Fashion* report, Parliament's Environmental Audit Select Committee recommended that government to take the following actions in order to reduce its environmental impact and improve human rights within its value chains:

- make fashion retailers take responsibility for the waste they create and reward companies that take positive action to reduce waste;
- ban incinerating or landfilling unsold stock that can be reused or recycled;
- introduce an EPR charge of one penny per garment on producers, which would raise approximately £35 million to invest in better clothing collection and sorting in the United Kingdom;
- consider whether a tax on virgin plastics should be applied to textile products that contain less than 50 percent recycled polyethylene terephthalate (PET) to pump-prime the market for recycled fibers;
- make compliance with the Sustainable Clothing Action Plan targets mandatory for all retailers with a turnover above £36 million;
- change the law to require due diligence checks across supply chains;
- work with industry to trace the sources of raw materials in garments in order to tackle social and environmental abuses in their supply chains;
- introduce a penalty for fashion firms that fail to report and comply with the Modern Slavery Act.

Landscape of Government Action in Fashion and Textiles Regulation, Spring 2023

The UK government did not act on any of the select committee's recommendations in the *Fixing Fashion* report. The initial government response emphasized the role of the voluntary initiative led by the waste charity WRAP—at that time under the banner of the Sustainable Clothing Action Plan (SCAP). We saw above how limited was the success of these initiatives.

The government did add textiles to a list of five priority waste streams to tackle in its Waste and Resources Strategy for England by 2025 (HM Government 2018). It subsequently promised to prioritize textiles and agreed to consult on ideas such as eco-design standards and an Extended Producer Responsibility scheme for textiles by 2022. In February 2023, the Secretary of State for Environment, Food and Rural Affairs, Therese Coffey, confirmed that there were no government plans for an EPR scheme for fashion and textiles in the near future, and in March 2023, no eco-design standards have been set. The coalition government published a review of waste policy in 2011 that pledged to "review the case for restrictions on sending other materials to landfill over the course of the Parliament, including looking specifically at textiles and biodegradable waste" (Defra 2011, 9). However, this has never been acted upon, and twelve years later, no restrictions are in place to prevent textiles from ending up in landfill.

Foreign Policy on the Horizon

While this chapter is intended to focus upon UK policy, it is worth noting other examples of recent/upcoming legislation from abroad that are likely to influence or have a direct impact upon the UK fashion industry.

First, the EU Strategy for Sustainable and Circular Textiles (March 2022) proposes actions for the entire life cycle of textile products, tying in with commitments made in the Circular Economy Action Plan, the European Green Deal, and EU Industrial Strategy. It addresses design methods and consumption patterns, including looking at sustainable technological solutions and innovative business models.

Some of the measures include

- new design requirements including mandatory minimums for recycled fibers in textiles;
- harmonized EU rules on EPR for fashion and textiles;
- addressing microplastics released from textiles;
- improved labeling of textiles and introduction of Digital Product Passports containing information on sustainability;
- strengthened controls around greenwashing;
- a roadmap for the industry to achieve its 2030 goals.

Meanwhile, the EU's new Corporate Sustainability Reporting Directive (CSRD) adopted in 2023 will require nearly 50,000 organizations and SMEs in various sectors, including fashion, to report on ESG metrics, verified with external audits.

In the United States, California's Garment Worker Protection Act, the Federal Fabric Act (which would be the first federal bill affecting the fashion industry), and New York's Fashion Sustainability and Social Accountability Act all signal a significant regulatory shift. The last, which was presented to the New York State senate in January 2022, requires supply-chain mapping as well as impact and due diligence disclosure. If passed, the bill would make New York the first state in the country to hold fashion brands with operations in the state (and US$100 million in annual revenue) accountable for their environmental and social impacts. That would include brands from Shein and Mango to LVMH. Penalties for noncompliance would be up to 2 percent of the company's global revenue. Maxine Bédat, founder and director of the New Standard Institute, which played an instrumental role in the bill's making said "The only way demonstrable progress is going to be achieved is through legislation, to make setting and meeting standards the requirement for doing business."[55]

Conclusion

In a world that, thanks to technology, is "changing faster than ever before" (Boston Consulting Group 2021),[56] it is essential to create strong yet agile governance frameworks that align corporate and political governance with planetary imperatives and the long-term public good.

While the UK policy landscape is slowly transforming in recognition of the need for adequate sustainability governance, there are key failings in legislation that are limiting progress in line with the Paris Agreement.

In summary, government must

- drive initiatives to define a common language around sustainability, industry-specific definitions in particular;
- be innovative and ambitious with strategies and timelines, leading policy implementation with the vigor required in an emergency;
- engage a multitude of stakeholders through diverse co-creation and collaboration in order to achieve truly integrated policy;

- introduce policy that covers the whole market;
- disincentivize unsustainable behavior by holding industry to account, using sanctions when science-based targets are not met;
- insist on transparent supply chains in all industries;
- be prepared to introduce mandatory legislation rather than rely on market forces;
- signal the importance of sustainability to industry and the public;
- embrace new metrics of success that do not just focus on endless growth;
- create a fertile landscape and adequate financial provision for innovation and data gathering;
- set a road map for a just transition;
- create mandatory minimum sustainability standards for every industry and outrightly ban damaging practices, toxins, and materials;
- consider using financial levers (taxation and/or subsidies) to level the playing field for sustainable businesses;
- implement EPR for fashion and textiles, creating strong incentives for eco-design that reduce waste and material consumption;
- regulate voluntary frameworks like Textiles 2030;
- take a long-term view and prioritize public good.

Clare Shine summarized her thoughts about contemporary public governance as follows:

> There is currently a shifting paradigm around people and power. Going forward, (and this is where technology can really help us) there is an opportunity for all kinds of innovation in the participatory sphere. We need to have a much nimbler approach to the way we think about governance, to enable a porous and receptive ecosystem for both the arrival of ideas and adoption of systems to manage their integration.[57]

The fashion industry and others have the potential to fix systemic material, supply chain, end-of-life, and overall consumption-level problems that are contributing to current global environmental and humanitarian crises. As this chapter makes clear, this will only be achieved through cohesive public governance that provides specific frameworks for tangible action.

Key Discussion Areas

- Impact of the international fashion industry on various global crises.
- Internal sustainability governance and the international governance framework for sustainable development.
- Laws and regulation in the United Kingdom to facilitate and promote sustainable development.
- Understanding the successes and failures of the Sustainability Governance and laws in the United Kingdom as well as other European Union (EU) countries through case studies from the fashion industry.
- Recommendations for the UK government for promoting sustainability practices.

Notes

1 Client Earth, "Historic High Court Ruling Finds UK Government's Climate Strategy 'Unlawful,'" July 18, 2022 press release, www.clientearth.org/latest/press-office/press/historic-high-court-ruling-finds-uk-government-s-climate-strategy-unlawful (accessed August 30, 2023)
2 Sustainable Government Commission, "Local Sustainable Development Lens: Final Proposal Overview Paper," www.sd-commission.org.uk/data/files/publications/SDCProposalLocalSDLens.pdf (accessed August 30, 2023).
3 United Nations Environment Programme (UNEP.org), The Montreal Protocol (accessed October 3, 2021).
4 United Nations Conference on Environment and Development, Rio de Janeiro, Brazil, June 3–14, 1992, www.un.org/en/conferences/environment/rio1992 (accessed October 2, 2021).
5 Convention on Biological Diversity, "2010 Biodiversity Target," December 21, 2020, www.cbd.int/2010-target/ (accessed August 30, 2023).
6 UNCC, "The Paris Agreement," https://unfccc.int/process-and-meetings/the-paris-agreement (accessed August 30, 2023).
7 Defra submission to the Environmental Audit Committee Fixing Fashion Follow-Up inquiry (FFFU0023), "Written Evidence from Defra," https://committees.parliament.uk/writtenevidence/15055/pdf.
8 Interview, October 22, 2021, Alan Wheeler, CEO at Textile Recycling Association UK.
9 Interview, September 28, 2021, Rachel Arthur, Sustainability Consultant for UN Environment Programme, Google and others.
10 www.globalfashionagenda.com/pulse-of-fashion-industry-2019-update-released/
11 Interview, October 13, 2021, Mary Creagh CBE, Former MP, Shadow Secretary of State for Transport, chair of the Environmental Audit Select Committee (UK Government).
12 Interview, October 13, 2021, Chief Sustainability Officer of well-known Global Fashion Brand.
13 Interview, October 18, 2021, Clare Shine, Director and CEO at Cambridge Institute for Sustainability Leadership (CISL), University of Cambridge.
14 Interview, September 28, 2021, Rachel Arthur, Sustainability Consultant for UN Environment Programme, Google and others
15 Ibid.
16 Interview, September 29, 2021, Abigail Morris, CEO at Compare Ethics.
17 Interview, October 18, 2021, Clare Shine, Director and CEO at Cambridge Institute for Sustainability Leadership (CISL), University of Cambridge.
18 Interview, October 28, 2021, Shailja Dubé, Institute of Positive Fashion Lead, British Fashion Council.
19 Interview, October 13, 2021, Mary Creagh CBE, Former MP, Shadow Secretary of State for Transport, chair of the Environmental Audit Select Committee (UK Government).
20 Sustainable Fashion Glossary, Condé Nast and the Centre for Sustainable Fashion, London College of Fashion, UAL, www.condenast.com/glossary.
21 Interview, October 18, 2021, Clare Shine, Director and CEO at Cambridge Institute for Sustainability Leadership (CISL), University of Cambridge.
22 Ibid.
23 Interview, October 13, 2021, Chief Sustainability Officer of well-known Global Fashion Brand.
24 Hannah Phang, Futerra, during Business of Fashion Podcast: www.businessoffashion.com/podcasts/sustainability/unpacking-fashions-role-in-slowing-global-warming.
25 Interview, October 13, 2021, Chief Sustainability Officer of well-known Global Fashion Brand.
26 Interview, October 19, 2021, Global Head of Material Sourcing at well-known luxury fashion brand.
27 Interview, October 13, 2021, Mary Creagh CBE, Former MP, Shadow Secretary of State for Transport, chair of the Environmental Audit Select Committee (UK Government).
28 Interview, October 18, 2021, Clare Shine, Director and CEO at Cambridge Institute for Sustainability Leadership (CISL), University of Cambridge.
29 Interview, October 13, 2021, Mary Creagh CBE, Former MP, Shadow Secretary of State for Transport, chair of the Environmental Audit Select Committee (UK Government).
30 Interview, October 28, 2021, Shailja Dubé, Institute of Positive Fashion Lead, British Fashion Council.

31 WRAP.org.uk, "What Is Textiles 2030? A New Ground-Breaking, Expert-Led Initiative" (accessed December 9, 2020).
32 WRAP (FFFU0014).
33 Interview, October 13, 2021, Mary Creagh CBE, Former MP, Shadow Secretary of State for Transport, chair of the Environmental Audit Select Committee (UK Government).
34 Ibid.
35 Hannah Phang, Futerra, during Business of Fashion Podcast: www.businessoffashion.com/podcasts/sustainability/unpacking-fashions-role-in-slowing-global-warming (accessed August 30, 2023).
36 Interview, October 13, 2021, Mary Creagh CBE, Former MP, Shadow Secretary of State for Transport, chair of the Environmental Audit Select Committee (UK Government).
37 Interview, October 28, 2021, Shailja Dubé, Institute of Positive Fashion Lead, British Fashion Council.
38 Interview, September 15, 2021, Paul Foulkes-Arellano, Circuthon Consulting.
39 WRAP (December 18, 2019) Summary of evidence on textile-derived microfiber.
40 Interview, September 29, 2021, Abigail Morris, CEO at Compare Ethics.
41 Interview, March 21, 2023, Abigail Morris, CEO at Compare Ethics.
42 Ibid.
43 Ibid.
44 European Commission, "The Environmental Footprint Pilots," https://ec.europa.eu/environment/eussd/smgp/ef_pilots.htm (accessed August 30, 2023).
45 Defra (FFFU0023).
46 Evidence submission from the Textiles Recycling Association (FFFU0009) to EAC's Fixing Fashion Follow-Up inquiry.
47 Interview, October 13, 2021, Mary Creagh CBE, Former MP, Shadow Secretary of State for Transport, chair of the Environmental Audit Select Committee (UK Government).
48 Ibid.
49 Interview, September 28, 2021, Rachel Arthur, Strategist for UN Environment Programme and Fashion Sustainability at Google.
50 Interview, October 8, 2021, Hannah Parris, Postdoctoral Research Associate at University of Cambridge.
51 Interview, October 13, 2021, Mary Creagh CBE, Former MP, Shadow Secretary of State for Transport, chair of the Environmental Audit Select Committee (UK Government).
52 Ibid.
53 Ibid.
54 Ibid.
55 www.forbes.com/sites/roxannerobinson/2022/01/11/fashion-industry-reacts-to-new-york-sustainability-legislation-that-could-upend-transparency-practices/?sh=584067aa39b3
56 www.bcg.com/publications/2020/challenge-of-slow
57 Interview, October 18, 2021, Clare Shine, Director and CEO at Cambridge Institute for Sustainability Leadership (CISL), University of Cambridge.

References

Australian Academy of Science. 2021. "The Risks to Australia of a 3°C Warmer World," www.science.org.au/files/userfiles/support/reports-and-plans/2021/risks-australia-three-deg-warmer-world-report.pdf (accessed August 30, 2023).

BBC News. 2018. "'Climate Apartheid' between Rich and Poor Looms, UN Expert Warns." June 25, 2019, www.bbc.co.uk/news/world-48755154 (accessed August 30, 2023).

Benjamin, A. 2021. "Stern: Climate Change a 'Market Failure'." *Guardian*, August 25, 2021, www.theguardian.com/environment/2007/nov/29/climatechange.carbonemissions (accessed August 30, 2023).

Berg, A., A. Granskog, L. Lee, and K. Magnus. 2020. "Fashion on Climate." *McKinsey & Company*, December 14, 2020, www.mckinsey.com/industries/retail/our-insights/fashion-on-climate (accessed August 30, 2023).

Bierney, Anna, Helen Clarkson, Peter Madden, Jonathon Porritt, and Ben Tuxworth. 2010. "Stepping Up: A Framework for Public Sector Leadership on Sustainability." *Forum for the Future: Action for a Sustainable World*, February 2010, www.criticaleye.com/inspiring/insights-servfile.cfm?id=2136 (accessed August 30, 2023).

Business of Fashion. 2021. "Inside Fashion: Unpacking Fashion's Role in Slowing Global Warming." December 13, 2021, www.businessoffashion.com/podcasts/sustainability/unpacking-fashions-role-in-slowing-global-warming (accessed August 30, 2023).

Ceballos, G., P. R. Ehrlich, and R. Dirzo. 2017. "Biological Annihilation via the Ongoing Sixth Mass Extinction Is Signaled by Vertebrate Population Losses and Declines." *Proceedings of the National Academy of Sciences* 114(30), https://doi.org/10.1073/pnas.1704949114.

Centre for Sustainable Fashion. 2020. *Rethinking Fashion Design Entrepreneurship: Fostering Sustainable Practices*. UAL: London College of Fashion, https://9dbc3c3f-8613-4a49-a8bb-a21c9f908f3d.usrfiles.com/ugd/9dbc3c_1be38405ba924d3d9418d641354cf249.pdf (accessed August 30, 2023).

Changing Markets Foundation (CMF). 2021. "Synthetics Anonymous." January, http://changingmarkets.org/wp-content/uploads/2021/07/SyntheticsAnonymous_FinalWeb.pdf (accessed August 30, 2023).

———. 2022. "License to Greenwash." March 24, 2022, http://changingmarkets.org/wp-content/uploads/2022/03/LICENCE-TO-GREENWASH-FULL-REPORT.pdf (accessed August 30, 2023).

Department for Business, Energy & Industrial Strategy. 2019. "Green Finance Strategy." *GOV.UK*, July 2, 2019, www.gov.uk/government/publications/green-finance-strategy (accessed August 30, 2023).

Department for Environment and Rural Affairs (Defra). 2011. *Government Review of Waste Policy in England 2011*. London: Defra, https://assets.publishing.service.gov.uk/government/uploads/system/uploads/attachment_data/file/69401/pb13540-waste-policy-review110614.pdf (accessed August 30, 2023).

Eggenberger, Katrin. 2022. "Has the UN Reached Its Sustainable Development Goals? Yes and No." *World Economic Forum*, November 10, 2022, www.weforum.org/agenda/2022/11/the-un-sustainable-development-goals-a-positive-perspective/ (accessed August 30, 2023).

Elkington, John. 2020. *Green Swans: The Coming Boom in Regenerative Capitalism*. New York: Fast Company Pr.

European Commission. 2019. *Mapping Sustainable Fashion Opportunities for SMEs*. UAL: London College of Fashion, Centre for Sustainable Fashion, www.sustainable-fashion.com/publications/mapping-sustainable-fashion-opportunities-for-smes (accessed August 30, 2023).

———. 2020. "EU Taxonomy for Sustainable Activities." March 7, 2020, https://ec.europa.eu/info/business-economy-euro/banking-and-finance/sustainable-finance/eu-taxonomy-sustainable-activities_en (accessed August 30, 2023).

Farra, E. 2019. "At the Copenhagen Fashion Summit, Kering's François-Henri Pinault Shares a Radical New Vision of Sustainability." *Vogue*, May 16, 2019, www.vogue.com/article/francois-henri-pinault-kering-sustainability-vision (accessed August 30, 2023).

Greenpeace. 2021. "The 'Just Transition': A Fairer Way to Fight Climate Change." January 15, 2021, www.greenpeace.org.uk/challenges/just-transition/ (accessed August 30, 2023).

Hickel, Jason (2021). "Less Is More: How Degrowth Will Save The World." Windmill Books.

HM Government. 2018. "Our Waste, Our Resources: A Strategy for England," https://assets.publishing.service.gov.uk/government/uploads/system/uploads/attachment_data/file/765914/resources-waste-strategy-dec-2018.pdf (accessed August 30, 2023).

———. 2023. "Strategic Framework for International Climate and Nature Action." March 2023, https://assets.publishing.service.gov.uk/government/uploads/system/uploads/attachment_data/file/1148323/2030-strategic-framework-for-international-climate-and-nature-action.pdf (accessed August 30, 2023).

House of Commons Environmental Audit Committee. 2018. "Greening Finance: Embedding Sustainability in Financial Decision Making." *House of Commons*, May 23, 2018, https://publications.parliament.uk/pa/cm201719/cmselect/cmenvaud/1063/1063.pdf (accessed August 30, 2023).

———. 2019. "Fixing Fashion: Clothing Consumption and Sustainability." *House of Commons*, February 19, 2019, https://publications.parliament.uk/pa/cm201719/cmselect/cmenvaud/1952/1952.pdf (accessed August 30, 2023).

Institute of Positive Fashion. n.d. "Stakeholder Actions and Connections." *Circular Fashion Ecosystem*, https://instituteofpositivefashion.com/Stakeholder_Actions_Connections/ (accessed August 30, 2023).

———. 2021. *The Circular Fashion Ecosystem: A Blueprint for the Future*. British Fashion Council, https://instituteofpositivefashion.com/uploads/files/1/CFE/Circular_Fashion_Ecosytem_Report.pdf (accessed August 30, 2023).

Intergovernmental Science-Policy Platform on Biodiversity and Ecosystem Services (IPBES). 2019. *Summary for Policymakers of the IPBES Global Assessment Report on Biodiversity and Ecosystem Services*. Bonn, Germany: IPEBS, https://ipbes.net/sites/default/files/2020-02/ipbes_global_assessment_report_summary_for_policymakers_en.pdf (accessed August 30, 2023).

Islam, S. Nazrul, and John Winkel. 2017. "Climate Change and Social Inequality." DESA Working Paper 152. United Nation Department of Economic and Social Affairs, October 17, 2017, www.un.org/development/desa/publications/working-paper/wp152 (accessed August 30, 2023).

Jackson, Tim. 2016. *Prosperity without Growth*, 2nd ed. London: Routledge.

Jordan, A., and V. Gravey. 2021. *Environmental Policy in the EU*, 4th ed. New York: Routledge.

Levin, K., B. Cashore, S. Bernstein, S., and G. Auld. 2012. "Overcoming the Tragedy of Super Wicked Problems: Constraining Our Future Selves to Ameliorate Global Climate Change." *Policy Sciences* 45(2): 123–52, https://doi.org/10.1007/s11077-012-9151-0.

Lucas, Caroline. 2022. "The Solution to Climate Change Is Already Here—We're Just Ignoring It." *Metro*, July 28, 2022, https://metro.co.uk/2022/07/28/the-solution-to-climate-change-is-already-here-were-just-ignoring-it-17082336/ (accessed August 30, 2023).

New Scientist. 2019. "We Need to Wake Up to the Potential Threat from Microplastics." December 4, 2019, www.newscientist.com/article/mg24432592-600-we-need-to-wake-up-to-the-potential-threat-from-microplastics/ (accessed August 30, 2023).

Puppis, M. 2010. "Media Governance: A New Concept for the Analysis of Media Policy and Regulation." *Communication, Culture & Critique* 3(2): 134–49, https://doi.org/10.1111/j.1753-9137.2010.01063.x.

Raworth, Kate. 2017. *Doughnut Economics: Seven Ways to Think Like a 21st-Century Economist*. London: Random House.

Ross, F. 2019. "Kate Raworth—Doughnut Economics: Seven Ways to Think Like a 21st Century Economist (2017)." *Regional and Business Studies* 11(2), https://doi.org/10.33568/rbs.2409.

Savage, M. 2021. "UK Can't Fight Climate Crisis with Austerity, Warns Expert." *Guardian*, August 25, 2021, www.theguardian.com/environment/2021/aug/14/uk-fight-climate-crisis-austerity-government-treasury-green-spending-net-zero-nicholas-stern (accessed August 30, 2023).

Thaler, Richard H., and Cass R. Sunstein. 2009. *Nudge*. New York: Penguin.

UK Parliament. 2019. "Fixing Fashion: Clothing Consumption and Sustainability." February 19, 2019, https://publications.parliament.uk/pa/cm201719/cmselect/cmenvaud/1952/full-report.html (accessed August 30, 2023).

UNFCCC Secretariat. 2021. "Nationally Determined Contributions under the Paris Agreement. Synthesis Report by the Secretariat." September 17, 2021, https://unfccc.int/documents/306848. 23 (accessed August 30, 2023).

United Nations. 2021. "Secretary-General Calls Latest IPCC Climate Report 'Code Red for Humanity', Stressing 'Irrefutable' Evidence of Human Influence." *Press Release*, August 9, 2021, www.un.org/press/en/2021/sgsm20847.doc.htm#:%7E:text=Today's%20IPCC%20Working%20Group%201,of%20people%20at%20immediate%20risk (accessed August 30, 2023).

White, Robyn. "SCAP 2020 Textile Waste Targets Missed." *Lets Recycle*, October 19, 2021, www.letsrecycle.com/news/wrap-misses-scap-2020-waste-targets/ (accessed August 30, 2023).

Wicker, A. 2020. "The Flawed Ways Brands Talk about Sustainability." *Vogue Business*, April 16, 2020, www.voguebusiness.com/sustainability/the-flawed-ways-brands-talk-about-sustainability-coronavirus (accessed August 30, 2023).

World Economic Forum. 2020. "These Facts Show How Unsustainable the Fashion Industry Is." January 31, 2020, www.weforum.org/agenda/2020/01/fashion-industry-carbon-unsustainable-environment-pollution/ (accessed August 30, 2023).

World Health Organization. 2021. "Air Quality and Health," www.who.int/teams/environment-climate-change-and-health/air-quality-and-health/ambient-air-pollution (accessed August 30, 2023).

WRAP. 2019. "Textiles Market Situation Report 2019," https://wrap.org.uk/sites/default/files/2021-03/WRAP-textiles-market-situation-report-2019.pdf (accessed August 30, 2023).

26

PROMOTING LONG-TERM HEALTHY AND SUSTAINABLE BUSINESSES THROUGH RESPONSIBLE AND PROACTIVE LEGAL PRACTICE

Aimée Girdwood and Christina Bartholomew

Do not think for one moment that you cannot change what exists. This world is a social construction; it can be reconstructed. This world was built; it can be rebuilt. Use everything that you accrue to reimagine the world.

(Clint Smith)

The biggest competitive advantage in business—either for a company or for an individual's career—is long-term thinking.

(James Cote)

Introduction: Our Operating Context

A good hockey player plays where the puck is. A great hockey player plays where the puck is going to be.

(Wayne Gretzky)

We live and work in a world of increasing uncertainty and escalating challenges further influenced by growing trends like the rise of artificial intelligence and technology: the "never normal," "VUCA max" world (World Economic Forum 2021; Berkhout et al. 2021; IPCC 2021; UN CBD 2020).[1]

The pace of change and the level of uncertainty make it difficult to understand the situation or predict the future. In addition, the Covid-19 pandemic and the resultant social and economic fallout demonstrated in a very tangible way what previously seemed theoretical and abstract: the interconnection between businesses' ability to operate and thrive; and the health of the society where it operates (King and Roberts 2021; Schwab and Vanham 2021; UN Global Compact 2019).[2]

DOI: 10.4324/9781003316077-32

What is the role of the legal profession in this unpredictable environment? Are lawyers responsible for tackling the challenges we face as a society? How can lawyers adapt and thrive in this new operating context and help their clients do the same? These are the questions that we seek to answer in this chapter.

This chapter focuses on the role of legal professionals in practice, because there seems to be relatively more information and support available for general counsel and in-house lawyers at writing (see Sherman 2021). That said, we hope our submissions will resonate in the many other settings in which lawyers work.

Transformational Governance: Importance, Meaning, History, and Status

The economy won't thrive unless people and planet are thriving.

(Polman and Winston 2021)

But now follows the difficult part: turning awareness and commitments into business reality.

(Erik Rasmussen)

Business and the competition and innovation it fosters play a vital role in society and has generated incredible economic and social progress (Donaldson and Walsh 2015). However, its focus on short-term benefits, as if disconnected from the world, has contributed to many of the converging crises we face (Tollefson 2021; Ramos and Hynes 2019). These social, economic, and environmental crises are a critical threat to all sectors of the economy. But with business as the primary employer, user, and generator of capital, and the primary investor in research, development, and innovation, it is also an essential partner in overcoming these challenges.[3]

Our global economic system and established way of doing business are no longer fit for purpose—if ever they were. Moreover, addressing the sustainability challenges we face presents companies with significant opportunities for long-term resilience (UN Global Compact 2019, 21).

What Does Transformational Governance Mean?

Transformational governance is not a new legal concept and does not require businesses to take on the role of governments (Koulias and Breslauer 2021) or charitable institutions. However, it requires companies to adopt a new perspective—shifting from short-term profit maximisation and superficial compliance to long-term value creation for both the business and its stakeholders, thereby safeguarding the resources and relationships essential to its success.

This requires that business be conducted respectfully and in a way that enhances positive long-term environmental, social, and governance (ESG)[4] impacts while ameliorating negative ESG impacts.

Transformational governance is, therefore, a philosophy that dictates that businesses lead with purpose by doing "not just what is legal but what is right" (UN Global Compact 2021; Koulias and Breslauer 2021): moving beyond legal compliance to implementing the highest standard of responsible business practices.

This approach to corporate governance backed by the UN Global Compact (Koulias and Breslauer 2021) and the World Economic Forum (Mayer 2020) recognizes the interdependence of thriving businesses, societies, and environments and dovetails with directors' fiduciary duties. These are to act in the best interests of the companies they serve, having regard to the material stakeholders' interests, needs, and expectations (Eccles 2021). Such an approach is also, circumstances and jurisdiction dependent, one that directors must adopt to be protected by the business judgment rule[5] and comply with the minimum disclosure requirements of corporations (Täger 2021).

Implementing transformational governance principles does not mean that businesses must be reorganized as charities. On the contrary, conducting business in a way that is mindful of its ESG impacts, both positive and negative, enables enterprises to take advantage of potential opportunities and mitigate financially material (including reputational) risks. Moreover, this approach can drive growth and profits and act as a precursor to long-term business success (Polman and Winston 2021).

Crucially, the adoption of transformational governance is increasingly linked to a businesses' ability to access finance, with the cost of that finance impacted by a corporates' understanding and disclosure of its ESG-related impacts and risks.[6]

Trade-offs between sustainability and profit may still exist, particularly in the short- to mid-term. Embracing transformational governance can therefore not rely on the business case alone. It must also, as the transformational governance approach suggests, be about conducting business ethically, with integrity and purpose (Le Menestrel et al. 2022).

The History of Transformational Governance

Transformational governance is about doing business to serve society while being profitable, rather than focusing only on maximizing profit in the short term and limiting legal liability.

This is not a new concept but has its roots in the founding purpose of the corporation in society, which regarded corporations as public or quasi-public institutions whose strategic priority was to balance the generation of shareholder profit against its public responsibility (Petrin and Choudhury 2020; Schwab and Vanham 2021; Stout 2002).

Over time, this purpose would be tested by the continuous tension between public good and private profit, ultimately resolving in favor of shareholder primacy.

For example, in the United States, the notion of shareholder primacy entered the common law in the case of Dodge v. Ford Motor Co.[7] Here, the court sided with shareholders against Henry Ford's decision to suspend dividends so that he could "employ still more men, to spread the benefits of this industrial system to the greatest possible number, [and] to help them build up their lives and their homes."[8] Corporate profits couldn't be withheld, the court ruled, for the benefit of the general public.[9] "The business corporation is organized and carried on primarily for the profit of stockholders. The powers of the directors are to be employed for that end" (Hallorian 2018; Sundaram and Inkpen 2004).

In 1932, two preeminent legal scholars—Adolphe A. Berle and Merrick Dodd—revived this debate, articulating competing views on the corporation's purpose in a 1932 *Harvard Law Review*. Berle expressed the shareholder primacy view, believing that powers granted to the corporation are "exercisable only for the ratable benefit of all the shareholders as their interest appears" (Stout 2002). Dodd believed otherwise, arguing for a view of the corporation that encompassed social service, including more secure jobs for employees, better quality products for consumers, and more significant contributions to the community's welfare.

Ultimately, Milton Friedman's pronouncement that the social responsibility of business is to increase its profits (Friedman 1970) seems to have swayed business opinion to favor a shareholder primacy approach. What is lesser known is that Friedman himself placed a caveat on his doctrine. That is, in his famous 1970 letter, he made clear that the corporate responsibility to "make as much money as possible" is subject to the business "conforming to the basic rules of the society, both those embodied in law and those embodied in ethical custom." This suggests Friedman himself recognized that it is not enough for businesses to be profitable and legal. They must also meet society's expectations, which, as discussed above, are currently evolving rapidly, favoring the requirement that companies serve society while being profitable (British Academy 2019; Institute of Directors Southern Africa 2016; Schwab 2019).[10]

Where Are We Now?

> In the quest for sustainable development, the only thing more dangerous than the absence of progress is the illusion of it.
>
> *(EY 2022)*

Against a backdrop of increasing consumer, societal, investor, and regulatory pressure (Temple-West 2021; Climate Champions 2021) and action, there is an increasing understanding and recognition of the strategic importance of ESG risks and opportunities (Temple-West 2021; Dudek van Heel and Brahim 2021; Force for Good Initiative 2021). This pressure has translated into a "gold rush" in ESG and sustainability commitments by governments, the finance sector, and businesses.[11] ESG services and products are likewise also on the rise. This includes the legal community, where "ESG has come roaring" (Watchman and Hunt 2021; Temple-West 2021) as law firms scramble to meet the increasing ESG demands of clients and the evolving ESG requirements of regulators.

Despite this increasing activity around commitments and services, research shows a significant gap in the meaningful implementation of ESG. ESG risks are not yet fully grasped (PwC 2021), greenwashing[12] persists, levels of mistrust and misinformation are at an all-time high (Edelman 2021), and ESG competency and our progress on critical environmental and social issues remain low (United Nations 2021; IPCC 2021; UN CBD 2020; Austin 2021; EY 2022).[13]

Figure 26.1 illustrates the framework transformational governance provides for increasing levels of ambition for business to integrate sustainability for greater positive impact. These increasing levels of ambition require business "to be more accountable, ethical, inclusive, and transparent in order to drive responsible business conduct, improve ESG performance, and strengthen public institutions, laws and systems" (Koulias and Breslauer 2021).

What Does This Mean for Lawyers, and Why Must We Lead the Charge on Transformational Governance?

> *Governance and culture are certainly more entrenched, slower moving forces, but it is when these gears begin to turn that behaviour really starts to shift.*
>
> *(Duncan Austin 2021)*

Legal compliance mindset	**Proactive leadership mindset**	**Net positive leadership mindset**
- Avoid immediate unintended consequences / manage risk - Limit legal liability / "tick-box" compliance mentality	- Avoid becoming a barrier to positive ESG impact while ameliorating negative ESG impact - Avoid being in conflict with changing societal norms or values	- Highest standard of responsible business practices - Become (part of) the solution to the problems faced by people and planet while being profitable

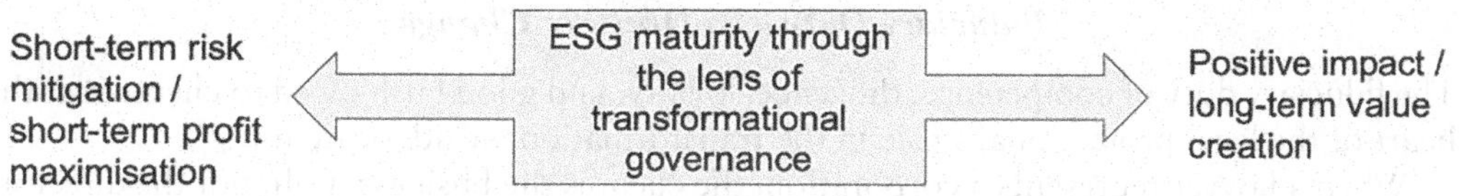

Figure 26.1 Thinking and Acting With Increasing Ambition to Drive Transformational Governance
Source: Adapted by authors from the work of Kania, Kramer, and Senge 2018.

> *They reflect upon the dual roles that attorneys play: as actors who perpetuate existing systems, as well as agents of systemic change.*
>
> *(Tomar Pierson-Brown)*

> *If the first 20 years of corporate sustainability amounted to the normalisation of sustainability within the mainstream corporate narrative, the next 20 years need to amount to realisation.*
>
> *(EY 2022)*

Why Must Lawyers Lead?

We are in a race against time (World Economic Forum 2023; IPCC 2021; EY 2022). The pace of change needed in "how business gets done" is urgent and aggressive (Tollefson 2021). "Structural and cultural changes"[14] in the economy and corporate sustainability are necessary.

Closing the gap between ESG commitments, action, and impact requires understanding what ESG means for each business and taking meaningful and substantive action to embed it into the core of how businesses and our economy function—in every organization, every department, and every decision (Perlman, Goldberg, and Calviño 2021).

This requires critical reflection of existing legal and regulatory, institutional, and social systems and whether or not they work. It also means tackling big issues like effective collaboration,[15] dispute resolution, governance (see UN Global Compact 2021), funding (Dudek van Heel and Brahim 2021; Force for Good Initiative 2021; World Economic Forum 2021), strategy, and disclosure with "ambition, pragmatism, perseverance, and creativity" (Ruggie 2013).

Lawyers operate at the intersection of business, finance, and government, and in the heart of each of them. We create, teach, advise on, implement, enforce, or challenge (Lehmen 2021b) the law and accountability mechanisms that determine the structure and culture of our society and economy. Our role as skilled problem solvers at these intersection points makes us key leverage points[16] for effecting powerful change while maintaining the rule of law and ensuring access to justice.

Lawyers' education and training, decisions, and actions are therefore core to any change campaign (Pierson Brown 2020; Rubin and Bailey 1994) and the implementation of transformational governance in particular.

In the following sections, we set out in more detail the key (and interrelated) reasons for why lawyers must lead on transformational governance.

Fiduciary Duty as a Driver of Change

The fiduciary duty of competence, diligence, loyalty, and good faith owed to clients is at the heart of the legal professional's role in the transformation we advocate for.

When a lawyer represents a corporation, the client is the business itself, not the directors or managers who act on its behalf (Karmel 1988). In this sense, a corporation's governing body and the legal professionals who represent it share the same obligation: to ensure the business's long-term profitability even if it comes at the expense of immediate shareholder gains (Eccles 2021).

With this long-term perspective in mind, a business's strategy must incorporate the risks of climate change (Barker, Williams, and Cooper 2021) and biodiversity loss, and a "wider shift in expectations—at a global scale—toward more sustainable business, finance, and regulation" (Hutley and Davis 2019). This approach to fiduciary duties as they apply to climate change, and increasingly ESG more broadly, carries the backing and weight of opinion from lawyers in jurisdictions as diverse as Australia, Canada, Hong Kong,[17] New Zealand, Singapore, South Africa, the United Kingdom, and the United States.[18]

An Evolving Risk Landscape

Risks of all kinds are rapidly evolving due to an increasingly mandatory ESG regulatory environment and deepening soft law requirements, novel strategic litigation, and intense societal and activist scrutiny. Navigating this challenging terrain represents an opportunity for lawyers to look beyond short-term liability analysis and provide the strategic advice that enables client resilience in the mid-term to long term (Sherman 2021).

Law firms and their corporate clients operate in the same ecosystem and are interdependent. The long-term resilience of corporate clients is therefore vital to the stability and resilience of law firms themselves.

Growing Global Accountability

Global accountability is a strengthening trend that shifts soft, nonbinding law into hard law by codifying expectations, obligations, and responsibility for ESG impacts, thus enabling an economy that encourages ESG-positive practices.

France's Duty of Vigilance Act (2017) is such a law. Reflecting the United Nations' Guiding Principles on Business and Human Rights and the Paris Climate Agreement, it imposes a corporate duty of due diligence on large French companies. In addition, it requires the publication of a corporate "vigilance plan" that identifies, measures, and prevents severe impacts on human rights and the environment by the company and the actions of its subsidiaries and suppliers.[19] In January 2023, ClientEarth and French partners Surfrider Foundation Europe and Zero Waste France initiated legal action against Danone in the French courts for failing to provide an adequate plan to address risks related to the plastics pollution generated by their business activities. Germany and the Netherlands have followed suit with similar laws, and now, the European Union (EU) is considering requiring all its member states to pass vigilance legislation. Will it be long before the EU's trading partners enact their own versions of this due diligence duty? Indeed, for cross-jurisdictional businesses to thrive in an environment where ESG investment is rising, we will likely see increased laws adhering to global ESG standards and disclosure requirements (King and Roberts 2021; Latham & Watkins 2020).

Lawyers play a crucial role in advising their corporate clients on their power, responsibilities, and obligations in this evolving governance landscape.

Strategic and Novel Litigation

Strategic and novel litigation is a lever increasingly used by NGOs and activist groups to accelerate action and impact on key ESG issues (de Wit 2020; Setzer and Higham 2021; Lehmen 2021b). As ESG continues to gain momentum, we expect this litigation to grow and, in some ways, become self-perpetuating with ESG-related disclosures triggering claims based on those reports and disclosures (King and Roberts 2021; Latham & Watkins 2020).

As trusted advisors to organizations who bring an external, cross-jurisdictional, and cross-sector perspective to companies, lawyers can play an important role in helping their corporate clients maintain their social license to operate and reduce the risk of facing harmful litigation. This includes identifying the negative ESG impacts of a client, developing standards to mitigate them (Sherman 2021), and pushing their clients toward ethical behavior by making a compelling case for the business benefits of long-term thinking (King and Roberts 2021; Latham & Watkins 2020).

Box 26.1 Case Study: Board Member Liability

In March 2022, ClientEarth, a shareholder of Shell, alleged that Shell's Board breached its legal duties—both personal and corporate—when it failed to implement a climate strategy aligned to the Paris Climate Agreement (PCA) goal of keeping global temperature rise below 1.5°C by 2050. ClientEarth said that the directors had not acted in a way that promoted the company's success and had failed to exercise reasonable care, skill, and diligence as required under the UK Companies Act.

"The longer the board delays, the more likely it is that the company will have to execute an abrupt 'handbrake turn' to retain commercial competitiveness and meet the challenges of inevitable regulatory developments" (Hodgson and Wilson 2022). Insufficient targets to reduce Shell's emissions over the next three, five, and ten years undermine its ability to meet net-zero targets and secure the company's long-term value while protecting investors' capital.

While this action is in its early days, we can expect to see similar shareholder claims arising against board members where (1) companies purport to be addressing climate change while in practice fail to align with the 1.5°C PCA target[20] or (2) directors have failed to exercise their duty of care concerning ESG-related risks that result in harm to the company.

Source: Authors.

Opportunity Knocks

ESG represents an exceptional business opportunity for law firms.

A huge flow of investment funds into a broad range of ESG-aligned public and private offerings means that nearly every business sector is in the process of a transformation that requires legal assistance. The increased governance, regulatory, litigation, and mediation services arising from ESG-related matters represents exciting potential work for law firms and their clients.

Our Employees (Current and Future) Care

It's not enough for law firms to make ESG commitments or create ESG practice areas. Lawyers' significant societal duty creates an ethical obligation to demonstrate this commitment authentically. Stating their beliefs on the firm website or through press releases or CLE materials is only a starting point. For a firm to be genuinely focused on ESG outcomes, they need to demonstrate how this runs through their work with clients and how they use their skill sets to drive change. In addition, it is vital that law firms "walk the talk" on ESG, so they can become trusted advisors to their clients. This consistency is about aligning how a law firm does day-to-day business and the experiences of its staff with the firm's ESG commitments and credentials.

What Does Leading Look Like in Practice?

Lawyers must prepare for and accelerate this transformation as corporations implement long-term plans to promote governance that balances stakeholder interests with profit.

It takes time and commitment to make an authentic commitment to ESG and build a robust implementation of ESG approaches in law firms and their legal practices. Below are some examples of exciting work by lawyers to drive transformational governance.

Box 26.2 How Law Societies and Bar Associations Can Lead

Law societies are vital to building an ESG-conscious approach to legal practice. For example, the International Bar Association has published an ESG Toolkit for Law Firms,[21] and the International Bar and American Bar Associations were early adopters of the UN Guiding Principles on Business and Human Rights. The American Bar Association has further enshrined the

Principles' spirit through guidelines that encourage lawyers to advise not only on the law but also on moral and ethical considerations.[22] Furthermore, the Law Society of England and Wales has published a climate change resolution to urge solicitors and the companies or firms they work for to adopt science-based targets for operations and "take climate change into account when providing legal services."[23] This resolution is backed up with a social-media awareness campaign and resources for solicitors.

Source: Authors.

Common Understanding

Leadership from legal professionals can take many paths. Education and training to promote an awareness and a shared understanding of lawyers' role in bringing about change are critical.

Part of this education and training involves equipping young lawyers with the skills necessary to be resilient entrepreneurial, and to work well with people—all vital skills to delivering client-focused value offerings—and, importantly, to build the well-being and health of legal professionals and therefore the profession as a whole. The College of Legal Practice and O Shaped Skills is an example of two organizations who have partnered to develop such training.[24]

From a technical legal skills perspective, law school curriculums are critical for developing ESG awareness and providing new lawyers with the ethical and practical guidance to balance long-term societal interests with short-term client demands. In addition, the trending legal curriculum addresses corporate governance, human rights, and climate change. The University of California, Berkeley School of Law has encouragingly partnered with the firm Paul, Weiss, Rifkind, Wharton, and Garrison to launch a research initiative centered on ESG.

Furthermore, codes of responsibility in countries like Canada and Japan, as well as some in Europe, acknowledge that lawyers must act as gatekeepers for the interests of courts and society (Sherman 2012).

As lawyers vie to position themselves as experts in this fast-developing space, law societies might also consider implementing standards for ESG legal expertise or firm disclosure requirements with consequences for greenwashing.[25]

"Walking the Talk"

Incorporation of ESG Into Practice

For firms to credibly offer advice on transformational governance, they must ensure that their house is in order.[26]

Obtaining ISO 14000 Certification, for example, exemplifies commitment to managing environmental footprint, similar to how adhering to the United Nations' Guiding Principles on Business and Human Rights reflects a commitment to responsible management of talent and suppliers. Publishing a policy statement stipulating their human rights expectations for talent, suppliers, and business partners is a good first step. In addition, establishing a robust diversity, equity, and inclusion program and aligning pro bono activities and charitable efforts around social and environmental development goals is an excellent start to becoming a transformation partner to business clients.

Some scholars and practitioners have also advocated for the profession's reconsideration of the pervasive billable hours ("eat-what-you-kill") compensation model, which discourages a lawyer's investment in self-education, information sharing, or leadership activities beneficial to the entire firm (Bartel, Cardiff-Hicks, and Shaw 2017). It can also entrench outdated ways of thinking. Instead, growing evidence suggests that reimagined firm models, rewarding output rather than hours, can lead to more multidisciplinary, diverse, and agile operations (Cohen 2019) better aligned to a purpose-driven business strategy.

Thought Leadership

Ongoing legal education is necessary for all corporate lawyers to provide robust counsel incorporating hard and soft law impacts. Linklaters, for example, provides both internal and client-facing training aimed at human rights risks and opportunities in the operations of multinational corporations.[27] A growing number of law firms have identified a market opportunity for ESG services and responded by creating dedicated practice areas[28] or boutique offshoot firms[29] to address this sophisticated and interdisciplinary speciality (Lehmen 2021b). Firms implementing compensation structures and metrics with sufficiently ambitious ESG targets have the most credibility in this area.

Nevertheless, lawyers must move beyond law-review scholarship toward actual ESG capacity building and practical thought leadership to play a critical role in transformational governance.

The landmark Freshfields Report of 2005 and Linklaters' UN Global Compact Guide for General Counsel on Corporate Sustainability in 2015 have been seminal in this regard (Parsons, Watchman, and Wood 2020b), and top firms now regularly publish ESG-related guidance and insights through their platforms. For example, Hong Kong–based Ben McQuhae & Co. have committed to making their "journey to become a sustainable law firm" open source.[30]

Unfortunately, however, resource-stretched mid- and small-sized firms are less likely to share ESG know-how on their websites, which may suggest a worrisome gap for our governance ambitions to reach mid- and small-sized businesses.

Client Counsel

Accelerating transformational governance requires lawyers to engage in challenging, even uncomfortable, client conversations.

Firms should state their ESG-related expectations during initial discussions of a potential client mandate (Food and Agriculture Organization of the United Nations 2019, 36) and build into their client agreements their intention to terminate their mandate if a client refuses to act on their advice regarding these matters. However, even without this forewarning, lawyers are entitled to withdraw representation when clients ignore legal advice.

We acknowledge the debate concerning whether lawyers' applying such leverage can lead to the over-identification of lawyers with their clients, undermining the lawyer's independence and social role in the administration of justice.[31] This debate must be approached carefully while keeping in mind competing interests, understanding the consequences of divesting from clients with a negative ESG impact (therefore losing the ability to influence change by "having a seat at the table"), and lawyers' professional and ethical responsibilities to lead in the implementation of transformational governance. Guidance from law societies in this regard would be welcome.

In the United States, the government has regulated through the Sarbanes-Oxley Act of 2002 (and the Securities Exchange Commission rules implementing it) that "noisy" withdrawal by legal professionals is permitted where in contravention of legal advice, a client has engaged in fraud, or a substantial injury to investors has occurred.[32]

For lawyers who operate under a dual-bar system, it is worth highlighting that the cab rank rule only applies to barristers in limited circumstances (Higgins 2017). Furthermore, we submit that the access to justice argument is tenuous in cases where the client is a large corporation with a substantial budget that continues to knowingly operate to the detriment of society, the environment, or other stakeholders.

Box 26.3 Client Mandates

Refusing work that will likely result in negative ESG impact sends a powerful signal to a corporation that it is insufficiently ESG-focused. For example, Ben McQuhae & Co. only accepts clients aligned with the UN Sustainable Development Goals. By providing management consulting services to those who wish to address the shortcomings addressed by the SDGs, the firm amplifies ESG-positive impact.[33] Furthermore, decision-making regarding the acceptance or refusal of new client mandates that incorporates robust debate and transparency increases acceptance of decisions and protects firms against reputational risk.

Source: Authors.

Scaling Net-Zero Contracts and Human Rights Due Diligence

To accelerate progress, the legal profession must find ways to scale impact.

The Chancery Lane Project,[34] for example, is a collective pro bono effort by lawyers worldwide to develop open-source tools for drafting a range of net zero–aligned commercial agreements. With nearly a hundred contract clauses and multiple tools to assist with issue-spotting and mapping, the project offers practitioners of all stripes a path toward advising on contracts with climate change in mind.

Similarly, the Shift Project,[35] a legacy of John Ruggie's work with the UN to develop the Guiding Principles on Business and Human Rights, offers practical guidance and scholarship around human rights due diligence.

Impact Through Strategic Litigation

Litigation can be a powerful governance instrument for change when advice, influence, and problem-solving fail to encourage transformational governance.

An example of successful strategic litigation is Brazil's Climate Fund Case. Plaintiffs filed the action to challenge a governing body's unwillingness to release funds that had already been allocated to further Brazil's climate action policy (Lehmen 2021a). In the summer of 2022, the case culminated in the Brazil Supreme Court's recognition of the PCA as a human rights treaty—a move with implications for international law. Furthermore, the court ordered the state to properly reactivate the fund and to prepare and present annual plans for allocating resources and disbursing funds to projects aimed at cutting carbon emissions (Kamisky 2022).

Conclusion

"ESG is DNA, not a new practice area."

(Professor Paul Watchman)

Except in special circumstances (e.g., where a sophisticated legal client demands only technical legal advice), the day of narrowly couched technical legal advice should be over. Orison Marden's 'responsible professional and public citizen,' in today's world, has at least an aspirational obligation to counsel clients—beyond law—about practical considerations, likely public perceptions, and reactions, and generally, about doing the right thing.[36]

(Commissioner Harvey J. Goldschmid)

The practical implementation of transformational governance requires transparency and accountability. Lawyers play a critical role, but achieving ESG integration and positive impact at the scale transformational governance demands will not be easy.

That said, great lawyers (and law firms) exist to help their clients solve complicated and pertinent challenges. In doing so, we must value progress over perfection. We are all starting our journey to scale transformational governance at a different place.

But we must also be authentic—in the commitments we make and the actions we take. Our credibility matters.

This chapter contributes to the evolving conversation on transformational governance, the leading role lawyers must play in scaling impact, the challenges encountered in doing so, and how we might overcome these challenges. Our findings are by no means definitive. Instead, this chapter describes where we are now and what we hope can happen.

Every lawyer can lead. So, what is your ambition for our world? And what are you going to do to take action?

Key Discussion Areas

- The history, concept, and significance of transformational governance
- The importance of lawyers leading in the implementation of transformational governance through their advice to clients, in line with, and while having regard to, their professional and fiduciary duties
- The role lawyers can play in encouraging their corporate clients to adopt and exercise an environmental, social, and governance (ESG) net positive impacts approach

Notes

1 "Never normal" refers to an environment of constant change and uncertainty. Also referred to as VUCA (i.e., volatile, uncertain, complex, and ambiguous). These terms refer to the many challenges we face as a society including social and economic instability and fragmentation, human-led climate change, environmental degradation, and biodiversity loss.

2 See also, "Resources Overview," The Value Reporting Foundation, www.valuereportingfoundation.org/#integrated-thinking-principles.

3 Speech by P. Polman: "A New Era of Business," Grantham Institute of Research on Climate Change and the Environment, London School of Economics, London, November 26, 2018.

4 "ESG" and "sustainability" are notoriously difficult to define: they may have different meanings to different people and organizations, and what amounts to ESG and "sustainability" may vary depending on the context. For the purposes of this chapter, the acronym ESG refers to environmental, social, and governance issues, as well as the impact, risks, and/or opportunities of a business or project ("Introduction to ESG," https://corpgov.law.harvard.edu/2020/08/01/introduction-to-esg/, accessed March 3, 2023). We define sustainability by the achievement of the UN Sustainable Development Goals, a set of interlinked global goals. You can read more about these at "The 17 Goals," sdgs.un.org/goals (accessed March 3, 2023).

5 The business judgment rule is a rule that enables directors to make decisions they believe to be in the best interests of the company, without fear of liability. This rule exists in some form in many countries.

6 For example, consider the increasing impact of the Task Force on Climate-Related Disclosures (TCFD).

7 Dodge v. Ford Motor Col, 204 Mich. 459, 507 (1919).

8 Dodge v Ford Motor Co. at 505.

9 Dodge v Ford Motor Co. at 507–10.

10 See also Business Roundtable updated statement, August 19, 2019, www.businessroundtable.org/business-roundtable-redefines-the-purpose-of-a-corporation-to-promote-an-economy-that-serves-all-americans; https://enactingpurpose.org/assets/epi-report-final.pdf (accessed March 3, 2023).

11 For example, by March 2021, "more than a fifth of the world's largest public companies had committed to achieving net zero greenhouse gas emissions" (Vincent 2021).

12 Greenwashing refers to claims about environmental performance that are misleading or unsubstantiated.

13 See also "Tackling Biodiversity and Climate Crises Together and Their Combined Social Impacts," United Nations, June 10, 2021, www.un.org/sustainabledevelopment/blog/2021/06/tackling-biodiversity-climate-crises-together-and-their-combined-social-impacts/ (accessed March 3, 2023); PwC 2021; "The Sustainability Board Report 2020," https://a89c8240-f3c4-4e8b-b920-fae532b127b6.filesusr.com/ugd/f6724f_323dfac850ca46d09705c8db9ba97321.pdf (accessed March 3, 2023).

14 "Rewiring the Economy: Ten Tasks, Ten Years," Cambridge Institute for Sustainability Leadership, 2015, updated 2017, www.cisl.cam.ac.uk/resources/cisl-frameworks/rewiring-the-economy (accessed March 3, 2021).

15 See SDG17; "Rewiring the Economy: Ten Tasks, Ten Years"; Drier, Nabarro, and Nelson 2019; Understanding Our Systems Together, *Race to Zero Initiative*, 2020; "SDG 16: A Legal Guide," *A4Aid*, June 2021 (accessed September 15, 2021).

16 Donella Meadows defines leverage points as "places within a complex system (a corporation, an economy, a living body, a city, an ecosystem) where a small shift in one thing can produce big changes in everything," www.scrummaster.dk/lib/AgileLeanLibrary/People/DonellaMeadows/donellameadows.org-Leverage%20Points%20Places%20to%20Intervene%20in%20a%20System.pdf (accessed March 3, 2023).

17 Legal Opinion on Hong Kong Directors Obligations and Climate Change, October 19, 2021, https://ccli.ubc.ca/wp-content/uploads/2021/10/Hong-Kong-Directors-obligations-and-climate-change.pdf (accessed March 3, 2023).

18 Hutley and Davis 2019; "Fiduciary Obligations with Respect to Climate Change-Carol Hansell and Catherine McCall," video, https://digitalcommons.osgoode.yorku.ca/ccli_webinars/2/ (accessed March 3, 2023); "Legal Opinion on Fiduciary Duties and Climate Change, by Chapman Tripp," video, www.youtube.com/watch?v=QdeR2MNTYEM (accessed March 3, 2023); "Company

Directors in Singapore Urged to Consider Climate Change Risks," Morgan Lewis, www.morganlewis.com/pubs/2021/04/company-directors-in-singapore-urged-to-consider-climate-change-risks (accessed March 3, 2023); Barker, Williams, and Cooper 2021.

19 "France's Duty of Vigilance Law," www.business-humanrights.org/en/big-issues/corporate-legal-accountability/frances-duty-of-vigilance-law (accessed March 3, 2023). In September 2021, France's Supreme Court relied on the law to rule that a company could be charged with complicity for knowingly backing a terrorist group responsible for the killing of innocent people. "Due Vigilance for Global Corporations," *Christian Science Monitor,* October 12, 2021, www.csmonitor.com/Commentary/the-monitors-view/2021/1012/Due-vigilance-for-global-corporations (accessed March 3, 2023).

20 Importantly, the majority of climate-related litigation is happening in the United States. Of the 1,841 ongoing or concluded cases of climate change litigation from around the world (as of May 2021), 1,387 were filed before courts in the United States. Findings and insights taken from Setzer and Higham 2021.

21 ESG Toolkit for Law Firms, International Bar Association, September 2021, https://s3.documentcloud.org/documents/21045191/law-students-for-climate-accountability-report.pdf (accessed June 14, 2022).

22 American Bar Association, Model Rule of Professional Conduct 2.1: Advisors, commentary notes, www.americanbar.org/groups/professional_responsibility/publications/model_rules_of_professional_conduct/rule_2_1_advisor/ (accessed March 3, 2023).

23 "Creating a Climate Conscious Approach to Legal Practice," The Law Society of England and Wales, October 28, 2021, www.lawsociety.org.uk/topics/climate-change/creating-a-climate-conscious-approach-to-legal-practice#download-the-resolution (accessed March 3, 2023).

24 "O Shaped Skills," The College of Legal Practice, www.collegalpractice.com/our-programmes/developing-legal-professionals-programme/o-shaped-skills (accessed March 3, 2023).

25 McQuhae, B. Interview with Girdwood, A. and Bartholomew, C. October 21, 2021.

26 "One common misperception that law firms have, according to Amity Advisory founder and CEO Pamela Cone, is a 'sense of immunity' that they can advise clients on these issues without ensuring that their own house is in order" (Packel 2021).

27 UN Global Compact: Communication on Progress, Linklaters, https://lpscdn.linklaters.com/-/media/digital-marketing-image-library/files/02_about-us/responsibility/2020/march/linklaters-cop-2020.ashx?rev=fb1e6cc8-b7ea-45cf-b4d9-137ecd5c2fa4&extension=pdf&hash=69FC6136E608F550ACE184A97B9CC9AB (accessed March 3, 2023).

28 For example, Linklaters International Business and Human Rights practice. In 2020, Linklaters launched an ESG Recruitment Webinar that attracted 700 candidates (see Parsons, Watchman, and Wood 2020a).

29 For example, the sustainability practice Mischon Purpose, launched by Mischon de Reya in April 2020.

30 "Our Guiding Principles," Ben McQue, https://bmcquhae.com/en/sustainability/ (accessed: October 16, 2021).

31 IBA, American Bar Association (ABA) and CCBE, *A Lawyer's Guide to Detecting and Preventing Money Laundering* (October 2014); see also Quack 2006.

32 Specifically, Section 205.3(d)(2).

33 McQuhae, B. Interview with Girdwood, A. and Bartholomew, C. October 21, 2021.

34 "Start Using Climate Aligned Clauses in Your Contracts," Chancery Lane Project, https://chancerylaneproject.org (accessed October 16, 2021).

35 Shift Project, https://shiftproject.org (accessed March 3, 2023).

36 Speech by SEC Commissioner: "A Lawyer's Role in Corporate Governance: The Myth of Absolute Confidentiality and the Complexity of the Counseling Task," November 17, 2003, New York, www.sec.gov/news/speech/spch111703hjg.htm (accessed March 3, 2023).

References

Austin, Duncan. 2021. "Market-Led Sustainability Is a 'Fix That Fails' . . . Part 1." *Responsible Investor,* October 25, 2021, www.responsible-investor.com/market-led-sustainability-is-a-fix-that-fails/ (accessed March 3, 2023).

Barker, S., C. Williams, and Alex Cooper. 2021. "Fiduciary Duties and Climate Change in the United States," *Commonwealth Climate and Law Initiative (CCLI)*, October 20, 2021, https://ccli.ubc.ca/wp-content/uploads/2021/11/Fiduciary-duties-and-climate-change-in-the-United-States.pdf (accessed March 3, 2023).

Bartel, A. P., B. Cardiff-Hicks, and K. Shaw. 2017. "Incentives for Lawyers Moving away from 'Eat What You Kill.'" *ILR Review* 70(2): 336–58, https://doi.org/10.1177/0019793916650450.

Berkhout, Esmé, Nick Galasso, Max Lawson, Pablo Andrés Rivero Morales, Anjela Taneja, and Diego Alejo Vázquez Pimentel. 2021. *The Inequality Virus: Global Report*. Oxford: Oxfam International, https://d1ns4ht6ytuzzo.cloudfront.net/oxfamdata/oxfamdatapublic/2021-01/The%20Inequality%20Virus%20-%20Global%20Report%20%282021%29-3.pdf?N03OMRi1S_PWAiXig7D34AiDJ6ibPSOP (accessed March 3, 2023).

British Academy. 2019. "Principles for Purposeful Business: How to Deliver the Framework for the Future of the Corporation," www.thebritishacademy.ac.uk/publications/future-of-the-corporation-principles-for-purposeful-business/ (accessed March 3, 2023).

Climate Champions. 2021. "GFANZ: Net Zero Financial Alliance Launches." *Race to Zero, UNFCCC*, April 21, 2021, https://racetozero.unfccc.int/net-zero-financial-alliance-launches/ (accessed March 3, 2023).

Cohen, M. A. 2019. "Are Law Firms Sustainable? It's the Model That Matters." *Forbes*, August 18, 2019, www.forbes.com/sites/markcohen1/2019/08/19/are-law-firms-sustainable-its-the-model-that-matters/?sh=63c758e4628f (accessed March 3, 2023).

de Wit, Elisa. 2020. "Climate Change Litigation Update." *Norton Rose Fulbright*, December 2020, www.nortonrosefulbright.com/en-za/knowledge/publications/0c9b154a/climate-change-litigation-update (accessed March 3, 2023).

Donaldson, T., and J. P. Walsh. 2015. "Toward a Theory of Business." *Research in Organizational Behavior* 35: 181–207, https://doi.org/10.1016/j.riob.2015.10.002.

Drier, L., D. Nabarro, and J. Nelson. 2019. "Systems Leadership for Sustainable Development: Strategies for Achieving Systemic Change." Harvard Kennedy School Corporate Responsibility Imitative, www.hks.harvard.edu/sites/default/files/centers/mrcbg/files/Systems%20Leadership.pdf (accessed March 3, 2023).

Dudek van Heel, O., and E. Brahim. 2021. "Deploying Capital as a Force for Good: A No-brainer?" *Freshfields Bruckhaus Deringer*, October 20, 2021, https://sustainability.freshfields.com/post/102h8x5/deploying-capital-as-a-force-for-good-a-no-brainer (accessed March 3, 2023).

Eccles, Robert G. 2021. "Yes, Even U.S. Board Directors (and Their Attorneys) Need to Worry about Climate Change." *Forbes*, October 24, 2021, www.forbes.com/sites/bobeccles/2021/10/24/yes-even-us-board-directors-and-their-attorneys-need-to-worry-about-climate-change/?sh=7a235337f338 (accessed March 3, 2023).

Edelman. 2021. "Edelman Trust Barometer," www.edelman.com/sites/g/files/aatuss191/files/2021-03/2021%20Edelman%20Trust%20Barometer.pdf (accessed March 3, 2023).

EY. 2022. "Enough. A Review of Corporate Sustainability in a World Running Out of Time." June 2022, https://assets.ey.com/content/dam/ey-sites/ey-com/en_au/pdfs/ey-au-enough-report-june_2022.pdf (accessed March 3, 2023).

Food and Agriculture Organization of the United Nations. 2019. "Due Diligence, Tenure, and Agricultural Investment: A Guide on the Dual Responsibilities of the Private Sector Lawyers in Advising on the Acquisition of Land and Natural Resources." May 23, 2019, https://books.google.co.uk/books?id=u2i1DwAAQBAJ&source=gbs_navlinks_s (accessed March 3, 2023).

Force for Good Initiative. 2021. "Capital as a Force for Good: Capitalism for a Sustainable Future," www.forcegood.org/report-2021 (accessed March 3, 2023).

Friedman, Milton. 1970. "A Friedman Doctrine—the Social Responsibility of Business Is to Increase Its Profits." *New York Times*, September 13, 1970, www.nytimes.com/1970/09/13/archives/a-friedman-doctrine-the-social-responsibility-of-business-is-to.html (accessed March 3, 2023).

Hallorian, T. 2018. "A Brief History of the Corporate Form and Why It Matters." *Fordham Journal of Corporate and Financial Law*, November 18, 2018. https://news.law.fordham.edu/jcfl/2018/11/18/a-brief-history-of-the-corporate-form-and-why-it-matters/

Higgins, A. 2017. "Rebooting the Cab Rank Rule as a Limited Universal Service Obligation." *Legal Ethics* 20(2): 201–23, https://doi.org/10.1080/1460728x.2017.1292623.

Hodgson, Camille, and Tom Wilson. 2022. "Climate Group Prepares Legal Action against Shell Directors." *Financial Times*, March 15, 2022, www.ft.com/content/d7feaa8a-7555-47ae-828b-274527c6f89c (accessed March 3, 2023).

Hutley, N., and S. H. Davis. 2019. "Climate Change and Directors' Duties." *Centre for Policy Development,* March 26, 2019, https://cpd.org.au/wp-content/uploads/2019/03/Noel-Hutley-SC-and-Sebastian-Hartford-Davis-Opinion-2019-and-2016_pdf.pdf (accessed March 3, 2023).

Institute of Directors Southern Africa. 2016. "King IV: Report on Corporate Governance for South Africa 2016," www.adams.africa/wp-content/uploads/2016/11/King-IV-Report.pdf (accessed March 3, 2023).

Intergovernmental Panel on Climate Change (IPCC). 2021. "Climate Change 2021: The Physical Science Basis." August 6, 2021, www.ipcc.ch/report/sixth-assessment-report-working-group-i/ (accessed March 3, 2023).

Kamisky, I. 2022. "Brazilian Court World's First to Recognise Paris Agreement as Human Rights Treaty." *Climate Home News*, July 7, 2022, www.climatechangenews.com/2022/07/07/brazilian-court-worlds-first-to-recognise-paris-agreement-as-human-rights-treaty/ (accessed March 3, 2023).

Kania, J., M. Kramer, and P. Senge. 2018. "The Water of Systems Change." *FSG*, June 4, 2018, www.fsg.org/blog/new-article-water-systems-change/ (accessed March 3, 2023).

Karmel, Roberta S. 1988. "Duty to the Target: Is An Attorney's Duty to the Corporation a Paradigm for Directors?" *Hastings Law Journal* 29(677): 677–98, https://core.ac.uk/download/pdf/228601646.pdf (accessed March 3, 2023).

King, M., and Roberts, L. 2021. *The Healthy Company*. Kenwyn, SA: Juta & Co. Ltd.

Koulias, C., and M. Breslauer. 2021. "Introduction." In *SDG 16 Business Framework: Inspiring Transformational Governance*. UN Global Compact, https://sdg16.unglobalcompact.org/ (accessed March 3, 2023).

Latham & Watkins. 2020. "ESG Litigation Roadmap," www.lw.com/admin/upload/SiteAttachments/ESG-Litigation-Roadmap.pdf (accessed March 3, 2023).

Le Menestrel, Marc, Julian Rode, Nicolai Heinz, and Gert Cornelissen. 2022. "Encouraging Sustainability Why the Business Case Isn't Enough." *Insead*, August, 15, 2022, https://knowledge.insead.edu/responsibility/encouraging-sustainability-why-business-case-isnt-enough (accessed March 3, 2023).

Lehmen, A., 2021a. "Advancing Strategic Climate Litigation in Brazil." *German Law Journal*. Cambridge University Press (upcoming).

———. 2021b. "The Rise of ESG Law: In Search of Lost Time." *Academia Letters*, www.academia.edu/49924799/The_rise_of_ESG_Law_in_search_of_lost_time (accessed March 3, 2023).

Mayer, Colin. 2020. "It's Time to Redefine the Purpose of Business. Here's a Roadmap." *World Economic Forum*, January 7, 2020, www.weforum.org/agenda/2020/01/its-time-for-a-radical-rethink-of-corporate-purpose/ (accessed March 3, 2023).

Packel, D. 2021. "Clients Scrutinize Law Firm ESG Practices and Look for Red Flags." *Law.com*, August 3, 2021, www.law.com/international-edition/2021/08/03/clients-are-aware-of-these-red-flags-within-law-firm-esg-practices-378-175484/?fbclid=IwAR3I60I2XXtZU75_JCL3gPTP-D8xRZ50L2o23UJSU3Gr46rZ1GOoZOf0pUn0 (accessed March 3, 2023).

Parsons, Carla, Paul Watchman, and Vanessa Wood. 2020a. "The Rise of ESG Law Firms Part I: ESG Law Gets 'Hot' and CEOs Get Bothered, Leading to Integrated ESG Legal Practices." *Responsible Investor,* October 26, 2020, www.responsible-investor.com/the-rise-of-esg-law-firms-part-i-esg-law-gets-hot-and-ceos-get-bothered-leading-to-integrated-esg-legal-practices/ (accessed March 3, 2023).

———. 2020b. "The Rise of ESG Law Firms Part II: General Counsel Respond to the Regulation Tsunami and Litigation Goes Viral." *Responsible Investor*, October 27, 2020, www.responsible-investor.com/the-rise-of-esg-law-firms-part-ii-general-counsel-respond-to-the-regulation-tsunami-and-litigation-goes-viral/ (accessed March 3, 2023).

Perlman, R., S. Goldberg, and I. Calviño. 2020. "Environmental, Social & Governance Law 2021 | ESG and Corporate Strategy: A Cross-Sectoral View." *The International Comparative Legal Guides*, December 15, 2020, https://iclg.com/practice-areas/environmental-social-and-governance-law (accessed March 3, 2023).

Petrin, Martin, and Barnali Choudhury. 2020. "Corporate Purpose and Short-Termism." In *Research Handbook on Comparative Corporate Governance*, edited by Afra Afsharipour and Martin Gelter. Edward Elgar Publishing, forthcoming. Published online March 9, 2020, https://papers.ssrn.com/sol3/papers.cfm?abstract_id=3538156 (accessed March 3, 2023).

Pierson Brown, Tomar. 2020. "(Systems) Thinking Like a Lawyer." *Clinical Law Review, New York University*, March 9, 2020, www.law.nyu.edu/sites/default/files/Tomar%20Pierson-Brown%20-%20%28Systems%29%20Thinking%20Like%20a%20Lawyer.pdf (accessed March 3, 2023).

Polman, P., and Winston, A., 2021. "The Net Positive Manifesto: Is the World Better Off Because Your Company Is In It?" *Harvard Business Review*, September–October 2021, https://hbr.org/2021/09/the-net-positive-manifesto (accessed March 3, 2023).

PwC. 2021. "The Director's New Playbook: Taking on Change." Annual Corporate Directors Survey. Governance Insights Center, www.pwc.com/us/en/services/governance-insights-center/assets/pwc-2021-annual-corporate-directors-survey.pdf (accessed March 3, 2023).

Quack, Sigrid. 2006. "Who Fills the Legal 'Black Holes' in Transnational Governance? Lawyers, Law Firms and Professional Associations as Border-Crossing Regulatory Actors." In *Global Governance and the Role of Non-State Actors*, edited by Gunnar Folke Schuppert. Baden-Baden: Nomos-Verl.-Ges.https://www.econbiz.de/Record/global-governance-and-the-role-of-non-state-actors-schuppert-gunnar-folke/10003270813

Ramos, Gabriela, and William Hynes. 2019. "Beyond Growth: Towards a New Economic Approach." Report of the Secretary General's Advisory Group on a New Growth Narrative. Organisation for Economic Co-operation and Development, September 12, 2019, www.oecd.org/officialdocuments/publicdisplaydocumentpdf/?cote=SG/NAEC(2019)3&docLanguage=En (accessed March 3, 2023).

Rubin, P. H., and M. J. Bailey. 1994. "The Role of Lawyers in Changing the Law." *Journal of Legal Studies* 23(2): 807–31.

Ruggie, J., 2013. *Just Business: Multinational Corporations and Human Rights*. New York, NY: W.W. Norton & Company.

Schwab, K. 2019. "Davos Manifesto 2020: The Universal Purpose of a Company in the Fourth Industrial Revolution." *World Economic Forum*, December 2, 2019, www.weforum.org/agenda/2019/12/davos-manifesto-2020-the-universal-purpose-of-a-company-in-the-fourth-industrial-revolution/ (accessed March 3, 2023).

Schwab, K., and Vanham, P. 2021. *Stakeholder Capitalism*. Hoboken, NJ: John Wiley & Sons, Inc.

Setzer, Joana, and Catherine Higham. 2021. "Global Trends in Climate Litigation: 2021 Snapshot." Grantham Research Institute on Climate Change and the Environment, www.lse.ac.uk/granthaminstitute/wp-content/uploads/2021/07/Global-trends-in-climate-change-litigation_2021-snapshot.pdf (accessed March 3, 2023).

Sherman John F. III. 2012. "Professional Responsibility of Lawyers under the Guiding Principles." *Shift*, April 2012, https://shiftproject.org/professional-responsibility-of-lawyers-under-the-guiding-principles/ (accessed March 3, 2023).

———. 2021. "The Corporate General Counsel Who Respects Human Rights." *Legal Ethics* 24(1): 49–72. doi : 10.1080/1460728x.2021.1979731.

Stout, Lynn A. 2002. "Bad and Not-So-Bad Arguments for Shareholder Primacy." *Cornell Law School*, November 19, 2002, https://papers.ssrn.com/sol3/papers.cfm?abstract_id=331464 (accessed March 3, 2023).

Sundaram, A. K., and A. C. Inkpen. 2004. "The Corporate Objective Revisited." *Organization Science* 15(3): 350–63.

Täger, Matthias. 2021. "'Double Materiality': What Is It and Why Does It Matter?" Grantham Institute on Climate Change and the Environment, April, 21, 2021, www.lse.ac.uk/granthaminstitute/news/double-materiality-what-is-it-and-why-does-it-matter/ (accessed March 3, 2023).

Temple-West, Patrick. 2021. "Calls to Action on ESG Boost Demand for Legal Expertise." *Financial Times*, October 14, 2021, www.ft.com/content/ab23e76b-2497-4655-865e-c90c34d3e1b5 (accessed March 3, 2023).

Tollefson, Jeff. 2021. "COP26 Climate Summit: A Scientists' Guide to a Momentous Meeting." *Nature*, October 25, 2021, www.nature.com/immersive/d41586-021-02815-w/index.html?utm_source=Nature+Briefing&utm_campaign=7a8f0a1880-briefing-dy-20211026&utm_medium=email&utm_term=0_c9dfd39373-7a8f0a1880–43722373 (accessed March 3, 2023).

UN Convention on Biological Diversity (CBD). 2020. "The Global Biodiversity Outlook 5 (GBO-5)." *UN Environment Programme*, September 15, 2020, www.unep.org/resources/report/global-biodiversity-outlook-5-gbo-5?_ga=2.34486310.649028595.1634823085-461105125.1634823085 (accessed March 3, 2023).

UN Global Compact. 2019. "1.5° Business Leadership: Solutions, Strategies, and Mindsets for Our Only Future." *Special Edition Report for the UN Secretary-General's Climate Action Summit*, September 23, 2019, https://goexplorer.org/wp-content/uploads/1.5-degree-Business-Leadership.pdf (accessed March 3, 2023).

———. 2021. "Executive Summary: SDG 16 Business Framework Inspiring Transformational Governance," https://ungc-communications-assets.s3.amazonaws.com/docs/publications/EXECUTIVE-SUMMARY-SDG-16-Business-Framework-Inspiring-Transformational-Governance.pdf (accessed March 3, 2023).

Vincent, Matthew. 2021. "Can Business Deliver on Their Climate Promises." *Financial Times*, May 26, 2021, www.ft.com/content/70b675de-d15d-4bbf-8c35-e4e1f46a8756?shareType=nongift (accessed March 3, 2023).

Watchman, P., and P. Clements Hunt. 2021. "The Rise of the ESG Law Firm: Chasing the Dragon'," https://businessbeyondcovid19.org/wp-content/uploads/2021/03/ChasingThe-Dragon_120321_0050.pdf (accessed March 3, 2023).

World Economic Forum. 2021. *The Global Risks Report 2021*, 16th ed., https://www3.weforum.org/docs/WEF_The_Global_Risks_Report_2021.pdf (accessed October 19, 2021).

———. 2023. *The Global Risks Report 2023*, 18th ed., https://www3.weforum.org/docs/WEF_Global_Risks_Report_2023.pdf (accessed February 20, 2023).

27

ESG MATURITY MAPPING

Sustainability in Legacy, New Age, and Start-Up Organizations

Preeti Shroff-Mehta, Sukaran Thakur, Vijay Viswanathan, and Parker Lemal-Brown

Introduction

Environmental, social, and governance (ESG) sustainability is purpose and compliance driven. It is strongly influenced by national, regional, and global policies as well as internal and external stakeholders. According to PricewaterhouseCoopers (2022a):

> **'In March 2022, the SEC [U.S. Securities and Exchange Commission] proposed new rules for cyber and climate-related disclosures. While they are not yet final and are open for public comments, the SEC is likely to advance rules that obligate companies to describe in detail the processes through which the board of directors provides oversight of cybersecurity and climate related risks and expertise.'**

According to Brookings (2022) report: ESG investments are likely to reach US$50 trillion in assets by 2025. In April 2021, the EU released a Corporate Sustainability Reporting Directive (CSRD) that has mandated rigorous disclosure standards to enhance the coverage and reliability of sustainability reporting for streamlining corporate reporting.

Since then, many more directives have defined various performance and accounting standards for reporting ESG policies and achievements. Clearly, there is a convergence of consumers, investment, and compliance-driven forces to mainstream ESG across start-ups, legacy, and New Age companies (European Commission 2023).

ESG sustainability is a critical framework originating in the international standards and policy guidance but now adopted by legacy to start-up organizations as a direct response to customer awareness about the relationship between products, people, and the planet. The key question is: is sustainability perceived to be cost prohibitive, or will it generate shared value, and how?

SEC Required Sustainability Reporting: Alignment Across the Business Value Chain

Businesses around the world are integrating sustainability as a key priority for business strategy, growth, and impact. Environmental, Social and Governance—ESG sustainability

DOI: 10.4324/9781003316077-33

is rooted in the deeper systemic transformation defined by "Circular Economy" (CE) principles. It moves the economy and society away from "Extract-Use-Throw" model of unsustainable waste creating to reuse, repurpose and regenerate principles across industries.

> Though renewable actions can extend the lifespan of a resource, there is still a clear endpoint in mind. Circular keeps a resource' lifespan rolling forward. When created with circularity in mind, there isn't a pre-determined endpoint to a resource's usefulness.
>
> *(Deloitte 2024)*

> It is useful to emphasize collaborative relationship between stakeholders and creating differential values based on British Standards institution proposed guiding principles as an essential basis for decision making towards the implementation of CE.
>
> *(Bertassinni et al. 2022)*

- Systemic Thinking
- Innovation
- Stewardship
- Collaboration
- Value Optimization
- Transparency

There are global, regional, national, and local standards (mandatory and voluntary) that must be addressed while reporting business ESG strategy and performance. There are five critical areas that require alignment in business sustainability/ESG reporting and communications for being responsive to multiple global compliance requirements.

1. Strategic alignment (vision and values alignment for ESG)
2. Systemic alignment across the value chain (circular economy and sustainability indicators for business and societal impact)
3. Supply-chain alignment (all touch points in procurement—production—distribution—marketing and sales value chain across countries)
4. Stakeholder alignment (internal and external stakeholder communication and engagement)
5. Social-media alignment (consistency in brands' sustainability strategy and ESG reporting across social-media platforms and channels)

The SEC-defined ESG disclosure categories and businesses with the largest percentage increase (2021–2022) are as follows, followed by multiple reporting frameworks adopted by companies (Gez et al. 2022).

- Environmental (sustainability, recycling, renewable energy)
- Human-capital management (Form 10-K)
- E&S targets and goals
- Corporate culture
- Board oversight of E&S issues
- Social impact and community
- E&S issues in shareholder engagement

Reporting frameworks and standards are defined around materiality, Scope 1, Scope 2, and Scope 3 compliance requirements for direct and indirect ESG related indicators. Companies also define their own proxy standards for reporting as they prepare for SEC filing and compliance.

- SASB: Sustainability Accounting Standards Boards
- TCFD: Taskforce on Climate-Related Financial Disclosures
- GRI: Global Reporting Initiative
- CDP: Climate Disclosure Project
- UN Standards (UNSDGs, UN Global Compact, UN Guiding Principles Reporting Framework)

The crucial verifications will involve company's SEC filing, investors' reports with reviews and approvals by CEO, CFOs, and governing board. The same will apply for consistency across all customer/stakeholder communications rooted in compliance guidelines and reporting data requirements. There are several existing models for mapping ESG maturity as companies implement and evolve policies to address environmental, social, and governance issues. Legacy organizations are beginning to implement more ESG policies, whether due to stakeholder demand, company values, and/or compliance regulations. Meanwhile, emerging and innovative start-ups—interviewed for this study—such as Latitude, enter and develop their ESG values and vision from the ground up for nurturing green and restorative communities, social inclusion, and collaborative stakeholder governance. While focusing on green, regenerative, and restorative community-building real estate, the founders of Latitude explained that People-Planet-Purpose-centered shared value orientation is critical in the real-estate industry.

> ***There is a critical need for the policy, financial and transactional side of the real estate industry to change and provide better counsel to real estate buyers and sellers. We want to help catalyze a change in our homes and habitats, community ecosystem to help both people and the planet thrive.***
>
> *(Collins 2021)*

With more flexible organizational structures and smaller value chains than traditional companies, start-ups have more potential to achieve comprehensive ESG maturity, in which environmental, social, and governance factors are equally and significantly prioritized. Furthermore, start-up founders have introduced a critical fourth factor in ESG: the role of the individual's passion/purpose within the organization, and how the organization shapes the individual. While start-ups often lack the capital that powers the impact of larger legacy organizations, these smaller companies could radically change the ESG landscape and, in some cases, could be considered more mature in ESG than the established titans.

Major corporations are now actively addressing ESG topics and are required to report policy changes. However, many of these companies are only focusing on partial solutions, mainly environmental aspects, while ignoring social or governance issues. Based on maturity mapping models, most legacy and New Age organizations could not be considered ESG mature due to incomprehensive approaches to ESG and ineffective or partial policies that do not transform value chains or internal supply chains and organizational governance in ways that will significantly impact the world. On the other hand, nascent purpose-driven companies show deeper ESG maturity by crafting new environmental, social, and governance approaches from the ground up. Despite having a smaller global impact compared to larger corporations, these start-ups could have something to teach legacy organizations on how to fully embrace every factor in ESG.

Literature Review: Purpose and Perception Motivate ESG

The rising collective passion and interest in the purpose and value of ESG are reflected in the push from internal and external stakeholders—customers, investors, and legal bodies (national, regional such as the EU, global)—for adopting and declaring ESG measures. There are financial rewards and incentives for adopting green processes (Jensen 2000). Even as customers, choosing sustainable products and services is not merely measured in fiscal cost and benefit, it is also about the purpose of the company and the way it defines its values. Investors have also taken a keen interest in this, as they believe ESG forms a part of good business ethics as well as long-term sustainability. This helps sail through turbulent times and manage risks, more so in this ongoing pandemic era.

According to Polman and Winston (2021):

> **Finding personal and organizational meaning is not a soft-hearted, anti-business strategy. In fact, satisfying basic human needs is a powerful path to business success. A net positive company will work to satisfy all four drives (acquire, defend, to bond with others, to comprehend our world) for its employees. It will improve their lives by giving them good paying jobs, of course, but mainly by helping to discover and unlock their purposes—letting them connect heart and brain.**

Globally, there have been a recognition and trend toward adoption of long-term sustainability goals, instead of short-term "myopic" goals usually centered around profit maximization (Chelawat and Trivedi 2016). While the literature is limited, research shows that a positive correlation exists between financial performance and ESG compliance. In fact, stocks portfolios of ESG-sensitive organizations outperform the blue-chip stock portfolio by absolute rate of return over a period of five years (Goyal and Aggarwal 2014).

The Environmental Kuznets Curve (EKC) hypothesis has long noted that initial economic growth causes negative ecological impact, which continues to increase until a turning point, after which environmental damage stabilizes and economy continues to grow (Stern 2004); considering the climate reports and social-inequality index performances, it has been noted that this turning point has not yet arrived for larger countries such as India (Dalal and Thaker 2019).

Like all global-scale events, the ESG performance of organizations has been impacted by the global financial crisis of 2007 as well as the Covid-19 pandemic. After the global financial crisis, organizations that complied with environmental, social, and governance laws performed better financially than the organizations that did not (Singh 2013). Similarly, ESG performance positively contributed to returns during the Covid-19 pandemic period, wherein ESG score was found to be positively related to cumulative raw returns and market adjusted returns (Beloskar and Rao 2022).

As an example, organizations in India usually disclose information around ESG compliance in annual reports and in sustainability reports, with the government using corporate social responsibility (CSR) reporting as a marker to ascertain the level of ESG activities

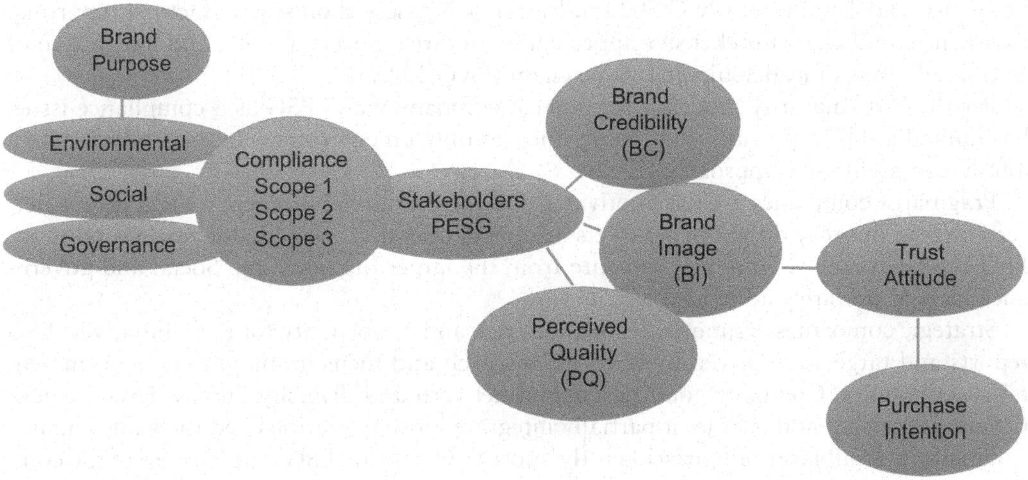

Figure 27.1 Brand Purpose–Perception–Purchase Linkages

Source: Adapted from Koh, Burnasheva, and Suh 2022.

(Sharma, Panday, and Dangwal 2020). The size of an organization and environmental certification are the only significant variables associated with the Environmental Disclosure Index (Chaklader and Gulati 2015). Organizations benefit from such disclosures not just from a policy perspective but also from a consumer and investor perspective (Chaklader and Gulati 2015), mainly because stakeholders pay attention to this disclosure information for making product and service purchase as well as investment decisions.

In fact, it has been long observed that environmental consciousness helps organizations fare better in both the consumer market and the stock market (Toms 1999). Thus, most corporate leaders view these sustainability efforts primarily as a way to enhance organizational reputation and attract socially aware consumers, employees, and investors (Porter, Serafeim, and Kramer 2019). This relationship runs deep, and directly impact brand credibility, image, and perceived quality, with a positive relation between social and governance dimensions of people perceived ESG (PESG) on the aforementioned parameters (Koh, Burnasheva, and Suh 2022) as demonstrated in Figure 27.1.

Ultimately, there is a deeply intertwined relationship between business purpose, performance, and environmental, social, and governance concerns (Henisz, Koller, and Nuttall 2019). Annual Reports and ESG reports reviewed for the purpose of this study offer a detailed insight into not just the activities that an organization is undertaking but also of how self-aware it is, as well as how it would like to be perceived.

ESG Rating and Maturity Mapping

Now that there is widespread impetus for corporations to address ESG, new models and ratings guides have emerged to measure ESG effectiveness and maturity. For ESG scoring, MSCI has created a *ratings framework* to assess the ESG initiatives of global companies across all industries (MSCI 2022). PricewaterhouseCoopers (PwC) has published a *mapping framework* that breaks down ESG maturity into four profiles: Minimalist, Pragmatist,

Strategist, and Trailblazer (PwC 2022a). Maturity is assessed on several factors: reporting, experience in ESG, comprehensive approach to all three aspects of ESG, and integration of ESG at all levels of leadership and value chain (PwC 2022b).

Per the PwC maturity model, a Minimalist company views ESG as a compliance issue, has limited public reporting, and mainly focuses only on environmental issues rather than a fully comprehensive approach.

Pragmatist companies are risk-motivated and have sustainability reports and maybe net-zero targets, but they do not base targets in current scientific research; the responsibility for ESG lies below the C-Suite and separate from the larger organization. Social and governance factors are rarely addressed.

Strategic companies are motivated by both risk and opportunity for ESG initiatives. ESG reports and targets are driven by scientific research and focus on more than environmental sustainability. Company goals go beyond net-zero and diversity quotas. ESG includes C-Suite leadership and is at least partially integrated into operations and the value chain.

Finally, a Trailblazer organization is the most ESG mature. ESG is at the core of the company mission and integrated into every aspect of operations, strategy, and organizational design. The CEO is primarily responsible for ESG strategies, and ESG metrics are used in all company reports. Most crucially, Trailblazer companies publicly advocate for ESG practices and help to develop new industry standards and regulations. In these organizations, ESG is synonymous with all company practices.

This framework gives a solid base on what ESG ideally looks like in practice. However, little research currently maps these profiles to existing organizations. There are many types of firms and industries, which impacts how ESG looks from company to company. While compliance reporting has become widespread, there is not much data on how companies are evolving their ESG practices and how effective these policies are.

The other relevant framework focuses on strategy, data, compliance and regulations, and supply chain. The recently organized Reuters—Responsible Business USA 2024 conference for U.S. business/brand leaders—focused on five key pillars of responsible business.[1]

Field Research Methodology

In order to understand the range of maturity stages of companies, we researched key questions on how the corporate world looks at ESG: Are they committed to the purpose or is it just a checkbox? When is a company considered mature for ESG? How self-aware are they? For comprehensive research and analysis, we undertook both primary and secondary data collection.

Primary Research: We reached out to one hundred selected companies based on their size, scale, and industry and interviewed over thirty companies. In-depth interviews were conducted with the help of a discussion guide based on suitable questions related to ESG goals for a company and how they impact its performance. The interviews were taken with various representatives from the companies, both national and local, which helped us gather direct insights, candid statements, and valuable data figures for the research. Supporting data was also taken from secondary reports, annual statements, and company websites.

The companies interviewed have been categorized into three firm types: Legacy, New Age Digital, and Start-Up. Legacy organizations are over fifty years old, publicly traded, and often operating in multiple industries. New Age companies are mainly digital organizations

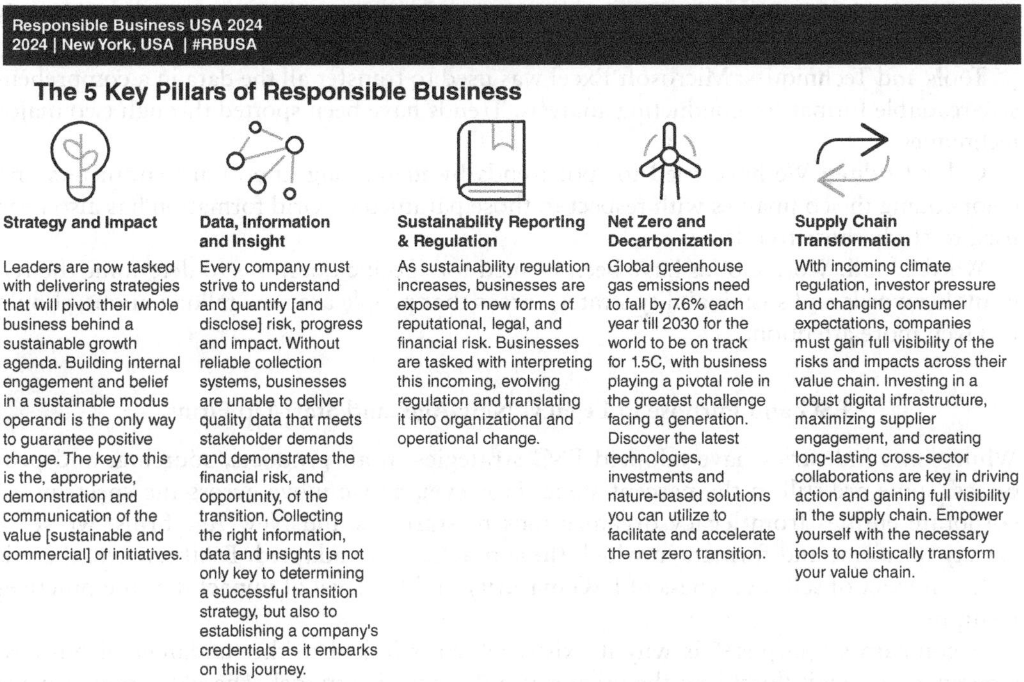

Figure 27.2 The Five Pillars of Sustainability

Source: Responsible Business USA.

founded within the last fifty years but are publicly traded and have global impact. New Age companies such as Netflix and Amazon were founded as start-up digital companies, but now have significantly greater impact on global industry. Finally, Start-Ups are nascent companies that do not have IPOs and have a minimal global impact but may quickly grow into larger organizations.

Secondary Research: To further strengthen the primary research, we attempted to understand the good practices of the industry by analyzing the existing company documents and assessing where they stand using the ESG maturity profiles by PwC, as described in section 1.2.

In addition, we used the MSCI ESG Ratings Framework (MSCI 2022), which provides annual ESG scores. The MSCI score is based on ten themes and thirty-five key issues under the environmental, social, and governance pillars. These themes include climate change, natural capital, pollution and waste, environmental opportunities, human capital, product liability, stakeholder opposition, social opportunities, corporate governance, and corporate behavior. MSCI provides a comprehensive score for individual companies, as well as performance analysis of different aspects of ESG.

A comprehensive literature review was also conducted for areas in and around ESG, as well as research around big companies like Amazon and Netflix and their recent ESG-related initiatives. More than fifteen prominent and recent articles were studied in detail from verified sources such as McKinsey, CRISIL ESG Compendium, Motilal Oswal, Cambridge, and PwC. A compiled report of all literature reviews and insights generated from these articles has been made, keeping in mind the emerging themes, topics, and trends around ESG.

Tools and Techniques: Microsoft Excel was used to transfer all the data in a comprehensive readable format for conducting analysis. Trends have been spotted through two major techniques.

Color Coding: We have tried to spot trends by identifying important parameters and color coding the companies with respect to those parameters. Grid formation has also been used to study those trends.

Word Cloud: Word clouds have been formed for specific questions to determine the relevant keywords and sustainability strategy areas that people are now talking about, should be given more attention.

ESG and Purpose in Legacy, New Age, and Start-Up Firms

While some industries have adopted ESG strategies in all products, sourcing, and processes, some are still in the nascent stage. However, as we move across the spectrum of corporate entities from legacy organizations to start-ups and New Age firms, we see a variety of norms and formats in which these practices are adapted. Furthermore, there is a clear impact of self-awareness of ESG maturity and the level of impact that the practices result in.

A company's "purpose" is why it exists, which is linked to the fundamental business strategy and how it flows into the organization's operating model. The ESG commitments then deliver on the goals the purpose sets. In an article by Sean Brown and Robin Nuttall (2022), the recommendations on how to align ESG commitments and how to embed them in the company's DNA help us understand more about how the corporate world is heading toward adopting and mainstreaming the "Green Governance and Diversity" principles for defining the purpose.

Any company, regardless of the industry, can be driven by purpose—it is a simple articulation of what issues affecting the people and planet they are trying to solve. Company purpose is no longer just a marketing initiative but reflects a shift in the stakeholder attitude: The pressure to focus on ESG is coming from employees, customers (millennials, a generation Z especially), and investors and regulators (like the European Union and SEC). Regarding ESG and value creation, strong links have been observed between purposeful activity and productivity and performance improvements. Win-win situations are created with the advantages of a better relationship with regulators, higher resource efficiency with a green supply chain, and higher employee engagement.

For seamless adoption of the purpose, experts (PwC 2022a) advise aligning executive rewards and incentives with the corporate purpose of measuring social and people metrics, then communicating the purpose and having it recognized by investors. Anchoring in purpose and ensuring that ESG commitments are followed as part of the organizational strategy, instead of chasing after big ESG issues, are more impactful. Investors don't expect a business to change overnight; having a road map with milestones and a trajectory to improvement is the way to go about imbibing the Green Purpose. Also, while appointing sustainability officers is increasingly popular among firms, doing so at an operational level and developing the purpose and ESG jointly with business unit leaders is a key indicator of ESG maturity.

Box 27.1 SCORE Framework

S—Simplify (make sure purpose is simple and convincing)
C—Connect (ensure that purpose connects with practice)
O—Own (make sure that board owns company's purpose)
R—Reward (Incentivize and track purposeful behavior)
E—Exemplify (Tell Great Stories About Purpose)

Source: Brown and Nuttall 2022.

Governments, NGOs, and corporations alone cannot be held accountable for the environment. There is a call for corporate climate action to fill the gaps left in the policy and initiatives. In an article by Robert A. Ritz (2020), titled "Climate Targets, Executive Compensation and Corporate Strategy," the rationale behind linking executive pay to climate metrics is discussed in order to mainstream climate action and results as well as accountability. This school of thought has been gaining traction as all efforts of the companies are now being reviewed for their measurable impact on the planet.

In the energy industry, for example, institutional investors yield significant pressure regarding ESG. The issue will also become increasingly acute for other emissions-intensive sectors like airlines and aluminum, cement, and steel manufacturers. Legacy businesses can be re-optimized to extract their remaining value through more sustainable production, while investing in new low-carbon products and technologies for future growth (Ritz 2020). Climate-linked incentives can be useful in several ways to businesses in the long term. Apart from addressing the pressure from investors, they can strengthen the alignment between high-level corporate strategy and management incentives in the organization. Increasing the weight attached to ESG metrics in the company's balanced scorecard will also send a positive message to investors and potential employees about the future of the business.

Sustainability efforts tend to be the first stage of ESG initiatives for most companies, due to stakeholder pressure and government regulations. This has prioritized the environmental aspect of ESG, while social and governance factors lack equal attention within organizations. The trend can be seen even within ESG reports, by the amount of research and policies offered for each segment. Environmental action is critical, but it is often misconstrued as the core of ESG rather than one of three interconnected elements.

L&T India (Legacy)

The company report analyzed various aspects in which L&T is moving toward a more sustainable future. The following are the key highlights:

- 19.4 million INR was invested in various energy-efficient projects, which could translate into potential energy savings of 9.8L kWh over one year.
- 26.4 percent of the energy for offices now comes from renewable sources.
- 70 percent area of India operations now follow green building standards.

- 152,025 trees were planted through CSR.
- 4,116 tons of CO2 were mitigated through energy conservation and green power procurement.
- 2,000 acres of land were irrigated through water conservation programs.
- Energy conservation initiatives along with low occupancy due to pandemic helped in reducing energy consumption by 63.2 percent.

However, L&T is reported to be implicated in a 2.2°C rise in global temperatures due to its business practices.[2] MSCI rates L&T as a laggard in ESG for its industry, with a score of B. The clean target only covers 0.08 percent of the company carbon footprint. And while it is a leader in clean tech, L&T lags in corporate governance. Due to this, we cannot consider L&T to be a mature ESG company, likely falling into the Minimalist profile of the PwC model.

Netflix (New Age)

The popular streaming and production company Netflix dominates the media and entertainment sector globally with a presence in over 190 countries. As discussed below, their 2020 ESG Report captures the snapshot of their initiatives and performance as per the SASB benchmark standard (Netflix 2021).[3]

Environment: "Netflix will act to reduce, retain, and remove carbon in concert with nature to achieve net zero emissions by the end of 2022, and every year thereafter."

In an attempt to do so, they have taken up a few initiatives:

1. hired a sustainability officer and created a sustainability office
2. aligned the management board to their strategy
3. aligned ESG report with financial reporting
4. mapped the major sources by business activity and attempting to reduce carbon footprint.

Social and Governance: "To entertain our members, who come from all around the world, we need to work with a diversity of creators as well as have a diverse workforce."

- Their hiring initiatives reflect their commitment toward inclusion and equitable pay.
- They are cautious and compliance driven about data privacy and security.
- Operating in a dynamic industry, their governance structure is unconventional, providing the board unfettered access to management to ensure long-term value while managing business ethically.
- They also regard intellectual property protection as important to their success.

What Drives Them to Adopt ESG?

Netflix's dedication reflects, in their content (titles related to sustainability), how they produce content (their partnerships across the value chain), and their stand to take responsibility for their emissions (even of the productions they don't manage directly) in an attempt to create a positive ripple effect across the industry. However, it is clear in the Netflix ESG report that environmental factors take priority as it fills the majority of the report. Governance is only given two pages of the report. The MSCI ESG rating for Netflix is BB (average).

	CONTENT CREATION	CORPORATE OPERATIONS	STREAMING DELIVERY
OPTIMIZE	Hire local crew to avoid travel and lodging.	Provide employee commuting options (shuttles, transit passes, van pools, etc.)	Install content delivery caches close to members, reducing traffic on transmission networks
ELECTRIFY	Install additional power at stages and use clean and silent mobile battery units, reducing the need for diesel generators.	Offer free charging and parking for electric vehicles.	Already 100% electrified.
DECARBONIZE	Opt into local renewable energy programs to power offices.	Install onsite photovoltaics and 100% renewable energy green tariffs in select locations.	Encourage data center and other technology partners to continue decarbonizing their energy supply and disclose details to their customers.

Figure 27.3 Netflix ESG Strategy Components

Source: Authors.

While a leader in reducing carbon emissions, Netflix is only average in corporate governance and human-capital development. It lags behind industry peers in corporate behavior despite stated concerns and care for privacy and data security.[4]

Amazon (New Age)

Per Amazon's ESG report, the company is committed to and invested in sustainability and is working toward reducing the carbon footprint across all its business operations. They have been the world's largest corporate purchasers of renewable energy and are leading the way for other companies to decarbonize worldwide. According to their sustainability strategy, they might issue green, social, or sustainability bonds in the future to enable investors to join them in the good cause. The sales from these bonds will be used to fund the sustainability projects in five areas:

- renewable energy
- clean transportation
- sustainable buildings
- affordable housing and
- socioeconomic advancement and empowerment

Amazon's commitment to sustainability are as follows:

1. Net-zero carbon: Reaching net-zero carbon across Amazon by 2040, one decade ahead of the Paris Agreement
2. 100,000 electric delivery vehicles: purchasing 100,000 electric delivery vehicles
3. Hundred percent renewable energy: becoming hundred renewable energy company by 2025
4. Shipment zero: delivering 50 percent of all shipments with net-zero carbon by 2030
5. Climate pledge fund: Investing to support the scalability and development of technologies and services that facilitate the transition to a low-carbon economy
6. Right now, climate fund: Investing in nature-based solutions
7. Affordable housing: Supporting innovative housing affordability initiatives
8. Advancement and empowerment: Increasing opportunities for underrepresented groups and investing in skill training programs

Amazon ESG efforts received a BBB rating from MSCI, which is average among industry peers.[5] As one of the largest retailers in the world, Amazon has a massive impact on global emissions and the millions of workers employed by the company. Despite their ESG sustainability commitments, Amazon is implied to be responsible for a 2.1°C rise in global temperature, which is misaligned with current global climate goals. Amazon also lags in labor management and corporate behavior. Per the PwC maturity model, Amazon may not be considered more than a Strategic Company at best due to the lack of focus on social and governance issues across retail, data and cloud, media, and entertainment industry sectors.

Proctor & Gamble (Legacy)

The recent report discusses in detail Proctor & Gamble's (P&G's) plan for Ambition 2030—an initiative undertaken by the different brands under P&G that are aiming to solve problems for the better via sustainable offerings and solutions.[6] It also discusses the various measures brands at P&G have taken as a part of their sustainable efforts in terms of reusable packaging, responsible consumption for energy saving, and water-efficient products. The supply-chain bit is also described in detail—how the brand is trying to minimize its footprint at every stage:

- purchasing 100 percent renewable electricity in the United States and Canada, and most of Europe except Russia and Ukraine, which currently have not established renewable energy markets
- third-party certification for 100 percent of the virgin wood pulp purchased
- ninety-nine percent of the volume reported by suppliers were either recycled or third-party-certified virgin content
- P&G increased transparency of their supply chain by publishing both palm oil supplier names and a detailed list of the Palm Oil Mills in our supply chain
- seventy percent of all washing machine loads have been turned into energy-efficient cycles
- water-efficient products were provided to 1 billion people
- truck transportation was reduced by 20 percent
- thirteen percent of energy is from renewable sources
- absolute GHG emissions were reduced by 25 percent.

MSCI rates P&G as average (A) in ESG practices. P&G is a leader in corporate governance, but it lags in corporate behavior and supply-chain standards. The ESG Ratings range from leader (AAA, AA), average (A, BBB, BB), to laggard (B, CCC).[7]

Global Trends

In 2022, McKinsey & Company examined how ESG has become an important part of company goals and objectives, especially after the pandemic. Notably, the social part of the ESG concept is often overlooked by companies. The most important factors to consider under the social umbrella include treating workers fairly; giving them disposable incomes beyond just paying for food and rent; and investing in employee skills, training programs, diversity, equity, and inclusivity; and creating sustainable products. There has also been a trend of movement from brands to stands. Inconsistency between company values and products/services have seen large numbers of people boycotting products and shifting to new brands.

Many companies have a purpose statement that is not goal-driven. Companies need to know their vulnerability and strengths in the ESG space before making any such claims. Take the example of PayPal, who identified its strength and vulnerability to understand the current problems with employees and create a full-fledged employee benefits program. According to Franz Paasche (senior vice president and chief corporate affairs officer at PayPal), "companies need to focus on the full financial and health security of employees to create value across the spectrum of stakeholders as it would affect every community and the way our economies work." Having brands in the portfolio that are tailored in terms of affinity with the customer or communities that produce the products see consumers switch to them faster and show higher loyalty, as can be seen with Unilever's portfolio. There is a clear intersection of purpose and profit. One cannot survive without the other, and the PayPal example has been a benchmark for companies that this combination has proved to be a strategic strength and will immensely improve the bottom line.

There is clearly a meaningful and evolving role of the private sector to maintain sustainable development. Corporations have shifted from lobbying and evil practices to striving toward becoming genuine partners. They believe sustainable development is essential not just for the future of their business but for the planet. But still, there is a long way to go. There is an increase in impact investment, which focuses on making investments that achieve social and environmental impact along with financial returns. Currently, the approach to achieving sustainability has been limited to reducing negative and social impacts by the private sector, but is minimizing harm enough or does this only prolong the inevitable decline of the natural and social systems?

Sustainability-Oriented Hybrid Organizations (SOHOs) combine social, environmental, and commercial logics and aim to create regenerative equity. It is important for private sector partners to establish sustainable profitability-driven ventures that not only reduce the environmental impact but also achieve holistic sustainable and equitable transformation with the help of innovative mechanisms. A lot of untapped potential and a gap remain in this area to answer the question of a trade-off between profitability and sustainability or an intersection between the two.

Value Propositions

To be able to fully act on ESG goals, organizations need to internally define environmental, social, and governance impacts and how the three elements are interlinked with each

	Strong ESG proposition (examples)	**Weak ESG proposition** (examples)
Top-line growth	Attract B2B and B2C customers with more sustainable products Achieve better access to resources through stronger community and government relations	Lose customers through poor sustainability practices (eg, human rights, supply chain) or a perception of unsustainable/unsafe products Lose access to resources (including from operational shutdowns) as a result of poor community and labor relations
Cost reductions	Lower energy consumption Reduce water intake	Generate unnecessary waste and pay correspondingly higher waste-disposal costs Expend more in packaging costs
Regulatory and legal interventions	Achieve greater strategic freedom through deregulation Earn subsidies and government support	Suffer restrictions on advertising and point of sale Incur fines, penalties, and enforcement actions
Productivity uplift	Boost employee motivation Attract talent through greater social credibility	Deal with "social stigma," which restricts talent pool Lose talent as a result of weak purpose
Investment and asset optimization	Enhance investment returns by better allocating capital for the long term (eg, more sustainable plant and equipment) Avoid investments that may not pay off because of longer-term environmental issues	Suffer stranded assets as a result of premature write-downs Fall behind competitors that have invested to be less "energy hungry"

Figure 27.4 Value Creation Parameters for ESG Proposition

Source: Henisz, Koller, and Nuttall 2019.

other for the overall growth of the company. If utilized properly, all three elements help in creating a higher value proposition for any company. A strong ESG proposition links to value creation in five essential ways: top line growth, cost reductions, regulatory and legal interventions, productivity uplift, and investment and asset optimization. Each of these five parameters should be a part of any leader's strategy while creating an ESG proposition (Henisz, Koller, and Nuttall 2019).

For leaders who are seeking out new ESG growth opportunities for their organization and want to shift from traditional work culture, they must keep in mind the following three mandates:

Get specific: It is very important for the company to choose the ESG goals that align with the company mission, vision, and values. Priority initiatives should be clearly articulated, and the number should be no more than five.

Get practical: Companies' ESG priorities must link to the value created backed up by hard metrics. Setting up vague and inconsistent goals will eventually help no one. Research should be conducted to find out the untapped areas where the maximum impact lies.

> Get real: Overdoing ESG can cost a leader's time, and under-doing it is even worse. In the past few years, multiple companies with a weak ESG proposition saw double-digit declines in market capitalization in the days and weeks after their missteps came to light. Being thoughtful and transparent about ESG risk enhances long-term value—even if doing so can feel uncomfortable and engender some short-term pain.

The boards of directors of high-sustainability companies are more likely to be formally responsible for sustainability, and top executive compensation incentives are more likely to be a function of sustainability metrics. High-sustainability companies are more likely to have established processes for stakeholder engagement, to be more long term oriented, and to exhibit higher measurement and disclosure of nonfinancial information. Finally, high-sustainability companies significantly outperform their counterparts over the long term, both in terms of the stock-market and accounting performance.

Field Research Insights

In an effort to contextualize the ESG horizon, a number of questions emerge: How do corporate entities look at ESG? Are they committed to the purpose? Is it just a checkbox? When is a company mature for ESG? How aware are they and how do they implement ESG?

To answer these questions, ground-level data needs to be analyzed. From a pool of one hundred companies based on their size, scale, and industry, thirty companies were chosen for an in-depth analysis. Conversations with key resources within these organizations help develop greater understanding related to company ESG goals and how they impact its performance.

Furthermore, secondary reports, annual statements, and company websites add a holistic picture to the work done in this sphere. When key organizational resources are questioned about the understanding of ESG, we see words like company, corporate social responsibility, environment, climate change, natural resources, and carbon neutrality were prominent. This points out the one-dimensional focus of the firms on the environment ESG aspect.

On being asked or researched whether the company has ESG implementation as a part of its brand positioning, words like shared value, core value, and sustainable growth were prominent. So, whatever might be the reality of a firm's execution, ESG finds a place in the mission statement, vision statement, or values on which the brand claims to stand for. The variations are evident in implementation approach and indicators.

Most of the innovations implemented in these organizations were focused on reducing the carbon footprint and implementing renewable energy policies. As far as the implementation of ESG in the value chain is concerned, firms are focusing on sustainable packaging, responsible supply-chain management, and the fulfillment of mandatory green certification requirements. Similarly, ESG implementation on the products and services side focuses on the conservation of environmental resources.

When enquired about the impact of ESG implementation on financial performance, words like financial returns, costs, sustainability, and revenue were dominant. Also, in the literature review, the new concept of ESG investing has been mentioned in detail. As far as the community and social impact are concerned, companies contributed to existing government schemes and helped in the implementation of skill development and education facilities for the less privileged. Almost every organization, particularly the well-established legacy corporation, has a CSR committee, which includes people occupying top positions in

Table 27.1 Restorative, Sustainable, Regenerative, and Green Companies

India study: Company categories	*Restorative*	*Sustainable (adding no additional harm)*	*Regenerative*	*Green*
Legacy	Asian Paints, Titan, Larson & Toubro, Dabur, Nestle, Honeywell, GSK, Proctor and Gamble, Tata Steel, TVS	Marico, TATA Power, Aditya Birla Grasim, Reliance Industries, Apollo Hospitals, Infosys	Mahindra, EY	Mott MacDonald, Tata Chemicals, Berger Paints, Jindal Steel
Start-Up	Love, The World Today, Refillable, Terra Foods	Happy Healthy Organic, Verdant Agro Foods	NA	Bummer
New Age	NA	HDFC	NA	IPG Mediabrands

Source: Authors.

the organization, formed largely because it is mandatory to have such a committee as per the law in India. The Covid-19 pandemic and climate change came out to be the most significant constraints in the implementation of ESG practices. Other common words were skill training as per the changing times, dealing with supply-chain disruptions and awareness.

Recommendations

Established companies are set in the organizational structure so much that they focus on one component of ESG and do not address the other two. Start-up ideas and companies, on the other hand, are more fluid and flexible in their evolution and hence better positioned to achieve ESG in values and in practice.

In all of our conversations with companies from each organizational type, there is clarity on environmental sustainability but not always on the social and governance practices needing to be undertaken. S and G require substantial analysis and rethinking of the organizational hierarchy from the ground to the C-Suite, which can be a complex and political process. Governance itself could be thought of as not a separate element but the crucial skeleton needed to fully transform the environmental and social elements of a company.

Start-ups, such as Latitude, are rethinking the governance structure and its power dynamics as the company begins to build and find financing. This approach may be unique to nascent companies, but the time dedicated to the G in ESG could exponentially impact future company practices and policies. These types of companies have the potential to be Trailblazers in ESG maturity, even if the scope of impact is smaller than larger, more established industry firms.

There are still many questions to investigate. Is there a new type of model that could map ESG maturity with more nuance, or use a matrix to compare ESG policies to the size and age of the companies itself? Connect ESG with leadership and organizational culture. How can we fully measure the financial, cultural, and environmental impact of ESG practices on global industry and the consumer economy? Can all aspects of ESG even be quantified? How can legacy organizations learn and adapt the practices of New Age and start-up companies? The New Age companies are able to adopt digital governance and data for purpose-driven communications very well. The Start-up companies are much more dynamic and flexible to adapt to evolving ESG policies and compliance. The legacy companies need to overcome silos and strategically promote integration across structural and functional vertices.

Regardless of organizational size, ESG is at its heart a practice of self-improvement and the way of life for internal and external stakeholders. Organizations are made of individuals, and it is individual action that creates the purpose and practices of an organization. In order to achieve full ESG maturity, organizations must deeply reflect on the governance aspect and how equitable the internal structure is for all individuals of the company. Even individuals themselves need to focus on their own self-governance, making equitable, respectable, and sustainable choices in their own lives. Without comprehensive understanding of all aspects of ESG, there can be no significant change.

Appendix
ANNEXURE 1

Link to questionnaire:

https://docs.google.com/document/d/1dKB0hI1FFLeYWccTrxdiLol3m5VPYQGr/edit
Link to Primary Research Data & Findings:
https://docs.google.com/spreadsheets/d/1ETjEE7m-XODwHnYW7fAkK5uFL85Yw2xYMYd8ty-voC5k/edit#gid=787882639

Key Discussion Areas

- ESG evolution across legacy to start-up organizations.
- ESG strategy and maturity scale.
- Compliance.
- ESG leadership and self-transformation.
- Stakeholder and user centricity for an integrated ESG-I approach.

Notes

1 Reuters Events, "Responsible Business USA 2024," March 26–27, 2024, https://events.reutersevents.com/sustainable-business/responsible-business-usa (accessed October 1, 2023).
2 MSCI L&T Report, ESG Ratings & Climate Search Tool, www.msci.com/our-solutions/esg-investing/esg-ratings-climate-search-tool/issuer/larsen-and-toubro-limited/IID000000002173528 (accessed October 1, 2023).
3 Global ranking of Netflix in ESG available at www.sustainalytics.com/esg-rating/netflix-inc/1007910258 (accessed October 1, 2023), and www.sustainable.com/companies/netflix (accessed October 1, 2023).
4 MSCI Netflix Report, ESG Ratings & Climate Search Tool, www.msci.com/our-solutions/esg-investing/esg-ratings-climate-search-tool/issuer/netflix-inc/IID000000002177083 (accessed October 1, 2023).

5 MSCI Amazon Report, ESG Ratings & Climate Search Tool, www.msci.com/our-solutions/esg-investing/esg-ratings-climate-search-tool/issuer/amazoncom-inc/IID000000002157075 (accessed October 1, 2023).
6 P&G, "Environmental," www.pginvestor.com/esg/environmental/environmental-overview (accessed October 1, 2023).
7 MSCI P&G Report, ESG Ratings & Climate Search Tool, www.msci.com/our-solutions/esg-investing/esg-ratings-climate-search-tool/issuer/the-procter-gamble-company/IID000000002180249 (accessed October 1, 2023).

References

Beloskar, Ved Dilip, and S. V. D. Nageswara Rao. 2022. "Did ESG Save the Day? Evidence from India during the COVID-19 Crisis." *Asia-Pacific Financial Markets*, April 17, 2022, https://link.springer.com/article/10.1007/s10690-022-09369-5 (accessed May 23, 2023).

Bertassinni Caolina Ana, Lucas Gabriel Zanon, Jean Guiherme Azarias, Mateus Cecilio Gerolamo and Aldo Roberto Ometto. 2022. "Circular Business Ecosystem Innovation: A Guide For Mapping Staekholders, Capturing Values, and Finding New Opportunities." *Sustainable Production and Consumption* 27: 436–48.

Brown, S., and R. Nuttall. 2022. "The Role of ESG and Purpose." *McKinsey & Co.*, January 4, 2022, www.mckinsey.com/capabilities/strategy-and-corporate-finance/our-insights/the-role-of-esg-and-purpose (accessed May 23, 2023).

Chaklader, Barnali, and Puja Aggarwal Gulati. 2015. "A Study of Corporate Environmental Disclosure Practices of Companies Doing Business in India." *Global Business Review* 16(2): 321–35, https://doi.org/10.1177/0972150914564430.

Chelawat, Hemlata, and Indra Vardhan Trivedi. 2016. "The Business Value of ESG Performance: The Indian Context." *Asian Journal of Business Ethics* 5: 195–210.

Collins, Neal. "The Rise of Regenerative Real Estate with Latitude." *Trim Tab*, February 17, 2021, https://trimtab.living-future.org/blog/the-rise-of-regenerative-real-estate-with-latitude/ (accessed May 23, 2023).

Dalal, Karishma K., and Namit Thaker. 2019. "ESG and Corporate Financial Performance: A Panel Study of Indian Companies." *IUP Journal of Corporate Governance* 18(1): 44–59.

Deloitte. 2024. "Supply Chain And The Circular Economy." www2.deloitte.com

European Commission. 2023. "European Sustainability Reporting Standards—First Set." July 31, 2023, https://ec.europa.eu/info/law/better-regulation/have-your-say/initiatives/13765-European-sustainability-reporting-standards-first-set_en (accessed October 1, 2023).

Gez, M., E. Angnosti, T. Pullins, and White & Case LLP. 2022. "ESG Disclosure Trends in SEC Filings," *Harvard Law School Forum on Corporate Governance,* July 16, 2022, https://corpgov.law.harvard.edu/2022/07/16/esg-disclosure-trends-in-sec-filings (accessed May 23, 2023).

Goyal, M., and K. Aggarwal. 2014. "ESG Index Is Good for Socially Responsible Investor in India." *Asian Journal of Multidisciplinary Studies* 2(11): 92–96.

Henisz, Witold, Tim Koller, and Robin Nuttall. 2019. "Five Ways That ESG Creates Value." *McKinsey Quarterly*, November 14, 2019, www.mckinsey.com/capabilities/strategy-and-corporate-finance/our-insights/five-ways-that-esg-creates-value (accessed May 23, 2023).

Jensen, Michael C. 2000. "Value Maximization and Stakeholder Theory." *Harvard Business Review*, July 24, 2000, https://hbswk.hbs.edu/item/value-maximization-and-stakeholder-theory (accessed May 23, 2023).

Koh, Hee-Kyung, Regina Burnasheva, and Yong Gu Suh. 2022. "Perceived ESG (Environmental, Social, Governance) and Consumers' Responses: The Mediating Role of Brand Credibility, Brand Image, and Perceived Quality." *Sustainability* 14(8): 4515, https://doi.org/10.3390/su14084515.

MSCI. 2022. "MSCI ESG Ratings Methodology Executive Summary," www.msci.com/documents/1296102/21901542/ESG-Ratings-Methodology-Exec-Summary.pdf (accessed December 1, 2022).

Netflix. 2021. "Environmental Social Governance Report 2021," https://s22.q4cdn.com/959853165/files/doc_downloads/2022/03/30/2021-SASB-Report-FINAL.pdf (accessed May 23, 2023).

Polman, P. and A. Winston. 2021. *Net Positive: How Courageous Companies Thrive by Giving More Than They Take*. Boston, MA: Harvard Business Review Press.

Porter, Michael E., George Serafeim, and Mark Kramer. 2019. "Where ESG Fails." *Institutional Investor*, October 16, 2019, www.institutionalinvestor.com/article/b1hm5ghqtxj9s7/Where-ESG-Fails (accessed May 23, 2023).

PricewaterhouseCoopers. 2022a. "ESG Oversight: The Corporate Director's Guide." March 2022, www.pwc.com/us/en/services/governance-insights-center/library/esg-corporate-directors-guide.html (accessed December 1, 2022).

———. 2022b. "The Four Profiles of ESG Maturity." *PwC Canada,* www.pwc.com/ca/en/today-s-issues/environmental-social-and-governance/four-profiles-of-esg-maturity.html (accessed December 1, 2022).

Ritz, Robert. 2020. "Climate Targets, Executive Compensation, and Corporate Strategy." Working Papers EPRG2029, Energy Policy Research Group. Cambridge Judge Business School, University of Cambridge.

Sharma, Preeti, Priyanka Panday, and R. Dangwal. 2020. "Determinants of Environmental, Social and Corporate Governance (ESG) Disclosure: A Study of Indian Companies." *International Journal of Disclosure and Governance* 17(4): 208–17.

Singh, R. 2013. "Standard & Poor's Environmental, Social and Governance (ESG) India Index- during and Post Global Financial Crisis." *Global Journal of Management and Business Studies* 3(10): 1205–12.

Stern, David. 2004. "Environmental Kuznet's Curve." In *Encyclopedia of Energy*, 517–25. Science Direct. New York, US: Rensselaer Polytechnic Institute, Troy, www.sciencedirect.com/science/article/abs/pii/B012176480X00454X (accessed May 23, 2023).

Toms, S. 1999. "Financial Incentives for Corporate Greening: Some UK Evidence." *Social and Environmental Accounting* 19(1): 5–7.

28
HEALTH SYSTEM GOVERNANCE
Making Health-Care Systems More Accessible and Sustainable

K. V. Ramani

Introduction

The origin of health system governance can be traced back to the World Health Organization's (WHO) 1978 Alma Ata declaration,[1] "Health for All." The Alma Ata declaration stated:

> Governments have a responsibility for the health of their people which can be fulfilled only by the provision of adequate health and social measures. The people have the right and duty to participate individually and collectively in the planning and implementation of their health care.

The conference also highlighted the crucial role of primary health care[2] and the involvement of many other social and economic sectors in addition to the health sector in the attainment of health for all. The Alma Ata declaration has been and continues to be the focus for strengthening health systems

Health systems comprise all organizations, institutions, and resources that produce actions whose primary purpose is to improve the health of the population it serves. Its actors include the health sector and all other sectors contributing to health improvements and overall development, such as education, nutrition, drinking water, and environment.[3] The primary goals of any national health system are to provide health-care services that are effective, responsive to population needs, and affordable ("fairness in health financing") for all the population groups. Health system performance continues to be a topic of importance to health policy-makers, since any health policy has to address the roles of all the actors contributing to health and developments.

Universal health coverage (UHC) is recognized as a unifying platform for achieving health system goals. The WHO report on *Health Systems Governance for Universal Health Coverage* (WHO 2014a) is an action plan toward the attainment of health for all. Achieving UHC is also one of the targets of the Sustainable Development Goals.[4] People in countries that progress toward UHC[5] will have a better quality of life and more effectively contribute toward economic and social development of their countries.

DOI: 10.4324/9781003316077-34

Health system governance is a complex task. It involves developing a framework for improving health system performance to the satisfaction of sectoral and intersectoral stakeholders. The WHO report *Health Systems: Improving Performance* (WHO 2000) introduced the concept of "stewardship" in health system governance. The UN declarations on Millennium Development Goals (MDGs) in 2000 and the Sustainable Development Goals (SDGs) in 2015 highlighted the importance of health system governance. Health system governance should also provide a framework for health systems to be resilient and responsive to meet the population needs in pandemics (such as the Covid-19 outbreak) and other emergencies.

Health Systems

Health and socioeconomic developments are so closely intertwined that it is impossible to achieve one without the other. The Alma Ata conference highlighted the role of intersectoral planning in a nation's health system to achieve health for all. Evelyne de Leeuw (2017) discusses the importance of health system engagement by sectors other than health for a successful integration of health governance, policy, and action. Figure 28.1 provides a conceptual view of a nation's health system.

The primary aim of any national health system is to ensure availability and access to good and affordable health-care services to all population groups as and when needed. Hence, the health system's goals are

1. effective health-care services (good quality medical services);
2. responsive health-care services (meet the expectations of its population groups);
3. fairness in financing (affordable by all population groups).

Effective Health-Care Service

Effective health-care service focuses on the medical quality of interventions, and the degree to which good quality and evidence-based health-care interventions lead to improvements in health outcomes. Effective health service delivery requires an enabling environment, such as trained staff, medicines and drugs, medical devices and equipment, and adequate financing. Effective health-care service delivery should also ensure patient safety, which refers to the risk of patient death due to preventable medical errors (also known as hospital acquired infections)[6] and is a serious global public health concern. Medical interventions should be evidence-based, ensure patient safety, be centered on patient needs, and achieve the desired outcomes. Assessing the effectiveness of health-care service delivery is challenging, since it is multidimensional in nature. The Organization for Economic Co-Operation and Development (OECD) has identified thirteen indicators (OECD 2019) that could be used in several of its countries to assess the quality of health-care delivery. The Quality Improvement Project sponsored by the U.S. Agency for International Development (USAID) has proposed a set of indicators with specific care standards as well as outcome indicators for specific diseases. Alexander Rowe and colleagues (2018) discuss evidence-based recommendations for research on improving health-care provider practices in low-income and middle-income countries.

Figure 28.1 Health System—A Conceptual Overview
Source: Author.

Responsive Health-Care Services

Responsiveness is fundamental, because it relates to basic human rights. Responsive health-care service is the degree to which a health system responds to the non-health-enhancing aspects of the health system. Communities (patients, their relatives, and friends) expect the health system to offer access to quality care, affordability, prompt service, and service with dignity; encourage good and friendly communications with their health-care providers; facilitate their role in decisions about their care; and assure that they keep medical records confidential. The WHO (2000) defines responsiveness as "the ability of the health system to meet the population's legitimate expectations regarding their interaction with the health system, apart from expectations for improvements in health or wealth." Indicators of health system responsiveness need to address the twin objectives of (i) what happens when health-care providers interact with their patients and (ii) the patients' expectations (perceptions) of what happens. Health system responsiveness is usually assessed through a sample survey of the population it serves. When assessing health system responsiveness, both the level of achievement (average over the whole population) and the distribution (equitable spread of this achievement to all segments of the population) must be measured. Nicole Valentine and colleagues (2003) provide a detailed understanding of the measurements of health system responsiveness.

Fairness in Health Financing

Health financing includes government funding, private funding, mandatory insurance, voluntary insurance, and out-of-pocket payments by individuals. The out-of-pocket payment (financing) component in health financing is a major concern in many developing countries.

For example, out-of-pocket payment for health services accounts for 65 percent of the total health financing in India. High out-of-pocket payment puts an enormous financial burden on poor households. Globally, more than 150 million individuals face financial catastrophe as a direct result of having to pay out-of-pocket expenses for health-care every year. If the out-of-pocket payments were proportional to the disposable income of each household, then such out-of-pocket payments could be considered as fair in financing the national health system. Financial protection for the poor against any financial catastrophe in health is a key health system objective and an important component in the Sustainable Development Goal 3.8. Per the Institute of Medicine (2001), "fairness in health financing is an important indicator of health equity."[7] Fairness in health financing ensures affordable care over and above effective and responsive health-care services to all. It is based on the concept of (i) risk pooling between the healthy and the sick and (ii) risk-sharing across income levels.

The efficiency of a health system is estimated by its utilization of scarce and expensive resources to produce good outcomes. It is a measure of the level of performance relative to the resources consumed for a given output.

Christopher J. L. Murray and Julio Frenk (1999) discuss a WHO framework for health system performance assessment as a function of all three intrinsic goals of health systems: effective health services, responsive health services, and fairness in financing Effectiveness in health services (medical quality of health-care services) and responsiveness of health-care services (quality of nonmedical services perceived by the community) together define the quality of health-care services. Effectiveness and responsiveness are assessed on both levels and fairness of the distribution of services. Health system goals can therefore be summarized as shown in Table 28.1. Achieving health system goals is fundamental to health system governance.

Health outcomes continue to be unacceptably low across many developing countries. Lack of health-care financing is often cited as a major reason for the poor functioning of the health system in developing countries (WHO 2001). Developing countries also face challenges in overcoming nonfinancial barriers in delivering effective and equitable services. Nonfinancial barriers include shortage of doctors and health workers, lack of essential medicines at health-care facilities, and poor capital investment in medical equipment and devices for evidence-based diagnosis and treatment.

UHC is recognized as a unifying platform for achieving health system goals.

Universal health coverage (UHC) means that all people have access to the full range of quality health services they need, when and where they need them, without financial hardship. It covers the full continuum of essential health services, from health promotion to prevention, treatment, rehabilitation, and palliative care across the life course.[8]

Table 28.1 Health System Goals

Intrinsic Goals	*Level*	*Distribution*
Effectiveness in health services	✓	✓
Responsiveness in health-care services	✓	✓
Fair in health-care financing		✓
	Quality	Equity

Source: Author.

The 2015 Sustainable Development Goal 3.8 (SDG 3.8) states "*Achieve universal health coverage, including financial risk protection, access to quality essential health-care services and access to safe, effective, quality and affordable essential medicines and vaccines for all.*" The SDG target on universal health coverage set out specific indicators to monitor progress in coverage of essential health-care services and financial protection. UHC was identified as a priority for international development by the G20, the World Health Organization, and the United Nations.

Above all, health systems should also be resilient to delivering health-care needs during emergencies, such as the ongoing Covid-19 pandemic. The Global Health Security Index is a useful indicator to measure the preparedness of each country in the face of globally catastrophic biological events (Bell and Nuzzo 2021). Covid-19 highlighted the underpreparedness of all countries, many of which had to divert their health system resources to address emergency Covid-19 services. This led to a drop in routine immunization services for children, which could result in increased child deaths from vaccine-preventable diseases. Also, many health facilities could not provide routine consultation for patients with noncommunicable diseases (NCDs), which raises serious questions on the global commitment to meet the SDG target on preventing premature mortality from NCDs.

The USAID (2021) emphasizes the need of system-based approaches for building resilient health systems.

Health Policy

Health policy is defined by the WHO as the "decisions, plans, and actions that are undertaken to achieve specific health-care goals."

The general goal of health policy is to improve the health of the population while providing accessible and quality health-care services. Any national health policy sets target for health outcomes and outlines the priorities and expected roles of different groups to achieve the stated outcomes. Health policies cover topics of financing and delivery of health care, access to care, quality of care, and health equity. Unfortunately, many health policies are silent on intersectoral cooperation for health equity, even though the WHO highlighted the role of intersectoral cooperation in the Alma Ata conference in 1978, and subsequently emphasized in its report on *Intersectoral Action for Health* (1986) by asking all its member countries to regularly monitor specific equity-oriented targets expressed in terms of health improvements among the population, with a special focus on disadvantaged groups. The UN declaration of Sustainable Development Goals in 2015 also emphasizes the importance of intersectoral coordination to achieve the stated goals.

Health policy-making is very complex, as it involves many sectoral and intersectoral actors. UHC finds a prominent place in the national health policies of many countries, and it is recognized as a unifying platform for improving population health. UHC is the aspiration that all people can obtain the health services they need, of good quality, without suffering financial hardship when paying for them. Health services under UHC include promotion, prevention, treatment, rehabilitation, and palliative care. The SDG 3.8 states "Achieve universal health coverage, including financial risk protection, access to quality essential health-care services and access to safe, effective, quality and affordable essential medicines and vaccines for all." The SDG target on universal health coverage set out specific indicators to monitor progress in coverage of essential health-care services and financial protection. The importance of strengthening primary health-care systems and equity in service delivery for achieving UHC is highlighted by Gerald Bloom and colleagues (2019). The roles of primary care and intersectoral coordination need better focus in health policies, especially in developing countries. UHC was identified as a priority for international development by the Group of Twenty (G20) countries, the World Health Organization, and the United Nations.

Health Policy and Systems Research (HPSR) is an emerging field that seeks to understand how different actors interact in the policy and implementation processes to contribute to policy outcomes. The WHO strategy on HPSR is to strengthen the process of developing evidence-based health policy through a wide network of health systems actors, researchers, policy-makers, managers, and implementers.

Health in All Policies (HiAP) is a term coined by the European Union in 2006 with the aim of collaborating across sectors to achieve common goals. "HiAP recognizes that health is created by a multitude of factors beyond health-care and promotes a collaborative approach that integrates and articulates health considerations into policy-making across sectors to improve the health of all communities and people."[9] HiAP includes an emphasis on the consequences of public policies on health systems, determinants of health, and well-being. Building and implementing HiAP would strengthen the potential that other sectors have for health (de Leeuw 2017). It improves accountability of policy-makers for health impacts at all levels of policy-making. The process to achieve intersectoral cooperation in the HiAP policy is not very different from the approach suggested by the WHO in its 1986 report. The WHO conference in Helsinki (2014b) proposed a framework for enhancing a coherent approach to HiAP, particularly at a national level.

A well-designed Health Management Information System (HMIS) is integral to framing an evidence-based national health policy. HMIS is a planned system of collecting, processing, storing, disseminating, and using health-related information to carry out management functions. It is crucial for policy-formulation, planning, implementation, and evaluation of health programs. It would also facilitate establishing a framework for an appropriate utilization of health system resources at all levels of the health system.

Health System Governance

The primary role of health system governance is to provide a framework for the health system to achieve its goals. Pyone Thidar, Helen Smith, and Nynke van den Broek (2017) offer a review of frameworks to assess health system governance and provide an overview of the concept of governance as applied to health systems.

Stewardship refers to the role of the state in the health sector. Debates on this topic have covered a wide variety of technical and political dimensions. Though there are several views on this topic (see WHO 2000; Travis et al. 2002; Kass 1990; Saltman and Ferroussier-Davis 2000; Kapoor, Kumar, and Thakur 2014), there seems to be a common agreement to align the role of the state authorities with the desired policy objectives. The existence of a strategic policy framework with effective oversight, regulation, and accountability ensures that all the decisions and actions by the steward (trustee of the national health system) are governed by laws, rules, and regulations in the functioning of the health system in achieving its goals. Stewardship gives an overarching responsibility and accountability of governance over the functioning of the health system.

In a 2003 report, the World Bank argued that, for services such as education and health-care, there is no direct accountability by the service providers to their clients (people), since these services are provided by the government. Hence accountability is explained by building a triangular relationship involving government policy-makers, service providers, and their clients (people). The clients as citizens influence the policy-makers (for services that are responsive and fairness in financing) and the policy-makers, in turn, influence the service providers (for effective and responsive service delivery).

The WHO Report *Everybody's Business* (2007) mirrors the above observations around the following three core stakeholders:

- the state (government at central and subnational level)
- health service providers (public and private sectors)
- health service beneficiaries (the public who become service users)

A framework for health system governance based on the governance triangle involving the state, service providers, and service beneficiaries is presented in Figure 28.2 (see also Bigdeli et al. 2020; Brinkerhoff and Bossert 2014).

State includes politicians and policy-makers at the national and subnational levels, as well as regulatory bodies. Policy-makers in health systems include several actors, with the ministry of health playing the role of the steward. Stewardship, as per the WHO, covers six domains, closely related to governance: generating intelligence, formulating strategic policy direction, ensuring tools for implementation, building coalition and partnerships, developing synergy between policy objectives and organizational structures and culture, and ensuring accountability.

The link between service providers and service beneficiaries is crucial. Service providers include all medical and paramedical staff, administrators/managers, and organizations responsible for service delivery such as primary, secondary, and tertiary care units, pharmacies, and diagnostic centers. Service beneficiaries include people, communities, citizen representatives, and civil society organizations., The WHO report on health system governance for UHC proposes an action plan for strengthening health-care financing, since fairness in financing is a key determinant of UHC. Accordingly, any framework for health system governance should address the following challenges:

- resource generation
- resource allocation to competing demands
- ensuring fairness in financing

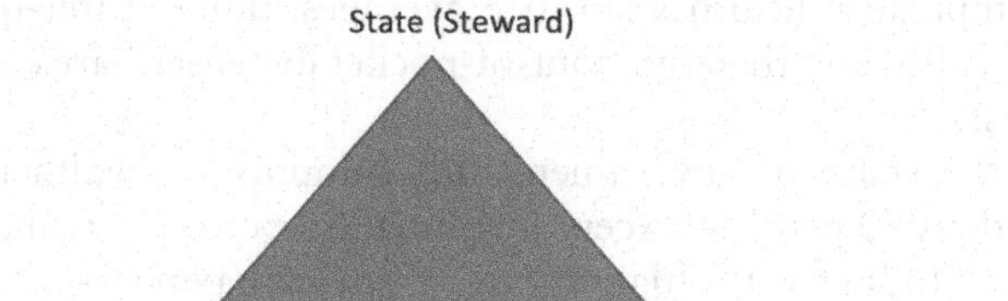

Figure 28.2 The Health-System Governance Triangle

Source: Author.

Resource generation schemes raise revenues to pay health care for the population. Allocation of resources should ensure effective, responsive, and equitable services for all. Fairness in financing, which calls for appropriately linking out-of-pocket payments with the individual's capacity to pay, is a requirement for achieving UHC.

The System of Health Accounts developed by the OECD for its member countries is an excellent source to analyze the impact of health expenditure on health system performance. This system of accounts has been adapted by the WHO and the World Bank with minor modifications for developing countries. The OECD publication *Health at a Glance* (2019) provides the latest comparable data and trends over time on population health and health system performance across OECD members and partner countries (Brazil, Russia, India, China, and South Africa [BRICS]).

Figure 28.3 provides an overview of total health expenditure as a percentage of gross domestic product (GDP).

It can be seen from Figure 28.3 that

- the average OECD countries spend about 8.8 percent of GDP on health care;
- the United States, which spends 16.9 percent of its GDP on health care, tops the list of OECD countries;
- in comparison, developing countries spend much less on health care.

Figure 28.4 displays the composition of the total health-care expenditure by type of financing. Government schemes and compulsory health insurance form the principal financing arrangement in all OECD countries.

1. All spending by private health insurance companies in the United States is reported under compulsory health insurance (Affordable Care Act, popularly known as Obamacare 2014).
2. Health payment schemes unable to be disaggregated into voluntary health insurance, non-profit institutions serving households (NPISH) and enterprise financing are reported under other.
3 Voluntary payments schemes unable to be disaggregated are reported under voluntary health insurance

It can be seen from Figure 28.4 that

- in OECD countries, the government contribution to health care from government schemes and compulsory health insurance averages almost three-quarters of the total expenditure on health, and thereby, "out-of-pocket expenses" are considerably less than in most countries;
- in comparison, the share of government and compulsory health insurance in BRICS countries is less than 50 percent; except in China (55 percent); resulting in high "out-of-pocket payments." India has the highest out-of-pocket payments (65 percent); this is due to the dominant role played by the private health sector.

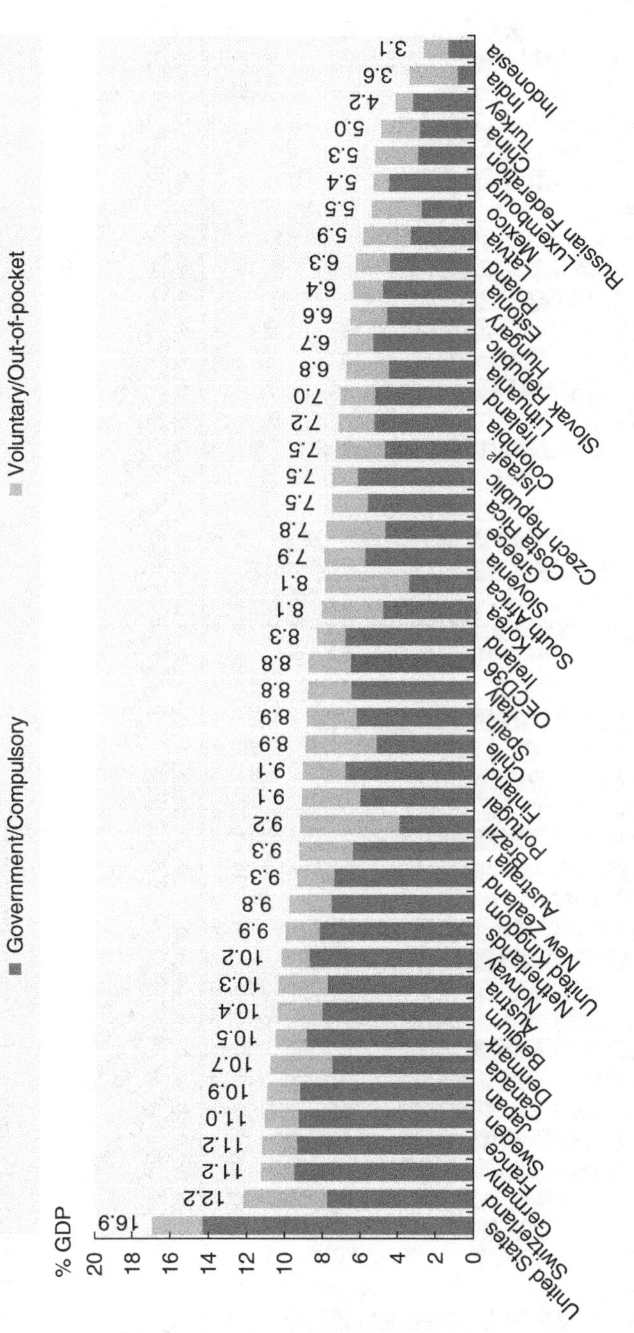

Figure 28.3 Health Expenditure as a Percentage of GPD 2018 (or Nearest Year)

Source: OECD 2019. *For comparison, GDP of all the countries is converted to a common currency (U.S. dollar) and expressed in PPP (purchasing power parity).*

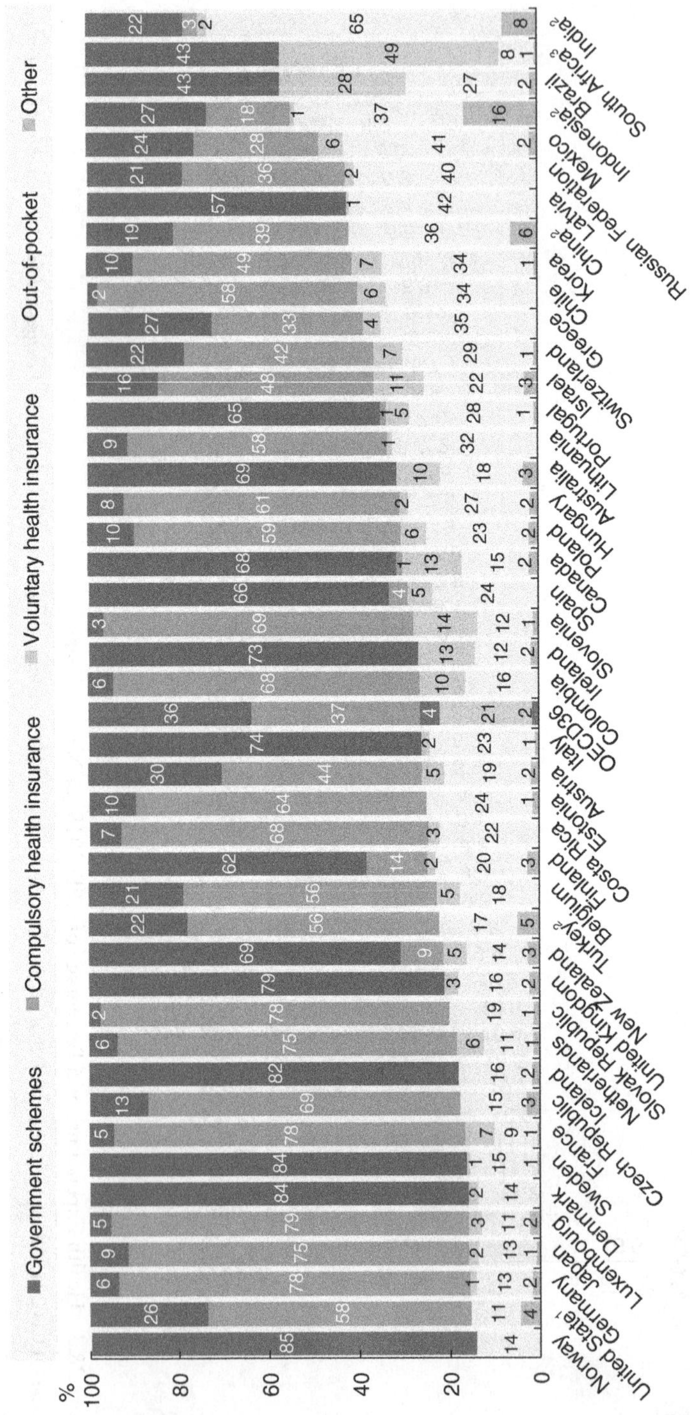

Figure 28.4 Health Expenditure by Type of Financing

Source: OECD 2019.

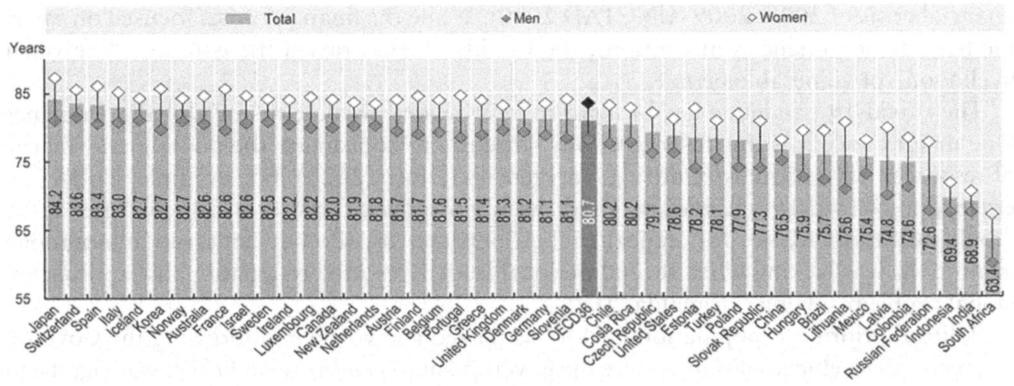

Figure 28.5 Life Expectancy at Birth

Source: OECD 2019.

The impact of health expenditure on health system performance is given below. For illustration, Figure 28.5 shows the average life expectancy at birth (often used as an indicator of population health).

It can be seen from Figure 28.5 that

- life expectancy at birth is around eighty-four years for OECD countries, while developing countries lag behind by ten to twenty years;
- countries that spend about 8 percent of the GDP on health care report high levels of life expectancy at birth (except for the United States, which has not implemented UHC completely).

A better indicator of health system performance is DALE (disability adjusted life expectancy), proposed by the WHO working group (Murray and Lopez 1996). DALE estimates the equivalent number of healthy life expectancy based on mortality and morbidity, while life expectancy at birth is based only on mortality. However, DALE requires enormous data on the disease(s) that cause morbidity/disability and the severity of disability.

To conclude, health-care financing (resource generation and fairness in financing) is a critical component of any framework for health system governance for UHC. Evidence from several countries that have achieved UHC shows that policy entrepreneurs in relatively stable institutional environments were able to mobilize allies, overcome opposition, and implement UHC (Tangcharoensathien et al. 2020). Siddiqi and colleagues (2009) provide a framework for assessing health system governance in developing counties. Lucy Gilson Lucy and Irene Akua Agyepong (2018) offer good suggestions for strengthening health system leadership for better governance.

Covid-19 and Beyond

Covid-19 is an unprecedented public health emergency. Monetarily, the impact of Covid-19 on global value chains, trade, and investment is possibly worse than that from the global financial crisis of 2008–2009 (UNCTAD 2020). While the financial crisis focused on saving the lives of rich financial institutions, the Covid-19 crisis raised the issues of "life versus livelihood" of vulnerable people.

The Covid-19 pandemic has brought to light several weaknesses of global governance. One major concern is the absence of any structure to coordinate the pooling and sharing of resources across countries during emergencies (Lancet 2020). For example, global governance for Covid-19 vaccines exposed the fragmented efforts by many countries in the development of vaccines for clinical trials. Coordinated collective action by international institutions was lacking when several political leaders resorted to a nationalist approach to global problem-solving (Grimalda 2020).

Political priority to population health has played a key role in addressing the Covid-19 emergency. Developed nations where the government expenditure on health was significant were more successful in addressing the challenges of revenue generation and deployment of finance and the health workforce to reconfigure health service delivery. Nations with poor allocation of resources to health systems paid a heavy price in debating life versus livelihood concerns.

The Covid-19 pandemic has shown us the way forward to reorient global governance. Any framework for future global governance should be adaptive and responsive to the pooling and sharing of resources to combat any future emergency—whether they be another virus, a migration crisis, or climate change. We should be prepared for more zoonotic diseases as human contact with animals has increased due to massive deforestation and human encroachment on wildlife habitat. Tropical diseases are on the rise due to climate change. Judging from the political response to Covid-19, it will be very challenging to develop a standardized response to emergencies, acceptable to all countries, unless the WHO takes an initiative in global disease governance. The World Bank (2021) has recently launched its Global Governance Program to support innovative activities at the global, regional, and country levels that are aimed at addressing extraordinary challenges such as Covid-19.

Health is political, and the best political choice at the moment would be to strengthen the WHO's legal power—not destroy it (Kickbusch 2020). One of the recommendations of the Independent Panel for Pandemic Preparedness and Response to Covid-19 (set up by the World Health Assembly in May 2020) is to elevate pandemic preparedness and response to the highest level of political leadership (Sirleaf and Clark 2021).

Conclusion

Successful implementation of health system governance requires intersectoral coordination between (i) central and local administrative levels; (ii) public and private sectors in health systems; and (iii) public health and primary, secondary, and tertiary health services for achieving UHC. It may be necessary to rely on e-governance, which uses information and communication technologies at various levels of the government and the public sector and beyond, and to strengthen intra- and intersectoral coordination, which is critical for a successful implementation of health system governance. To take up the WHO's famous "Health for all" declaration made in Alma Ata in 1978, we must now take up e-health for all by 2030.

Key Discussion Areas

- Health systems and their goals.
- Health policies and universal health coverage.
- Guidelines and frameworks for health system governance.
- The impact of Covid-19 on the health systems and the aspects in need of improvement.

Notes

1 The WHO declaration on "Health for All" was made at the international conference on primary health care held in Alma Ata, Kazakhstan, in September 1978. This conference was attended by virtually all the member nations of the World Health Organization (WHO) and UNICEF. See "WHO Called to Return to the Declaration of Alma-Ata," www.who.int/teams/social-determinants-of-health/declaration-of-alma-ata (accessed March 4, 2023).
2 Primary health care is the first level of contact of individuals, family, and community with the national health system bringing health care as close as possible to where people live and work and constitutes the first element of a continuing health care process.
3 Education creates an awareness of good lifestyle habits to remain healthy, which leads to more productivity in the workplace and at home and improves quality of life. Nutrition and water play important roles in the development of maternal and child health, building a strong immune system and lowering the risk of many diseases. Unsafe drinking water is responsible for all diarrheal diseases, which account for 10 percent of child deaths. Poor air quality carries the risk of respiratory diseases, which affect the working of the heart and lungs.
4 The Sustainable Development Goals are a collection of seventeen interlinked global goals designed to be a "blueprint to achieve a better and more sustainable future for all." Health has a central place in SDG "Ensure healthy lives and promote well-being for all at all ages," underpinned by thirteen targets that cover a wide spectrum of the WHO's work. Almost all of the other sixteen goals are related to health or their achievement will contribute to health indirectly. See United Nations, https://sdgs.un.org/goals (accessed March 3, 2023).
5 UHC is aimed at ensuring affordability and access to good quality health care for all.
6 As per the WHO report on patient safety, the risk of patient death occurring due to a preventable medical accident, while receiving health care, is estimated to be one in 300, much higher than the one in three million risk of dying while traveling by airplane.
7 Equity in health care, as per the IOM, is "providing care that does not vary in quality because of personal characteristics such as gender, ethnicity, geographic location, and socioeconomic status."
8 "Universal Health Coverage," WHO, www.who.int/health-topics/universal-health-coverage#tab=tab_1 (accessed March 3, 2023).
9 "Health in All Policies," Centers for Disease Control and Prevention, www.cdc.gov/policy/hiap/index.html (accessed March 3, 2023).

References

Bell, Jessica A., and Jennifer B. Nuzzo. 2021. "Global Health Security Index: Advancing Collective Action and Accountability Amid Global Crisis." *Nuclear Threat Initiative,* www.ghsindex.org/wp-content/uploads/2021/12/2021_GHSindexFullReport_Final.pdf (accessed March 4, 2023).

Bigdeli, Maryam, Benjamin Rouffy, Benjamin Downs Lane, Gerad Schmets, and Agnes Soucat. 2020. "Health Systems Governance: The Missing Link." *BMJ Global Health* 5: e002533, https://doi.org/0.1136/bmjgh2020-002533.

Bloom, Gerald, Yasushi Katsuma, Krishna D. Rao, Saeda Makimoto, Jason D. C., and Gabriel M. Leung. 2019. "Universal Health Coverage: Next Steps Towards Universal Health Coverage Call for Global Leadership." *BMJ* 365: l210, https://doi.org/10.1136/bmj.l2107.

Brinkerhoff, D. W., and T. J. Bossert. 2014. "Health Governance: Principal-Agent Linkages and Health System Strengthening." *Health Policy Plan* 29(6): 685–93, https://doi.org/10.1093/heapol/czs132.

de Leeuw, Evelyne. 2017. "Engagement of Health Other Than Health in Integrate Health Governance, Policy and Action." *Annual Review of Public Health* 38: 329–49, www.annualreviews.org/doi/abs/10.1146/annurev-publhealth-031816-044309.

Gilson, Lucy, and Irene Akua Agyepong. 2018. "Strengthening Health System Leadership for Better Governance What Does It Take? *Health Policy and Planning* 33(2), July 8, 2018, https://academic.oup.com/heapol/article/33/suppl_2/ii1/5050013 (accessed March 4, 2023).

Grimalda, Gianluca. 2020. "Lessons for Global Cooperation from the Covid-19 Pandemic." *IDOS German Institute of Development and Sustainability*, April 1, 2020, https://blogs.idos-research.de/2020/04/01/lessons-for-global-cooperation-from-the-covid-19-pandemic/ (accessed March 4, 2023).

Institute of Medicine. Committee on Quality of Health Care in America. 2001. *Crossing the Quality Chasm: A New Health System for the 21st Century*. Washington: National Academies Press.

Kapoor, Neelesh, Dewesh Kumar, and Nivedita Thakur. 2014. "Core Attributes of Stewardship; Foundation of Sound Health System." *International Journal of Health Policy Management* 3(1): 5–6.

Kass, H. D. 1990. "Stewardship as a Fundamental Element in Images of Public Administration." In *Images and Identities in Public Administration*, edited by Kass H. D. and B. Catron. London: Sage.

Kickbusch, Iona. 2020. "COVID-19 Is Smoke and Mirrors—What Matters Is International Law." *Think Global Health*, April 15, 2020, www.thinkglobalhealth.org/article/covid-19-smoke-and-mirrorswhat-matters-international-law.

Lancet. 2020. "Global Governance for COVID-19 Vaccines." *Lancet* 395(10241) (June 20): P1883, www.thelancet.com/journals/lancet/article/PIIS0140-6736(20)31405-7/fulltext (accessed March 4, 2023).

Murray, Christopher J. L., and Julio Frenk. 1999. "Global Programme on Evidence for Health Policy. A WHO Framework for Health System Performance Assessment." World Health Organization, https://apps.who.int/iris/handle/10665/66267 (accessed March 4, 2023).

Murray, Christopher J. L., and Alan D. Lopez, eds. 1996. *The Global Burden of Disease: A Comprehensive Assessment of Mortality and Disability from Diseases, Injuries, and Risk Factors in 1990 and Projected to 2020*. Harvard School of Public Health/World Health Organization/World Bank, https://apps.who.int/iris/bitstream/handle/10665/41864/0965546608_eng.pdf (accessed March 4, 2023).

OECD. 2019. *Health at a Glance 2019: OECD Indicators*. Paris: OECD Publishing, https://doi.org/10.1787/4dd50c09-en (accessed March 4, 2023).

Pyone T., H. Smith, and N. van den Broek. 2017. "Frameworks to Assess Health Systems Governance: A Systematic Review." *Health Policy Plan* 32(5): 710–22, https://doi.org/10.1093/heapol/czx007.

Rowe, A. K., S. Y. Rowe, D. H. Peters, K. A. Holloway, J. Chalker, and D. Ross-Degnan. 2018. "Effectiveness of Strategies to Improve Health-Care Provider Practices in Low-Income and Middle-Income Countries: A Systematic Review." *Lancet Global Health* 6(11): e1163–75, https://doi.org/10.1016/S2214-109X(18)30398-X.

Saltman, R. B., and O. Ferroussier-Davis. 2000. "The Concept of Stewardship in Health Policy." *Bulletin of the World Health Organization* 78(6): 732–39.

Siddiqi S., T. I. Masud, S. Nishtar, D. H. Peters, B. Sabri, K. M. Bile, and M. A. Jama. 2009. "Framework for Assessing Governance of the Health System in Developing Countries: Gateway to Good Governance." *Health Policy* 90(1): 13–25, https://doi.org/10.1016/j.healthpol.2008.08.005.

Sirleaf, E. J., H. and Clark. 2021. "Report of the Independent Panel for Pandemic Preparedness and Response: Making COVID-19 the Last Pandemic." *Lancet* 398(10295): 101–03, https://doi.org/10.1016/S0140-6736(21)01095-3.

Tangcharoensathien V., A. Mills, W. Patcharanarumol, and W. Witthayapipopsakul. 2020. "Universal Health Coverage: Time to Deliver on Political Promises." *Bulletin of the World Health Organization* 98(2): 78–78A, https://doi.org/10.2471/BLT.20.250597.

Travis, Phyllida, Dominique Egger, Philip Davies, and Abdelhay Mechbal. 2002. "Towards Better Stewardship: Concepts and Critical Issues." *World Health Organization*, https://apps.who.int/iris/handle/10665/339291 (accessed March 3, 2023).
United Nations Conference on Trade and Development (UNCTAD). 2020. "Impact of the COVID-19 Pandemic on Global FDI and GVCs: Updated Analysis. Investment Trends Monitor Special Issue, March," https://unctad.org/en/PublicationsLibrary/diaeiainf2020d3_en.pdf (accessed March 4, 2023).
U.S. Agency for International Development (USAID). 2021. "USAID Vision for Health System Strengthening." Washington, www.usaid.gov/sites/default/files/2022-05/USAID_OHS_VISION_Report_FINAL_single_5082.pdf (accessed March 3, 2023).
Valentine, N. B., A. De Silva, K. Kawabata, C. Darby, C. J. L. Murray, and D. Evans. 2003. "Health System Responsiveness: Concepts, Domains and Operationalization." In *Health Systems Performance Assessment: Debates, Methods and Empiricism*, edited by C. J. L. Murray and D. B. Evans. Geneva: World Health Organisation.
World Bank. 2003. "Making Services Work for Poor People." *World Bank*, https://openknowledge.worldbank.org/handle/10986/5986 (accessed March 3, 2023).
———. 2021. "Global Governance Program," https://thedocs.worldbank.org/en/doc/bc4d7580e7ed8bb430153cea939663cb-0060052021/original/ggp-program-doc-v4.pdf (accessed March 4, 2023).
World Health Organization (WHO). 1986. "Intersectoral Action for Health: The Role of Intersectoral Cooperation in National Strategies for Health for All." *World Health Organization*, https://apps.who.int/iris/handle/10665/41545 (accessed March 4, 2023).
———. 2000. "World Health Report 2000: Health Systems: Improving Performance," https://reliefweb.int/report/world/world-health-report-2000-health-systems-improving-performance (accessed March 4, 2023).
———. 2001. "Investing in Health for Economic Development: Report of the Commission on Macroeconomics and Health," https://apps.who.int/iris/handle/10665/42435 (accessed March 4, 2023).
———. 2007. "Everybody's Business: Strengthening Health Systems to Improve Health Outcomes."
———. 2014a. "Health Systems Governance for Universal Health Coverage; Action Plan." *Department of Health Systems Governance and Financing*, www.who.int/publications/i/item/WHO-HSS-HSF-2014.01 (accessed March 4, 2023).
———. 2014b. "Health in All Policies: Helsinki Statement. Framework for Country Action," www.who.int/healthpromotion/frameworkforcountryaction/en/ (accessed March 4, 2023).

29

CLIMATE CHANGE, HEALTH, AND GOVERNANCE

The Ultimate Challenge

Henry Falk

Introduction

Environmental health is a particularly difficult challenge for governance, beyond the usual complexities of the health system. Virtually all diseases related to the environment require multiple sectors of society and relevant government agencies outside of the health sector for resolution. Air pollution, for example, is responsible for approximately 15 percent of global cardiovascular disease (Rajagopalan 2021) which is treated medically like that from any other source, but its prevention is almost entirely the domain of environment, energy, commerce, transportation and other sectors of society beyond health. Because of the complexity of the governance issues, resolution of environmental disease may take decades or longer, even though the causes are clear. Tobacco was linked to lung cancer more than a half century ago, but the end of this epidemic is nowhere in sight (Nilsson 2009). Although there are no advocates for promoting cardiovascular and respiratory disease of any type, society benefits from the key risk factors for these diseases (such as convenient travel, cheap energy, and behavioral preferences), and entrenched stakeholders (such as auto manufacturers, energy companies, and tobacco industry) strongly advocate for the status quo. As a result, progress in reducing or eliminating such diseases can be haltingly slow.

If the magnitude of the health problem is large enough, as we have experienced with the Covid-19 pandemic, governance becomes essentially a whole of society response that is breathtakingly complex, as seen with broad societal and economic lockdowns, and with pervasive policies and mandates to curb transmission of the virus. From a global governance perspective, we have fallen far short in our response to the pandemic. In addition to the factors resisting change mentioned above, the forceful assertion of civil liberties by key activist groups and others leads to resistance to vaccines, mandates, masks, and other preventive measures (Omer 2021). We have also seen a pronounced bias by many people against advice from scientists, experts, and health officials, which is amplified by opinion leaders through social media. The governance challenges are at many levels.

Climate change threatens to surpass all of the above as the ultimate challenge at the interface of health and governance due to the magnitude, duration, and global impact of its

DOI: 10.4324/9781003316077-35

health risks; the extensive societal and international coordination required for their resolution; the deeply entrenched voices in society resisting the changes, effort, and sacrifice necessary to respond; and the potential for disaster if the issues are not successfully addressed within a comparatively short period of time. This chapter provides an overview of both the health and complex governance issues related to climate change.

Health Effects of Climate Change

The broad outlines of the anticipated effects from climate change have been well described since the 1990s (McMichael 2006; McMichael 2013; Patz 2014; USGCRP 2016). What has changed in the past several years is the public perception that such change is already occurring based on dramatic natural disasters and emergency events (Gibbens 2021; Levitt 2021; NOAA National Centers for Environmental Information 2022); fig 1, for example, from the National Oceanic and Atmospheric Administration (NOAA), highlights the distribution of major U.S. disasters in 2021 that are discussed in detail in the following section. Scientific journals are no match for the pervasive reach of mass and social media in getting through to the public. Also, there is now a very concerted effort, amplified at the 26th Conference of the Parties (COP26) of the UN Framework Convention on Climate Change held at Glasgow in 2021, to frame climate change as a public health issue, with the hope that doing so would lead to greater resonance with the public (Whitmee 2021; WHO 2021). There is also a growing understanding of the need to better address these issues in low- and middle-income countries (LMICs) who may be the most affected by climate change but also where the issues are least studied (Ebi and Luchters 2021).

Direct Health Effects (Extreme Weather Events)

Heat

There are places that expect periodic heat waves. One region that doesn't is the Pacific Northwest, including the states of Oregon and Washington in the Unites States, and British Columbia in Canada, whose extreme weather in the summer of 2021 shattered records in each of those areas (maximum temperatures of 121.3°F in Lytton, Canada; 116°F in Portland, OR; and 108°F in Seattle, WA). Preliminary death tolls were at least 1,500 for Canada, and hundreds more in the United States; final tolls including excess mortality statistics will probably be even higher. In Europe, Sicily, Italy, reached 119.8°F (Gardener 2021; WMO 2021a).

A Global Burden of Disease modeling study estimates that extreme heat and cold are associated with seventeen causes of death, particularly metabolic (including heat stroke) and cardiovascular disease, but also suicide and some types of injuries. A Lancet series on heat and health provides a detailed review of the physiology, epidemiology and behavioral risks for heat related morbidity and mortality (*Lancet* 2021; Ebi et al. 2021). The elderly and those who are poor and isolated are at particular risk.

The long-term threat from heat relates not only to the increased frequency and severity of heat waves in many parts of the world depending on the degree of global warming but also to the impact of sustained extreme temperatures in vulnerable parts of the world, such as South Asia and the Middle East, which would dramatically affect habitability, economic viability and disease rates in the most impacted areas (Mani 2018).

Wildfires

The United States watched the unfolding drama of the wildfires approaching the pristine and beautiful Lake Tahoe, just one of the many wildfires raging across California in recent years. Wildfires are also dramatically transforming large parts of Alaska (Jandt 2021). A recent review summarizes the direct effects of wildfires, including burns, injuries, mental health effects, and mortality from heat and flames; it particularly emphasizes the short- and long- term health effects from wildfire smoke (Xu et al. 2020). An article in *the Journal of the American Medical Association* (JAMA) summarizes the outcome of a National Academies of Science, Engineering, and Medicine (NASEM) meeting, highlighting (1) the increasing frequency, intensity, and magnitude of climate change-induced wildfires; (2) the unpredictable and therefore dangerous course of current extreme wildfires; (3) the potential health effects, including from toxic chemicals in the smoke, and the prominent effects on people with preexisting chronic conditions; (4) the impact on vulnerable and marginal groups in society, many without the resources to rebuild their lives after such disasters; (5) the effects of the Covid-19 pandemic which has both exacerbated and highlighted the limited resources available for fighting the multitude of forest fires as well as the need to protect from Covid-19, which hampers the operations of the firefighters as well as the functioning of the shelters for evacuees; and (6) the need to come up with far better approaches to preventing and preparing for wildfires, and also for more successful post-fire recovery strategies (Kizer 2020; Cornwall 2021a). As wildfires grow ever more dangerous, firefighting becomes ever more perilous; this is an area in dire need of major technological advances (O'Connor 2021).

Globally, the toll from the Australian wildfires in early 2020 was striking, to the extent of heavily impacting a very respected health system (Johnson 2020; Lancet 2020a). In addition, serious wildfires have appeared in multiple areas across the globe in recent years, such as in Indonesia where recurrent wildfires have repeatedly blanketed parts of the country and adjacent parts of southeast Asia in smoke (McCall 2019).

Floods, Storms, and Sea-Level Rise

Violent weather, storms, and floods have always been with us, but in recent years, exacerbated by climate change, they appear more threatening. Fig. 2 points to the increasing frequency and severity of major storms in the United States. Warmer seas and more moisture in a warmer atmosphere are fueling intense hurricanes, heavy rainfall events, and flooding (Francis and Ross 2021). Hurricane Harvey in 2017 seemed like a game changer, settling over Houston, Texas, for five days and delivering as much as five feet of rain in some areas (Pennisi 2017). That same year, Hurricane Maria assaulted the weakened infrastructure of Puerto Rico, leading to thousands of deaths (recounts kept increasing the toll as more sophisticated epidemiologic approaches were applied), and the Federal Emergency Management Agency (FEMA) was stretched beyond capacity (Mazzei 2019). The summer of 2021 saw one shockingly unexpected flooding event after another, first in western Germany and Belgium, then in Zhengzhou, China, followed by Tennessee, and finally Hurricane Ida which in our new climate change circumstances grew from a Category 1 hurricane to Category 4 in less than twenty-four hours (Cornwall 2021b; Francis and Ross 2021). All these storms easily overwhelmed existing infrastructure, which was not capable of dealing with so much rapidly delivered water.

In the United States and elsewhere, disaster planning in recent decades has made great strides at predicting the trajectory of storms, rapidly evacuating large vulnerable populations, creating a disaster response system capable of rapidly responding with needed resources, and reinforcing vulnerable housing and infrastructure to withstand storm winds. We are now discovering the limits of our infrastructure to deal with seemingly endless amounts of water delivered by moisture laden storms fueled by climate change. Satchit Balsari and colleagues point out that from a public health perspective there is a strong need to rethink and upgrade preparedness and response to disasters, including increased mapping of baseline vulnerabilities, use of enhanced and innovative data systems, greater coordination within the medical community, and the availability of more resources (Balsari 2021).

In addition to discrete floods from storms, climate change is leading to the urgent reality of a long-term threat to coastlines, heavily populated coastal cities, and large stretches of low-lying inland areas from rising seas. Compounding this challenge are major demographic shifts to rapidly growing coastal megacities, depletion of protective natural shorelines for absorbing water, land subsidence as aquifers are depleted, and a lack of barriers and adequate infrastructure for flood protection (Folger 2013). NOAA has just released a report on anticipated sea-level rise of approximately one foot on average for U.S. coastlines by the year 2050 which can be expected to hamper economies, cause more dramatic and more frequent flooding, inundate freshwater areas with salt, and cause a plethora of additional problems (Sweet et al. 2022). Furthermore, there are enough uncertainties about the future of glaciers to add significant anxiety about the extent of future sea-level rise (Moon 2017). A recent dramatic report suggests that a key Antarctic ice shelf is within years of failure (Voosen 2021).

By this point, we are moving well beyond the general statements above. In 2018, a *Bloomberg Businessweek* article expressed fears of Miami going underwater at some point, perhaps preceded by the loss of its drinking water (Flavelle 2018). In 2019, the New Yorker ran an article asking whether engineers could save the Louisiana coastline; the subtext is what would happen to New Orleans (Kolbert 2019). Similar articles speak about protecting New York City and the New Jersey coast from flooding after the Hurricane Sandy experience and of protecting the Boston waterfront (Schwartz 2018). Indonesia is moving its capital away from Jakarta because of serious land subsidence and the threat of rising seas and flooding (Paddock 2019). Across the globe, coastal cities must address the new reality; solutions will likely be very costly in dollar and human terms (Herrera-Garcia et al. 2021).

Drought

Climate change will alter global water distribution patterns. While some parts of the world will live in the conditions described in the previous paragraphs, others will be experiencing major droughts, compounded by depleted groundwater aquifers (Ault 2020; Jasechko 2021). Major cities such as Cape Town, South Africa, and Chennai, India, have been very close to the brink of depleting such resources (Le Page 2018). Many LMICs such as Iraq and Syria face severe drought (Devi 2021), and Taherah Asmall and colleagues have reviewed the adverse health effects of drought in Africa (Asmall 2021). The Western United States is living through its worst drought in 1,200 years, presenting difficult challenges to all States involved (Hobbins 2020; Williams 2022). Again, serious questions are looming with an urgent need for new ideas, solutions, and technology.

Indirect Health Effects

This chapter focuses heavily on the direct health effects of climate change, since in the year 2021, they particularly dominated the news cycle and social media, and they pose urgent needs for public health, technology, infrastructure, funding, and governance. From the perspective of global public health and disease, the indirect health effects that are mediated by an altered environment resulting from climate change are equally important, and their magnitude will become more apparent as climate change proceeds (Patz 2014; USGCRP 2016).

> Changing patterns of disease vectors will result in increases of very specific infectious diseases, such as dengue fever, Chikungunya, malaria, a variety of water-borne diseases from various pathogens, food-borne diseases, and fungal diseases; this is potentially a very long list.
>
> *(Cisse 2019)*

Changes in habitats, geographic spread, virulence, and other risk factors for pathogens, vectors, media, and hosts, will lead in many instances to expanding risk for threatened populations. For example, a recent review of historical and future health risks from dengue details how environmental factors like temperature, precipitation, and humidity alter the global distribution of this rapidly spreading viral disease (Altizer 2013; Soneja 2021). Changing patterns of vegetation will affect pollen and respiratory irritants and can clearly lead to increases in asthma and allergic diseases (Eguiluz-Gracia 2020; Schramm et al. 2021a). Changing atmospheric patterns will lead to increases in specific air pollutants, primarily particulate matter (PM), but others as well. In countries like India which already have striking levels of air pollution, this can only exacerbate existing challenges. Air pollution can lead to increases in many diseases, particularly cardiovascular and respiratory diseases, but can also affect many other conditions such as adverse birth outcomes and a lengthening list of other conditions such as dementia and cataracts (Mitra 2021). Changing agricultural patterns and impact on fisheries and livestock will lead to dramatic changes in food security and nutrition, with the resulting expected impact on health and development, particularly in children and vulnerable groups (Myers 2017; Plaganyi 2019; Springmann 2016). Changing exposures to toxic chemicals and hazardous conditions, due to population, industrial, agricultural, and environmental shifts will lead to new or more challenging exposures to toxic chemicals, hazardous occupations, pesticides, occupational hazards, and other environmental diseases.

Complex Pattern Health Effects

Included in this section is a brief overview of health effects related to major societal shifts likely to result from climate change, including overlapping direct and indirect effects.

Mental Health

A variety of mental health disorders such as post-traumatic stress disorder (PTSD), depression, anxiety, and even suicide, are regularly seen after all types of disasters, whether acute or long-term emergencies. This is the most consistently seen health impact after disasters, though the effects are challenging to study methodologically, as disasters occur in various settings without warning and often without an opportunity to set up valid follow-up investigations. Nevertheless, these mental health disorders are regularly found after all major disasters, whether caused by the shock and trauma of the disaster event itself, or by the challenging and prolonged repercussions during the recovery period (Falk 2014; Marazziti 2021).

Vulnerable Populations, Equity, and Global Social Medicine

A recent *Lancet* perspective article (Adams 2021) highlights the impact of disasters on vulnerable populations such as the disabled and those with chronic diseases as they experience and recover from the disruptive impact of the disasters. Beyond individual infirmities, marginalized communities resulting from poverty, racism, or environmental degradation are at great risk from the disaster itself and in attempting to recover post-disaster. Public health programs place great emphasis on addressing health disparities and inequities. Among various age groups, children are invariably at greater risk in virtually all disaster situations (Philipsborn 2018; Rubin 2019). The U.S. Environmental Protection Agency (EPA) recently provided a detailed overview on the disproportionate impact of climate change among socially and economically vulnerable populations in the United States (EPA 2021). Also, in the United States, Native American Tribes are distinct population groups that require special attention and planning (Schramm et al. 2020a). Networks for support and caregiving that operate beyond the immediate disaster response through the period of recovery are particularly important to the functional restoration of these at-risk groups. In addition to direct care, physicians and health workers can be a conduit for directing adequate social services for those in need.

The scope of this issue cannot be underestimated. Billions of people live in poverty or in marginalized settings or have disabilities or chronic diseases. A recent viewpoint in *JAMA* (Ross, Zaman, and Clemens 2019) highlights the health concerns of the global urban slum population, which is estimated to grow from one billion to two billion by 2030. Health for this major portion of humanity is already severely challenged and will only be greatly magnified by climate change.

Migration and Health

Climate change will lead to large-scale migration from heavily impacted areas as a result of adaptive responses, resettlement efforts, and even forcible displacement of populations at risk (McMichael 2012). A recent *Lancet* editorial (Lancet 2020b) summarizes the magnitude of several projections by official world bodies, such as an UN estimate of potentially one billion climate migrants by 2050 and a European Parliament estimate of 26.4 million people displaced by weather events every year since 2008. A recent series of articles highlights the interconnected role governance and science will play in improving climate-related decision-making related to migration and relocation issues (Wible 2021). The world is not ready for migration at this scale, which will leave lasting health effects for all, but particularly for the ill, vulnerable, poor, and marginalized segments of society.

Climate Change, Conflict, and Health

While it seems likely that dwindling access to resources such as water and food, accompanied by migration, health impacts, and social traumas, will lead to increased conflict in high-risk areas, there is still insufficient data on this issue (Bohannon 2013; Hsiang 2013). This is likely to be a huge governance challenge going forward, and if it occurs, the impact of violence will trigger major health effects in all affected areas.

Climate Change and Economic Impact

A report in *Science* (Hsiang 2017) estimated the economic damage in the United States across multiple sectors (agriculture, crime, coastal storms, energy, human mortality, and labor) and predicted major impacts among the poorest third of U.S. counties later this century. More research is needed in this area, but there can be little doubt that from a global perspective worsening poverty cannot be good for global health.

Climate Change Governance

The Covid-19 pandemic has clearly illustrated just how challenging it is to mount a unified, effective response at all levels to a disaster that has reached every corner of the globe. The governance challenges for climate change are even greater. The goal, to the extent possible, is to mitigate (prevent) and/or adapt (respond) to the many impacts of climate change. Although there is no formal governance structure to respond to these impacts, there are myriad efforts working toward this goal. This section on governance will provide, without attempting to be exhaustive, a framework for thinking holistically about the diverse approaches to governance of climate change, starting at the global scale, and then working down to regional, national, state/city/local, health care/public health, and individual and community level efforts. It will focus particularly on the overview of the governance structure rather than the very exhaustive task of systematically summarizing everything that is happening in all these programs. From the health perspective, many programs to reduce greenhouse-gas emissions have the ancillary benefit of simultaneously improving health (Haines 2009).

Today, governance faces new challenges. As noted in an editorial in *Science*:

> Since the end of WWII, scientists have clung to the idea that if they stay objective and state the science, then the rest of the world will follow. As climate change rages and the pandemic cycles on, it's time to face the fact that this old notion is naïve.
>
> *(Thorp 2021)*

A likely explanation follows:

> Arguably, the greatest challenge that scientists must address as a community, stems from a fundamental change in how scientific information gets shared, amplified, and received in online environments . . . the societal balance of power for scientific information has shifted away from legacy media, government agencies, and the scientific community. Now, social media platforms are the central gatekeeper of information and communication about science. The scientific community has been slow to react.
>
> *(Brossard 2022)*

An earlier publication provided a detailed overview of how the rise of digital media reshaped the coverage of climate change (Boykoff 2013).

A recent study (Vosoughi 2018) concluded that falsehoods or "fake news" diffuses significantly farther, faster, deeper, and more broadly than the truth in all categories of information, aided by appearing novel, and enhanced when politics is engaged (Woolhandler 2021). And, as is well known, one doesn't have to outright lie to distort the scientific record. The artful choice of topics for study, framing the question to reach a predetermined conclusion, weak protocols, and deliberate distortions of data analysis and presentation are equally effective in misrepresenting the truth (Bailar 2006).

On the plus side, we are in an era when digital technologies offer tremendous promise for improving health and the response to challenges such as climate change. A recent *Lancet and Financial Times* Commission on Governing Health Futures 2030 report emphasizes that digital access, and the quality of that access, must now be recognized as a key determinant of health (Kickbusch et al. 2021). Health-care-related artificial intelligence interventions will play an important role in addressing health inequities at the individual patient, health system, and population health levels (Hosny and Aerts 2019).

Global Level

IPCC

The Intergovernmental Panel on Climate Change (IPCC) leads the global effort to track the status of climate change, advise on its risks, and assess progress for mitigation efforts and achievement or lack thereof in meeting global targets. It is perhaps the most visible and well-known part of the global effort to combat climate change. IPCC was created in 1988 as a joint effort of the World Meteorological Organization (WMO) and the UN Environment Program (UNEP). It has released six major assessment reports (ARs) since then (IPCC 2021; the remaining parts of the sixth AR will be concluded by 2023). The Working Group II contribution to the fifth AR, on "Impacts, Adaptation, and Vulnerability" (IPCC 2014) was a critical update on health and adaptation. The effort to produce these assessments is extraordinary in scope, having involved perhaps thousands of authors, contributors, and editors over time in a sophisticated process that has been described as the largest scientific assessment process in history (Woodward 2014). Indeed, it has taken just such a massive effort to successfully convince the bulk of world leaders, scientists, and citizens that climate change is happening, that abrupt and irreversible changes could occur, that it is unequivocal that warming is largely attributable to human input, and that the time to act is now if we are to reach global targets for limiting temperature increases to 1.5°C or 2°C (Oreskes 2021; Sherwood 2021). A very concise overview of the developing understanding of the health risks of climate change, including key findings from the first five IPCC ARs is available (Ebi 2017).

WMO and UNEP

WMO and UNEP also provide global leadership through their own annual reports. The *State of Global Climate 2021-WMO Provisional Report* for example details the major climate data for the year, including concentrations of major greenhouse gases, global mean temperature, global sea-level rise, ocean heat content, and data about the major global weather disasters for the year (WMO 2021a). It also produces many other critical reports such as the *2021 State of Climate Services-Water* which addresses the critical issue of global water scarcity and resources (WMO-Water 2021b). UNEP's *Emissions Gap Report 2021* assesses the shortfall between announced country pledges and plans for emissions reductions and what is actually occurring (UNEP 2021).

WHO

The World Health Organization (WHO) assesses climate change as the greatest health threat facing humanity, and in response to the most recent IPCC report and in anticipation of the COP26 meeting in Glasgow released the *COP26 Special Report on Climate Change and Health: The Health Argument for Climate Action* (WHO 2021). The report bolstered the effort at COP26 to frame climate change as a health issue, and it provides ten recommendations for priority health actions to be undertaken globally.

UNFCCC and COP26

The UN Framework Convention on Climate Change (UNFCCC) began in 1994 and has been ratified by 197 countries. Its goal is to stabilize greenhouse-gas emissions and prevent dangerous anthropogenic interference with the climate system. It is the framework through which countries make national contributions and pledges to reduce emissions and provide support to global emissions reduction efforts. Key global treaties and agreements have been reached at their annual meetings, generally referred to by the location of the meetings (e.g., Kyoto and Paris). The 26th meeting of the Conference of the Parties, COP26, was held in Glasgow, United Kingdom, in October 2021. There were new and updated pledges on emission reductions from some key countries, but the vagueness and lack of immediate timetables for achieving them in some countries left considerable uncertainty about meeting global climate goals. Other major efforts, such as funding climate change programs in developing countries or the phaseout of coal as an energy source, received only partial support, leading to disappointment among many (Washington Post 2021; O'Grady 2021a, 2021b).

Other (Nonofficial) Global Efforts

Major global foundations/philanthropies (e.g., Gates, Bloomberg, Wellcome Trust) and NGOs have major ongoing or planned programs to address climate change and its health impact (Koh 2018). In the private sector, several large multinational corporations are taking the lead in responding to climate change with very impressive efforts to reduce emissions (Esty 2018). At this point, for example, virtually all the largest automotive manufacturers have major new programs to produce electric-powered vehicles to eventually replace conventional fossil fuel-powered vehicles. This is a multi-decade effort that will lead to profound changes in climate impacts on society. In many countries, governmental regulations are promoting this shift. In other industries, such as energy, there is only a mixed response to date (Dietz et al. 2021). There are also research efforts underway involving both the public and private sectors to develop affordable technologies to remove carbon dioxide from the atmosphere; this is still in a very early stage (Conniff 2019; Service 2021).

Many scientific, academic, and professional groups are leading participants and advocates for climate change programs. The *Lancet* Countdown on Health and Climate Change has been a leader in this effort. The journal has established a very detailed set of indicators (forty-four in the 2021 countdown) covering five domains: climate change impacts, exposures, and vulnerabilities; adaptation, planning, and resilience for health; mitigation actions and health co-benefits; economics and finance; and politics and governance, which represent the consensus thinking of leading researchers from dozens of academic institutions and UN agencies, for both advocating and tracking progress in climate change and health (Romanello et al. 2021a; Watts et al. 2018). In another example, just prior to COP26, the editors of health journals worldwide issued a joint call for urgent action to limit global temperature increases and for health professionals to assist in the transition to a sustainable, fairer, more resilient, and healthier world (New England Journal of Medicine 2021).

In general, the official programs described above have made a remarkable effort at data development, governmental coordination, scientific updates, and advocacy, but they lack the ability to regulate or assure compliance with climate change efforts. Many of the nonofficial programs, within their own spheres, can be strong advocates as well as leaders in promoting climate change actions. All are necessary for successfully reaching climate change targets.

Regional Levels

Lancet Regional Countdown and Regional Organization Efforts

The *Lancet* regional countdown program tracks national and regional responses with sets of indicators closely linked to the *Lancet* global countdown; recent reports such as from the Europe, China, and Australia programs highlight progress as well as shortcomings in those efforts (Romanello et al. 2021b; Zhang et al. 2018; Cai et al. 2021). In another approach to assist coordinated policy development across regions, the InterAcademy Partnership (IAP), a global network of more than 140 academies of science, engineering, and medicine, is bringing together evidence from Africa, the Americas, Asia, and Europe to evaluate climate change effects on health and to assess policy priorities for adaptation and mitigation (Fears et al. 2021). Regional organizations also have active roles in supporting climate and health initiatives. In Southeast Asia, the Asian Development Bank and the Asia-Pacific Regional Forum on Health and Environment both support such efforts, each with their own specific mix of expertise and resources (Gilfillan 2018).

Emerging Regional Governance Issues

Perhaps nowhere is this better illustrated than in the Arctic region. As the ice melts and the oceans thaw, access to the incredible resources of the Arctic becomes a crucial issue for all the countries that border on the region. The governance issues regarding boundaries, access, control, and ownership are formidable. Many fear the potential for conflict as the future of the Arctic unfolds. Clearly, issues of environment and health will be caught up within this larger governance challenge (Berkman 2009; Fischetti 2019).

National Level

The key governance decisions are going to be made at the national level-this is where the global leadership must come from. Of course, there are many competing issues vying for attention in every country. During the pandemic, for example, Covid-19 consumed much of the available oxygen; the pandemic deeply affected the global economy and constrained resources everywhere. As noted earlier, in addition to the well-known resource limits, the pandemic heightened political and ideological divisions which further exacerbated climate change responses. In addition, democracies face a challenge in policy continuity over the long term due to the frequent change in elected governments, which can lead to loss of policy and climate action momentum.

A recent report has elaborated on three key aspects of governance at the national level: coordination challenges, building consensus, and strategy development. All are key for a successful government response to climate change, and yet there is considerable diversity worldwide in how various countries create the institutional structure to accomplish this. To address the coordination challenge, nations have developed four broad approaches: (1) layer climate coordination responsibilities onto an existing ministry such as the environment ministry; (2) reorganize existing bureaucracies to reallocate climate responsibilities to a new or redesigned department; (3) establish new inter-ministerial coordination committees; and (4) create climate laws which subsume coordination within a framework of target setting and compliance. There are varying degrees of success with all these approaches (Dubash et al. 2021). Kristie Ebi has highlighted that governance and the effectiveness of institutions are among the key variables that determine the success of health systems in responding to climate change (Ebi 2020). Multiple reports emphasize the importance of a systems approach to analyzing and understanding the complex relationships between climate and health and for informing adaptation and mitigation decisions (Pongsiri 2021).

I will use the United States as illustrative of issues at this level, although future success is heavily dependent on actions in many other countries, including Australia, Brazil, China, India, Russia, and African and European countries. Several recent articles review climate risks and challenges in specific LMICs (Ahmed, Zounemat-Kermani, and Scholz 2020; Bush 2011; Opoku et al. 2021; Swaminathan 2020; Wright et al. 2021).

The United States

Each of the last three administrations have produced dramatic shifts in U.S. climate policy. The changes are exhilarating to their proponents but unnerving to outside observers concerned about the long-term consistency of policy. On his first day in office, President Joe Biden announced the United States would rejoin the Paris Agreement and began to establish a new climate path for the United States, including new priorities, leadership, laws, regulations, programs, and funding decisions.

Key highlights of the Biden administration's efforts to combat climate change are as follows:

1. New climate leaders were appointed, including Gina McCarthy as National Climate Advisor and John Kerry as a cabinet-level Special Envoy for Climate Change, and strong climate leadership appointed in key cabinet positions such as Transportation, Energy, and Interior, as well as the Environmental Protection Agency (Mervis 2021).
2. At the Department of Health and Human Services, the administration created a new Office for Climate Change, Health, and Equity which will provide leadership for climate progress in the health sector.
3. Congress passed a bipartisan roughly US$1 trillion infrastructure bill, which contains approximately US$50 billion for issues such as climate resilience and weatherization to help reduce the toll from climate-related disasters.

4. The administration initially proposed an approximately US$2 trillion Build Back Better legislative bill with far greater climate funding to reduce greenhouse-gas emissions which was not approved by Congress; however, Congress subsequently approved the US$350+ billion Inflation Reduction Act primarily focused on climate change.
5. The administration advanced multiple regulations to support renewable sources of energy and electric vehicles, while scaling back the use of fossil fuels.
6. The administration set a final target of reaching carbon neutrality in the United States by 2050, and put forth an agenda for achieving such a goal.
7. The administration developed climate plans for each of twenty-one major U.S. Agencies.
8. The administration developed major initiatives in the transportation sector as the largest emitter of CO2 in the United States.
9. The administration supported major global initiatives including funding assistance for LMICs to enable country climate change initiatives. The president personally participated at COP26.

Time will tell the extent to which this effort can be sustained beyond this administration. The main takeaway here is just how much climate governance is dependent on national leadership in key countries, both for in-country efforts and for the support of global initiatives.

State/City/Local Levels

In the United States, not unlike many other countries, the dollars will flow from the national government, but key decisions about how to spend the money will be made at the state and local levels, often with heavy support from local stakeholders in academia, business, NGOs, and others.

To illustrate the magnitude of decisions being considered at these levels, several of the largest coastal cities within the United States, including Boston, Miami, and New York, are all engaged with complex decision-making about how to protect their cities from rising sea level, hurricanes, flooding, and land subsidence (Barnard 2020; Klinenberg 2013; Mazzei 2021; Roush 2020). New Orleans has been engaged in coastal restoration, levee, and seawall discussions for decades, and these efforts became more urgent after the devastation from Hurricane Katrina. These are projects that could cost tens of billions of dollars, take decades to implement, and have an enormous impact on the future safety and habitability of these cities. As populations keep growing in coastal megacities worldwide, similar challenges await across the globe, and are already being painfully addressed as noted earlier in cities such as Jakarta.

Cities in the future will have to address not just potential catastrophic events from climate change but numerous urban design changes related to energy, transportation, construction, homes, water, food, sanitation, and wastewater. Two excellent series of articles, one in *Science* (Wigginton et al. 2016) and the other in *Scientific American* (McDonough 2017), explore the range of issues facing the cities of the future in diverse parts of the globe. Two major city networking alliances which have focused on climate change are the Cities Alliance (www.citiesalliance.org/) and the C40 global network of mayors (www.c40.org/).

From a governance perspective, indicators for state- and local-level use have been developed to monitor and assess both environmental health and adaptation responses to climate change (Doubleday et al. 2020; English 2009); these are similar in the concept to the *Lancet* countdowns discussed earlier but adapted to state and local use. Recent articles also discuss the levels and types of support that local jurisdictions will need from central governments (Austin et al. 2019), the use of health impact assessments to optimize climate change policies (Dannenberg, Rogerson, and Rudolph 2019 the lessons learned from city-level mitigation strategies and implementation (de Oliveira, Puppim, and Doll 2016), and how Native American Tribes are adapting to climate change (Schramm et al. 2020b).

Health-Care Facilities and Public Health

In 2015, the WHO released the *Operational Framework for Building Climate Resilient Health Systems*, proposing ten areas of intervention. Some relate to climate change, vulnerability, and adaptation assessments as well as limiting emissions from health-care facilities. Others are focused on assuring that health facilities are sustainable and resilient to be able to function in the face of climate change impacts. The conditions for achieving sustainability and resilience include adequate resources to respond to environmental challenges, safe management of water and wastes, sustainable energy sources, and appropriate infrastructure (Corvalan et al. 2020). Several recent reports provide guidance for training clinicians and medical residents to respond to climate change issues (Lemery et al. 2020; Philipsborn et al. 2021). At this point, many major medical schools, schools of public health, and their universities have active and innovative climate change programs for training, research, reducing emissions, and providing significant support to their communities and local stakeholders in promoting effective responses to climate change.

The Centers for Disease Control and Prevention (CDC) has adapted the classic ten essential services of public health to the climate change situation and incorporated that into a model for public health response. CDC also provides funding, technical assistance, and an adaptation framework to assist states and localities with climate planning and adaptation activities (Schramm et al. 2020b, 2021b). The current public health capacity, infrastructure, resources, and statutory authority are inadequate for the scope of the climate change response (Moulton 2020). The Covid-19 pandemic has brought the weaknesses of the U.S. public health system into sharp relief; in addition to the complex structure and decision-making process, the information technology and data capacity, a core issue for public health, are very dated and inadequate for current needs (Wallace 2022). Finally, Kristie Ebi and others have summarized key lessons learned from public health to inform the process of climate change adaptation (Ebi et al. 2006).

Several key health NGOs in the United States are the Council of State and Territorial Epidemiologists (CSTE), the American Public Health Association (APHA), the Association of State and Territorial Health Officers (ASTHO), and the National Association of County and City Health Officials (NACCHO) (Breysse et al. 2021).

Individuals and Communities

Here are steps we can all take as individuals and within our local neighborhoods to combat climate change: (1) promote a sensible approach to air conditioning; (2) promote smart land use decisions about parks and open spaces; (3) promote better building strategies with natural ventilation, heat reflectors, shade, conservation of rainwater, use of solar energy, and many other climate-friendly decisions; (4) promote climate-friendly, community-wide energy, transportation, and other local policies; (5) develop heat action plans and building guidelines for community institutions such as homes for the elderly and facilities for children (schools, daycare); (6) promote climate-friendly hospitals and other municipal institutions; and (7) develop educational programs for children and adults (see Appendix Table 29.1 for website lists and additional individual guidance from key institutions).

Postscript

This chapter was submitted at the end of 2021. The broad outlines of the health and governance issues related to climate change are essentially unchanged and continue to be relevant and valuable. However, important events, policies, reports, and more continue to occur at a rapid pace. For example, the specific climate-related disasters in 2022 and in succeeding years are obviously different than those in 2021 and add to our understanding, but don't negate the lessons learned in this chapter. On the governance side, updated material can often easily be found by looking at subsequent reports from the same groups that were cited here, such as the newer reports from the IPCC or the *Lancet* Countdown, the annual reports from UNEP and WMO, the results of COP27 and subsequent years, recent legislation in the United States such as the Inflation Reduction Act, updates on various reference websites such as the cited city alliances and the agencies such as WHO, CDC, and EPA. I hope that this chapter, although it is in a rapidly evolving area, can nevertheless provide a clear structure for understanding the scope of the health and governance issues and a roadmap to finding updated information for the interested reader.

Appendix

Table 29A.1 To-Do Lists for Individuals to Help Fight the Climate Crisis

A-UNEP list, 2021: www.unep.org/news-and-stories/story/10-ways-you-can-help-fight-climate-crisis

1 spread the word
2 keep up political pressure
3 transform transport
4 rein in power use
5 tweak your diet
6 shop local and buy sustainable
7 don't waste food
8 dress (climate) smart
9 plant trees
10 focus on planet-friendly investments

B-Grantham Institute, Imperial College, London list: www.imperial.ac.uk/stories/climate-action/

Make your voice heard by those in power

1 eat less meat and dairy
2 cut back on flying
3 leave the car at home
4 reduce your energy use
5 respect and protect green spaces
6 invest your money responsibly
7 cut consumption-and waste
8 talk about the changes you make

Source: Author.

Note: See the web sites for added details and supplementary materials—sites were accessed on February 19, 2022.

Key Discussion Areas

- Direct, indirect, and complex patterns of human health.
- Multiple global approaches toward mitigating climate change and adapting to its negative impacts.
- Actions taken by the United States and others to mitigate and adapt to the health impact of climate change at the national, state, city, community, and local levels.

References

Adams, Vincanne, Saudi Garcia, and David S. Jones. 2021. "Climate Disasters and Global Social Medicine." *Lancet* 398: 656–57.

Ahmed, Toqeer, Mohammad Zounemat-Kermani, and Miklas Scholz. 2020. "Climate Change, Water Quality and Water-Related Challenges: A Review with Focus on Pakistan." *International Journal of Environmental Research and Public Health* 17, https://doi.org/10.3390/ijerph17228518 (accessed April 7, 2023).

Altizer, Sonia, Richard C. Ostfeld, Pieter T. J. Johnson, Susan Kutz, and C. Drew Harvell. 2013. "Climate Change and Infectious Diseases: From Evidence to a Predictive Framework." *Science* 341: 514–19.

Asmall, Taherah, Amber Abrams, Martin Roosli, Gueladio Cisse, Kirsty Carden, and Mohamed Aqiel Dalvie. 2021. "The Adverse Health Effects Associated with Drought in Africa." *Science of the Total Environment* 793: 148500, https://doi.org/10.1016/j.scitotenv.2021.148500 (accessed April 7, 2023).

Ault, Toby R. 2020. "On the Essentials of Drought in a Changing Climate." *Science* 368: 256–60.

Austin, Stephanie E., James D. Ford, Lea Berrang-Ford, Robert Biesbroek, and Nancy A. Ross. 2019. "Enabling Local Public Health Adaptation to Climate Change." *Social Science and Medicine* 220: 236–44.

Bailar, John C. 2006. "How to Distort the Scientific Record Without Actually Lying: Truth, and the Arts of Science." *European Journal of Oncology* 11(4): 217–24.

Balsari, Satchit, Mathew V. Kiang, and Caroline O. Buckee. 2021. "Data in Crisis—Rethinking Disaster Preparedness in the United States. *New England Journal of Medicine* 385(16): 1526–30.

Barnard, Anne. 2020. "The $119 Billion Sea Wall That Could Defend New York . . . or Not." *New York Times*, January 17, 2020, updated August 21, 2021.

Berkman, Paul Arthur, and Oran R. Young. 2009. "Governance and Environmental Change in the Arctic Ocean." *Science* 324: 339–40.

Bohannon, John. 2013. "Study Links Climate Change and Violence, Battle Ensues." *Science* 341: 444–46.

Boykoff, Maxwell T., and Tom Yulsman. 2013. "Political Economy, Media, and Climate Change: Sinews of Modern Life." *WIREs Climate Change* 4: 359–71, https://doi.org/10.1002/wcc.233 (accessed April 7, 2023).

Breysse, Pat, Kathleen Dolan, Paul Schramm, and Marcus Plescia. 2021. "Approaching Climate Change: The Role of State and Territorial Health Agencies." *Journal of Public Health Management and Practice* 27: 615–17.

Brossard, Dominique and Dietram A. Scheufele. 2022. "The Chronic Growing Pains of Communicating Science Online- Scientists Have Not Yet Adapted to New Information Environments." *Science* 375: 613–14.

Bush, Kathleen F., George Luber, S. Rani Kotha, R. S. Dhaliwal, Vikas Kapil, Mercedes Pascual, Daniel G. Brown, et al. 2011. "Impacts of Climate Change on Public Health in India: Future Research Directions." *Environmental Health Perspectives* 119(6): 765–70.

Cai, Wenjia, Chi Zhang, Shihui Zhang, Siqi Ai, Yuki Bai, Junzhe Bao, Bin Chen, et al. 2021. "The 2021 China Report of the *Lancet* Countdown on Health and Climate Change: Seizing the Window of Opportunity." *Lancet Public Health*, November 7, 2021, https://doi.org/10.1016/S2468-2667(21)00209-7 (accessed April 7, 2023).

Cisse, Gueladio. 2019. "Food-borne and Water-borne Diseases Under Climate Change in Low- and Middle-income Countries: Further Efforts Needed for Reducing Environmental Health Exposure Risks." *Acta Tropica* 194: 181–88.

Conniff, Richard, and Liz Tormes. 2019. "The Last Resort." *Scientific American* 320: 52–59, January 2019.

Cornwall, Warren. 2021a. "Clearing the Tinderbox." *Science* 373: 1300–3.

———. 2021b. "Europe's Deadly Floods Leave Scientists Stunned." *Science* 373: 372–73.

Corvalan, Carlos, Elena Villalobos Prats, Aderita Sena, Diarmid Campbell-Lendrum, Josh Karliner, Antonella Risso, Susan Wilburn, et al. 2020. "Towards Climate Resilient and Environmentally Sustainable Health Care Facilities." *International Journal of Environmental Research and Public Health* 17, https://doi.org/10.3390/ijerph17238849 (accessed April 7, 2023).

Dannenberg, Andrew L., Bethany Rogerson, and Linda Rudolph. 2020. "Optimizing the Health Benefits of Climate Change Policies Using Health Impact Assessment." *Journal of Public Health Policy* 41: 139–54.

de Oliveira, Jose A. Puppim, and Christopher N. H. Doll. 2016. "Governance and Networks for Health Co-Benefits of Climate Change Mitigation: Lessons from 2 Indian Cities." *Environment International* 97: 146–54.

Devi, Sharmila. 2021. "Syria and Iraq Facing Severe Drought." *Lancet* 398: 1395.

Dietz, Simon, Dan Gardiner, Valentin Jahn, and Jolien Noels. 2021. "How Ambitious Are Oil and Gas Companies' Climate Goals." *Science* 374: 405–8.

Doubleday, Annie, Nicole A. Errett, Kristie L. Ebi, and Jeremy J. Hess. 2020. "Indicators to Guide and Monitor Climate Change Adaptation in the US Pacific Northwest." *American Journal of Public Health* 110(2): 180–88.

Dubash, Navroz K., Aditya Valiathan Pillai, Christian Flachsland, Kathryn Harrison, Kathryn Hochstetler, Matthew Lockwood, Robert MacNeil, et al. 2021. "National Climate Institutions Complement Targets and Poliicies." *Science*: 690–93.

Ebi, Kristie L. 2020. "Mechanisms, Policies, and Tools to Promote Health Equity and Effective Governance of the Health Risks of Climate Change." *Journal of Public Health Policy* 41: 11–13.

Ebi, Kristie L., Anthony Capon, Peter Berry, Carolyn Broderick, Richard de Dear, George Havenith, Yasushi Honda, et al. 2021. "Hot Weather and Heat Extremes: Health Risks." *Lancet* 398: 698–708.

Ebi, Kristie L., and Jeremy Hess. 2017. "The Past and Future in Understanding the Health Risks of and Responses to Climate Variability and Change." *International Journal of Biometeorology* 61(Suppl 1): S71–80.

Ebi, Kristie L., and Stanley Luchters. 2021. "Most Affected by Climate Change; Least Studied." *Environmental Health Perspectives* 129(11), https://doi.org/10.1289/EHP10384 (accessed April 7, 2023).

Ebi, Kristie L., Joel Smith, Ian Burton, and Joel Scheraga. 2006. "Some Lessons Learned from Public Health on the Process of Adaptation." *Mitigation and Adaptation Strategies for Global Change* 11: 607–20.

Eguiluz-Gracia, Ibon, Alexander G. Mathioudakis, Sabine Bartel, Susanne J. H. Vijverberg, Elaine Fuertes, Pasquale Comberiati, Yutong Samuel Cai, et al. 2020. "The Need for Clean Air: The Way Air Pollution and Climate Change Affect Allergic Rhinitis and Asthma." *Allergy* 75: 2170–84.

English, Paul B., Amber H. Sinclair, Zev Ross, Henry Anderson, Vicki Boothe, Christine Davis, Kristie Ebi, et al. 2009. "Environmental Health Indicators of Climate Change for the United States: Findings from the State Environmental Health Indicator Collaborative." *Environmental Health Perspectives* 117: 1673–81.

EPA. 2021. *Climate Change and Social Vulnerability in the United States: A Focus on Six Impacts*. Washington: U.S. Environmental Protection Agency, EPA 430-R-21–003, www.epa.gov/system/files/documents/2021-09/climate-vulnerability_september-2021_508.pdf (accessed April 7, 2023).

Esty, Daniel C., and Michelle L. Bell. 2018. "Business Leadership in Global Climate Change Responses." *American Journal of Public Health* 108(Suppl. 2): S80–4.

Falk, Henry. 2014. "Natural Disasters, Environmental Emergencies, and Children's Health." In *The Oxford Textbook of Children's Environmental Health*, edited by Philip J. Landrigan and Ruth A. Etzel. New York: Oxford University Press.

Fears, Robin, Khairul Annuar B. Abdullah, Claudia Canales-Holzeis, Deoraj Caussy, Andy Haines, Sherilee L. Harper, Jeremy N. McNeil, Johanna Mogwitz, and Volker ter Meulen. 2021. "Evidence-Informed Policy for Tackling Adverse Climate Change Effects on Health: Linking Regional and Global Assessments of Science to Catalyse Action." *PLoS Med* 18(7): e1003719, https://doi.org/10.1371/journal.pmed.1003719 (accessed April 7, 2023).

Fischetti, Mark, and Peter Horvath. 2019. "Arctic Ambitions—Divide or Conquer." *Scientific American* 321: 26–36, August 2019.

Flavelle, Christopher, and Anastasia Samoylova. 2018. "Before the Flood." *Bloomberg Businessweek*, September 3, 2018.

Folger, Tim, and George Steinmetz. 2013. "Rising Seas." *National Geographic* 224: 30–57, September 2013.

Francis, Jennifer A., and Mark Ross. 2021. "Vapor Storms." *Scientific American* 325: 26–33, November 2021.

Gardener, James Ross. 2021. "Under the Dome: A Chronicle of a Climate Disaster in Slow Motion." *New Yorker*, October 18, 2021.

Gibbens, Sarah. 2021. "2021's Weather Disasters Brought Home the Reality of Climate Change." *National Geographic*, December 6, 2021.

Gilfillan, Daniel. 2018. "Regional Organizations Supporting Health Sector Responses to Climate Change in Southeast Asia." *Globalization and Health* 14, https://doi.org/10.1186/s12992-018-0388-z (accessed April 7, 2023).

Haines, Andy, Anthony J. McMichael, Kirk R. Smith, Ian Roberts, James Woodcock, Anil Markandya, Ben G. Armstrong, et al. 2009. "Public Health Benefits of Strategies to Reduce Greenhouse-Gas Emissions: Overview and Implications for Policy Makers." *Lancet* 374: 2104–14.

Herrera-Garcia, Gerardo, Pablo Ezquerro, Roberto Tomas, Marta Bejar-Pizarro, Juan Lopez-Vinielles, Mauro Rossi, Rosa M. Mateos, et al. 2021. "Mapping the Global Threat of Land Subsidence." *Science* 371: 34–6.

Hobbins, Mike, and Joseph Barsugli. 2020 "Threatening the Vigor of the Colorado River." *Science* 367(2020): 1192–93.

Hosny, Ahmed and Hugo J. W. L. Aerts. 2019. "Artificial Intelligence for Global Health." *Science* 366: 955–56.

Hsiang, Solomon M., Marshall Burke, and Edward Miguel. 2013. "Quantifying the Influence of Climate on Human Conflict." *Science* 341: 1212, http://dx.doi.org/10.1126/science.1235367 (accessed April 7, 2023).

Hsiang, Solomon M., Robert Kopp, Amir Jina, James Rising, Michael Delgado, Shashank Mohan, D. J. Rasmussen, et al. 2017. "Estimating Economic Damage from Climate Change in the United States." *Science* 356: 1362–69.

IPCC. 2014. "Summary for Policymakers." In *Climate Change 2014: Impacts, Adaptation, and Vulnerability. Part A: Global and Sectoral Aspects. Contribution of Working Group II to the Fifth Assessment Report of the Intergovernmental Panel on Climate Change*, edited by C. B. Field, V. R. Barros, D. J. Dokken, K. J. Mach, M. D. Mastrandrea, T. E. Bilir, M. Chatterjee, et al. New York: Cambridge University Press.

———. 2021. "Summary for Policymakers." In *Climate Change 2021: The Physical Science Basis. Contribution of Working Group I to the Sixth Assessment Report of the Intergovernmental Panel on Climate Change*, edited by Masson-Delmotte, V., P. Zhai, A. Pirani, S. L. Connors, C. Pean, S. Berger, et al. New York: Cambridge University Press.

Jandt, Randi, and Alison York. 2021. "Alaska Burning." *Scientific American* 325: 42–49, October 2021.

Jasechko, Scott, and Debra Perrone. 2021. "Global Groundwater Wells at Risk of Running Dry." *Science* 372: 418–21.

Johnson, Edward. 2020. "Chronicle of a Fire Foretold." *Bloomberg Businessweek*, January 13, 2020.

Kickbusch, Ilona, Dario Piselli, Anurag Agrawal, Ran Balicer, Olivia Banner, Michael Adelhart, Emanuele Capobianco, et al. 2021. "The *Lancet* and *Financial Times* Commission on Governing Health Futures 2030: Growing Up in a Digital World." *Lancet* 398: 1727–76.

Kizer, Kenneth W. 2020. "Extreme Wildfires—A Growing Population Health and Planetary Problem." *Journal of the American Medical Association* 324(16): 1605–6.
Klinenberg, Eric. 2013. "Adaptation." *New Yorker*, January 7, 2013.
Koh, Howard K., and Gina A. McCarthy. 2018. "Private and Public Sector Responses to Climate Change." *Journal of the American Medical Association* 319: 1756–57.
Kolbert, Elizabeth. 2019. "Under Water." *New Yorker*, April 1, 2019.
Lancet. 2020a. "Australia on Fire." *Lancet* 395(2020): 165.
———. 2020b. "Climate Migration Requires a Global Response." *Lancet* 395: 839.
———. 2021. "Health in a World of Extreme Heat." *Lancet* 398: 641.
Le Page, Michael. 2018. "A City Without Water." *New Scientist*, February 17, 2018.
Lemery, Jay, John Balbus, Cecilia Sorensen, Caitlin Rublee, Caleb Dresser, Satchit Balsari, and Emile Calvello Hynes. 2020. "Training Clinical and Public Health Leaders in Climate and Health." *Health Affairs* 39(12): 2189–96.
Levitt, Zach, and Bonnie Berkowitz. 2021. "Cold, Heat, Fires, Hurricanes, and Tornadoes: The Year in Weather Disasters." *Washington Post*, December 15, 2021.
Mani, Muthukumara, Sushenjit Bandyopadhyay, Shun Chonabayashi, Anil Markandya, and Thomas Mosier. 2018. *South Asia's Hotspots: The Impact of Temperature and Precipitation Changes on Living Standards*. South Asia Development Matters. Washington: World Bank, https://doi.org/10.1596/978-1-4648-1155-5 (accessed April 7, 2023).
Marazziti, Donatella, Paolo Cianconi, Federico Mucci, Lara Foresi, Ilaria Chiarantini, and Alessandra Della Vecchia. 2021. "Climate Change, Environment Pollution, COVID-19 Pandemic and Mental Health." *Science of the Total Environment* 773: 145182, https://doi.org/10.1016/j.scitotenv.2021.145182 (accessed April 7, 2023).
Mazzei, Patricia. 2019. "Hunger and an Abandoned Hospital: Puerto Rico Waits as Washington Bickers." *New York Times*, April 7, 2019.
———. 2021. "A 20-Foot Sea Wall? Miami Faces the Hard Choices of Climate Change." *New York Times*, June 2, 2021. Updated August 21, 2021.
McCall, Chris. 2019. "Indonesian Forest Fires Raise Concerns About Health." *Lancet* 394: 1699–700.
McDonough, William. 2017. "How Cities Could Save Us." *Scientific American* 317: 44–48, July 2017.
McMichael, Anthony J. 2013. "Globalization, Climate Change, and Human Health." *New England Journal of Medicine* 368(14): 1335–43.
McMichael, Anthony J., Rosalie E. Woodruff, and Simon Hales. 2006. "Climate Change and Human Health: Present and Future Risks." *Lancet* 367: 859–69.
McMichael, Celia, Jon Barnett, and Anthony J. McMichael. 2012. "An Ill Wind? Climate Change, Migration, and Health." *Environmental Health Perspectives* 120(5): 646–54.
Mervis, Jeffrey. 2021. "Biden Breaks New Ground with Science Team Picks." *Science* 452–53.
Mitra, Esha, and Rhea Mogul. 2021. "A Silent Killer is Choking India's Capital. For Millions, There's No Choice but to Breathe It In." *CNN World*, November 23, 2021, www.cnn.com/2021/11/23/india/air-pollution-delhi-residents-intl-hnk-dst/index.html (accessed April 7, 2023).
Moon, Twilla. 2017. "Saying Goodbye to Glaciers." *Science* 356: 580–81.
Moulton, Anthony D. 2020. "Needed: New Authority to Build Public Health System Capacity for Climate Change Health Threats." *Journal of Public Health Policy* 41: 14–23.
Myers, Samuel S., Matthew R. Smith, Sarah Guth, Cristopher D. Golden, Bapu Vaitla, Nathaniel D. Mueller, Alan D. Dangour, and Peter Huybers. 2017. "Climate Change and Global Food Systems: Potential Impacts on Food Security and Undernutrition." *Annual Review of Public Health* 38: 259–77.
Nilsson, Maria, Robert Beaglehole, and Rainer Sauerborn. 2009. "Climate Policy: Lessons from Tobacco Control." *Lancet* 374: 1955–56.
New England Journal of Medicine. 2021. "Call for Emergency Action to Limit Global Temperature Increases, Restore Biodiversity, and Protect Health." *New England Journal of Medicine* 385: 1134–37.
NOAA National Centers for Environmental Information. 2022. "Billion-Dollar Weather and Climate Disasters," www.ncdc.noaa.gov/billions (accessed April 7, 2023).
O'Connor, M. R. 2021. "Towering Infernos: What It's Like to Fight a Megafire." *New Yorker*, November 15, 2021.

O'Grady, Cathleen. 2021a. "New Pledges Could Keep Global Warming Below 2°C Target." *Science* 374: 801–2.

———. 2021b. "Glasgow Pact Leaves 1.5°C Goal on Life Support." *Science* 374: 920–21.

Omer, Saad B., Regina M. Benjamin, Noel T. Brewer, Alison M. Buttenheim, Timothy Calaghan, Arthur Caplan, Richard M. Carpiano, et al. 2021. "Promoting COVID-19 Vaccine Acceptance: Recommendations from the Lancet Commission on Vaccine Refusal, Acceptance, and Demand in the USA." *Lancet* 398: 2186–92.

Opoku, Samuel Kwasi, Walter Leal Filho, Fudjumdjum Hubert, and Oluwabunmi Adejumo. 2021. "Climate Change and Health Preparedness in Africa: Analysing Trends in Six African Countries." *International Journal of Environmental Research and Public Health* 18, https://doi.org/10.3390/ijerph18094672 (accessed April 7, 2023).

Oreskes, Naomi. 2021. "IPCC, Your Job is Partly Done." *Scientific American* 325: 70, November 2021.

Paddock, Richard C., and Muktita Suhartono. 2021. "Indonesia's Capital is Sinking, Polluted, and Crowded. It's Leaders Want to Build a New One." *New York Times*, November 26, 2019. Updated May 9, 2021.

Patz, Jonathan A., Howard Frumkin, Tracey Holloway, Daniel J. Vimont, and Andrew Haines. 2014. "Climate Change: Challenges and Opportunities for Global Health." *Journal of the American Medical Association* 312(15): 1565–80.

Pennisi, Elizabeth, and David Malakoff. 2017. "Record Storm Puts Gulf Resilience to the Test." *Science* 357: 954.

Philipsborn, Rebecca Pass, and Kevin Chan. 2018. "Climate Change and Global Child Health." *Pediatrics* 141: e20173774.

Philipsborn, Rebecca Pass, Perry Sheffield, Andrew White, Amanda Osta, Marsha S. Anderson, and Aaron Bernstein. 2021. "Climate Change and the Practice of Medicine." *Academic Medicine* 96(3): 355–67.

Plaganyi, Eva. 2019. "Climate Change Impacts on Fisheries." *Science* 363: 930–32.

Pongsiri, Montira J., and Andrea M. Bassi. 2021. "A Systems Understanding Underpins Actions at the Climate and Health Nexus." *International Journal of Environmental Research and Public Health* 18, https://doi.org/10.3390/ijerph18052398 (accessed April 7, 2023).

Rajagopalan, Sanjay, and Philip J. Landrigan. 2021. "Pollution and the Heart." *New England Journal of Medicine* 385(20): 1881–92.

Romanello, Marina, Alice McGushin, Claudia Di Napoli, Paul Drummond, Nick Hughes, Louis Jamart, Harry Kennard, et al. 2021a. "The 2021 Report of the *Lancet* Countdown on Health and Climate Change: Code Red for a Healthy Future." *Lancet* 398: 1619–62.

Romanello, Marina, Kim van Daalen, Josep M. Anto, Niheer Dasandi, Paul Drummond, Ian G. Hamilton, Slava Jankin, et al. 2021b. "Tracking Progress on Health and Climate Change in Europe." *Lancet* 6: e858–65.

Ross, Allen G. P., Khaleku Zaman, and John D. Clemens. 2019. "Health Concerns in Urban Slums: A Glimpse of Things to Come." *Journal of the American Medical Association* 321(20): 1973–74.

Roush, Wade. 2020. "Dollars for Dikes." *Scientific American*, March 2020.

Rubin, I. Leslie, Henry Falk, and Abby D. Mutic. 2019. "Natural Disasters and Vulnerable Populations: A Commentary." *International Journal of Child Health and Human Development* 12: 303–18.

Schramm, Paul J., Munerah Ahmed, Hannah Siegel, Jamie Donatuto, Larry Campbell, Kristin Raab, and Erik Svendsen. 2020a. "Climate Change and Health: Local Solutions to Local Challenges." *Current Environmental Health Reports* 7: 363–70.

Schramm, Paul J., Angelica L. Al Janabi, Larry W. Campbell, Jamie L. Donatuto, and Shasta C. Gaughen. 2020b. "How Indigenous Communities are Adapting to Climate Change: Insights from the Climate-Ready Tribes Initiative." *Health Affairs* 39: 2153–59.

Schramm, Paul J., C. L. Brown, S. Saha, K. C. Conlon, A. P. Manangan, J. E. Bell, and J. J. Hess. 2021a. "A Systematic Review of the Effects of Temperature and Precipitation on Pollen Concentrations and Season Timing, and Implications for Human Health." *International Journal of Biometeorology* 65: 1615–28.

Schramm, Paul J., Amy Cordero, Pam Protzel Berman, Trevor McCoy, Christy Gaines, Erik Svendsen, Josephine Malilay, et al. 2021b. "Building a Comprehensive Approach in CDC's National Center for Environmental Health to Address the Health Effects of Climate Change." *Journal of Climate Change and Health* 4: 100071.

Schwartz, Jen, and Grant Delin. 2018. "Under Water." *Scientific American* 319: 44–55, August 2018.

Service, Robert F. 2021. "Carbon Capture Marches Toward Practical Use." *Science* 371: 1300.

Sherwood, Steven, and Brian Hoskins. 2021. "Clarion Call from Climate Panel." *Science* 373: 719.

Soneja, Sutyajeet, Gina Tsarouchi, Darren Lumbroso, and Dao Khanh Tung. 2021. "A Review of Dengue's Historical and Future Health Risk from a Changing Climate." *Current Environmental Health Reports* 8: 245–65.

Springmann, Marco, Daniel Mason-D'Croz, Sherman Robinson, Tara Garnett, H. Charles J. Godfrey, Douglas Gollin, Mike Rayner, Paola Ballon, and Peter Scarborough. 2016. "Global and Regional Health Effects of Future Food Production Under Climate Change: A Modelling Study." *Lancet* 387: 1937–46.

Swaminathan, Soumya, and Poornima Prabhakaran. 2020. "The Future of Health in a Climate Crisis." In *Weather Report: The Crisis of Climate Change*, edited by Omita Goyal. New Delhi, India: India International Centre (IIC) Quarterly. 46(2019–2020): ISSN: # 0376-9771.

Sweet, William V., Benjamin D. Hamlington, Robert E. Kopp, et al. 2022. "Global and Regional Sea Level Rise Scenarios for the United States: Updated Mean Projections and Extreme Water Level Probabilities Along U.S. Coastlines." In *NOAA Technical Report NOS 01*. Silver Spring, MD: National Oceanic and Atmospheric Administration, National Ocean Service, https://oceanservice.noaa.gov/hazards/sealevelrise/noaa-nos- techrpt01-global-regional-SLR-scenarios-US.pdf (accessed April 7, 2023).

Thorp, H. Holden. 2021. "Time to Unfriend Facebook." *Science* 374: 9.

UNEP. 2021. *The Heat Is On: A World of Climate Promises Not Yet Delivered*. Nairobi: United Nations Environment Program.

USGCRP. 2016. *The Impacts of Climate Change on Human Health in the United States: A Scientific Assessment*. Edited by Crimmins, A., J. Balbus, J. L. Gamble, C. B. Beard, J. E. Bell, D. Dodgen, R. J. Eisen, et al. Washington: U.S. Global Change Research Program, http://dx.doi.org/10.7930/JOR49NQX (accessed April 7, 2023).

Vosoughi, Soroush, Deb Roy, and Sinan Aral. 2018. "The Spread of True and False News Online." *Science* 359: 1146–51.

Voosen, Paul. 2021. "Key Antarctic Ice Shelf is Within Years of Failure." *Science* 374: 1420–21.

Wallace, Megan, and Joshua M. Sharfstein. 2022. "The Patchwork U.S. Public Health System. *New England Journal of Medicine* 386: 1–4.

Washington Post. 2021. "The Glasgow Climate Pact, Annotated." *Washington Post*, November 13, 2021, www.washingtonpost.com/climate-environment/interactive/2021/glasgow-climate-pact-full-text-cop26/?no_nav=true (accessed April 7, 2023).

Watts, Nick, Markus Amann, Sonja Ayeb-Carlsson, Kristine Belasova, Timothy Bouley, Maxwell Boykoff, Peter Byass, et al. 2018. "The *Lancet* Countdown on Health and Climate Change: From 25 Years of Inaction to a Global Transformation for Public Health." *Lancet* 391: 581–630.

Whitmee, Sarah, Rosemary Green, Joy Phumaphi, Helen Clark, and Andy Haines. 2021. "Bridging the Evidence Gap to Achieve a Healthy, Net Zero Future." *Lancet* 398: 1551–53.

WHO. 2021. *COP26 Special Report on Climate Change and Health: The Health Argument for Climate Action*. Geneva: World Health Organization. Licence: CC BY-NC-SA 3.0 IGO.

Wible, Brad. 2021. "Out of Harm's Way." *Science Special Section: Climate-Induced Relocation* 372: 1275–300.

Williams, A. Park, Benjamin I. Cook, and Jason E. Smerdon. 2022. "Rapid Intensification of the Emerging Southwestern North American Megadrought in 2020–2021." *Nature Climate Change*, www.nature.com/articles/s41558-022-01290-z (accessed April 7, 2023).

Wigginton, Nicholas S., Julia Fahrenkamp-Uppenbrink, Brad Wible, and David Malakoff. 2016. "Cities Are the Future." *Science* Special Section 352: 904–45.

WMO. 2021a. *State of the Global Climate 2021: WMO Provisional Report*. Geneva: World Meteorological Organization.

———. 2021b. *State of Climate Services—Water*. Geneva: World Meteorological Organization.

Woodward, Alistair, Kirk R. Smith, Diarmid Campbell-Lendrum, Dave D. Chadee, Yasushi Honda, Qiyong Liu, Jane Olwoch, et al. 2014. "Climate Change and Health: On the Latest IPCC Report." *Lancet* 383: 1185–89.

Woolhandler, Steffie, David U. Himmelstein, Sameer Ahmed, Zinzi Bailey, Mary T. Bassett, Michael Bird, Jacob Bor, et al. 2021. "Public Policy and Health in the Trump Era." *Lancet* 397: 705–52.

Wright, Caradee Y., Thandi Kapwata, David Jean du Preez, Bianca Wernecke, Rebecca M. Garland, Vusumuzi Nkosi, Willem A. Landman, Liesl Dyson, and Mary Norval. 2021. "Major Climate Change-Induced Risks to Human Health in South Africa." *Environmental Research* 196, https://doi.org/10.1016/j.envres.2021.110973 (accessed April 7, 2023).

Xu, Rongbin, Pei Yu, Michael J. Abramson, Fay H. Johnston, Jonathan M. Samet, Michelle L. Bell, Andy Haines, Kristie L. Ebi, Shanshan Li, and Yuming Guo. 2020. "Wildfires, Global Climate Change, and Human Health." *New England Journal of Medicine* 383(22): 2173–81.

Zhang, Ving, Paul J Beggs, Hilary Bambrick, Helen L Berry, Martina K Linnenluecke, Stefan Trueck, Robyn Alders, et al. 2018. "The *MJA-Lancet* Countdown on Health and Climate Change: Australian Policy Inaction Threatens Lives." *Medical Journal of Australia* 209: 474e1–21.

PART 6

Community and Faith-Based Governance

Community and faith are two peas in a pod. Community needs faith to establish normative behavior (faith-based governance), and faith needs the congregation for its survival and growth. Both are incubated and sustained by external ecology, including technology. For example, the printing press spread biblical texts beyond local communities, and as a result, Christianity became a global religion. This is true not only for the Bible but also for the Qur'an, the Bhagavad Gita, and the Torah.

The printing press, radio, and television have all expanded the reach of faith-based institutions to a national and even a global scale. However, the impact of digital technology—especially social media—on both community and faith is simply transformative, especially with respect to governance. Communities are more bonded across geographic locations because of the global reach of social media and digitization, which enable different communities to interact and share information across geographic boundaries. At the same time, social media such as YouTube and TikTok are generating user content that influences governance. Along with greater participation, there is greater democratization of governance. The typical hierarchical structure in most faiths is shifting toward a more participatory governance. Finally, greater transparency spotlights the good, the bad, and the ugly conduct in many faiths, increasing the need for accountability and transparency.

Katherine Marshall's thoughtful chapter on digital transformation and democratic reforms argues that interfaith and intergovernmental governance is increasingly at least as important as governance within religious communities. Faith-based governance is both local and global at the same time. Marshall also believes that religion can play a significant role in implementing the seventeen Sustainable Development Goals (SDGs) of nongovernment institutions such as the United Nations, the World Bank, and the International Monetary Fund. Therefore, religious leaders should be invited and encouraged to enable the United Nations to successfully execute both programs and engagement.

Tine Vekemans focuses on the impact of social media on the practice of Jainism. As a religion, Jainism has advocated a life devoid of use of technology and material possessions. In fact, traditionally it has frowned upon the use of electricity or automobiles. Consequently, the priest and the congregation remained local in small villages and towns. This is now dramatically changing with the use of social media. Most preachers cannot live

DOI: 10.4324/9781003316077-36

without a cell phone, and today they travel and preach all over the world. The power of the priest who uses social media has grown exponentially, and those who refuse to embrace digital technology have remained local. With the rise of access to both the rituals and the philosophy of Jainism on the internet and cable television, Jainism as a location-bound and time-bound religion is today able to extend anytime and anywhere through the borderless world of social media. Jainism uses social media to raise funds for building temples or start new social programs. Probably, the single most significant consequence of social media is to reach any Jain in any part of the earth for social interaction. It has also created a growing interest in the religion by the younger generation.

Barak Cohen in his chapter describes the dramatic transformation of Judaism since the dawn of the internet. Judaism has become universally accessible to Jews and non-Jews all over the world. For example, the chebad.org website boasts 52 million annual visitors and holds more than 10,000 video and 14,000 audio classes. Similarly, Torah Anytime is a repository of over 70,000 lectures on topics across the Jewish spectrum. The use of digital media has not only made the teachings of the Torah even more accessible at a time when printed books are rapidly replaced by digital texts but also generated three types of religious digital creatives. The first are digital entrepreneurs such as Sefaria, an open-source platform that encourages user-generated content similar to Wikipedia. Second are digital spokespersons who have greater impact such as chebad.org mentioned earlier. Third are digital strategists who use digital tools to advance a religious objective even though they often stand outside of a specific denomination or institution.

Nadereh Chamlou's chapter on the origin and spread of Islam shows how Islam is anchored to adaptation to local context (Think Global, Act Local) and at the same time governed by sharia law, albeit interpreted differently in different parts of the world. Chamlou focuses on two areas of great importance: Islamic finance and gender inequality. Significant progress has been made in providing financing to lower- and middle-income families and small businesses based on sharia laws, which forbid charging interest and speculating on investment. All financial transactions are backed by assets, and there are profit-and-loss sharing mechanisms for the investor. It is estimated that today there is more than US$2 trillion of investment capital worldwide anchored to Islamic finance. Gender inequality, however, will continue to be an issue, especially with respect to defining the role of women as mothers and wives. While more rights are granted to women in policy formulations (and in practice), including voting rights, employment, and ownership of wealth—the biggest mechanism to reduce gender inequality is through education, and especially the college education. It is likely that both online education and social media will also narrow the gender gap over time.

The final chapter by Arpen Yagnik presents a conceptual model of faith-based governance. After defining faith as trust in God or some other concept, Yagnik suggests that there are five dimensions that make us biased from a neutral position or zone. The dimensions exist across continuums of ignorance–arrogance; apathy–sympathy; self-centered–other centered; planet centered–human centered; and alternate reality–alternate reality. The extremes of these five dimensions act as gravitational pulls against neutrality. Through faith, one can strive for neutrality and avoid any of the five extreme dimensions of will toward prejudice.

Digital technology is truly transformative of the community and faith-based governance. In general, it has democratized participation and social engagement on a global basis. At the same time, it has generated more acrimony and virulent attacks, especially by extreme groups in each faith or the community. The power of social media and user-generated content will be long-lasting and will result in deep transformations. Religions and faith will influence policy and governance from the outside of traditional hierarchical/authority frameworks and can serve as a substitute for society's lack of trust in other governance spheres.

30

DIGITAL TRANSFORMATION AND DEMOCRATIC REFORMS—RELIGIONS AT TABLES

Contributing to Global Governance

Katherine Marshall

Introduction: How Is Religion Relevant for Global Governance?

A widely cited Pew Research Center (2012) figure indicates that some 84 percent of the world's population has a religious affiliation, highlighting the importance of this widespread life dimension. The bewildering array of religious institutions that are part of this wide gamut of individual and community affiliations commonly crosses many boundaries: national, sectoral, and others. They clash and cooperate with each other and with national and transnational authorities in different ways. Many religious institutions, the Catholic Church most notably, have truly global governance structures, present in far corners of the globe. They count among the most ancient of contemporary global institutions. To address both clash and cooperation, an array of interreligious organizations spans a range from global to local, intellectual and theological, to abstract and aspirational, esoteric and firmly planted on the ground.

The Covid-19 pandemic has presented new challenges to many forms of relationships and to expectations for governance. Given the remarkable realities of the visible global interconnections that have emerged in light of the crisis, transnational responses take on particular prominence today, as do the institutional structures behind them. This applies to the roles of religious and interreligious institutions and approaches, with a notable focus on peace and conflict resolution, public health, and climate change, but also for issues that affect those who are most vulnerable and their positions within and across societies—forced migrants, including refugees, for example.

Differing approaches to religious engagement as a facet of global governance—within the UN context and through entities such as the World Bank, Group of Twenty (G20), and Group of Seven (G7)—reflect the growing awareness of the complex and multiple roles that both religious institutions and beliefs play in global affairs. At a practical level, questions turn on which institutions and individuals are engaged in policy discussions, how, and how far: thus, who sits at which tables where policies are discussed and decided upon? Who should be? And how might their roles most constructively be defined?

DOI: 10.4324/9781003316077-37

Religious Roles in Transnational Affairs

A first step in untangling the immensely complex questions around religion in global affairs is to appreciate governance relationships among different religious communities and institutions and between such communities and pertinent government institutions, national and transnational. Alongside that is the need to build from local and national religious involvement in governance in different forms of global institutions. A third set of questions probes the contemporary challenges posed by Covid-19, with the often-expressed hope to "build back better" and "fairer" that accompanied the pandemic response. That wish might be expressed also as "building back more inclusively." Discussion of religious engagement during the Covid-19 emergencies links to the volume's central theme of digital governance. The pandemic highlighted sharply the challenges around information and especially misinformation, with links to its divisive and distracting character and the matter of hate speech and its transnational permutations. Finally, given the complex and fraught history and present realities of tensions around religious roles, for example in security matters but also health and education, some blue-sky reflections on the matter are appropriate, looking both to current debates and even some "ideal" notions of religious roles at global governance tables today.

Debates, Perceptions, and Realities

There is a simple, rather simplistic, narrative about how religious institutions and leaders have and have not been part of global governance debates and realities. Not that long ago, religion and governance were so intricately connected that separating one from the other made little sense to those who lived in those times. Authority to govern was commonly expressed in religious terms; religious institutions raised and ran armies, taxed their communities, provided education, and held power over many facets of personal lives. Conflicts also were defined in religious terms—for example, as a crusade. Then, in Europe and later in its colonies, bitter religious conflicts and wars resulted in deliberate decoupling of religious power in most aspects of governance. In this secular age, new forms of boundaries—legal and well-established, sometimes less formal—took precedence and often curtailed religious influence in politics and power. Recent magazine covers, however, have announced that "God is dead." Indeed, in many situations, communist nations and France as notable examples, religious institutions were relegated to the margins of governance from the early twentieth century. In academic institutions that prepared diplomats and other international actors, religion was essentially invisible. But then world events, notably in Muslim-majority countries, catapulted religion in many forms back into global affairs. Different governments took notice, with action programs on religious engagement, debates about the meaning of the human right to Freedom of Religion or Belief (FoRB), programs to enhance religious literacy, and various forms of dialogue and engagement. A Transatlantic Policy Network on Religion and Diplomacy[1] brings together diplomats with specific responsibility for religious affairs; the United Nations established a Multifaith Advisory Council in 2018;[2] the World Bank has pursued various threads aimed at linking religion and development since 1998 (Marshall 2021); and the U.S. Agency for International Development (USAID) in October 2020 organized an ambitious "Evidence Summit on Strategic Religious Engagement."[3]

The historical and present realities are far more complex than this simplistic narrative of religious domination, neglect, and then rediscovery as suggested by many programs.

Religious influence has never disappeared, even in highly secular states; the few theocracies in today's world confront considerable nonreligious influences. A close examination of constitutional arrangements in different countries reveals the complex arrangements hammered out over time, for example shaping health and education policies, family law, and land rights. Heated tensions around religious authority, as well as the integration of religious principles and history in national identity, continue. Religious nationalism in different forms presents complex challenges. Inclusion and pluralism are both well-articulated ideals and topics that can generate heated debate and action. In short, there is today a complex pattern of politicization of religion and its mirror image, religionization of politics, both of which extend from very local to very global contexts.

Transnational aspects of religious engagement reflect the play of politics, ideologies, and historical legacies. It is telling that Samuel Huntington's (1993) article in *Foreign Affairs*, "The Clash of Civilizations?" may still be the magazine's most-read article ever. It argued that ideological struggles around core civilizational values (largely driven by religious differences) would replace Cold War tensions as forces driving future conflicts. Hotly debated, the clash of civilizations narrative still shapes many of the complex exchanges about how religious ideas and power shape global affairs.

Interreligious Relationships

Hans Küng, a Swiss Catholic theologian who died in 2021, advanced the hypothesis that there could be no peace among nations without peace among religions. Religious tensions, which scourge over so many eons of history, could and must be brought to an end with dialogue, leading to understanding. This and other threads of reasoning have contributed to a host of very different interreligious efforts that also encompass efforts and institutions within religious traditions (ecumenical—Anglican Orthodox within Christianity, for example, Shia-Sunni within Islam) and those beyond specifically theological frameworks, termed by some "dialogue among worldviews." My report *Interfaith Journeys: An Exploration of History, Ideas, and Future Directions* (2017) traces the history of the many religious initiatives and institutions that have supported dialogue and different forms of action. Indeed, peace has been the anchor for many efforts, but the scope and ambition have widened, encompassing curiosity, efforts to benefit from the richness that plural societies can bring to specific programs, and advocacy efforts for social, political, or economic change with truly global scope. A prime example was the religiously inspired Jubilee 2000 alliances that were led by religious actors (notably the Catholic and Anglican churches), with a mission to change international approaches to poor country debt.

Interreligious efforts today span the full range, from local efforts, even within a family but more commonly local communities, to global institutions. A prominent example of a global body is Religions for Peace (RfP), founded in 1970. Based in New York City, across from the UN headquarters buildings, RfP works through regional and national interreligious councils and an elaborate representative body of co-presidents as well as trustees. RfP today defines peace broadly, well beyond the goal of absence of conflict, and indeed describes itself as the United Nations of religions. It aspires to engage with the full range of the Sustainable Development Goals (SDGs) approved by the UN General Assembly in 2015. Other prominent interreligious bodies with global scope include the Parliament of the World's Religions, which traces its history to the first such Parliament event in 1893 in Chicago, and the United Religions Initiative (URI), which prides itself on a local structure based on Cooperation Circles (CCs), which set their agendas according to local needs (Parliament of the World's Religions 2015). The King Abdallah bin Abdulaziz Centre for Interreligious and Intercultural Dialogue (KAICIID), an intergovernmental interreligious body founded by Saudi Arabia, Austria, Spain, and the Vatican (as founding observer), focuses in particular on engaging Muslim institutions and communities in dialogue to build peace.

Interreligious dialogue in its various forms plays especially critical roles in times of crisis. Leaders from different religious traditions standing side by side after, say, a church bombing or riots targeting Muslims symbolize their common commitment to building peace. Likewise, persistent efforts to help communities know and understand each other better can ease tensions and, ideally, work toward genuine social cohesion. However, such efforts can be met with cynicism—one leader recently referred to the phenomenon of "kisses and candles," and the anthem song "Kumbaya" has taken on the significance of naïve goodwill that does not produce much. Evaluation of interfaith work is especially difficult, and the counter-factual—what would have happened had dialogue efforts not taken place—can never be readily established. Many astute commentators testify to the important benefits of creative, determined work to bridge divides and to understand and act to resolve bitter memories and tensions. Addressing different forms of extremism, especially when it involves incitement to violence or direct violent action, is a central, difficult, and important theme in interreligious dialogue, as are efforts to address and calm social tensions that can incite violence and cause indelible harm, especially to minority communities.

Interreligious approaches can play significant roles in working toward democracy, even if many religious institutions themselves are not renowned for democratic approaches. Most significant and far from straightforward are religious roles in the promotion of human rights. Here, the picture is decidedly mixed. Many religious traditions, perhaps best distilled in the global ethic that Hans Kung and colleagues presented at the 1993 Parliament of the World's Religions, again in Chicago, lay claim to support core human rights principles and indeed to fundamental roles in shaping the underlying principles that lie behind them. Gender equality, not to speak of denunciation of racism, can be sticking points, but the notions of freedom of conscience and belief are seen as the very core and anchor of human rights. Divisions on issues such as rights for LGBT people and women's equality (including reproductive rights) can run deep. So can the prejudicial treatment of religious minorities in different settings and the ugly faces of antisemitism and Islamophobia.

Hate speech, which of course extends far beyond religious communities, has taken on new forms in the digital age. Addressing hate speech and incitement to violence (at best seeking to address underlying causes) are central themes for many interreligious initiatives.

An issue closely associated with democratic values is the human right to freedom of religion or belief (FoRB), or as it is more commonly known in the United States, religious freedom. The freedom to practice one's faith, to an individual's and a community's beliefs, but also the freedom to propound and to change one's affiliation are embedded in the Universal Declaration of Human Rights and other international conventions. However, the consensus on what FoRB involves and its limits is fragile, and there are distinctly polarized views on the topic (including, notably, the right to seek to convert others to one's faith and understandings of blasphemy in relation to freedom of speech). Religious freedom is thus a common theme in interreligious dialogue at many levels (see Petersen and Marshall 2019). And proselytizing is a tense topic in many settings where it is seen to undermine social cohesion.

Religion and Governance: National and Regional Arrangements

The previous discussion has focused on relationships among different religious traditions (or within them). Interreligious initiatives grapple with the challenges of assuring that different religious communities can live together in harmony in today's increasingly plural societies. These challenges vary considerably among different places and even within them. In Latin America, for example, the growing role of evangelical Christian churches can involve tensions, especially with the Catholic institutions that have long dominated the landscape. In Southeast Asia, tensions between Buddhist and Muslim communities have led to violence and forced migration, notably in Myanmar; similar tensions exist between Buddhists and Hindus in Sri Lanka. In Nigeria, religious and ethnic tensions overlap and blend in complex ways. The issues and relationships among religious communities are invariably complex, and deeply felt truth claims can make harmony among those whose claims differ hard to achieve. But in many places, with or without formal interreligious institutional mechanisms, different communities succeed in living peacefully side by side, though tensions can flare up rapidly and unexpectedly.

The backdrop of interreligious relationships impinges in various ways on the relationships between religious institutions and national governments (Marshall 2013). These relationships vary from state to state and, quite often, among local communities within a nation-state. History and power, as well as the ethos and values of each nation, play significant roles in shaping how governments and religious communities relate. Formal relationships (including whether there is an established religion that enjoys special status and privileges) are often set out in national constitutions and regulated by law, but informal relationships can also prevail. Approaches will invariably differ among countries where census data indicates that all citizens share a common religious identity, where a range of communities have long lived together, and where there is no formal reference to religious communities and institutions in any form. In several countries national identity is formally and quite tightly tied to a religious identity—Cambodia, Mauritania, and Zambia, for example. These approaches can change over time. In Latin America, for example, the formal, legal, and constitutional roles of the Catholic Church today are less prominent in constitutions than they were several decades ago.

Situations vary widely, ranging from hostile or simply ignoring religious actors to well-elaborated and established links (legally or informally). And in some situations (Iran, Afghanistan) where the political system is essentially a theocracy, religious authorities govern. Many different countries have specific mechanisms that take different forms to engage religious bodies in governance. These can apply to representative bodies like parliaments or to legal and judicial systems. The United Kingdom's relationship with the Church of England is an example, with bishops represented in the House of Lords and established government roles for approval of many religious appointments. Other areas of links on governance include nations where religious communities govern family law (Bangladesh, Israel) and collaboration in the management of health (Ghana, Zambia) and education (Ireland, the Netherlands). There are specific religious or interreligious councils in some countries that have clear links to governments, with more or less well-articulated mechanisms to assure representation of elements of the communities and the definition of processes and areas of responsibility. In many situations, governance arrangements can be worked out on an ad hoc basis, perhaps in response to a crisis or to parallel developments elsewhere.

Several regional institutions have specific provisions in their formal governance arrangements to engage with religious communities, though these are by no means universal. While the European Union (EU), for example, is a secular body with no specific religious identity or formal relationships, there are arrangements for dialogue with churches, religious associations or communities, and philosophical and non-confessional organizations. The goal is to allow an open exchange of views on policies between EU institutions and parts of European society. Few other regional organizations have comparable formal arrangements.

Transnational Governance and the United Nations

The roles of religious representation and authority in the UN orbits have been a topic of discussion since its establishment in the 1940s. Broadly, the United Nations has neither a religious identity as such nor formal mechanisms to engage religious communities in the major governance structures. But in different ways religious institutions and of course religious ideas and values are forged as part of the United Nations' history and contemporary reality. Nation-states with differing relationships with religious institutions are member states, and this variety quite often colors the different positions that nation-states take, even if they are not expressed as such. The relationships involved can be complex, with religious affiliations and power relationships at the national level coloring discourse and action at the transnational level. The most prominent examples turn around reproductive health issues and gender rights, but deeply embedded issues around security and peace-building have central importance. Debates about women's rights, the role of the United Nations in family planning, and domestic violence are among those often influenced by religious roles and are often influenced by active engagement. And religious representatives tend to be among the most active in civil society debates around the work and roles of UN agencies.

The nonreligious character of the United Nations needs, nonetheless, to be viewed with some nuance, as religious factors are rarely, if ever entirely, absent from the work of UN institutions. The Holy See, as a sovereign state, has observer status alongside member governments. The UN Educational, Scientific, and Cultural Organization (UNESCO) has a mandate that includes engagement with religious and spiritual topics (though it has exercised these with caution over the years). In the wake of the September 11, 2001, attacks on the United States, initiatives to bridge religious and "civilizational" divides and to engage religious actors in, for example, genocide prevention have led to the establishment of different mechanisms, prominently the UN Alliance of Civilizations (UNAOC). Many nongovernmental institutions with clear religious links and identities are accredited to the United Nations and participate in deliberations as part of civil society as well as in the implementation of programs.

The formal relationships of religious bodies in the United Nations have taken on new forms in recent decades. From the very outset, some argued for formal religious roles (and power) within the United Nations, with the notion of a "spiritual council" alongside the "security council" mooted (an idea that has never gained much traction). Some relationships at an "institutional" level have included a tripartite mechanism (member states, religious NGOs, and specialized agencies), an interfaith harmony week, an interagency task force that relates to religious actors, and a multifaith advisory group.

Several UN operational agencies have long-established relationships with specific religious communities. The UN Children's Fund (UNICEF) has an analytic record going back several decades documenting country-level engagement centered on protecting children and promoting their welfare. The refugee organization (UNHCR) and the World Food Program (WFP) also have worked quite closely on faith-linked operational organizations, although rarely did these partnerships explore consciously how religious beliefs and networks might be relevant for the work. The United Nations Development Program (UNDP) has a mixed history, with some administrators reaching out to religious organizations while others were less inclined to do so. This pattern of "stop and start" has been a characteristic of engagement: quite often, the focus and priority are determined in large measure by the interest of the leader.

A similar comment applies to the multilateral development banks, notably the World Bank, as well as the International Monetary Fund (IMF). The author's experience at the World Bank, with responsibility for engaging in dialogue with religious organizations from 2000 to 2006, was inspired by the World Bank's then president, James D. Wolfensohn, who launched a dialogue process in 1998. When he brought this to the attention of the Bank's Executive Directors representing member countries, with his plan to expand and institutionalize the dialogue, he met stiff resistance that reflected a wide variety of concerns, including notably the political nature of religion and its association with negative approaches to development priorities, especially gender equality and private investment as strategic pillars. Interestingly, the IMF and the Inter-American Development Bank both engaged in quite prominent dialogue processes with religious actors that did not result in a similar stir.

Religious involvement in development debates and work, both within the UN operational agencies and the multilateral banks and institutions, merits specific attention. An argument often advanced by religious actors is that they were involved in development and anti-poverty work long before today's international institutions emerged and will remain there long after the demise of these global institutions. There is some truth to this, for example looking at education and health. But the active engagement of specific groups in debates took on new features with the turn of the millennium in 2000, with its large conferences, the development of millennium development goals (MDGs), and, after the deadline of 2015 passed, seventeen Sustainable Development Goals (SDGs). This international architecture and emphasis on partnerships shone more light on the historic and present roles of religious organizations and, in turn, prompted both debate and collaboration in many areas, food security among them. This work offers the promise of shifting some focus from security and violent extremism toward the broader and more positive roles of religious communities, especially their shared concern for vulnerable communities and those mired in the deepest poverty. It would be a stretch to describe a shared vision in the form of the SDGs, and many inside and outside religious communities see them as "instrumentalizing" religious bodies by expecting them to adopt them as a mantra, but the definitions of specific goals and debates around them do provide the scaffold for both dialogue and cooperation.

In short, the involvement of religious institutions and communities in transnational governance arrangements varies quite widely. The question of formal arrangements remains ambiguous, in part because some member states have little willingness to support such formal arrangements, but practical arrangements, notably in fragile states where religious organizations tend to play especially significant roles, are seen quite frequently, generally adapted to the specific history and needs of each specialized agency and the pertinent religious actors.

An example of a United Nations–led initiative that has drawn on active and explicit religious involvement is the Rabat Plan of Action (OHCHR 2013). It centers on a set of proposals hammered out through various workshops in different regions and designed as "a practical tool to combat incitement to hatred." The challenges addressed are discrimination, hostility, and violence (outlined in article 20 of the International Covenant on Civil and Political Rights). Leadership came from the UN High Commissioner for Human Rights (OHCHR) and the Office of Genocide Prevention. The Rabat Plan of Action on the prohibition of advocacy of national, racial, or religious hatred that constitutes incitement to discrimination, hostility, or violence recommends the adoption of comprehensive nation-by-nation anti-discrimination legislation, with preventive and punitive action to combat incitement to hatred effectively. It also addresses the empowerment of minorities and vulnerable groups. The effort has involved UN special rapporteurs (Frank La Rue, special rapporteur on freedom of opinion and expression; Heiner Bielefeldt, special rapporteur on freedom of religion or belief; Adama Dieng; Mutuma Ruteere, UN special rapporteur on racism, racial discrimination, xenophobia, and related intolerance), Agnes Callamard, executive director of article 19, as well as forty-five experts from different cultural backgrounds and legal traditions.

Another UN initiative specifically focused on religious communities, this one in relation to human rights, is the Faith for Rights declaration, which has resulted in the articulation of specific commitments. In March 2017, the OHCHR launched the initiative at an expert workshop in Beirut. The aim is to "provide space for a cross-disciplinary reflection on the deep, and mutually enriching, connections between religions and human rights" and thus to "foster the development of peaceful societies, which uphold human dignity and equality for all and where diversity is not just tolerated but fully respected and celebrated" (OHCHR 2017). Religious leaders are described as potentially important human rights actors in view of their considerable influence on the hearts and minds of millions of people. The two efforts highlight the interwoven nature of religious UN relationships and common efforts to address transnational challenges.

Some religious communities have sought seats at the tables of specific global governance bodies, notably the G20 and the G7/8.[4] Informal to date to a large extent, the G20 Interfaith Forum is seeking a more formal status as an official "engagement group." Such a status would imply recognition of the significance of interreligious groups as a constituency entitled to a voice and heighten both scrutiny and communication about the views and recommendations presented.[5] For both G7/8 and G20, religious networks and communities have in different ways been part of the civil society coalitions that track meetings and processes, with a formula of leadership shared by the host country bodies and a continuing international hub. With the plethora of voices seeking to be heard in these settings, especially around the annual leaders' summits, the effort to engage, while challenging, offers a disciplined opportunity to draw on the many religiously linked or inspired networks that address different topics (refugees, climate change, and health, for example) and engage explicitly in the framing and tone of global discussions. An aspiration is to contribute not only to specifics on the agenda for particular moments and events but also more broadly to the framing of these global agendas.

Challenges Arising from Covid-19 Emergencies

The ongoing crises linked to the Covid-19 pandemic have highlighted significant issues that involve relationships between governing institutions and arrangements and religious communities and institutions at global, regional, and national levels. In some instances, a central theme has been cooperation and clarification of partnerships, while in others the dominant focus has been on tension and conflict, played out in operational matters, in the courts and legislatures, and even, in some places, in violent protests and conflicts. The testing of relationships is likely to shine a new set of spotlights on the roles that religious institutions and approaches play in the future, including in global governance arrangements (see Marshall 2020).

Public health regulations have been a centerpiece of the pandemic, especially those affecting religious gatherings in many places, as well as certain religious practices. Early understandings of the roles of large gatherings in facilitating the spread of Covid-19 infections highlighted the roles of a specific church community's gathering in South Korea and also of large assemblies of the transnational Muslim body Tablighi Islam. These events were seen as "super-spreaders," and that recognition directed attention to similar gatherings, most significantly the Hajj pilgrimage in Saudi Arabia but also others that drew large numbers of people from across the world. Decisions to restrict (Saudi Arabia) or to continue (e.g., Senegal's Mouride Magal) have affected millions, often with resounding effects. As lockdowns in various forms emerged as a central means of flattening the curve of infection spread, questions arose as to the roles of places of worship: Were they subject to public health restrictions? (Yes, in virtually all cases.) How did the communities themselves participate in decisions about the scope and duration of lockdowns? (In practice, very little.) How did communities cope with shifts to online worship? (Very differently.) What were and are lasting effects? Public health regulations (mask wearing) and recommendations were generally accepted, but significant minorities of different communities contested them or refused to follow guidelines. While in most countries, government restrictions on religious behaviors in the interests of public safety form part of agreed governance authorities, the lockdowns in particular presented these provisions in a new light and thus opened new debates.

Different religious practices have been affected by Covid-19 restrictions, with funerals and rites around death the most prominent. Government requirements to cremate the bodies of those who died from Covid-19 roused objections in Sri Lanka because of Muslim prohibitions on cremation. More broadly, the widely shared inability across many communities to mark death with traditional rituals and personal engagement has left bitter legacies, which include recriminations against what can be seen as arbitrary government interference in spiritual and pastoral care.

The active role of countless religious communities in supporting people and communities affected by the Covid-19 emergencies has opened debates about responsibilities for social protection, including its scope, financial provisions, and accountability.

Issues playing out at national levels about religious roles and responsibilities and their relationships with governments have echoed in several national and international institutions, most specifically the World Health Organization (WHO). This body has a long history of engagement but also disengagement with religious communities. Broadly, health care involves religious communities in many different ways, including direct management by religious bodies of hospitals and clinics as well as the health repercussions of different religious practices. Dialogue and engagement of various religious communities (especially Christian) have thus had obvious links to governance arrangements. The links have, however, generally been reflected in partial understandings (with gaps in knowledge and information) and arrangements that vary widely and have many fuzzy definitions and boundaries. During the Covid-19 emergencies, the WHO has focused more explicitly on religious roles, both positive (communication of messages, in particular) and negative (misinformation, vaccine resistance). The organization has taken pains to engage some religious actors both to gain from their experience and knowledge but also to avoid the common charge of using them rather than engaging them as true partners (instrumentalization).

Pandemic preparedness has been a central concern during the Covid-19 pandemic. Many epidemiologists have commented on the irony or tragedy that a disease like Covid-19 was well known to be highly likely to occur, but even so, strategic and practical preparations fell far short of what they should have been. An area of shortfall was the failure to engage religious communities, who in many situations are the primary responders in situations of crisis. Limited efforts to draw operational and policy lessons from the 2014 to 2015 Ebola pandemic in West Africa and, more broadly, HIV/AIDS are cases in point. Engaging religious communities in disaster preparedness emerges as an obvious area for future attention.

Looking Ahead?

Religious institutions and communities are very much part of global governance approaches, mechanisms, and institutions, especially when they are broadly defined. For many people and communities, religious beliefs, teachings, and practices shape relationships, attitudes toward community and authority, and the ways in which individuals and communities view life and "others," near and far. It is thus unwise, for any topic on global agendas, to leave aside or ignore religious dimensions. These dimensions are, however, commonly interwoven with other identity markers and institutional arrangements, some of which fall under the headings of culture, ethnicity, and class. The links and influencing factors may be straightforward in some instances, for example where a specific religious minority community is central to a conflict or a legal instrument, but far more often the roles are interwoven and complex. Defining what roles religious factors play in a place or on a topic is rarely straightforward.

More specifically and narrowly, religious roles in formal transnational institutions and mechanisms vary widely. This chapter has focused on the ways in which national governance arrangements influence and shape the roles that religious institutions, actors, and beliefs affect or are part of global governance institutions, notably the United Nations and its operational arms as well as regional institutions and entities like the G7/8, G20, and even the G7+ (fragile states). These arrangements vary from formal (the UN Alliance of Civilizations or Interfaith Harmony Week) to far less formal and firmly established. They tend to be quite dynamic (rather than stable and well defined), changing over time.

Some transnational religious bodies can be viewed as part of an overall portrait of contemporary global governance. Specific religious communities exert considerable influence on global affairs. The Catholic Church plays significant roles, through its communications and moral sway but also its diplomatic arm. The Organization of the Islamic Community (OIC) is not a religious institution but is influenced both by religious teachings and power structures. The World Council of Churches (WCC) seeks to influence and shape significant agendas, for example on food security. The International Network of Engaged Buddhists (INEB) aims precisely at that—engagement—both to shape the underlying values behind governance and to address specific policies, like dam construction and educational curricula. Interreligious institutions, notably RfP, aspire to be part of global governance structures at many levels, exemplified in its commitment to human rights and to the framework of the UN SDGs, which address wide-ranging global agendas.

It is often and aptly asserted that religion is "part of the problem" and "part of the solution." Sorting out which is which is fraught with political and ethical challenges. The religious landscape includes a wide array of ideas, institutions, and leaders that reflect the community governance (often crossing nation-state boundaries) of their adherents. Many seek to influence laws or to govern specific areas (family law, for example). Some religious communities, especially interreligious institutions, seek more active engagement in global affairs. Their authority and the objectives they seek are contested, for example if they might involve incitement to violence or go against the international norms reflected in the Universal Declaration of Human Rights. Religious institutions also are, in practice, significant actors in many areas of governance, with health, climate change, and peace being the most readily appreciated examples. These challenges do spill over into the broader questions of why and how religious institutions belong at global governance tables.

Right-sizing and mainstreaming religious engagement in global governance is thus a continuing challenge. Areas for reflection necessitate efforts to engage in the full complexity and diversity, past and present, of the religious landscape. Assuring both meaningful "religious literacy" among global governors and "governance literacy" for engaged religious leaders is an essential prerequisite for strategic action on the topic, alongside savvy awareness of the complex political dimensions that are involved. As a broad comment, the many aspects of religious engagement in global governance institutions are better addressed on a case-by-case basis, rather than seeking or aspiring to an overall approach.

Key Discussion Areas

- Examination of the ways in which national governance arrangements influence and shape the roles that religious institutions, actors, and beliefs affect or are a part of global governance institutions.
- Religion and religious beliefs addressed and involved in UN actions and decisions.
- Indispensability of considering religion and religious beliefs and ritual when designing a program or implementing a policy.
- Roles played by religious rituals in the spread of Covid-19 and highlighting the importance of integrating religious actors to successfully implement policies.

Notes

1 Religion and Diplomacy, https://religionanddiplomacy.org/ (accessed September 1, 2023).

2 "Multi-faith Advisory Council Hosts Global Conference on 75th Anniversary of the United Nations," www.peacemakersnetwork.org/multi-faith-advisory-council-hosts-global-conference-on-75th-anniversary-of-the-united-nations/ (accessed September 1, 2023).

3 "2020 Evidence Summit on Strategic Religious Engagement," USAID, last updated April 28, 2021, www.usaid.gov/faith-and-opportunity-initiatives/2020-evidence-summit-strategic-religious-engagement (accessed September 1, 2023).

4 The G8 was an intergovernmental political forum from 1997 to 2014 that incorporated Russia into the G7.

5 The author is a vice president of the G20 Interfaith Association.

References

Huntington, Samuel. 1993. "The Clash of Civilizations?" *Foreign Affairs*, Summer 1993, www.foreignaffairs.com/articles/united-states/1993-06-01/clash-civilizations (accessed September 1, 2023).

Marshall, Katherine. 2013. *Global Institutions of Religion: Ancient Movers, Modern Shakers*. New York: Routledge.

———. 2017. "Interfaith Journeys: An Exploration of History, Ideas, and Future Directions." *Berkley Center, Georgetown University*, February 23, 2017, https://berkleycenter.georgetown.edu/publications/interfaith-journeys-an-exploration-of-history-ideas-and-future-directions (accessed September 1, 2023).

———. 2020. "What Religion Can Offer in the Response to COVID-19." *World Politics Review*, May 26, 2020, www.worldpoliticsreview.com/religion-and-covid-19-faith-during-a-pandemic/ (accessed September 1, 2023).

———. 2021. "Religion and Development." In *Handbook on Religion and International Relations*, edited by Jeffrey Haynes. Cheltenham, UK: Edward Elgar Publishing.

Office of the UN High Commissioner for Human Rights (OHCHR). 2013. "Between Free Speech and Hate Speech: The Rabat Plan of Action, a Practical Tool to Combat Incitement to Hatred." *United Nations*, February 21, 2013, www.ohchr.org/en/stories/2013/02/between-free-speech-and-hate-speech-rabat-plan-action-practical-tool-combat (accessed September 1, 2023).

———. 2017. "The Beirut Declaration and Its 18 Commitments on Faith for Rights." *United Nations*, https://jliflc.com/resources/the-beirut-declaration-and-its-18-commitments-on-faith-for-rights/ (accessed September 1, 2023).

Parliament of the World's Religions. 2015. "Towards a Global Ethic: An Initial Declaration," https://parliamentofreligions.org/global-ethic/towards-a-global-ethic-an-initial-declaration/ (accessed September 1, 2023).

Petersen, Marie Juul, and Katherine Marshall. 2019. "The International Promotion of Freedom of Religion or Belief: Sketching the Contours of a Common Framework." *Danish Institute for Human Rights*, April 5, 2019, www.humanrights.dk/research-project/report-international-promotion-freedom-religion-belief-sketching-contours-common (accessed September 1, 2023).

Pew Research Center. 2012. "The Global Religious Landscape." December 18, 2012, www.pewforum.org/2012/12/18/global-religious-landscape-exec/ (accessed September 1, 2023).

31

GOOGLING RELIGIOUS GUIDANCE

Digitally Renegotiated Lay–Ascetic Relations in Contemporary Jainism

Dr. Tine Vekemans

Introduction: The Internet as a Market of Ideas

In the initial frenzy of positivity that surrounded the rise of the commercial internet, this new technology was heralded as a democratizing force, allowing voices to be heard that would otherwise remain censured and bypassing existing hierarchies of wealth and power to profoundly level the playing field of ideas. However, this early unbridled enthusiasm was tempered as time and research indicated that the internet was being shaped by human and corporate agents. As such, in large part, the internet mirrors society as it exists offline (Laidlaw 2015, 3). Although digital media have certainly opened up possibilities for certain voices to be amplified, to become more accessible or even omnipresent, it is often rich and powerful organizations that are able to invest more in an extensive and professionally constructed online presence. Subsequently, the digital realm also reproduces and reinforces existing hierarchies: individuals and smaller groups presenting countercurrents and alternative interpretations find themselves as stuck in the digital margins as they had been on the offline fringe. In addition to the degree to which the creation and maintenance of a digital presence is prioritized and professionalized, online visibility and findability are dependent on the algorithms behind search engines, which contain certain biases pertaining to language, geo-location, and moment of entry—biases that combine to favor older, English-language websites hosted in the United States above others (Halavais 2009; Vaughan and Thelwall 2004). While it did not universally mature into the nonhierarchical and open space of ideas wished for by some, the internet and subsequent digital technologies did impact the ways in which information and knowledge could be found and shared and greatly facilitated transnational communication. As such, the extent to which the rise of digital media changed not only the cultural, economic, social but also religious lives of people around the world cannot be overestimated.

The impact of the internet and digital media on religious organization and experience has been an expanding topic of research since the early days of internet research (for an overview, see Wagner 2012 and Campbell and Altenhofen 2016). The ongoing development, increased accessibility, and functional diversification of digital media have prompted

DOI: 10.4324/9781003316077-38

a continually evolving body of literature. Whereas the earliest works dealt with various forms of discussion groups (Helland 2005; Krüger 2005), subsequent waves of research looked into websites (Scheifinger 2008, 2018), social media (Cheong et al. 2012), and apps (Campbell et al. 2014; Wagner and Accardo 2014; Cheong 2014; Fewkes 2019). The subfield of digital religion also includes work on aspects of South Asian religious traditions, such as Buddhism (Grieve and Veidlinger 2014), Hinduism (Balaji 2018; Zeiler 2019), Sikhism (Kumar 2012), and Jainism (Vekemans 2014, 2019a, 2020; Vekemans and Vandevelde 2018). This body of research indicates that more and more adherents of a variety of traditions, as well as students, policy-makers, and others, use digital media to look for religious information, community, resources, and guidance, rendering the question of which information is most easily available or visible online especially pertinent. In this light, the field of religious media studies has also examined the democratizing versus conservative potential of digital technologies (e.g., Campbell 2007; Cheong 2013). Such research reveals how the tendency toward a mirroring of offline hierarchies and power balances intersects with the fact that the attitudes of religious actors and organizations regarding digital media differ, with some seeking to reap their full benefits immediately, some adopting new technologies hesitantly after doctrinal scrutiny, and others stressing perceived negative aspects of digital technologies and remaining weary or aloof. As such, more progressive, reform-minded organizations and organizations already engaging or seeking to engage a geographically broad, international membership are often more inclined to focus on the potential benefits and invest in a solid digital media presence.

Media Innovations and Religious Repositioning in South Asia

Arguably, the introduction of each new media form has had an impact on religious life and the transmission of religious and other ideas. Discussing earlier media innovations (print, comics, recordings, television, and film) and their impact on South Asian religious traditions, Lawrence Babb points out that these media have greatly increased the physical and social mobility of religious ideas and concepts ("information-bearing symbols") in South Asia (Babb 1995, 3–4). Babb further indicates that "mechanical or electronic exigencies particular to a given medium" may affect the content transmitted and that the embedding of traditional content within a new medium is likely to affect audience perception (Babb 1995, 4). More than a quarter century after Babb's assessment was first written, the processes he describes remain valid. The digital content discussed in this chapter illustrates a further—perhaps exponential—increase in mobility. At the same time, the representation of religious content in digital media entails a selection and restructuring of the information and symbols governed by the idiosyncrasies and biases inherent to digital media, on the one hand, and the uneven adoption of digital technology by religious actors, on the other. Just like the introduction of the printing press, the adoption of the internet and subsequent digital technologies has, thus, impacted the way a religious tradition is defined, studied, experienced, organized, and transmitted. Given the scale and scope of digital media today, the impact of these technologies is particularly high.

Subsequently, digital media are likely to—subtly or radically—alter the way religious actors are positioned with regard to others—proximate others, such as other sectarian groups, teachers, and followers belonging to the same tradition, and external others, such as religious actors belonging to different traditions or academic and government "outsiders" looking in. This dual internal and external repositioning corresponds with a bifurcation in scholarly work on religion and governance—that is, works dealing with governance as internal management of religious organizations, groups, and communities (e.g., Wirtz 2017; Keplinger and Feldbauer-Durstmüller 2016) and those dealing with governance in the sense of religious actors spreading views of how public life and the state should be managed (e.g., Metcalf 2010; Pal and Tok 2019). The remainder of this chapter examines the impact of digital media on lay–ascetic relationships past and present within the South Asian religious tradition of Jainism. It therefore deals mostly with religious governance in the internal sense—that is, it examines potential shifts in power balances within mendicant orders and within this specific religious community. However, as will become clear throughout the discussion of Jainism's engagement with digital media presented here, the digital realm has also become an important platform for spreading broader societal views based on Jain principles, connecting the material closer to the second, external interpretation of religion and governance.

The proposed case study is particularly interesting to the study of religion and media in general, as it illustrates how religious customs and traditional injunctions can muddy the digital waters, at once inhibiting digital media use and amplifying its impact. It shows digital media as spaces where religious content as well as religious relationships reemerge in—subtly or radically—altered, negotiated, and reconstituted forms. After an exploration of the religious injunctions that complicate engagement with digital technologies in Jainism, this chapter will provide an overview of digital content and practices relating to Jain mendicants and present some insights on the use and impact of these new digital forms in the lives of lay Jains. In the concluding section, this chapter will reiterate the findings presented in this chapter and draw tentative conclusions regarding the impact of mendicant digital engagement on the internal dynamics of the Jain tradition and the way it is perceived by others.

Lay–Ascetic Relations in the Jain Tradition

Jainism[1] became prominent in South Asia from the sixth century BCE. It has a strong focus on the individual soul's path of purification toward enlightenment and the escape from further cycles of reincarnation. Although Jains have always been a minority in South Asia,[2] the tradition has endured and thrived up to the present day, generating important contributions to the philosophical and literary life in South Asia. It has continued to evolve and develop into two main sub-traditions,[3] which are further subdivided into a myriad of smaller groups. The emphasis on austerities and asceticism found in many doctrinal texts and early mendicant-centered accounts of Jainism has determined much of the academic work on the tradition. However, this focus risks leaving large parts of the actual practices and day-to-day customs of both the lay and mendicant community undiscussed. More recent anthropological and lived religion approaches have worked to correct this historical myopia.[4]

Sociologically, the Jain community is said to consist of four groups: the male and female lay community—often termed "householders," and male and female renouncers.[5] Although the principles[6] Jainism stands for are identical for lay Jains and ascetics alike, the way these principles are translated into rules and vows differs significantly. The rules set forth for lay adherents are to an extent flexible to facilitate their responsibilities to family and society. The rules for those who choose a life of asceticism and seek initiation into a monastic order are more stringent. For example, whereas the vow of *aparigraha* means that a layperson is encouraged not to make more profit than they need and not to become attached to material goods, *aparigraha* for the ascetic community translates into an injunction against the handling of money as well as the ownership of any personal property at all and the necessity to lead a peripatetic existence for most of the year. Whereas the cardinal value of nonviolence, or *ahiṃsā*, results in a strict vegetarian (and increasingly, vegan) diet for the lay community, it informs the wearing of face masks for most Jain ascetics, as well as a number of various injunctions prohibiting Jain ascetics from cooking, traveling by mechanical means, and so on. Within both the lay and ascetic communities, customs and behavior can vary quite widely. Although all Jains hold to very similar soteriological categories and beliefs, there is no central governing body or authority in Jainism to set binding rules.

Traditionally, the lay and ascetic communities are intertwined through their mutual service. Lay people give alms of food to wandering ascetics, provide services as needed, and supply them with medication when necessary. Monks and nuns of any rank are venerated by the lay community as symbols of the Jain path, as they are said to have advanced further on the way to liberation than regular householders can. In addition, some monks and nuns are very learned and are often sought out for both worldly and spiritual guidance (Babb 2016, 54, 62–63). Although the two parts of the Jain community are thus intricately connected, the extent to which Jain monks and nuns should be involved in lay affairs is also a point of discussion, with some groups within the tradition emphasizing the individuality of the spiritual path and counseling against mendicant involvement in worldly affairs, and others stressing the important role monks and nuns can play in guiding the lay community in addressing their personal and societal problems. Early Jain texts seem to have taken the former stance (Dundas 2002, 173). This discussion also has a clear impact on aspects of hierarchy and governance in Jainism. However, even when the value of ascetic involvement in the lay community is promoted, the potential role ascetics can take up in this regard is traditionally limited by practical constraints brought on by their limited numbers[7] and peripatetic lifestyle.[8] Especially in smaller towns and places with a limited number of Jains, sightings and contact with monks or nuns could be a rare occasion for lay Jains. Devoted lay Jains could of course seek out mendicants by following them on their wanderings or visiting them where they spend the rainy season. However, this requires a significant effort on the part of the lay devotee. There have always been ways in which lay Jains could engage with mendicants in their absence, namely—on an intellectual or ideological level—through the philosophical and literary works written by Jain mendicants and—on a devotional level—in the form of funerary monuments (*padukas*) and statues, as well as paintings of popular monks.

Questions of Propriety and Compromise in the Use of Digital Devices

As technology developed, these traditional modes of interaction-in-absence transformed and multiplied. Calendars and pictures of monks and nuns appeared on the market, as did first printed, then audio-recorded, and ultimately video-recorded *pravachans* (lectures, preaching) (Little 1995, 254–83). As discussed previously, this greatly increased the mobility of religious symbols. The coming of digital technology has further facilitated this kind of circulation, expanding the scope of both the type of content that can be shared and the scale on which it can be made available. It also enabled new kinds of mediated contact with mendicants through mobile phones, WhatsApp, live streams, and so on. However, as with previous new technologies, the adoption of digital technologies within the Jain community is an open-ended and uneven process of negotiation. In the absence of a central governing body or overarching authority, each mendicant group—each individual Jain even—delineates their own permitted mode of digital engagement.

First, media use between the lay and ascetic communities differs greatly, and, second, there are significant differences between sects and groups of ascetics or mendicants. The Jain lay community in India as well as overseas, in the diaspora, is generally highly educated and technologically savvy. By contrast, Jain ascetics traditionally do not make use of technology. The reason for this is dual. First, upon entering the monastic state, Jain ascetics forsake all worldly possessions (with the exception of bare essentials such as robes, a water pot, and a brush), making ownership of a personal computer or smartphone impossible. Second, the use of electricity, considered a form of fire, is seen as something that inherently involves violence and is to be minimized or avoided entirely by mendicants (Cort 2001, 55). As such, the use of microphones, cameras, computers, and mobile phones by mendicants, and by lay followers at the request of mendicants, has been a point of fierce debate. However, the degree to which ascetics avoid any electrical appliances (microphones, lights, and fans) and digital devices (computers and smartphones) now varies from individual to individual and from ascetic order to ascetic order.

Those orders that allow their initiates to make use of digital devices and develop a digital presence usually circumvent the injunction against personal property (an application of the principle of *aparigraha*) by having a lay follower be the official owner of the device or putting such a lay follower in charge of making, updating, and running websites and social media accounts. The objections based on the implications of electricity (related to the principle of *ahiṃsā*) are more difficult to work around. The reason for allowing the use of technology is that the potential positive effects the (indirect) use of some electrical equipment by monks and nuns, their digital media presence, and their global accessibility can have in the lives of the lay community outweigh the degree of *hiṃsā* caused. As such, these allowances are often part of a package of reforms undertaken by groups seeking to play a more active role in lay society and to reach out beyond the subcontinent to Jains living in the diaspora. Indeed, in such cases, a robust (negotiated) digital media presence and digitally accessible religious or spiritual leadership are often combined with a loosening travel restriction for (some) mendicants and the organization of educational programs that actively engage the lay community. Groups that combine these types of reforms include the Amar Muni Sampradāy,[9] the Śvetāmbar Terāpanth,[10] and various guru-led movements.[11] However, many groups that otherwise uphold traditional customs regarding travel do make some allowances for technology, and indeed, many of the most popular mendicants on YouTube belong to sects and groups not otherwise considered especially reformist or heterodox. The use of microphones and recording materials, once rare, has become widespread, and slowly the use of mobile phones and computers is also gaining ground. In some cases, the development of a more engaged digital presence may be a strategy to keep the more traditional groups within Jainism relevant to lay Jains with limited face-to-face access to ascetics.

Mendicant Media Presence

Digital Resources on Jain Mendicants

Photographs of monks and nuns, sometimes with descriptions of their mendicant lineage and background, were present on some of the earliest websites on Jainism (e.g., Jainworld.

com, launched in 1996). Wallpapers and audio and video recordings of mendicants preaching, leading meditation sessions, or singing devotional songs followed as technology developed. The resources described here can be conceptualized as passive forms of media involvement on the part of Jain mendicants. Some content is produced without them taking an active part in the creative process at all, but in the case of pictures, audio recordings, or video recordings, the mendicant is fully involved at the time the content is created. However, after their creation and initial launch or broadcast, the content acquires a life of its own, beyond the control and intent of its creators. After its first launch, a video *pravachan* is likely to be shared through official and private channels, popping up in different contexts and eliciting various responses from different audiences.

Whereas websites were the main event until the first decade of the twenty-first century, social media platforms and mobile applications have recently become the main repository of such materials. This shift is of course informed by the development of new technologies, but the opportunities for collaboration and interaction social media provide also fit well into the strategies of organizations and actors who want to appeal to a broader, global audience. Additionally, the use of smartphones as primary internet devices, which is especially salient in India, is likely to reinforce the move toward apps and social media platforms, as they are often easier to access and content-wise better geared toward use on smaller screens in an on-the-go environment. As illustrated in the examples given below, clusters of content occurring across different platforms are very common, either because content is shared and reposted by different users or because the same individual or organization shares content on different platforms, hosting a website and a mobile application, as well as maintaining social media pages and channels.

Websites dedicated to a single ascetic tend to be developed by individual devotees. Lay followers with the necessary technological skills may undertake the development of such a personal page unbidden, as an act of piety and devotion toward their guru, but this is more often done at the request of the ascetic. Often, such websites become miniature portal sites (e.g., shantivijay.org), including the monk's life story, audio and video links, digital versions of books and pamphlets, and many pictures. Some Jain organizations led by mendicants, or those that have "resident" or inspirational monks or nuns, also provide similar information and resources. These websites are usually professionally maintained. One example is Digambar Jain Trilok Shodh Sansthan's (Digambara Jain Institute of Cosmographic Research) website, www.jambudweep.org, dedicated to a Digambara Jain pilgrimage destination at Hastinapur, near Delhi. A significant portion of the website consists of resources on Gyanmati Mataji, a Digambara Jain nun, and her first disciple Chandanamati Mataji, including their writings, biographies, lectures, and devotional songs. Another example is Veerayatan's website veerayatan.org, which, although focusing on the organization's charity and education activities, also includes a section on ācārya Shri Chandanaji and the other nuns, as well as publications. Lastly, some large general websites on Jainism include basic information on Jain mendicants from different traditions, with some including features that facilitate traditional in-person lay-mendicant interactions such as Jain mendicant locators and information on the area the mendicant is traveling through or the city in which they are spending *cāturmās*.

It is clear that many of these websites are no longer updated regularly or have become defunct altogether. Indeed, although the Śvetāmbara Terapanth is generally well-represented and active in the digital realm, their self-proclaimed official site, www.terapanthinfo.com, which presents a wealth of resources on the order's current ācārya Mahashraman, has not been updated for some years. This is indicative of a shift in digital media use, away from large, static, and often text-heavy websites, toward social media platforms with interactional, multimedia, and dynamic content features on the one hand and mobile applications with their signature focus on a single functionality and tendency toward very little text on the other.

Indeed, Facebook pages and YouTube channels dedicated to Jain monks and nuns and their teachings have become very prolific. Again, we can differ between pages, channels, and apps dedicated to an individual monk or nun, and pages, channels, and apps belonging to a Jain organization but containing a significant portion of Jain ascetic-related content. In the first category, the Ratnaworld channel[12] shares and broadcasts videos of Śvetāmbara ācārya Vijay Ratnasundersuri Maharaj Saheb. New content is added daily, and the channel has 149,000 subscribers. It is not uncommon for a new video to reach 4,000 views within 24 hours. Another very popular channel was that of Digambara Monk Tarun Sagar, on which his discourses were shared up until his death in 2018.[13] On Facebook, pages devoted to individual mendicants are common. For example, Digambara ācārya Shree Vasunandiji has a group, an organizational page, and a public figure page.[14] Organizational channels that contain ascetic-related content are legion, especially since the sudden move toward online and virtual events brought on by the Covid-19 pandemic (Vekemans 2021; Maes 2021). Many Jain *sanghs* in India and beyond have taken to recording or livestreaming lectures, for example the *pravachans* delivered during the *paryuṣaṇ*[15] festival. The Śvetāmbara Terapanth YouTube channel (active since 2015)[16] has more than 80,000 followers, with some videos—mostly *pravachans*—getting close to 500,000 views. New content is uploaded several times a day. The channel also refers to a mobile application for both iOS and Android operating systems,[17] which provides a selection of videos and a wealth of other types of resources relating to Jain ascetics and Jainism in general. Parasdham's channel[18] mostly features *pravachans* by the Śvetāmbara ācārya Namramuni Maharaj Saheb and has more than 72,000 subscribers. The organization also features a website and two apps with similar content.[19]

Digitally Mediated Personal Contact

Moving one step further, digital media also enable new forms of direct contact between lay Jains and Jain ascetics. As a growing minority of mendicants starts to make use of mobile phones and laptops, they can be contacted by and engage with lay followers regardless of their respective location. This further loosens the constraints their peripatetic lifestyle imposed on contact and personal involvement with lay followers. With digital devices in the hands of lay attendants, Jain mendicants can stay in touch with and provide guidance for followers in Mumbai, Dubai, or London while walking from village to village in Rajasthan. Different types of digitally mediated communication are used, including phone calls and email. However, WhatsApp remains perhaps the most popular platform.

Digitally mediated communication between ascetics and laypeople can take different forms. It can be a top-down one-to-many speech on WhatsApp, Zoom, Facebook Live, or YouTube live broadcast, which differs from a prerecorded YouTube video due to its feeling of closeness stemming from the synchronicity of the event and the (often limited) opportunity for interaction with the speaker through the comments or chat function, or through verbal interpellations (depending on the allowances of the platform used). On these same platforms, we find more interactional events geared toward multidirectional communication, such as Q&A sessions or group discussions that include Jain mendicants. Whereas recordings of many such larger-scale instances of digitally mediated communication with Jain mendicants end up available online for asynchronous viewing and become a digital resource akin to the ones described above, one-on-one communication usually remains private. It is through such digitally mediated contact—which can take the form of email correspondence, text messages, WhatsApp chats, or video chat—that individual guidance is usually sought and personal relationships are developed. As ethnographic research on this matter is limited in scope, it is impossible at this point to quantify this type of communication. However, in my own limited-scope fieldwork in India and the Jain diaspora, I encountered different mendicants who used a digital device (carried by a lay follower who traveled with the mendicant group) to interact with laypeople in different ways, and the vast majority of my lay Jain respondents (over 80 percent) indicated that they knew of mendicants that could be reached this way. In about 25 percent of these cases, they had actually experienced digitally mediated communication with mendicants. Most of those who had not experienced such interactions said they did not see the need to instigate such conversations, as they had other avenues for seeking guidance or advice (Vekemans 2019b, 10–12). Only a minority felt that digitally mediated communication with mendicants was inappropriate.

Lay Appraisals of Digital Interactions

> Because we go to India for a short time, so you don't have that much interaction, you don't get to go to a lot of discourses. So I think those monks and nuns that are using electronic media . . . you know, traditionally they might be against it but obviously they've adopted it. . .. For us from our perspective, in the west. It is a really good thing.

The excerpt from an interview I conducted with a lay Jain in London illustrates that lay Jains too are aware of the tenuous relationship between mendicants and technology. What is more, the rigid adherence to doctrine by those individual ascetics and monastic orders that do not engage with technology or digital media at all tends to be admired by laypeople. However, this admiration does not translate into a rejection of the online resources and digitally mediated avenues of communication that are now available. Indeed, their popularity is evidenced by the number of dedicated websites, channels, pages, and apps, as well as the number of views, downloads, and shares, and by ethnographic research (Vekemans 2019b, 2020). However, metrics such as the number of views tell us little about how lay Jains and others are interacting with the digital artifacts or how they experience digitally mediated contact with mendicants.

Arguably, it is precisely the modalities of these interactions that are important vectors when seeking to describe changes in the lay-ascetic relationship and assessing their overall impact. Babb touched on these modalities when emphasizing the need to consider audience perception of religious content embedded within a new medium but also pointed out that, despite fears of a total disengagement or loss of meaning due to the dis-embedding from traditional ritual and social contexts, most research reported only limited distortive effects (Babb 1995, 4). Limited work has been done trying to investigate what the potential distortive effects of the re-embedding of religious content in the digital realm actually are. My own small scale ethnographic work in India, but mostly in the Jain diaspora in the United Kingdom and North America (2014–2020), revealed a wide range of reasons that motivate lay Jains to go online and find pictures or watch *pravacans*, examined their search and selection strategies, and indicated a number of aspects traditionally attributed to religious activities and interactions that my respondents felt to be distorted or lost in the digital realm.

The reasons my respondents watched *sādhūs* and *sādhvīs pravacans* were often a combination of different factors. Some approached them mainly on an intellectual level, as a means of accessing doctrinal teachings and Jain philosophy, whereas others integrated videos and other resources into their regular devotional praxis, often performed in a designated prayer room or house temple. Some respondents in the diaspora emphasized the emotional support they found while watching or listening to recordings of *pravacans*. For such viewings, devotional attachment or intellectual content are less relevant, and they do not require a religious or devotional setting. Indeed, one exchange student indicated he watched this type of video while studying to make him feel less homesick and lonely and stay motivated. Another respondent was in the habit of listening to *pravacans* while cooking, because it made her feel connected to Jain culture and the community she grew up in.

Although the set-up and semiotics of watching an online *pravacan* are arguably rather different from the devotional, ritual, and social dimensions of attending a live *pravacan* in person, devotional, ritual, and social aspects are nonetheless still present in most reported uses of the YouTube *pravacans*, albeit not always to the same extent, and in a somewhat reconstituted way. For some, the nature of the digital devices themselves detracts from the atmosphere of solemnity and concentration necessary for serious religious engagement. For others, communal and social aspects, or indeed the multisensory experiences that come with attending in-person events, are lacking. The sharp rise in digital events brought on by the Covid-19 pandemic provided additional insight into what aspects of religious activity are felt to be distorted or missing online. However, as pointed out above, such objections did not as a rule keep people from taking part and interacting with these online resources, although they do impact the ways in which lay Jains experience these interactions.

Interestingly, what is available seems to be a more important factor than sectarian background when it comes to selecting *pravachans* to watch, and although some respondents stick to videos by a favorite ascetic, many follow and/or watch content by different mendicants from various traditions.

> I listen to the *samaṇī-jīs*. And I listen quite frequently to Rakeshbhai [Rakesh Jhaveri of SRCMD] and I find him very, very, very interesting. He uses a lot of humor, a lot of wit and because he's traveled around the world, he understands the lifestyle here. I also listen to Ācārya Ratnasunder Mahārāj . . . and a little bit to Namramuni but I like Ratnasundar more.

Although this respondent identifies as a Digambar Kāñjī Svāmī Panth devotee, he names Śvetāmbara *samaṇīs* and monks, as well as a lay guru, among his favorite speakers. This crossing of traditional sectarian boundaries is not uncommon, in line with Babb's conclusions regarding social mobility, and in some cases perhaps also informed by pan-sectarian tendencies popular in parts of the Jain diaspora. It can also be interpreted as a side effect of the partial dis-embedding of content from its traditional sectarian and devotional context.

Conclusion

Digital media have made it easier to access and share religious content. They have made the resources discussed above available 24/7 to anyone with a digital device. Those that feel the need to can regularly communicate with Jain mendicants year-round. This proliferation of information about Jain ascetics and their teachings, as well as a significant rise in the accessibility of some of them, arguably brings the ascetic community into the world of lay Jainism, and into the broader society, in new and more intense ways. This chapter set out to probe the impact of the round-the-clock online availability of lectures and teachings, and the increased personal accessibility of some Jain ascetics to their lay constituents on the traditional relationships that govern the fourfold Jain community. It started out by examining how religious customs and sensibilities have influenced the adoption of digital media in Jainism. Based on data derived from ethnographic fieldwork and an analysis of online content available on different platforms, it provided the reader with an overview of different types of digital engagement by Jain mendicants today and discussed the way lay Jains respond to these types of engagements.

Although ethnographic work in different locations in India and the diaspora, as well as an analysis of online content, has confirmed a gradual and partial adoption of technology—passive and active—by Jain mendicants, as well as an increase in digitally mediated communication between lay Jains and mendicants, it is difficult to quantify the changes in lay-mendicant relationships such technology has brought about. The popularity of broadcasted lectures on television and YouTube and the rate at which they are shared on WhatsApp and similar platforms indicate a significant, global audience year-round. The semiotics of watching a YouTube lecture on a mobile phone screen arguably differ from the traditional set-up of a mendicant's *pravachan*. Although these "digital artefacts" lose some degree of the devotional, ritual, and intentional aspects of real-life lay-mendicant interactions, they do acquire a life of their own, beyond the control or intent of the mendicant or indeed the producer, circulating and arousing intellectual, devotional reactions in the audiences they encounter.

In a clear departure from the traditional patterns of contact between the lay and mendicant communities, temporal and spatial limitations stemming from rules regarding a mendicant's mostly peripatetic lifestyle become less relevant in the digital realm, and interactions are often—though not always—more casual and less ritualized than they would be if taking place in person. The ease of access, degree of anonymity, and limited range of content available also influence the composition of digital audiences, which tends to transcend sectarian boundaries (attracting Jains belonging to different groups, but also non-Jains) much more easily than traditional in-person events would.

All of this points to a significant influence of digital media on lay-mendicant relationships in Jainism, as well as on the way Jainism is likely to be encountered and perceived by others. As some mendicants and mendicant orders have negotiated traditional injunctions, allowing them to engage with digital media, mendicants have become much more visible, their teachings much more accessible, and their taking up an active role in lay-society much more likely. The fact that not all groups within Jainism have taken to digital media in equal measure does mean that some voices and interpretations are more pervasive online, whereas others may be absent altogether. Taking into account just how many Jains at least occasionally use the internet to engage with the tradition, this digital self-selection process is likely to affect the power balance between different sects and interpretations at present and in the foreseeable future.

Although some Jain organizations have a clear and well-thought-out strategy regarding their digital presence, and actively seek to be more visible and appeal to larger audiences, others maintain a more amateur, ad-hoc approach to digital media (as evidenced by the significant number of defunct or semi-defunct websites and irregularly updated social media pages and apps). There is no overarching plan to use digital media to drive the Jain tradition in any particular direction. Indeed, as Jainism knows no central hierarchy or overarching authority, such an organized endeavor seems highly unlikely to ever occur. Rather, any changes in the course of Jainism influenced by mendicants' digital presence will occur as the result of large numbers of individual decisions regarding the opportunities, allowances, and challenges posed by digital media in a religious setting. As this process is ongoing, and taking into account the increasing importance of digital media as a means by which people seek to engage meaningfully with different aspects of religion—that is, to study, practice, find resources, connect with coreligionists, and so on—it is vital to keep an eye on these developments, as they are and will remain an important factor in shaping contemporary Jainism.

Key Discussion Areas

- The expected and real impact of the internet in democratizing the backward and unheard sectors of society.
- The role and the extent of acceptance of media in religious spaces and people.
- A case study of Jainism and the impact of religious customs and traditional injunctions to digital media.
- The use of emerging technology by religious groups to connect with people with similar beliefs from across the world.

Notes

1 For a robust general introduction into most aspects pertaining to Jainism and the Jain tradition, I refer to the handbook by Paul Dundas (2002). More specialized content can be found in Bril's recent *Encyclopedia of Jainism* (Cort et al. 2020).

2 The last census of India, conducted in 2011, consultable on censusindia.gov.in, reported Jainism to be the religion of 0.37 percent of the population (just under 4.5 million individuals). However, there are concerns that not all Jains report their religion unambiguously in the census. In addition to this, it is assumed that between 250,000 and 300,000 Jains live outside India, in the diaspora (Jain 2011).

3 The tradition has split into Digambara and Śvetāmbara sub-traditions. Although the two now differ on quite a few doctrines and practices, one of the most significant differences is reflected in the names: Digambara (literally "clad in sky") refers to the fact that this sub-tradition's monks are naked, whereas Śvetāmbara ("clad in white") refers to the white garments worn by monks and nuns of this sub-tradition.

4 The anthropological turn in the study of Jainism, with scholars combining the study of texts with ethnographical methods, gained momentum at the turn of the twenty-first century. Important contributions along this line are John Cort's *Jains in the World* (2001), Whitney Kelting's *Singing to the Jinas* (2001), and Marcus Banks's *Organizing Jainism in India and England* (1992).

5 I use the gender-neutral terms "ascetic" and "mendicant" interchangeably to refer to Jains who have taken full initiation as monks and nuns. The terms most commonly used to denote monks and nuns in Śvetāmbara Jainism are *sādhū* and *sādhvī*, respectively, whereas Digambara Jainism tends to speak of *muṇi* and *āryikā*.
6 Jainism puts forth five main values, which translate into vows and rules of conduct for the entire community. These five fundamental principles are *ahiṃsā* (nonviolence), *satya* (truth), *asteya* (non-stealing), *brahmacharya* (chastity), and *aparigraha* (nonpossession).
7 Kirsti L. Wiley mentions 11,000 Śvetāmbara ascetics (2,400 monks and 8,600 nuns) and 1,000 Digambara ascetics as of 1999 (2004, 17). It is generally assumed that the numbers have been growing steadily since then.
8 Even though not all Jain sects put this rule into full practice, it is considered proper for Jain monks and nuns to wander around, seeking alms from pious Jain families and preaching as they go. Only during the rainy season of *cāturmās* are they allowed to spend some sedentary time. For the lay-community, these four months are a chance for closer contact with the ascetic community (cf. Wiley 2004, 66; Dundas 2002, 216).
9 Progressive *Śvetāmbara Sthānakvāsī* mendicant lineage established by Amar Muni. After his death, this was the first group to appoint a female ascetic—Chandanā-jī—to the rank of ācarya. This group has founded the Veerayatan charity, which runs a number of medical, environmental, and educational programs in India and abroad. The senior ascetics of this group occasionally travel abroad and take on an active role in the charity's projects.
10 Śvetāmbar Sthānakvāsī ascetic group, founded in the eighteenth century by ācārya Bhikṣu, and, uniquely, still unified under one ācārya. This order has given rise to a number of organizations, of which Jain Vishva Bharati, a Jain educational charity, is the most prominent one. The Śvetāmbara Terāpanth also includes an intermediate-level novice ascetic called *samaṇ* (m.) and *samaṇī* (v.). These monks and nuns take most of the vows full ascetics take but do not have to lead a peripatetic life, and are allowed to travel, handle money and digital devices, and provide their own food if necessary. This enables them to study at universities, visit Jain communities in the diaspora, etc. After some time, mostly at their own request and after receiving permission from the order's ācārya, most *samaṇ* and *samaṇī*s take full initiation.
11 These are a special category that is tangential to the discussion presented in this chapter, as the gurus who lead these movements are laypeople who are considered to have reached a state of complete self-realization but are not bound by the injunctions and customs that govern Jain mendicancy. However, as they tend to be very active online, cultivate a global following, and rely on a—mostly digitally mediated—personal relationship between the guru and each follower, guru-led groups deserve to be mentioned here for completeness' sake. The currently most prominent ones are both inspired by the figures of Śrīmad Rājchandra: Shrimad Rajchandra Mission Dharampur, led by Rakesh Jhaveri, and Rajsaubhag, led by Bhaishree.
12 www.youtube.com/c/Ratnaworld (accessed September 3, 2023).
13 www.youtube.com/channel/UCQ2-NYg2edCXQTgCPfAM0ew (accessed September 3, 2023).
14 www.facebook.com/groups/vasunandiji/ (accessed September 3, 2023).
15 An eight-to-ten-day festival during the rainy season, during which Jains invest extra time in religious observances and meditation. Digambars refer to this festival as *Das Lakṣaṇa*.
16 www.youtube.com/c/Terapanth (accessed September 3, 2023).
17 https://play.google.com/store/apps/details?id=com.santronix.terapanth (accessed September 3, 2023).
18 www.youtube.com/c/parasdhamtv/featured (accessed September 3, 2023).
19 Namramuni Mahārāj Saheb is a Śvetāmbara Sthānakvāsī ascetic (*Gondal sampradāya*). In addition to the YouTube channel mentioned here, his organization, Parasdham, has a website (www.parasdham.org), a WhatsApp group, and mobile applications for both Android and iOS operating systems

References

Babb, Lawrence A. 1995. "Introduction." In *Media and the Transformation of Religion in South Asia*, edited by Lawrence A. Babb and Susan A. Wadley. Delhi: Motilal Banarsidass Publishers.

———. 2016. *Understanding Jainism*, Indian edition. Mumbai: Hindi Granth Karyalay.

Balaji, Murali, ed. 2018. *Digital Hinduism: Dharma and Discourse in the Age of New Media*. London: Lexington Books

Banks, Marcus. 1992. *Organizing Jainism in India and England*. Oxford: Clarendon Press.

Campbell, Heidi A. 2007. "Who's Got the Power? The Question of Religious Authority and the Internet." *Journal of Computer-Mediated Communication* 12(3): 1043–62.

Campbell, Heidi A., and Brian Altenhofen. 2016. "Methodological Challenges, Innovations and Growing Pains in Digital Religion Research." In *Digital Methodologies in the Sociology of Religion*, edited by Sariya Cheruvallil-Contractor and Suha Shakkour. London: Bloomsbury Publishing.

Campbell, Heidi A., Brian Altenhofen, Wendi Bellar, and Kyong James Cho. 2014. "There's a Religious App for That! A Framework for Studying Religious Mobile Applications." *Mobile Media & Communication* 2(2): 154–72.

Cheong, Pauline H. 2013. "Authority." In *Digital Religion: Understanding Religious Practice in New Media Worlds*, edited by Heidi A. Campbell. London: Routledge.

———. 2014. "From Cyberchurch to Faith Apps Religion 2.0 on the Rise?" In *Feminist Cyberethics in Asia: Religious Discourses on Human Connectivity*, edited by Agnes M. Brazal. New York: Palgrave Macmillan.

Cheong, Pauline H., Peter Fischer-Nielsen, Stefan Gelfgren, and Charles Ess, eds. 2012. *Digital Religion, Social Media and Culture: Perspectives, Practices and Futures*. New York: Peter Lang.

Cort, John A., Paul Dundas, Knut A. Jacobsen, and Kristi L. Wiley, eds. 2020. *Brill's Encyclopedia of Jainism*. Leiden, the Netherlands: Brill.

Cort, John E. 2001. *Jains in the World: Religious Values and Ideology in India*. Oxford: Oxford University Press.

Dundas, Paul. 2002. *The Jains*, 2nd ed. London: Routledge.

Fewkes, Jacqueline, ed. 2019. *Anthropological Perspectives on Religion and Mobile Apps*. London: Palgrave Macmillan.

Grieve, Gregory P., and Daniel Veidlinger, eds. 2014. *Buddhism, the Internet and Digital Media: The Pixel in the Lotus*. London: Routledge.

Halavais, Alexander. 2009. *Search Engine Society*. Cambridge: Polity Press.

Helland, Christopher. 2005. "Online Religion as Lived Religion, Methodological Issues in the Study of Religious Participation on the Internet." *Heidelberg Journal of Religions on the Internet* 1(1): 1–16.

Jain, Prakash C. 2011. *Jains in India and Abroad, A Sociological Introduction*. New Delhi: ISJS.

Kelting, Whitney. 2001. *Singing to the Jinas: Jain Laywomen, Mandal Singing, and the Negotiations of Jain Devotion*. New York: Oxford University Press.

Keplinger, K., and B. Feldbauer-Durstmüller. 2016. "Monastic Approach to Governance and Leadership: A Literature Review." *International Journal of Strategic Management* 16(1): 39–60.

Krüger, Oliver. 2005. "Discovering the Invisible Internet: Methodological Aspects of Searching Religion on the Internet." *Heidelberg Journal of Religions on the Internet* 1(1): 1–27.

Kumar, Priya. 2012. "Sikh Narratives: An Analysis of Virtual Diaspora Networks." Working Paper. Prais: e-Diasporas Atlas.

Laidlaw, E. B. 2015. *Regulating Speech in Cyberspace: Gatekeepers, Human Rights and Corporate Responsibility*. Cambridge: Cambridge University Press.

Little, John T. 1995. "Video Vacana: Swadhyaya and Sacred Tapes." In *Media and the Transformation of Religion in South Asia*, edited by Lawrence A. Babb and Susan A. Wadley. Delhi: Motilal Banarsidass Publishers.

Maes, C. 2021. "Jain Life Reimagined: An Examination of Jain Practice and Discourse during the Covid-19 Pandemic." *Entangled Religions* 12(3), https://doi.org/10.46586/er.12.2021.9179.

Metcalf, Barbara. 2010. "Religion and Governance in India—A Comment." *South Asia Journal of South Asian Studies* 33(1): 1–12, https://doi.org/10.1080/00856401003592446.

Pal, Leslie A., and M. Evren Tok, eds. 2019. *Global Governance and Muslim Organizations*, 1st ed. London: Palgrave Macmillan.

Scheifinger, Heinz. 2008. "Hinduism and Cyberspace." *Religion* 38(3): 233–49.

———. 2018. "The Significance of Non-Participatory Digital Religion: The Saiva Siddhanta Church and the Development of Global Hinduism." In *Digital Hinduism: Dharma and Discourse in the Age of New Media*, edited by Murali Balaji. Lanham: Lexington Books.

Vaughan, Liwen, and Mike Thelwall. 2004. "Search Engine Coverage Bias: Evidence and Possible Causes." *Information Processing & Management* 40(4): 693–707.

Vekemans, Tine. 2014. "Double-Clicking the Temple Bell: Devotional Aspects of Jainism Online." *Heidelberg Journal of Religions on the Internet* 6: 126–43.

———. 2019a. "From Self-Learning Pathshala to Pilgrimage App: Studying the Expanding World of Jain Religious Apps." In *Anthropological Perspectives on Religion and Mobile Apps*, edited by Jacqueline Fewkes. London: Palgrave Macmillan.

———. 2019b. "Roots, Routes, and Routers: Social and Digital Dynamics in the Jain Diaspora." *Religions* 10(3): 252, https://doi.org/10.3390/rel10040252.

———. 2020. "Jainism on the Internet". In *Brill's Encyclopedia of Jainism*, edited by John E. Cort, Paul Dundas, Knut A. Jacobsen, and Kristi L. Wiley. Leiden, the Netherlands: Brill.

———. 2021. "Crisis and Continuation: The Digital Relocation of Jain Socio-Religious Praxis during the COVID-19 Pandemic." *Religions* 12(5): 342, https://doi.org/10.3390/rel12050342.

Vekemans, Tine, and Iris Vandevelde. 2018. "Digital Derasars in Diaspora: A Critical Examination of Jain Ritual Online." In *Technology and Religion in Historical and Contemporary South Asia*, edited by Knut A. Jacobsen and Kristina Myrvold. London: Routledge.

Wagner, Rachel. 2012. *Godwired: Religion, Ritual and Virtual Reality*. New York: Routledge.

Wagner, Rachel, and Christopher Accardo. 2014. "Buddhist Apps: Skillful Means or Dharma Dillution?" In *Buddhism, the Internet, and Digital Media: The Pixel in the Lotus*, edited by Gregory Price Grieve and Daniel Veidlinger. London: Routledge.

Wirtz, Peter. 2017. "Governance of Old Religious Orders: Benedictines and Dominicans." *Journal of Management History* 23(3): 259–77, https://doi.org/10.1108/JMH-02-2017-0007.

Zeiler, Xenia, ed. 2019. *Digital Hinduism*. London: Routledge.

32

FIVE-DIMENSIONAL MATRIX OF FAITH-BASED GOVERNANCE

Arpan Yagnik

Introduction

Faith-Based Governance (FBG) is a macro-level manifestation and expansion of an innate consciousness beginning from the self and extending to the society and beyond. FBG is the need of the hour because the incessant disintegration of morals and integrity in governance and the rampant myopia in regards to the forms and purpose of governance are impacting living and nonliving entities in the most unfortunate way. The intellectual faculty of sentient beings, especially humans, is becoming obsessively concentrated toward disproportionate and mercurial "having" and "possessing." The five-dimensional matrix conveys a way of self and societal governance that inspires newer, more evolved forms of governance.

This chapter introduces the reader to examples of faith-based governance (FBG). To do so, it starts in the south of India, moves to the Vatican, then back to the north of India. This chapter briefly elaborates on the understanding of the construct of faith and the faithfuls before sharing the vision and guiding principles of FBG. In addition, this chapter also expands the scope of faith by relieving the construct of its strict adherence to theistic scholarship.

This chapter also introduces the five-dimensional matrix of FBG, with its core focus on neutrality as a selected lens for such governance. It introduces five spectrums to understand the pulls that individuals and groups have on them that take them away from a pure form of FBG. This chapter ends with a hope for increased harmony and progression toward enhanced consciousness and encourages the reader to explore and imagine the manifestation of the five-dimensional matrix in several twenty-first-century global governance scenarios.

From India to the Vatican and Back

The following three examples of FBG cover a broad time period of human history. Their uniqueness gives the reader an insight into the vast breadth of FBG—its scope, intensity, and nature as it manifests in different parts and times across the globe.

DOI: 10.4324/9781003316077-39

Auroville

On February 28, 1968, four sentences were scribbled on a chit of paper. The chit was written in French and titled "Charter d'auroville" (the Auroville Charter), as shown in Figure 32.1.

For the next half a century, these four sentences that form the Auroville charter would go on to successfully demonstrate a different, plural, and possible way of governance to the world.

Auroville is a town with an experimental form of governance in the south of India that still runs today. The Mother, who was the spiritual successor of Sri Aurobindo and whose signature you see in Figure 32.1, was instrumental in creating Auroville. Auroville is situated in Pondicherry (now Puducherry), which was colonized by the French. And even today, many streets are referred to as rues, just like in France. Auroville is a unique form of FBG in that it does not have much to do with conventional aspects of faith. There is no real or concrete notion of God or religion that drives this endeavor. Rather, such governance is driven by an understanding of a divine[1] consciousness that pervades the cosmos and its living beings such as us. To what extent it manifests within a human varies extensively. Auroville exists as a recognized and celebrated entity within the jurisdiction of the Republic of India.

Translation of the Auroville Charter

1. Auroville belongs to nobody in particular. Auroville belongs to humanity as a whole. But, to live in Auroville, one must be a willing servitor of the Divine Consciousness.
2. Auroville will be the place of an unending education, of constant progress, and of youth that never ages.
3. Auroville wants to be the bridge between the past and the future. Taking advantage of all discoveries from without and from within, Auroville will boldly spring toward future realizations.
4. Auroville will be a site of material and spiritual research for a living embodiment of actual human unity.

Faith in the divine consciousness drives Auroville's system of governance. According to its official website, "Aurovilians apply the ideas of the Auroville Charter in their daily life, in policy-development, and decisions, big and small."[2] Although physically located in the Republic of India, at the time of Auroville's conception, representatives from 124 different nations and 23 Indian states got together to deposit a handful of their native soils into an urn as a symbol of the global nature of Auroville.

The fact that the town can belong to nobody in particular: even if you are granted a space of land for building your home, once you pass away, it goes back to Auroville. This system established a solid foundation for eliminating much of the trouble arising from different forms of accumulation for oneself and for one's near and dear ones. The clear and definitive aim of making Auroville a place for unending lifelong learning and exploration sustains it and preserves it as a testimony of human-enabled harmony and progress. These four principles and faith in these principles have given the world a fine example of FBG working toward the development and achievement of human consciousness devoid of nativist[3] compulsions.

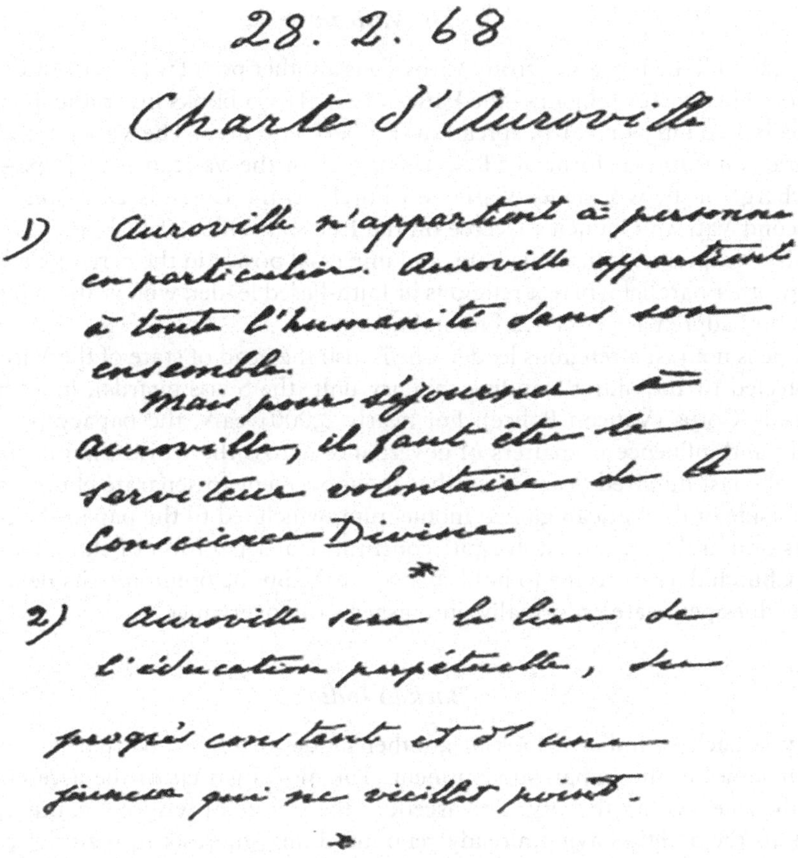

28. 2. 68

Charte d'Auroville

1) Auroville n'appartient à personne en particulier. Auroville appartient à toute l'humanité dans son ensemble.
Mais pour séjourner à Auroville, il faut être le serviteur volontaire de la Conscience Divine.

*

2) Auroville sera le lieu de l'éducation perpétuelle, du progrès constant et d'une jeunesse qui ne vieillit point.

*

3) Auroville veut être le pont entre le passé et l'avenir.
Profitant de toutes les découvertes extérieures et intérieures, elle veut hardiment s'élancer vers les réalisations futures.

*

4) Auroville sera le lieu des recherches matérielles et spirituelles pour donner un corps vivant à une unité humaine concrète.

Figure 32.1 Charter d'auroville

Source: www.auroville.org.

The Vatican

Roughly 7,252 kilometers away from Auroville is another popular form of FBG, in this case one anchored in a major religion—the Vatican City. Trivia books invariably list the Vatican as the smallest country on earth, spread over a 0.44 km^2 area. The Vatican is considered a much more conventional form of FBG. The leader of the Vatican—the pope—is the ultimate in charge of the worldwide Catholic Church. In the *Christus Dominus*, also known as the Second Vatican Council's Decree on the Pastoral Office of Bishops, it is stated that the pope has "supreme, full, immediate, and universal power in the care of souls." There is hardly any other parallel where a religious or faith-based leader, who is also a human, holds such a level of supremacy over 1.2 billion humans.[4]

The pope is not just a religious leader—he is also the head of state of the Vatican. Hence, he is protected by the oldest standing military unit (the Swiss guards), in addition to the Gendarmerie Corps (Vatican Police). For nearly 2,000 years, the papacy possessed a lot more clout and influence in matters of governance across the world than it does today. It is only in the last hundred years or so that the movement to separate church and state in nations outside of the Vatican gained momentum, which led to the papacy being restricted to matters of morality and faith. Despite constitutional separation of church and state, the Catholic Church does continue to hold sway over the public opinion of its believers, which sometimes does permeate, informally, into aspects of governance.

Back to India

We take you back to India to look at another model of FBG, one that has existed since the ancient times in the Indian subcontinent. The model is that of the ascetic outside the city and the ruler within the city. The ascetic is the source of wisdom, counsel, and direction. Due to the ascetic having already renounced any interests in material pursuits, the ascetic was believed to be a genuine well-wisher of the kingdom with no vested interests. The ascetic also did not have an interest in ruling or governing. Hence, the ascetic was endowed with respect; the ruler or king showed utmost faith in the ascetic and the counsel they offered in matters pertaining to governance. A high level of faith was bestowed on the ascetic essentially for displaying stern courage in making the unimaginable sacrifice of renouncing any and every aspect of material pursuits.

Another important aspect was that wise and deeply spiritual people were living outside of a kingdom and guiding a king for the overall welfare of his people. By virtue of their power of knowledge/wisdom, they would sometimes prevail over the king's wrong decisions and ensure a course correction. The last time a major kingdom conducted its affairs based on ascetic counsel—only three hundred years ago—was during the reigns of Chhatrapati Shivaji and Swami Ramdas. The *Ramayana* and *Mahabharata*, the two Sanskrit epics of Indian literature, serve as excellent examples from ancient India of FBG.

Faith

Most discussions of faith are often about and within theistic religious literature and practice, and generally they stand for faith in God. But at a generic level, faith signifies a concept of trust—trust or confidence in a thing or concept and described in a context independent of theistic belief systems. It can stand for participation, devotion, and love for an object or concept.

Faith is "a planetary human characteristic involving the capacity to perceive, to symbolize, and live loyally and richly in terms of, a transcendental dimension to human life" (Smith 1979). Some of the many dimensions of the concept of faith, according to the *Stanford Encyclopedia of Philosophy*, include affective, cognitive, and evaluative dimensions.

Affective: Faith is a feeling of existential confidence and an affective psychological state (i.e., a feeling of trust).

Cognitive: Faith is a knowledge of certain aspects of truth. In organized religion this is the truth as revealed in the religious literature.

Evaluative: This dimension identifies faith as a type of belief.

The concept of faith may be somewhat relieved from its general application in theistic religious traditions. In secular, humanistic, and nontheistic contexts, it may be seen as "an outcome of the inborn propensity to self-conservation and self-betterment which is a part of human nature" (Tennant 1943/1989, 111). It is a universal human value, we argue, because it has independently flourished among geographically distant individuals and groups with no connection to each other whatsoever. Faith is a type of universal human value that "ventures beyond the apprehension and treatment of data to supposition, imagination and creation of ideal objects, and justifies its audacity and irrationality" (Tennant 1943/1989, 110).

Faith also needs to be discussed in conjunction with spirituality, which is defined as something greater than an individual. It is related to the spirit of the holistic nature of the universe, which is cosmic. Human spirituality has three aspects: relationships, values, and life purpose. Therefore, faith involves experiencing a certain type of spirituality, which encompasses a sense of connection with the rest of humanity, nature, and the cosmos.

Who Are the Faithful?

Scholars and practitioners of faith have described the faithful as those who have faith in the human community and the evolving human potential and prospects of their cognitive growth and morality. This may also include the grand and thoughtful passions of life and a life lived according to those passions. The faithful see the world around them as "benign and life as meaningful." (Solomon 2002). The faithful adhere firmly and devotedly to

1. the welfare of all beings including nonhuman entities,
2. equality,
3. freedom in the sense that people should have an opportunity to live full and meaningful lives,
4. genuine democracy, and
5. the belief that people should be active agents in creating a just and inclusive world and cosmos.

Individuals and communities that identify and live according to the above are to be construed as the faithful in the context of this chapter.

Faith-Based Governance

Faith-based governance is a macro-level manifestation and expansion of an innate consciousness beginning from the self and extending to the society and beyond. The beauty of FBG is that it is neither exclusively present in the individual nor in society. It simultaneously occurs in both and in their dynamic interaction.

Vision of Faith-Based Governance

In the vision of FBG, each unit is a self-organizing unit in accordance with the highest ideal(s) it can envision and collaborates with other (neighboring) units for harmony, growth, joy, and expansion of ideals. FBG encompasses all aspects and units of human society on the entire planet.

It is critical that proper understanding and this chapter's definition of certain terms are explicitly stated to avoid misinterpretation.

Unit: Unit of a human society is a conscious entity of relevance. Units include individual, family, clan, and self-organizing groups and associations; groups whose members have common characteristics or interests; businesses and corporations; institutions of education, health services, law and order, and scientific pursuits; political units and government bodies at the local to the global level; nations; international organizations; and more.

Ideals: An ideal is perceived and set in human consciousness as something not yet achieved but worth striving for. Ideals, in which we put our faith, are derived from the partial or complete realization of intuitive and self-evident truth that the entire universe, with its animate and inanimate objects, is the manifestation of one balancing entity.

The balancing entity: The balancing entity supports, guides, enters, and upholds the universe from within a unit. It has also come to mean the constantly evolving universe, of which human society is a conscious peak. The balancing entity or force is also the pluralistic interpretation of the unmanifested that is conceptualized by different religions in their highest revelations, which they have termed the Divine, God, Goddess, Allah, Brahman, Vishnu, Shiva, Krishna, Satchidananda, Tao, and more.

Aspects of human society: Aspects of human society include physical, ethical, moral, emotional and sentimental, mental and intellectual, religious, spiritual, and more.

Guiding Principles for the Framework of Faith-Based Governance

The following are recommendations for guiding principles that can serve as a framework for a version of FBG:

- Harmony and joy exist for all, excluding none, recognizing that human existence is intricately and inseparably linked to the welfare of subhuman animal and plant life.
- All are my sisters and brothers, and the entire world is my family.
- All cherish freedom as I do: to live, to set ideals and pursue them, to conceptualize and worship the balancing entity (divine) according to the level of consciousness.
- Knowledge, power and authority, and physical resources are to be viewed in their ultimate origin as divine and have to be used only for overall benefits to human society, recognizing that physical resources are not unlimited, nor are they evenly available or produced in all regions of the earth.

- Governance must be truly democratic nature, where each member of each unit has equal rights and representation and has a mechanism to exercise those rights and representation.
- It must be truly self-organizing, in that each member of each unit is aware of and consciously carrying out their duties toward their unit.
- Education and training on "Guiding Principles for the Framework of FBG" is a continuous process for all.

Five-Dimensional Matrix of Faith-Based Governance

The five-dimensional matrix of faith-based governance (5D-FBG) offers a nuanced version of FBG. 5D-FBG is made up of dimensions with spectrums that draw attention to aspects of humans and humanity. These spectrums are intrinsically pertinent to global governance. Global governance is no longer only a matter of regulation of trade and commerce-related transactions, cooperating on matters of peace and security, or collaborating on innovations for making human existence easy; rather, it is a mindful state of existence that is persistently fighting the gravitational pull of the pleasures of the aspects on the spectrum.

The dimensions and their extremities on the spectrums are the given labels (for example, sympathy and apathy are the two extremities in the spectrum of one of the five dimensions). As a reader, refrain from applying the literal or denotative meaning of the words to the labels because these are simply labels and symbols. A complete reading of these discussions is a prerequisite for grasping the holistic view of the meanings behind the matrix, the spectrums, and the labels. Labels such as arrogance and ignorance refer to a state of social and individual being with several in-depth nuances.

Figure 32.2 provides a visual representation of the 5D matrix. Each line is a different in color and structure because it is a symbol and provides a certain meaning. The appearance

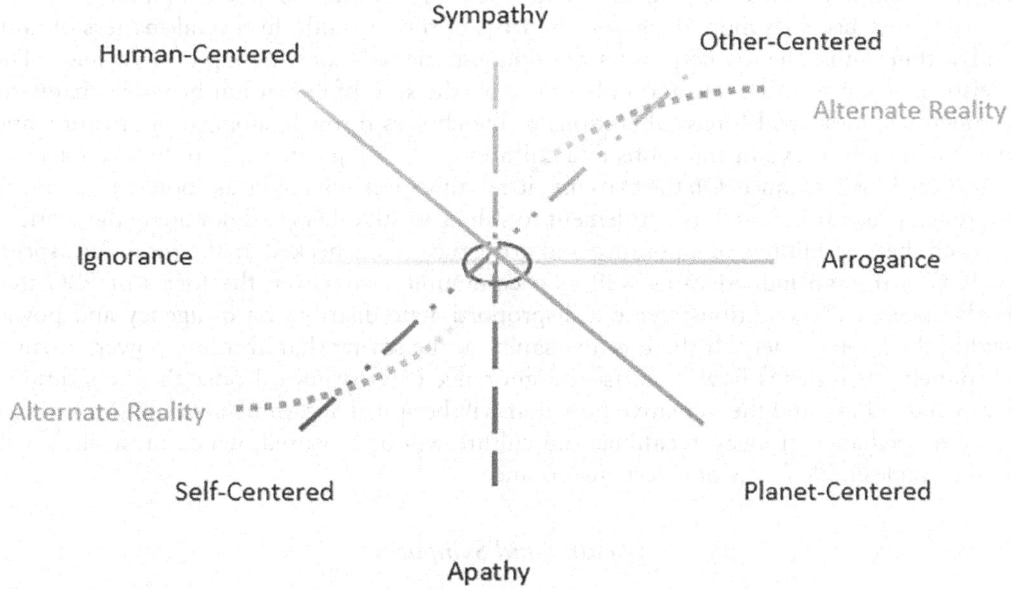

Figure 32.2 Five-Dimensional Matrix of Faith-Based Governance

Source: Author.

and the disappearance of the line, too, are symbolic, as is the presence of the solid line and that of the dotted line. The colors of the line, too, are carefully chosen.

Ignorance and Arrogance

The spectrum representing ignorance and arrogance relates to the presence or the absence of—as well as the abundance or dearth of—awareness, knowledge, comprehension, realization, and cognizance. A thorough lack of the above can be referred to as a state of ignorance. Hence, the line fades and ultimately disappears. Being in a state of ignorance is perilous because one cannot effectively sift between what is true and what is false or what is right and what is wrong.

The state of ignorance effectively nullifies critical thinking and processing. It gives importance to authority, and as long as the source is some kind of authority, an ignorant will put faith in it. Blind faith in many anachronistic practices and rituals is most likely a result of ignorance mixed with some aspects of pressure and respect within a given cultural setting. Ignorance can be in a particular field/area or in several fields/areas. Ignorance does not have to be a "thorough absence" of awareness. One can be on different levels of ignorance, as suggested by the fading lines.

Arrogance, which is on the other side of the spectrum, emerges from an abundance of awareness, knowledge, comprehension, realization, and cognizance. The condition of arrogance blocks change and transforms faith from fluid to solid as well as less amenable. The condition of arrogance comes about when dogmas and other forms of unquestionable tenets are formed. In the short run and in exceptional circumstances, the condition of arrogance can act as a saving grace—but that will never be the case in the long run. Arrogance is believed to come into existence not just when there is an abundance of knowledge and awareness; it can also manifest itself when one mistakenly believes that one has or knows it all.

Arrogance becomes more dangerous in areas of theistic faith. In several matters of faith and within faiths, the divine powers are unquestionable—contributing to arrogance. The theistic arrogance of the one and only one sows the seed of expansion bias that manifests through conquests and forced alterations of life choices through subjugation, torture, and the elimination of extant traditions and cultures of the subjugated group. Ego can also be substituted for arrogance. On the extreme side of this spectrum are ideas about a given race's supremacy over others and its entitlement to subjugate all others and dominate the world.

Both these conditions of ignorance and arrogance, if unchecked, make room for aspects of FBG within an individual as well as a community. However, the forms of FBG that evolve from such conditions create a disproportionate distribution of agency and power within the larger society. If there is any sanity in the saying that absolute power corrupts absolutely, then this is how it starts—in ignorance or arrogance. Under these conditions, many individuals and their creative potential will be stifled and suffocated. Notions of free and fair exchange of ideas, meaning, and culture will be censored, which most likely will lead to undesirable forms of macro governance.

Apathy and Sympathy

The conditions of apathy and sympathy apply to an individual more so than to a society. Both labels here signify the different decision-making choices and the probable consequences resulting from them. The condition of apathy signifies a decision-making process that is devoid of emotion or attachment. Such decisions are based on logic, reason, evidence, reality, and facts. Apathy arises from a lack of connectedness, a lack of some relationship. It is a form of indifference and does not consider the sentiments, emotions, and attachments of others because it sees them as obstructions in the way of linear progress. Historical injustices and current prejudices are all outcomes of such apathy. In the condition of apathy, an individual embraces a linear nature of progress.

The condition of sympathy is where an individual rejects the linear nature of progress. The nature and route of progress or development can be circuitous or stagnant as long as the decisions are providing sufficient or at times unreasonable amounts of consolation and relief for the sentiments, attachments, and emotions of others according to an individual. Notions of revenge that require one to have an eye for an eye and a life for a life would qualify to be part of the sympathy extreme of this spectrum.

Sympathy can cloud judgment if too many emotions are involved. It is well known that killing other people is not going to bring back the person you have lost, but when the sympathy condition has a sufficient gravitational pull on a person, they will be unable to make a reasonable choice. Another aspect is that an individual will not think twice before compromising the aims and goals of good governance for the sake of sympathy his kin.

Other-Centered and Self-Centered

The other-centered and self-centered labels apply to and are restricted to humans only. This spectrum draws parallels with aspects of individualistic cultures and collectivistic cultures. Unlike the other spectrum of planet-centered and human-centered labels, the self-centered and other-centered spectrum does not extend to species, organisms, and extant natural resources of the planet. The label "self-centered" reflects a state of existence where an individual and their expressions, manifestations, outputs, entitlements, and even whims reign supreme. This supremacy may, at times, extend to other individuals of a person's choosing, which is most likely going to be the people that look and behave like them. As long as there is abundance and bounty, this approach survives with negligible conflicts. But as soon as scarcity raises its ugly head, dynamics change. People that will gang up and seek refuge in numbers will be the ones that will initially prevail over the lone wolves. But eventually this too will lead to conflicts between groups over resources because there is no prevailing attitude for compromising or sharing.

The other-centered approach is where the needs, happiness, desires, whims, and more of other humans take precedence. But the other-centered label goes beyond where every policy and every governance-related decision puts the needs of others front and center. This extremity comes with its own set of challenges. When everyone is willing to forgo their own needs, there is an uncanny vacuum. There is natural cohesion where all can rally and put themselves behind chasing a certain need. All this also creates a lack of direction. This lack of direction can also likely lead to frustration and angst, but a solution is unlikely to emerge rapidly. The lines of the spectrum and their colors are representative of the nature of this particular spectrum. The line toward other-centered ends with a light-colored dot, whereas the line toward self-centered ends with a dark, solid chunk of line.

Human-Centered and Planet-Centered

The planet-centered label is for a state of existence where the needs and requirements of the planet are front and center for every policy and every decision. Much of the consumerism that is prevalent would not have come into being if humans were governed by a planet-centered approach, because most of the products are not what the planet needs or gains from—on the contrary, they exist at the cost of the stability and sustainability of the planet.

The planet-centered approach here would consistently strive to not disrupt a natural order in whatever form it exists. It is likely that this would come at the cost of certain aspects of human progress. An individual or a community would strive to live much more in harmony with nature and other species. Such harmony is possible from an individual's or a community's side, but how do we know if it is reciprocated equally by other species as well? Our limited ability to communicate with and understand other species has not yet led us to believe that an extreme version of this approach would be beneficial for the survival and sustenance of humankind.

The human-centered approach, by contrast, is a state of being where human needs and priorities gain precedence over that of the planet. There is no hesitation or reluctance in looking at the planet and its resources as mere tools for human progress, not as companions in coexistence. The human-centered label further extends challenges by unwillingly creating gradations and preferences among our companion species. The ones that help us, support us, and nourish us will be given extra care and be considered a strategic ally, whereas the rest are treated with indifference.

The essential piece that the human-centered state of existence misses out on is that each and every entity, from the most microscopic to the most gigantic, is here for a reason and plays an integral part in keeping ecological sanctity. From a governance point of view, this approach will lead to rapid progress but will also be equally dangerous because, as of yet, we humans do not have anywhere but this planet to inhabit.

Alternate Reality and Alternate Reality

Alternate reality is a label for the infinite variations of possibilities other than the current one in which one lives. On both sides are possibilities that vary in intensity from a given current possible reality. Alternate reality is represented as an S-shaped curve and not a straight line because it is fluid and not linear. The reason for it is that it can bend and take different shapes depending on the imaginative capability of a unit or a collection of units. It exists in possibilities but not in reality. Hence, the line starts disappearing as it approaches reality. As soon as the alternate reality stops being a possibility, it also stops being alternate reality and instead becomes the reality.

The pull to challenge and alter the status quo is an inherent drive and characteristic of humanity. This fits well in the model because although in FBG one puts faith in something static—be it ideals or a version of the balancing entity—it is always at play in catalyzing to prioritize progress and evolution. The staticity of reality is always at odds with the dynamism of the alternates.

(0,0,0,0,0) AKA Neutrality

Each of the ten labels exerts a natural gravitational pull over individuals and communities, where they get drawn to one or some of these conditions in different intensities. Individuals, communities, societies, and nations keep moving in different positions in the matrix with the passage of time in different patterns and trends. Some individuals oscillate between two, whereas others keep revolving. Some move gradually, while some jump from one position to land in another position. The bottom line is that hardly anyone is able to fight the outward gravitational pull of the extremes of the matrix. But it is the element of compassion, as explicated in the first three guiding principles of FBG, as well as in the characterization of the faithful, that is the game changer here. Compassion of a spiritual nature goes above and beyond the individual or the unit itself and supplies the needed superhuman avidity and ardor to balance priorities and actions for the self in conjunction with others.

FBG in its purest form can never lie in any other position but in neutrality(0,0,0,0,0). This is where an individual or a community has successfully been able to nullify the pulls of the labels. The area denoted by the red circle is graphically and mathematically represented by (0,0,0,0,0). And that is the operationalization as well as the definition of neutrality.

Neutrality comes into existence when any unit is able to withstand the pull of the dimensions and, with indifference to the dimensions, is able to sustain itself in the (0,0,0,0,0) coordinates. When the dimensions have no sway over the unit and its decisions, actions, policies, and pursuits, neutrality comes into existence. Absolute and thorough neutrality is the fertile ground for FBG to survive and thrive. This is where one can hope to achieve the vision of FBG and transcend toward the elevation of the collective conscience, where the achievement is collective, and the expression is individual.[5]

Summary

Clearly, neutrality is the key to FBG. Without neutrality, all versions of FBG remain biased and skewed by unduly advantaging a being or a group of beings over others and by disadvantaging the remaining some or all. A foundational crack in governance is bound to, over time, develop into a fissure, bringing much dismay and disorder to the units. Neutrality is the way to avoid foundational cracks. Neutrality is difficult to achieve but not impossible. It is also energy-consuming because one must constantly fight against the pull of the dimensions.

Neutrality has to permeate individual life and consciousness. The trust form of faith must now operate within units to believe and be loyal to the notion that the other unit is doing its utmost best and is loyal to manifesting the sentiment of neutrality within its life and consciousness. This is the tricky part, because although the achievement is collective, the expression of the upliftment of consciousness and adherence to neutrality must happen at the individual level. The individual or a unit may not see any direct benefit in doing or being so, but the collective of units will realize the benefits of it.

Neutrality in its many forms is quintessential for the uncorrupted and untarnished governance of units and for encouraging them to learn and realize the highest ideals that their extant consciousness can make available to them.

The present is the maker of the future, and at the same time, the present is also a barrier in the formation of the desired future.[6] The five dimensions and their perennial existence will continue to present themselves as a barrier, but through neutrality units can harmonize. Once harmonized, steady progress can be made toward identifying the pulls of the dimensions and addressing them in multiple aspects of governance.

I ask individuals and leaders that are involved in governance and are interested in its evolution to chart their current governance style, policies, plans, and pursuits on the five-dimensional matrix. Once you get the coordinates, the path forward is clear. The destination is (0,0,0,0,0). The red circle or the zone of neutrality is where the purest version of faith-based governance can come into being.

Acknowledgement

I want to acknowledge the foundational and sustaining support of Parashar Dwivedi to this project. I thank Abhinav Dwivedi for not only being there throughout the project but also in guiding me to find my footing when I could not, while in pursuit of unpacking faith-based governance. I also thank Priti Dave and Kalpesh Naik for indulging at length with me in dialogues that helped me refine and crystalize many ideas presented in this chapter. Lastly, I want to thank Srinivas Melkote, my respected adviser, for diving into these deep waters and co-discovering a few pearls on the way.

Key Discussion Areas

- An overview of faith.
- The vision of faith-based governance.
- Guiding principles of faith-based governance.
- Dimensions and neutrality in the faith-based governance model.

Notes

1 We consider the use of the term "divine" as not necessarily in reference to God as referred to in religious literature; it connotes something "of superhuman or surpassing excellence."
2 www.auroville.org.
3 A nativist philosophy argues for the existence of ideas that are biologically, genetically, or socially learned and not as a manifestation of the original constitution of the human mind.
4 "Catechism of the Catholic Church," www.vatican.va/archive/ENG0015/__P2A.HTM (accessed March 25, 2023), www.vatican.va/archive/hist_councils/ii_vatican_council/documents/vat-ii_decree_19651028_christus-dominus_en.html (accessed March 25, 2023).
5 "Laws or Principles of Social Development," Mother's Service Society, www.motherservice.org/node/104 (accessed March 25, 2023).
6 Ibid.

References

Smith, Wilfred Cantwell. 1979. *Faith and Belief*. Princeton, NJ: Princeton University Press.
Solomon, Robert., 2002. *Spirituality for the Skeptic: The Thoughtful Love of Life*. Oxford: Oxford University Press.
Tennant, Frederick. Robert. 1943/1989. "Faith." In *Faith*, edited by Terence. Penelhum. London: Collier Macmillan.

33

TORAH TRANSMISSION IN A DIGITAL AGE

Barak Cohen

Introduction

What does it mean to be the People of the Book at a time when printed books are rapidly being replaced by digital texts? Contained within this question is both the practical question of Judaism's evolution in a digital age and the less obvious core governance assumption on which this chapter rests—that the Jewish people are indeed a people "of the book," a people whose history and modern life are governed to lesser or greater extents through the ongoing interpretation and engagement of the Torah, or Hebrew Bible. That is "the Book." But as we will see in the pages ahead, the Torah is not simply a book—or many books—of wisdom, history, or morals, despite containing aspects of all three. It is rather an evolving blueprint for a people's relationship with G-D that has spanned millennia and the foundation of countless explanations, interpretations, codifications, and adaptations that have guided Jewish history and continue to govern many facets of Jewish life to this day.

An early version of this study explored the three pillars of Jewish faith, as described by the great scholar Rabbi Akiva (50–135 CE), as they are being established in the digital realm. The pillars—Torah (Jewish learning, covered in this paper), Avodah (divine service or "Jewish work"), and G'milut Hasadim (acts of human kindness)—are all being transformed by digital tools, a process greatly accelerated by Covid-19. In the end, I chose to begin with Torah, not only because it is the first of the three pillars and warrants a lengthy chapter of its own but also and primarily because every feature of Jewish life has Torah embedded in it.

Indeed, the term *Torah* comes from the root that means to "teach" or "guide." That is also why this paper is, at its core, about governance, even as it diverges from more familiar conceptions. The authority and guidance that the Torah provides to traditional Jews makes it a primary source for governance decisions, and it also makes the governance structures behind digital Torah sources particularly important.

What we are witnessing today is a major transition and transformation in the way that Torah learning is made available for the Jewish people and for the world. For over a decade, I have been listening to pre-recorded lectures on Torah subjects in transit to and from work each day. This amounts to hundreds of hours of learning afforded to me by the apps and

DOI: 10.4324/9781003316077-40

websites accessible on my smartphone. While sitting in the waiting room at the doctor's office or in a lobby awaiting a meeting, both the deeply committed and the simply curious have thousands of years of Jewish scholarship—in the original languages or in translation—available for study. The five-minute gaps that pepper our days can now be filled with the study of Torah.

This proliferation of Torah learning resources—and listeners eager to tune in—stems from the very teaching of the Torah itself: there is no more important action one can take, no greater deed one can perform, than the study of the Torah. Why the preoccupation? The short answer is that the Torah itself tells us that there is no greater act one can undertake than the study of the Torah. First thing every morning, as a part of the opening prayers of the day, a section from the Mishne Zeraim (1:1), known as Mishne Peah, is recited, which establishes the primacy of Torah learning among life's sacred acts: "Honoring one's father and mother/The performance of righteous deeds/And the making of peace between a person and his friend/But the study of the Torah is equal to them all." Rabbi Moses ben Maimon (1138–1204), one of the most prolific and influential scholars in Jewish history, in *Mishneh Torah*, elaborates in detail—as do countless other sages throughout all generations of Jewish history—on the paramount importance of spending time daily engaged in Torah study. And today, every Jew, regardless of their background or level of observance, has both access and the ability to fill their days with Torah.

But This Was Not Always the Case

For much of Jewish history, numerous prerequisites existed for accessing Jewish text and law. To begin with, approaching the foundational works required a command of the Hebrew language—and often Aramaic and Yiddish as well. A rabbi was needed for Torah insights, legal rulings, and guidance in religious practice. If one chose to take study more seriously, religious education could be found in a full-time *yeshiva* (for men), with access to and understanding of texts available largely to the scholarly elite. One might also take advantage, if they were available, of learning opportunities offered by *kollels*,[1] community centers, local Jewish organizations, traveling scholars, and, beginning in the twentieth century, universities. The common denominator among all these Torah experiences is that they take place *in person* and/or demand a teacher or skill set not always easily attainable, certainly not for more secular segments of a Jewish community. Additionally, women were largely left out of the structures of formal learning for most of Jewish history.

Scholars and rabbis continue to play critical functions in the Jewish world and the lives of their communities. At the same time, sources for Jewish learning are available in abundance and are accessible to all without requiring the gatekeepers they once did.

The process of digitizing Torah commentary and teaching took its first major step forward with the introduction of the searchable text database by the Bar Ilan University Responsa Project in the late 1960s. This database continued to grow, and the technology evolved from university servers (1970s) to CD-ROMS (1990s) to the internet (2007). The DBS Master Library provided a similar tool. The 1980s saw a proliferation of Torah and Hebrew language study on VHS, beta, and cassette tapes, with "over 100 Jewish educational software titles" by 1986, according to one accounting (Neiss 2017).

In the 1980s and 1990s, the Artscroll publishing house and a wide range of Jewish educational institutions introduced multimedia educational packages that paired books and pamphlets with CDs and later, DVDs. These years also brought email distribution lists, blogs, and other subscription services, creating a new level of accessibility to Torah and online educational communities.

Today, however, with the prominence and convenience of smartphones, Torah is available everywhere (with the right data plan!) and at all times. This new tool, developed in our lifetimes, produced a leap forward in the dissemination of Torah learning and accessibility, unparalleled except by, perhaps, the printing press. Before diving deeper into a few of the prominent platforms where Torah resides today, it is important to first review why the Jewish world might care about access to Torah and the nuances of its contemporary vehicle, Jewish digital learning platforms, in the first place.

The Torah, to the Jewish people, is not simply a historical document that teaches Jews how to live better, holier lives, but rather the foundation on which Jewish lives and their relationship with G-D are built and adapted to every historical age. In this way, it serves more like the U.S. Constitution. Its study and the application of its principles to the challenges of each generation of Jews are what give Torah its unparalleled and permanent role at the center of Jewish life. It is for this reason that the gatekeepers and moderators of the Jewish relationship with Torah have historically been, and still are, so very important. In every generation, those leaders whose interpretations of Torah, and whose legal rulings based on Torah, are most widely and devotedly embraced become the transmitters and transcribers of *Torah Sh'Baal Peh*, or the Oral Law, for that generation and historical moment.

The Written Law, *Torah Sh'Bichtav*, is what is most often referred to as the Hebrew Bible and consists of the three Masoritic texts known by the acronym *TaNaKh*—Torah (Five Books of Moses), Nevi'im (Prophets), and Ketuvim (Writings). There are twenty-four total books included in Tanakh. The Oral Law, on the other hand, is the tradition passed down by word of mouth, from parents to children and teachers to disciples, which explains how to live by the principles of the Written Law. Initially codified and written down by Rabbi Judah the Prince during the second century CE in the text of the Mishne, each subsequent generation of Jewish leaders and scholars has taken upon themselves the task of interpreting and issuing rulings on the particular challenges of their age, based on the Written Law *and* the preceding oral traditions. Together, the Written and Oral Laws govern the personal, communal, and national behavior of the Jewish people. And it is for this reason that the Jewish people cannot ignore—and should in fact understand and evaluate—the motivations of those who oversee the tools for accessing, understanding, and disseminating Torah in each generation.

Today, critical to the discussion of Torah transmission is the reality that technology can amplify the influence of a particular institution or teacher far beyond any geographic or ideological boundaries previously known. Digitization can also disseminate teachings well beyond the actual (official, institutional, etc.) bona fides of a platform's teachers, scholars, and editors. Students of media will recall the famous words of Marshall McLuhan, "the medium is the message" (1964).

Indeed, significant, if often unrecognized, social processes unfold across digital platforms due to their digital nature, even before we have considered the content. From McLuhan's perspective, the digital platform, whether an app or a website, is what holds the primary power and influence. The content is secondary.

During his lifetime, McLuhan often cited the use of the telephone as a simple example of this phenomenon. What is said on the telephone, in any given conversation, is far less consequential than the impact of the telephone system and infrastructure on the lives of its users. Likewise with digital communication technologies today. From a religious vantage point, we can now carry the entire text of Tanakh, its commentaries, our liturgy, rabbinic counsel, our study partners, and even the audience for our own interpretations in our pant pockets and purses.

As we explore the individual digital platforms that comprise the case studies of this chapter, it is particularly relevant to note the philosophical position of the platform's founders and leadership vis-à-vis the medium itself, whether spoken or implied, and its practical implications. Unlike the telephone, television, or any prior medium for that matter, digital media today permit developers to make source material available to the public, allowing the posting of user-generated content, enabling engagement between users, and facilitating other features unfamiliar to earlier forms of media. As we will soon see, how digital platforms choose to engage with these opportunities is both consequential for the user experience and indicative of how they view Torah learning *and* Torah creation. These governance choices set the boundaries of the learning experience and in many ways come to define what it means to engage Torah in modern times.

A superficial review reveals hundreds of digital platforms performing different functions and representing a variety of Jewish practices and denominations. Making sense of this landscape required the limiting of sources to a small but meaningful sampling of these online tools, as well as a theoretical framework for classifying them and fitting them into the broader field of digital media studies.

Enter Religious Digital Creatives

The Religious Digital Creative (RDC) framework, developed by Heidi Campbell in *Digital Creatives and the Rethinking of Religious Authority* (2021), takes the well-known marketing concept of a "digital creative" and applies it to those who pursue digital innovation *on behalf* of their church or Christian denomination or from a place of *personal* religious conviction. In her introduction, she observes a governance challenge posed by digitization that features prominently in the world of Jewish digital creatives as well, namely how "non-hierarchical or flattening features of the internet" empower individuals "outside traditional religious power structures" (Campbell 2021, 10). These individuals and institutions are RDCs. An exploration of the purpose, policies, and governance structure of four prominent Jewish examples of RDCs forms the central, qualitative section of this study.

The defining characteristics of the RDC subsets—digital entrepreneurs (DEs), digital spokespersons (DSPs), and digital strategists (DSTs)—elucidate how these large Jewish online platforms emerge to "become unintentional authorities by creating new spaces for religious engagement" (Campbell 2021, 13). Their positions of authority are often, but not always, earned, as opposed to appointed. And while not necessarily in conflict with established religious institutions, many of these digital creatives bypass "recognized offline religious authorities" in pursuit of their mission.

The characteristics of the three categories of RDC are as follows:

1. Campbell's DEs are early adopters of technologies who come to marry their faith and religious ideals with a professional, technical skill set. She builds her definition of a DE upon the concept of "creole pioneers" developed by Benedict Anderson in his pioneering 1983 work, *Imagined Communities: Reflection on the Origins and Spread of Nationalism*. This unique form of pioneer helped to successfully bring about a sentiment and

experience of national identity because they carried the culture, language, and tools of the country of origin into the distant community. Campbell uses Jon Anderson's (1999) application of this term to trends in Islamic media to guide the concept of creolization into media studies. Anderson (1999) recognized that those who pioneered new media and digital technologies in the 1990s for the purpose of promoting Islam were not traditional religious leaders but rather early adopters of new technologies motivated to use them to explore or promote their faith. Campbell's DEs follow a similar pattern of being largely non-clergy professionals with the technical skills to apply to their religious interests or hobbies (Campbell 2021, 49).

In this chapter, we explore Sefaria as an example of a DE. Sefaria is a text-based platform developed by Silicon Valley entrepreneurs. It was not founded by Orthodox entrepreneurs nor by individuals deeply immersed in Torah and acting out of a sense of religious obligation, but rather by Jewish DEs who recognized an opportunity and an invaluable contribution that they could make to Jewish learning. They endeavored to create an open-source platform that would make Jewish texts easily and widely accessible as part of the Jewish people's "collective inheritance." In early 2021, Sefaria hit a record 500,000 users per month and currently hosts over 300,000 user-generated source sheets in addition to its library of over 250,000,000 words. They are a clear example of the DE.

2. Campbell's DSPs attempt to speak in the accepted language and frameworks of a traditional entity or authority. In other words, they use new technologies to express the positions and advance the missions of existing, non-digital organizations, movements, or philosophies. Jewish DSPs, such as Chabad.org in this study, adhere to the mission and guidelines set by their particular brand of Judaism.

   In Chabad.org, we find perhaps the oldest Jewish website with the widest scope of impact. Launched in 1988 as a digital discussion board enabling Jews to ask questions of Chabad rabbis, Chabad.org and its subsites today boasted 52,000,000 annual visitors in 2020, hosting 10,000 video, and 14,000 audio classes. The website's vision is guided by the teachings of Chabad-Lubavitch Hasidism generally and the mission of their most recent leader, Rabbi Menachem Mendel Schneerson (1902–1994), in particular. It exists largely as an outreach tool and serves as the DSP for the Chabad-Lubavitch Movement worldwide.

3. Finally, DSTs, while not necessarily religious authorities themselves, are most often religious "insiders" representing a particular religious movement or affiliation. They employ their skills with "new technological tools or opportunities" (Campbell 2021, 16) to advance the religious objectives of a specific denomination or institution and maintain a clear affiliation. In this study, we will consider two very different DSTs: Torah Anytime and My Jewish Learning.

   Torah Anytime (TAT) is a digital repository for, as of 2020, over 70,000 lectures on topics across the Jewish spectrum. Founded by Orthodox Jews, TAT is motivated by a desire to make Torah learning available anytime and anywhere, with a particular concern for the elderly, sick, geographically isolated, exceedingly busy, or those uncomfortable or unfamiliar with traditional Orthodox text study. It hosts audio and video classes by over 1,000 Orthodox Torah teachers. According to their website, over 350 classes are uploaded weekly, and they see 300,000 visits per month from 120 countries. As it has a clear Orthodox religious agenda, even without mandate from any specific institution, Torah Anytime fits into the DST framework.

A very different type of DST, My Jewish Learning, hosted over 10,000 articles as of 2020 "on all aspects of Jewish life, religion, and history." MJL's content spans the full Jewish learning spectrum—from Jewish ritual to Jewish cooking, to the challenges facing the modern State of Israel. A secular, North American Jewish philanthropist initiated the project in 2002, and the site continues to uphold its commitment to pluralistic Judaism in the North American model. Their mission is to "spread knowledge of Jewish religion, history, values, traditions and culture in a manner that is meaningful and accessible to people of all backgrounds." Although it is hard to place—and definitionally problematic—to declare a formal authority over pluralistic Judaism, I would offer this unique brand of Judaism as the umbrella philosophy of secular Jewry in North America. My Jewish Learning takes up this mantle and advances its ideals.

The examples of digital Jewish learning explored in this paper walk different paths and follow different rules in their dissemination of information. It is worth noting, however, that Benedict Anderson's concept of imagined communities provides an interesting framework through which to view the output of RDC and religious digital culture generally. These new sources of cultural authority, despite their differences from one another, all create conceptions of community out of individuals who often do not know each other nor live in face-to-face communities but who are tied by bonds of language/print culture. These are the familiar factors that led to the creation of national identity and solidarity in Anderson's study. Perhaps future studies will explore the possibility that digital religious communities have additional similarities to cultural imaginaries like the nation-state.

Through a combination of primary sources and interviews, the following pages will sketch the origins, ideological underpinnings, content creation, editorial controls, funding sources, and trajectories of this small but impactful group of Jewish learning platforms, adding meaningful insights to the discourse on the evolution of Torah learning and its governance in our unique digital moment.

The coming pages provide snapshots of four prominent Jewish digital platforms used today in our unique Covid-19 pandemic moment. Although other examples and models exist, those explored here are among the largest and most dominant in today's marketplace. These four platforms made their analytics, history, and policy information *and* themselves—in the form of interviews and responses to email requests—accessible and available for this study. Much of the information was gleaned from the websites themselves. Additionally, contact was made, questions presented, and interviews conducted with one or more of the site's founders, directors, or senior staff members. While significant Jewish learning platforms declined to participate in this study, the four explored here had the size, prominence, and digital reach (in terms of amount of content and number of users), accessibility (in terms of governance and structural transparency and willingness to be interviewed), and relevance to the theoretical framework (three categories of RDCs) to fit nicely into this study.

Sefaria

According to the Sefaria website, their platform was created with the mission "to shepherd our texts from print to digital in a way that can expand their impact in new and unprecedented ways." At its core a text-based platform, Sefaria is in its essence a free Jewish library containing all available (accessible and purchasable) texts from the extensive, multi-millennial canon of Jewish literature.

In 2011, the concept for Sefaria was developed by the unlikely pairing of Brett Lockspieser, a former Google employee, and Joshua Foer, an author and former USA Memory Champion. The two set off, in the words of Lockspieser, to create a tool "for engaging the texts of Judaism and interlinking them in conversation with one another."[2] In many ways, this mission reflected their personal life experiences. Lockspeiser followed a path from a nonreligious but spiritual and intellectually curious Jewish home to an Orthodox Yeshiva education in Israel and today identifies as a secular Jew who maintains "a Jewish practice."

Foer grew up in a conservative household where he ate only Kosher meat in their home, had a traditional weekly Shabbat dinner on Friday nights, and attended non-Jewish school supplemented with extracurricular Hebrew school. Today, Foer considers himself an "observant Jew." In light of his journey, Lockspeiser came to recognize that the beauty of Jewish texts and the ability to navigate them were important enough to "dedicate his career to," while in Foer's words (in the course of email correspondence), the craving to know more coupled with an "inadequate Jewish education" produced the tension that helped to spur Sefaria's creation.

The first task the pair would undertake was to upload the core canon of Torah literature to serve as the platform's foundation. Their first 1,000 texts were what they determined to be the texts most used by those engaged in Torah study, or, as Lockspeiser described, "95 percent of the texts that 95 percent of people learn 95 percent of the time." The sections of the library mirror the traditional divisions of Jewish text and commentary, including Tanakh, Mishne, Talmud, Midrash, Halakhah, Kabbalah, and more.

As of early 2021, Sefaria was logging over 500,000 users per month. The metrics in July 2021 showed over 5,000 "index records" (the closest data point to a "book"), with 270 million words in the library and 2.8 million intertextual links between Sefaria sources.

In addition to the permanent library hosted by Sefaria, users are also able to generate and post their own content in the form of source sheets. Deeply committed to the democratization of Torah learning, Sefaria allows anyone to create source sheets, which inevitably leads to nontraditional content. These source sheets are not included as a part of the "official" Sefaria library but are almost never removed from the user-generated section of the website, even when they contain challenging or controversial content. Today, these source sheets number over 300,000—with 30,000 shared publicly and the remainder created for private use. Fierce internal debates regarding censorship have taken place among the Sefaria professional team, almost all of which ended with the content (including justifications of the Capitol riots in January 2021, explorations of LGBT-related topics, and references to Jesus and Christianity) being allowed to remain on the site.

But there is quite a bit more to Sefaria's guiding philosophy than simply an acceptance of a wide range of users and their opinions. Sefaria was born out of and reflects hacker culture. Its foundational governance decision was to make its content open-source and available for anyone and any purpose. This is central to the concept of "free Torah" described by Sefaria Senior Product Engineer Russel Neiss and an echo of programmer and free software activist Richard Stallman's definition of free software. The core values, according to Neiss, include:

1. Freedom to use Torah as you wish for any purpose
2. Freedom to study how Torah works so you can do with it what you wish
3. Freedom to redistribute Torah so that you can help your neighbor
4. Freedom to distribute *your* Torah to others

In these ways, the free Torah of Sefaria operationalizes a principle derived from the value of liberty, not connected to money or the cost of a product or service. In Neiss's words, it is free like "free speech," not like "free beer."[3] But the nod to personal liberty is more than a simple attempt to clarify the meaning of the word "free." Indeed, it is raising the value of this principle in digital innovation to the level of *halacha*, or law. It has become a type of *hacker halacha* guiding the governance and policy decisions at Sefaria.

Opening up Torah interpretation and teaching—not simply learning—to everyone introduces the agenda of Torah democratization, which constitutes an ideology radically different from that of more traditional, Orthodox Torah-learning institutions. But, while one might be tempted to see Sefaria's success as a DE as simply a win for progressive Judaism, it is important to note that their passion for inclusivity applies to non-liberal viewpoints as well. According to their annual report,[4] in 2020 Sefaria sources were used by and linked to Orthodox sites including Aish HaTorah, Orthodox Union, and YUtorah.org. Additionally, the library of texts offered includes most, if not all, of the core curricula of Orthodox yeshivas, which includes many decidedly non-liberal commentaries. For this reason, it seems likely that while Sefaria's philosophical and operational values may be progressive, a meaningful percentage of its users and its texts are not.

Lockspeiser describes the algorithms behind Sefaria as different from more familiar social media algorithms. Sefaria uses "relevance algorithms" that present material based on sheet rank, or how often a particular source sheet is sighted, and page rank, which prioritizes the pages that are linked to most often. In addition, there are popular traditional commentaries, such as that of Rabbi Shlomo Yitzchaki, the medieval French rabbi better known as Rashi, that are always "pinned at the top." These choices for presenting content, together with the laws of *hacker halacha* that create an almost religious commitment to open-source principles, stand at the center of governance at Sefaria. Decision-making, both strategic and related to specific content, is guided by principles unique to the digital realm. Content oversight is minimal. Algorithms largely determine what you do and don't see. Anyone can contribute to the platform (albeit not to the formal library). And the materials are available for anyone to link to or to take freely to do with as they please. As it wades into uncharted waters for Jewish learning, Sefaria's preference for accessibility over religious ideology situates it squarely in the theoretical framework of the DE.

When it comes to the funding behind Sefaria, a registered 501c(3), in addition to soliciting donations from users who wish to "support the future of Torah," Sefaria's website also lists Jewish foundations as its top donors. The first four include the Jim Joseph Foundation, William Davidson Foundation, Koschitzky Family, and Maimonides Fund.

It is no surprise that these well-known names in North American Jewish Philanthropy committed funding for developing the "future of Jewish learning in an open and participatory way . . . allowing more people to engage with the textual treasures of our tradition."[5] And Sefaria truly has emerged as the primary source for Jewish texts for a digital generation.

Torah Anytime

In 2006, the founders of Torah Anytime (TAT) set out to create a collection of Torah lectures accessible to anyone, anywhere, who was interested in learning Torah. Yosef Davis, along with brothers Shimon and Rubin Kolyako, sought to "give their friends and family the ability to experience Torah classes wherever they were, whenever they wanted."[6]

As most of their friends and family were, like themselves, Orthodox Jews, these recorded lectures were intended to replace daily in-person study in the *Beit Midrash* (house of learning, or Jewish study hall). Davis, currently TAT CEO and director, described the desire to "make a lasting contribution to the Jewish people" as the driving force behind his effort to create TAT. This endeavor followed an impactful, if unusual, detour for young Orthodox North Americans: service in the Israel Defense Forces.

At the conclusion of his military service, Davis was eager to pursue a career that would tie him meaningfully to Judaism and set out to create a library of recorded Torah lectures that would be easily accessible to the busy professional or parent, the geographically isolated, the sick and bedridden, the elderly and immobile, and the Jew uncomfortable—for whatever reason—with the Orthodox study hall or synagogue setting.

The website for Torah Anytime, home to over 70,000 Torah recordings by over 1,000 speakers in 2021, was the outgrowth and evolution of a modest library of CD recordings. According to their "About Us" webpage, TAT records and posts roughly 350 classes weekly and claims the title of the "largest library of originally recorded Torah videos in the world." Torah Anytime users spend 7,500,000 hours annually engaged in the Torah learning made available through the platform.

In the theoretical framework of RDCs, Torah Anytime fits the category of DST. There is no parent organization, synagogue, or institution behind Torah Anytime, but their objectives and content choices reflect a clear affiliation with Orthodox Judaism. They serve as a mouthpiece for a strictly observant and *halachically* committed segment of the Jewish population.

According to Davis, all of the speakers uploaded to the website are vetted and approved by a board.[7] Gaining permission to upload lectures to the site requires the submission of a questionnaire and a process Davis describes as similar to an admissions process at a school. A rabbinic advisory board, entirely Orthodox but representative of Ashkenazi, Sephardi, Hasidic, Mizrahi, and other traditional Jewish divisions, evaluates whether the speaker represents "an authentic Jewish voice." And, once approved, they are able to upload their own content freely. Davis spoke of no disagreement among the rabbinic advisory board as to what voices did or did not qualify for inclusion, which in itself reveals a form of consensus unique to Orthodoxy.

Looking across the digital Torah learning landscape as a whole, Davis insists that there is space for everyone and that there should be no competition between all those working for the same "Boss, with a capital 'B.'" There is plenty of bandwidth—literally and figuratively(!)—in the digital sphere for all types of Torah. That said, the highly controlled, ideologically consistent environment of Torah Anytime exists and is maintained by design. TAT is not interested in making its content open source or sharing a diverse range of nontraditional perspectives, and implements strong controls to maintain their standards of what "is or is not" authentic Torah.

While from a governance standpoint, Torah Anytime leaves content control in the hands of the rabbinic advisory board, the website is presented as a "project" of three institutions: Mishkan Yechezkel, Lev Echad Foundation, and the Ach Tov V'Chessed Foundation. According to Davis, these organizations provide no more than 10 percent of Torah Anytime's funding and play no meaningful governance role. However, given the prominent credit offered (in the footer of every page of the website), it seems likely that these institutions do maintain an important function, which, if not related to funding or active governance, perhaps comes from the credibility they provide to TAT's content.

Torah Anytime is a 501c(3), and their website recognizes that donations are their "main source of funding." While a full list of donors was not accessible through the website, there is ongoing recognition of individual donors by way of a home page ticker. On August 31, 2021, for example, it read, "Today's learning is sponsored as a *refuah sheleimah* [which in Hebrew means a 'complete recovery'] for Idan Ben Shoshana."

My Jewish Learning

At the age of seventy-four, philanthropist and former CEO of Seagram Ltd. Edgar Bronfman founded My Jewish Learning in order to "leverage the internet and other new media to spread knowledge of Jewish religion, history, values, traditions and culture in a manner that is meaningful and accessible to people of all backgrounds."[8] Since its establishment in 2002, My Jewish Learning has grown to become "the leading pluralistic website of Jewish information and education," hosting, as of May 2021, over 10,000 articles and logging over 1,500,000 monthly web users, 196,000 social media followers, and 136,000 daily email subscribers.[9]

Unlike the other digital Torah sources presented here, MJL is one product among a family of brands living under a large digital media organization, 70 Faces Media. This parent nonprofit company oversees a portfolio of brands that includes websites dedicated to Jewish food, parenting, culture, youth, and current events/news. This cross-section of websites fits well into the model of Jewish pluralism in America, a form of Judaism that recognizes that most American Jews do not affiliate with any Jewish denomination and their particularistic guidelines for living a religious Jewish life.[10]

Pluralistic Judaism begins with the premise that Jewish identity does not need to be defined by a particular lifestyle or practice but can be expressed through any cultural, educational, social, or spiritual engagement that contains Jewish meaning. Indeed, the name 70 Faces Media itself is derived from a quotation from Numbers Rabbah 13:15–16 referring to the many possible interpretations (i.e., the faces) of Torah.

A number of content-related differences between MJL and the other digital learning platforms are quickly and easily observable on the menu bar of their website. Jewish engagement via MJL is divided into six primary categories: Celebrate (Jewish holidays), Eat (Jewish food), Live (Jewish milestones), Mourn (the passing of loved ones in a Jewish way), Pray (Jewish prayers), and Study (Jewish texts and topics). Within each of these categories, a variety of voices can be heard—some articulating the explanations and positions of MJL's staff writers and others the viewpoint of outside contributors.

According to an MJL editor interviewed in August 2021, the website has an editorial team that both curates and edits its content. Whether solicited or pitched by internal staff writers, requested from outside scholars and academics, or submitted by outside contributors, MJL content is approved or rejected by media professionals. Content is treated much like content is handled by traditional newspapers. Articles are expected to be intriguing and enticing to a viewing audience, generate traffic, and bring in advertising dollars. Advertising options through MJL include website and social media advertising, as well as sponsored content/paid posts. Importantly, submissions must fit into the ideological framework of the website, Jewish pluralism, which respects diverse Jewish perspectives and practices.

While most content is created internally, the MJL editor interviewed for this study insisted that when external content must be solicited, it is expected to be "factual and fair-minded."[11] The website does not host opinion pieces, nor will it post "restrictive perspectives" that raise questions or doubts about any form of Jewish practice. As such, Orthodox perspectives that prefer one type of practice over another, or that cast doubt on the appropriateness of non-halachic traditions, are not included.

In light of MJL's organizational structure, as well as the way in which content is created and controlled, they are appropriate to the DST theoretical framework. They embody the ideology of Jewish pluralism, which has no governing body. There are no rabbis or religious leaders at their core. At the same time, MJL earns its authority through the popularity and reliability of its content, the fact that it speaks the language and considers the sensibilities of North American Jewry, and the skill with which it wields its digital tools.

In addition to generating advertising revenue, MJL is a 501c(3) nonprofit under its parent media company, 70 Faces Media. Funding for MJL, according to their donor page, comes from many well-known, largely progressive North American Jewish Foundations, including the William Davidson Foundation, Maimonides Fund, Charles and Lynn Schusterman Family Philanthropies, Jim Joseph Foundation, and Samuel Bronfman Foundation, among others. It is interesting to note that three out of the four top donors to Sefaria are also among MJL's top donors.

Chabad.org

Chabad-Lubavitch defines itself as "a philosophy, a movement, and an organization."[12] And, indeed, depending on where you come across Chabad, you might see it fitting any one of these definitions. A movement within the Hasidic branch of Orthodox Judaism, Chabad finds its origins in the teachings of the eighteenth-century mystic, Rabbi Israel Ben Eliezer, known as the *Baal Shem Tov* (Good Master of the Name), as understood and interpreted by Rabbi Shneur Zalman of Liadi (1745–1812), known in Chabad circles as the *Alter Rebbe* (Old Rabbi). The modern incarnation of Chabad and its global renown are largely attributed to the efforts of the seventh and most recent leader of the Chabad dynasty, Rabbi Menachem Mendel Schneerson (1902–1994), known within Chabad as the *Rebbe*.

Today, Chabad summarizes the movement's mission as imparting an "understanding and recognition of the Creator, the role and purpose of creation, and the importance and unique mission of each creature." Leading with this ideological and educational mandate, Chabad-Lubavitch has grown to become the spiritual headquarters for "over 5,000 full-time emissary families . . . (who) direct more than 3,500 institutions . . . dedicated to the welfare of the Jewish people worldwide." But, beyond the emissary families (known as *shlichim*) who run in-person prayer services, schools, holiday celebrations, Kosher food offerings, and Torah classes across the globe, Chabad-Lubavitch offers many additional services, including, in the digital realm, Chabad.org. The website serves as the mouthpiece of the movement and primary outreach tool, and as such, it finds itself playing the role of DSP for Chabad-Lubavitch.

Begun initially as an "Ask the Rabbi" discussion forum on Fidonet in 1988, the Chabad internet presence was the brainchild of Rabbi Yosef Yitzchak Kazen and predates the invention of the World Wide Web. As of 2021, Chabad.org had a major web presence, claiming the title of "the largest faith-based website," with 52 million unique annual visitors, over 102,000 unique pages of content, and "over 20,000 multimedia titles." In conversation with Rabbi Zalman Shmotkin, director of Chabad.org, he spoke enthusiastically about the *Rebbe's* worldview that guides their website and its content choices.[13] Technology, according to the *Rebbe's* teachings, exists primarily to introduce new ways of connecting to the divine purpose of creation. The internet, and by extension Chabad.org, is an example of this. According to Shmotkin, digital tools allow users to see new layers of Torah and appreciate the interconnectedness of Torah with all facets of life. The internet "connects the dots," helping to show how the Torah is "living and breathing" and relevant to every experience and decision.

The Chabad.org website contains hundreds of topics and subsites, what Shmotkin describes as smaller "organizations" within Chabad.org, built for everything from basic "Judaism 101," to personal mentoring from Rabbis, to Jewish world news, and advanced Kabbalistic concepts. Its user numbers and wealth of content attest to the fact that, as related by Shmotkin, for the better part of "20 years all (Jewish-related) Google searches led to Chabad.org." Content is also offered in eight languages.

Chabad.org lists sixty men and women who make up the Chabad.org team and four additional Rabbis who serve as the Lubavitch HQ Internet Committee. While content is primarily generated internally, Shmotkin describes a process by which topics are often chosen by combing through the keywords left behind by users: "Users turn to us and ask us things, a lot of our content was created in response to public questions. . . . We're seeing queries in our search engine . . . and we answer." This is a part of what Shmotkin calls their nonlinear approach to talent and content, which also consists of accepting free articles submitted by users, commissioning content from external writers, and encouraging creative input from "staff who recognize a need or have a specific passion." While the sources are diverse, as long as they are aligned with "Torah Judaism and Orthodox Judaism," says Shmotkin, "we're fine with it." Of course, the rabbis offering consultation via the Ask the Rabbi feature are all Orthodox Chabad rabbis.

Editorial control is largely limited to ensuring that the articles are well written (copy editing), rejecting content that is too similar to that which already exists on the site, and moving or separating sections of articles for placement across different areas of the site. However, when sensitive Jewish topics are addressed, the process turns serious. According to Schmotkin:

> [While] we don't have each article go under the scrutiny of a whole editorial board, very foundational things dealing with *hashkafa* [Jewish worldview], or *Yiddishkeit* [Jewish forms of custom/practice], have a very rigorous group of reviewers . . . and we put authors through the wringer.

The donation page on Chabad.org invites individual contributors to dedicate their gifts "in memory" or "in honor" of someone, as well as to have the gift publicized through the homepage "Partners Ticker Display." The homepage itself bears a dedication as well, made possible by a significant donation. Individual gifts of varying sizes provide the operating support for Chabad.org. Shmotkin explained that website users donate "in gratitude and recognition . . . of all it does for them" and that no money is received from the Chabad-Lubavitch headquarters. Additionally, the website hosts no advertisements because "ads take you off the site and we work very hard to keep people on the site."

With this basic sketch of our four digital platforms, the following section provides a brief look inside to see how one might practically experience their differences. Approaching these four websites with a Jewish question, in pursuit of a Torah perspective, what does one find?

Four Searches: A (Very) Short Case Study on the Pandemic Prayer Quorum Dilemma of 2020

In 2020, when the Covid-19 global pandemic forced much of the world into quarantine, Jewish authorities were faced with unfamiliar circumstances and a population looking for guidance on a range of ritual and spiritual matters. One well-known example that finds wide variance between the liberal and conservative ends of the religious continuum is that of the permissibility of virtual prayer quorums.

Traditionally, the Jewish prayer quorum, known in Hebrew as a *minyan*, is made up of ten adult men and is a requirement for the recitation of certain prayers. Many, if not all, non-Orthodox streams of Judaism also include women in the prayer quorum. While the origins and evolution of the prayer quorum are interesting topic, our primary concern is the way in which Jewish digital platforms respond to the question of whether *minyanim* can be constituted virtually or only when physically together.

Searches conducted on each of our four websites for the terms "virtual minyan" or "virtual prayer" yielded quite different results as they relate to the boundaries of online prayer and the creation of a virtual quorum.

Not surprisingly, the Sefaria search yields no results in its formal library. The great historical texts of the Jewish canon did not wrestle directly with dilemmas related to anything virtual, of course. There are, however, eleven user-generated source sheets that contain much of the relevant source material for making a *halachic* determination as to the acceptability of virtual prayer quorums. (This is done via the application of related precedents and legal rulings to the modern dilemma.)

In other words, Sefaria will show you how others (those who wish to share with you) have chosen to study the topic. You can peruse them for your own edification or entertainment, or perhaps to help determine how to approach the issue.

A similar search on Torah Anytime produced five results in the form of presentations on the topic—between 4:15 and 34:00 minutes in length—by two Orthodox rabbis. Neither commented on the acceptability of virtual or zoom prayer on the Sabbath or holidays—the answer was perhaps too obvious to warrant mentioning. Halachically observant Jews do not turn on or off electric devices at all on the Sabbath, let alone participate in web gatherings.

Both rabbis go into detail regarding the rulings issued by the top Orthodox rabbinic authorities and quote many of the sources used to come to these decisions (the same ones found in Sefaria's source sheets on the topic).

The answer they give regarding participating in a virtual prayer quorum is that one *is permitted*, in extenuating circumstances, to join services, to say the prayers together with others, and to respond "amen" to prayers virtually. However, one must be joining an existing *in-person* quorum of ten men. One cannot be counted as a part of this quorum digitally but can participate in many of the prayers, together with a quorum that is physically together.

There are, however, certain prayers, such as the Mourner's Kaddish, that they do not permit one to say virtually, regardless of whether there is a live quorum taking place. So, it seems that TAT's scholars present the intricacies of the *halachic* debate and conclude with the answer "Yes, but. . . ." It was also interesting to note that one of these rabbis who posted a video on this topic also hosted a virtual *minyan* in coordination with and live streamed by Torah Anytime.

Virtual prayer, for My Jewish Learning, is presented as the obvious solution for the lack of in-person prayer. Just as Torah Anytime's place of departure—their "given"—is that virtual prayer on Sabbath and holidays is not an option, the MJL presumption is that it is. Indeed, the first link that showed up in my query was "High Holiday Zoom Services: How to Get the Most out of Them."[14] In addition to the assumed permissibility of streaming synagogue services online on holidays, MJL goes on to make suggestions as to how to create a more meaningful virtual experience (streaming prayer services on a large-screen television, creating a festive holiday backdrop behind the screen, etc.).

MJL also provides the option of virtually reciting the Mourner's Kaddish every weekday at 4:00 p.m. EST following a live Torah class. As referenced in the TAT example, nearly all Orthodox rabbinic authorities prohibit saying this prayer unless it is done live, with an in-person quorum.

Chabad.org showed 172 results for a search for "virtual minyan." Most, of course, had one of these two keywords in them but did not address our particular question. The ones that did provided a predictable answer. As an Orthodox platform, they oppose the idea of virtually reciting the Mourner's Kaddish or other prayers requiring a quorum and do not entertain the idea of virtual Sabbath or holiday prayers at all. They do not mention the more complex, nuanced option of participating in prayers virtually while avoiding certain prayers that must be said in person. Perhaps that would prove confusing for users who are new to navigating the details and subtleties of rabbinic rulings.

One does find, interestingly, that Chabad.org provides a solution for mourners unable to attend a prayer quorum in person because of Covid-19. Fill out a short form, and a group of Chabad volunteers will say the prayer and memorialize your loved one for you, with a safe and Covid-free quorum.

Discussion

The digital Torah learning platforms described above are much more than their unique governance decisions and organizational structures. Each of them alone has an audience that would be the envy of history's greatest Jewish sages. They are making editorial choices and selecting content that addresses the most challenging and sensitive topics of the moment. They employ the latest digital technologies, present innovative programming, and are redefining Jewish participation for a generation being shaped by the Covid-19 global pandemic. They are at the center of the evolving story of the Jewish people's engagement with both their inherited *and* their ever-emerging wisdom. As such, the governance of these platforms and the choices made by each of these and other RDCs embody far more than just nuanced differences between websites.

Content Control Preferences

Editorial control, when it comes to the dissemination of Torah, takes on greater meaning than it might for a different type of digital or print publication. Indeed, the great authors and scholars of Jewish history have often codified, organized, and made Torah wisdom more easily accessible, rather than promoting their own novel interpretations. Similarly, Jewish RDCs today are creating the tools for encountering and engaging Torah for a large swath of the Jewish world.[15]

Some RDCs control their content with a mind toward "online identity curation" (Campbell 2021, 199), as one would expect from an outreach-oriented organization like Chabad-Lubavitch. Others display, and often themselves define, a different set of motivations behind their editorial decisions. My Jewish Learning is committed to being a "nondenominational Jewish media" source, while its tight control over messaging and its pluralistic self-image limit the perspectives that MJL is prepared to present.

Likewise with Torah Anytime. Ideology governs content selection and is established by a council of Orthodox rabbis. When they approve or reject certain teachers, they work to ensure the ideological consistency of their content. This selection process ensures that the color and flavor of their Torah conform to strict religious standards, even as the individual submissions of the selected teachers are posted without editorial review.

Sefaria, for all of its commitment to algorithmic authority, requires the input of an editorial team in the selection of texts and collections for inclusion in their library. The library contains thousands of traditional texts, innovatively organized, interlinked, and filtered algorithmically. However, the decision as to what texts do and do not belong to this canon is a choice left to the discretion of the Sefaria professional leadership. The almost nonexistent filtering of the user-generated source sheets, together with the commitment to making their open-source library available to all for any use, reflects a clear partiality for light-handed governance of Torah wisdom generally, preferring ease of access and open participation.

Negotiating With the User

Sefaria's opening of access to Jewish texts and the interlinking of texts to one another has been an innovation of generational proportions. Additionally, their source sheet concept removed entry barriers for publicly engaging in Jewish discourse. But, despite its commitment to openness and the sacred algorithms of hacker culture, Lockspeiser nonetheless expressed a fear of being deemed *treif*, or unkosher, by traditional religious authorities. Interested (and perceptive!) visitors might notice how well separated the user-generated, unfiltered content is from the core library of Jewish texts that make up the Sefaria collection. Despite the existence of user-generated content that would surely be uncomfortable for certain Jewish populations, the separation between the core library and the source pages ensures that sensitive users can engage with Sefaria's content without stumbling across something they may find offensive. This careful negotiation between the values of the organizational leadership and the religious public served by the platform is perhaps most pronounced at Sefaria, but it is manifest in all of the platforms explored.

For its part, Torah Anytime is walking a line between the rejection of the internet by the strictest circles of Jewish practice—for its unhealthy content and lifestyle implications—and the value of the internet as a tool for disseminating Torah. Perhaps the other side of this coin is the North American model of pluralistic Judaism represented by My Jewish Learning, which seeks to advance the understanding of Jewish history, life, and ritual but stops short of presenting the many stringent, more traditional positions and interpretations that their target users might find disagreeable. As a DSP, Chabad.org is likely the least preoccupied with filtering its content to suit its end users, spending its editorial energies instead on generating lots of content consistent with the ideology and mission of the movement. It does, however, spend significant energy responding to inquiries and answering its users' questions, which is logical in light of its outreach agenda.

As Campell notes in the final pages of her study of Christian RDCs, there is an effort among religious digital platforms to "create discourse that stresses the ways technology is compatible with Christian mission and how it can reflect core religious goals" (2021, 196). This can be said of Jewish RDCs as well, although the effort is not simply to showcase the value of digital technology for religious missions. That goal is obvious. The Jewish RDCs are also, each in their own way, proving their religious bona fides—be they ideologically conservative or progressive—to their target audiences. Indeed, in all of our cases, the authoritative role played by RDCs is, as Campbell describes it in Christian contexts, "negotiated" with a user from whom they seek validation and support.

Authority Earned, Not Ordained

In a 2013 interview conducted with Eric van den Berg, a leading Dutch Catholic RDC, Campbell quotes him as stating: "I am not official, but I am authoritative" (2021, 198). The same may be said for the Jewish RDCs discussed here, with the exception, perhaps, of Chabad.org, which functions as an official spokesperson for a formal religious organization. However, all four websites have earned their popularity, and by extension their authority, by providing a highly desirable product, via the most effective medium, at an opportune time.

It would be challenging to locate individual Jewish leaders who can wield the religious influence of the RDCs described in this study. With annual visitor data available for only three out of the four websites discussed in this paper, the number of yearly users still tops 75 million! While these are certainly not all Jewish users, and perhaps many are repeat and not unique users, these numbers are nonetheless staggering. As of the writing of this chapter, the total population of Jews in the world was just over 14 million.

Sefaria draws its authority from the number and quality of texts it has acquired—and that it presents in an innovative fashion and for free—as well as the quantity of users it has generated. Although they worry about staying in the good graces of broader religious and social structures, they do not rely on them for their authority.

My Jewish Learning and Torah Anytime are not officially affiliated with any particular religious organization, but both can be viewed as "institutional affiliates" (Campbell 2021, 200) of their respective brands of Jewish practice, whose missions and priorities they serve.

Torah Anytime advances the agenda of Orthodox Judaism, and My Jewish Learning the agenda of pluralistic Judaism. Neither speaks authoritatively on behalf of any formal religious body, and yet both exert influence within *and* beyond their streams of Judaism in greater measure than their earned or ordained religious jurisdiction.

It is also important to note that all of these digital creatives were asked about the source of their funding and the possible influence of their funders. All insisted that their donors defer full policy and editorial control to the professional leadership. The large North American foundations supporting Sefaria and My Jewish Learning certainly keep track of their grant recipients' progress, review annual reports, renew funding on a regular basis, and generally follow the formalities of large, well-organized philanthropic bodies. Chabad.org and Torah Anytime showcase individual donors, who give in smaller increments, on their websites. The names of larger donors are not easily accessible, if they exist at all. Annual reports were also unavailable digitally for these two organizations. Despite the differences in sources of funding and the transparency of that funding, the donors to these websites do not appear, on the surface, to play a meaningful governance role. A future study should explore in greater depth the influence of funding sources on the governance decisions made by RDCs.

Looking to the Future

The individuals interviewed for this study were asked to "play prophet" and share their thoughts, from their unique vantage point, on where Torah learning is heading in the coming years and what the digitization of Torah and Jewish learning might mean for the Jewish world at large. Not everyone was willing to answer, but the few that did are worth summarizing here.

When thinking about Torah Anytime's contribution to Torah learning and where this digital age might be headed, Josef Davis quoted a rabbinic source that prophesied that "in the times of Moshiach [the messianic age anticipated in Jewish tradition] we will be learning not from books, but from bits of data and information." While he was unclear as to the source of this idea, Davis sees this revelation being fulfilled in his lifetime and takes pride in the role that TA is playing to actualize it and to bring "more G-dliness into the physical world."

When asked specifically about the future of Jewish learning and Sefaria's role in it, Lockspeiser shared the following thoughts:

> Sefaria's purpose is to play a guiding and positive role in shaping the future of Torah. We try to stay humble and remind ourselves that we simply do not know what the future will look like, even if we have a lot of intuitions and evidence that point in one direction or another. This mindset is why we're an open-source organization—we don't want to claim that we alone know or know better than others what the shape of the future of Torah will be, so we want to make sure as many people as possible are empowered to help us explore and experiment and build so we can all get there faster and better.

Outside of the Jewish context, as a result of Sefaria's success, Lockspeiser and Foer have begun to think about and test their software in other domains, "applying the practice of Torah to non-Jewish texts." One prototype provides the Sefaria treatment to the library of American democracy, with the interlinking of constitutional texts with philosophical sources, presidential speeches, case law, and other related sources.[16]

For Chabad.org, the internet and digital technologies are a means for spreading Torah. In their view, the path toward greater enlightenment and, ultimately, redemption is interwoven with the advancement of technology, and in Shmotkin's words, it should reveal Torah "always, all day, everywhere—in the mundane." So long as Chabad.org has the "money and manpower," they can be expected to continue to advance this mission.

Finally, it is worth noting that all of the platforms explored perceive great value in what both they *and* the other Jewish learning platforms are contributing to Jewish history at large. These are idealistic entrepreneurs, spokespeople, and strategists who are motivated by the potential of their efforts to change lives. Unified by a love of their faith and the wisdom it offers both fellow Jews and the world, the digital creatives explored here, in addition to the clergy and institutional leadership who advised and guided my thinking on this project, take a decidedly nonconfrontational, noncompetitive approach to the dissemination of Torah. All expressed variations of "the more the merrier," or perhaps in this case, "the more the holier."

Concluding Thoughts

It is my hope that this study can shed modest light on the importance of exploring the governance and decision-making behind Judaism's digital resources. While rabbis are unquestionably central to Jewish practice, basic information on Judaism and answers to Jewish questions are increasingly in the realm of search engines on smartphones. This form of inquiry has, of course, become almost a reflex for our generation. Our hands automatically move to our phones to answer medical questions and home repair quandaries, as well as to look up historical facts, define unfamiliar words, and locate vegetarian restaurants within five miles. Given the quantity, variety, and reliability of religious sources available online, Torah learning and Jewish information seem poised to go the same way. Indeed, the large number of users of the four sites explored here seems to imply that that ship has sailed and that the democratization of Torah is at hand.

While this paper has offered some points of interest, most of the questions related to the evolution of Judaism in a digital age remain to be explored. How will formal Jewish institutions/historical structures be impacted by digitization? Certainly, today's RDCs are shaping Jewish life for Millennials and Gen-Zers and will continue to impact the transmission of Torah for the increasingly digitized generations to come. They will need to navigate the range of digital platforms, but also make choices at the intersection between digital engagement and in-person Jewish experience. They will make profoundly historically consequential decisions between the institutional and the nonconventional, with some choosing both and others none at all.

The Covid-19 global pandemic compounded and accelerated the shift toward digital religious engagement. The Jewish relationship to many of the cornerstones of Jewish life looks different today it has at any point in Jewish history. This study, as I mentioned in the introduction, might have gone on to explore the other pillars of Jewish faith described by Rabbi Akiva (50–135 CE) in his well-known formulation. Indeed, there is much to be said about the digital evolution of the other two pillars of Jewish faith (in addition to Torah): *Avodah* and *G'milut Hasadim*. While I chose to look first at Torah due to its role as the source for all other features and traditions of Jewish life, it stands to reason that the democratization we have observed in Torah transmission would follow the same trend through the other two categories as well. A superficial review of new resources and practices for marking Jewish life-cycle events, visiting the sick and the mourning, engaging philanthropic opportunities, lay leadership and board participation, organization of meetings and seminars, and other Jewish communal work point to the major shifts underway as well.

Many of the clergy and institutional leadership I spoke with over the course of my research celebrated the creativity and innovation brought on by the pandemic. Some saw five or ten times greater attendance at annual gatherings and other events when offered digitally instead of in person. But they also unanimously lamented the missing human contact around weddings, funerals, holiday celebrations, classes, and other occasions that are so meaningful to participants and that work to strengthen community and interpersonal bonds. And, although it didn't quite fit into this paper, the feedback on digital Torah received from many rabbis, representing a range of denominations, is worthy of further exploration.

Might the radical democratization of knowledge provided by digital platforms impact or change the role of rabbi as teacher/expert?

And what of the institutions of traditional Jewish learning? Will they all maintain their value in this new era?

Will the Jewish schools and *Yeshivot*, where barriers to entry are high, accessibility limited, and authority consolidated, continue to thrive in a world where anyone can learn from the great teachers of our generation, pour over Judaism's classic texts, and have questions answered (from one's preferred/most palatable perspective) with the tap of a finger?

Jewish communities around the world contend now, as a result of the pressures and adaptations that took place during the pandemic period, with the lure of a more convenient and comfortable, albeit solitary, spiritual practice that can take place from the comfort of home, with a cup of coffee, and in pajamas. Additionally, what does the future of the local synagogue look like if I can stream a better Jewish experience from another part of the world, joining a distant congregation digitally that offers better production value—a more prestigious and engaging rabbi, a professional and polished choir, more advanced multimedia capabilities, and better programmatic or content offerings than the congregation in my hometown?

These potential shifts in Torah access, authority, and practice have significant meaning for the Jewish world and will, I hope, be the source of much consideration and research in the years ahead. This paper offers more observations than implications, but hopefully others will continue to think through these trends and the paths they chart for the future of Jewish life.

Appendix

Table 33A.1 Summary of Key Data Points

	Theoretical framework	*Key analytics*	*Mission*	*Affiliation/ ideology*	*Primary medium*	*Content creation*	*Editorial control*	*Funding*
Sefaria	Digital Entrepreneur	• 6 mm yearly users • 5k "index records" (~books) and 270 mm words in library • 2.8 mm intertextual links • 300k user-created source sheets	Source Material	Independent	Texts and source sheets	• Uploading of traditional texts and full collections • User-generated source sheets	• Core library curated and algorithmically linked • User-generated source sheets lightly filtered	• Individual Donations • Large foundation support
Torah Anytime	Digital Strategist	• 7.5 mm hours of classes heard annually • 70k Torah class recordings • 1k+ speakers	Access to classes	Orthodox	Video and audio recordings	Approved rabbis and teachers	Scholars approved by rabbinic council, then free to upload without controls	• Donations
My Jewish Learning	Digital Strategist	• 18 mm yearly users • 10k articles • social media users	Judaism Basics/ Facts	Pluralistic	Articles and videos	• Staff writers • External writers/ experts • Paid content • Article submissions	Editorial oversight and approval	• Individual donations • Large foundation support • Advertising • Paid content
Chabad.org	Digital Spokesperson	• 52 mm yearly users • 102k content pages • 23k multi-media files	Outreach	Hasidic Orthodox	Articles and videos	• Staff writers • External contributors • Response to user inquiries	• Rabbinic oversight • Editorial approval	• Individual donations

Source: Author.

Key Discussion Areas

- Ways in which digital media is being used to facilitate Jewish learnings and rites to Jews across the globe
- Key websites and their products and services developed specifically to serve a Jewish audience
- Online platforms as a helping hand in mitigating the lack of access to religious worship, rites, and rituals by the community during the Covid-19 pandemic

Notes

1 Organizations that establish and support groups of rabbis and their families in a given community to promote the study of traditional Torah texts and exposure and recruitment to more observant Jewish lifestyles.
2 Virtual interview conducted with Brett Lockspeiser, February 4, 2021.
3 Interview with Russel Neiss, March 31, 2021.
4 Sefaria Annual Report 2020, www.sefaria.org/annualreport/2020 (accessed February 25, 2023).
5 "About Sefaria," www.sefaria.org/about (accessed February 25, 2023).
6 Interview with Yosef Davis, April 15, 2021.
7 Interview with Yosef Davis, April 15, 2021.
8 "History of the Organization," 70 Faces Media, parent organization of My Jewish Learning.
9 "Illuminate, Connect, Inspire: The Jewish Outcomes of 70 Faces Media," www.70facesmedia.org/wp-content/uploads/2021/07/70-Faces-Media-Jewish-Outcomes-Final-Report-20210527RC-3.pdf (accessed February 25, 2023).
10 "Jewish Pluralism," Harvard University, https://pluralism.org/jewish-pluralism (accessed February 25, 2023).
11 Anonymous MJL editor, interviewed August 2021.
12 "About Chabad-Lubavitch," www.chabad.org/library/article_cdo/aid/36226/jewish/Overview.htm (accessed February 25, 2023).
13 Interview with Rabbi Zalman Shmotkin, September 13, 2021.
14 www.myjewishlearning.com/article/make-the-most-of-high-holidays-on-zoom/ (accessed February 25, 2023).
15 One limitation to this study is that it only reviewed English-language digital platforms. More Jews live in Israel today (6,738,500) than anywhere else in the world, including the United States (5,700,000). Of the more than 14 million Jews in the world, nearly half live in Israel and speak Hebrew as their mother tongue. ("Jewish Population by State," World Population Review, https://worldpopulationreview.com/state-rankings/jewish-population-by-state, accessed February 25, 2023.)
16 The American Democracy Library, https://democracy.sefaria.org/ (accessed February 25, 2023).

References

Anderson, Jon. 1999. "The Internet and Islam's New Interpreters." In *New Media in the Muslim World: The Emerging Public Sphere*, edited by D. F. Eickleman. Bloomington: Indiana University Press

Campbell, Heidi. 2021. *Digital Creatives and the Rethinking of Religious Authority*. New York: Routledge.

McLuhan, Marshall. 1964. *Understanding Media: The Extensions of Man*. New York: McGraw Hill.

Neiss, Russel. 2017. "The Potential Impact of Educational Technology on Jewish Education: A History of the 'Future of Jewish Education'." *Jewish Funders Network*, June 12, 2017, www.jfunders.org/potential_impact_edtech_jewish_education (accessed February 25, 2023).

34

ISLAM AND GLOBAL GOVERNANCE

Nadereh Chamlou

Introduction

There are approximately 1.8 billion Muslims—defined as those who were either born to Muslim parents or converted to Islam—making up 24 percent of the world's population. Muslims are the second-largest religious group after Christians (31.2 percent) (Hackett and McClendon 2017).[1] Geographically, they are widely dispersed, as seen in Figure 34.1, in either Muslim-majority countries or minorities in countries that are nominally dominated by other religions, for instance China, France, the United Kingdom, and even the United States. As such, the beliefs and practices of nearly a quarter of the world's population will undoubtedly have an impact on global governance and institutions. This chapter strives to describe the development of Islamic governance, if such a thing could be said, and its strengths and challenges.

Origins of Islam

While other Abrahamic religions were mostly concentrated in or around Palestine, Islam originated in the beginning of the seventh century in the city of Mecca, close to the shores of the Red Sea, and on historic trade routes between the civilizations bordering the coasts of the Indian Ocean and the empires of the Middle East and Europe. Besides communities of Christians and Jews, the region was also crisscrossed by numerous Bedouin tribes from around the Arabian Peninsula with varying beliefs and customs. Some tribes were monotheistic, some were Christian or Jewish, and others worshiped diverse deities. The Ka'ba, the cubic black structure that is today the symbol of Mecca and Islam, was for millennia before Islam, the repository of tribal gods and religious symbols. The clans convened in Mecca during certain times of the year to trade and perform religious rituals, setting aside tribal feuds and conflicts. As such, Mecca was a thriving cultural melting pot marked by the existence of long-practiced conventions, which allowed its diverse population some degree of peaceful coexistence.

It is against this backdrop that the prophet Mohammed (peace be upon him) was born around 570 CE into one of the monotheistic tribes that followed the prophet Abraham. He lost

DOI: 10.4324/9781003316077-41

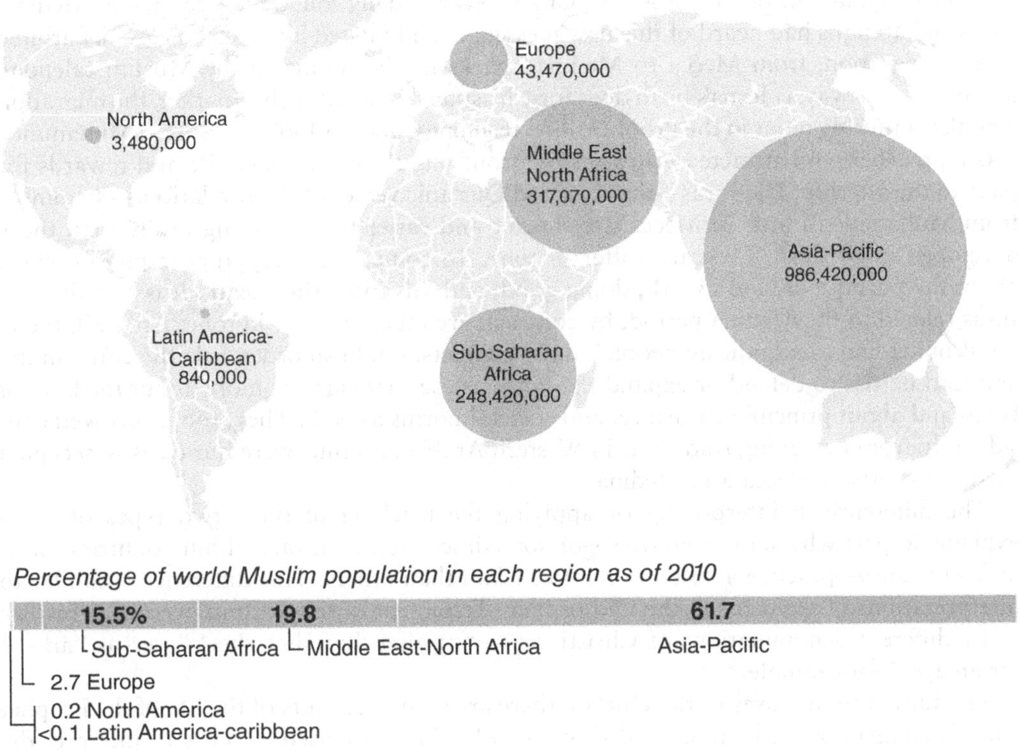

Figure 34.1 Regional Distribution of Muslims
Source: Pew Research Center.

his parents in early childhood, and relatives raised him, albeit in poverty. He began to work at an early age as an attendant on trade caravans. The trips would take him to Palestine and the Levant and expose him to other peoples and religions, such as Christianity, Judaism, and Zoroastrianism, in addition to the prevailing culture of the administrations of the Roman and Sassanian empires, which incorporated vast domains. Hence, Mohammed's experience was far more global than his biblical predecessors. One of his employers was a powerful and prominent Meccan woman merchant and entrepreneur, Khadija, who had considerable wealth. Despite being older than him (some say as much as fifteen years), she proposed to him, married him, and was his sole wife until she died. She had significant influence on the rise of Islam and has been an important female role model, as I elaborate later in this chapter.

Calling and Migration—Hijra

In 610 CE, Mohammad reportedly received his calling to be the messenger of God. Khadija was his first convert, and she used her considerable influence within Meccan society to support her husband's new religion. She died nine years later. Heralding a new socioreligious order based on allegiance to one God—Allah—was unpopular among some of the leaders of Mecca, who threatened the lives of Muhammed and his followers, so much so that they were forced to migrate out of Mecca in 622 CE. They eventually found a new home in Medina, whose inhabitants had heard of this new messenger and invited him to be their chief arbiter.

The migration, from Mecca to Medina, marks the beginning of the Muslim calendar, much the same way as Jesus's birth does for Christians. Beyond such a marker, the migration was also a turning point in the Prophet's life, teachings, and outlook. In Mecca, Muhammed was a preacher who attracted followers by promising a more fulfilled life and rewards for piety in the afterlife. The suras—the recorded Qur'anic verses of the revelations—stemming from Muhammed's time in Mecca are shorter and easier to pass along orally than those developed in Medina. They are softer in tone. To some, they may appear philosophical about the purpose of God's work, doing good, and salvation after death. It is said that the suras related to the Medina period, by contrast, are much harsher in tone. After all, there, the Prophet had to adjudicate people's daily conflicts, establish order, rule the community, and lead battles to defend or expand the faith. These suras are far more about the laws of Islam and about principles, warfare, and societal norms as well. They, too, borrowed considerably from prevailing traditions in Western Arabia and thus were more easily accepted by the converts in Mecca and Medina.

The difference in interpreting or applying the teaching of these two types of suras explains in part why some countries—or sometimes even divisions within countries, or at different times—practice a stricter or softer Islam than others. This difference is similar to interpretations of segments in the Old or New Testament during certain periods in history or by different denominations of Christianity—"turning the other cheek" versus "an eye for an eye," for example.

In addition to the suras of the Qur'an, there are many accounts of the life of the Prophet and his companions, which are called the hadiths. They are used at times to interpret the tenets of Islam and how Muslims should lead their spiritual and worldly lives, otherwise known as the Shari'a or Islamic law. Naturally, there are different understandings of these very same texts—as similar in other religions—so that at least five different schools have evolved. The Shi'a school is called Jafari, and the Sunni ones are Hanbali, Maliki, Shafi'i, and Hanafi. The five differ in how literally they interpret the texts from which Shari'a law is derived. Interpretations can also be nuanced by local culture and customs, which means that even the same school of the Shari'a may be interpreted differently in different countries.

Regardless of adherence to a specific school of the Shari'a, all Muslims accept the five main pillars of Islam: (1) belief in only one God and in Muhammed as his messenger; (2) praying five times per day; (3) paying a share of one's income to the poor; (4) fasting during Ramadan; and (5) making a pilgrimage to Mecca. Beyond these, there are secondary principles that may differ between various schools, though some commonalities exist, such as belief in the afterlife and justice on the day of judgment. It is important to note that Islam accepts Christianity and Judaism, since Mohammed is said to be the continuation of, and the last in the line of, biblical prophets. And there exist considerable congruencies in teachings between the three faiths. It would also be interesting to point out that the only woman named in the Qur'an is the Virgin Mary, to whom an entire *sura* with ninety-eight verses is dedicated.

The Evolution of Islamic Governance

Shortly after the Prophet's death in 632 CE, his followers began to expand Islam by way of conquest. One of the early territories on their site was the Sassanian Empire (see Figure 34.2), which was defeated in 651 CE after a twenty-year war. While the Medina period had established some broad concepts of governance among the Prophet's followers and within its immediate domain, the new Muslim conquerors found themselves to rule and administer a vast expanse of territories that was inhabited by diverse cultures, languages, and peoples, which were distinctly different than those of Western Arabia. Other than the relatively thin layer of Arab rulers, who claimed lineage to the Prophet, most, if not all, institutions continued as before and were administered by locals. For instance, generations of the prominent Persian Barmaki family held high positions in the courts of the Abbasid Khalifs and played an important role early on in shaping the nature of their statecraft. Sassanian government and administration were over time integrated into the institutional structure of the Califates (Haidari 2018), albeit given a Muslim validation—much the same way as Roman institutions prevailed in the West long after the fall of Rome.

A similar course took place in the subsequent conquests of North Africa and Iberia. Islam brought with it a certain unifying supra-structure across the territories it subjugated, such as a common belief and language, but also adapted itself to the circumstances it found on the ground. Even Islam's most holy ritual of the hajj—the pilgrimage to Mecca—is said to replicate and build on existing ceremonies practiced over centuries, presumably from the time of the Prophet Abraham (Philips 2013).

But, except for the above-mentioned conquests, the gradual spread of Islam into Africa or Asia happened through trade and economic interactions. Indeed, the proximity to ancient pre-600 CE trade networks, such as the land-based and maritime Silk Roads, is a robust predictor of today's Muslim communities (Michalopoulos, Naghavi, Prarolo 2017). People of the same religion trust each other more than someone from a different faith, and this is significantly correlated to economic and political outcomes both within and across countries (Guiso, Sapienza, and Zingales 2006). For this reason, Muslim liturgy evolved and

> became quite extensive on the workings of markets and the role of government in bringing about material and spiritual happiness for the *umma*—the community of believers. Functioning markets played a central role in the Islamic economic system and was deemed quite justifiable to a large part because the Prophet and his wife Khadija were themselves traders. Prices in the market are metaphorically set by God (similar to Adam Smith's "invisible hand" of several centuries later) and represent a contract between God and the faithful that must not be reneged on. Merchants must set their prices inside the market and in public view (an early attempt to thwart non-competitive behavior or insider trading). Islam upholds the sanctity of contracts and respects private property. Trade and cross-national alliances were encouraged, thus recognizing the concept of comparative advantage, and hence supportive of globalization. The required pilgrimage to Mecca, which was obligatory for every Muslim who could afford it, was an opportunity to be exposed to the faithful from other regions and exchange goods and ideas—a kind of annual meeting of the wealthy and powerful believers.
>
> *(Chamlou 2014)*

Justice and charity played a strong role, since Islam does not consider scarcity to be a binding constraint at the level of humanity, only at the level of the individual. That is, God has provided for all, and compliance with rules should assure in normal times that everyone receives his/her "equitable" share. Individuals may face limitations, and noncompliance with God-given rules, such as hoarding, creates distortions and shortages that result in unfairness. Islam shuns excesses and encourages moderation and generosity. Therefore, wealth, which has been generated, must be purified through the payment of religious taxes that are then redistributed to the needy. Adhering to such rules, internalizing the rules prescribed, and being conscious of the presence of the creator (equivalent to today's regulators), was thought to guide people in conducting their economic and social affairs (Mirakhor and Askari 2010). For centuries these rules functioned well and led to a Golden Age of these societies, during which the exchange of ideas, science, and arts flourished across countries.

But the rules also provided for institutions, which had good intentions but in practice impeded the accumulation and agglomeration of capital. The Turkish economist Timur Kuran (Kuran 2010) argues that Islamic law, particularly inheritance laws, led to the fragmentation of assets. He explains that for centuries, the waqfs, religious endowments to which believers bequeathed their wealth, took out of circulation vast amounts of contiguous resources. Furthermore, inheritance rules distributed the wealth of any individual among all his male and female relatives, with men receiving two-thirds and women one-third. This broke up wealth into suboptimal portions, while the institution of primo-geniture in Europe, whereby the eldest child—usually the son—inherited all and the rest nothing, allowed for keeping properties consolidated generation after generation, even though it may have seemed unfair among siblings. Kuran argues that Muslims could not accumulate such a volume of intergenerational wealth, while the West could safeguard large estates and compound vast amounts of resources. This trend became much more pronounced by the sixteenth century when, through the establishment of large joint stock companies, such as the East India Company, the West could generate economies of scale that became the engines of the Western industrial revolution and progress. The fragmentation of estates in Muslim lands could not keep pace, which Kuran sees as the cause of the decline of the East (Chamlou 2014).

When Jesus spoke, "give to Caesar what is Caesar's, and to God what is God's," he arguably laid the groundwork for the separation of church and state. Such a delineation was blurred during the life of the Prophet, since he was the spiritual leader as well as the governing ruler of the community. This combination continued during the subsequent Omayyad and the Abassid Caliphates, and later transferred to the Ottoman Sultans, who were the leaders of the Sunni faith.

In Iran, the situation evolved differently. Two centuries after the defeat of the Persian Sassanid Empire, Iranians drove out the Arab conquerors, and a series of dynasties/families ruled these territories. The kings were solely the secular rulers, and Iranian Muslims were Sunni. But in the sixteenth century, the rise of the Ottomans posed an existential threat to Iran. It led the prevailing Safavid rulers to create a distinction between Iranians and Ottomans because, in battles, they could not command the warriors to fight against their spiritual leader. They declared the Shi'a faith as Iran's official religion—which at that time constituted a relatively small share of Muslims who believed that the rightful successor to the Prophet was his cousin Ali and his subsequent heirs, rather than those that historically ruled. This split allowed Iran to create a separate identity from the Sunni Ottomans, and the population was forced to accept the Shi'a faith, often by force of the sword. Nonetheless, to bestow upon the kings the necessary religious legitimacy, an arrangement of mutual support was reached between the crown and the Shi'a clergy, similar to the pledge between King Saud, the founder of Saudi Arabia, and the Wahabi faith, for mutual respect and support. In Iran, this pact existed, and the clergy and monarch protected each other for centuries, up until the modernizing efforts and policies of the Pahlavi Shahs (1925–1979), which were seen as distancing Iran from Islam. It led to an alienation of the clergy. The 1979 Revolution abolished the secular monarchy, and the two roles of spiritual and governing ruler were combined in Ayatollah Khomeini's concept of *Velayat-e Faghih*—the rule of the Islamic Jurist.

Islamic Governance in Today's Global Context

One could address this topic by posing two questions: To what extent do Muslim countries comply with, or deviate from, international governance conventions or institutions? And, to what extent do they comply with, or deviate from, what experts consider Islamic?

If global governance is defined as institutions that mediate transnational interactions, set rules for cooperation, dispute resolution, and help address collective problems, one could review if and how soon Muslim-majority countries signed on to international conventions or became members of international bodies, such as the United Nations and its precursor, the League of Nations, the Bretton Woods institutions of the World Bank or International Monetary Fund (IMF), or international conventions like the UN Convention on the Law of the Sea, or the Universal Declaration of Human Rights, and so on. The only countries that are generally absent from such international agreements are North Korea and Cuba. Muslim countries not only signed on these accords, but like every member, they also had to have them ratified by their parliaments and opinions by their highest legal bodies. Hence, Islamic principles do not seem to object to global governance concepts, even in those countries whose governing laws comply with their respective school of the Shari'a. Even the 1979 Convention on the Elimination of Discrimination against Women (CEDAW) has been signed by all Muslim countries (except Iran) and had to be ratified by parliaments. Although the parliaments initially did so with some reservations, they gradually dropped any objections. Interestingly, the United States has signed but so far refused to ratify the CEDAW.

If there are disagreements with the design or implementation of any global governance principle, these were usually of a technical or political nature—much the same way as those that non-Muslim countries may have raised. Furthermore, governance principles normally offer a band of acceptable actions or interpretations that can guide the implementation phase. For instance, it is common to see international organizations strive to adapt their programs and projects to local and national conditions, mainly to improve the effectiveness of such interventions. To this end, local cultural considerations may be integrated into the design of the activities. But this applies to all countries, not just Muslim ones. A community development project in Egypt should design its components based on the social and cultural realities on the ground. This could be different than a similar project targeted at Bolivian highlanders.

The second question about Muslim countries' adherence to true Islamic principles is more complicated. As mentioned earlier in this chapter, Islam adapted itself to its underlying cultures. For instance, the traditions of Muslims in Sumatra are considerably different than those in the Atlas Mountain areas of Morocco; Chinese Muslims are decidedly more Chinese than their Ethiopian brethren. Local customs play as much of a role in the evolution of Muslim norms in each country as do historical trajectories, colonial legacies, or lack thereof, and political movements and systems. And, since every country, every population, and every society claim to practice Islam in its rightest way, even despite vast differences, Islamic principles can range from the draconian interpretation by the Taliban or that of the Islamic Republic of Iran to the softer versions of Albania or Tunisia.

A relatively recent approach, first developed by Scheherazade Rehman and Hossein Askari (2010) and since updated by other researchers, has defined an Islamicity index and ranking. It examines a country's performance against stated tenets and aspirations of Islam, such as absence of corruption, rule of law, justice, social inclusion, absence of poverty, respect for private property, and sanctity of contracts. Askari, an MIT-trained economist, states his motivation to construct such an index as a desire to generate a debate among Muslims about the deeper meaning of their religion than its mechanical requirements (2019). By presenting a measure of how these universal aspirations are manifested in any community or country, a road map can be provided for economic, social, and legal reforms. He believes that such an index would offer quantifiable targets that serve for setting policies and monitoring them over time.

Rehman and Askari calculated the index for 208 Muslim and non-Muslim countries and territories. They found that Islamic countries, defined as those that belong to the Organization of Islamic States (OIS), perform quite poorly, even though they are presumably Islamic in their stated outlook. In their first round, New Zealand, Ireland, and Denmark obtained the highest rankings, seemingly more in line with the presumed underlying aspirations of Islam (2010, 17–22). Table 34.1 lists the 2020 rankings of the top ten countries plus those of the fifty-six OIS states. Few, if any, marked changes with Rehman/Askari's 2010 round of results. Even Saudi Arabia, the cradle of Islam, ranks ninety-third. The results give credence to the words of Muhammad Abduh, the late nineteenth-century scholar and Grand Mufti of Egypt, who said, "I went to the West and saw Islam, but no Muslims; I got back to the East and saw Muslims, but no Islam."

Skepticism about the results that placed Muslim countries in the lower ranks of the Islamicity Index and well below dozens of non-Muslim countries has fueled some criticism about its approach and methodology (Cook 2019). Critics argued that the methodology internalized values and concepts that are dominant in the West rather than applying a very specific convention for the interpretation of the Shari'a (Abdeldayem and Aldulaimi 2018).

Table 34.1 2020 Islamicity Index

		2020 Islamicity Index					
Top ranking				*Organization of Islamic States*			
New Zealand	1	Malaysia	43	Azerbaijan	89	Guinea	127
Iceland	2	UAE	47	Saudi Arabia	93	Egypt	128
Netherlands	3	Qater	51	Kyrgyzstan	94	Turkmenistan	130
Sweden	4	Albania	53	Morocco	96	Iran	132
Norway	5	Kazakstan	59	Turkey	100	Pakistan	134
Denmark	6	Indonesia	62	Sierra Leon	108	Nigeria	135
Ireland	7	Oman	63	Lebanon	114	Mauritania	140
Switzerland	8	Kuwait	65	Burkina Faso	115	Iraq	141
Canada	9	Bosnia Hercegovina	74	Uzbekina Faso	116	Libya	142
Finland	10	Bahrain	75	Tajikistan	117	Sudan	149
		Jordan	84	Bangla desh	129	Afghanistan	150
USA	26	Tunisia	85	Algeria	121	Syria	151

Source: Islamicity Indices, https://islamicity-index.org/wp/latest-indices-2020 (accessed September 3, 2023).

Others have come to the defense of the authors of the index, and a foundation was established to sustain the work that they started. Nevertheless, it must be stressed that regardless of which proclamations or interpretations reflect the essence of Islam—a debate that can be endless—Muslims are not exceptions in wishing for, and aspiring to, the same outcomes as anyone else in the world, independent of their faith or religious adherence. Muslims want an absence of corruption, rule of law, justice, social inclusion, access to opportunity, peace, and physical and economic security, among others. Many Muslims believe that these are attainable within the teachings of Islam. Yet, Muslim countries rank low on indices of these measures because of poor internal governance frameworks, weak institutions, and lack of democracy. A 2003 World Bank report for the Middle East and North Africa region highlights that better governance could have raised growth rates by at least one percent per year—not insignificant—and enabled more socially and economically inclusive societies. The failure to do so ultimately led to the 2010 Arab Spring upheavals, which nonetheless caused formidable violence and disruption, and few positive outcomes so far, if any.

Two topics have attracted attention: Islamic finance and gender equality, which will be covered below.

Islamic Finance

An area that has seen considerable dynamism and an effort to reevaluate and reframe Islamic concepts relates to banking and financial products. Though still relatively small in terms of total assets in relation to global finance, Islamic finance has been recognized as a fast-growing market. The motivation for a reinterpretation of Islamic tenets in the financial realm comes from the need to have access to, and to stay in step with, international financial trends. It is equally critical to provide access to a considerable number of believers who would otherwise remain un-banked or underserved in terms of financial products, such as home mortgages or insurance, because they fear overstepping their religious duties.

So, what is Islamic finance, and why is it different? The five fundamental pillars that govern the regulation and religious validity (Shari'a compliance) of any Islamic economic and financial activity are: (1) a ban on charging interest (*ribà*); (2) a ban on speculating (*maysìr*) and introducing elements of uncertainty in contracts (*ghàrar*); (3) a ban on the use of, trade, and investment in prohibited assets or activities (*haram*); (4) a requirement for profit and loss sharing; and (5) an obligation for real assets to back all financial transactions (for instance, they prohibit short sales, which are central to the functioning of financial markets).

These requirements impact anything from savings accounts to home mortgages or insurance products. The essence is that parties must share the risks and rewards of a business transaction, and the transaction should have a real economic purpose without undue speculation, and not involve any exploitation of either party. Otherwise, they are considered harmful to society. Islamic finance claims to be equity-based, asset-backed, ethical, sustainable, and environmentally and socially responsible. It strives to promote risk sharing, connects the financial sector with the real economy, and emphasizes financial inclusion and social welfare. Products currently encompass banking, leasing, securities (Sukuk) and equity markets, investment funds, insurance (Takaful) and micro finance, but the banking and Sukuk assets represent about 95 percent of total Islamic finance assets (IMF 2017).

Since Islamic financial products must be cleared as permissible—halal—Shari'a compliant institutions have a two-tier governance, that is, a regular board of directors and a

Shari'a supervisory board, which includes religious jurists (*fuqaha*) and experts in relevant fields. This group examines the financial aspects of the products and the sponsoring company's compliance vis-à-vis the Shari'a. It can also explore and certify the adherence of new products to Shari'a requirements. For instance, insurance incorporates uncertainty (*ghàrar*), which is prohibited. But, by interpreting the rules governing blood money conventions that were customary in tribal Arabia, an interpretation could be found. When a member of one tribe killed someone from another tribe, compensation had to be paid to the tribe to which the victim belonged. This amount was expressed in terms of a significant number of camels. But, if the offender himself could not come up with the requisite compensation, members of the tribe pooled their resources, camel by camel, to pay the victim's tribe. Such a comparison of sharing of resources to pay for an adverse event, which is the task of the insurance company among its clients, can recast the mechanics of this product within the context of Shari'a and make it permissible (Khan 2017).

In 2015, the World Bank estimated the size of the Islamic financial assets to be around US$2 trillion and projected a growth of 10–12 percent annually (Alawode 2015). It emerged as an effective tool for development finance globally and mainstreamed within the global financial system, with the potential to address the challenges of poverty and help boost shared prosperity.

> In many majority Muslim countries, Islamic banking assets have been growing faster than conventional banking assets. There has also been a surge of interest in Islamic finance from non-Muslim countries such as the UK, Luxembourg, South Africa, and Hong Kong.

It must be noted that this rapid development is owed to the broad-based effort of the Muslim clergy to review 1400-year-old Islamic tenets and interpret and adapt them to today's global realities. In other words, when there is a will, there is a way for creativity and adaptation. Unfortunately, such an effort is still missing on the issue of gender equality, even though there is robust evidence and considerable literature that women's economic inclusion contributes significantly to economic growth and addresses income inequality, when and where gender-based discrimination, which is often justified in the name of religion, can be overcome.

Gender Equality

The position of women within and outside the family has generally been circumscribed by religion in nearly all societies, and their roles have been defined as wives and mothers. This resulted in limitations on women's access to the public sphere. No religion has afforded women the same rights as men. From Confucius to Jesus, from Moses to Hinduism, from Zoroaster to the Baha'i faith, from Catholics to Southern Baptists, men can rise to positions that women cannot and have rights that women do not. Even ancient Athens, which worshiped six gods and six goddesses and was named after the Goddess Athena, excluded women from decision-making in history's first experience with democracy.

The degree and nature of discrimination have varied from society to society and ebbed and flowed within the same society from time to time. Even today and in every country, women are a minority among judges, corporate leaders, politicians, and decision-makers. But when gender inequality comes to mind, one finds that fingers are quickly pointed to

Islam and substantiated by the examples of the Taliban in Afghanistan, the Islamic Republic of Iran, or women's ban on driving in Saudi Arabia. By the standards of the Gender Gap Index, which is produced by the World Economic Forum, most Muslim countries indeed rank low. This section cannot cover this extensive field in detail but only highlights that, as elsewhere, there is a need for reforms. In some countries this process has been faster than others. To put gender issues in Muslim countries into perspective, it behooves to stress that women's rights have only recently progressed in the West (see Box 34.1).

Box 34.1 Women's Rights in England (Excerpts from *The Narrow Corridor* by Daron Acemoglu and James Robinson)

The evolution of liberty is a protracted process, especially for groups, such as women, who have been systematically discriminated against and suffer heavy restrictions on their social and economic behavior. The 1632 compilation, *The Lawes Resolutions of Women's Rights*, stated, "*That which the husband hath is his own. That which the wife hath is the husband's.*" . . . William Blackstone, the great British legal scholar, summarized the common law situation in his [1765] *Commentaries on the Laws of England*:

> *By marriage, the husband and wife are one person in law: that is, the very being or legal existence of the woman is suspended during the marriage. Everything was under the control of the husband "under whose wing, protection, and cover, she performs everything."*

In 1854, Caroline Norton published *English Laws for Women*, [outlining] the inequity and hypocrisy of the legal status quo:

> *A married woman in England has no legal existence: her being is absorbed in that of her husband. Years of separation [or] desertion cannot alter this position . . . the legal fiction holds her to be "one" with her husband, even though she may never see or hear of him. She has no possessions . . . her property is his property. . . . An English wife has no legal right even to her clothes or ornaments; her husband may take them and sell them if he pleases, even though they be the gifts of relatives or friends or bought before marriage. An English wife cannot make a will. . . . An English wife cannot legally claim her own earnings. Whether wages for manual labour, or payment for intellectual exertion, whether she weed potatoes, or keep a school, her salary is the husband's. . . . An English wife may not leave her husband's house. Not only can he sue her for "restitution of conjugal rights," but he has a right to enter the house of any friend or relation with whom she may take refuge, and who may "harbour her,"—as it is termed,—and carry her away by force, with or without the aid of the police.*

In 1857 Parliament passed the *Matrimonial Causes Act*, establishing grounds for which women could sue for divorce. The cause of liberty for women subsequently acquired an influential supporter in the British philosopher John Stuart Mill, whose 1869 book, *The Subjection of Women*, was a powerful call for complete equality for women in legal, economic, and political life. . .. In 1870 came the *Married Women's Property Act*. . . . Norton's victories and the support of figures such as Mill signaled a fundamental change in norms. But they still left women without the right to vote and political representation. Women still suffered massive economic discrimination. This started to change in 1918, when women over the age of 30 got the vote, and finally in 1928, all adult women were enfranchised. These political fruits came after intense mobilization and protests by the suffragettes. Predictably, norms and economic relations changed more slowly. The Equal Pay Act of 1970 establishing the legal principle of gender equality in the workplace was an important step, but equal economic opportunities and pay for women are still a work in progress in Britain as elsewhere.

Source: Acemoglu and Robinson 2019, 191–94.

But it was not too long ago that Muslim women fared better than their peers in the rest of the world, as they enjoyed economic rights that were progressive for their time. Contrary to the views of extremists such as the Taliban, Islam is said to encourage women to receive an education and be economically active—perhaps in recognition of the quintessential role that Khadija played at the dawn of Islam and the unquestioned female role model that she has imprinted on believers. Women must keep their own name, hence their own identity and lineage. They have three unequivocal rights that are significant considering what existed in pre-modern times even in the West (per box above). A Muslim woman can own and inherit property, transact and sign contracts in her own name, and have uncontested control over her assets. She has the liberty to buy, sell, mortgage, lease, borrow, lend, donate, act as trustee, own a business, and sign legal documents regardless of her marital status. What belongs to her does not belong to her husband. Any of her male kin must not interfere with these rights—unless she explicitly permits them to do so. She can dispose of her earnings as she pleases. Good evidence of this practice are the historical records in Ottoman and other Muslim territories that show that the *waqfs*—religious trusts—obtained a considerable share of their endowments from women who bequeathed their wealth to them.

Women enjoyed other economic rights during marriage that were to ensure that they not be exploited, and taken care of, by their husbands. According to Islamic traditions, a woman keeps all her pre-marriage possessions. Any income she may receive during the marriage belongs to her. Upon marriage she is entitled to a "dower" (*mahr*) from the husband, a financial gift, and retains control over it in case she is divorced. A woman is entitled to a standard of living as before marriage; in other words, if a man marries the daughter of a rich family, he must ensure that he provides for her similarly. The husband is responsible for all household expenses, and he must pay/compensate his wife for all the household work she performs—going as far as paying her for nursing their child. This indicates that her contribution has a monetary, and not just a moral, value and cannot be taken for granted. He must also provide for her upkeep (*nafaqa*), which is separate and in exchange for his conjugal rights (*tamkin*), and he is permitted to withhold *nafaqa* if she refuses his rights. Upon divorce, she receives the pre-marriage negotiated settlement—like pre-nuptials in the West. Hence, in relative terms, Muslim women had significant protections in terms of property rights and economic security.

The Qur'an refers to men and women with equal frequency, such as the men and women who are truthful, the men and women who fast, the men and women who give alms, and so on, will be rewarded by Allah and receive their rewards, suggesting their spiritual equality before God. It also dedicates an entire 176-verse sura to women, their role, duties, and rights ("An-Nisa"–"Women"). Yet, two seemingly innocuous words would alarm any Muslim feminist: these are "complementarity" and "equity," which religious jurists (*foqaha*) apply to justify sex-based and gender-based differential treatment. In 2012, Tunisian women fought hard to remove the word "complementarity" from the country's first post-Arab Spring constitution. The term stems from the notion that men and women complete one another and that neither can live without the other. To achieve harmony and equilibrium, each is assigned different roles and separate social functions. Over time, women's sphere of influence became the home, and that of the man the outside world. Despite this, some women managed to take a public role as sultanas, queens, elected heads of state, and wealthy businesswomen.

Women have also been bound by other sex and gender-based differential treatment that has impeded their social status and presence. Within the framework of complementary roles and men's access to economic opportunities outside the home, they bear the duty to provide for the family. It is argued that each person needs to be given equitable resources for the level of responsibility he/she shoulders vis-à-vis others. Since men bear a heavier financial obligation, they should receive a bigger share. The issue of unequal inheritance comes up frequently. The oft-heard justification that Muslim jurists use for why women should receive less inheritance is that what is a man's belongs to the whole family, and what the woman owns or earns is hers alone. However, male and female advocates for gender equality argue that this may have been the case in the past, but in the modern world the concept of complementarity has changed and that men can no longer shoulder alone, and women contribute a steady share of the household expenses in officially male-headed ones, as well as being the head of the growing number of female-headed households. With the blurring of lines between male–female roles and responsibilities, justice is not served by sticking to outdated and no longer realistic delineations.

A woman inherits from her parents, siblings, and other near relatives in prescribed shares. Though her share is technically half of her male relative, her inheritance cannot be denied to her. Most other religions and cultures stay silent on the issue of female inheritance, which often results in women inheriting nothing. But the silence on this matter has left the door open for reform. However, because Islam details inheritance rights in clear terms, changing the goal posts has proven difficult. Shari'a inheritance rules apply to cases where the diseased leaves no will. But a Muslim is free to bequeath his/her wealth in part or totally as he/she wishes, in equal shares to their children, favoring daughters over sons and vice versa, or give to religious foundations (*waqf*).

While inheritance laws in any society are relevant for men and women who come from families with means, there are other domains that affect women of all backgrounds and classes. Compensation for a woman's life—blood money—is half of that of a man, which some clerics justify based on the equity argumentation presented above. This has had important implications not only in the case of death but also during the lifetime, say in the case of a loss of a limb or other physical injuries. This notwithstanding, increasingly most Muslim-majority countries have found ways to reinterpret these tenets and bypass them as much as possible. The testimony of two women is also equal to that of one man, unless the woman testifies as an expert, not as a witness. For instance, a female ophthalmologist's opinion in a court case is equivalent to that of her male peer.

So, where else does the commonly known inequality of Muslim women seem to originate? And what are women's rights activists trying to change? The central issue is that by making men responsible for providing for women, women have been in affect placed under the guardianship of men, which entitles men to have authority over women. This belief has reinforced the prevailing cultures of the patriarchy and manifests itself in two important legal realms.

The first legal realm is in family laws or what is commonly known as personal status codes. Divorce and custody laws discriminate against women. A man has the primary right to divorce, but a woman does not, and only in cases of probable cause and in exchange for forfeiting the *mahr*—the pre-marriage gift. This inequality is compounded by custody rules, which give the father and not the mother the right to keep the children since he is to provide for them. These differential rights create an imbalance in bargaining power within the marriage and the household. Modern mechanisms to counter these rules have been to agree in advance on these arrangements in the marriage contract. While such a practice may be a band-aid on the problem, activists strive to change family laws so that the rights to divorce and custody are applied equally to men and women. Activists seek also to outlaw polygamy, that is, incidences where a man can have more than one wife at a time—since in Islam men are allowed to have up to four wives simultaneously if the man can afford them financially and treat his wives emotionally equally—which is hardly possible. Even the Prophet, who had nine concurrent wives, is said to have had a favorite.

The second area where male authority over women can be demonstrated is in a host of civil laws that were integrated into the body of legislation as part of the modernization efforts of the late nineteenth and early twentieth centuries. These laws can range from labor laws, pension laws, citizenship laws, nationality laws, and passport laws, among others, which did not exist in Islam per se. Most civil laws were modeled after Western codes. But, since they were introduced into Muslim countries during a period when there was extensive gender inequality in the West, as shown in the case of England, such discriminatory treatment of women made their way into the legislations of Muslim societies as well. For instance, until the 1960s and 1970s, European women needed their husband's permission to work, a requirement that no longer exists but is still on the books of many Muslim countries that copied these laws. Reforming them will take time, particularly because the opponents to reforms attempt to find Islamic tenets, such as the husband's responsibility to provide for his wife, hence guardianship, to justify and retain these Western-originated limitations (Nabli and Chamlou 2004).

The World Bank's Women, Business, and Law program, which reviews regulations affecting women's economic participation, finds the highest numbers of legal barriers among Muslim-majority countries—though the severity changes significantly from country to country, substantiating the argument presented earlier that Muslim legal systems are not monolithic and lend themselves to be interpreted as desired. IMF research finds that more equal laws boost female labor force participation (Gonzales et al. 2015). This in turn improves the level and quality of growth, increases productivity, reduces income inequality, as well as promotes industrial and export diversification (Lagarde and Ostry 2018). Female labor force participation rates are low in most Muslim-majority countries, despite considerable gains in education and a marked reduction in fertility rates. It reflects the many barriers that married women in particular face when working outside the home.

On the other hand, women's entrepreneurship is a brighter spot in Muslim countries, perhaps because emulating a role model like Khadija offered an acceptable path. Saudi

Arabia has enacted considerable gender reforms in recent years. The Khadija Center in Jeddah, which opened in 2004 to support businesswomen, played a critical role in opening the public Saudi space for women (Akeel 2004). It initiated the debate about the necessity of a modern role for women and convened those who could effectively advocate for reform. Similar centers for women entrepreneurs have long existed in other corners of the Muslim world and were critical in building the momentum for change.

A 2008 World Bank study that analyzed large samples of enterprises found that female ownership of enterprises was widespread (Chamlou 2008). Roughly one in seven enterprises in the eight Middle East and North Africa (MENA) countries covered in the survey were female owned. More importantly, the share of large female-owned firms was as high as their male counterparts. They also operated in similar sectors. Nonetheless, the study found that these firms still faced discrimination that was statistically significant, and which impacted their profitability. Consequently, a large component of the World Bank gender agenda for the MENA region consisted of highlighting this phenomenon and showcasing women entrepreneurs. It was seen as a gateway to expand the debate about the need for more gender-inclusive policies that would address such discrimination. This effort gave rise to a considerable movement to highlight women's entrepreneurship, beyond the well-trodden path of micro finance, not only within the World Bank, or MENA, but also in other regions. No longer seen as exceptions and outliers, *Forbes Magazine* now regularly features powerful women business leaders from MENA.

While reforms, which have been hampered by conflict and a rise of fundamentalism, may be slow, a bright future lies ahead. Female education has risen considerably. In most Muslim societies, the gender gap in education among the younger generations has closed or is narrowing fast; in many of these countries, women outnumber men at university levels—and do so in technical and STEM fields. Steve Levitt of the University of Chicago and Roland Fryer of Harvard (Fryer and Levitt 2010) studied the link between math scores and the gender gap across countries. They found a consistent trend that boys scored better than girls in math, but that gap narrowed in societies with greater gender equality. The exception was in the Middle East and North Africa, where the gender gap in math was reversed, meaning that girls did better; the results were statistically significant.

The growing female talent pool has indeed changed perspectives within several Muslim countries. Besides women who at one point or another were heads of states (Bangladesh, Indonesia, Pakistan, Singapore, Turkey, etc.), many governments now include more women ministers in key portfolios (Algeria, Egypt, Jordan, Lebanon, Malaysia, Tunisia, the United Arab Emirates, etc.) and are represented by women ambassadors in coveted diplomatic posts (Jordan, Morocco, Saudi Arabia, etc.). They integrate gender issues into their development agenda and budgets. These women pioneers can undoubtedly accelerate the pace of reform in Muslim countries.

Conclusion

This chapter reviewed with a broad brush the origin and evolution of what can be termed Islamic governance, which in one way or another impacts a quarter of the world's population. The cradle of Islam was a cultural melting pot, and as such it incorporated many varied influences shaped into a new world order. While the initial spread of Islam was through war, the territories it conquered had considerable influence in defining how governments should function within the proper territories, and beyond. As such, as Islam was adopted in diverse societies, it adapted itself to the prevailing circumstances. In later periods, Islam spread largely through trade. Therefore, the economic content of Islamic institutions evolved and became quite intensive for its time, since they provided trust and confidence among believers half a world away.

With few exceptions, in today's world, Muslim-majority countries exhibit hardly any religiously motivated differences with global governance structures and institutions. They belong to international organizations and have signed and ratified nearly all international laws and conventions. However, on their domestic fronts, these countries appear to fall short on the expectations of their citizens and what Islam is said to aspire to, such as the absence of corruption, rule of law, justice, social inclusion, access to opportunity, peace, and physical and economic security.

Two areas attract the limelight with regard to the Muslim world: Islamic finance and gender inequality. Regarding the former, there has been a dynamic and concerted effort to respond to the growing need of Muslims for financial services by modifying financial products and access to comply with Islamic principles. Islamic finance has tried to emerge as an effective tool for development finance globally and mainstreamed within the global financial system, with the potential to address the challenges of poverty and help boost shared prosperity.

An area of slower progress is gender equality. Nearly all Muslim countries lag, though at different paces and levels compared to their peers. Gender issues and the reinterpretation and recasting of some Muslim tenets with modern realities have not yet seen the kind of dynamism that can be witnessed in Islamic finance. Even legal domains that have no grounding in Islam and were imported from European codes, which were gender discriminatory at the time of their adoption, need considerable efforts to reform. Nevertheless, Muslim countries have made steady progress on educating girls, and women constitute an ever larger share of modern human capital. This has led many countries to begin integrating more women seriously in their decision-making processes. These trends in the coming decades will undoubtedly change the dynamics in every family, in every neighborhood, society, and country.

Disclaimer

I write this article from the perspective of a woman born into a Muslim family, raised mostly in a Muslim culture, and who worked for an extensive period in Muslim-majority countries. I had to learn and understand Islam from a practical aspect and navigate and negotiate my way therein personally and professionally. I believe that my perspective, which is that of an average person, much the same way as a Christian or Jew, also represents the views of a great majority, which could be more relevant for this topic than someone whose knowledge is largely academic or scholarly.

Key Discussion Areas

- The origins of Islam.
- Factors influencing Islamic governance.
- Islamic finance and its practices.
- Gender equality in Muslim societies.

Note

1 The sizes of other major religion include the Hindus (15 percent) Buddhists (7 percent), and adherents of other religions, including Jews (0.2 percent), while about 16 percent profess to have no religion.

References

Abdeldayem, Marwan Mohamed, and Saeed Aldulaimi. 2018. "The Economic Islamicity Index, between Islamicity and Universality: Critical Review and Discussion." March 2018, www.researchgate.net/publication/323604408_The_Economic_Islamicity_Index_between_Islamicity_and_Universality_Critical_Review_and_Discussion (accessed September 1, 2023).

Acemoglu, Daron, and James A. Robinson. 2019. *The Narrow Corridor: States, Societies, and the Fate of Liberty*. New York: Penguin.

Akeel, Maha. 2004. "Khadija Center Helping Businesswomen," *Arab News*, October 6, 2004, www.arabnews.com/node/256202 (accessed September 1, 2023).

Alawode, Abayomi A. "Islamic Finance." *World Bank*, March 31, 2015, www.worldbank.org/en/topic/financialsector/brief/islamic-finance (accessed September 1, 2023).

Askari, Hossein. 2019. "Islamicity Indices: A Moral Compass for Reform and Effective Institutions." *International Journal of Islamic Economics*. August 26, 2019, https://e-journal.metrouniv.ac.id/index.php/IJIE/article/view/1574 (accessed September 1, 2023).

Chamlou, Nadereh. 2008. "The Environment for Women's Entrepreneurship in the Middle East and North Africa." *World Bank*, https://openknowledge.worldbank.org/handle/10986/6479 (accessed September 1, 2023).

———. 2014. "The Economics of Happiness and Anger in North Africa." WIDER Working Paper 60/2014. Helsinki, Finland: UN University World Institute for Development Economics Research, www.wider.unu.edu/publication/economics-happiness-and-anger-north-africa (accessed September 1, 2023).

Cook, Erin. 2019. "The Most Islamic Country Is . . . New Zealand?" *IslamiCity*, November 3, 2019, www.islamicity.org/20554/the-most-islamic-country-is-new-zealand (accessed September 1, 2023).

Fryer, Roland G. Jr., and Steven D. Levitt. 2010. "An Empirical Analysis of the Gender Gap in Mathematics." *American Economic Journal: Applied Economics* 2(2): 210–40, www.aeaweb.org/articles?id=10.1257/app.2.2.210 (accessed September 1, 2023).

Gonzales, Christina, Sonali Jain-Chandra, Kalpana Kochhar, and Monique Newiak. 2015. "Fair Play: More Equal Laws Boost Labor Force Participation." *International Monetary Fund*, www.imf.org/external/pubs/ft/sdn/2015/sdn1502.pdf (accessed September 1, 2023).

Guiso, Luigi, Paola Sapienza, and Luigi Zingales. 2006. "Does Culture Affect Economic Outcomes?" *Journal of Economic Perspectives* 20(2): 23–48, www.jstor.org/stable/30033649 (accessed September 1, 2023).

Hackett, Conrad, and David McClendon. 2017. "Christians Remain World's Largest Religious Group, but They Are Declining in Europe." *Pew Research Center*, April 5, 2017, www.pewresearch.org/fact-tank/2017/04/05/christians-remain-worlds-largest-religious-group-but-they-are-declining-in-europe (accessed September 1, 2023).

Haidari, Mansoor. 2018. "The Influence of the Ancient Persian Administration, Structure on Post-Islamic Governmental Bureaus." *International Journal for Modern Trends in Science and Technology* 4(8), www.ijmtst.com/volume4/issue8/3.IJMTST040803.pdf (accessed September 1, 2023).

International Monetary Fund. 2017. "Islamic Finance and the Role of the IMF." February 2017, www.imf.org/external/themes/islamicfinance/ (accessed September 1, 2023).

Khan, Ibrahim. "Insurance: Is It Haram or Halal?" *Islamic Finance Guru*, January 4, 2017, www.islamicfinanceguru.com/articles/personal-finance/insurance-haram-halal (accessed September 1, 2023).

Kuran, Timur. 2010. *The Long Divergence: How Islamic Law Held Back the Middle East*. Princeton, NJ: Princeton University Press.

Lagarde, Christine, and Jonathan D. Ostry. 2018. "Economic Gains from Gender Inclusion: Even Greater Than You Thought." *International Monetary Fund Blog*, November 28, 2018, www.imf.

org/en/Blogs/Articles/2018/11/28/blog-economic-gains-from-gender-inclusion-even-greater-than-you-thought (accessed September 1, 2023).

Michalopoulos, Stelios, Alireza Naghavi, and Giovanni Prarolo. 2017. "Trade and Geography in the Spread of Islam." *Economic Journal* 128(616): 3210–41, https://doi.org/10.1111/ecoj.12557.

Mirakhor, Abbas, and Hossein Askari. 2010. *Islam and the Path to Human and Economic Development*. London: Palgrave Macmillan.

Nabli, M., and Nadereh Chamlou. 2004. *Gender and Development in the Middle East and North Africa: Women in the Public Sphere*. Washington, DC: World Bank, https://documents1.worldbank.org/curated/en/976361468756608654/pdf/281150PAPER0Gender010Development0in0MNA.pdf (accessed September 1, 2023).

Philips, Bilal. 2013. "Haj in Pre-Islamic Times." *Arab News*, September 20, 2013, www.arabnews.com/news/465223 (accessed September 1, 2023).

Rehman, Scheherazade S., and Hossein Askari. 2010. "An Economic IslamicityIndex (EI^2)." *Global Economy Journal* 10(3), https://hossein-askari.com/wordpress/wp-content/uploads/islamicity-index.pdf (accessed September 1, 2023).

INDEX

Note: Page numbers in *italics* indicate a figure and page numbers in **bold** indicate a table on the corresponding page.